Lecture Notes in Computer Science   9886

Commenced Publication in 1973
Founding and Former Series Editors:
Gerhard Goos, Juris Hartmanis, and Jan van Leeuwen

More information about this series at http://www.springer.com/series/7407

Alessandro E.P. Villa · Paolo Masulli
Antonio Javier Pons Rivero (Eds.)

Artificial Neural Networks and Machine Learning – ICANN 2016

25th International Conference on Artificial Neural Networks
Barcelona, Spain, September 6–9, 2016
Proceedings, Part I

 Springer

Editors
Alessandro E.P. Villa
University of Lausanne
Lausanne
Switzerland

Antonio Javier Pons Rivero
Universitat Politècnica de Catalunya
Terrrassa
Spain

Paolo Masulli
University of Lausanne
Lausanne
Switzerland

ISSN 0302-9743   ISSN 1611-3349   (electronic)
Lecture Notes in Computer Science
ISBN 978-3-319-44777-3   ISBN 978-3-319-44778-0   (eBook)
DOI 10.1007/978-3-319-44778-0

Library of Congress Control Number: 2016948233

LNCS Sublibrary: SL1 – Theoretical Computer Science and General Issues

Printed on acid-free paper

This Springer imprint is published by Springer Nature
The registered company is Springer International Publishing AG Switzerland

Preface

It is our honor and our pleasure to present this two-volume proceedings of the 25th International Conference on Artificial Networks (ICANN 2016) held during September 6–9, 2016, in Barcelona, Spain, and organized by the Universitat Politècnica de Catalunya and the Universitat Pompeu Fabra. The annual ICANN is the flagship conference of the European Neural Network Society (ENNS). After 25 editions, it is clear that ICANN's is a story of success. The field has grown and matured during all these years and the conference series has maintained its rank among the most prestigious conferences in the world. A special social gathering brought together all ENNS members to celebrate its 25th anniversary. Professor Teuvo Kohonen was the first president of ENNS serving the term 1990–1992. The office was then taken by John G. Taylor, Errki Oja, Wlodek Duch, and Alessandro Villa, who comes to the end of his last term. A new president of ENNS was elected and Barcelona is a very appropriate location for this anniversary edition. It has a long tradition in neuroscience going back to Santiago Ramón y Cajal, more than one century ago, who, after moving to the University of Barcelona, made his pioneering neuroanatomical studies in this city. We are sure that such a nice environment and intense program of activities will leave a positive trace in our memories.

The field of artificial neural networks evolved tremendously in the past quarter of a century, but the goal to bring together researchers from two worlds, i.e., information sciences and neurosciences, is still fresh and necessary. The conference gathers people not only from Europe but also from the rest of the globe. The 25th ICANN united presenters from 42 countries from all continents. ICANN 2016 was tightly organized in partnership with ENNS. This governance has been guided by not-for-profit procedures that allowed us to keep very low congress fees compared with international standards. Moreover, we consolidated the practice of offering a subscription to ENNS to all ICANN delegates who present a scientific communication.

The Scientific and Reviewing Committee selected 169 contributions, after a peer-review process of 227 submissions, which are published in these two proceedings volumes. The variety of topics covered by all these contributions proves the maturity and, at the same time, the vitality of the field of artificial neural networks. Besides, this year, we introduced short extended abstract contributions in order to encourage top-level scholars to join the conference without the need to submit a full paper. This opportunity appeared very attractive also to researchers who are interested in presenting results that could not justify a full paper submission. Hence, the implementation of this scheme eventually produced 122 full papers and 47 short extended abstracts.

The type of submission was not the ultimate criterion in assigning the submitters to an oral or a poster presentation. Papers were equally good and attributed to 94 oral and 75 poster presentations following, in the vast majority of the cases, the preference expressed by the authors. The proceedings of the 47 short presentations have been grouped together following the rules of the Publisher. Oral presentations were divided into 18 sessions following the usual dual track, initially intended as the brain-inspired computing track and machine-learning research track. As in the past editions the dual track became track A and track B, because many papers presented an interdisciplinary approach and track C for the posters. In addition, ICANN had eight plenary talks by internationally renowned speakers, in particular one lecture sponsored by ENNS, the John G. Taylor Memorial Lecture given by Errki Oja, past president of ENNS. Several satellite workshops completed the intensive program of ICANN 2016.

This scientific event would not have been possible without the participation of many people. We want to thank everyone who contributed, in one way or another, to the success of the conference and the publication of the proceedings. We want to express our deepest gratitude to the members of the Executive Committee of the ENNS, who have accepted the proposal of Barcelona organizing the event. We are grateful for the work of the Scientific and Reviewing Committee and all reviewers who worked under strong time constraints during the compilation of the proceedings. The conference would have been impossible without the contribution of all members of the Organizing Committees. We want to thank the outstanding work by the ENNS, UPC, and UPF personnel. We want to thank, particularly, the work of Paolo Masulli, Lara Escuain, and Daniel Malagarriga. The conference would not have been a reality without the help of Caroline Kleinheny. Finally, we would like to thank Anna Kramer, Frank Holzwarth, and Alfred Hofmann from Springer for their help with the tough publication project. We acknowledge, too, all authors who contributed to the volumes and shared their ideas during the conference. We are sure that the papers appearing in these volumes will contribute to the field of artificial neural networks with many new and inspiring ideas that will help other concepts flourish in the future.

July 2016

Alessandro E.P. Villa
Paolo Masulli
Antonio Javier Pons Rivero

Organization

General Chair

Antonio Javier Pons Rivero   Universitat Politècnica de Catalunya, Spain

Honorary Chair

Alessandro E.P. Villa   University of Lausanne, Switzerland

Local Co-chairs

Jordi Garcia-Ojalvo   Universitat Pompeu Fabra, Spain
Paul F.M.J. Verschure   ICREA-Universitat Pompeu Fabra, Spain

Communications Chair

Paolo Masulli   University of Lausanne, Switzerland

Registration Chair

Caroline Kleinheny   ENNS Secretariat, Switzerland

Scientific and Reviewing Committee

Javier Martín Buldú   Center for Biomedical Technology, Spain
Jérémie Cabessa   Université Panthéon-Assas - Paris 2, France
Joan Cabestany   Universitat Politècnica de Catalunya, Spain
Stephen Coombes   University of Nottingham, UK
José R. Dorronsoro   Universidad Autónoma de Madrid, Spain
Jordi Garcia-Ojalvo   Universitat Pompeu Fabra, Spain
Petia Georgieva   University of Aveiro, Portugal
Barbara Hammer   Bielefeld University, Germany
Petia Koprinkova-Hristova   Bulgarian Academy of Sciences, Bulgaria
Věra Kůrková   Czech Academy of Sciences, Czech Republic
Alessandra Lintas   University of Lausanne, Switzerland
Francesco Masulli   University of Genoa, Italy
Paolo Masulli   University of Lausanne, Switzerland
Claudio Mirasso   IFISC, Spain
Juan Manuel Moreno Arostegui   Universitat Politècnica de Catalunya, Spain
Günther Palm   Universität Ulm, Germany

Jaakko Peltonen	Aalto University Helsinki, Finland
Antonio Javier Pons Rivero	Universitat Politècnica de Catalunya, Spain
Jordi Soriano	Universitat de Barcelona, Spain
Paul F.M.J. Verschure	ICREA-Universitat Pompeu Fabra, Spain
Alessandro E.P. Villa	University of Lausanne, Switzerland

Program and Workshop Committee

Grégoire Montavon	Technische Universität Berlin, Germany
Antonio Javier Pons Rivero	Universitat Politècnica de Catalunya, Spain
Jordi Soriano	Universitat de Barcelona, Spain
Paul F.M.J. Verschure	ICREA-Universitat Pompeu Fabra, Spain

Secretariat and Communications

Ana Calle	Universitat Politècnica de Catalunya, Spain
Lara Escuain-Poole	Universitat Politècnica de Catalunya, Spain
Caroline Kleinheny	ENNS Secretariat, Switzerland
Daniel Malagarriga	Universitat Politècnica de Catalunya, Spain
Paolo Masulli	University of Lausanne, Switzerland

ENNS Travel Grant Committee

Barbara Hammer	Bielefeld University, Germany
Antonio Javier Pons Rivero	Universitat Politècnica de Catalunya, Spain
Alessandro E.P. Villa	University of Lausanne, Switzerland

Additional Reviewers

Amr Abdullatif	University of Genoa, Italy
Takeshi Abe	Okinawa Institute of Science and Technology Graduate University, Japan
Waqas Waseem Ahmed	Universitat Politècnica de Catalunya, Spain
Hisanao Akima	Tohoku University, Japan
Tetiana Aksenova	CEA, France
Carlos M. Alaíz	KU Leuven, Belgium
Bruno Apolloni	University of Milan, Italy
Daniel Araújo	Universidade Federal do Rio Grande do Norte, Brazil
Yoshiyuki Asai	Okinawa Institute of Science and Technology Graduate University, Japan
Pragathi Priyadharsini Balasubramani	Indian Institute of Technology, India
Alessandro Barardi	Universitat Politècnica de Catalunya, Spain
Pablo Barros	University of Hamburg, Germany
Lluís A. Belanche	Universitat Politècnica de Catalunya, Spain
Alexandre Bernardino	IST University of Lisbon, Portugal

Daniel Brunner	Université Pierre et Marie Curie, France
Javier Martín Buldú	Center for Biomedical Technology, Spain
Jérémie Cabessa	Université Panthéon-Assas - Paris 2, France
Joan Cabestany	Universitat Politècnica de Catalunya, Spain
Anne Canuto	Federal University of Rio Grande do Norte, Brazil
Elena Cerezuela-Escudero	University of Seville, Spain
Youcef Chibani	University of Science and Technology Houari Boumédiene, Algeria
Chris Christodoulou	University of Cyprus, Cyprus
Laura Cohen	EPFL, Switzerland
Albert Compte	IDIBAPS, Spain
Stephen Coombes	University of Nottingham, UK
Omid E. David	Bar-Ilan University, Israel
Sergey Dolenko	M.V. Lomonosov Moscow State University, Russia
Manuel J. Domínguez-Morales	University of Seville, Spain
José R. Dorronsoro	Universidad Autónoma de Madrid, Spain
Hiroshi Dozono	Saga University, Japan
David Díaz-Vico	Universidad Autónoma de Madrid, Spain
Víctor M. Eguiluz	IFISC, Spain
Wolfram Erlhagen	University of Minho, Portugal
Lara Escuain-Poole	Universitat Politècnica de Catalunya, Spain
Ángela Fernández	KU Leuven, Belgium
Ingo Fischer	IFISC, Spain
Jordi Garcia-Ojalvo	Universitat Pompeu Fabra, Spain
Philippe Gaussier	University of Cergy Pontoise, France
Petia Georgieva	University of Aveiro, Portugal
Michele Giugliano	University of Antwerp, Belgium
Ana González	Universidad Autónoma de Madrid, Spain
André Grüning	University of Surrey, UK
Gianpaolo Gulletta	University of Minho, Portugal
Tatiana V. Guy	Czech Academy of Sciences, Czech Republic
Christina Göpfert	Bielefeld University, Germany
Barbara Hammer	Bielefeld University, Germany
Kazuyuki Hara	Nihon University, Japan
B. Somashekar Harish	SJCE, India
Robert Haschke	Bielefeld University, Germany
Stefan Heinrich	Universität Hamburg, Germany
Ramon Herrero Simon	Universitat Politècnica de Catalunya, Spain
Babak Hosseini	Bielefeld University, Germany
Juan Huo	Zhengzhou University, China
Axel Hutt	Inria Nancy, France
Brian Hyland	University of Otago, New Zealand
Maciej Jedynak	Universitat Politècnica de Catalunya, Spain
Ryo Karakida	University of Tokyo, Japan
Okyay Kaynak	Bogazici University, Turkey

Monji Kherallah	University of Sfax, Tunisia
Stefanos Kollias	NTUA, Greece
Petia Koprinkova-Hristova	Bulgarian Academy of Sciences, Bulgaria
Irena Koprinska	University of Sydney, Australia
Kostadin Koroutchev	UAM, Spain
Maciej Kusy	Rzeszow University of Technology, Poland
Markus Kächele	University of Ulm, Germany
Věra Kůrková	Czech Academy of Sciences, Czech Republic
Alessandra Lintas	University of Lausanne, Switzerland
Sheng Luo	Hasso Plattner Institute, Germany
Rania Maalej	National Engineering School of Sfax, Tunisia
Maciej Majewski	Koszalin University of Technology, Poland
Daniel Malagarriga	Universitat Politècnica de Catalunya, Spain
Thomas Martinetz	University of Lübeck, Germany
Paolo Masulli	University of Lausanne, Switzerland
Francesco Masulli	University of Genoa, Italy
Fernanda Matias	Universidade Federal de Alagoas, Brazil
Maurizio Mattia	Istituto Superiore di Sanità, Italy
Corrado Mencar	University of Bari A. Moro, Italy
Claudio Mirasso	IFISC, Spain
Juan Manuel Moreno Arostegui	Universitat Politècnica de Catalunya, Spain
Javier Márquez Ruiz	Universidad Pablo de Olavide Seville, Spain
Taishin Nomura	Osaka University, Japan
Dimitri Nowicki	National Academy of Science of Ukraine, Ukraine
Adil Omari	Universidad Autónoma de Madrid, Spain
Silvia Ortin	IFISC, Spain
Sebastian Otte	University of Tuebingen, Germany
Günther Palm	Universität Ulm, Germany
Juan Pardo	Universidad CEU Cardenal Herrera, Spain
Jaakko Peltonen	Aalto University Helsinki, Finland
Ernesto Pereda	University of La Laguna, Spain
Luis Pesquera	Instituto de Física de Cantabria, Spain
Gordon Pipa	University of Osnabrück, Germany
Angel Ricardo Plastino	Universidad del Noroeste de la Provincia de Buenos Aires, UNNOBA-Conicet, Argentina
Antonio Javier Pons Rivero	Universitat Politècnica de Catalunya, Spain
Yifat Prut	Hebrew University, Israel
Irene Rodriguez-Lujan	Universidad Autónoma de Madrid, Spain
João Rosa	Universidade de São Paulo, Brazil
Stefano Rovetta	University of Genoa, Italy
Ariel Ruiz-Garcia	Coventry University, UK
Vicent Sala	MCIA Research Center - UPC, Spain
Maria V. Sanchez-Vives	ICREA-IDIBAPS Barcelona, Spain
Friedhelm Schwenker	University of Ulm, Germany
Sugandha Sharma	University of Waterloo, Canada

Hua Shen	RenMin University of China, China
Jordi Soriano	Universitat de Barcelona, Spain
Alberto Suarez	Universidad Autónoma de Madrid, Spain
Hakaru Tamukoh	Kyushu Institute of Technology, Japan
Alberto Torres-Barrán	Universidad Autónoma de Madrid, Spain
Bryan Tripp	University of Waterloo, Canada
Alicia Troncoso	University Pablo de Olavide Seville, Spain
Vassilis Vassiliades	University of Cyprus, Cyprus
Paul F.M.J. Verschure	ICREA-Universitat Pompeu Fabra, Spain
Alessandro E.P. Villa	University of Lausanne, Switzerland
Julien Vitay	TU Chemnitz, Germany
Roseli Wedemann	Universidade do Estado do Rio de Janeiro, Brazil
Stefan Wermter	University of Hamburg, Germany
Francisco Zamora-Martinez	Universidad CEU Cardenal Herrera, Spain

Contents – Part I

From Neurons to Networks

Improved Chaotic Multidirectional Associative Memory.   3
  Hiroki Sato and Yuko Osana

Effect of Pre- and Postsynaptic Firing Patterns on Synaptic Competition 11
  Nobuhiro Hinakawa and Katsunori Kitano

Asymmetries in Synaptic Connections and the Nonlinear Fokker-Planck
Formalism 19
  Roseli S. Wedemann and Angel R. Plastino

Synaptogenesis: Constraining Synaptic Plasticity Based on a Distance Rule . . . 28
  Jordi-Ysard Puigbò, Joeri van Wijngaarden, Sock Ching Low,
  and Paul F.M.J. Verschure

A Sensor Fusion Horse Gait Classification by a Spiking Neural Network
on SpiNNaker. 36
  Antonio Rios-Navarro, Juan Pedro Dominguez-Morales,
  Ricardo Tapiador-Morales, Manuel Dominguez-Morales,
  Angel Jimenez-Fernandez, and Alejandro Linares-Barranco

Multilayer Spiking Neural Network for Audio Samples Classification
Using SpiNNaker 45
  Juan Pedro Dominguez-Morales, Angel Jimenez-Fernandez,
  Antonio Rios-Navarro, Elena Cerezuela-Escudero,
  Daniel Gutierrez-Galan, Manuel J. Dominguez-Morales,
  and Gabriel Jimenez-Moreno

Input-Modulation as an Alternative to Conventional Learning Strategies 54
  Esin Yavuz and Thomas Nowotny

A Potential Mechanism for Spontaneous Oscillatory Activity in the
Degenerative Mouse Retina 63
  Kanako Taniguchi, Chieko Koike, and Katsunori Kitano

Striatal Processing of Cortical Neuronal Avalanches – A Computational
Investigation. 72
  Jovana J. Belić and Jeanette Hellgren Kotaleski

Networks and Dynamics

Mapping the Language Connectome in Healthy Subjects and Brain Tumor
Patients   83
  Gregory Zegarek, Xerxes D. Arsiwalla, David Dalmazzo,
  and Paul F.M.J. Verschure

Method for Estimating Neural Network Topology Based
on SPIKE-Distance   91
  Kaori Kuroda and Mikio Hasegawa

Dynamics of Evolving Feed-Forward Neural Networks
and Their Topological Invariants   99
  Paolo Masulli and Alessandro E.P. Villa

Scaling Properties of Human Brain Functional Networks   107
  Riccardo Zucca, Xerxes D. Arsiwalla, Hoang Le, Mikail Rubinov,
  and Paul F.M.J. Verschure

Attractor Dynamics Driven by Interactivity in Boolean Recurrent
Neural Networks   115
  Jérémie Cabessa and Alessandro E.P. Villa

Training Bidirectional Recurrent Neural Network Architectures
with the Scaled Conjugate Gradient Algorithm   123
  Michalis Agathocleous, Chris Christodoulou, Vasilis Promponas,
  Petros Kountouris, and Vassilis Vassiliades

Learning Multiple Timescales in Recurrent Neural Networks   132
  Tayfun Alpay, Stefan Heinrich, and Stefan Wermter

Investigating Recurrent Neural Networks for Feature-Less Computational
Drug Design   140
  Alexander Dörr, Sebastian Otte, and Andreas Zell

Inverse Recurrent Models – An Application Scenario for Many-Joint Robot
Arm Control   149
  Sebastian Otte, Adrian Zwiener, Richard Hanten, and Andreas Zell

Population Coding of Goal Directed Movements   158
  Andreas G. Fleischer

Body Model Transition by Tool Grasping During Motor Babbling
Using Deep Learning and RNN   166
  Kuniyuki Takahashi, Hadi Tjandra, Tetsuya Ogata, and Shigeki Sugano

Centering Versus Scaling for Hubness Reduction   175
  Roman Feldbauer and Arthur Flexer

High Integrated Information in Complex Networks Near Criticality   184
Xerxes D. Arsiwalla and Paul F.M.J. Verschure

Comparison of Graph Node Distances on Clustering Tasks   192
Felix Sommer, François Fouss, and Marco Saerens

Higher Nervous Functions

Influence of Saliency and Social Impairments on the Development
of Intention Recognition   205
Laura Cohen and Aude Billard

A System-Level Model of Noradrenergic Function   214
Maxime Carrere and Frédéric Alexandre

Phenomenological Model for the Adapatation of Shape-Selective Neurons
in Area IT   222
Martin A. Giese, Pradeep Kuravi, and Rufin Vogels

Deliberation-Aware Responder in Multi-proposer Ultimatum Game   230
Marko Ruman, František Hůla, Miroslav Kárný, and Tatiana V. Guy

From Cognitive to Habit Behavior During Navigation,
Through Cortical-Basal Ganglia Loops   238
*Jean-Paul Banquet, Souheïl Hanoune, Philippe Gaussier,
and Mathias Quoy*

Fast and Slow Learning in a Neuro-Computational Model
of Category Acquisition.   248
Francesc Villagrasa, Javier Baladron, and Fred H. Hamker

Realizing Medium Spiny Neurons with a Simple Neuron Model.   256
Sami Utku Çelikok and Neslihan Serap Şengör

Multi-item Working Memory Capacity: What Is the Role
of the Stimulation Protocol?.   264
Marta Balagué and Laura Dempere-Marco

Plasticity in the Granular Layer Enhances Motor Learning
in a Computational Model of the Cerebellum   272
*Giovanni Maffei, Ivan Herreros, Marti Sanchez-Fibla,
and Paul F.M.J. Verschure*

How Is Scene Recognition in a Convolutional Network Related to that
in the Human Visual System?.   280
Sugandha Sharma and Bryan Tripp

Hybrid Trajectory Decoding from ECoG Signals for Asynchronous BCIs. . . .   288
  Marie-Caroline Schaeffer and Tetiana Aksenova

Dimensionality Reduction Effect Analysis of EEG Signals
in Cross-Correlation Classifiers Performance.   297
  Jefferson Tales Oliva and João Luís Garcia Rosa

EEG-driven RNN Classification for Prognosis of Neurodegeneration
in At-Risk Patients   306
  *Giulio Ruffini, David Ibañez, Marta Castellano, Stephen Dunne,
  and Aureli Soria-Frisch*

Competition Between Cortical Ensembles Explains Pitch-Related
Dynamics of Auditory Evoked Fields   314
  Alejandro Tabas, André Rupp, and Emili Balaguer-Ballester

Dynamics of Reward Based Decision Making: A Computational Study   322
  Bhargav Teja Nallapu and Nicolas P. Rougier

Adaptive Proposer for Ultimatum Game.   330
  František Hůla, Marko Ruman, and Miroslav Kárný

Dynamical Linking of Positive and Negative Sentences to Goal-Oriented
Robot Behavior by Hierarchical RNN   339
  Tatsuro Yamada, Shingo Murata, Hiroaki Arie, and Tetsuya Ogata

Neuronal Hardware

Real-Time FPGA Simulation of Surrogate Models of Large Spiking
Networks   349
  Murphy Berzish, Chris Eliasmith, and Bryan Tripp

Randomly Spiking Dynamic Neural Fields Driven by a Shared
Random Flow.   357
  Benoît Chappet de Vangel and Bernard Girau

Synfire Chain Emulation by Means of Flexible SNN Modeling on a SIMD
Multicore Architecture.   365
  Mireya Zapata and Jordi Madrenas

Towards Adjustable Signal Generation with Photonic Reservoir Computers . . .   374
  Piotr Antonik, Michiel Hermans, Marc Haelterman, and Serge Massar

Hierarchical Networks-on-Chip Interconnect for Astrocyte-Neuron
Network Hardware   382
  Junxiu Liu, Jim Harkin, Liam McDaid, and George Martin

Restricted Boltzmann Machines Without Random Number Generators
for Efficient Digital Hardware Implementation   391
   Sansei Hori, Takashi Morie, and Hakaru Tamukoh

Compact Associative Memory for AER Spike Decoding in FPGA-Based
Evolvable SNN Emulation   399
   Mireya Zapata and Jordi Madrenas

Learning Foundations

Combining Spatial and Parametric Working Memory in a Dynamic Neural
Field Model   411
   Weronika Wojtak, Stephen Coombes, Estela Bicho,
   and Wolfram Erlhagen

C4.5 or Naive Bayes: A Discriminative Model Selection Approach   419
   Lungan Zhang, Liangxiao Jiang, and Chaoqun Li

Adaptive Natural Gradient Learning Algorithms for Unnormalized
Statistical Models   427
   Ryo Karakida, Masato Okada, and Shun-ichi Amari

Octonion-Valued Neural Networks   435
   Călin-Adrian Popa

Reducing Redundancy with Unit Merging for Self-constructive
Normalized Gaussian Networks   444
   Jana Backhus, Ichigaku Takigawa, Hideyuki Imai, Mineichi Kudo,
   and Masanori Sugimoto

Learning to Enumerate   453
   Patrick Jörger, Yukino Baba, and Hisashi Kashima

Pattern Based on Temporal Inference   461
   Zeineb Neji, Marieme Ellouze, and Lamia Hadrich Belguith

Neural Networks Simulation of Distributed Control Problems
with State and Control Constraints   468
   Tibor Kmet and Maria Kmetova

The Existence and the Stability of Weighted Pseudo Almost Periodic
Solution of High-Order Hopfield Neural Network   478
   Chaouki Aouiti, Mohammed Salah M'hamdi, and Farouk Chérif

Sparse Extreme Learning Machine Classifier Using Empirical
Feature Mapping   486
   Takuya Kitamura

Three Approaches to Train Echo State Network Actors of Adaptive
Critic Design   494
   Petia Koprinkova-Hristova

Increase of the Resistance to Noise in Data for Neural Network Solution
of the Inverse Problem of Magnetotellurics with Group Determination
of Parameters   502
   Igor Isaev, Eugeny Obornev, Ivan Obornev, Mikhail Shimelevich,
   and Sergey Dolenko

Convergence of Multi-pass Large Margin Nearest Neighbor Metric
Learning   510
   Christina Göpfert, Benjamin Paassen, and Barbara Hammer

Short Papers

Spiking Neuron Model of a Key Circuit Linking Visual and Motor
Representations of Actions   521
   Mohammad Hovaidi Ardestani and Martin Giese

Analysis of the Effects of Periodic Forcing in the Spike Rate and Spike
Correlation's in Semiconductor Lasers with Optical Feedback.   523
   Carlos Quintero-Quiroz, Taciano Sorrentino, M.C. Torrent,
   and Cristina Masoller

Neuronal Functional Interactions Inferred from Analyzing Multivariate
Spike Trains Generated by Simple Models Simulations Using Frequency
Domain Analyses Available at Open Platforms   524
   Takeshi Abe, Yoshiyuki Asai, and Alessandro E.P. Villa

Controlling a Redundant Articulated Robot in Task Space
with Spiking Neurons   526
   Samir Menon, Vinay Sriram, Luis Kumanduri, Oussama Khatib,
   and Kwabena Boahen

Onset of Global Synchrony by Application of a Size-Dependent Feedback. . .   528
   August Romeo and Hans Supèr

Identification of Epileptogenic Rhythms in a Mesoscopic Neuronal Model. . .   529
   Maciej Jedynak, Antonio J. Pons, Jordi Garcia-Ojalvo,
   and Marc Goodfellow

Modulation of Wave Propagation in the Cortical Network
by Electric Fields   530
   Pol Boada-Collado, Julia F. Weinert, Maurizio Mattia,
   and Maria V. Sanchez-Vives

Investigation of SSEP by Means of a Realistic Computational Model
of the Sensory Cortex   532
   Elżbieta Gajewska-Dendek and Piotr Suffczyński

Exploration of a Mechanism to Form Bionic, Self-growing
and Self-organizing Neural Network   533
   Hailin Ma, Ning Deng, Zhiheng Xu, Yuzhe Wang, Yingjie Shang,
   Xu Yang, and Hu He

Living Neuronal Networks in a Dish: Network Science
and Neurological Disorders   534
   Sara Teller, Elisenda Tibau, and Jordi Soriano

Does the Default Network Represent the 'Model' in Model-Based
Decision-Making?   535
   Raphael Kaplan and Gustavo Deco

Experimental Approaches to Assess Connectivity in Living
Neuronal Networks   536
   Lluís Hernández-Navarro, Javier G. Orlandi, Jaume Casademunt,
   and Jordi Soriano

Spectral Analysis of Echo State Networks   537
   Pau Vilimelis Aceituno, Gang Yan, and Yang-Yu Liu

Adaptive Hierarchical Sensing   538
   Henry Schütze, Erhardt Barth, and Thomas Martinetz

Across-Trial Dynamics of Stimulus Priors in an Auditory
Discrimination Task   539
   Ainhoa Hermoso-Mendizabal, Alexandre Hyafil,
   Pavel Ernesto Rueda-Orozco, Santiago Jaramillo, David Robbe,
   and Jaime de la Rocha

Artificial Neural Network-Based Control Architecture: A Simultaneous
Top-Down and Bottom-Up Approach to Autonomous Robot Navigation   540
   Dalia-Marcela Rojas-Castro, Arnaud Revel, and Michel Ménard

Realization of Profit Sharing by Self-Organizing Map-Based Probabilistic
Associative Memory   541
   Takahiro Katayama and Yuko Osana

State-Dependent Information Processing in Gene Regulatory Networks   542
   Marçal Gabaldà-Sagarra and Jordi Garcia-Ojalvo

Patent Citation Network Analysis: Topology and Evolution of Patent
Citation Networks   543
   Péter Érdi

Patent Citation Network Analysis: Ranking: From Web Pages to Patents   544
Péter Érdi and Péter Bruck

Multistable Attractor Dynamics in Columnar Cortical Networks
Transitioning from Deep Anesthesia to Wakefulness   545
*Cristiano Capone, Nuria Tort-Colet, Maurizio Mattia,
and Maria V. Sanchez-Vives*

Modulation of Cortical Intrinsic Bistability and Complexity
in the Cortical Network   547
*Maria V. Sanchez-Vives, Julia F. Weinert, Beatriz Rebollo,
Adenauer G. Casali, Andrea Pigorini, Marcello Massimini,
and Mattia D'Andola*

A Neural Network for Visual Working Memory that Accounts
for Memory Binding Errors   548
João Barbosa and Albert Compte

Single-Neuron Sensory Coding Might Influence Performance
in a Monkey's Perceptual Discrimination Task   549
*Pau de Jorge, Verónica Nácher, Rogelio Luna, Jordi Soriano,
Ranulfo Romo, Gustavo Deco, and Adrià Tauste Campo*

Modelling History-Dependent Perceptual Biases in Rodents   550
Alexandre Hyafil, Ainhoa Hermoso Mendizabal, and Jaime de la Rocha

Applicability of Echo State Networks to Classify EEG Data
from a Movement Task   551
Lukas Hestermeyer and Gordon Pipa

Data Assimilation of EEG Observations by Neural Mass Models   553
Lara Escuain-Poole, Jordi Garcia-Ojalvo, and Antonio J. Pons

Functional Reorganization of Neural Networks Prior to Epileptic Seizures . . .   554
*Adrià Tauste Campo, Alessandro Principe, Rodrigo Rocamora,
and Gustavo Deco*

Attractor Models of Perceptual Decisions Making Exhibit Stochastic
Resonance   555
Genis Prat-Ortega, Klaus Wimmer, Alex Roxin, and Jaime de la Rocha

VLSI Design of a Neural Network Model for Detecting Planar Surface
from Local Image Motion   556
*Hisanao Akima, Satoshi Moriya, Susumu Kawakami, Masafumi Yano,
Koji Nakajima, Masao Sakurabah, and Shigeo Sato*

Learning Method for a Quantum Bit Network....................... 558
  Yoshihiro Osakabe, Shigeo Sato, Mitsunaga Kinjo, Koji Nakajima,
  Hisanao Akima, and Masao Sakuraba

Information-Theoretical Foundations of Hebbian Learning 560
  Claudius Gros and Rodrigo Echeveste

Artificial Neural Network Models for Forecasting Tourist Arrivals
to Barcelona... 561
  Bulent Alptekin and Cagdas Hakan Aladag

Experimental Study of Multistability and Attractor Dynamics in Winnerless
Neural Networks.. 562
  Ashok Chauhan and Alain Nogaret

Author Index 563

Contents – Part II

Deep Learning

Video Description Using Bidirectional Recurrent Neural Networks 3
  Álvaro Peris, Marc Bolaños, Petia Radeva, and Francisco Casacuberta

Tactile Convolutional Networks for Online Slip and Rotation Detection. 12
  Martin Meier, Florian Patzelt, Robert Haschke, and Helge J. Ritter

DeepPainter: Painter Classification Using Deep Convolutional
Autoencoders 20
  Omid E. David and Nathan S. Netanyahu

Revisiting Deep Convolutional Neural Networks for RGB-D Based
Object Recognition 29
  Lorand Madai-Tahy, Sebastian Otte, Richard Hanten, and Andreas Zell

Deep Learning for Emotion Recognition in Faces 38
  *Ariel Ruiz-Garcia, Mark Elshaw, Abdulrahman Altahhan,
  and Vasile Palade*

Extracting Muscle Synergy Patterns from EMG Data Using Autoencoders . . . 47
  *Martin Spüler, Nerea Irastorza-Landa, Andrea Sarasola-Sanz,
  and Ander Ramos-Murguialday*

Integration of Unsupervised and Supervised Criteria for Deep Neural
Networks Training 55
  Francisco Zamora-Martínez, Javier Muñoz-Almaraz, and Juan Pardo

Layer-Wise Relevance Propagation for Neural Networks with Local
Renormalization Layers 63
  *Alexander Binder, Grégoire Montavon, Sebastian Lapuschkin,
  Klaus-Robert Müller, and Wojciech Samek*

Analysis of Dropout Learning Regarded as Ensemble Learning. 72
  Kazuyuki Hara, Daisuke Saitoh, and Hayaru Shouno

The Effects of Regularization on Learning Facial Expressions
with Convolutional Neural Networks. 80
  Tobias Hinz, Pablo Barros, and Stefan Wermter

DeepChess: End-to-End Deep Neural Network for Automatic Learning
in Chess. 88
  Omid E. David, Nathan S. Netanyahu, and Lior Wolf

A Convolutional Network Model of the Primate Middle Temporal Area   97
  Bryan P. Tripp

Pseudo Boosted Deep Belief Network   105
  Tiehang Duan and Sargur N. Srihari

Keyword Spotting with Convolutional Deep Belief Networks and Dynamic
Time Warping   113
  Baptiste Wicht, Andreas Fischer, and Jean Hennebert

Computational Advantages of Deep Prototype-Based Learning   121
  Thomas Hecht and Alexander Gepperth

Deep Convolutional Neural Networks for Classifying Body Constitution   128
  Haiteng Li, Bin Xu, Nanyue Wang, and Jia Liu

Feature Extractor Based Deep Method to Enhance Online Arabic
Handwritten Recognition System.   136
  Mohamed Elleuch, Ramzi Zouari, and Monji Kherallah

On Higher Order Computations and Synaptic Meta-Plasticity
in the Human Brain.   145
  Stanisław Ambroszkiewicz

Compression of Deep Neural Networks on the Fly   153
  Guillaume Soulié, Vincent Gripon, and Maëlys Robert

Blind Super-Resolution with Deep Convolutional Neural Networks   161
  Clément Peyrard, Moez Baccouche, and Christophe Garcia

DNN-Buddies: A Deep Neural Network-Based Estimation Metric
for the Jigsaw Puzzle Problem   170
  Dror Sholomon, Omid E. David, and Nathan S. Netanyahu

A Deep Learning Approach for Hand Posture Recognition from Depth Data   179
  Thomas Kopinski, Fabian Sachara, Alexander Gepperth,
  and Uwe Handmann

Action Recognition in Surveillance Video Using ConvNets and Motion
History Image.   187
  Sheng Luo, Haojin Yang, Cheng Wang, Xiaoyin Che,
  and Christoph Meinel

Classification and Forecasting

Bi-Modal Deep Boltzmann Machine Based Musical Emotion Classification   199
  Moyuan Huang, Wenge Rong, Tom Arjannikov, Nan Jiang,
  and Zhang Xiong

StreamLeader: A New Stream Clustering Algorithm not Based
in Conventional Clustering...................................... 208
   Jaime Andrés-Merino and Lluís A. Belanche

Comparison of Methods for Community Detection in Networks 216
   Hassan Mahmoud, Francesco Masulli, Stefano Rovetta,
   and Amr Abdullatif

A Robust Evolutionary Optimisation Approach for Parameterising a Neural
Mass Model... 225
   Elham Zareian, Jun Chen, and Basabdatta Sen Bhattacharya

Kernel Depth Measures for Functional Data with Application
to Outlier Detection... 235
   Nicolás Hernández and Alberto Muñoz

Nesterov Acceleration for the SMO Algorithm 243
   Alberto Torres-Barrán and José R. Dorronsoro

Local Reject Option for Deterministic Multi-class SVM................ 251
   Johannes Kummert, Benjamin Paassen, Joris Jensen, Christina Göpfert,
   and Barbara Hammer

Palmprint Biometric System Modeling by DBC and DLA Methods
and Classifying by KNN and SVM Classifiers 259
   Raouia Mokni and Monji Kherallah

Ensemble Models of Learning Vector Quantization Based
on Bootstrap Resampling... 267
   Fumiaki Saitoh

Cluster Ensembles Optimization Using Coral Reefs
Optimization Algorithm.. 275
   Huliane M. Silva, Anne M.P. Canuto, Inácio G. Medeiros,
   and João C. Xavier-Júnior

Classification of Photo and Sketch Images Using Convolutional
Neural Networks.. 283
   Kazuma Sasaki, Madoka Yamakawa, Kana Sekiguchi,
   and Tetsuya Ogata

Day-ahead PV Power Forecast by Hybrid ANN Compared to the Five
Parameters Model Estimated by Particle Filter Algorithm.............. 291
   Emanuele Ogliari, Alberto Bolzoni, Sonia Leva, and Marco Mussetta

Extended Weighted Nearest Neighbor for Electricity Load Forecasting 299
   Mashud Rana, Irena Koprinska, Alicia Troncoso,
   and Vassilios G. Agelidis

Using Reservoir Computing and Trend Information for Short-Term
Streamflow Forecasting   308
   Sabrina G.T.A. Bezerra, Camila B. de Andrade,
   and Mêuser J.S. Valença

Effect of Simultaneous Time Series Prediction with Various Horizons
on Prediction Quality at the Example of Electron Flux in the Outer
Radiation Belt of the Earth.   317
   Irina Myagkova, Vladimir Shiroky, and Sergey Dolenko

A Time Series Forecasting Model Based on Deep Learning Integrated
Algorithm with Stacked Autoencoders and SVR for FX Prediction   326
   Hua Shen and Xun Liang

Multivariate Dynamic Kernels for Financial Time Series Forecasting.   336
   Mauricio Peña, Argimiro Arratia, and Lluís A. Belanche

Recognition and Navigation

Symbolic Association Using Parallel Multilayer Perceptron   347
   Federico Raue, Sebastian Palacio, Thomas M. Breuel, Wonmin Byeon,
   Andreas Dengel, and Marcus Liwicki

Solution of an Inverse Problem in Raman Spectroscopy
of Multi-component Solutions of Inorganic Salts
by Artificial Neural Networks.   355
   Alexander Efitorov, Tatiana Dolenko, Sergey Burikov, Kirill Laptinskiy,
   and Sergey Dolenko

Sound Recognition System Using Spiking and MLP Neural Networks.   363
   Elena Cerezuela-Escudero, Angel Jimenez-Fernandez,
   Rafael Paz-Vicente, Juan P. Dominguez-Morales,
   Manuel J. Dominguez-Morales, and Alejandro Linares-Barranco

Using Machine Learning Techniques to Recover Prismatic Cirrus Ice
Crystal Size from 2-Dimensional Light Scattering Patterns   372
   Daniel Priori, Giseli de Sousa, Mauro Roisenberg,
   Christopher Stopford, Evelyn Hesse, Emmanuel Salawu, Neil Davey,
   and Yi Sun

25 Years of CNNs: Can We Compare to Human Abstraction Capabilities?. . .   380
   Sebastian Stabinger, Antonio Rodríguez-Sánchez, and Justus Piater

A Combination Method for Reducing Dimensionality in Large Datasets   388
   Daniel Araújo, Jhoseph Jesus, Adrião Dória Neto, and Allan Martins

Two-Class with Oversampling Versus One-Class Classification
for Microarray Datasets   398
   Beatriz Pérez-Sánchez, Oscar Fontenla-Romero,
   and Noelia Sánchez-Maroño

Polar Sine Based Siamese Neural Network for Gesture Recognition   406
   Samuel Berlemont, Grégoire Lefebvre, Stefan Duffner,
   and Christophe Garcia

Day Types Identification of Algerian Electricity Load Using an Image
Based Two-Stage Approach   415
   Kheir Eddine Farfar and Mohamed Tarek Khadir

SMS Spam Filtering Using Probabilistic Topic Modelling and Stacked
Denoising Autoencoder   423
   Noura Al Moubayed, Toby Breckon, Peter Matthews,
   and A. Stephen McGough

Improving MDLSTM for Offline Arabic Handwriting Recognition
Using Dropout at Different Positions   431
   Rania Maalej and Monji Kherallah

A Neural Network Model for Solving the Feature Correspondence Problem . . .   439
   Ala Aboudib, Vincent Gripon, and Gilles Coppin

The Performance of a Biologically Plausible Model of Visual Attention
to Localize Objects in a Virtual Reality   447
   Amirhossein Jamalian, Frederik Beuth, and Fred H. Hamker

Pose-Invariant Object Recognition for Event-Based Vision with Slow-ELM . . .   455
   Rohan Ghosh, Tang Siyi, Mahdi Rasouli, Nitish V. Thakor,
   and Sunil L. Kukreja

Learning V4 Curvature Cell Populations from Sparse Endstopped Cells   463
   Antonio Rodríguez-Sánchez, Sabine Oberleiter, Hanchen Xiong,
   and Justus Piater

Recognition of Transitive Actions with Hierarchical Neural Network
Learning   472
   Luiza Mici, German I. Parisi, and Stefan Wermter

Rotation-Invariant Restricted Boltzmann Machine Using Shared
Gradient Filters   480
   Mario Valerio Giuffrida and Sotirios A. Tsaftaris

Improving Robustness of Slow Feature Analysis Based Localization
Using Loop Closure Events   489
   Benjamin Metka, Mathias Franzius, and Ute Bauer-Wersing

Self-Organizing Map for the Curvature-Constrained Traveling
Salesman Problem.   497
   Jan Faigl and Petr Váňa

Non-negative Kernel Sparse Coding for the Analysis of Motion Data   506
   Babak Hosseini, Felix Hülsmann, Mario Botsch, and Barbara Hammer

Effect of Neural Controller on Adaptive Cruise Control.   515
   Arden Kuyumcu and Neslihan Serap Şengör

Intelligent Speech-Based Interactive Communication Between Mobile
Cranes and Their Human Operators.   523
   Maciej Majewski and Wojciech Kacalak

Short Papers

Orthogonal Permutation Linear Unit Activation Function (OPLU).   533
   Artem Chernodub and Dimitri Nowicki

Smartphone Based Human Activity and Postural Transition Classification
with Deep Stacked Autoencoder Networks.   535
   *Luke Hicks, Yih-Ling Hedley, Mark Elshaw, Abdulrahman Altahhan,
   and Vasile Palade*

Accuracies and Number of Rules Extracted Using the Re-RX Algorithm
Family from a Pareto-Optimal Perspective   537
   Yoichi Hayashi, Guido Bologna, and Riku Hashiguchi

Finding an Hidden Common Partition in Duplex Structure-Function
Brain Networks.   539
   Casimiro Pio Carrino and Sebastiano Stramaglia

A Novel Quasi-Newton-Based Training Using Nesterov's Accelerated
Gradient for Neural Networks.   540
   Hiroshi Ninomiya

Use of Ensemble Approach and Stacked Generalization for Neural Network
Prediction of Geomagnetic Dst Index.   541
   Vladimir Shiroky, Irina Myagkova, and Sergey Dolenko

Artificial Neural Network for the Urinary Lithiasis Type Identification   542
   *Yasmina Nozha Mekki, Nadir Farah, Abdelatif Boutefnouchet,
   and KheirEddine Chettibi*

Artificial Neural Network-Based Modeling for Multi-scroll
Chaotic Systems   544
   Mohammed Amin Khelifa and Abdelkrim Boukabou

Detailed Remote Sensing of High Resolution Planetary Images by Artificial
Neural Network 545
   Marzieh Foroutan

Sentiment Analysis Using Extreme Learning Machine with Linear Kernel . . . 547
   Shangdi Sun and Xiaodong Gu

Neural Network with Local Receptive Fields for Illumination Effects 549
   Alejandro Lerer, Matthias S. Keil, and Hans Supèr

ROS Based Autonomous Control of a Humanoid Robot 550
   Ganesh Kumar Kalyani, Zhijun Yang, Vaibhav Gandhi, and Tao Geng

A Robotic Implementation of Drosophila Larvae Chemotaxis 552
   Daniel Malagarriga, Ivica Slavkov, James Sharpe, and Matthieu Louis

Author Index 553

From Neurons to Networks

Improved Chaotic Multidirectional Associative Memory

Hiroki Sato and Yuko Osana$^{(\boxtimes)}$

Tokyo University of Technology, 1401-1 Katakura, Hachioji, Tokyo, Japan
osana@stf.teu.ac.jp

Abstract. In this paper, we propose an Improved Chaotic Multidirectional Associative Memory (ICMAM). The proposed model is based on the Chaotic Multidirectional Associative Memory (CMAM) which can realize one-to-many associations. In the conventional CMAM, the one-to-many associative ability is very sensitive to chaotic neuron parameters. Moreover, although the Chaotic Multidirectional Associative Memory with adaptive scaling factor of refractoriness can select appropriate scaling factor of refractoriness α based on internal states of neurons automatically, their one-to-many association ability is lower than that of well-tuned Chaotic Multidirectional Associative Memory with variable scaling factor of refractoriness when the number of layers is large. In the proposed model, one-to-many association ability which does not depend on the number of layers is realized by dividing internal states of neurons by the number of layers. We carried out a series of computer experiments in order to demonstrate the effectiveness of the proposed model, and confirmed that the one-to-many association ability of this model almost equals to that of well-tuned Chaotic Multidirectional Associative Memory with variable scaling factor of refractoriness even when the number of layers is large.

1 Introduction

In the field of neural networks, a lot of associative memories have been proposed. However, most of these models can deal with only one-to-one associations [1,2]. In contrast, as the model which can realize one-to-many associations, some models which are based on the chaotic neuron models [3] or chaotic neuron-based models [4,5] have been proposed [6–11]. However, the association ability of neural networks composed of chaotic neuron models or chaotic neuron-based models are very sensitive to chaotic neuron parameters such as scaling factor of refractoriness α and damping factor k and so on. And, in these models, appropriate parameters have to determined by trial and error. Although the Chaotic Multidirectional Associative Memory with adaptive scaling factor of refractoriness [12] can select appropriate scaling factor of refractoriness α based on internal states of neurons automatically, their one-to-many association ability is lower than that of well-tuned Chaotic Multidirectional Associative Memory with variable scaling factor of refractoriness when the number of layers is large.

© Springer International Publishing Switzerland 2016
A.E.P. Villa et al. (Eds.): ICANN 2016, Part I, LNCS 9886, pp. 3–10, 2016.
DOI: 10.1007/978-3-319-44778-0_1

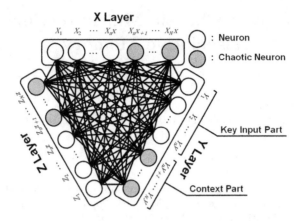

Fig. 1. Structure of proposed ICMAM.

In this paper, we propose an Improved Chaotic Multidirectional Associative Memory (ICMAM). In the proposed model, one-to-many association ability which does not depend on the number of layers is realized by dividing internal states of neurons by the number of layers.

2 Improved Chaotic Multidirectional Associative Memory

Here, we explain the proposed Improved Chaotic Multidirectional Associative Memory (ICMAM). The proposed ICMAM is based on the conventional Chaotic Multidirectional Associative Memory [7], and can realize one-to-many association of M-tuple binary patterns.

2.1 Structure

The proposed model has three or more layers as similar as the conventional Chaotic Multidirectional Associative Memory. Figure 1 shows the structure of the proposed model which has three layers. Each layer consists of two parts; (1) Key Input Part composed of conventional neuron models and (2) Context Part composed of chaotic neuron models [3]. Since chaotic neuron models in the Context Part change their states by chaos, plural patterns corresponding to the input common term can be recalled, that is, one-to-many association can be realized.

2.2 Learning Process

In the proposed model, pattern sets are memorized by the orthogonal learning. In the proposed model which has M layers, the connection weights from the layer x to the layer y is given by

$$\boldsymbol{w}^{yx} = \boldsymbol{X}_y(\boldsymbol{X}_x^T\boldsymbol{X}_x)^{-1}\boldsymbol{X}_x^T \tag{1}$$

$$\boldsymbol{w}^{xy} = \boldsymbol{X}_x(\boldsymbol{X}_y^T\boldsymbol{X}_y)^{-1}\boldsymbol{X}_y^T \tag{2}$$

and $\boldsymbol{X}_x$ and $\boldsymbol{X}_y$ are given by

$$\boldsymbol{X}_x = \{\boldsymbol{X}_x^{(1)}, \cdots, \boldsymbol{X}_x^{(p)}, \cdots, \boldsymbol{X}_x^{(P)}\} \tag{3}$$

$$\boldsymbol{X}_y = \{\boldsymbol{X}_y^{(1)}, \cdots, \boldsymbol{X}_y^{(p)}, \cdots, \boldsymbol{X}_y^{(P)}\} \tag{4}$$

where P is the number of the training pattern sets, and $\boldsymbol{X}_x^{(p)}$ is the pattern p which is stored in the layer x, $\boldsymbol{X}_y^{(p)}$ is the pattern p which is stored in the layer y. Each element of training patterns takes -1 or 1.

In the orthogonal learning, since the stored common pattern causes superimposed pattern in the recall process, the pattern sets including one-to-many relation can not be memorized. In the proposed model, each learning pattern is memorized together with its own contextual information in order to memorize the training set including one-to-many relations as similar as the conventional CMAM. Here, the contextual information patterns are generated randomly.

2.3   Recall Process

In the recall process of the proposed model, only neurons in the Key Input Part receives input in the first step. This is because we assume that contextual information is usually unknown for users. In the proposed model, since the chaotic neurons in the Context Part change their states by chaos, plural patterns corresponding to the input common pattern can be recalled.

Step 1: Input to Layer x
The input pattern is given to the key input part in the layer x.
Step 2: Propagation from Layer x to Other Layers
The information in the layer x is propagated to the key input part in other layers. The output of the neuron k in the key input part of the layer y ($y \neq x$) at the time t, $x_k^y(t)$ is calculated by

$$x_k^y(t) = f\left(\sum_{j=1}^{N^x} w_{kj}^{yx} x_j^x(t)\right) \tag{5}$$

where N^x is the number of neurons in the layer x, w_{kj}^{yx} is the connection weight from the neuron j in the layer x to the neuron k in the layer y, and $x_j^x(t)$ is the output of the neuron j in the layer x at the time t.
Step 3: Propagation from Other Layers to Layer x
The information in other layers is propagated to the layer x. The output of the neuron j in the Key Input Part of the layer x, $x_j^x(t+1)$, is given by

$$x_j^x(t+1) = f\left(\frac{1}{M-1}\sum_{y\neq x}^{M}\left(\sum_{k=1}^{n^y} w_{jk}^{xy} x_k^y(t)\right) + vA_j^x\right) \tag{6}$$

where M is the number of layers, n^y is the number of neurons in the key input part of the layer y, w_{jk}^{xy} is the connection weight from the neuron k in the layer y to the neuron j in the layer x, and v is the connection weight from the external input.

A_j^x is the external input to the neuron j in the layer x and is given by

$$
A_j^x = \begin{cases} 0 & (t < t_{in}) \\ \hat{x}_j^x(t_{in}) & (t_{in} \leq t) \end{cases}
\tag{7}
$$

$$
t_{in} = \min \left\{ t \left| \sum_{j=1}^{n^x} (\hat{x}_j^x(t) - \hat{x}_j^x(t-1)) = 0 \right. \right\}
\tag{8}
$$

$$
\hat{x}_j^x(t) = \begin{cases} 1 & (0 \leq x_j^x(t)) \\ -1 & (x_j^x(t) < 0) \end{cases}
\tag{9}
$$

where $\hat{x}_j^x(t)$ is the quantized output of the neuron j in the layer x at the time t.

The output of the neuron j of the Context Part in the layer x, $x_j^x(t+1)$ is given by

$$
x_j^x(t+1) = f \left(\frac{1}{M-1} \sum_{y \neq x}^{M} \left(\sum_{k=1}^{n^y} w_{jk}^{xy} \sum_{d=0}^{t} k_m^d x_k^d(t-d) \right) \right.
$$
$$
\left. - \alpha(t) \sum_{d=0}^{t} k_r^d x_j^x(t-d) \right)
\tag{10}
$$

where k_m and k_r are damping factors. And, $\alpha(t)$ is the scaling factor of refractoriness at the time t, and it is given by

$$
\alpha(t) = a + b \sin \left(c \cdot \frac{\pi}{12} \cdot t \right)
\tag{11}
$$

Step 4: Repeat
    Steps 2 and **3** are repeated.

3   Computer Experiment Results

Here, we show the computer experiment results in order to demonstrate of effectiveness of the proposed ICMAM. The experimental conditions is shown in Table 1. In the experiments, the N binary random pattern sets which have 1-to-N relation were memorized, and the common pattern is given to the network.

3.1   One-to-Many Association Ability

Here, we compared the one-to-many association ability in the 3~7-layered proposed ICMAM with the well-turned 3~7-layered conventional Chaotic Multidirectional Associative Memory with variable scaling factor of refractoriness

(Adjusted Model) and conventional Chaotic Multidirectional Associative Memory with adaptive scaling factor [12] (Conventional Model).

Figure 2 shows the one-to-many association ability of the proposed model, the adjusted model and the conventional model. As shown in this figure, the one-to-many association ability of the proposed model almost equals to that of the adjusted model. Moreover, the one-to-many association ability of the proposed model is superior to that of the adjusted model when the number of stored patterns are large.

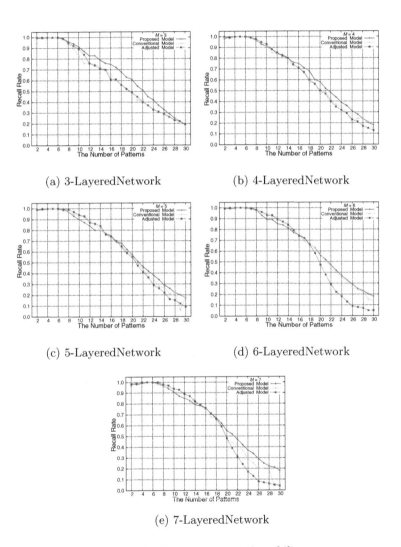

Fig. 2. One-to-many association ability.

3.2   One-to-Many Association Ability in Various Size Networks

Figure 3 shows the one-to-many association ability of the various size proposed model. In this experiments, we used the network composed of 300 or 400 or 500 neurons in the Key Input Part and 100 neurons in the Context Part.

From these results, we confirmed that the proposed model in various size has good one-to-many association ability as similar as in the result shown in Fig. 2.

Figure 4 shows the one-to-many association ability in the network which has 8 or 9 layers. In the conventional model, when the number of layers is large,

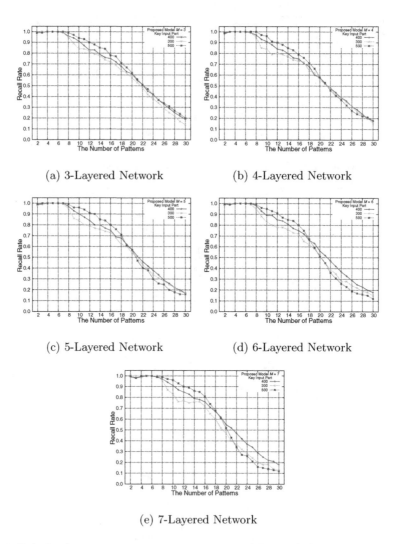

(a) 3-Layered Network

(b) 4-Layered Network

(c) 5-Layered Network

(d) 6-Layered Network

(e) 7-Layered Network

Fig. 3. Relation between one-to-many association ability and the number of neurons in key input part.

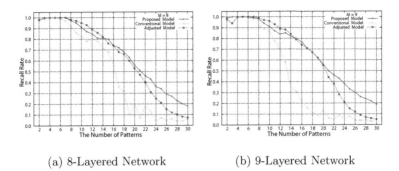

(a) 8-Layered Network (b) 9-Layered Network

Fig. 4. One-to-many association ability in 8 or 9-layered network.

Table 1. Experimental conditions

The number of neurons in key input part		400
The number of neurons in context part		100
Damping factor	k_m	0.86
Damping factor	k_r	0.89
Coefficient in scaling factor	a	0.9
Coefficient in scaling factor	b	0.47
Coefficient in scaling factor	c	2
Steepness parameter	ε	0.013
Connection weight from external input	v	10

one-to-many association ability decreases. In contrast, as shown in Fig. 4, one-to-many association ability of the proposed ICMAM which has 8 or 9 layers is almost similar as that of the proposed ICMAM when the number of layers are small.

4 Conclusion

In this paper, we have proposed the Improved Chaotic Multidirectional Associative Memory (ICMAM). The proposed model is based on the Chaotic Multidirectional Associative Memory (CMAM) [7] which can realize one-to-many associations. In the proposed model, one-to-many association ability which does not depend on the number of layers is realized by dividing internal states of neurons by the number of layers.

We carried out a series of computer experiments and confirmed that the proposed model has following features.

(1) One-to-many association ability of the proposed model is almost equal to that of the well-tuned Chaotic Multidirectional Associative Memory with variable scaling factor of the refractoriness.

(2) The parameters can be determined appropriately in various size networks even when the number of layers is large.

References

1. Kosko, B.: Bidirectional associative memories. IEEE Trans. Syst. Man Cybern. **18**(1), 49–60 (1988)

2. Hagiwara, M.: Multidirectional associative memory. In: Proceedings of IEEE and INNS International Joint Conference on Neural Networks, Washington, D.C., vol. 1, pp. 3–6 (1990)

3. Aihara, K., Takabe, T., Toyoda, M.: Chaotic neural networks. Phys. Lett. A **144**(6–7), 333–340 (1990)

4. Nakada, M., Osana, Y.: Chaotic complex-valued associative memory. In: Proceedings of International Symposium on Nonlinear Theory and Its Applications, Vancouver (2007)

5. Osana, Y.: Chaotic quaternionic associative memory. In: Proceedings of IEEE and INNS International Joint Conference on Neural Networks, Brisbane (2012)

6. Osana, Y., Hattori, M., Hagiwara, M.: Chaotic bidirectional associative memory. In: Proceedings of IEEE International Conference on Neural Networks, pp. 816–821 (1996)

7. Osana, Y., Hattori, M., Hagiwara, M.: Chaotic multidirectional associative memory. In: Proceedings of IEEE International Conference on Neural Networks, Washington, D.C., vol. 2, pp. 1210–1215 (1997)

8. Yano, Y., Osana, Y.: Chaotic complex-valued bidirectional associative memory. In: Proceedings of IEEE and INNS International Joint Conference on Neural Networks, Atlanta (2009)

9. Shimizu, Y., Osana, Y.: Chaotic complex-valued multidirectional associative memory. In: Proceedings of IASTED Artificial Intelligence and Applications, Innsbruck (2010)

10. Chino, T., Osana, Y.: Chaotic complex-valued multidirectional associative memory with adaptive scaling factor. In: Proceedings of IEEE and INNS International Joint Conference on Neural Networks, Dallas (2013)

11. Osana, Y.: Chaotic quaternionic associative memory. In: Proceedings of IEEE and INNS International Joint Conference on Neural Networks, Brisbane (2012)

12. Hayashi, N., Osana, Y.: Chaotic multidirectional associative memory with adaptive scaling factor of refractoriness. In: Proceedings of IEEE and INNS International Joint Conference on Neural Networks, Killarney (2015)

13. Osana, Y.: Recall and separation ability of chaotic associative memory with variable scaling factor. In: Proceedings of IEEE and INNS International Joint Conference on Neural Networks, Hawaii (2002)

Effect of Pre- and Postsynaptic Firing Patterns on Synaptic Competition

Nobuhiro Hinakawa[✉] and Katsunori Kitano

Department of Human and Computer Intelligence, Ritsumeikan University,
1-1-1 Nojihigashi, Kusatsu, Shiga 5258577, Japan
h@cns.ci.ritsumei.ac.jp, kitano@ci.ritsumei.ac.jp

Abstract. Synaptic plasticity is known to depend on the timing of pre and postsynaptic spikes, a.k.a. spike-timing-dependent plasticity (STDP). This implies that outcomes brought about by STDP should be sensitive to the dynamic properties of pre and postsynaptic neuron activity. Furthermore, because the classical model of STDP does not consider the effect of various pre and postsynaptic spike patterns on the outcome, it fails to reproduce the dependence of the synaptic plasticity polarity, namely the long-term potentiation or depression, on firing rates. In this study, we investigated the interplay between realistic pre and postsynaptic dynamic property models and a modified STDP model, reproducing the firing rate dependency. Our results showed that strengthened synapses depend on a combination of pre and postsynaptic properties as well as input firing rates, suggesting that a postsynaptic neuron may favor specific spike statistics and input firing rates may facilitate this tendency.

Keywords: STDP · Synaptic competition · Inter-spike intervals · MAT model

1 Introduction

Neurons in the brain connect with each other through a vast number of synapses responsible for neural information transfer. It is known that a synapse undergoes change in strength depending on the pre and postsynaptic neural activities, which is called Hebbian synaptic plasticity. In addition, it is supposed that this type of synaptic plasticity should be a neural substrate of higher-order functions, such as learning and memory.

The amount of change in synaptic strengths is determined by the timing of pre and postsynaptic spikes as well as their firing rates [1–3]. This suggests that the strengths should be sensitive to dynamic characteristics of pre and post-synaptic neurons. Indeed, a variety of spike statistic classes have been found, depending on the cortical regions and layers [4]. In most computational studies, however, theoretically-tractable assumptions have been imposed on such characteristics; presynaptic spike trains are characterized by a Poisson process whereas

© Springer International Publishing Switzerland 2016
A.E.P. Villa et al. (Eds.): ICANN 2016, Part I, LNCS 9886, pp. 11–18, 2016.
DOI: 10.1007/978-3-319-44778-0_2

postsynaptic spiking activity can be reproduced using the leaky integrate-and-fire (LIF) neuron model. A previous study introduced more realistic characteristics by using Gamma spike trains and the multi-timescale adaptive threshold (MAT) model [5,6]. The results of the study showed that the outcomes of synaptic competition through spike-timing-dependent plasticity (STDP) depend on combinations of pre and postsynaptic characteristics [5]. However, the dependence of the outcomes on firing rates was inconsistent with known experimental evidence that high frequency inputs induce long-term potentiation (LTP), whereas low frequency inputs induce long-term depression (LTD). This result was due to the nature of the STDP model [7] used. Therefore, the outcome of the interplay between the characteristics of pre and postsynaptic activity, and the more realistic STDP rule, on reproducing the firing rate dependence is still unclear.

In our research, we addressed this issue by incorporating the STDP rule proposed by Pfister and Gerstner (2006) into the previous study [9]. The STDP rule takes into consideration additional synaptic spikes, not solely a pair of a pre and a postsynaptic spikes. This successfully reproduces the firing rate dependence. We investigated the type of features that are preferred and strengthened by pre and postsynaptic spikes through synaptic competition under the STDP rule defined by the time between spikes, which we term spike patterns.

2   Methods

2.1   Postsynaptic Neuron Model

The dynamics of the postsynaptic neuron can be represented by the MAT model, which reproduces cortical spike patterns more accurately than any other neuron model, such as LIF model [6]. The membrane potential V of the MAT model obeys the following linear differential equation

$$\tau_\mathrm{m}\frac{dV}{dt} = V_\mathrm{rest} - V + \sum_i^{1000} g_i^\mathrm{ex}(t)\,(E_\mathrm{ex} - V) + \sum_i^{200} g_i^\mathrm{in}(t)\,(E_\mathrm{in} - V), \qquad (1)$$

where τ_m, V_rest, E_ex, and E_in are the membrane time constant, the resting membrane potential, and the reversal potential of excitatory and inhibitory synapses, respectively. $g_i^\mathrm{ex}(t)$ and $g_i^\mathrm{in}(t)$ are the conductance of the ith excitatory synapse and the ith inhibitory synapse, respectively. In addition, when the membrane potential V reaches the time-varying threshold $\theta(t)$, the neuron generates a neural spike without resetting the membrane potential. $\theta(t)$ is described in time as follows:

$$\theta(t) = \omega + \sum_l (\alpha_1 \mathrm{e}^{-(t-t_l)/\tau_1} + \alpha_2 \mathrm{e}^{-(t-t_l)/\tau_2}), \qquad (2)$$

where α_j and τ_j are the amount and the decay time constants of the threshold increase, respectively. ω is the time-invariant threshold. Each time-varying component of $\theta(t)$ increases simultaneously at spike time t_l by α_1, α_2 and then exponentially decays.

2.2   Synapse Model

The dynamics of the synaptic conductance is modeled by

$$\frac{dg_i^X}{dt} = -\frac{g_i^X}{\tau_X} + \hat{g}_i^X \sum_l \delta(t - t_l) \quad (X = \text{ex, in}), \tag{3}$$

where τ_X, $\hat{g}_i^X$, and $\delta(\cdot)$ are the time constant, the peak synaptic conductance, and the Dirac's delta function, respectively. While the peak conductance of inhibitory synapses was constant, the excitatory synapses changed according to the following description:

$$\hat{g}_i^{\text{ex}} \rightarrow \hat{g}_i^{\text{ex}} + g_{\max} w_i(t), \tag{4}$$

where $g_{\max}$ is the maximal synaptic conductance and $w(t)$ defines an amount of synaptic plasticity. To implement the STDP rule in our study, a triplet-based model with all-to-all interactions was used [9], in which the variable $w(t)$ changed as described below. The presynaptic spike, generated at time t_{pre}, triggers a change depending on the postsynaptic variable o_1 and the second presynaptic variable r_2 as follows:

$$w(t) \rightarrow w(t) - o_1(t)\left[A_2^- + A_3^- r_2(t - \epsilon)\right]. \tag{5}$$

Similarly, the postsynaptic spike, generated at time t_{post}, triggers a change depending on the presynaptic variable r_1 and the second postsynaptic variable o_2 as follows:

$$w(t) \rightarrow w(t) + r_1(t)\left[A_2^+ + A_3^+ o_2(t - \epsilon)\right]. \tag{6}$$

A_2^- and A_2^+ are the weight change amplitudes whenever there is a post-pre pair and pre-post pair, respectively. Similarly, A_3^- and A_3^+ are the triplet term amplitudes for depression and potentiation, respectively. If a presynaptic spike is generated, the presynaptic detectors r_1 and r_2 are updated by $r_1 = r_1 + 1$ and $r_2 = r_2 + 1$. Otherwise, the presynaptic detectors r_1 and r_2 decay in the following manner:

$$\frac{dr_1(t)}{dt} = -\frac{r_1(t)}{\tau_+}, \tag{7}$$

$$\frac{dr_2(t)}{dt} = -\frac{r_2(t)}{\tau_x}. \tag{8}$$

Similarly, if a postsynaptic spike is generated, the postsynaptic detectors o_1 and o_2 are updated by $o_1 = o_1 + 1$, and $o_2 = o_2 + 1$. Otherwise, the postsynaptic detectors o_1 and o_2 decay exponentially.

$$\frac{do_1(t)}{dt} = -\frac{o_1(t)}{\tau_-}, \tag{9}$$

$$\frac{do_2(t)}{dt} = -\frac{o_2(t)}{\tau_y}. \tag{10}$$

τ_+, τ_x, τ_-, and τ_y are the time constants of the corresponding variables.

2.3 Presynaptic Spike Trains

Inter-spike intervals (ISIs) of a presynaptic spike train obey a gamma distribution. An ISI $T_l = t_l - t_{l-1}$ was drawn from a gamma distribution;

$$T_l \sim p(T; k, \lambda) = \frac{\lambda^k T^{k-1} e^{-\lambda T}}{\Gamma(k)}. \tag{11}$$

k is the shape parameter, λ is the rate parameter, and $\Gamma(k)$ is the gamma function. The mean ISIs, $\bar{T}$, is $\bar{T} = \frac{k}{\lambda}$. The shape parameter k defines the shape of the distribution. If $k = 1$, the distribution is an exponential distribution generating a Poisson spike train. The presynaptic spike train shows nearly periodic firing for larger k, whereas it shows burst firing for a smaller $k(<1)$.

2.4 Numerical Simulations

In order to examine how synaptic competition is affected by interplay between presynaptic inputs and postsynaptic dynamics, we compared different combinations of pre and postsynaptic characteristics. Input spikes were generated by the gamma distribution with various values for the shape parameter. The LIF and MAT models were implemented to represent the postsynaptic neuron (results shown below are obtained using the MAT model). In our final investigation, 1,000 excitatory synapses were divided into 4 subgroups (250 synapses per a subgroup). Synapses in each subgroup delivered spike trains generated by gamma distributions with an identical shape parameter; the parameter for the i-th group was set to $k = 2^{i-1}$.

The parameters of the MAT model were the same as those used in a previous study [5]. Other model parameters were taken from another previous study [9].

3   Results

For various input firing rates, we conducted numerical simulations using our computational model until the distribution of synaptic strengths reached a stationary state. We focused on the stationary distribution of synaptic strengths and postsynaptic firing characteristics, firing rate, and coefficients of variation (Cv) of the postsynaptic neuron ISIs, as a function of the presynaptic spike trains.

3.1 Inputs with an Identical Value of k

We first examined synaptic competition in the case where input spike trains were generated by a gamma distribution with identical shape parameter values ($k = 1$) for all excitatory synapses. Figure 1 shows the stationary distribution of synaptic strengths for various input firing rates and the spike statistics of the postsynaptic neurons in the stationary state. Figures 1a–d show that all distributions exhibited bimodal shapes, in which there existed two populations

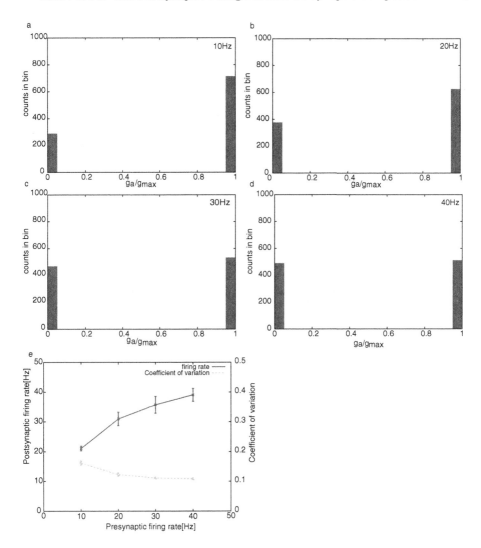

Fig. 1. Synaptic competition and activity regulation when the MAT model received Poisson spike trains ($k = 1$). **a.** Stationary distributions of synaptic strengths for an input firing rate of 10 spikes/s. The abscissa indicates the normalized synaptic conductance. **b**, **c**, and **d** are similar to **a**, but for 20 spikes/s, 30 spikes/s, and 40 spikes/s, respectively. **e.** Dependencies of postsynaptic firing rates and coefficients of variation (Cv) of postsynaptic ISIs on the input firing rates.

of strengthened synapses (around 1) and weakened synapses (around 0). As the input firing rate was increased, the population of strengthened synapses became smaller, and the population of weakened ones became larger. However, the change in the fraction of the two populations could be seen with an increase in the input firing rate of up to 30 spikes/s. Figure 1e shows the postsynaptic firing rate and coefficients of variation (Cv) of the postsynaptic ISIs. The firing rate of postsynaptic neurons increased moderately, suggesting that the activity regulation by the STDP was successful, but weak. The Cv of postsynaptic ISIs were kept low due to the dynamic nature of the MAT model.

Figures 2a–d show the mean synaptic conductances as a function of the input firing rate for various values of the shape parameter ($k = 0.5, 1, 4,$ and 8). When $k = 0.5$ and 1, averaged synaptic strengths monotonically decreased with an increase in input firing rates. In contrast, for $k = 4$ and 8, they differently depended on the input firing rates, suggesting that the interplay between the postsynaptic dynamics and the input spike patterns modulated the process of synaptic competition.

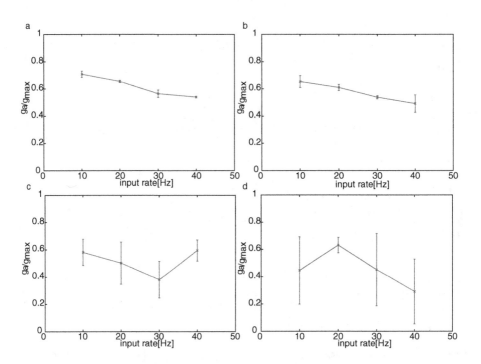

Fig. 2. Averaged synaptic strengths when the MAT model received Gamma spike trains. **a.** The averaged synaptic strengths if input spikes were generated by the Gamma distribution with $k = 0.5$ and various input firing rates. The abscissa axis indicates the input firing rate. **b, c,** and **d** are similar to **a**, but for $k = 1$, $k = 4$, and $k = 8$, respectively.

3.2   Inputs with Different Values of k

Next, in order to see if synapses delivering a specific spike train were selectively potentiated, we examined synaptic competition in the case where input spikes were generated by a mixture of spike trains with different regularity (see Methods). While synapses in the subgroup 1 provided spike trains with $k = 1$, namely

Poisson spike trains, those in subgroup 4 did so with more regular spike trains. Figure 3a shows averaged synapse strengths within a subgroup for different input firing rates. For the lower input firing rates (*le* 20 spikes/), the averaged synaptic strengths for the subgroup with a smaller k seemed more increased. In contrast, for increased input firing rates ($\geq$30 spikes/s), synapses in the subgroup with a larger k was likely to be more potentiated. In Fig. 3b, the postsynaptic firing rate and coefficients of variation (Cv) of postsynaptic ISIs are shown as a function of the input firing rate. The change in the postsynaptic firing rate was similar to that in Fig. 1, and activity regulation worked moderately for this condition as well. However, the ISI Cvs decreased with an increase in the input firing rate.

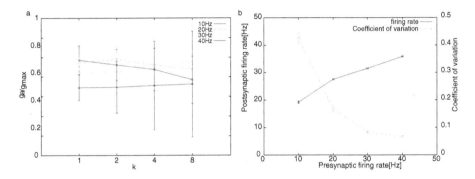

Fig. 3. Synaptic strengths and postsynaptic spike statistics when the MAT model received a mixture of Gamma spike trains with different regularity ($k = 1, 2, 4,$ and 8). **a.** The averages of synaptic strengths within a subpopulation for various input firing rates. The abscissa indicates the values of the shape parameter k. **b.** Dependencies of postsynaptic firing rates and coefficients of variation (Cv) of postsynaptic ISIs on the input firing rates.

4   Discussion

If the shape parameter k is identical for all input spike trains, we obtain results similar to those in the previous study. Both methodologies give the distribution of synaptic strengths, the shift between strengthened and weakened populations with an increase in input firing rates, and a moderate increase in the postsynaptic firing rate [7]. Thus, employing the STDP rule did not cause differences under this condition.

However, in the case of mixture spike trains with different spike patterns (k), the STDP rule could strengthen the synapses delivering spike trains with larger k, that is, more periodic spike trains with an increase in the input firing rate. If the dynamics of the postsynaptic neuron was modeled by the LIF neuron, such a preference was not seen for any input firing rates (data not shown). These results suggest that the determination of which synapses are potentiated is determined by a combination of the presynaptic spike train structure (k) and the dynamic property of the postsynaptic neuron (This is found using either the LIF or MAT models).

Thus, we conclude (i) the dynamic feature of postsynaptic neurons could favor a specific spike pattern through synaptic competition brought about by STDP and (ii) such a preference depends on input firing rates. Although the former conclusion was already obtained by the previous study applying the classical STDP rule [5,7], the latter was achieved only through our use of the employed STDP rule.

References

1. Markram, H., Lubke, J., Frotscher, M., Sakmann, B.: Regulation of synaptic efficacy by coincidence of postsynaptic APs and EPSPs. Science **275**, 213–215 (1997)
2. Bi, G.-Q., Poo, M.-M.: Synaptic modifications in cultured hippocampal neurons: dependence on spike timing, synaptic strength, and postsynaptic cell type. J. Neurosci. **18**, 10464–10472 (1998)
3. Bliss, T.V., Lomo, T.: Long-lasting potentiation of synaptic transmission in the dentate area of the anaesthetized rabbit following stimulation of the perforant path. J. Physiol. **232**, 331–356 (1973)
4. Shinomoto, S., Miyazaki, Y., Tamura, H., Fujita, I.: Regional and laminar differences in in vivo firing patterns of primate cortical neurons. J. Neurophysiol. **94**, 567–575 (2005)
5. Ito, H., Kitano, K.: Pre- and postsynaptic properties regulate synaptic competition through spike-timing-dependent plasticity. In: Wermter, S., Weber, C., Duch, W., Honkela, T., Koprinkova-Hristova, P., Magg, S., Palm, G., Villa, A.E.P. (eds.) ICANN 2014. LNCS, vol. 8681, pp. 733–740. Springer, Heidelberg (2014)
6. Kobayashi, R., Tsubo, Y., Shinomoto, S.: Made-to-order spiking neuron model equipped with a multi-timescale adaptive threshold. Front. Comput. Neurosci. **3**, 9 (2009)
7. Song, S., Miller, K.D., Abbott, L.F.: Competitive Hebbian learning through spike-timing-dependent synaptic plasticity. Nat. Neurosci. **3**, 919–926 (2000)
8. Cateau, H., Fukai, T.: A stochastic method to predict the consequence of arbitrary forms of spike-timing-dependent plasticity. Neural Comput. **15**, 597–620 (2003)
9. Pfister, J.P., Gerstner, W.: Triplets of spikes in a model of spike-timing-dependent plasticity. J. Neurosci. **26**, 9673–9682 (2006)

Asymmetries in Synaptic Connections and the Nonlinear Fokker-Planck Formalism

Roseli S. Wedemann[1(✉)] and Angel R. Plastino[2]

[1] Instituto de Matemática e Estatística, Universidade do Estado do Rio de Janeiro,
Rua São Francisco Xavier, 524, Rio de Janeiro, RJ 20550-900, Brazil
roseli@ime.uerj.br
[2] CeBio, Universidad del Noroeste de la Provincia de Buenos Aires,
UNNOBA-Conicet, Roque Saenz Peña 456, Junin, Argentina
arplastino@unnoba.edu.ar

Abstract. In previous work we have developed illustrative, neuro-computational models to describe mechanisms associated with mental processes. In these efforts, we have considered mental processes in phenomena such as neurosis, creativity, consciousness/unconsciousness, and some characteristics of the psychoses. Memory associativity is a key feature in the theoretical description of these phenomena, and much of our work has focused on modeling this mechanism. In traditional neural network models of memory, the symmetry of synaptic connections is a necessary condition for reaching stationary states. The assumption of symmetric weights seems however to be biologically unrealistic. Efforts to model stationary network states with asymmetric weights are mathematically complex and are usually applied to restricted situations. This has motivated us to explore the possibility of a new approach to the synaptic symmetry problem, based on its analogies with some features of the nonlinear Fokker-Planck formalism.

Keywords: Mental functions · Memory · Asymmetry · Nonlinear Fokker-Planck equation

1 Introduction

Much of our previous work [1–3] regards the search for neuronal network mechanisms, whose emergent states underlie behavioral aspects traditionally studied by psychiatry, psychoanalysis and neuroscience [4–9]. A working hypothesis in neuroscience is that human memory is encoded in the neural net of the brain, and associativity is frequently used to describe mental processes, both in normal and pathological functioning. Neuronal models of associative memory [10] have therefore formed a central component of our descriptions.

In traditional neural network models of memory, such as the Hopfield model [10], the symmetry of synaptic connections is a necessary mathematical requirement for reaching stationary states (memory) [10,11]. This is the case both

© Springer International Publishing Switzerland 2016
A.E.P. Villa et al. (Eds.): ICANN 2016, Part I, LNCS 9886, pp. 19–27, 2016.
DOI: 10.1007/978-3-319-44778-0_3

when using the Boltzmann Machine (BM) procedure, as when employing more recent approaches based on the Generalized Simulated Annealing (GSA) algorithm [12]. Real biological neural networks, however, do not seem to comply with the synaptic symmetry condition. We then face the curious situation that the main mathematical-mechanistic neural models for memory are based on an assumption that is at odds with biological reality. There have been efforts to model stationary memory attractor states with asymmetric weights, but they are mathematically complex and usually applicable only to restricted situations [13,14]. In spite of these interesting attempts, and even though memory modeling with neural networks has been an active field of research for decades, the (a)symmetry issue remains largely an unexplored (and almost forgotten) open problem. This indicates the need to consider new alternative approaches to this subject. Our main aim in the present exploratory work is to point out basic similarities between the synaptic symmetry problem and some aspects of the nonlinear Fokker-Planck (NLFP) dynamics. These connections may lead to a new possible way to address the symmetry problem in neural networks. Here we advance the first steps in the development of a formalism based on the nonlinear Fokker-Planck equation, which we summarize in this paper, along with some preliminary results. A more detailed discussion is being prepared for an extended publication.

In previous work, we have used the Boltzmann Machine [10] and Generalized Simulated Annealing [12] to simulate memory. In the BM and GSA, pattern retrieval on the net is achieved by a simulated annealing (SA) process, where the temperature T is gradually lowered by an annealing schedule α. For a BM or GSA network with N nodes, where each node i has a discrete state S_i in $\{-1, 1\}$, it is a necessary condition for the network to have stable states that synaptic weights between nodes i and j obey $w_{ij} = w_{ji}$. One can then define an Energy function, representing the potential energy corresponding to the interactions between neurons,

$$E(\{S_i\}) = -\frac{1}{2} \sum_{ij} w_{ij} S_i S_j, \tag{1}$$

and stored memories correspond to minimum energy (stable) states, which are attractors in the memory retrieval mechanism (SA process).

In the SA process, the energy surface is sampled according to the following transition probabilities. For the Boltzmann Machine (BM)

$$P_{BG}(S_i \rightarrow -S_i) = \frac{1}{1 + \exp \frac{(E(\{-S_i\}) - E(\{S_i\}))}{T}}, \tag{2}$$

and for the Generalized Simulated Annealing or Tsallis Machine (GSA) [12]

$$P_{GSA}(S_i \rightarrow -S_i) = \frac{1}{\left[1 + (q-1)\frac{(E(\{-S_i\}) - E(\{S_i\}))}{T}\right]^{\frac{1}{q-1}}}. \tag{3}$$

These transition probabilities tend to take the system from a current state towards a final, more favorable minimum energy state (although energy may increase at intermediate steps).

In Sect. 2, we briefly review neural network models as related to basic theory of Dynamical Systems. We then introduce basic aspects of the Fokker-Planck formalism. In Subsect. 4.2, we show that it is possible to introduce a drift or force term not arising from the gradient of a potential, which is related to asymmetric couplings, and still achieve stationary states for the probability density function, in the phase space describing the system. We also mention further developments and present our conclusions in the last section.

2   Dynamical Systems and Neural Networks

For a continuous deterministic dynamical system with phase space variables $\{X_1, X_2, \cdots, X_N\}$, considering that there is no noise, the equations of motion can be expressed as

$$\frac{dX_1}{dt} = G_1(X_1, X_2, \cdots X_N)$$

$$\vdots$$

$$\frac{dX_N}{dt} = G_N(X_1, X_2, \cdots X_N), \tag{4}$$

which in self-explanatory vector notation is expressed as $\frac{d\mathbf{X}}{dt} = \mathbf{G}(\mathbf{X})$, with $\mathbf{X}, \mathbf{G} \in \Re^N$. That is, the time evolution of the system's state $\mathbf{X}$ is described by a phase space flux given by the vectorial field $\mathbf{G}$. Neural networks have been widely studied within this framework [10]. In neural network models, the synaptic weight w_{ij} expresses the intensity of the influence of neuron j on neuron i (the coupling). So the net signal input to neuron i is given by

$$u_i = \sum_j w_{ij} V_{O_j}, \tag{5}$$

where V_{O_j} is the output signal of neuron j.

It is possible to generalize the McCulloch-Pitts (discrete activation) neural model, in order to consider continuous state variables [10,11], so that V_{O_i} (in equilibrium) is updated by a continuous function of u_i,

$$V_{O_i}(t + \Delta t) = g(u_i(t)). \tag{6}$$

In Eq. (6), the activation function $g(u)$ is usually nonlinear and saturates for large values of $|u|$, such as a sigmoid or $\tanh(u)$. One possible continuous-time rule for updating the V_{O_i} [11,15], is the set of differential equations

$$\frac{dV_{O_i}}{dt} = \frac{-V_{O_i} + g(u_i)}{\tau_i} = G_i(V_{O_1}, V_{O_2}, \ldots), \tag{7}$$

where τ_i are suitable time constants.

In traditional neural network models of memory, such as the Hopfield model, BM and GSA, $w_{ij} = w_{ji}$ is a necessary condition for reaching stationary states (memory). This symmetry restriction seems to be biologically unrealistic. In this contribution we comment on the similarities between the synaptic symmetry problem and some features of the nonlinear Fokker-Planck dynamics, which may shed new light on this problem and suggest possible ways to tackle it.

3   Fokker-Planck Equation

We now consider an ensemble of identical systems, each consisting of N elements, that evolve from different initial conditions. This ensemble is described by a time-dependent probability density in phase space $\mathcal{P}(X_1, \cdots, X_N, t)$ obeying the Liouville equation

$$\frac{\partial \mathcal{P}}{\partial t} + \sum_{i=1}^{N} \frac{\partial(\mathcal{P}G_i)}{\partial X_i} = 0. \tag{8}$$

If the system presents noisy behavior, it is necessary to add a new diffusion-like term in Eq. (8), which results in the Fokker-Planck equation (FPE)

$$\frac{\partial \mathcal{P}}{\partial t} = D \left(\sum_{i=1}^{N} \frac{\partial^2 \mathcal{P}}{\partial X_i^2} \right) - \sum_{i=1}^{N} \frac{\partial(\mathcal{P}G_i)}{\partial X_i}, \tag{9}$$

where D is the diffusion coefficient and the second term on the right, involving the field G, is referred to as the *drift* term. We shall call G the *drift* field. If

$$G_1 = -\partial V / \partial X_1,$$
$$\vdots$$
$$G_N = -\partial V / \partial X_N, \tag{10}$$

for some potential function $V(\boldsymbol{X})$, there is a Boltzmann-Gibbs-like stationary solution to Eq. (9),

$$\mathcal{P}_{BG} = \frac{1}{Z} \exp\left[-\frac{1}{D} V(\boldsymbol{X}) \right], \tag{11}$$

where Z is an appropriate normalization constant. That is, $\mathcal{P}_{BG}$ satisfies (9) with $\frac{\partial \mathcal{P}_{BG}}{\partial t} = 0$. The distribution $\mathcal{P}_{BG}$ maximizes the Boltzmann-Gibbs entropy S_{BG} under the constraints of normalization and the mean value $\langle V \rangle$ of the potential V.

Note that a dynamical system with a flux in phase space of the form (10) (gradient form) corresponds to a system that evolves so as to minimize V, *i.e.* *down-hill* along the potential energy surface. For a field G of the form (10) one has,

$$\frac{\partial G_i}{\partial X_j} = \frac{\partial G_j}{\partial X_i} = \frac{\partial^2 V}{\partial X_i \partial X_j}. \tag{12}$$

In the case of a Hopfield Neural Network, if the activation $g(u)$ is linear, for example in Eq. (7), $G_i \propto \sum_j w_{ij} X_j$ (corresponding to linear forces),

$$\frac{\partial G_i}{\partial X_j} = w_{ij}, \tag{13}$$

and therefore, by Eq. (12), $w_{ij} = w_{ji}$. We see that the general condition (12), that guarantees that the Fokker-Planck dynamics evolves towards a stationary Boltzmann-Gibbs distribution (11), is very similar to the synaptic symmetry requirement, necessary for a neural network to evolve towards minima of an energy surface. This similarity is, of course, also closely related to the fact that the simulated annealing technique provides a useful algorithm to find the minima of the network's energy landscape. In the Fokker-Planck case, however, it is possible to relax the condition (12), considering more general drift fields, and still have a dynamics that leads to a stationary Boltzmann-Gibbs distribution. This suggests that the Fokker-Planck scenario with non-gradient drift fields may be relevant to the synaptic symmetry problem. In the following sections we explore some basic aspects of this scenario, within the more general context of the nonlinear Fokker-Planck equation.

4   Nonlinear Fokker-Planck Equation

In [16], Ribeiro, Nobre and Curado state: "The linear differential equations in physics are, in many cases, valid for media characterized by specific conditions, like homogeneity, isotropy, and translational invariance, with particles interacting through short-range forces and with a dynamical behavior characterized by short-time memories". It is possible to introduce a nonlinear diffusion term to the FPE to describe a physical ensemble of interacting particles, so that the nonlinearity is an effective description of the interactions [16–20]. Physical systems characterized by spatial disorder and/or long-range interactions seem to be natural candidates for this formalism, which has recently attracted considerable attention from the complex systems research community.

We thus use the nonlinear Fokker-Planck equation (NLFP)

$$\frac{\partial \mathcal{P}}{\partial t} = D \left[\sum_{i=1}^{N} \frac{\partial^2}{\partial X_i^2} \left(\mathcal{P}^{2-q} \right) \right] - \sum_{i=1}^{N} \frac{\partial (\mathcal{P} G_i)}{\partial X_i}, \tag{14}$$

to study systems which may deviate from the linear description. Since we need to model stable properties of interesting physical systems, such as the stored memory states in a neural network, we search for possible stationary solutions to Eq. (14).

4.1   Stationary Solution - G of Gradient Form

In the most frequently studied case, where the field G is of the gradient form (10), the stationary solution of the NLFP is found by solving,

$$D\left[\sum_{i=1}^{N}\frac{\partial^2}{\partial X_i^2}\left(\mathcal{P}^{2-q}\right)\right] - \sum_{i=1}^{N}\frac{\partial(\mathcal{P}G_i)}{\partial X_i} = 0, \tag{15}$$

considering the Tsallis ansatz [20]

$$\mathcal{P}_q = A[1 - (1 - q)\beta V(\boldsymbol{X})]^{\frac{1}{1-q}}, \tag{16}$$

where A and β are constants to be determined. One finds that the ansatz given by Eq. (16) is a stationary solution of the NLFP equation, if

$$A = [(2 - q)\beta D]^{\frac{1}{q-1}}. \tag{17}$$

We call Eq. (16) the q-exponential ansatz. As already mentioned, it constitutes a stationary solution of the NLFP equation, when G is minus the gradient of a potential V (Eq. (10)), and A and β satisfy Eq. (17). The distribution $\mathcal{P}_q$ is also called a q-maxent distribution because it optimizes the nonextensive q-entropy S_q, under the constraints of normalization and the mean value of the potential V [17,20]. In the limit $q \to 1$, the q-maxent stationary distribution (16) reduces to the Boltzmann-Gibbs one (11), with $\beta = 1/D$.

4.2   Stationary Solution - G Not of the Gradient Form

Now we consider the NLFP equation, with a drift term not arising from the gradient of a potential and with the form

$$\boldsymbol{G} = \boldsymbol{F} + \boldsymbol{E}, \tag{18}$$

where $\boldsymbol{F}$ is equal to minus the gradient of some potential $V(\boldsymbol{X})$, while $\boldsymbol{E}$ does not come from a potential function (that is, we have $\partial E_i/\partial X_j \neq \partial E_j/\partial X_i$). We then substitute this G and $\mathcal{P}_q$ (Eq. (16)) in the stationary NLFP Eq. (15) and obtain

$$D\left[\sum_{i=1}^{N}\frac{\partial^2}{\partial X_i^2}\left(\mathcal{P}_q^{2-q}\right)\right] - \left[\sum_{i=1}^{N}\frac{\partial(\mathcal{P}_q F_i)}{\partial X_i}\right] - \left[\sum_{i=1}^{N}\frac{\partial(\mathcal{P}_q E_i)}{\partial X_i}\right] = 0. \tag{19}$$

The first two terms in Eq. (19) vanish, because we know that $\mathcal{P}_q$ is a stationary solution of Eq. (15), when only the gradient field $\boldsymbol{F}$ is present. In order for $\mathcal{P}_q$ to satisfy (19), we then require $\sum_{i=1}^{N}\partial(\mathcal{P}_q E_i)/\partial X_i = 0$. If this relation is satisfied, then $\mathcal{P}_q$ is also a stationary solution of the full NLFP equation, including the non-gradient term corresponding to $\boldsymbol{E}$. We therefore require

$$\sum_{i=1}^{N}\frac{\partial}{\partial X_i}\left(E_i[1 - (1 - q)\beta V]^{\frac{1}{1-q}}\right) = 0, \tag{20}$$

This equation constitutes a consistency requirement that the potential function V, the non-gradient field $\boldsymbol{E}$, the inverse temperature β, and the entropic parameter q have to satisfy in order that the nonlinear Fokker-Planck equation admits a stationary solution of the q-maxent form. In the most general β-dependent situation, the condition given by Eq. (20) leads to a rather complicated relation between the non-gradient component E and the potential V. However, there are cases where a β-independent set of constraints can be obtained. We illustrate this with a two-dimensional example. Consider two-dimensional fields F and G with components of the form,

$$
\begin{aligned}
(F_1;\ F_2) &= (-w_{11}X_1 - w_{12}X_2;\ -w_{22}X_2 - w_{12}X_1) \\
(E_1;\ E_2) &= (h_{11}X_1 + h_{12}X_2;\ h_{21}X_1 + h_{22}X_2),
\end{aligned}
\tag{21}
$$

with the w_{ij} and h_{ij} constant real parameters. The field F is minus the gradient of the potential

$$
V(X_1, X_2) = \frac{1}{2}\left(w_{11}X_1^2 + 2w_{12}X_1X_2 + w_{22}X_2^2\right).
\tag{22}
$$

It can be verified after some algebra that the q-maxent distribution (16) is a stationary solution of the NLFP equation, if the parameters characterizing the potential V and the (non-gradient) drift term E satisfy,

$$
\begin{aligned}
h_{11} &= h_{22} = w_{12} = 0, \\
w_{11}h_{12} &+ w_{22}h_{21} = 0.
\end{aligned}
\tag{23}
$$

We see that we have a family of noisy dynamical systems (described by NLFP equations) characterized by 3 independent parameters, that have q-maxent stationary solutions in spite of having drift fields not necessarily arising from a potential. This can be appreciated from the fact that the constraints (23) are compatible with $h_{12} \neq h_{21}$. Therefore, the drift field given by Eq. (21) does not necessarily comply with the symmetry restriction described by Eq. (12), which is akin to the standard symmetry condition in neural networks.

We are preparing an extended manuscript with a more detailed and general discussion of the ideas that we presented here briefly, due to space limitations. There we plan to explore systematically the conditions for having a q-maxent stationary state in more general scenarios described by NLFP equations, where the deterministic part of the concomitant dynamics involves a phase space flux not having the gradient form.

5   Conclusions

Inspired on the symmetry problem in neural networks, we explored properties of multi-dimensional NLFP equations endowed with drift fields not arising from a potential. We considered drift fields having both a gradient term and a non-gradient contribution. The non-gradient component of the drift field exhibits asymmetric features akin to those associated with the dynamics of neural networks with asymmetric synaptic weights. We identified cases where a NLFP equation having a non-gradient drift field still has a stationary solution of the q-maxent form (*i.e.* a q-exponential of the potential associated with the gradient part of the drift field). In future contributions, we plan to continue exploring the connections between the NLFP equation and the synaptic symmetry problem in the dynamics of neural networks, in order to apply the formalism of a non-potential drift term to account for attractor states in neuronal circuits, with asymmetric synaptic interactions.

Acknowledgments. We acknowledge financial support from the Brazilian National Research Council (CNPq), the Rio de Janeiro State Research Foundation (FAPERJ) and the Brazilian agency which funds graduate studies (CAPES).

References

1. Vidal de Carvalho, L.A., Quintella Mendes, D., Wedemann, R.S.: Creativity and delusions: the dopaminergic modulation of cortical maps. In: Sloot, P.M.A., Abramson, D., Bogdanov, A.V., Gorbachev, Y.E., Dongarra, J., Zomaya, A.Y. (eds.) ICCS 2003, Part I. LNCS, vol. 2657, pp. 511–520. Springer, Heidelberg (2003)
2. Wedemann, R.S., Donangelo, R., Vidal de Carvalho, L.A.: Generalized memory associativity in a network model for the neuroses. Chaos **19**(1), 015116 (2009)
3. Wedemann, R.S., Vidal de Carvalho, L.A.: Some things psychopathologies can tell us about consciousness. In: Villa, A.E.P., Duch, W., Érdi, P., Masulli, F., Palm, G. (eds.) ICANN 2012, Part I. LNCS, vol. 7552, pp. 379–386. Springer, Heidelberg (2012)
4. Freud, S.: Introductory Lectures on Psycho-Analysis, Standard Edition. W. W. Norton and Company, New York, London (1966). First German edition (1917)
5. Kandel, E.: Psychiatry, Psychoanalysis, and the New Biology of Mind. American Psychiatric Publishing Inc., Washington, D.C., London (2005)
6. Shedler, J.: The efficacy of psychodynamic psychotherapy. Am. Psychol. **65**(2), 98–109 (2010)
7. Cleeremans, A., Timmermans, B., Pasquali, A.: Consciousness and metarepresentation: a computational sketch. Neural Netw. **20**, 1032–1039 (2007)
8. Taylor, J.G., Villa, A.E.P.: The "Conscious I": a neuroheuristic approach to the mind. In: Baltimore, D., Dulbecco, R., Francois, J., Levi-Montalcini, R. (eds.) Frontiers of Life, pp. 349–368. Academic Press (2001)
9. Taylor, J.G.: A neural model of the loss of self in schizophrenia. Schizophrenia Bull. **37**(6), 1229–1247 (2011)
10. Hertz, J.A., Krogh, A., Palmer, R.G. (eds.): Introduction to the Theory of Neural Computation. Lecture Notes, vol. 1. Perseus Books, Cambridge (1991)
11. Cohen, M.A., Grossberg, S.: Absolute stability of global pattern formation and parallel memory storage by competitive neural networks. IEEE Trans. Syst. Man Cybern. **13**, 815–826 (1983)
12. Tsallis, C., Stariolo, D.A.: Generalized simulated annealing. Phys. A **233**, 395–406 (1996)
13. Parisi, G.: Asymmetric neural networks and the process of learning. J. Phys. A Math. Gen. **19**, L675–L680 (1986)

14. Xu, Z.B., Hu, G.Q., Kwong, C.P.: Asymmetric hopfield-type networks: theory and applications. Neural Netw. **9**(3), 483–501 (1996)
15. Hopfield, J.J.: Neurons with graded responses have collective computational properties like those of two-state neurons. Proc. Nat. Acad. Sci. U.S.A. **81**, 3088–3092 (1988)
16. Ribeiro, M.S., Nobre, F., Curado, E.M.F.: Classes of N-dimensional nonlinear Fokker-Planck equations associated to Tsallis entropy. Entropy **13**, 1928–1944 (2011)
17. Plastino, A.R., Plastino, A.: Non-extensive statistical mechanics and generalized Fokker-Planck equation. Phys. A **222**, 347–354 (1995)
18. Tsallis, C., Buckman, D.J.: Anomalous diffusion in the presence of external forces: Exact time-dependent solutions and their thermostatistical basis. Phys. Rev. E **54**(3), R2197–R2200 (1996)
19. Franck, T.D.: Nonlinear Fokker-Planck Equations: Fundamentals and Applications. Springer, Heidelberg (2005)
20. Tsallis, C.: Introduction to Nonextensive Statistical Mechanics. Approaching a Complex World. Springer, New York (2009)

Synaptogenesis: Constraining Synaptic Plasticity Based on a Distance Rule

Jordi-Ysard Puigbò[1]([⊠]), Joeri van Wijngaarden[1], Sock Ching Low[1],
and Paul F.M.J. Verschure[1,2]

[1] Laboratory of Synthetic, Perceptive, Emotive and Cognitive Science (SPECS),
DTIC, Universitat Pompeu Fabra (UPF), Barcelona, Spain
jordiysard.puigbo@upf.edu
[2] Catalan Research Institute and Advanced Studies (ICREA), Barcelona, Spain

Abstract. Neural models, artificial or biologically grounded, have been used for understanding the nature of learning mechanisms as well as for applied tasks. The study of such learning systems has been typically centered on the identification or extraction of the most relevant features that will help to solve a task. Recently, convolutional networks, deep architectures and huge reservoirs have shown impressive results in tasks ranging from speech recognition to visual classification or emotion perception. With the accumulated momentum of such large-scale architectures, the importance of imposing sparsity on the networks to differentiate contexts has been rising. We present a biologically grounded system that imposes physical and local constraints to these architectures in the form of synaptogenesis, or synapse generation. This method guarantees sparsity and promotes the acquisition of experience-relevant, topologically-organized and more diverse features.

Keywords: Machine learning · Connections · Biologically constrained

1 Introduction

Typically, artificial networks of learning nodes, or neurons, have been conceived as all-to-all connected. There are two reasons to begin with this approach. First, at a low scale, biological neurons are strongly connected with most of their neighbors, small networks being approximated in this way. Second, the flow of information among plastic networks is usually computed through dot products. This leads to fully disconnected networks becoming fully connected with the slightest amount of noise. This becomes equivalent to having all to all connections between all nodes, regardless of some weights trending towards 0. These two assumptions have been implicitly used for several years. Still the exponential increase in computational power is limited by this approach, as the complexity in the data increases, affecting the stability of the network.

A.E.P. Villa et al. (Eds.): ICANN 2016, Part I, LNCS 9886, pp. 28–35, 2016.
DOI: 10.1007/978-3-319-44778-0_4

1.1 Sparseness in Artificial Networks

State of the art approaches to neural computation, which has been gaining momentum, has discovered the benefits of sparsity and local connectivity patterns:

Convolutional Networks (ConvNets) approaches the problem by defining local sets of weights (or kernels) shared by all or part of the other neurons. These kernels are limited in size, limiting the effect of one neuron to the others, and are convolved over the network. This implies that neurons are locally connected to just a small fraction of other neurons, dramatically reducing the amount of connections to below 5 % of all possible connections and, by extension, the computational power needed.

Reservoir Computing (RC) considers pools of units with complex temporal dynamics, that are randomly connected. The idea is that a sufficiently large and complex pool would contain potentially useful features. With it, one could use simple, shallow classifiers that read from the pool (or reservoir) and learn combinations of such features for a range of different tasks. One of the principal requirements for the convergence of these networks is having a spectral radius smaller than one [1], what is strongly influenced by the degree of sparsity of the network.

Deep architectures, combined with other techniques, are currently a trend that is used under the lemma of reusing features from previous layers, indirectly increasing the sparsity of the whole network. This occurs because the number of connections existing in the layered architecture could be reconverted into a shallow network which would have lost most of the initial connections.

Sparsity, then, is a feature present in State of the Art machine learning, typically imposed through architectural constraints. Still, the techniques are usually designed artificially, occasionally with inspiration from biology.

1.2 Sparseness in Biological Systems

The connections between and within areas of the brain have been widely studied in order to understand what makes it so unique. One of the most outstanding regions of the brain in this sense is the neocortex. The neocortex is the larger extension of neurons in the primate brain. Over its long extension, rich, functional heterogeneity at large scale levels conflicts with apparently strong structural homogeneity among cortical areas at a neuronal level. This introduces a dichotomy that is present also at the level of connectivity: long range, inter-areal connectivity matrices seem to be very dense [2] with over 90 % of possible connections existing. This does not mean that the connections are evenly distributed in terms of weight. Additionally, at the neuronal level, neurons strongly exhibit lots of short range, local connections to their neighbors, and the longer the distance, the lower the probability of connecting 2 neurons, which results in very sparse networks as they scale up. Kennedy et al. has proposed that cortical connections must follow a distance rule that determines their level of neighboring connectivity [3]. We therefore present a model of how such a distance rule can generate new network topologies driven by external activity patterns.

1.3 Synaptogenesis

Connections are functionally critical for neurons: how neurons connect to each other determines the way the neural network would operate. Synaptogenesis occurs not only in neurons grown during the embryonic and neonatal stages of life, but also in adult-grown neurons. In the case of adult neurogenesis, it is necessary for newly-grown neurons to not only create synapses with older neurons but also do so in a manner that would not disrupt the preexisting network. However, adult neurogenesis in mammals is relatively uncommon and occurs mainly in specific regions of the brain, like the olfactory bulb [4] and the dentate gyrus [5]. Regardless of when the neurons exhibiting synaptogenesis are grown, synapses' proliferation and survival are of scientific interest as they offer insight on how the brain processes stimuli.

Synaptogenesis has been shown to be dependent on activity of the neuron [6] and genetic traits. In addition, the distances between neurons could also play a significant role in synaptogenesis. Particularly in the cortex, most connections within the area are local, with approximately 80 % of connections in the V1, V2 and V4 stemming from intra-areal sources [2], with 95 % of these intrinsic connections arising from within 1.9 mm. Such evidence suggest that the brain's neural network is composed of clusters of densely connected neurons which are then connected to each other by sparse, long-range connections [3].

Moreover, tone directionality and frequency tuning are characteristics that identify receptive fields in primary auditory cortex (A1) [7]. As receptive fields are shaped by the connections between neurons, these phenomena should also be reflected by synaptogenesis. While it is also possible that neurogenesis could contribute to their formation, the low rate of occurrence of adult neurogenesis in the cortex suggests that synaptogenesis is a plausible mechanism for the early formation of receptive fields. Other plastic mechanisms at the level of neuron receptors might then have a more important role on their later fine tunning. This paper attempts to propose a model of synaptogenesis that can describe the structure and function of the cortex, in particular A1.

2 Methods

We propose a model of a cortical layer that uses Izhikevich neurons with spike time dependent plasticity (STDP) to update connections and a distance rule to model how connections are formed during development.

2.1 Spiking Cortical Dynamics

Cortical dynamics were modeled using python scripts. The network consisted of 800 excitatory and 200 inhibitory Izhikevich neurons in total, that together represent part of the primary auditory cortex [8]. The neuron's membrane potential v and membrane recovery variable u follow two differential equations:

$$\frac{dv}{dt} = 0.04v^2 + 5v + 140 - u + I \tag{1}$$

$$\frac{du}{dt} = a(bv - u) \tag{2}$$

With $a = .02/.10$ for E/I, $b = .2$, after-spike membrane reset $c = -65$ and after-spike recovery reset $d = 2.0$. Both populations had a rectangular shape with a ratio of 2:1 (*i.e.*, 40 × 20) with a randomly initialized connectivity matrix (see Table 1 for initialization values). The network was first trained using real-world auditory signals, consisting of 7 different songs converted to input signals with the multi-taper fast Fourier Transformation (FFT), that gives the music's power spectrum over time. Songs covered different genres, including 70's and 80's pop, rock and metal, and lasted approximately 34 min. The FFT's spanned 100 frequencies in the range of 150–650 Hz, and were normalized at each time point such that the maximum input value was always 1. This input was then mapped to the 800 excitatory neurons in a 1:10 ratio with small overlap using Gaussian smearing over both the x- and y-axis. Simulations ran at a temporal resolution of 1 ms, and the connectivity matrix was updated at each iteration based on Synaptic Time-Dependent Plasticity (STDP) principles. These principles constitute temporal asymmetric Hebbian learning, where synapse strength increases as a pre-synaptic action potential is followed by a post-synaptic spike and decreases vice versa. This was implemented on a population level through two variables M(t) and P(t) that either increase or decrease synaptic weights based on the order of spikes:

$$\tau_+ \frac{dP}{dt} = P + a_+ \quad and \quad \tau_- \frac{dM}{dt} = -M + a_- \tag{3}$$

This implementation was based on [9], with τ_+ and τ_- being the time constants of synaptic potentiation and depression respectively and a_+ and a_- their amplitude. Where weights W_{ij} are updated for each spiking neuron:

$$W_{ij} = W_{ij} + M_{ij} + P_{ij} \tag{4}$$

Alternatively an artificial network was trained using the same setup but using a different learning rule. A rate version of STDP was extracted from [10] and used as a learning rule for the rate approximation of the same system as:

$$W_{ij} = W_{ij} + \eta(W_M - W_{ij})(W_m - W_{ij})x_i x_j + W_e \epsilon (W_M - W_{ij})W_{ij} \tag{5}$$

Table 1. Model parameter values

Neuron	a	b	c	d
E	.02	.20	−65	2.0
I	.10	.20	−65	2.0

Where $W_{e\epsilon}$ corresponds to the integral of the STDP rule, W_M and W_m are the maximum and minimum thresholds for the weights, making the learning rule bi-stable and with a homeostatic decay. The rule is in function of the spiking rates of the presynaptic (x_i) and postsynaptic (x_j) neurons.

2.2 Synaptogenesis

In order to model synaptogenesis, a distance matrix has been computed in order to identify the position of each neuron of the space. In order to do this, the neurons have been distributed along two axis and given a normalized distance of 1 unit. From that, the probability of forming a connection from a neuron i to a neuron j given their distance d_{ij} is:

$$P(C_{ij}|d_{ij}) = \frac{1}{1 + kd_{ij}^2} \qquad (6)$$

Where k is a scaling constant that defines the range connections will reach. The exponential has been chosen squared standing for the distribution gradient a typical fluid will suffer on a 2D medium (see Fig. 1 for reference). This rule was extended in two ways:

- The probability of a connection between neuron i and j being created is influenced by nearby existing connections to neurons k. With the probability distribution in Eq. 6, scaled by the weight between the origin neuron i and the neighbor neuron k, in order to promote clusters of specialized neurons and rich-club effects. The computation is then equivalent to a dot product like:

$$P(C_{new}|W, P) = WP \cdot P^T \qquad (7)$$

Where C corresponds to the Boolean connectivity matrix, W is the weights matrix and P is the probability matrix obtained from Eq. 6 and shown in Fig. 1a.

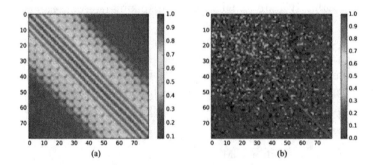

Fig. 1. (a) Sample distribution of probabilities extracted from Eq. 6. The network was initialized with size 20×40 neurons and considered a 2D layer of interconnected excitatory neurons. Parameters: k: 0.1, network size: $10x5$. (b) Connectivity matrix W of the model using synaptogenesis. One can observe the weights organized in clusters, spatially concentrated around the low frequencies (neurons 10–20).

– The connection probability was then scaled by the plasticity rule. It increases the weight as defined by the STDP rule above, promoting the formation of only relevant connections between the input and cortical layers and filtering out random ones.

3   Results

3.1   Synaptogenesis Creates Sparse Networks

In order to understand the sparsity of the receptive fields, we trained our STDP and rate networks for around 30 min of real music. We observed higher degrees of sparsity in the model using synaptogenesis as compared to the model without (Fig. 2).

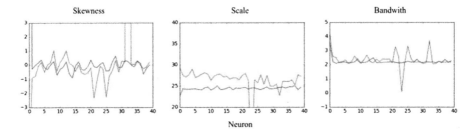

Fig. 2. Synaptogenesis (red) produces more variety (higher standard deviation) in skewness, bandwidth and scale than raw STDP (blue). Y axis show the fitting value of the data in a skewed Gaussian distribution. This data was generated using the rate based model. (Color figure online)

3.2   Synaptogenesis Converges to Richer Receptive Fields

We aimed to reproduce the data observed in [7], who found a high variability in the cortex, in terms of skewness, scale and bandwidth, and which corresponds to the three main parameters describing a skewed Gaussian distribution. We selected 10 evenly distributed frequencies and tested the network trained in the previous experiment for 10 trials. We then computed the rate of subpopulations of the network by summing the number of spikes in bins of 25 neurons, selected accordingly from the 2 dimensional pool. We extracted the spectral receptive fields for each population of neurons, as shown in Fig. 3. In order to extract the receptive fields we used the same methodology typically used in the study of the auditory cortex [7]. This showed slight differences between the receptive fields of the different neurons, where using synaptogenesis usually led to more dissimilar receptive fields among the neurons of the population. The minimal differences observed in Fig. 3 are attributed to the use of too strong inputs during testing, and the task of producing more realistic background noise and auditory input in order to show more relevant differences is left out of the scope of

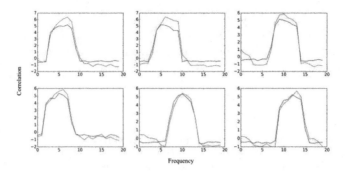

Fig. 3. Examples of the variety of receptive fields found. Top row shows three sample neurons with receptive fields that show greater variability in skewness and scale, whereas the bottom row shows neurons that have similar receptive fields for both approaches. The data was generated using the rate based model. Blue: STDP, red: synaptogenesis (Color figure online)

this paper. Finally, in order to test the relevance of these small differences, we fit a skewed Gaussian curve to the receptive fields. We observed increased variability (standard deviation) in the measures of skewness, bandwidth and scale of the model with synaptogenesis, relative to the model without synaptogenesis. We then conclude that additional work should show significant differences on the trends observed.

4   Conclusions

We have proposed a model of synapse generation, or synaptogenesis, based on a distance rule. This rule promotes the formation of a richer family of receptive fields, specializing neurons for variations in bandwidth, skewness and intensity. We have shown this variations comparing plasticity rules for rate and spiking neurons, with and without the synaptogenesis process.

We have shown that this process leads to sparser networks, a characteristic highly valued in state of the art artificial neural networks. Nonetheless, the capacity of this process to filter out redundant information and keep just relevant connections has yet to be shown. A big improvement to this model would involve the addition of apoptosis, or neural death, what would help prune connections that have become irrelevant. Still, the processes underlying apoptosis are mostly unknown and good measures to guide the pruning are still under debate.

We have proposed this experimental setup as a potential substrate of a single cortical layer. In this sense, the layer has a realistic ratio of excitatory and inhibitory neurons. Moreover, our model has been trained on auditory data, allowing the generation of a richer variety of features which is already observed in the auditory cortex of the ferret [7]. Next steps include completing the cortical model with several layers and a better set of neuron types. Moreover, the input was mathematically modeled as observations in the A1 of the ferret (described in [11]), but in order to account for a real model of the cortex, the input should be filtered through attentional processes mainly driven by thalamo-cortical connections.

References

1. Schrauwen, B., Verstraeten, D., Van Campenhout, J.: An overview of reservoir computing: theory, applications and implementations. In: 15th European Symposium on Artificial Neural Networks, pp. 471–482 (2007)
2. Markov, N., Misery, P., Falchier, A., Lamy, C., Vezoli, J., Quilodran, R., Gariel, M., Giroud, P., Ercsey-Ravasz, M., Pilaz, L., et al.: Weight consistency specifies regularities of macaque cortical networks. Cereb. Cortex **21**(6), 1254–1272 (2011)
3. Ercsey-Ravasz, M., Markov, N.T., Lamy, C., Van Essen, D.C., Knoblauch, K., Toroczkai, Z., Kennedy, H.: A predictive network model of cerebral cortical connectivity based on a distance rule. Neuron **80**(1), 184–197 (2013)
4. Luskin, M.B.: Restricted proliferation and migration of postnatally generated neurons derived from the forebrain subventricular zone. Neuron **11**(1), 173–189 (1993)
5. Kuhn, H.G., Dickinson-Anson, H., Gage, F.H.: Neurogenesis in the dentate gyrus of the adult rat: age-related decrease of neuronal progenitor proliferation. J. Neurosci. **16**(6), 2027–2033 (1996)
6. Kelsch, W., Sim, S., Lois, C.: Watching synaptogenesis in the adult brain. Ann. Rev. Neurosci. **33**, 131–149 (2010)
7. Wang, K., Shamma, S.A., Byrne, W.J.: Noise robustness in the auditory representation of speech signals. In: IEEE International Conference on Acoustics, Speech, and Signal Processing, ICASSP 1993, vol. 2, pp. 335–338. IEEE (1993)
8. Izhikevich, E.M., et al.: Simple model of spiking neurons. IEEE Trans. Neural Netw. **14**(6), 1569–1572 (2003)
9. Song, S., Miller, K.D., Abbott, L.F.: Competitive Hebbian learning through spike-timing-dependent synaptic plasticity. Nat. Neurosci. **3**(9), 919–926 (2000)
10. Abbott, L., Gerstner, W.: Homeostasis and learning through spike-timing dependent plasticity. In: Summer School in Neurophzsics, no. LCN-PRESENTATION-2007-001 (2003)
11. Wang, K., Shamma, S.: Self-normalization and noise-robustness in early auditory representations. IEEE Trans. Speech Audio Process. **2**(3), 421–435 (1994)

A Sensor Fusion Horse Gait Classification by a Spiking Neural Network on SpiNNaker

Antonio Rios-Navarro[✉], Juan Pedro Dominguez-Morales,
Ricardo Tapiador-Morales, Manuel Dominguez-Morales,
Angel Jimenez-Fernandez, and Alejandro Linares-Barranco

Robotic and Technology of Computers Lab,
Department of Architecture and Technology of Computers,
University of Seville, Seville, Spain
arios@atc.us.es,
http://www.rtc.us.es

Abstract. The study and monitoring of the behavior of wildlife has always been a subject of great interest. Although many systems can track animal positions using GPS systems, the behavior classification is not a common task. For this work, a multi-sensory wearable device has been designed and implemented to be used in the Doñana National Park in order to control and monitor wild and semi-wild life animals. The data obtained with these sensors is processed using a Spiking Neural Network (SNN), with Address-Event-Representation (AER) coding, and it is classified between some fixed activity behaviors. This works presents the full infrastructure deployed in Doñana to collect the data, the wearable device, the SNN implementation in SpiNNaker and the classification results.

Keywords: SpiNNaker · Spiking neural network · Pattern classification · Horse gait · IMU · Integrate-and-fire · Caffe

1 Introduction

The animal behaviour classification is a challenge for biologists who try to get some patterns from the acts of different animals. There are certain commercial devices that can track animals using GPS and detect their activity level offering some numerical values based on their position. The challenge of the system presented in this paper is to classify the animal behaviour into different patterns, which are previously trained, proposed by biologists. Currently there are some mechanisms like Neural Networks (NNs), SVM (Support Vector Machines), statistical algorithms, among others, that are trained to extract some patterns from large amount of data. These mechanisms are usually implemented on computers but other hardware platforms like [1, 2] have been designed to develop SNNs easily and with better throughput than conventional computers.

The work presented in this paper is part of the Andalusian Excellence project MINERVA, which main aim is to study and classify the wildlife behaviour inside

© Springer International Publishing Switzerland 2016
A.E.P. Villa et al. (Eds.): ICANN 2016, Part I, LNCS 9886, pp. 36–44, 2016.
DOI: 10.1007/978-3-319-44778-0_5

Doñana National Park [3]. To achieve this goal, a hierarchical wireless sensor network capable of gathering and transmitting information from the animals has been deployed and tested inside the park. A low-power collar device attached to the animal, which has an IMU (Inertial Measurement Unit) and a GPS as main sensors, collects the animal information. It sends data throw a ZigBee network of motes to a base station, where this information is classified and uploaded into a cloud server database, using a Wi-Fi link. Biologists can access those reports through a web application, where processed and raw data from animal collars is shown. This paper focuses on the behaviour classification task of horse gaits using SpiNNaker [1], a neuromorphic hardware platform where SNNs can be deployed. The SpiNNaker board is placed in a base station and it receives the collected data from a mini PC (NUC) that interfaces with the ZigBee network using a ZigBee-to-USB bridge board. The raw sensor data is processed by the SNN on SpiN-Naker after this information is sent from the collars to the base station and, then, the classification results are sent to the server. This work is focused on horse gaits, but thanks to the configurability of the developed architecture, this classification system can be either extended to other animals or even improved easily by only changing the parameters involved in the training step without the need to catch the animal, which is not possible on the commercial devices that already exist (they only give position and activity level).

The rest of the paper is structured as follows: Sect. 2 describes the hardware platforms involved in this work. Section 3 presents the spiking neural network (SNN) model implemented and its training process. In Sect. 4 the accuracy results of the SNN are shown. Finally, Sect. 5 presents the conclusions.

2   Hardware Platforms

For this work, four different platforms have been designed. They are, from lower to higher operating range: collar, sniffer, base station and central server (see Fig. 1). The collar is the end device, which is attached to the animal. The sniffer device is an easy-to-carry device used by biologists and animal handlers to find a particular animal and obtain its information. Base stations (BS) are placed inside Doñana National Park and they are used as beacons to receive the information transmitted by the collars to classify animal's behavior and send results to a server. Finally, the central server receives the information from BS and stores it into an accessible format through web applications.

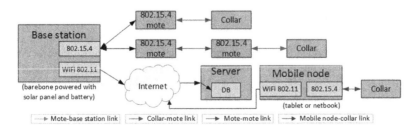

Fig. 1. MINERVA communication topology architecture

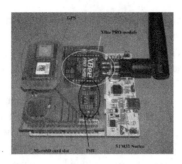

Fig. 2. Collar device prototype

Next, from all these hardware platforms, we will focus on those ones that take part more actively in the SNN classification: collar and BS will be detailed deeply.

2.1 Collar

This device collects information from the environment using multiple sensors. These sensors are a GPS, which gives the position and time; and an inertial movement unit (IMU), which combines 3 different sensors: accelerometer, gyroscope and magneto-meter. The IMU has 3 axes for each sensor: (X, Y, Z). These parameters will be taken into account in the SNN for learning and classification steps.

A low power microcontroller is in charge of the measurements. Furthermore, the collar includes a Zigbee module that can transmit data through the network in a wireless way. If the device is out of range from the network, it carries an SD card where the information is always stored; so the animal behavioural information can be accessed later in an offline way, avoiding data loss (see Fig. 2).

2.2 Base Station

The main task of the BS is to receive data packets from collars and to retransmit them to a remote web server via 802.11 Wi-Fi connection. If the collar is out of range, it stores everything in the SD card until it reaches the BS. Moreover, the main impact of these stations is the inclusion of a SNN classifier that allows to know the animal activity. This NN classifier uses the sensors' raw data collected by the collars to obtain the animal behavior, which is later uploaded to the server. Hence, the classification is not done in real time, but in an offline way. This is due to the fact that both the power consumption of the SpiNNaker board and its size are not small enough to be embedded on the collar, which on the other hand leads to implement a simpler firmware on this device.

BS is composed of: the Bridge board, which contains the sensors (i.e. temperature, humidity, luminosity, accelerometer and battery amperimeter) and Zigbee module, which is used to communicate with collars. BS is USB-connected to an Intel NUC [4]. And a battery, a solar panel and a regulator allows the BS to be installed close to wild-animals habitat to charge the battery during daylight (see Fig. 3).

Fig. 3. Bridge board (left) and base station (right)

2.3 Synthetic Spikes Generator (RB-SSG)

A Synthetic Spikes Generator (SSG) will transform digital words into a stream of rate-coded spikes to feed SpiNNaker hardware. This element is necessary for transforming digital sensors information into spikes because the output of these sensors are not spike-coded. There are several ways to implement a SSG as presented in [5]. A SSG should generate a synthetic spikes stream, whose frequency should be proportional to a constant (kSpikesGen) and an input value (x), according to next equation:

$$SSG(x)_{SpikesRate} = k_{SpikesGen} * x \tag{1}$$

The SSG used in this work implements the Reverse-Bitwise (RB) method (details in [6]) for synthetic spikes generation. Figure 4 shows the internal components of the RB-SSG. It uses a continuous digital counter, whose output is reversed bitwise and compared with the input absolute value $(ABS(x))$. If the input absolute value is greater than reversed counter value, a new spike is sent. RB-SSG ensures a homogeneous spikes distribution along time, thanks to reversing bitwise counter output. Since a sensor value can be negative, it is necessary to generate positive and negatives spikes. A demultiplexer is used to select the right output spike port, where selection signal is the input sign $(X(MSB))$. Finally, a clock frequency divider is included to adjust RB-SSG gain. This element will activate a clock enable (CE) signal, for dividing the clock frequency, according to a frequency divider signal $(genFD)$. So RB-SSG gain $(k_{BWSpikesGen})$ can be calculated as in (2):

$$K_{BWSpikesGen} = \frac{F_{CLK}}{2^{N-1}(genFD + 1)} \tag{2}$$

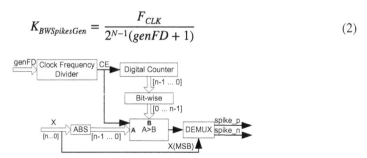

Fig. 4. Reverse Bitwise Synthetic Spikes Generator block diagram.

Where *Fclk* represents system clock frequency, *N* the RB-SSG bits length, and *genFD* clock frequency divider value. These parameters can be modified in order to set up RB-SSG gain according with design requirements.

2.4   Spiking Neural Network Architecture (SpiNNaker)

SpiNNaker is a parallel multi-core computing system designed for modelling very large SNNs in real time. Each SpiNNaker consists of chips (both system architecture and chip are designed by the Advanced Processor Technologies Research Group [7] in Manchester), with eighteen 200 MHz ARM968 cores each. In this work, a SpiNNaker 102 machine, plus PACMAN software was used to implement and test a SNN architecture, presented in the next section. This board has 4 SpiNNaker chips (72 ARM processor cores, where typically are 64 application cores, 4 are monitor cores and there are 4 spare cores) and it requires a 5 V 1A power supply. The control and I/O data is sent through a 100 Mbps Ethernet link. See Fig. 5.

Fig. 5.   SpiNNaker 102 machine.

3   Spiking Neural Network Configuration

3.1   Network Architecture

The SpiNNaker platform allows fast and easy SNNs implementation using PyNN [8], which is a Python package for simulator-independent specification of SNN models. PyNN provides a set of different spiking neuron models. However, integrate-and-fire neurons (IF) have been used in this work due to the fact that it is one of the simplest and most widely used models for pattern classification in SNNs. The implemented architecture consists of 3 layers. The input layer receives the stream of spikes (coded in AER [9]) related to the sensor information which was captured with the collar and (converted into aedat files by the SSG) for a specific horse gait [10]. This layer has 9 IF neurons (one per IMU's axis).

Both the hidden and the output layers have the same number of neurons as the desired number of classes to be classified. Three different horse gaits were investigated in this work (motionless, walking and trotting), hence these layers should consist of three IF neurons. Figure 6 shows the SNN architecture implemented on the SpiNNaker board. Two set of connections between consecutive layers of the network are presented: (1) connections between the input and the hidden layers. These connections are trained using a spike-rate based algorithm which is described in the next section. And (2) connections between the hidden and the output layers. These connections inhibit the unwanted signal from the classification output obtained in the hidden layer.

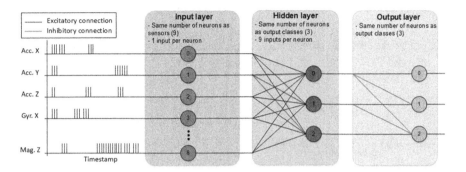

Fig. 6. Spiking neural network architecture using a horse gait aedat file sample as input.

3.2   Training Phase

The weights of the first set of SNN connections are obtained using an offline and supervised spike-rate based training algorithm. These weights are calculated from the normalization of the spike firing activity for each IMU signal using a set of aedat files. These files were generated from a 20-samples frame variance of the raw data obtained in Doñana from the collar while a horse was performing the three different gaits that want to be classified (motionless, walking and trotting). The aim of this training is to obtain the weights of the SNN connections. After that, according to the neuron labels shown on Fig. 6, when the horse is motionless, the only firing neuron in the hidden layer is the number 2; when it is walking, both number 1 and 2 neurons fire; and, in case of trotting, the three of them. Hence, connections between the neurons in the input layer and the neuron 2 of the hidden layer have greater weight values than the connections between the inputs and the number 1, and so on.

The firing rate of a specific degree of freedom ($FRate_{dol[i]}$) is calculated by dividing the number of AER events fired during a certain time period by that time period. Then, the firing rate of a specific sensor (accelerometer, gyroscope or magnetometer) ($FRate_{sensor[i]}$) is the maximum firing rate value of its axes. Finally, $FRate_{dol[i]}$ is normalized using its corresponding $FRate_{sensor[i]}$ value, obtaining (3).

$$FRate_{dol[i]} = \left(\sum AERevents \right) / T_{sample} \tag{3}$$

$$FRate_{sensors[i]} = \max \left(FRate_{dol[x]}, FRate_{dol[y]}, FRate_{dol[z]} \right) \tag{4}$$

$$FRate_{dol[i]\_normalized} = FRate_{dol[i]} / FRate_{sensors[i]} \tag{5}$$

As seen in Fig. 7 (left), the highest event rate for each axis is obtained when the horse is trotting (collar in constant motion), hence variance values are greater. However, setting the weights of the connections with the results obtained from (3) after using these numbers of AER events leads to a firing output in the hidden layer that is the opposite of what was expected. To solve this problem, the normalized firing rate values are inverted (see Fig. 7 right) and used as weights for the connections between input and hidden layers.

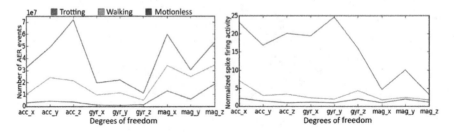

Fig. 7. AER events fired (left) and normalized activity (right) for each IMU degree of freedom

The connections between hidden and output layers are configured such as the first neuron of the hidden layer inhibits the last two neurons of the output layer. However, the second neuron of the hidden layer only inhibits the last neuron of the output layer. With this configuration, when the horse is performing one of the gaits that want to be classified, only its corresponding output neuron fires.

4   Results

The information required for training and testing the SNN has been collected with the collar placed on a horse. This specie was chosen due to the weight of the collar prototype. For the testing scenario, the collar collects information continuously from on-board sensors and send it to a computer application. The information is stored in different files depending on the behaviour.

The information is obtained by a biologist managing the animal while a user captures each behaviour in different files: 6000 samples for each behaviour have been collected. Next, the dataset is pre-processed by calculating the variance using 20-sample windows. Finally, 300 samples per behaviour are used for training (200) and testing (100) the SNN after converting them to spikes. Figure 8 shows the accuracy results of this test.

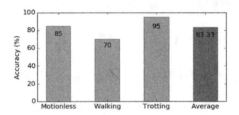

Fig. 8. Accuracy results for the SNN SpiNNaker implementation

The network proposed in this paper has been compared with a modification of the LeNet5 [11] ConvNet, which has been trained and tested using Caffe [12] (Convolutional Architecture for Fast Feature Embedding). This network is well known for its high accuracy results for image recognition, so data samples have been converted to frames. The network is fed with these frames, using the same train and test ratio of the whole dataset. Each frame has been composed as Fig. 9-left shows.

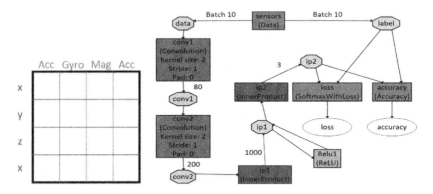

Fig. 9. (left) Frame structure using sensor variance. Column: IMU sensor, Row: coordinate. (right) Network topology from Caffe

Figure 9-right shows the modified LeNet5 network where pooling operations have been removed in both convolutional stages because input frames have low pixel resolution. After training and testing this network, an 81.2 % average accuracy value is obtained.

5   Conclusions

In this manuscript, a novel SNN for horse gait classification was implemented and tested using SpiNNaker. For that purpose, a collar with a low-power microcontroller and a 9-axis IMU has been developed along with a desktop application for collecting the data. This data was obtained in Doñana National Park from different horses in three different seasons of the year. After transforming the collected sensor information into spike-streams using the RB-SSG, the SNN was trained. And then, several classification tests were performed on the SpiNNaker board, obtaining an 83.33 % accuracy on average. These tests were also performed using a modified LeNet ConvNet implemented in Caffe to compare the results, obtaining an 81.2 % accuracy. The SpiNNaker board has allowed modeling, implementing and testing a SNN for this purpose in an easy and fast way, proving its versatility and efficiency when deploying SNNs in hardware platforms.

Acknowledgement. The authors would like to thank the Advanced Processor Technologies (APT) Research Group of the University of Manchester for instructing us on the SpiNNaker platform on the 5th SpiNNaker Workshop. This work is supported by the Spanish government grant BIOSENSE (TEC2012-37868-C04-02) and by the excellence project from Andalusian Council MINERVA (P12-TIC-1300), with support from the European Regional Development Fund.

References

1. Painkras, E., et al.: SpiNNaker: A 1-W 18-core system-on-chip for massively-parallel neural network simulation. IEEE J. Solid-State Circ. **48**(8), 1943–1953 (2013)
2. Merolla, P.A., et al.: A million spiking-neuron integrated circuit with a scalable communication network and interface. Science **345**(6197), 668–673 (2014)
3. Doñana National Park: http://whc.unesco.org/en/list/685
4. Intel NUC. http://www.intel.com/content/www/us/en/nuc/nuc-kit-d54250wykh.html
5. Gomez-Rodriguez, F., Paz, R., Miro, L., Linares-Barranco, A., Jimenez, G., Civit, A.: Two hardware implementations of the exhaustive synthetic AER generation method. In: Cabestany, J., Prieto, A.G., Sandoval, F. (eds.) IWANN 2005. LNCS, vol. 3512, pp. 534–540. Springer, Heidelberg (2005)
6. Paz, R., et al.: Synthetic retina for AER systems development. In: AICCSA 2009, pp. 907–912 (2009)
7. A.P. Techonologies Research Group: http://apt.cs.manchester.ac.uk/projects/SpiNNaker
8. Davison, A.P.: PyNN: a common interface for neuronal network simulators. Front. Neuroinform. **2**, 11 (2008)
9. Sivilotti, M.: Wiring Considerations in analog VLSI Systems with Application to Field-Programmable Networks. California Institute of Technology, Pasadena CA (1991)
10. Harris, S.E.: Horse Gaits. Balance and Movement (1993)
11. LeCun, Y., et al.: Gradient-based learning applied to document recognition. Proc. IEEE **86**(11), 2278–2323 (1998)
12. Jia, Y., et al.: Caffe: Convolutional Architecture for Fast Feature Embedding. In: Proceedings of the ACM International Conference on Multimedia, pp. 675–678 (2014)

Multilayer Spiking Neural Network for Audio Samples Classification Using SpiNNaker

Juan Pedro Dominguez-Morales[✉], Angel Jimenez-Fernandez, Antonio Rios-Navarro, Elena Cerezuela-Escudero, Daniel Gutierrez-Galan, Manuel J. Dominguez-Morales, and Gabriel Jimenez-Moreno

Robotic and Technology of Computers Lab,
Department of Architecture and Technology of Computers,
University of Seville, Seville, Spain
{jpdominguez,ajimenez,arios,ecerezuela,
dgutierrez,mdominguez,gaji}@atc.us.es
http://www.atc.us.es

Abstract. Audio classification has always been an interesting subject of research inside the neuromorphic engineering field. Tools like Nengo or Brian, and hardware platforms like the SpiNNaker board are rapidly increasing in popularity in the neuromorphic community due to the ease of modelling spiking neural networks with them. In this manuscript a multilayer spiking neural network for audio samples classification using SpiNNaker is presented. The network consists of different leaky integrate-and-fire neuron layers. The connections between them are trained using novel firing rate based algorithms and tested using sets of pure tones with frequencies that range from 130.813 to 1396.91 Hz. The hit rate percentage values are obtained after adding a random noise signal to the original pure tone signal. The results show very good classification results (above 85 % hit rate) for each class when the Signal-to-noise ratio is above 3 decibels, validating the robustness of the network configuration and the training step.

Keywords: SpiNNaker · Spiking neural network · Audio samples classification · Spikes · Neuromorphic auditory sensor · Address-Event Representation

1 Introduction

Neuromorphic engineering is a discipline that studies, designs and implements hardware and software with the aim of mimicking the way in which nervous systems work, focusing its main inspiration on how the brain solves complex problems easily. Nowadays, the neuromorphic community has a set of neuromorphic hardware tools available such as sensors [1, 2], learning circuits [3, 4], neuromorphic information filters and feature extractors [5, 6], robotic and motor controllers [7, 8]. In the field of neuromorphic sensors, diverse neuromorphic cochleae can be found [2, 9, 10]. These sensors are able to decompose the audio in frequency bands, and represent them as streams of short pulses, called spikes, using the Address-Event Representation (AER) [11] to interface with other neuromorphic layers. On the other hand, there are several software tools in the community for spiking neural networks (SNN) simulation, i.e. NENGO [12] and

© Springer International Publishing Switzerland 2016
A.E.P. Villa et al. (Eds.): ICANN 2016, Part I, LNCS 9886, pp. 45–53, 2016.
DOI: 10.1007/978-3-319-44778-0_6

BRIAN [13]; or jAER [14] for real-time visualization and software processing of AER streams captured from the hardware using specific interfaces [15]. Hardware platforms like the SpiNNaker board [16] allows to develop and implement complex SNN easily using a high-level programming language such as Python and the PyNN [17] library.

This manuscript presents a novel multilayer SNN architecture built in SpiNNaker which has been trained for audio samples classification using a firing rate based algorithm. To test the network behavior and robustness, a 64-channel binaural Neuromorphic Auditory Sensor (NAS) for FPGA [10] has been used together with an USB-AER interface [15] (Fig. 1) and the jAER software, allowing to produce different pure tones with frequencies varying from 130.813 Hz to 1396.91 Hz, record the NAS response storing the information in aedat files through jAER and use these files as input for the SNN that has been implemented in the SpiNNaker board.

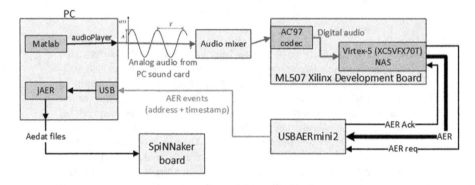

Fig. 1. Block diagram of the system

The paper is structured as follows: Sect. 2 presents the number of neurons, layers and connections of the SNN. Then, Sect. 3 describes the training algorithm used in every layer for the audio samples classification. Section 4 describes the test scenario, including information about the input files. Then, Sect. 5 presents the experimental results of the audio samples classification when using the inputs described in Sect. 4. Finally, Sect. 6 presents the conclusions of this work.

2   Hardware Setup

The standalone hardware used in this work consists of two main parts: the 64-channel NAS connected to the USB-AER interface for generating a spike stream for each audio sample, and the SpiNNaker for back-end computation and deployment of the SNN classifier.

2.1   Neuromorphic Auditory Sensor (NAS)

A Neuromorphic Auditory Sensor (NAS) is used as the input layer of our system. This sensor converts the incoming sound into a train of rate-coded spikes and processes them using Spike Signal Processing (SSP) techniques for FPGA [5]. NAS is composed of a set of Spike Low-pass Filters (SLPF) implementing a cascade topology, where SLPF's correlative spike outputs are subtracted, performing a bank of equivalent Spikes Band-pass Filters (SBPF), and decomposing input audio spikes into spectral activity [10]. Finally, SBPF spikes are collected using an AER monitor, codifying each spike using the Address-Event Representation, and propagating AER events through a 16-bit parallel asynchronous AER port [11].

NAS designing is very flexible and fully customizable, allowing neuromorphic engineers to build application-specific NASs, with diverse features and number of channels. In this case, we have used a 64-channel binaural NAS, with a frequency response between 20 Hz and 22 kHz, and a dynamic range of +75 dB, synthesized for a Virtex-5 FPGA. Figure 1 shows a NAS implemented in a Xilinx development board, and a USB-AER mini2 board, that implements a bridge between AER systems and jAER in a PC (Fig. 2).

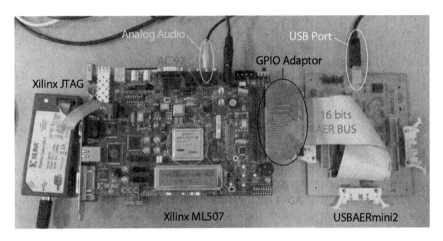

Fig. 2. 64-channel binaural NAS implemented in a Xilinx ML507 FPGA connected to an USB-AER mini2 board.

2.2 Spiking Neural Network Architecture (SpiNNaker)

SpiNNaker is a massively-parallel multi-core computing system designed for modelling very large spiking neural networks in real time. Each SpiNNaker chip comprises 18 general-purpose ARM968 cores, running at 200 MHz, communicating via packets carried by a custom interconnect fabric. Packets are transmitted and their transmission is brokered entirely by hardware, giving the overall engine an extremely high bisection bandwidth. The Advanced Processor Technologies Research Group (APT) [18] in Manchester are responsible for the system architecture and the design of the SpiNNaker chip itself.

In this work, a SpiNNaker 102 machine was used. The 102 machine, Fig. 3, is a 4-node circuit board and hence has 72 ARM processor cores, which are typically deployed as 64 application cores, 4 Monitor Processors and 4 spare cores. The 102 machine requires a 5 V 1 A supply, and can be powered from some USB2 ports. The control and I/O interface is a single 100 Mbps Ethernet connection.

Fig. 3. SpiNNaker 102 machine.

3   Leaky Integrate-and-Fire Spiking Neural Network

The SpiNNaker platform allows to implement a specific spiking neuron model and use it in any SNN deployed on the board thanks to the PyNN package. Leaky Integrate-and-Fire (LIF) neurons have been used in a 3-layer SNN architecture for audio samples classification.

- **Input layer.** This layer receives the stream of AER events fired for the audio samples captured as aedat files through jAER. The number of input neurons is equal to the number of channels that the NAS has. As a 64-channel NAS (64 different AER addresses) was used in this work, the input layer consists of 64 LIF neurons.
- **Hidden layer.** The hidden layer has the same number of neurons as the desired number of classes to be classified in the output layer. As an example, this layer should consist of eight LIF neurons if eight different audio samples are expected to be classified.
- **Output layer.** As the previous layer, this also has as many neurons as output classes. The firing output of the neurons in this layer will determine the result of the classification.

Figure 4 shows the SNN architecture. Connections between layers are achieved using the FromListConnector method from PyNN, meaning that the source, destination and weight of the connection are specified manually. Using other connectors from this package will result on having the same weight in all the connections between consecutive layers, instead of a different value for each. In this architecture, each neuron in a layer is connected to every neuron in the next layer, and the weight value is obtained from the training step, which is described in Sect. 4. The threshold voltage of the neurons in the hidden layer is 15 mV, while this voltage is 10 mV in the neurons in the output layer.

Decay rate and refractory period are the same for both layers: 20 mV/ms and 2 ms, respectively.

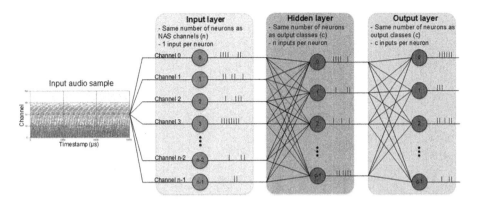

Fig. 4. SNN architecture using an audio sample aedat file as input.

4   Training Phase for Audio Classification

In the previous section, each of the three layers comprising the network were described. The training phase is performed offline and supervised. The main objective of this training is to obtain the weight values of the connections between the input and the hidden layer and between the hidden and the output layers for further audio samples classification. Therefore, two different training steps need to be done.

The weights of the first step of the training phase are obtained from the normalized spike firing activity for each NAS channel using a set of audio samples similar to those to be recognized (same amplitude, duration and frequencies). The firing rate for a specific channel ($FR_{channel\_i}$) is obtained by dividing the number of events produced in that channel by the NAS firing rate (FR_T), which is the number of events fired in the NAS in a particular time period.

$$FR_T = \left(\sum AERevents \right) / T_{sample} \qquad (1)$$

$$FR_{channel\_i} = \left(\sum AERevents(i) \right) / FR_T \qquad (2)$$

Figure 5 shows the normalized spike firing activity for a set of eight pure tones with frequencies that range from 130.813 Hz to 1396.91 Hz, logarithmically spaced.

The weights of the second step of the training phase are obtained from the firing output of each neuron in the hidden layer when using the set of audio samples as input after loading the weights calculated in the previous step into the connections between the input and the hidden layer. These firing outputs are normalized by dividing each of them by the maximum value. The results obtained are the weight values that will be used in the connections between the hidden and the output layer.

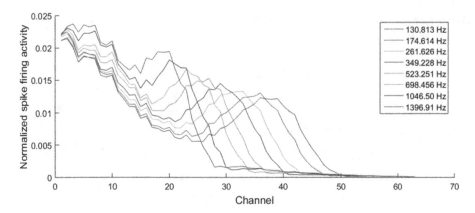

Fig. 5. Normalized spike firing activity for each NAS channel per audio sample.

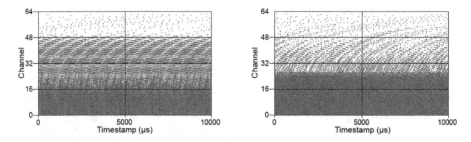

Fig. 6. First 10 ms cochleogram of the 130.813 Hz (left) and 1396.91 Hz (right) pure tones.

5   Test Scenario

In this work, the SNN architecture and training algorithm presented are tested using eight different audio samples. These output classes correspond to eight different pure tones with frequencies that range from 130.813 Hz to 1396.91 Hz, logarithmically spaced (130.813, 174.614, 261.626, 349.228, 523.251, 698.456, 1046.50 and 1396.91 Hz). These samples have a duration of 0.5 s and were generated using the audioplayer function from Matlab with a sampling rate of 48 KHz and a peak-to-peak voltage value of 1 V. After the signal is sent to the mixer, it propagates the sound to NAS input and sends an AER stream to the PC through the AER-USB interface. The jAER software running on the PC is able to capture this stream and save it as an aedat file. Figure 6 shows the cochleograms for the 130.813 Hz and the 1396.91 Hz pure tones after capturing them.

The first step of the training phase can be achieved by applying the equations presented in Sect. 4 to the set of eight aedat files corresponding to each pure tone. This will generate a CSV file containing the weights for the 64 × 8 connections between the input and the hidden layers of the SNN based on the firing rate of the spike streams for each audio sample. As described in the previous section, loading those weights into the corresponding connections and using the eight pure tones as input will result on a firing output on the second layer neurons that will be used for training the connections between the second and the output layers of the SNN.

After the weights are set on these connections, new sets of the same pure tones (same frequencies) are recorded using different Signal-to-Noise Ratio (SNR) values and tested on the network, calculating the hit rate percentage for each class.

6 Experimental Results

Different pure tone sets with the same frequencies and properties (0.5 s and 0.5 V amplitude) as the ones used in this work were captured and used to test the network robustness and effectiveness. A 100 % hit rate was obtained for every class when the signal was a pure sine wave. Moreover, the network has also been tested by adding a noise signal consisting of random values to the pure tones original signals, obtaining audio samples with different SNR values (from 35.2 dB to 0 dB). The hit rate percentage for every class using the previous SNR values are listed in Table 1.

Table 1. Hit rate percentage of the audio samples classification SNN for different SNR values.

SNR (dB)	Pure tone frequency (Hz)							
	130.813	174.614	261.626	349.228	523.251	698.456	1046.5	1396.91
No noise	100 %	100 %	100 %	100 %	100 %	100 %	100 %	100 %
35.1993	100 %	100 %	100 %	100 %	100 %	100 %	100 %	100 %
21.3363	100 %	83 %	96 %	100 %	100 %	100 %	100 %	100 %
13.2273	100 %	81 %	92 %	100 %	100 %	100 %	100 %	96 %
7.4733	100 %	86 %	100 %	100 %	100 %	100 %	100 %	95 %
3.0103	74 %	90 %	100 %	98 %	100 %	100 %	100 %	98 %
2	93 %	88 %	20 %	32 %	16 %	92 %	32 %	97 %
1	10 %	5 %	0 %	0 %	0 %	88 %	26 %	94 %
0	0 %	0 %	0 %	0 %	0 %	76 %	22 %	91 %

The results show very high hit rate percentages when the SNR is above 3 dB. However, when the SNR falls below 3 dB and approaches zero dB (the amplitude of the pure tone is the same as the amplitude of the noise signal) the network is not able to classify every input signal as its corresponding class.

7 Conclusions

In this paper, a novel multilayer spiking neural network architecture for audio samples classification implemented in SpiNNaker has been presented. To achieve this goal, an optimized training phase for audio recognition has been described and specified in two different steps, which allow obtaining the weights for the connections between the input and the hidden layers and between the hidden and the output layers. The network was trained using eight pure tones with frequencies between 130.813 Hz and 1396.91 Hz and tested by adding a noise signal with SNR values between 35.1993 and 0 dB.

The hit rate values obtained after many tests confirm the robustness of the network and the training, which make it possible to classify every pure tone with a probability over 74 % even when the SNR value is 3 dB, obtaining almost a 100 % probability for every input when the SNR is above that value.

Finally, the SpiNNaker board has allowed to model and develop a leaky integrate-and-fire spiking neural network for this purpose in an easy, fast, user-friendly and efficient way, proving its potential, and promoting and facilitating the implementation of SNNs like these in real hardware platforms. The PyNN code used to test the SNN presented in this work is available at [19].

Acknowledgements. The authors would like to thank the APT Research Group of the University of Manchester for instructing us in the SpiNNaker. This work is supported by the Spanish government grant BIOSENSE (TEC2012-37868-C04-02) and by the excellence project from Andalusian Council MINERVA (P12-TIC-1300), both with support from the European Regional Development Fund.

References

1. Lichtsteiner, P., Posch, C., Delbruck, T.: A 128×128 120 dB 15 μs latency asynchronous temporal contrast vision sensor. IEEE J. Solid-State Circ. **43**, 566–576 (2008)
2. Chan, V., Liu, S.C., van Schaik, A.: AER EAR: a matched silicon cochlea pair with address event representation interface. IEEE Trans Circ. Syst. I **54**(1), 48–59 (2007)
3. Häfliger, P.: Adaptive WTA with an analog VLSI neuromorphic learning chip. IEEE Trans. Neural Netw. **18**, 551–572 (2007)
4. Indiveri, G., Chicca, E., Douglas, R.: A VLSI array of low-power spiking neurons and bistable synapses with spike-timing dependent plasticity. IEEE Trans. Neural Netw. **17**, 211–221 (2006)
5. Jiménez-Fernández, A., Jiménez-Moreno, G., Linares-Barranco, A., et al.: Building blocks for spikes signal processing. In: International Joint Conference on Neural Networks, IJCNN (2010)
6. Linares-Barranco, A., et al.: A USB3.0 FPGA event-based filtering and tracking framework for dynamic vision sensors. In: Proceedings of IEEE International Symposium on Circuits and Systems, pp. 2417–2420 (2015)
7. Linares-Barranco, A., Gomez-Rodriguez, F., Jimenez-Fernandez, A., et al.: Using FPGA for visuo-motor control with a silicon retina and a humanoid robot. In: IEEE International Symposium on Circuits and Systems, pp. 1192–1195 (2007)
8. Jimenez-Fernandez, A., Jimenez-Moreno, G., Linares-Barranco, A., et al.: A neuro-inspired spike-based PID motor controller for multi-motor robots with low cost FPGAs. Sensors **12**, 3831–3856 (2012)
9. Hamilton, T.J., Jin, C., van Schaik, A., Tapson, J.: An active 2-D silicon cochlea. IEEE Trans. Biomed. Circ. Syst. **2**, 30–43 (2008)
10. Jimenez-Fernandez, A., Cerezuela-Escudero, E., Miro-Amarante, L., et al.: A binaural neuromorphic auditory sensor for FPGA: a spike signal processing approach. IEEE Trans. Neural Networks Learn. Syst. **1**(0) (2016)
11. Boahen, K.: Point-to-point connectivity between neuromorphic chips using address events. IEEE Trans. Circ. Syst II Analog Digit Sig. Process. **47**, 416–434 (2000)

12. Bekolay, T., et al.: Nengo: a Python tool for building large-scale functional brain models. Front Neuroinform. **7**, 48 (2014)
13. Goodman, D., Brette, R.: Brian: a simulator for spiking neural networks in python. Front Neuroinform. **2**, 5 (2008)
14. jAER Open Source Project. http://jaer.wiki.sourceforge.net
15. Berner, R., Delbruck, T., Civit-Balcells, A., Linares-Barranco, A.: A 5 Meps $100 USB2.0 address-event monitor-sequencer interface. IEEE International Symposium on Circuits and Systems (2007)
16. Painkras, E., et al.: SpiNNaker: A 1-W 18-core system-on-chip for massively-parallel neural network simulation. IEEE J. Solid-State Circ. **48**, 1943–1953 (2013)
17. Davison, A.P.: PyNN: a common interface for neuronal network simulators. Front Neuroinform. **2**, 11 (2008)
18. SpiNNaker Home Page. http://apt.cs.manchester.ac.uk/projects/SpiNNaker
19. Dominguez-Morales, J.P.: Multilayer spiking neural network for audio samples classification using Spinnaker Github page. https://github.com/jpdominguez/Multilayer-SNN-for-audio-samples-classification-using-SpiNNaker

Input-Modulation as an Alternative to Conventional Learning Strategies

Esin Yavuz[✉] and Thomas Nowotny

School of Engineering and Informatics, University of Sussex,
Falmer, Brighton BN1 9QJ, UK
{e.yavuz,t.nowotny}@sussex.ac.uk
http://www.sussex.ac.uk

Abstract. Animals use various strategies for learning stimulus-reward associations. Computational methods that mimic animal behaviour most commonly interpret learning as a high level phenomenon, in which the pairing of stimulus and reward leads to plastic changes in the final output layers where action selection takes place. Here, we present an alternative input-modulation strategy for forming simple stimulus-response associations based on reward. Our model is motivated by experimental evidence on modulation of early brain regions by reward signalling in the honeybee. The model can successfully discriminate dissimilar odours and generalise across similar odours, like bees do. In the most simplified connectionist description, the new input-modulation learning is shown to be asymptotically equivalent to the standard perceptron.

Keywords: Reinforcement learning · Olfactory system · Spiking neural network

1 Introduction

Reinforcement learning is a learning paradigm in which appropriate actions are associated to sensory input guided by an evaluative feedback signal [16]. In computational models, this feedback is often considered to lead to modifications of the synapses between the outputs of the sensory processing cascade and the pre-motor regions that give rise to behaviour.

There are a number of regions associated with stimulus-reward associations in the human brain, and many different pathways are involved. On the other hand, insects are also capable of performing quite complex tasks even though their brains have much fewer brain regions and less than a million neurons. Honeybees, for example, rely on stimulus-reward associations for foraging, which is essential for their survival. Because of their extraordinary capabilities of solving complex learning tasks and the small size of their brains, they are a good animal model for studying the neural correlates of reinforcement learning [12].

The main brain regions of the honeybee olfactory system are the antennae, the antennal lobe (AL) and the mushroom bodies (MB). The olfactory receptor

© Springer International Publishing Switzerland 2016
A.E.P. Villa et al. (Eds.): ICANN 2016, Part I, LNCS 9886, pp. 54–62, 2016.
DOI: 10.1007/978-3-319-44778-0_7

neurons (ORNs) in the antennae respond to olfactory stimuli and make synapses with projection neurons (PNs) and local interneurons (LNs) in the AL. PNs then rely this stimulus-related information to the MBs. Even though the MBs are considered to be the main regions of stimulus identification and learning, bees have been shown to be capable of performing acquisition, but not consolidation, of elementary stimulus-reward associations even when the MBs are ablated [11] or their spiking activity is suppressed [3]. Moreover, injecting octopamine, a neurotransmitter which is known to mediate reward signalling in the insect brain, into the AL just after presenting an odour has been shown to be sufficient for conditioning [7]. Other studies have found that associative learning induces changes in the spiking activity of the neurons in the AL [2,5,15], not only in the MBs. These experiments suggest that reinforcement learning can be induced and evokes changes in the very early stages of the olfactory system, the AL, and that the MBs are not essential for simple elemental associative learning tasks.

Based on these observations, we have developed a spiking neural network model of the early olfactory system of the honeybee that does not require MBs to learn simple associations for appetitive absolute conditioning. The model uses elements of an earlier olfaction model [14], and includes additional mechanisms for reward modulation in the AL. Stimulus-reward associations are stored in plastic ORN-PN connections governed by a three-factor learning rule.

2   Model

The network connectivity is shown in Fig. 1. The model has four main layers: ORNs, PNs and LNs in the AL, and detector neurons (DNs), presumably located in the lateral protocerebrum. We have included 450 ORNs, 150 PNs, 30 LNs and 2 DNs, modelling roughly 1/5, or 30 glomeruli, of the AL. This choice was guided by the availability of experimental data for 30 glomeruli that are located dorsally and hence easily accessible for imaging [14]. Each glomerulus has five PNs and one LN associated to it. We have interpreted this as the substrate for five potential behaviours, and modify only the ORN-PN synapses of one of the PNs in response to reward. Others may be modified by other signals, e.g. in response to punishment. LN-LN and LN-PN synapses are inhibitory, all the other synapses are excitatory.

Each ORN expresses only one receptor type and each ORN type projects to the same glomerulus. ORN responses are modelled as Poisson spike trains with input-dependent rate. The rates are calculated as a function of the identity and concentration of odour input, in a rate model of binding, unbinding, activation and inactivation of receptors [13]. Details can be found in a previous study [14].

PNs and LNs are modelled as Hodgkin-Huxley type conductance based neurons [17], tuned to reproduce the electrophysiological data from honeybees [10]. We only modelled the homogeneous LNs which provide all-to-all inhibition, and excluded the heterogeneous LNs which connect to only a subset of glomeruli.

The membrane potential V_i of neuron i is given by:

$$C\dot{V}_i = -I_{\text{Na},i} - I_{\text{K},i} - I_{\text{L},i} - I_{\text{DC},i} - I_{\text{syn},i}, \tag{1}$$

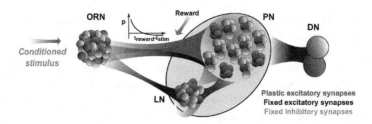

Fig. 1. Network connectivity. Presynaptic populations are at the light end of the synapses, and the postsynaptic populations are at the dark end. Each 5 PNs (and 1 LN) are members of the same glomeruli, and one of them makes reward-modulated plastic synapses with ORNs. LN-LN and LN-PN connections are inhibitory.

where C is the membrane capacitance, and $I_{\mathrm{DC},i}$ is a direct current injected into the neuron. The leak current is $I_{\mathrm{L},i} = g_{\mathrm{L}}(V_i - E_{\mathrm{L}})$ and the ionic currents $I_{\mathrm{Na},i}$, $I_{\mathrm{K},i}$ and $I_{\mathrm{M},i}$ are described by

$$I_{\mathrm{Na},i}(t) = g_{\mathrm{Na}} m_i(t)^3 h_i(t)(V_i(t) - E_{\mathrm{Na}}) \tag{2}$$

$$I_{\mathrm{K},i}(t) = g_{\mathrm{K}} n_i(t)^4 (V_i(t) - E_{\mathrm{K}}) \tag{3}$$

$$I_{\mathrm{M},i}(t) = g_{\mathrm{M}} z_i(t)^4 (V_i(t) - E_{\mathrm{K}}). \tag{4}$$

The synaptic current $I_{\mathrm{syn},i}$ received by neuron i is given by

$$I_{\mathrm{syn},i}(t) = (V_{\mathrm{syn}} - V_i(t)) \sum_j g_{\mathrm{syn},ij}(t) S_{ij}(t) \tag{5}$$

with a reversal potential of $V_{\mathrm{syn}} = 0$ mV for excitatory and -80 mV for inhibitory synapses. The synaptic activation variable S_{ij} is governed by

$$\dot{S}_{ij} = -\frac{S_{ij}}{\tau_{\mathrm{syn},ij}} + \sum_k \delta(t - t_j^{(k)}), \tag{6}$$

where $t_j^{(k)}$ is the time stamp of the kth spike of the presynaptic neuron j. Each activation and inactivation variable $m_i(t), h_i(t), n_i(t), z_i(t)$ satisfied first-order kinetics exactly as described in [14], Eqs. (10) and (11).

The plastic synapses between ORNs and learning PNs were updated by a 3-factor learning rule. The "eligibility trace" p_{ij} is updated according to $p_{ij} \mapsto p_{ij} + F_{\mathrm{STDP}}(\Delta t_{\mathrm{spike}})$ whenever a pre- or post-synaptic spike occurs and otherwise decays exponentially according to $\dot{p}_{ij} = -(p_{ij} - p_{base})/\tau_p$. For simplicity, the STDP function was set to a constant, $F_{\mathrm{STDP}} = A$, if $-20 < \Delta t < 30$ and $= 0$ otherwise. The time window was chosen to match the STDP time window observed in locust Kenyon cells [1]. p_{ij} then drives changes in the synaptic conductance $g_{\mathrm{syn},ij}$ in conjunction with the reward signal R according to

$$\dot{g}_{\mathrm{syn},ij} = \frac{R \cdot p_{ij}}{\tau_{\mathrm{learn}}} - \frac{g_{\mathrm{syn},ij}}{\tau_{\mathrm{forget}}} \tag{7}$$

R is determined by the external experimental protocol in the form of a reward signal value $R_{\text{target}}(t)$ to which R approaches exponentially with a given time scale τ_{reward}:

$$\dot{R} = \frac{R_0 + R_{\text{target}} - R}{\tau_{\text{reward}}} \qquad (8)$$

Here, R_0 is a negative baseline value for reward that causes responses in the absence of reward to lead to depression of $g_{\text{syn},ij}$ and hence extinction of previous memories. In a steady state without reward, both R and p_{ij} are negative; therefore the total effect on $g_{\text{syn},ij}$ is positive, resulting in recovery. The model behaviour is summarised in Table 1.

Table 1. Model behaviour as a function of reward (R) and eligibility (p)

	R < 0	R > 0
p < 0	+ (recovery)	− (inactivation)
p > 0	− (extinction)	+ (reinforcement)

The model was simulated on the GeNN GPU-accelerated modelling framework [18][1].

3   Results

In order to test the performance of the model for discrimination and generalisation when forming associations between odours and reward, we tested responses to 2-Hexanol (2-Hex) against responses to 1-Hexanol (1-Hex) and 2-Octanol (2-Oct). According to behavioral [6] and calcium imaging [4] studies, 2-Hex and 1-Hex are similar and should lead to generalisation and 2-Oct is dissimilar and should be discriminated. When tested against 2-Hex conditioning, the behavioral generalisation probability of bees was 75.0 % for 1-Hex and 37.5 % for 2-Oct [6].

The absolute conditioning protocol used here consists of five consecutive presentations of an odour paired with a reward signal (A+). The odour is presented for 4 s, and the reward signal is introduced 2 s after the stimulus onset. The reward is presented for 3 s. After the five consecutive presentations of A+, a second odour is presented without any reward (B−). Following B−, the first odour is presented again three times without sugar pairing (A−).

As a result of conditioning, the glomeruli that are active during A+ increase their firing, while the glomeruli that are not active decrease their firing. The temporal evolution of the PN responses during the absolute conditioning protocol is shown in Fig. 2 for dissimilar odours, and in Fig. 3 for similar odours. Glomerulus 15 responds to 1-Hex but not to 2-Hex, therefore its synapses are

---

[1] The code and the parameter values are available at https://github.com/esinyavuz/Input-Modulation-Learning.

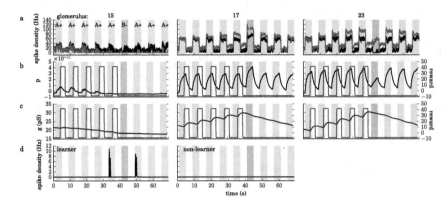

Fig. 2. Glomerular responses and corresponding learning parameters in time, during the absolute conditioning protocol for 2-Hex as the conditioning odour (A) and 2-Oct as the test odour (B), for three glomeruli. **(a)** PN responses as spike density function of spike trains. Responses of the neuron that has learning synapses is shown in green, other neurons with simple synapses is shown in black. **(b)** Eligibility traces and the reward signal. **(c)** ORN-PN conductances **(d)** DN responses. (Color figure online)

weakened during A+, which results in suppression of this glomerulus during B− (Fig. 3a, left). On the other hand, glomerulus 23 responds to 2-Hex and 1-Hex but not to 2-Oct, therefore learning results in a slight increase of its response to 2-Oct (Fig. 2a, right). Other glomeruli that have average response levels are slightly modulated, according to their eligibility that depends on the level of their activity (Fig. 2b). The resulting change in conductance is shown in Figs. 2 and 3c. Changes in the spiking activity is then detected by the learner DN: it starts to fire after the 4th or the 5th conditioning trial (Figs. 2 and 3d), due to random initialisation of the conductances. During the test trial, it responds to the similar odour (Fig. 3d) but not to the dissimilar odour (Fig. 2d), which shows that the model could successfully learn to discriminate the dissimilar odour while it generalises to the similar odour. After the first A− trial, the DN stops to respond as the odour is not associated with reward anymore, which is a phenomenon known as extinction.

4   Discussion

We presented a novel model for associative learning which involves modulation of AL activity by plasticity. This is much more akin to sensory learning than to usual associative learning models, like the classical perceptron. There are a number of alternative mechanisms that could underlie this type of learning. It could be based on recurrent network activity which provides a type of short-term memory and would facilitate the recurrent activation of PNs relevant to a rewarded stimulus. However, this is somewhat unlikely given that persistent spiking activity is not observed neither in calcium imaging, nor in electrophysiological recordings [4,10]. Another alternative hypothesis would be changes in

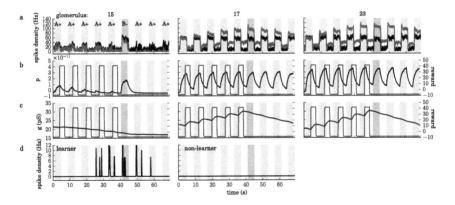

Fig. 3. Same as Fig. 2, for 2-Hex as odour A and 1-Hex as odour B.

neuronal properties of involved PNs or LNs, as has been observed in the snail feeding system [9]. The most likely substrate, however, are synaptic changes either between ORNs and PNs, as assumed here, or in the local network of the AL. This view is supported by the observation that associative learning induces changes in the spiking activity of the neurons in the AL [2,5,15].

The model of associative learning presented here is unusual compared to classical models such as the perceptron. In essence, this novel learning model is like a perceptron in which the input neurons learn to respond differently to rewarded inputs and so encode the knowledge of the world rather than modifying the synapses towards output neurons to achieve this. Figure 4 illustrates the essence of the two different solutions. It is natural to ask whether the two solutions are related and how they compare in classifying an input pattern against a backdrop of non-rewarded background patterns. To show this, we reduce the two models to a minimal connectionist description with binary variables as in [8].

For the perceptron, the responses are given by $y_i = \Theta\left(\sum_j w_{ij}x_j - \theta_{DN}\right)$, where the input neurons x_j are the PNs, w_{ij} is a binary connection matrix, and θ_{DN} the firing threshold. The PNs governed by $x_j = \Theta(c_j \sum_k r_{jk} - \theta_{PN})$, and $r_{jk} \in \{0,1\}$ are the responses of ORNs of type j, $k = 1, \ldots, N_{ORN}$, and c_j is a synaptic connection strength from ORNs to PNs, the same for all k (and potentially also all j). θ_{PN} is the firing threshold of PNs. Learning takes place through changes in w_{ij}, e.g. by applying this simple stochastic binary learning rule [8] for a rewarded stimulus:

$$w_{ij}(t+1) = \begin{cases} 1 & \text{with probability } p_+ \text{ if } y_i = 1 \text{ and } x_j = 1 \\ 0 & \text{with probability } p_- \text{ if } y_i = 1 \text{ and } x_j = 0 \\ w_{ij}(t) & \text{otherwise} \end{cases} \qquad (9)$$

It is straightforward to see that if the same pattern $\hat{\mathbf{x}} = (\hat{x}_j)$ is applied repeatedly and paired with an activation of y_i, then, eventually, the connectivity will equal $\hat{\mathbf{x}}$, i.e. $w_{ij} = \hat{x}_j$ for all j [8]. The separation of the target input $\mathbf{x}$ from other inputs $\mathbf{x}$ then depends on the overlap of the other inputs with $\mathbf{x}$ and the value of

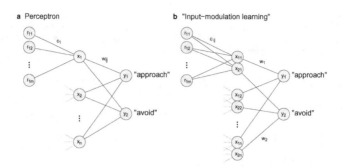

Fig. 4. Perceptron (**a**) compared to "input modulation learning" (**b**) introduced here. In the perceptron, the weights w_{ij} change during learning and there is only one copy of the "input pattern" in the PNs, and hence only one set of input neurons. In **b**, there are multiple copies of PNs, and learning takes place in the input synapses, c_{ij}.

θ_{DN}. In particular, the total input to y_i for an input pattern $\mathbf{x} = (x_j)$, is given by $\sum_j \hat{x}_j x_j$ or, equivalently, $\hat{\mathbf{x}} \cdot \mathbf{x}$.

On the other hand, for the learning system presented here, the responses are given by $y_i = \Theta\left(w_i \sum_j x_{ij} - \theta_{\mathrm{DN}}\right)$, the PN activitiy is $x_{ij} = \Theta\left(c_{ij} \sum_k r_{jk} - \theta_{\mathrm{PN}}\right)$, and it is the input conductances c_{ij} that change during learning. In the same minimalistic connectionist manner as above [8], an appropriate simplified description of the learning rule would be that, if reward is present,

$$c_{ij}(t+1) = \begin{cases} 1 & \text{with probability } p_+ \text{ if } r_{ij} = 1 \text{ and } i \text{ is the "reward pathway"} \\ 0 & \text{with probability } p_- \text{ if } r_{ij} = 0 \text{ and } i \text{ is the "reward pathway"} \\ c_{ij}(t) & \text{otherwise} \end{cases}$$

$$(10)$$

If no reward is present, all synaptic strengths c_{ij} remain unchanged. This scheme assumes, that there is one output neuron y_i per reward or punishment pathway, or, equivalently, each type of action, e.g. "approach" and "avoid". With the same argument as in [8] for the learning rule (9), the outcome of repeated i type reward for a single input pattern $\hat{\mathbf{r}}$ would be $c_{ij} = \hat{r}_j$ for all j. In such a case, we can assume that θ_{PN} is such that $r_{jk} = 1$ would lead to $x_{ij} = c_{ij}$, i.e. PNs x_{ij} spike if the corresponding receptors r_{jk} are active and $c_{ij} = 1$. If either the receptors are silent or $c_{ij} = 0$, no input will be received and no spiking will occur. The total input to an output neuron y_i hence depends essentially on the overlap of an input $\mathbf{r} = (r_j)$ with $\hat{\mathbf{r}}$, in particular, this input strength is $\sum_j \hat{r}_j r_j$ or the scalar product $\hat{\mathbf{r}} \cdot \mathbf{r}$, which is the same expression as above for the perceptron.

Our results suggest that input-modulation and the standard perceptron lead to the same results in their essentially reduced form, therefore the two approaches are equivalent. This indicates that learning can happen via different mechanisms than the traditionally studied ones. Investigating different strategies could provide insights to why the bees evolved to use this unusual mechanism, which is promising for development of novel algorithms for reinforcement learning.

Acknowledgments. This work is supported by the EPSRC (Green Brain Project, grant number EP/J019690/1) and Human Frontiers Science Program, grant number RGP0053/2015.

References

1. Cassenaer, S., Laurent, G.: Hebbian STDP in mushroom bodies facilitates the synchronous flow of olfactory information in locusts. Nature **448**(7154), 709–713 (2007)
2. Denker, M., Finke, R., Schaupp, F., Grün, S., Menzel, R.: Neural correlates of odor learning in the honeybee antennal lobe. Eur. J. Neurosci. **31**(1), 119–133 (2010)
3. Devaud, J.M., Blunk, A., Podufall, J., Giurfa, M., Grünewald, B.: Using local anaesthetics to block neuronal activity and map specific learning tasks to the mushroom bodies of an insect brain. Eur. J. Neurosci. **26**(11), 3193–3206 (2007)
4. Ditzen, M.: Odor concentration and identity coding in the antennal lobe of the honeybee Apis Mellifera. Ph.D. thesis, Freie Universität Berlin (2005)
5. Faber, T., Joerges, J., Menzel, R.: Associative learning modifies neural representations of odors in the insect brain. Nat. Neurosci. **2**(1), 74–78 (1999)
6. Guerrieri, F., Schubert, M., Sandoz, J.C., Giurfa, M.: Perceptual and neural olfactory similarity in honeybees. PLoS Biol. **3**(4), e60 (2005)
7. Hammer, M., Menzel, R.: Multiple sites of associative odor learning as revealed by local brain microinjections of octopamine in honeybees. Learn Mem. **5**(1), 146–156 (1998)
8. Huerta, R., Nowotny, T., Garcia-Sanchez, M., Abarbanel, H.D.I., Rabinovich, M.I.: Learning classification in the olfactory system of insects. Neural Comput. **16**, 1601–1640 (2004)
9. Kemenes, I., Straub, V.A., Nikitin, E.S., Staras, K., O'Shea, M., Kemenes, G., Benjamin, P.R.: Role of delayed nonsynaptic neuronal plasticity in long-term associative memory. Curr. Biol. **16**(13), 1269–1279 (2006)
10. Krofczik, S., Menzel, R., Nawrot, M.P.: Rapid odor processing in the honeybee antennal lobe network. Front Comput. Neurosci. **2**, 1–13 (2008)
11. Malun, D., Giurfa, M., Galizia, C.G., Plath, N., Brandt, R., Gerber, B., Eisermann, B.: Hydroxyurea-induced partial mushroom body ablation does not affect acquisition and retention of olfactory differential conditioning in honeybees. J. Neurobiol. **53**(3), 343–360 (2002)
12. Menzel, R.: The honeybee as a model for understanding the basis of cognition. Nat. Rev. Neurosci. **13**(11), 758–768 (2012)
13. Münch, D., Schmeichel, B., Silbering, A.F., Galizia, C.G.: Weaker ligands can dominate an odor blend due to syntopic interactions. Chem. Sens. **38**, 293–304 (2013). bjs138
14. Nowotny, T., Stierle, J.S., Galizia, C.G., Szyszka, P.: Data-driven honeybee antennal lobe model suggests how stimulus-onset asynchrony can aid odour segregation. Brain Res. **1536**, 119–134 (2013)
15. Rath, L., Galizia, C.G., Szyszka, P.: Multiple memory traces after associative learning in the honey bee antennal lobe. Eur. J. Neurosci. **34**(2), 352–360 (2011)

16. Sutton, R.S., Barto, A.G.: Reinforcement Learning: An Introduction. MIT press, Cambridge (1998)
17. Traub, R.D., Miles, R.: Neuronal Networks of the Hippocampus, vol. 777. Cambridge University Press, Cambridge (1991)
18. Yavuz, E., Turner, J., Nowotny, T.: GeNN: a code generation framework for accelerated brain simulations. Sci. Rep. **6**, 18854 (2016)

A Potential Mechanism for Spontaneous Oscillatory Activity in the Degenerative Mouse Retina

Kanako Taniguchi[1]([✉]), Chieko Koike[2], and Katsunori Kitano[1]

[1] Department of Human and Computer Intelligence,
Ritsumeikan University, Kyoto, Japan
kanako@cns.ci.ritsumei.ac.jp, kitano@ci.ritsumei.ac.jp
[2] College of Pharmaceutical Sciences, Ritsumeikan University,
1-1-1 Nojihigashi, Kusatsu, Shiga 5258577, Japan
koike@fc.ritsumei.ac.jp

Abstract. Spontaneous oscillation, which does not occur in the normal retina, is observed in the retina of the retinal degeneration mutant rd1 mouse, and provides insight into some details of the retinal network. The simple model by Trenholm *et al.* (2012) explained a mechanism for the oscillation, but it is not clear whether this mechanism functions for a larger, real network. To explore important factors for such an oscillatory network, we constructed a computational model of the AII amacrine cell (AII-AC) network and investigated the factors that affected the AII-AC network state by the varying model parameters, such as the degree of hyperpolarization of AII-ACs, the connection range, and others. Our results revealed two major tendencies: the AII-AC network exhibited oscillation when AII-ACs were hyperpolarized sufficiently, and when the AII-AC network was made sparse. These results suggest that dysfunction of photoreceptor cells could prevent formation of the correct AII-AC network.

Keywords: Retina · AII amacrine cell · Spontaneous oscillation

1 Introduction

The retina is the front-end neural network responsible for conversion of light stimuli into electrical signals that are interpreted by the brain. Fundamental functions of the retina have been clarified, but much of the detail of how the retina processes visual information is still unclear, in part because of the large variety of cell types, and the multiple pathways that link them [1].

The typical responses of a normal retinal network, i.e., ON and OFF responses, are generated by the output cells of the retina, retinal ganglion cells. The ON response is evoked with the onset of light stimulus, whereas the OFF response is evoked by the offset of light stimulus. Ganglion cells exhibit low activity without any light stimulus. In contrast, the retina of the retinal degeneration rd1 mouse shows no response, even when a light stimulus is presented,

© Springer International Publishing Switzerland 2016
A.E.P. Villa et al. (Eds.): ICANN 2016, Part I, LNCS 9886, pp. 63–71, 2016.
DOI: 10.1007/978-3-319-44778-0_8

because the rd1 mouse retina completely loses photoreceptor function. Instead, the abnormal retina exhibits a spontaneous oscillation at a low frequency [2–7]. A previous study showed that Na$^+$ channels expressed on the membranes of AII amacrine cells (AII-AC), and gap junctions between the AII-ACs and ON cone bipolar cells largely contributed to the generation of oscillations in the rd1 retina, and the authors proposed a simple concept model for the generation of spontaneous oscillation [6]. However, it is unclear whether the proposed mechanism actually functions in real retinal networks, as the concept model consists of only three neurons: one bipolar cell and two AII-ACs.

In this study, we focused on the properties of the AII-AC network, considered the generator of the spontaneous oscillation, to see if the oscillation would persist when the network is composed of a larger number of AII-ACs. It is expected that the generation of the spontaneous oscillation is highly dependent on the network connectivity between AII-ACs through gap junctions, and on the heterogeneity of membrane properties of AII-ACs. This is because the dense network through gap junctions is likely to stabilize and smooth membrane potentials between neurons, which would prevent such spontaneous oscillation from occurring. Therefore, we investigated the dependence of the network state on parameters such as network connectivity to determine the parameters required for the generation of the spontaneous oscillation in the AII-AC network.

2   Methods

We constructed a model of the AII-AC network in a mouse retina based on the previously proposed model [6]. Our model consists of 20 AII-AC models, each of which is a single compartmental conductance-based model with the Hodgkin-Huxley formalism.

2.1   Neuron Model

Each AII-AC has a fast sodium current I_{Na}, a potassium current I_K, and a leakage current I_L [6]. The dynamics of the membrane potential of the ith AII-AC, V_i is described by

$$C_m \frac{dV_i}{dt} = -I_{Na} - I_K - I_L - \sum_j g(V_i - V_j) + I_{input}, \qquad (1)$$

$$I_{Na} = \bar{g}_{Na} m_\infty(V_i) h_i (V_i - E_{Na}), \qquad (2)$$

$$I_K = \bar{g}_K n_i (V_i - E_K), \qquad (3)$$

$$I_L = g_L (V_i - E_L), \qquad (4)$$

where $\bar{g}_X$ are the maximal ionic conductances and E_X are reversal potentials. m, h and n are the gating variables, the dynamics and functions of which are represented by the following equations:

$$\frac{dh}{dt} = \frac{h_\infty(V) - h}{\tau_h}, \tag{5}$$

$$\frac{dn}{dt} = \frac{n_\infty(V) - n}{\tau_n(V)}, \tag{6}$$

$$y_\infty(V) = \frac{1}{2}\left(1 + \tanh\left(\frac{V - V_{y1}}{V_{y2}}\right)\right), \quad y = m, h, n, \tag{7}$$

$$\tau_n(V) = \left(\phi \cosh\left(\frac{V - V_{n1}}{2V_{n2}}\right)\right)^{-1}. \tag{8}$$

ϕ is the time constant of the recovery process to the equilibrium state at V_i determined by Eq. (7). The fourth term of the right-hand side in Eq. (1) represents the sum of currents through gap junctions from all neurons connected with the i neuron [9]. The conductances of the gap junctions were all assumed to have an identical strength g. The last term of the right-hand side in Eq. (1) is the input current I_{input}, using a negative value to represent the hyperpolarizing current, depicting the loss of spontaneous release of excitatory neurotransmitter onto the AII-ACs.

The membrane capacitance is $C_m = 1\ \mu\text{F/cm}^2$. The reversal potentials are $E_L = -60$ mV, $E_{Na} = 40$ mV, and $E_K = -100$ mV. The parameters for the steady states and the time constants of the gating variables are $V_{m1} = -1.2$ mV, $V_{m2} = 20.5$ mV, $V_{n1} = 2$ mV, $V_{n2} = 15$ mV, $V_{h1} = -28$ mV, $V_{h2} = -1$ mV, $\phi = 0.039$ and $\tau_h = 2$ ms.

In order to incorporate heterogeneity into the membrane properties of AII-ACs, conductance of the leakage current and the fast sodium current were randomly set. The maximal ionic conductances used were $\bar{g}_L = 0.02$ to 0.035 mS/cm^2, $\bar{g}_{Na} = 0.36$ to 0.525 mS/cm^2 and $g_K = 0.1$ mS/cm^2. This heterogeneity yielded different base levels of the resting membrane potential.

2.2 Network Connectivity

A retina has a sheet-like structure and the AII-AC network is thought to spread in a plane parallel to the retinal sheet. Therefore, it could be assumed that AII-ACs were on a 2D plane. In our model, 20 AII-ACs were placed at randomly chosen grid points (out of $10 \times 10 = 100$ grid points) on the plane (Fig. 1a). If the distance between a pair of cells is smaller than the connection range parameter r, the cells are randomly coupled to one another with a gap junction. This manipulation was carried out for all pairs of cells to constitute the AII-AC network. If r is small, the network might have only sparse connections such that it is divided into disconnected subnetworks. As r is increased, each AII-AC tends to have multiple connections with other AII-ACs, that is, the AII-ACs would form a dense network.

2.3   Model Simulation

Simulation was conducted with the NEURON simulator [8]. The simulation time was 10000 ms. The hyperpolarizing condition was given at the latter half of the simulation time (5000–10000 ms) following the control condition (no hyperpolarizing input current, 0–5000 ms). The parameters we set out to investigate were the connection range parameter (r), gap junction conductance (g), and hyperpolarizing input current (I_{input}). The range of the parameters are $r = 0 - 10$, $g = 0.02 - 0.1$ nS and $I_{input} = -0.12 - 0$ pA.

The issues we looked to address are as follows:

- whether hyperpolarization of the AII-ACs induces a spontaneous oscillation, and
- how the spontaneous oscillation of the AII-AC network depends on the connection range parameter (r) and the gap junction conductance (g).

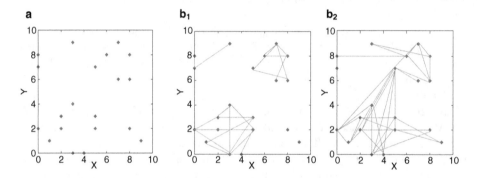

Fig. 1. Locations of cells and connection patterns of the AII-AC network with gap junctions. **a.** Locations of 20 AII-ACs on a 2D plane. Each cell (a red dot) was placed at a grid point that was randomly sampled out of $10 \times 10 = 100$ grid points. **b.** Connection patterns between the AII-ACs for different values of the connection range parameter r. If a pair of cells fell within the distance r, the cells were randomly connected. A green line indicates the gap connection between a pair of cells. **b$_1$.** The connection pattern for $r = 3$. **b$_2$.** The connection pattern for $r = 4$. (Color figure online)

3   Results

An example of the network used in the present study is shown in (Fig. 1). As shown in Fig. 1a, the locations of 20 AII-ACs were distributed uniformly, but randomly. Figure 1b demonstrates the network connectivity for the connection range parameter $r = 3$ and $r = 4$. Connections in the network with $r = 3$ (Fig. 1b$_1$) were sparse; the AII-ACs were divided into isolated cells and some clusters. On the other hand, if r was set to 4 (Fig. 1b$_2$), almost all the cells were connected to the network, and each the cell had more collateral connections than the $r = 3$ condition.

We conducted numerical simulations of the AII-AC network, varying the potentially influential parameters. From time courses of the membrane potentials in a steady state, we obtained amplitude signals from all the cells to determine if the conditions defined by the set of parameters had induced an oscillatory state. We found significant effects on the oscillatory state with three parameters: hyperpolarizing input currents I_{input}, the connection range parameter r, and the conductance of gap junctions g. To examine the effect of one of the parameters, we generally fixed the other parameters. We tried randomly generated different network patterns and obtained similar dependences of results on each parameter (data not shown).

3.1 Effect of Hyperpolarizing Input Currents

An example time course of the membrane potential of one of the AII-ACs is illustrated in Fig. 2a. No input was applied from 0–5000 ms; then a constant hyperpolarizing current with amplitude I_{input} was applied to all of the cells. As the current amplitude was increased, the spontaneous oscillations started, and the amplitude of the oscillation was gradually increased. Hyperpolarization brought about variability of resting membrane potentials due to different values of the leak conductance. Consequently, the varied resting membrane potentials initiated the oscillations through the effect of gap junctions and active channels. However, the oscillation was suppressed under very strong hyperpolarizing currents (data not shown). This is presumably because excessive hyperpolarization prevents Na^+ channels from being activated, which is consistent with the result in the previous study: blockade of Na^+ channels could stop the oscillation [6].

In Fig. 2b, the results of varying the hyperpolarizing input current are summarized: As the current gets stronger, it tends to enhance the spontaneous oscillation.

3.2 Effect of Network Connectivity of the AII-AC Network

Next we varied the connection range parameter (r) to reveal the relationship between network connectivity and generation of spontaneous oscillations. Figure 3 depicts the dependence of the amplitude of oscillation on the connection range parameter. When the hyperpolarizing current was weak (Fig. 3a), only AII-ACs in the $r = 3$ network model exhibited the oscillation; even so, the amplitudes remained very small. With a stronger hyperpolarizing current (Fig. 3b), the number of oscillating AII-ACs and the amplitudes of the oscillation were greatly increased for the networks where $r \leq 4$. In other words, even with a high hyperpolarizing current, densely connected networks with $r \geq 5$ failed to generate spontaneous oscillation.

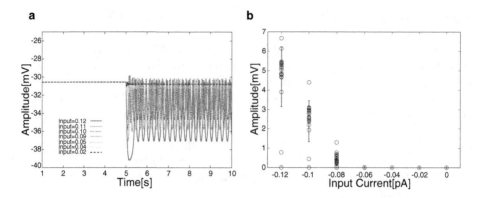

Fig. 2. Effect of hyperpolarizing input currents on generation of the spontaneous oscillation. The connection range parameter and the gap junction conductance were set to $r = 4$ and $g = 0.06$ nS, respectively. **a.** Time courses of the membrane potential of an AII-AC. Colors indicate different amplitudes of constant input currents. **b.** Dependence of oscillation amplitudes on the intensity of the hyperpolarizing input currents. An open circle illustrates an amplitude of an AII-AC whereas the error bars indicates the standard deviations over 20 AII-ACs.

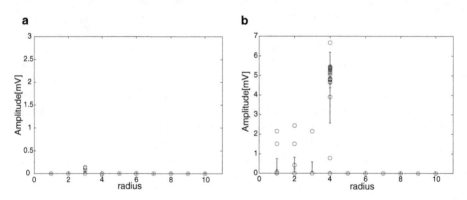

Fig. 3. Impact of the connection range on the oscillatory activity. The figures are similar to Fig. 2b except for the abscissa axis. The gap junction conductance was set to $g = 0.06$ nS. **a.** I_{input} set to -0.02 pA. **b.** I_{input} set to -0.12 pA.

3.3 Role of Gap Junctions Between AII-ACs

We varied the gap junction conductance to verify its role (Fig. 4). The spontaneous oscillation occurred for most values of g except $g = 0$. The oscillation amplitudes did not necessarily change systematically when the network connectivity was set to $r = 3$ (Fig. 4a). In this case, the largest amplitude was observed for $g = 0.01$ nS. In the case of the network with $r = 4$, shown in Fig. 4b, the oscillation occurred only for $g = 0.01$ nS, suggesting that in a more dense network, even slightly large gap junction conductances prevent the network from generating spontaneous oscillations.

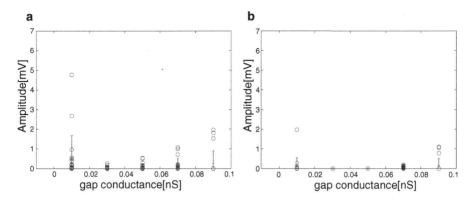

Fig. 4. Effect of the gap junction conductance on the oscillatory activity. I_{input} was set to -0.02 pA. **a.** Connection range parameter set to $r = 3$. **b.** Connection range parameter set to $r = 4$.

3.4   Dependence of the Frequency of the Parameters

Finally, we investigated what parameter determined the frequency of the oscillation (Fig. 5). The frequency only slightly changed depending on the connection range (Fig. 5a) whereas the change in the gap junction conductance had more effect on the frequency for this set of parameters (Fig. 5b). However, the frequency was determined by combinations of several parameters on the AII-AC network connectivity.

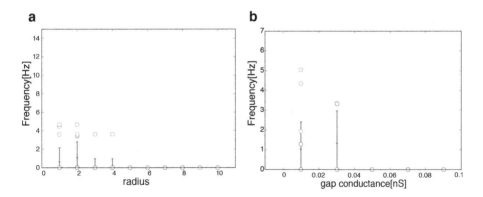

Fig. 5. Effect of the connection range and the gap junction conductance on the frequency of the spontaneous oscillation. ($I_{input} = -0.12$ pA). **a.** The dependence on the connection range parameter. ($g = 0.06$ nS) **b.** The dependence on the gap junction conductance. ($r = 3$)

4 Discussion

Our results show that as the intensity of the hyperpolarizing input current was increased, the number of oscillating neurons and the amplitude of the oscillation were increased, if the connection range parameter was set to specific values. From the results, we conclude that the hyperpolarization of AII-ACs is likely to trigger spontaneous oscillation. In addition, the connection range parameter has a strong impact on whether the AII-AC network exhibited spontaneous oscillation or not. In our model, the network with $r = 2$ to $r = 4$ exhibited spontaneous oscillation. Interaction by gap junctions was not strong for the network with a small r, because the number of connections was too few. For larger r ($r \geq 5$), the connections by gap junctions were dense. The balancing effect by the dense gap junctions was too strong to allow spontaneous oscillation. AII-ACs in the normal retina surely form a gap junction network, and normally exhibit no oscillation. This suggests that the degenerative mouse retina has a sparser AII-AC network than the normal retina; in other words, that the connection range of the degenerative mouse retina is smaller than that of the normal retina. Except for the network with $r = 3$, increased gap junction conductance tended to prevent the AII-ACs from oscillating. This is presumably because the increased gap junction conductance exerts a higher balancing effect to the membrane potentials between cells. From our model, the spontaneous oscillation observed in the degenerative mouse retina could be attributed to insufficient formation of the AII-AC network, particularly the loss of AII-AC collaterals to other AII-ACs, with their gap junctions and excitatory connections, stemming from the degeneration of the photoreceptor cells.

References

1. Asari, H., Meister, M.: Divergence of visual channels in the inner retina. Nat. Neurosci. **15**, 1581–1589 (2012)
2. Stasheff, S.F.: Emergence of sustained spontaneous hyperactivity and temporary preservation of off responses in ganglion cells of the retinal degeneration (rd1) mouse. J. Neurophysiol. **99**, 1408–1421 (2008)
3. Menzler, J., Zeck, G.: Network oscillations in rod-degenerated mouse retinas. J. Neurosci. **31**, 2280–2291 (2011)
4. Borowska, J., Trenholm, S., Awatramani, G.B.: An intrinsic neural oscillator in the degenerating mouse retina. J. Neurosci. **31**, 5000–5012 (2011)
5. Yee, C.W., Toychiev, A.H., Sagdullaev, B.T.: Network deficiency exacerbates impairment in a mouse model of retinal degeneration. Front. Syst. Neurosci. **6**, 8 (2012). doi:10.3389/fnsys.2012.00008
6. Trenholm, S., Borowska, J., Zhang, J., Hoggarth, A., Johnson, K., Barnes, S., Lewis, T.J., Awatramani, B.G.: Intrinsic oscillatory activity arising within the electrically coupled AII Amacrine-ON cone bipolar cell network is driven by voltage-gated Na$^+$ channels. J. Physiol. **590**(10), 2501–2517 (2012)
7. Choi, H., Zhang, L., Cembrowski, M.S., Sabottke, C.F., Markowitz, A.L., Butts, D.A., Kath, W.L., Singer, J.H., Riecke, H.: Intrinsic bursting of AII amacrine cells underlies oscillations in the rd1 mouse retina. J. Neurophysiol. **112**, 1491–1504 (2014)

8. Hines, M.L., Carnevale, T.: The NEURON simulation. Environment **9**(6), 1179–1209 (1997)
9. Vladimirov, N., Tu, Y., Traub, R.D.: Shortest loops are pacemakers in random networks of electrically coupled axons. Front. Comput. Neurosci. **6**, 17 (2011). doi:10.3389/fncom.2012.00017

Striatal Processing of Cortical Neuronal Avalanches – A Computational Investigation

Jovana J. Belić[1,2(✉)] and Jeanette Hellgren Kotaleski[1,3]

[1] School of Computer Science and Communication,
Royal Institute of Technology, Stockholm, Sweden
{belic,jeanette}@kth.se
[2] Bernstein Center Freiburg, University of Freiburg, Freiburg, Germany
[3] Department of Neuroscience, Karolinska Institute, Stockholm, Sweden

Abstract. In the cortex, spontaneous neuronal avalanches can be characterized by spatiotemporal activity clusters with a cluster size distribution that follows a power law with exponent –1.5. Recordings in the striatum revealed that striatal activity was also characterized by spatiotemporal clusters that followed a power law distribution albeit, with significantly steeper slope, i.e., they lacked the large spatial clusters that are commonly expected for avalanche dynamics. In this study, we used computational modeling to investigate the influence of intrastriatal inhibition and corticostriatal interplay as important factors to understand the experimental findings and overall information transmission among these circuits.

Keywords: Corticostriatal network · Neuronal avalanches · Striatum · Basal ganglia · Cortex

1 Introduction

Neuronal avalanches are a type of spontaneous activity first detected in vitro by recording local field potentials in cortical neural networks using slices of rat cortex as well as cultured networks [1]. It was observed that the sizes of these events (clusters), where the size was determined by the number of participating electrodes during each single activity burst, were distributed according to a power law with a characteristic exponent of –1.5. Power laws are ubiquitous in the brain on multiple scales, and this phenomenon has also been linked to many complex systems in nature, such as earthquakes, landslides, and forest fires [2].

Later on, neuronal avalanches have been shown to be the emerging dynamics at which various measures important for cortical information processing are maximized, such as dynamic range, burst pattern entropy and phase synchronization variability [3–6]. Neuronal avalanches display long-term stability and diversity [7], and it has been proposed that this type of activity reflects the transient formation of cell assemblies in the cortex [8].

Cortical networks in vivo are heavily connected to striatum, main input stage of the basal ganglia. The striatum is a recurrent inhibitory network, and how striatum responds to cortical inputs has crucial importance for clarifying the overall functions of the basal

© Springer International Publishing Switzerland 2016
A.E.P. Villa et al. (Eds.): ICANN 2016, Part I, LNCS 9886, pp. 72–79, 2016.
DOI: 10.1007/978-3-319-44778-0_9

ganglia. Our previous work revealed that striatal cluster size distributions were characterized by strongly reduced spatial correlations when compared to the cortex, and we also showed that one particularly high activation threshold of striatal nodes can reproduce power law-like distribution with a coefficient similar to the one found experimentally [9]. In this research, we extend our model in order to explore the role of intrastriatal inhibition, different activation thresholds, and increased cortical activity in shaping striatal responses to cortical neuronal avalanches. We tested different activation probabilities for the striatal nodes, from linear to highly skewed, and observed that the striatal network has to have an internal representation of the structure in the input space in order to reproduce the experimental results. By changing the ratio of excitation and inhibition in our cortical model, we saw that increased activity in the cortex strongly influenced striatal dynamics, which was reflected in a less negative slope of cluster size distributions in the striatum and increased firing of striatal nodes. Lastly, when we added inhibition to our model, cluster size distributions had a prominently earlier deviation from the power law distribution (lower probability for large events) compared to the case when inhibition was not present. Further, intrastriatal inhibition shapes striatal distribution by reducing the firing rate and duration of clusters.

2 Methods

2.1 Corticostriatal Network Model

First, we developed an abstract cortical model that reproduces statistics observed in experimental data [1, 3]. We set average connectivity between the N (N = 30; corresponding to the number of recording sites in experiments) cortical nodes to be 10 as suggested by the experimental data [3], and then applied the preferential attachment rule, where each node was attached to other nodes in proportion to the designated out-degrees of those nodes. In this way, we acquired a node degree linearly related to the average node strength for in and out degrees. Experimental data revealed that the weight distribution of the links has an exponentially decaying tail, demonstrating the presence of a few links with large traffic [3], thus we picked transmission probabilities p_{ij} (from node j to node i) from exponential distributions. In our model, there were neither any self-connections nor more than one connection between attached pairs. We scaled the weights, so the branching parameter σ (the average number of nodes activated in the next time step, given a single node being active in the current time step) for the entire network was set to 1:

$$p'_{ij} = p_{ij}/(\sum_i \sum_j p_{ij}) * N \qquad (1)$$

The probability that node i fired (reached the activation threshold) at time t + 1 was equal to:

$$p_{iJ} = \left(1 - \prod_{j \in J(t)} (1 - p'_{ij})\right), \tag{2}$$

where J(t) was the set of nodes that fired at time t. Only if $p_{iJ} > \epsilon$, where ϵ was a random number from a uniform distribution on [0, 1], node i fired in the next time step. Each of the N nodes in the striatum was randomly connected with a certain number of nodes in the cortex. We systematically varied the number of connections (N_k) between the cortex and striatum, assumed to be needed for evoking activity in the striatal nodes, in order to check how it influenced the observed striatal statistic. In the striatum, we had all-to-all or locally coupled nodes (without self-connections) where transmission probabilities ps_{ij} (from node j to node i) were randomly chosen from uniform distribution and were than scaled, so the striatal parameter σ_1 (where $\sigma_1 \leq 0$) for the entire network could be tested for different values:

$$ps'_{ij} = ps_{ij}/(\sum_i \sum_j ps_{ij}) * N * \sigma_1, \tag{3}$$

The probability that node i in the striatum fired at time t + 1 was equal to:

$$P_i(t + 1) = \sum \left(excitation_i(t + 1) - inhibition_i(t + 1)\right), \tag{4}$$

where i = 1,.., N. Node i fired at time t + 1 only if $P_i(t + 1) > \epsilon_1$ (ϵ_1 was also a random number from a uniform distribution on [0, 1]). Excitation was equal to 1 if the full pattern in the cortex assigned to node i was present; in the case of an uncompleted pattern, it was set to be very low (< 0.005). Probability of inhibition for node i was equal to:

$$inhibition_i(t + 1) = (1 - \prod_{j \in Js(t)} \left(1 - |Ps'_{ij}|\right)), \tag{5}$$

and Js(t) was the set of striatal nodes that fired at time t.

We elicited population events by randomly choosing and triggering a single node in the cortex while simultaneously collecting resulting activity in the cortex and striatum (this procedure was repeated 30,000 times for each trial).

2.2 Data Analysis

Power law exponents were estimated using the Kolmogorov-Smirnov (KS) statistic [10]. In cortical networks, the cut-off is typically at the system size, which is given by the number of electrodes in the cortical array [11]. Thus, cortical event size distributions were fitted on the range from 1 to the number of electrodes in the cortical array [9]. In most cases, striatal cluster sizes did not extend to the system size, in which case cluster size distributions were fitted from 1 to the maximum cluster size.

The KS test was used to determine whether the power law or exponential distribution was fitting the data better. Specifically, the distribution with the smallest KS distance between the model fit and data was considered the better fit.

We additionally estimated the degree of correlation between each pair of nodes with the Jaccard correlation coefficient, which shows the degree to which the positive events co-occur.

All values are expressed as mean ± standard error if not stated otherwise.

3   Results

We developed an abstract model of the corticostriatal network to investigate whether experimental findings regarding striatal processing of cortical avalanches can be explained by corticostriatal interactions and/or intrastriatal inhibition. First, we wanted to see how the sole connectivity pattern between cortex and striatum influences the observed dynamics by giving different activation probabilities to striatal nodes as a function of cortical activity. We did that by varying the number of cortical nodes (N_k) assigned to each striatal node. Simultaneously recorded activity in the cortex and striatum produced by the model has generally shown substantially more sparse activity in the striatum compared to the cortex (Fig. 1a). Similarly, experimental data have also revealed that the number of significantly negative local field potential (LFP) peaks was also much higher in the case of cortical LFP traces [9]. Thus, we set firing of these (N_k) cortical nodes as a precondition for the striatal node to fire, and in this way we obtained different activation probabilities for the striatal nodes, from linear to highly skewed (Fig. 1b). By increasing the number of cortical nodes assigned to each striatal node, we observed more negative estimations of the power law exponent (α) in the striatum (Fig. 1c and d). Under the assumption of a low activation threshold of striatal nodes ($N_k = 2$), the recorded distribution in the striatum was similar to the one found in the cortex. Specifically, under the assumption of a particular high activation threshold of striatal nodes ($N_k = 4$), we can reproduce power law-like distributions with a coefficient similar to the one found experimentally (Fig. 1e, upper plot, $p < 0.01$). The obtained distributions were also much more in favor of power law distributions compared to the exponential one (Fig. 1e, lower plot). Furthermore, average pairwise correlation was considerably higher in the cortex compared to the corticostriatal activity (Fig. 1f).

In order to investigate how additional striatal inhibition shapes observed striatal dynamics, we systematically varied the striatal parameter (σ_1) in our computational model. The value of σ_1 defines the probability of striatal nodes to be inhibited in the next time step by a single currently active presynaptic striatal node. We investigated two different striatal network topologies. In the first, the nodes were connected in an all-to-all fashion (Fig. 2a, left panel). The second network topology comprised nodes that were connected on a two-dimensional lattice with a nearest neighbor connectivity (four neighbors; Fig. 2a, right panel). Striatal nodes in this case were connected as a torus in order to avoid dissipation of activity due to border effects, and the connectivity strength between nodes was equal to $\sigma_1/4$. When inhibitory connections were imposed, cluster size distributions had a slightly decreased likelihood of occurrence of small events, but the decrease in the likelihood of medium and especially large events was prominent compared to the case when inhibition was not present. Kolmogorov-Smirnov statistics showed that power law distribution after introducing inhibition in the model became

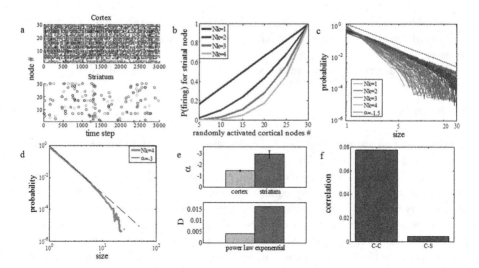

Fig. 1. Influence of activation threshold on striatal dynamics. (**a**) Raster of activity in the cortex and striatum produced by the model. (**b**) Probability of activation for striatal node depending on the number of randomly activated cortical nodes. (**c**) Cluster size distributions in the striatum for multiple runs. Black line indicates a power law with $\alpha = -1.5$ for comparison. (**d**) Average cluster size distributions in the striatum (averaged over 50 trials, $N_k = 4$). (**e**) Average power law exponent for cortex and striatal distribution given in (d) (Kolmogorov-Smirnov statistics, upper plot) and Kolmogorov-Smirnov distance for striatum (D, lower plot). (**f**) Average pairwise correlation in cortex and between cortex and striatum ($N_k = 4$).

steeper (-3.22 ± 0.36, $p < 0.01$, $\sigma_1 = -4$) compared to the control case without inhibition (-2.94 ± 0.27, Fig. 2b, upper plot). Inhibition also reduced the firing rate as well as duration of avalanches in the striatum (Fig. 2b, lower plot, $p < 0.05$).

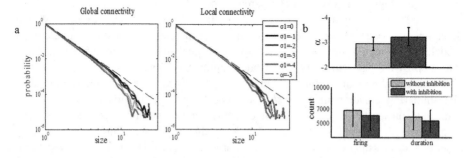

Fig. 2. Influence of intrastriatal inhibition on striatal dynamics. (**a**) Influence of intrastriatal inhibition on cluster size distributions in the striatum in the case of all-to-all (left panel) or local (right panel) connectivity in the striatum (50 trials, constant corticostriatal connectivity, Nk = 4, assumed). (**b**) Comparison between average power law exponent values (Kolmogorov-Smirnov statistics, upper plot) and firing and duration counts (lower plot) in the striatum in the case when inhibition is present ($\sigma_1 = -4$) and in the case without inhibition.

By changing the ratio of excitation and inhibition in our cortical model (σ), we wanted to test the influence of increased cortical activity on striatal dynamics. For $\sigma < 1$ an activated node triggers activity in less than one node, on average, resulting in a hypo-excitable state. For $\sigma > 1$, a node activates, on average, more than one node in the next time step, resulting in a hyperexcitable condition. When the system was hyperexcitable and inhibitory synaptic transmission was reduced, distribution had an increased likelihood for large activity clusters. Increased activity in the cortex influenced strongly striatal dynamics, which was reflected in a less negative slope of cluster size distributions in the striatum and increased firing of striatal nodes. We tested different values of the branching parameter in the cortex for two scenarios, without inhibition and with inhibition in the striatum (Fig. 3a). We observed in both cases that by increasing the value of σ, cluster size distributions in the striatum started to approach the power law distribution found in the cortex under normal conditions. Specifically, for a branching parameter in the cortex higher than 1.25, we observed a distribution in the striatum very similar to the one found in the cortex in the case of a balanced network ($\sigma = 1$, Fig. 3b).

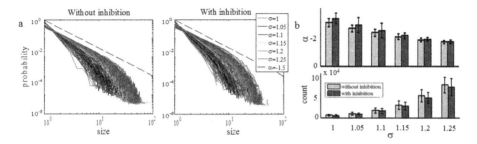

Fig. 3. Influence of input correlations on striatal dynamics. (**a**) Cluster size distributions in the striatum with and without intrastriatal inhibition for different values of excitation (σ) in the cortex ($\sigma_1 = -4$, $N_k = 4$). (**b**) Comparison between average power law exponent values (Kolmogorov-Smirnov statistics, upper plot) and firing counts (lower plot) for striatal distributions given in (a) for different values of excitation (σ) in the cortex.

4   Discussion

Medium spiny projection neurons (MSNs) are the dominant neuron type in the striatum, and they also have membrane properties that give them a high threshold for activation. A single striatal MSN receives input from more than 5,000 cortical neurons, which represent a massive convergence of cortical inputs [12]. Striatal MSNs tend to remain in a stabilized, silent state, except when they receive strong excitatory input. We have tested different connectivity patterns between cortex and striatum, from linear to those with a high threshold for activation of striatal nodes, in order to reproduce experimental data. Specifically, under the assumption of a particular high activation threshold of striatal nodes, we can reproduce power law-like distributions with a coefficient similar to the one found experimentally. How information is transferred among the circuits in the cortex and striatum has been unanswered, but our results suggest that the striatal network has to have an internal representation of the structure in the input space. Dimensionality reduction in the nervous system can be depicted as compression of the information encoded by a large neuronal population to a smaller number of neurons, and the number of corticostriatal neurons exceeds the number of striatal neurons by a factor of 10 [12]. This process is extremely useful, because it allows the transmission of a large amount of information within a limited number of axons. Other models have also assumed that the striatum performs dimensionality reduction and decorrelation of cortical information [13, 14]. In those models, lateral connections were only needed during the learning phase and become weak after a representation of the input statistics. Thus, striatum might be able to extract the correlation structure of high-dimensional cortical states after the network has achieved an internal representation of the cortical space.

There are at least two inhibitory circuits in the striatum that are activated by cortical inputs and which control firing in MSNs. The first is feedforward inhibition via the small population of fast spiking interneurons (FSIs), and the second is feedback inhibition from the axon collaterals of the MSNs themselves [15]. When we added inhibition to our model, cluster size distributions had a prominently earlier deviation from the power law distribution (lower probability for large events) compared to the case when inhibition was not present. The same statistics were observed in the case of globally as well as locally applied inhibition. Further, intrastriatal inhibition shapes striatal activity by decorrelating the output rate across striatal nodes as well as between cortical and striatal nodes, and this was reflected in reduced firing rate and duration of clusters.

Acknowledgements. The research leading to these results has received funding from the European Union Seventh Framework Programme (FP7/2007-2013) under grant agreement n°604102 (HBP), the Swedish Research Council, NIAAA (grant 2R01AA016022), Swedish e-Science Research Centre, and EuroSPIN – an Erasmus Mundus Joint Doctorate program. The authors are thankful to Andreas Klaus for helpful discussion.

References

1. Beggs, J., Plenz, D.: Neuronal avalanches in neocortical circuits. J. Neurosci. **23**, 11167–11177 (2003)
2. Bak, P.: How Nature Works: The Science of Self-organized Criticality. Copernicus Press, New York (1996)
3. Pajevic, S., Plenz, D.: Efficient network reconstruction from dynamical cascades identifies small-world topology of neuronal avalanches. PLoS Comput. Biol. **5**(1), e1000271 (2009)
4. Petermann, T., Thiagarajan, T., Lebedev, M., Nicolelis, M., Chialvo, D., Plenz, D.: Spontaneous cortical activity in awake monkeys composed of neuronal avalanches. Proc. Natl. Acad. Sci. U.S.A. **18**, 15921–15926 (2009)
5. Shew, W., Yang, H., Yu, S., Roy, R., Plenz, D.: Information capacity and transmission are maximized in balanced cortical networks with neuronal avalanches. J. Neurosci. **31**, 55–63 (2011)
6. Yang, H., Shew, W., Roy, R., Plenz, D.: Maximal variability of phase synchrony in cortical networks with neuronal avalanches. J. Neurosci. **32**, 1061–1072 (2012)
7. Beggs, J., Plenz, D.: Neuronal avalanches are diverse and precise activity patterns that are stable for many hours in cortical slice cultures. J. Neurosci. **24**, 5216–5229 (2004)

8. Plenz, D., Thiagarajan, T.: The organizing principles of neuronal avalanches: cell assemblies in the cortex? Trends Neurosci. **30**, 101–110 (2007)
9. Belić, J., Klaus, A., Plenz, D., Hellgren Kotaleski, J.: Mapping of cortical avalanches to the striatum. In: Liljenström, H. (ed.) Advances in Cognitive Neurodynamics, vol. 4, pp. 291–297. Springer, Dordrecht (2015)
10. Klaus, A., Yu, S., Plenz, D.: Statistical analyses support power law distributions found in neuronal avalanches. PLoS ONE **6**, e19779 (2011)
11. Yu, S., Klaus, A., Yang, H., Plenz, D.: Scale-invariant neuronal avalanche dynamics and the cut-off in size distributions. PLoS ONE **9**, e99761 (2014)
12. Zheng, T., Wilson, J.: Corticostriatal combinatorics: the implications of corticostriatal axonal arborizations. J. Neurophysiol. **87**, 1007–1017 (2002)
13. Bar-Gad, I., Havazelet-Heimer, G., Goldberg, A., Ruppin, E., Bergman, H.: Reinforcement-driven dimensionality reduction-a model for information processing in the basal ganglia. J. Basic Clin. Physiol. Pharmacol. **11**, 305–320 (2000)
14. Plenz, D., Kitai, S.: Adaptive classification of cortical input to the striatum by competitive learning. In: Brain Dynamics and the Striatal Complex, pp. 165–177 (2000)
15. Tepper, J., Koos, T., Wilson, C.: GABAergic microcircuits in the neostriatum. Trends Neurosci. **27**, 662–669 (2004)

Networks and Dynamics

Mapping the Language Connectome in Healthy Subjects and Brain Tumor Patients

Gregory Zegarek[1,2(✉)], Xerxes D. Arsiwalla[2],
David Dalmazzo[2], and Paul F.M.J. Verschure[2,3]

[1] Pritzker School of Medicine, University of Chicago, Chicago, IL, USA
gzegarek@uchicago.edu
[2] Synthetic Perceptive Emotive and Cognitive Systems (SPECS) Lab,
Center of Autonomous Systems and Neurorobotics,
Universitat Pompeu Fabra, Barcelona, Spain
x.d.arsiwalla@gmail.com, davmazo@gmail.com, paul.verschure@upf.edu
[3] Catalan Institute of Advanced Studies (ICREA), Barcelona, Spain
http://specs.upf.edu

Abstract. A crucial challenge for both clinical and systems neuroscience is reliable mapping of brain networks to higher-order cognitive functions in both health and disease. In this paper, we map the brain's emerging language network in the human connectome based on data from rTMS studies on healthy volunteers as well as brain tumor patients. The key finding is that cortical areas which are involved in the language network are more likely to be connected to Wernicke's and Broca's areas based on standard graph theoretic measures. In addition, the higher the connectivity of a particular area to the classic language areas, the more likely it is that region is involved in the language network. We comment on the clinical value that these structure-function connectome maps can have for planning and aiding neurosurgical procedures.

Keywords: Brain mapping · Connectomics · Neurosurgery

1 Introduction

In neurosurgery, eloquent cortex refers to the cortical area that is indispensable for a given function, such as language [18]. When a brain tumor occurs near language cortical areas, great care must be taken by the neurosurgical team to maximize the extent of the resection while avoiding any functional deficits. Localizing the areas of eloquent cortex is generally done presurgically or intra-operatively, utilizing methods such as Cortical Stimulation Mapping (CSM), functional Magnetic Resonance Imaging (fMRI), and repetitive navigated Transcranial Magnetic Stimulation (rTMS). While CSM remains the gold standard for peritumoral mapping, rTMS is gaining increasing importance in presurgical language mapping [15,17].

Evaluating eloquent cortex in regards to language function is particularly challenging due to a number of factors: (1) there is an extensive network of cortical areas which are involved in language, (2) there is considerable inter-individual

© Springer International Publishing Switzerland 2016
A.E.P. Villa et al. (Eds.): ICANN 2016, Part I, LNCS 9886, pp. 83–90, 2016.
DOI: 10.1007/978-3-319-44778-0_10

variation of the language network, and (3) any brain pathology, such as tumors, can lead to extensive reorganization of the language network [19]. While it is currently well-accepted that language processing in the brain is supported by an extensive network of many different regions [11], the traditional 19th century anatomical-based model of language still persists today. This model, which describes Wernicke's area as important for language comprehension and Broca's area as important for language production is the classic model still taught in medical schools and neurology textbooks [10]. We were interested in exploring a connection between the modern emerging language network and these classic anatomical areas.

In the context of the language network, positive brain regions were defined as those giving rise to any type of language error when that region was stimulated by TMS, and negative brain regions were defined as those that did not give rise to any language deficit when stimulated [15]. We hypothesized that (1) positive brain regions were more likely to be connected to Wernicke's and Broca's areas than negative brain regions, and that (2) the higher the induced language error rate in a given positive brain region, the more strongly connected that cortical area would be to Wernicke's and Broca's areas.

2   Methods

In order to explore the connectivity between the language network and the classic language areas, we utilized the functionality of BrainX^3 [2–4]. BrainX^3 is a large-scale simulation of the human brain with real-time interaction, rendered in 3D in a virtual reality environment [5–7,16]. BrainX^3 incorporates a large-scale simulation of the human connectome, grounded on structural connectivity data obtained from diffusion spectrum imaging [12].

2.1   rTMS Mapping

The cortical distribution of language areas in healthy subjects and brain tumor patients was based on the experiments done by Krieg et al. [15] and Rosler et al. [19], respectively. Repetitive navigated TMS was performed on 50 right-handed monolingual healthy volunteers and 50 right-handed patients with left-sided gliomas in the vicinity of language-eloquent areas. Healthy subjects underwent rTMS of the left hemisphere and Brain Tumor patients underwent rTMS of both hemispheres while performing an object-naming task provided by the Nexstim NexSpeech module. Frequency maps of elicited errors were created based on the Cortical Parcellation System, which parcellates the cortex into 37 anatomical areas bilaterally, making a total of 74 total cortical areas [9].

2.2   Efferent Mapping

Through Efferent Mapping, BrainX^3 allows the user to select the specific nodes making up the cortical regions in question and map the projections from those nodes to all other connected nodes. Figure 1 shows an example of efferent mapping from representative nodes within the language network of healthy individuals. All nodes, parcellated by the 74 areas were selected in a semi-automatic fashion, and the connected nodes and connection weights were outputted.

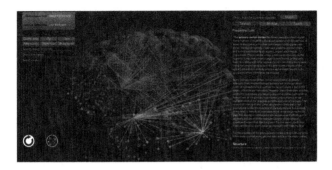

Fig. 1. Efferent mapping in BrainX^3. Connectome projections highlighted from representative points within regions with $> 25\%$ naming errors in healthy subjects.

2.3   Data Analysis

We analyzed the zone-zone connectivity from all 74 areas to Wernicke's and Broca's areas individually, as well as to Wernicke's or Broca's area collectively. Zone-zone connectivity was measured by three standard measures, shown in Eqs. 1 to 3 below [14].

$$C_{Zone}^{ACS}(A_i, A_j) = \sum_{\forall r_m \in N_i^s} \zeta_{r_m} + \sum_{\forall r_n \in N_j^s} \zeta_{r_n} \tag{1}$$

$$C_{Zone}^{ACD}(A_i, A_j) = \frac{C_{Zone}^{ACS}(A_i, A_j)}{|N_i^s| + |N_j^s|} \tag{2}$$

$$C_{Zone}^{ACP}(A_i, A_j) = \max\left(\max_{\forall r_m \in N_i^s} \zeta_{r_m}, \max_{\forall r_n \in N_j^s} \zeta_{r_n}\right) \tag{3}$$

Anatomical Connection Strength (ACS)is related to the cross sectional area of the fiber bundle connecting the two zones. Anatomical Connection Density (ACD) is a measure of the fraction of the surface area involved in the connection with respect to the total surface of both areas. Anatomical Connection Probability (ACP) is a measure of the probability of the two areas being connected at least by a single connection [14]. One-tailed T-tests were performed to compare the zone-zone connectivity from positive vs. negative brain regions to classic language areas along all 3 measures in order to test hypothesis 1. In order to test hypothesis 2, linear regressions were performed for all positive brain regions to compare their zone-zone connectivity to classic language areas vs. their error rate, defined as the percentage of all stimulations in that area that produced any kind of language error [19].

3   Results

3.1   The Language Connectome

Figure 2 demonstrates the Language Connectome in healthy subjects and patients with left-sided gliomas. Only nodes within positive brain regions were included, and only connections between included nodes are displayed. In reconciling rTMS language mapping with large-scale connectomics, we found that the language network spans across the frontal, temporal, and parietal lobes, wherein the classic language areas are major hubs. In addition, as it is well-documented in the literature [20], the left hemisphere is dominant for language in the vast majority of right-handed healthy individuals. Furthermore, it has also been well documented that patients with left-sided brain pathologies are more likely to have atypical language networks, and indeed to have functional language reorganization bilaterally due to plasticity, as seen in the bilateral distribution of nodes and connections in the brain tumor language connectome [1,13,19].

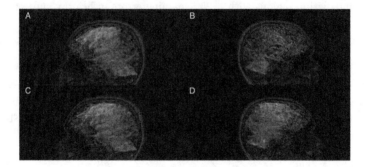

Fig. 2. The Language Connectome in Healthy Subjects (A, B) and Brain Tumor Patients (C, D). The number of nodes and connections within the left hemisphere of the healthy language connectome (A) is 169 and 3690, respectively. Right Healthy (B): 35, 280. Left Brain Tumor (C): 196, 4750. Right Brain Tumor (D): 197, 4750. Total available nodes and connections within the human connectome: 998 and 14,000.

3.2   Zone-Zone Connectivity from Modern Language Network to Classic Language Areas

Figures 3 and 4 target our first hypothesis. When viewed as connectivity to Wernicke's or Broca's area individually, positive brain regions in general have higher connectivity to the classic language areas with some exceptions. When analyzed as connectivity to either Wernicke's or Broca's area, positive brain regions always had significantly higher zone-zone connectivity to the classic language areas as compared with negative language areas, which was in line with our hypothesis. We interpret the higher statistical significance when connectivity

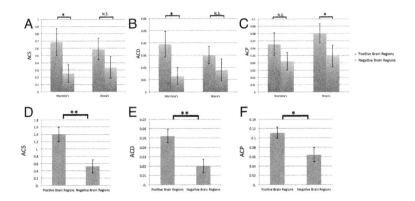

Fig. 3. A-C. One-tailed T-tests of positive vs. negative left hemisphere brain regions in zone-zone connectivity measures ACS, ACD, and ACP to unilateral Wernicke's and Broca's areas individually in healthy subjects. D-F. One-tailed T-tests of positive vs. negative left-sided brain regions in zone-zone connectivity measures to unilateral Wernicke's or Broca's areas collectively. P-values: A. p = .023, p = .110 B. p = .030, p = .148 C. p = .142, p = .049 D. p = .002 E. p = .004 F. p = .016

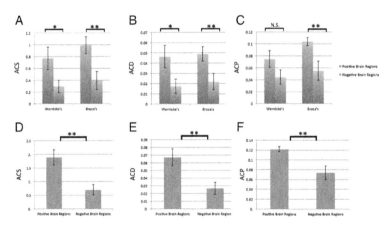

Fig. 4. A-C. One-tailed T-tests of positive vs. negative right hemisphere brain regions in zone-zone connectivity measures ACS, ACD, and ACP to unilateral Wernicke's and Broca's Areas individually in brain tumor patients. D-F. One-tailed T-tests of positive vs. negative right-sided brain regions in zone-zone connectivity measures to unilateral Wernicke's or Broca's areas collectively. P-values: A. p = .017, p = .003 B. p = .021, p = .006 C. p = .070, p = .004 D. p = .001 E. p = .004 F. p = .004

to either classic area is analyzed to be due to the fact that the object-naming task engages all three major language production functions: meaning, form, and articulation [15]. Figure 5 targets our second hypothesis, proving that there are graph theoretic measures of zone-zone connectivity to the classic language areas which correlate with rTMS-induced naming error rates, in health as well as in disease.

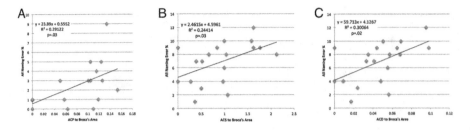

Fig. 5. Linear Regression models of positive brain regions Zone-Zone connectivity to classic language areas vs. all naming error percentage when that region is TMS stimulated. Each point on the graph represents a positive language area A. ACP to Broca's area in the left hemisphere of healthy subjects. B. ACS to Broca's area in the right hemisphere of brain tumor patients. C. ACD to Broca's area in the right hemisphere of brain tumor patients.

4   Discussion

In this paper, we have presented a novel method to aid in non-invasive language function localization. It is becoming more and more apparent that language functional organization in the cortex must be viewed as a large network of cortical areas which contribute to language function to different degrees. However, in clinical practice, neurosurgical patients with tumors near the classic language areas are thought to be at risk of damaging language function during surgery. In this paper, we investigated the connectivity between the language network and the classic language areas. We determined that language-positive regions are significantly more likely to be connected to Wernicke's or Broca's area both in the dominant left hemisphere in healthy subjects as well as in the expanded language network involving the right hemisphere in brain tumor patients. Furthermore, we have shown that regions with higher connectivity to the classic language areas also produce a higher language error rate when stimulated by rTMS.

   We interpret this finding as meaning that the more connected a particular area is to the classic language areas, the more likely it is that area is involved within the language network. This means that it is possible to predict the likelihood that a particular area is involved in the language network simply by analyzing it's zone-zone connectivity to the classic language areas. Although TMS is a very powerful tool, it has its limitations: it is impossible to determine exactly how much cortical area is affected with each TMS pulse, and only surface structures of the brain are accessible with TMS [8]. By building language networks within the connectome, it may be possible to predict areas that are involved in language function without relying on TMS. Prediction of language-involved cortex is very important, as it guides the surgeon in managing the risks involved in the surgery and accurately counseling the patient on those risks. The method of analysis presented in this paper can contribute to this prediction effort and aid in the introduction of connectomics to the clinical practice of neurosurgery.

Acknowledgments. This work has been supported by the European Research Council's CDAC project: "The Role of Consciousness in Adaptive Behavior: A Combined Empirical, Computational and Robot based Approach" (ERC-2013-ADG 341196).

References

1. Acioly, M.A., Gharabaghi, A., Zimmermann, C., Erb, M., Heckl, S., Tatagiba, M.: Dissociated language functions: a matter of atypical language lateralization or cerebral plasticity? J. Neurolog. Surg. Part A Central Eur. Neurosurg. **75**(1), 64–69 (2014)
2. Arsiwalla, X.D., Betella, A., Martínez, E., Omedas, P., Zucca, R., Verschure, P.: The dynamic connectome: a tool for large scale 3D reconstruction of brain activity in real time. In: 27th European Conference on Modeling and Simulation, ECMS Rekdalsbakken, W., Bye, R., Zhang, H. (eds.). Alesund, Norway (2013)
3. Arsiwalla, X.D., Dalmazzo, D., Zucca, R., Betella, A., Brandi, S., Martinez, E., Omedas, P., Verschure, P.: Connectomics to semantomics: addressing the brain's big data challenge. Procedia Comput. Sci. **53**, 48–55 (2015)
4. Arsiwalla, X.D., Zucca, R., Betella, A., Martinez, E., Dalmazzo, D., Omedas, P., Deco, G., Verschure, P.: Network dynamics with brainx3: A large-scale simulation of the human brain network with real-time interaction. Front. Neuroinformatics **9**(2) (2015) http://www.frontiersin.org/neuroinformatics/10.3389/fninf.2015.00002/abstract
5. Betella, A., Bueno, E.M., Kongsantad, W., Zucca, R., Arsiwalla, X.D., Omedas, P., Verschure, P.F.: Understanding large network datasets through embodied interaction in virtual reality. In: Proceedings of the 2014 Virtual Reality International Conference, pp. 23. ACM (2014)
6. Betella, A., Cetnarski, R., Zucca, R., Arsiwalla, X.D., Martínez, E., Omedas, P., Mura, A., Verschure, P.F.M.J.: BrainX3: embodied exploration of neural data. In: Proceedings of the 2014 Virtual Reality International Conference, VRIC 2014, pp. 37:1–37:4. ACM (2014) http://doi.acm.org/10.1145/2617841.2620726
7. Betella, A., Martínez, E., Zucca, R., Arsiwalla, X.D., Omedas, P., Wierenga, S., Mura, A., Wagner, J., Lingenfelser, F., André, E., et al.: Advanced interfaces to stem the data deluge in mixed reality: placing human (un) consciousness in the loop. In: ACM SIGGRApPH 2013 Posters, p. 68. ACM (2013)
8. Bolognini, N., Ro, T.: Transcranial magnetic stimulation: disrupting neural activity to alter and assess brain function. J. Neurosci. **30**(29), 9647–9650 (2010)
9. Corina, D.P., Loudermilk, B.C., Detwiler, L., Martin, R.F., Brinkley, J.F., Ojemann, G.: Analysis of naming errors during cortical stimulation mapping: implications for models of language representation. Brain Lang. **115**(2), 101–112 (2010)
10. Dronkers, N.F.: The pursuit of brain-language relationships. Brain Lang. **71**(1), 59–61 (2000)
11. Friederici, A.D., Gierhan, S.M.: The language network. Curr. Opin. Neurobiol. **23**(2), 250–254 (2013)
12. Hagmann, P., Cammoun, L., Gigandet, X., Meuli, R., Honey, C.J., Wedeen, V.J., Sporns, O.: Mapping the structural core of human cerebral cortex. PLoS Biol. **6**(7), e159 (2008)
13. Holodny, A.I., Schulder, M., Ybasco, A., Liu, W.C.: Translocation of broca's area to the contralateral hemisphere as the result of the growth of a left inferior frontal glioma. J. Comput. Assist. Tomogr. **26**(6), 941–943 (2002)

14. Iturria-Medina, Y., Canales-Rodriguez, E., Melie-Garcia, L., Valdes-Hernandez, P., Martinez-Montes, E., Alemán-Gómez, Y., Sánchez-Bornot, J.: Characterizing brain anatomical connections using diffusion weighted mri and graph theory. Neuroimage **36**(3), 645–660 (2007)
15. Krieg, S.M., Sollmann, N., Tanigawa, N., Foerschler, A., Meyer, B., Ringel, F.: Cortical distribution of speech and language errors investigated by visual object naming and navigated transcranial magnetic stimulation. Brain Structure and Function, pp. 1–28 (2015)
16. Omedas, P., Betella, A., Zucca, R., Arsiwalla, X.D., Pacheco, D., Wagner, J., Lingenfelser, F., Andre, E., Mazzei, D., Lanatá, A., et al.: Xim-engine: a software framework to support the development of interactive applications that uses conscious and unconscious reactions in immersive mixed reality. In: Proceedings of the 2014 Virtual Reality International Conference, pp. 26. ACM (2014)
17. Picht, T., Schmidt, S., Brandt, S., Frey, D., Hannula, H., Neuvonen, T., Karhu, J., Vajkoczy, P., Suess, O.: Preoperative functional mapping for rolandic brain tumor surgery: comparison of navigated transcranial magnetic stimulation to direct cortical stimulation. Neurosurgery **69**(3), 581–589 (2011)
18. Rosenow, F., Lüders, H.: Presurgical evaluation of epilepsy. Brain **124**(9), 1683–1700 (2001)
19. Rösler, J., Niraula, B., Strack, V., Zdunczyk, A., Schilt, S., Savolainen, P., Lioumis, P., Mäkelä, J., Vajkoczy, P., Frey, D., et al.: Language mapping in healthy volunteers and brain tumor patients with a novel navigated tms system: evidence of tumor-induced plasticity. Clin. Neurophysiol. **125**(3), 526–536 (2014)
20. Vikingstad, E.M., George, K.P., Johnson, A.F., Cao, Y.: Cortical language lateralization in right handed normal subjects using functional magnetic resonance imaging. J. Neurol. Sci. **175**(1), 17–27 (2000)

Method for Estimating Neural Network Topology Based on SPIKE-Distance

Kaori Kuroda[✉] and Mikio Hasegawa

Faculty of Engineering, Department of Electrical Engineering,
Tokyo University of Science, 6-3-1 Niijuku, Katsuhika-ku, Tokyo 125-8585, Japan
{kuroda,hasegawa}@ee.kagu.tus.ac.jp

Abstract. To understand information processing in the brain, it is important to clarify the neural network topology. We have already proposed the method of estimating neural network topology only from observed multiple spike sequences by quantifying distance between spike sequences. To quantify distance between spike sequences, the spike time metric was used in the conventional method. However, the spike time metric involves a parameter. Then, we have to set an optimal parameter in the spike time metric. In this paper, we used the SPIKE-distance instead of the spike time metric and applied a partialization analysis to the SPIKE-distance. The SPIKE-distance is a parameter-free measure which can quantify the distance between spike sequences. Using the SPIKE-distance, we estimate the network topology. As a result, the proposed method exhibits higher performance than the conventional method.

Keywords: Partialization analysis · SPIKE-distance · Neural network structure · Connectivity · Spike sequence

1 Introduction

In neural networks, neurons interact with other neurons, then very complicated behavior is often observed. To analyze, modelize, or predict such complicated behavior, it is important to understand the connectivity between neurons as well as the dynamics. Recent advances in measurement techniques make it possible to observe multiple spike sequences. Although many methods of estimating network structures for smooth and continuous time series have been proposed [1–4], spike sequences are discrete and discontinuous time series. Then, it is not straightforward to apply conventional measures to spike sequences, and it is important to develop a method of estimating connectivity between neurons from multiple spike sequences.

To resolve this issue, we have already proposed an estimation method of network structure only from observed multiple spike sequences [5,6]. In these method, we measured a distance between spike sequences by using the spike time metric which is proposed by Victor and Purpula [7]. The spike time metric

© Springer International Publishing Switzerland 2016
A.E.P. Villa et al. (Eds.): ICANN 2016, Part I, LNCS 9886, pp. 91–98, 2016.
DOI: 10.1007/978-3-319-44778-0_11

involves a parameter that sets the timescale. Therefore, we have to decide an optimal parameter value. Although we have proposed the method of how to decide the parameter [6], it is a heuristic method. In this paper, we use another measure the SPIKE-distance [8] instead of the spike time metric. The SPIKE-distance is a parameter-free measure which can quantify the distance between spike sequences [8].

At the same time, we cannot estimate the neural network topology only from the distance information because of the spurious correlation. To remove the spurious correlation, the partialization analysis is effective. Then, in the proposed method, we apply the partialization analysis to the SPIKE-distance.

To check the validity of the proposed method, we apply the proposed method to the observed multiple spike sequences from a mathematical neuron model. In numerical simulations, we show that the proposed method can estimate the neural network topology with higher estimation accuracy than the conventional method.

2   SPIKE-distance

SPIKE-distance is a parameter-free measure which can quantify distance between spike sequences [8]. Let us denote the kth spike timing in the ith spike sequence as $t_k^{(i)}$. We also denote the time of the preceding spikes as

$$t_P^{(i)}(t) = \max_k(t_k^{(i)} \mid t_k^{(i)} \le t), \tag{1}$$

and the time of the following spikes as

$$t_F^{(i)}(t) = \min_k(t_k^{(i)} \mid t_k^{(i)} > t), \tag{2}$$

and the instantaneous interspike interval as

$$x_{\mathrm{ISI}}^{(i)}(t) = t_F^{(i)}(t) - t_P^{(i)}(t). \tag{3}$$

We denote the instantaneous absolute differences of preceding and following spike times between the ith spike sequence and the jth spike sequence as

$$\Delta t_P^{(i)}(t) = \min_k(\mid t_P^{(i)}(t) - t_k^{(j)} \mid) \tag{4}$$

and

$$\Delta t_F^{(i)}(t) = \min_k(\mid t_F^{(i)}(t) - t_k^{(j)} \mid) \tag{5}$$

respectively. We denote the intervals to the previous and the following spikes for the ith spike sequence as

$$x_P^{(i)}(t) = t - t_P^{(i)}(t) \tag{6}$$

and

$$x_F^{(i)}(t) = t_F^{(i)}(t) - t. \tag{7}$$

The weighted distance for the spike time differences of the ith spike sequence reads

$$S_i(t) = \frac{\Delta t_P^{(i)}(t)x_F^{(i)}(t) + \Delta t_F^{(i)}(t)x_P^{(i)}(t)}{x_{\mathrm{ISI}}^{(i)}(t)}, \tag{8}$$

and similarly $S_j(t)$ is obtained for the jth spike sequence. Then, these local distances are weighted by the local interspike intervals and normalized by the mean interspike interval. This yields

$$S_{ij}(t) = \frac{S_i(t)x_{\mathrm{ISI}}^{(j)}(t) + S_j(t)x_{\mathrm{ISI}}^{(i)}(t)}{2\langle x_{\mathrm{ISI}}^{(n)}(t)\rangle_n^2}, \tag{9}$$

where $\langle x_{\mathrm{ISI}}^{(n)}(t)\rangle_n = \frac{1}{2}(x_{\mathrm{ISI}}^{(i)}(t) + x_{\mathrm{ISI}}^{(j)}(t))$. Finally, integrating over time leads to the distance between spike sequences i and j

$$D_{ij} = \frac{1}{T}\int_0^T S_{ij}(t)dt, \tag{10}$$

where T denotes the duration of the spike sequences. The SPIKE-distance D_{ij} takes a value between 0 and 1. If D_{ij} takes zero, the ith and jth spike sequences are identical spike sequences.

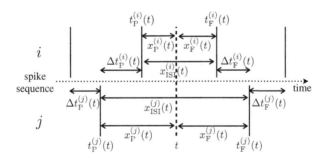

Fig. 1. Illustration of the SPIKE-distance. The definitions of interspike-intervals and time differences required for the calculation of the SPIKE-distance.

3 Partialization Analysis

To estimate the connectivity between neurons from spike sequences, we quantify the distance between two spike sequences. However, we cannot estimate the connectivity between neurons because of the spurious correlation.

For example, if two neurons, i and j, are not coupled, the distance between two spike sequences is close to one because these spike sequences are very different. However, if two neurons are driven by a common input, or indirectly connected but not directly connected, their spike sequences can have spurious correlation. To remove such a common influence, the partialization analysis is effective.

The most general measure in the partialization analysis is the partial correlation coefficient. The partial correlation coefficient can be calculated by using elements of the inverse matrix of the correlation matrix.

To apply the partialization analysis to the SPIKE-distance, the SPIKE-distance coefficient is defined as

$$C_{ij} = 1 - D_{ij}. \tag{11}$$

C_{ij} is similar to the correlation coefficient. It takes a value between 0 and 1. If ith and jth spike sequences are same, C_{ij} takes a value of one, otherwise, C_{ij} is close to zero.

However, it can be spuriously biased if the two neurons are driven by a common input from other neurons. To avoid such a bias, as in the case of deriving a partial correlation coefficient from the correlation coefficient, the partial SPIKE-distance coefficient (PSDC) between the ith and jth spike sequences is defined as

$$P_{ij} = \left| \frac{\alpha(i,j)}{\sqrt{\alpha(i,i)\alpha(j,j)}} \right|,$$

where $\alpha(i,j)$ is the (i,j)th entry of the inverse matrix of C_{ij}. The PSDC can reveal the unbiased correlation between the two spike sequences by removing any spurious correlation as the partialization analysis does. In other words, the PSDC works as a partial correlation coefficient between the two spike sequences based on the SPIKE-distance. Using the PSDC, we can find hidden relations between neurons and estimate the network structure.

4   Simulation

To evaluate the proposed method, we use a neural network constructed from a mathematical model, or the Izhikevich simple neuron model [9]. We generated multiple spike sequences using the Izhikevich simple neuron model. The dynamics of the ith neuron in the neural network is described by the following equations:

$$\dot{v}_i = 0.04v_i^2 + 5v_i + 140 - u_i + I_i,$$
$$\dot{u}_i = a_i(b_iv_i - u_i), \tag{12}$$
$$\text{if } v_i \geq 30[\text{mV}], \text{ then} \begin{cases} v_i \leftarrow c_i, \\ u_i \leftarrow u_i + d_i, \end{cases}$$

where v_i is the membrane potential, u_i is the membrane recovery variable and a_i, b_i, c_i and d_i are dimensionless parameters. We set $a_i = 0.02$, $b_i = 0.2$, $c_i = -65 + 15r_i^2$, and $d_i = 8 - 6r_i^2$ where r_i is uniform random numbers between $[0, 1]$. The network is heterogeneous; the neurons are regular spiking (RS), intrinsically bursting (IB), and chattering (CH) neurons. The variable I_i is the sum of the external and synaptic inputs from coupled neurons. The synaptic weight is set to six and the amplitude of the external inputs to five times G, where G is a Gaussian random number with a mean value and standard deviation of zero and unity, respectively. The neurons are mutually connected. We set delays between neurons to 2[ms] to 4[ms] randomly. For the sake of simplicity, the neural network is composed of only excitatory neurons.

We conducted numerical experiments according to the following procedures. First, we constructed the neural network whose elements are the Izhikevich simple neuron model (Eq. (12)), and observed multiple spike sequences. We generated a ring lattice network structure in which the number of edges is four. Then, the distance D_{ij} between spike sequences was calculated by using the SPIKE-distance. Next, we applied the partial SPIKE-distance coefficient to the observed multi spike sequences. If two neurons are coupled, P_{ij} might be large, otherwise it might be small. We calculated a threshold dividing the coupled or the uncoupled pairs. The threshold was decided by the Otsu thresholding [10] which is based on a linear discriminant analysis. We constructed an estimated network structure whether the values of P_{ij} take over the threshold or not. Finally, to confirm the estimation accuracy, we compared the structure of an estimated network with that of the original network. We used an index defined by

$$
E = \frac{\displaystyle\sum_{i,j=1}^{N} (\beta_{ij}\tilde{\beta}_{ij} + (1 - \beta_{ij})(1 - \tilde{\beta}_{ij}))}{N(N - 1)}, \tag{13}
$$

where β_{ij} and $\tilde{\beta}_{ij}$ are the (i, j)th element of the adjacency matrix of the original and the estimated network structure, respectively. If the ith and jth neurons are coupled, β_{ij} and $\tilde{\beta}_{ij}$ take unity. If they are not coupled, β_{ij} and $\tilde{\beta}_{ij}$ take zero. If E is close to unity, our method estimates the original network structure well.

5   Results

We compared the proposed method which uses the SPIKE-distance and the conventional method [6] which uses the spike time metric as the distance between spike sequences. Figure 2 shows the estimation accuracy E when the network size is changed. In the conventional method, the variance of E bocomes large as the network size become large. However, the estimation accuracy E in the proposed method is higher than the conventional method and variance of E is small for all network sizes.

Further, we investigated the estimation accuracy when the coupling strength is changed. The results are shown in Fig. 3. When the coupling strength is 4,

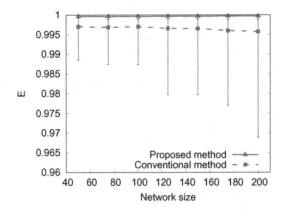

Fig. 2. Estimation accuracy of the network structure for several network sizes. We set the coupling strength is 6, and the temporal epoch is 50[s]. The solid line indicates the proposed method, and the dashed line indicates the conventional method. Error bars indicate minimum and maximum values with 10 trials.

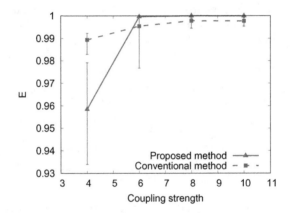

Fig. 3. Estimation accuracy of the network structure for several coupling strength. We set the network size is 100, and the temporal epoch is 50[s]. The solid line indicates the proposed method, and the dashed line indicates the conventional method. Error bars indicate minimum and maximum values with 10 trials.

the estimation accuracy E in the proposed method is lower than the conventional method. However, when the coupling strength is stronger than 6, the proposed method shows higher estimation accuracy than the conventional method.

We also examined how the estimation accuracy depends on the temporal epoch for observed spikes. The results are shown in Fig. 4. The estimation accuracy in both methods is close to unity as the temporal epoch is long. When the temporal epoch is 30[s], both methods exhibit almost same estimation accuracy. However, when the temporal epoch is longer than 30[s], the proposed method shows higher estimation accuracy than the conventional method.

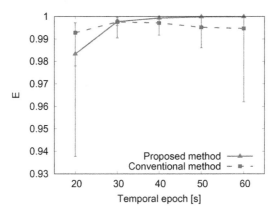

Fig. 4. Estimation accuracy of the network structure for several temporal epochs. We set the network size is 100, and the coupling strength is 6. The solid line indicates the proposed method, and the dashed line indicates the conventional method. Error bars indicate minimum and maximum values with 10 trials.

From the results, the proposed method exhibits very high estimation accuracy under certain conditions.

6   Conclusion

In this paper, we proposed a new method for estimating networr topology only from observed multiple spike sequences by using SPIKE-distance. In the conventional method, the spike time metric which involves a parameter is used for quantifying the distance between spike sequences, and we have to set the parameter in the spike time metric. Although we have proposed the method of how to decide the parameter, the decided parameter is almost appropriate but not optimal. Then, in the proposed method, we used the SPIKE-distance which is a parameter free measure for quantifying distance between spike sequences and applied the partialization analysis to the SPIKE-distance. As a result, the proposed method exhibits higher performance than the conventional method.

The research of KK was partially supported by Grant-in-Aid for Young Scientists (B) (No. 15K21232).

References

1. Schelter, B., Winterhalder, M., Dahlhaus, R., Kurths, J., Timmer, J.: Partial phase synchronization for multivariate synchronizing systems. Phys. Rev. Lett. **96**, 208103 (2006)
2. Smirnov, D., Schelter, B., Winterhalder, M., Timmer, J.: Revealing direction of coupling between neuronal oscillators from time series: phase dynamics modeling versus partial directed coherence. Chaos **17**, 013111 (2007)

3. Frenzel, S., Pompe, B.: Partial mutual information for coupling analysis of multivariate time series. Phys. Rev. Lett. **99**, 204101 (2007)
4. Eichler, M., Dahlhaus, R., Sandkuhler, J.: Partial correlation analysis for the identification of synaptic connections. Biol. Cybern. **89**, 289–302 (2003)
5. Kuroda, K., Hashiguchi, H., Fujiwara, K., Ikeguchi, T.: Reconstruction of network structures from marked point processes using multi-dimensional scaling. Phys. A **415**, 194–204 (2014)
6. Kuroda, K., Ashizawa, T., Ikeguchi, T.: Estimation of network structures only from spike sequences. Phys. A **390**, 4002–4011 (2011)
7. Victor, J., Purpura, K.: Metric-space analysis of spike trains: theory. Algorithms Appl. Netw. **8**, 127 (1997)
8. Kreuz, T., Chicharro, D., Houghton, C., Andrzejak, R.G., Mormann, F.: Monitoring spike train synchrony. J. Neurophysiol. **109**, 1457–1472 (2013)
9. Izhikevich, E.M.: Simple model of spiking neurons. IEEE Trans. Neural Networks **14**, 1569–1572 (2003)
10. Otsu, N.: A threshold selection method from gray level histograms. IEEE Trans. Syst. Man Cybern. **9**, 62–66 (1979)

Dynamics of Evolving Feed-Forward Neural Networks and Their Topological Invariants

Paolo Masulli$^{(\boxtimes)}$ and Alessandro E.P. Villa

NeuroHeuristic Research Group, University of Lausanne,
Quartier Dorigny, 1015 Lausanne, Switzerland
{paolo.masulli,alessandro.villa}@unil.ch
http://www.neuroheuristic.org

Abstract. The evolution of a simulated feed-forward neural network with recurrent excitatory connections and inhibitory forward connections is studied within the framework of algebraic topology. The dynamics includes pruning and strengthening of the excitatory connections. The invariants that we define are based on the connectivity structure of the underlying graph and its directed clique complex. The computation of this complex and of its Euler characteristic are related with the dynamical evolution of the network. As the network evolves dynamically, its network topology changes because of the pruning and strengthening of the onnections and algebraic topological invariants can be computed at different time steps providing a description of the process. We observe that the initial values of the topological invariant computed on the network before it evolves can predict the intensity of the activity.

Keywords: Graph theory · Network invariant · Directed clique complex · Recurrent neural dynamics · Synfire chain · Synaptic plasticity

1 Introduction

A network is a set of nodes satisfying precise properties of connectedness. This description allows the construction of topological spaces that can be studied with the tools of algebraic topology. Network theory aims to understand and describe the shape and the structure of networks, and the application of the tools developed within the framework of algebraic topology can provide new insights of network properties in several research fields.

The directed clique complex [6,13] is a rigorous way to encode the topological features of a network in the mathematical framework of a simplicial complex, allowing the construction of simple invariants such as the Euler characteristic and the Betti numbers and to make the constructions of persistent homology. These constructions have been applied successfully to the field of data science [4], proving to be a powerful tool to understand the inner structure of a data set by representing it as a sequence of topological spaces, and more recently to neuroscience [6,8,13,14].

© Springer International Publishing Switzerland 2016
A.E.P. Villa et al. (Eds.): ICANN 2016, Part I, LNCS 9886, pp. 99–106, 2016.
DOI: 10.1007/978-3-319-44778-0_12

In an evolving network, each node is represented by a unit whose activity is necessarily related to a set of precise rules defining the combined activity of the afferent nodes transmitted by the connecting edges. Re-entrant activity occurs in the presence of reciprocal connections between certain nodes. Selected pathways through the network may emerge because of dynamical processes that shape selected activity-dependent connection pruning. Hence, network topology and dynamics combine and play a crucial role in defining the evolution of a network [7]. In a previous study we introduced topological invariants [13] and suggested their application to integrate-and-fire recurrent neural networks with convergent/divergent layered structure [2] with an embedded dynamics of synaptic plasticity. Spontaneous development of synchronous layer activation in a self-organizing recurrent neural network model that combines a number of different plasticity mechanisms has been described [20]. However, the question to what extent the initial network topology can be predictive of the evolved circuit remains to be further investigated.

The current study extends further our previous investigation [13] because global background activity is introduced and inhibitory connections have now been included in the network. The results provide new evidence that the topological invariants presented here offer as a valid descriptor for predicting how a network may evolve under the effect of pruning dynamics. The family of network studied here represents an important step towards the direction of a simulation with more refined biologically-inspired models.

2   Methods

2.1   Graphs, Clique Complexes and Topological Invariants

An *abstract oriented simplicial complex* K [9] is the data of a set K_0 of vertices and sets K_n of lists $\sigma = (x_0, \ldots, x_n)$ of elements of K_0 (called *n-simplices*), for $n \geq 1$, with the property that, if $\sigma = (x_0, \ldots, x_n)$ belongs to K_n, then any sublist $(x_{i_0}, \ldots, x_{i_k})$ of σ belongs to K_k. The sublists of σ are called *faces*.

We consider a finite directed weighted graph $G = (V, E)$ with vertex set V and edge set E with no self-loops and no double edges, and denote with N the cardinality of V. Associated to G, we can construct its *(directed) clique complex* $K(G)$, which is the directed simplicial complex given by $K(G)_0 = V$ and

$$K(G)_n = \{(v_0, \ldots, v_n) \colon (v_i, v_j) \in E \text{ for all } i < j\} \quad \text{for } n \geq 1. \quad (1)$$

In other words, an n-simplex contained in $K(G)_n$ is a directed $(n+1)$-clique or a completely connected directed subgraph with $n + 1$ vertices. Notice that an n-simplex is though of as an object of dimension n and consists of $n+1$ vertices.

By definition, a directed clique (or a simplex in our complex) is a fully-connected directed sub-network: this means that the nodes are ordered and there is one source and one sink in the sub-network, and the presence of the directed clique in the network means that the former is connected to the latter in all the possible ways within the sub-network as illustrated by Fig. 1.

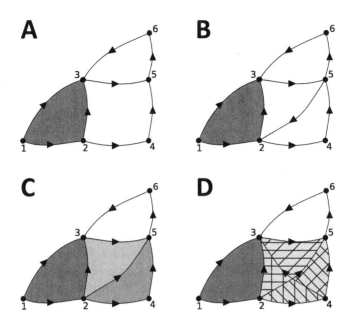

Fig. 1. The directed clique complex. (A) The directed clique complex of the represented graph consists of a 0-simplex for each vertex and a 1-simplex for each edge. There is only one 2-simplex (123). Note that '2453' does not form a 3-simplex because it is not fully connected. '356' does not form a simplex either, because the edges are not oriented correctly. (B) The addition of the edge (52) to the graph in (A) does not contribute to creating any new 2-simplex, because of its orientation. The edges connecting the vertices 2, 3 and 5 (respectively 2, 4 and 5) are oriented cyclically, and therefore they do not follow the conditions of the definition of directed clique complex. (C) By reversing the orientation of the new edge (25), we obtain two new 2-simplices: (235) and (245). Note that we do not have any 3-simplex. (D) We added a new edge (43), thus the subgraph (2435) becomes fully connected and is oriented correctly to be a 3-simplex in the directed clique complex. In addition this construction gives two other 2-simplices: (243) and (435).

The directed clique complex is the basic topological object that allows us to introduce invariants of the graph: the *Euler characteristic* of the directed clique complex $K(G)$ of G is the integer defined by $\chi(K(G)) = \sum_{n=0}^{N}(-1)^n |K(G)_n|$ or in other words the alternating sum of the number of simplices that are present in each dimension. The number of simplices in each dimension (in particular 1- and 2-simplices is also used as invariant of a network.

Notice that the construction of the directed clique complex of a given network G does not involve any choice, and therefore, since the Euler characteristic of a simplicial complex is a well-defined quantities for a simplicial complex [9], our constructions produce quantities that are well-defined for the network G, and we shall refer to them simply as the Euler characteristic of G.

2.2   Network Structure and Dynamics

The artificial recurrent neural networks consist of a finite number of Boolean integrate-and-fire (IF) neurons organized in layers with a convergent/divergent connection structure [2]. The networks are composed by 50 layers, each of them with 10 IF neurons.

The first layer is the layer that receives external stimulations (also referred to as the *input layer*) and all its 10 neurons get activated at the same time at a fixed frequency of 0.1, i.e. every 10 time steps of the history.

Each neuron in a layer is connected to a randomly uniformly distributed number of target neurons f belonging to the next downstream layer. The average distribution of the number of incoming connections is shown in Fig. 2. The networks include *recurrence* in their structure, meaning that a small fraction g of the neurons appears in two different layers. This means that a neuron k that is also identified as neuron l, is characterized by the union of the input connections of neurons k and l, as well as by the union of their respective efferent projections.

We extended the networks constructed in [13] to include inhibition and background activity. A fixed proportion (10%) of the neurons are inhibitory, the remaining (90%) are excitatory. The state $S_i(t)$ of a neuron i takes values 0 (inactive) or 1 (active) and all IF neurons are set inactive at the beginning of the simulation. The state $S_i(t)$ is a function of the its activation variable $V_i(t)$, such that $S_i(t) = \mathcal{H}(V_i(t) - 1)$. $\mathcal{H}$ is the Heaviside function, $\mathcal{H}(x) = 0 : x < 0$, $\mathcal{H}(x) = 1 : x \geq 0$, and neurons have a refractory period of one time step after activation. At each time step, the value $V_i(t)$ of the activation variable of the ith neuron is calculated with the formula $V_i(t + 1) = \sum_j S_j(t)w_{ji}(t) + b_i(t)$, where $b_i(t)$ is the background activity, $w_{ji}(t)$ are the weights of the directed connections from any j^{th} neuron projecting to neuron i. The background activity $b_i(t)$ is sampled from a Poisson distribution of parameter $\lambda = 1$ multiplied by a fixed factor of 0.15.

The weights of the excitatory connections have been limited to three values, i.e. $w_1 = 0.1$, $w_2 = 0.2$, and $w_3 = 0.4$. At the beginning of the simulations all connection weights are randomly uniformly distributed among the three possible values. On the opposite, all inhibitory connections are set to $w_4 = -0.2$. The weights of all excitatory connections are updated synchronously at each time step.

The network dynamics implements activity-dependent plasticity of the excitatory connections. Whenever the activation of a connection does not lead to the activation of its target neuron during an interval lasting a time steps, its weight is weakened to the level immediately below the current one. Whenever the weight of an excitatory connection reaches the lowest level without any increase in a time steps, then the connection is removed [10]. The pruning of the connections changes the topology of the network. Similarly, whenever an excitatory connection with a weight w_m is activated at least $m + 1$ consecutive time steps, the connection weight is strengthened to the level immediately higher than the current one. Note though that in the current implementation the inhibitory connections are never pruned and their weights remain constant.

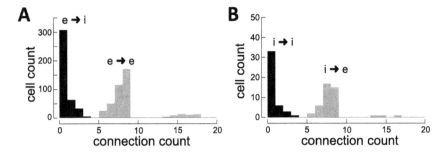

Fig. 2. Cumulative distributions of the efferences within one neural circuit at the begin of the simulation. Network parameters: layer-to-layer downstream connections: 90 %; fraction of recurrent neurons: 10 %; weakening dynamics threshold: 25 steps. (A) excitatory efferent connections to excitatory cells (e→e) and to inhibitory cells (e→i). (B) inhibitory efferent connections to excitatory cells (i→e) and to inhibitory cells (i→i).

Hence, the parameter space of our simulations was defined by three parameters: the number f of layer-to-layer downstream connections in the range 1–10 by steps of 3, the small fraction g of the neurons appearing in two different layers in the range 5–10 % by steps of 5 %, and the interval a of the weakening dynamics of the connections in the range 10–26 by steps of 8.

2.3 Implementation of the Simulations

The simulation software was implemented from scratch in Python. The network evolved with the dynamics explained above and the program computed the directed clique complex at each change of the network topology. The simulation was stopped after 200 time steps, or earlier if the activity died out because of the pruning. For the entire network, the directed clique complex was computed each time the connectivity changed because of pruning. For the sub-network of the active nodes, the computation was carried out at each step of the simulation.

The computed directed clique complexes were used to compute the Euler characteristic both for the complexes representing the entire network and for the sub-complexes of the active nodes. To compute the directed clique complex of a network, we used the algorithm implemented in the `igraph` Python package [5], adapted to find directed cliques, run in parallel on several CPUs using the tool GNU Parallel [16].

3 Results

We considered a directed graph with nodes representing individual neurons and oriented edges representing the connections between the neurons with a weight corresponding to the connection strength. The network topology is based on a simplified model of feed-forward neural network with convergent/divergent layered structure with few embedded recurrent connections and 10 % inhibitory units at the begin of the simulation. We have computed the Euler characteristic and its variation during the evolution of such networks in order to detect how the structure changes as the network evolves. The nodes of the input layer are activated at regular time intervals.

We observed that the Euler characteristic of the entire network could detect the pruning activity during the neural network evolution (Fig. 3). In particular, the step to step variation of the Euler characteristic matched the number of connections pruned over time. The Euler characteristic appears as a good estimator of the activity level within the network and of its topological changes.

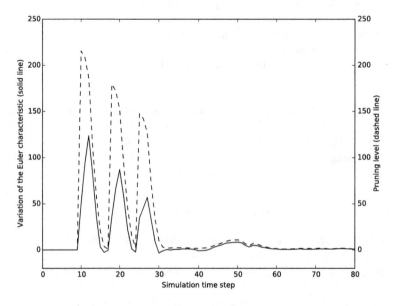

Fig. 3. The evolution of the Euler characteristic. The plot shows the variation of the Euler characteristic (averaged across all the networks in the family) over time during the network evolution (solid line), compared with the plot of the pruning activity (dashed line). We observe that the Euler characteristic of the direct clique complex of the entire network detects the changes in the network topology caused by the pruning activity.

Moreover, despite the more complex dynamics considered in the current simulation, we found new evidence in favor of the main finding of our previous study [13]: the type of dynamics undergoing the neural network evolution and the structure of the directed clique complex of that network at the very beginning of the simulation (i.e. before the occurrence of connection pruning) were correlated. In particular, the average number of active units during the simulation was correlated to the number of simplices, in the directed clique complex, of dimension two (Pearson correlation coefficient $r_{(190)} = 0.50$, $p < 0.001$) and dimension three ($r_{(190)} = 0.50$, $p < 0.001$).

Even in presence of different network dynamics, the initial connectivity structure of the network contains a algebraic-topological information that can be used to predict the type of evolution that the network is going to have. The rationale for it being correlated with the number of high (2 and 3) dimensional simplices is that directed cliques are fully connected sub-networks, i.e. sub-networks with an initial and a final node that are connected in the highest possible number of ways, and thus they contribute to the propagation of the activation.

4   Discussion

Network topology and dynamics are closely related: the convergent/divergent networks with neurons organised in layers in a feed-forward structure, which we considered here, are closely associated with synfire chains [1,2]. These networks are characterized by a highly correlated activity of the neurons within each later, propagated from a layer to the next one, which is the kind of behaviour that we observed in our simulations. The temporal patterns of activation displayed by synfire chains are of central importance in the transmission of neural information [11], and experimental results in electrophysiology show the emergence of precise patterns of activation [15,17], associated with neural functions such as sensory encoding and cognitive responses.

The networks considered here are a version of synfire chains, with the simplification that the chain structure forms the entirety of the network: for this reason we do not investigate the important problem of the emergence of synfire chains embedded in bigger networks. This question has been investigated in relation with several network features, as a function of network topology and plasticity rules [18–20]. Our simulations show that the excitatory-inhibitory and the background noise are central elements in the maintenance of a steady and irregular activity level [3,12]: the maintenance of a non-saturated activity level for the duration of the simulations is necessary in order to correlate the average activity of the networks with the topological invariants that we have presented here. The addition of inhibitory neurons and background activity with respect to our previous study [13] gave richer and more complicated dynamics, and yet we found that our tools can shed light on the links between network topology and pruning dynamics. The algebro-topological framework of analysis presented here appears as a very promising technique and deserves further study in order to investigate the deeper relations between temporal activation patterns and network topology in biologically inspired networks.

Acknowledgments. This work was partially supported by the Swiss National Science Foundation grant CR13I1-138032.

References

1. Abeles, M.: Local Cortical Circuits. An Electrophysiological Study. Studies of Brain Function, vol. 6. Springer, Heidelberg (1982)
2. Abeles, M.: Corticonics: Neural Circuits of the Cerebral Cortex. Cambridge University Press, Cambridge (1991)
3. Aviel, Y., Mehring, C., Abeles, M., Horn, D.: On embedding synfire chains in a balanced network. Neural Comput. **15**(6), 1321–1340 (2003)
4. Carlsson, G.: Topology and data. Bull. Am. Math. Soc. **46**(2), 255–308 (2009)
5. Csardi, G., Nepusz, T.: The igraph software package for complex network research. InterJ. Complex Syst. 1695 (2006). http://igraph.org
6. Dłotko, P., Hess, K., Levi, R., Nolte, M., Reimann, M., Scolamiero, M., Turner, K., Muller, E., Markram, H.: Topological analysis of the connectome of digital reconstructions of neural microcircuits. arXiv preprint arXiv:1601.01580 (2016)
7. Freeman, W.J.: Neural networks and chaos. J. Theor. Biol. **171**, 13–18 (1994)
8. Giusti, C., Ghrist, R., Bassett, D.S.: Two's company, three (or more) is a simplex: algebraic-topological tools for understanding higher-order structure in neural data. arXiv preprint arXiv:1601.01704 (2016)
9. Hatcher, A.: Algebraic Topology. Cambridge University Press, Cambridge (2002)
10. Iglesias, J., Villa, A.E.P.: Effect of stimulus-driven pruning on the detection of spatiotemporal patterns of activity in large neural networks. Biosystems **89**(1–3), 287–293 (2007)
11. Kumar, A., Rotter, S., Aertsen, A.: Spiking activity propagation in neuronal networks: reconciling different perspectives on neural coding. Nat. Rev. Neurosci. **11**(9), 615–627 (2010)
12. Litvak, V., Sompolinsky, H., Segev, I., Abeles, M.: On the transmission of rate code in long feedforward networks with excitatoryinhibitory balance. J. Neurosci. **23**(7), 3006–3015 (2003)
13. Masulli, P., Villa, A.E.P.: The topology of the directed clique complex as a network invariant. Springer Plus **5**, 388 (2016)
14. Petri, G., Expert, P., Turkheimer, F., Carhart-Harris, R., Nutt, D., Hellyer, P.J., Vaccarino, F.: Homological scaffolds of brain functional networks. J. R. Soc. Interf. **11**(101), 20140873 (2014)
15. Prut, Y., Vaadia, E., Bergman, H., Haalman, I., Slovin, H., Abeles, M.: Spatiotemporal structure of cortical activity: properties and behavioral relevance. J. Neurophysiol. **79**(6), 2857–2874 (1998)
16. Tange, O.: GNU parallel - the command-line power tool: login. USENIX Mag. **36**(1), 42–47 (2011)
17. Villa, A.E., Tetko, I.V., Hyland, B., Najem, A.: Spatiotemporal activity patterns of rat cortical neurons predict responses in a conditioned task. Proc. Nat. Acad. Sci. **96**(3), 1106–1111 (1999)
18. Waddington, A., Appleby, P.A., De Kamps, M., Cohen, N.: Triphasic spike-timing-dependent plasticity organizes networks to produce robust sequences of neural activity. Front. Comput. Neurosci. **6**, 88 (2012)
19. Zaytsev, Y.V., Morrison, A., Deger, M.: Reconstruction of recurrent synaptic connectivity of thousands of neurons from simulated spiking activity. J. Comput. Neurosci. **39**(1), 77–103 (2015)
20. Zheng, P., Triesch, J.: Robust development of synfire chains from multiple plasticity mechanisms. Front. Comput. Neurosci. **8**, 66 (2014)

Scaling Properties of Human Brain Functional Networks

Riccardo Zucca[1(✉)], Xerxes D. Arsiwalla[1], Hoang Le[2], Mikail Rubinov[3,4], and Paul F.M.J. Verschure[1,5]

[1] Laboratory of Synthetic Perceptive, Emotive and Cognitive Systems (SPECS), N-RAS, DTIC, Universitat Pompeu Fabra (UPF), Barcelona, Spain
{riccardo.zucca,paul.verschure}@upf.edu
[2] California Institute of Technology, Pasadena, USA
[3] Department of Psychiatry, Behavioural and Clinical Neuroscience Institute, University of Cambridge, Cambridge, UK
[4] Janelia Research Campus, Howard Hughes Medical Institute, Ashburn, VA, USA
[5] Catalan Institute of Advanced Studies (ICREA), Barcelona, Spain
http://specs.upf.edu

Abstract. We investigate scaling properties of human brain functional networks in the resting-state. Analyzing network degree distributions, we statistically test whether their tails scale as power-law or not. Initial studies, based on least-squares fitting, were shown to be inadequate for precise estimation of power-law distributions. Subsequently, methods based on maximum-likelihood estimators have been proposed and applied to address this question. Nevertheless, no clear consensus has emerged, mainly because results have shown substantial variability depending on the data-set used or its resolution. In this study, we work with high-resolution data (10 K nodes) from the Human Connectome Project and take into account network weights. We test for the power-law, exponential, log-normal and generalized Pareto distributions. Our results show that the statistics generally do not support a power-law, but instead these degree distributions tend towards the thin-tail limit of the generalized Pareto model. This may have implications for the number of hubs in human brain functional networks.

Keywords: Power-law distributions · Functional connectivity · Generalized pareto · Model fitting · Maximum likelihood · Connectome · Brain networks

1 Introduction

Much interest in theoretical neuroscience has revolved around graph-theoretic scaling properties of the network of structural and functional correlations in the human brain. Some authors have described the degree distribution of nodes in brain functional networks as scale-free; that is, these networks follow a power-law degree distribution $P(k) \sim k^{-\alpha}$ with an exponent close to 2 [7,11], indicating the

© Springer International Publishing Switzerland 2016
A.E.P. Villa et al. (Eds.): ICANN 2016, Part I, LNCS 9886, pp. 107–114, 2016.
DOI: 10.1007/978-3-319-44778-0_13

presence of a small number of hub-nodes that connect widely across the network. Other studies have suggested that functional brain networks are not scale-free, but instead are characterized by an exponentially truncated distribution [1,8,10]. The scaling characteristics of these networks are associated with the number and organization of network hubs and consequently may have implications with our understanding of how the brain responds to disease or damage [1,2]. This calls for a rigorous statistical methodology to infer underlying models that best describe the degree distribution of brain functional networks.

Initial studies were based on least-square fitting of log-log plots of frequency distributions to answer this question. This approach, although seemingly straightforward, is inadequate from a statistical point of view as elaborated in [6]. Least-square fitting may give systematically biased estimates of the scaling parameters and most of the inferential assumptions for regression are violated. Moreover, in all these studies no statistical testing was mentioned to measure the *goodness-of-fit* of each fitted degree distribution. As an alternative, Maximum Likelihood Estimation (MLE) of the scaling parameters should be used and alternative distributions should be also tested. In [6] an analytical framework for performing such tests for power-law models is provided, which has been subsequently extended for testing other distributions as well. However, it has been noted that results are still very much dependent on the way the data is preprocessed, how the network is extracted, its dimensions and whether one uses region or voxel-based networks. For instance, Hayasaka et al. [10] found that, although degree distributions of all analysed functional networks followed an exponentially truncated model, the higher the resolution, the closer the distribution was to a power-law.

In this work, as a first step to address this issue we analyzed the resting-state fMRI (rs-fMRI) data of 10 subjects obtained from the Human Connectome Project database. Using the MLE method, advocated in [6], we estimate the scaling parameters for the best possible fit for a model distribution and then check the *goodness-of-fit* for this distribution by comparing it to synthetic generated data. We do this for four model distributions: power-law, exponential, log-normal and generalized Pareto. The reason for choosing the generalized Pareto model is due to the fact that it interpolates between fat-tail and thin-tail distributions, including the power-law and exponential as special cases. In what follows, we find that at a resolution of 10 K nodes, the statistics favor the generalized Pareto thin-tail distributions.

2   Materials and Methods

2.1   Subjects, Imaging Data and Network Extraction

High-quality, high-resolution resting state fMRI scans of 10 subjects from the Human Connectome Project (Q1 data released by the WU-Minn HCP consortium in March 2013 [13]) were analysed in this study (age range: 26–35, 16.7 % male). Individual rs-fMRI data were acquired for ~15 min providing a total of

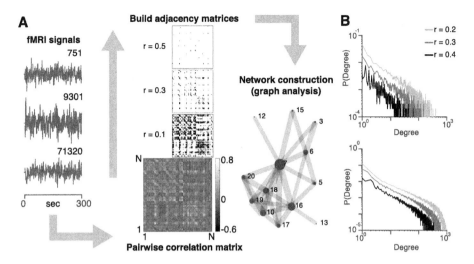

Fig. 1. A. Overview of the processing steps used to generate graph-based brain connectivity functional networks (see the main text for further details about the overall procedures). **B.** Degree distributions for three different values of the functional correlation threshold for a representative subject (top) and averaged over the 10 data-sets included in the study (bottom).

~98,300 grayordinates time–series of 1,200 time points each. A schematic illustration of the process used to build the networks is provided in Fig. 1A. Building and visualizing functional networks was done using the BrainX^3 platform [3–5]. For all the subjects, the original data-set was downsampled to ~10,000 nodes by averaging the time-series of neighbouring grayordinates within a 5 mm^3 cube.

Pearson's correlation coefficients were calculated between each possible pair of nodes to build a $N \times N$ functional connectivity matrix, which is symmetric by construction and with self-connections set to zero. The matrix was then thresholded to derive weighted undirected adjacency matrices. We examined a range of 18 different thresholds (R) between -0.7 and 0.8, at 0.1 steps. Outside this range, the functional matrices become too sparse for meaningful analysis. For a positive threshold, each entry in the correlation matrix is set to 0 if its value is less than the threshold value and maintains its value otherwise. For a negative threshold, absolute values of the entries less than the threshold are maintained, while others are set to 0. In a weighted network, the weighted degree of a node is defined as the sum of all weighted edges connected to that node. Figure 1B illustrates the degree distributions of extracted networks across three different thresholds for a representative subject and averaged over all 10 data-sets.

2.2 Fitting Parametric Models to Weighted Degree Networks

For every network generated from subject data, the vector of degrees $\mathbf{x} = [x_1, x_2, ..., x_n]$ is sorted in ascending order for each threshold. For every x_i, following [6], we use the method of maximum likelihood to estimate the scaling

Table 1. Fit results of the exponential $(p(x) = Ce^{-\lambda x})$ and the power law distributions $(p(x) = Cax^{-\alpha})$

	Exponential							Power law				
Thr	λ	x_{min}	TL	KS	p-value	TL_r		Thr	α	x_{min}	TL	KS	p-value	TL_r
+0.8	0.000	0.000	0.0	0.000	0.0000	0.714		+0.8	0.000	0.000	0.0	0.000	0.0000	0.655
+0.7	0.162	1.186	83.5	0.056	0.3125	0.500		+0.7	2.257	1.427	83.0	0.120	0.0005	0.437
+0.6	0.089	3.887	130.5	0.058	0.4840	0.306		+0.6	2.324	4.387	94.5	0.099	0.0070	0.336
+0.5	0.038	15.544	175.5	0.050	0.6170	0.187		+0.5	2.765	21.077	201.0	0.085	0.0275	0.141
+0.4	0.020	23.051	440.5	0.037	0.7305	0.160		+0.4	2.946	48.800	300.0	0.079	0.0020	0.099
+0.3	0.012	44.067	805.0	0.030	0.3305	0.167		+0.3	3.711	180.624	224.0	0.079	0.0650	0.045
+0.2	0.008	44.049	1552.5	0.024	0.0895	0.205		+0.2	5.541	360.395	281.5	0.079	0.0060	0.036
+0.1	0.006	25.520	4350.5	0.031	0.0015	0.433		+0.1	8.615	745.120	208.0	0.0666	0.1490	0.021
+0.0	0.007	545.110	1597.0	0.037	0.0290	0.159		+0.0	12.594	931.660	246.5	0.059	0.1810	0.025
-0.0	0.021	123.255	1678.0	0.021	0.0485	0.168		-0.0	5.303	142.645	1249.0	0.021	0.5085	0.124
-0.1	0.023	53.151	141.0	0.072	0.1835	0.014		-0.1	2.402	11.896	2352.5	0.044	0.0000	0.236
-0.2	0.095	7.104	123.0	0.170	0.0170	0.105		-0.2	2.417	3.349	521.5	0.052	0.0030	0.277
-0.3	0.348	0.330	95.5	0.224	0.0000	0.534		-0.3	2.367	1.089	118.5	0.088	0.0105	0.319
-0.4	0.000	0.000	0.0	0.000	0.0000	0.876		-0.4	0.000	0.000	0.0	0.000	0.0000	0.332
-0.5	0.000	0.000	0.0	0.000	0.0000	0.881		-0.5	0.000	0.000	0.0	0.000	0.0000	0.399
-0.6	0.000	0.000	0.0	0.000	0.0000	0.510		-0.6	0.000	0.000	0.0	0.000	0.0000	0.510
-0.7	0.000	0.000	0.0	0.000	0.0000	-		-0.7	0.000	0.000	0.0	0.000	0.0000	-
-0.8	0.000	0.000	0.0	0.000	0.0000	-		-0.8	0.000	0.000	0.0	0.000	0.0000	-

All data are expressed as median values. Legend: Thr, R threshold; λ, α model parameters; x_{min}, lower bound for model distribution; TL, length of the tail; KS, Kolgomorov-Smirnov statistic; p-value, plausibility of the model; TL_r, proportion of non-zero nodes in the tail.

parameter α providing the best possible fit for the hypothetical power-law distribution $P(x) \sim Cx^{-\alpha}$ for the tail of the observed data in the range x_i to x_n. Next, we calculate the Kolmogorov-Smirnov (KS) statistic for this power-law distribution with respect to x_i. Out of all possible x_i from the data, the one with the smallest KS statistic corresponds to the lower bound x_{min} for power-law behavior in the data. The next step is to verify whether this is indeed a good fit for the data. For that, a large number of synthetic data-sets are sampled from a true power-law distribution with the same scaling parameter α and bound x_{min} as the ones estimated for the best fit of the empirical data. We fit each synthetic data-set to its own power-law model and calculate the KS statistic for each one relative to its own model. An empirical p-value is then calculated as the fraction of the time the empirical distribution outperforms the synthetically generated ones (by having a smaller KS statistic value). If p-value $\leqslant 0.1$, the power-law hypothesis can be ruled out as a non plausible explanation of the data. Nevertheless, large p-values do not guarantee that the power-law is the best model and the power-law fit has to be compared to a class of competing distributions.

3   Results

Power-law testing was performed on Matlab (Mathworks Inc., USA) using [6]. Further, for testing exponential, log-normal and generalized Pareto models we adapted the framework provided in [6] to include these competing hypothesis. For each subject, we analyzed thresholds in the range -0.7 to 0.8, with 0.1 increments. The parametric *goodness-of-fit* test was conducted over 1,000 repetitions, ensuring precision of p-value up to two decimal digits.

Our results are summarized in Tables 1 and 2, respectively. An hypothesis is considered plausible if the p-value is larger than 0.1. Averaging over subjects, the

Table 2. Fit results of generalized Pareto distribution ($p(x) = \frac{1}{\sigma}(1 + k\frac{x - x_{min}}{\sigma})^{-1 - \frac{1}{k}}$) and of log-normal distribution ($C\frac{1}{x}exp[\frac{-(ln(x) - \mu)^2}{2\sigma^2}]$).

Generalized Pareto								Log normal							
Thr	k	σ	x_{min}	TL	KS	p-value	TL$_r$	Thr	μ	σ	x_{min}	TL	KS	p-value	TL$_r$
+0.8	0.000	0.000	0.000	0.0	0.000	0.0000	0.696	+0.8	0.000	0.000	0.000	0.0	0.000	0.0000	0.639
+0.7	0.000	3.663	1.539	58.5	0.049	0.1315	0.531	+0.7	0.618	0.599	1.141	58.0	0.039	0.1033	0.466
+0.6	0.118	11.094	2.943	172.5	0.048	0.3305	0.440	+0.6	1.804	0.957	2.589	110.5	0.040	0.1867	0.381
+0.5	0.031	28.656	20.072	338.5	0.034	0.7380	0.229	+0.5	3.363	0.794	15.167	246.5	0.033	0.7017	0.223
+0.4	0.001	62.035	34.191	372.5	0.027	0.6155	0.174	+0.4	3.459	0.799	24.044	543.5	0.027	0.4883	0.186
+0.3	-0.128	102.619	85.215	638.5	0.021	0.7975	0.176	+0.3	4.809	0.535	72.627	525.0	0.023	0.4633	0.114
+0.2	-0.178	152.365	136.945	938.5	0.014	0.8275	0.135	+0.2	5.754	0.434	209.015	759.5	0.023	0.3950	0.100
+0.1	-0.226	241.640	201.475	2387.0	0.010	0.7555	0.238	+0.1	6.143	0.299	418.120	852.0	0.019	0.6450	0.085
+0.0	-0.224	218.500	380.050	4681.5	0.009	0.6750	0.467	+0.0	6.299	0.236	472.295	1684.5	0.015	0.3150	0.168
-0.0	0.182	32.619	127.480	1195.5	0.012	0.8425	0.119	-0.0	4.298	0.588	81.662	4837.0	0.010	0.3500	0.482
-0.1	0.426	12.883	9.690	1469.0	0.020	0.1725	0.149	-0.1	2.176	1.197	7.105	1764.0	0.019	0.3600	0.180
-0.2	0.439	2.549	0.763	820.5	0.030	0.1890	0.457	-0.2	0.486	1.317	0.610	879.0	0.034	0.0167	0.599
-0.3	0.433	0.996	0.649	101.5	0.062	0.0105	0.405	-0.3	-0.243	1.237	0.543	106.0	0.072	0.0050	0.592
-0.4	0.000	0.000	0.000	0.0	0.000	0.0000	0.253	-0.4	0.000	0.000	0.000	0.0	0.000	0.0000	0.825
-0.5	0.000	0.000	0.000	0.0	0.000	0.0000	1.000	-0.5	0.000	0.000	0.000	0.0	0.000	0.0000	0.607
-0.6	0.000	0.000	0.000	0.0	0.000	0.0000	1.000	-0.6	0.000	0.000	0.000	0.0	0.000	0.0000	-Inf
-0.7	0.000	0.000	0.000	0.0	0.000	0.0000	-	-0.7	0.000	0.000	0.000	0.0	0.000	0.0000	-
-0.8	0.000	0.000	0.000	0.0	0.000	0.0000	-	-0.8	0.000	0.000	0.000	0.0	0.000	0.0000	-

All data are expressed as median values. Legend: Thr, R threshold; k, σ, μ model parameters; x_{min}, lower bound for model distribution; TL, length of the tail; KS, Kolgomorov-Smirnov statistic; p-value, plausibility of the model; TL$_r$, proportion of non-zero nodes in the tail.

p-values indicate that the power law hypothesis is rejected in the 83.3 % of the analyzed thresholds. Instead, 61.1 % of the examined thresholds are consistent with a generalized Pareto hypothesis, 55.6 % with a log-normal hypothesis and in 33.3 % of the cases with the exponential hypothesis, with several of these thresholds passing multiple tests. Median p-values are consistently larger for the generalized Pareto hypothesis (Fig. 2).

For each threshold examined, we then perform log-likelihood ratio tests to check which one among the consistent models is the most plausible in describing the empirical data. For all the positive thresholds up to 0.7 the evidence strongly goes in favor of the generalized Pareto distribution. Overall, the generalized Pareto model is outperforming the other candidate models in 41 % of the examined cases (all subjects and all thresholds). In a 13 % of the comparisons the log-normal distribution resulted in a better fit, 3 % were better fitted by an exponential model, 2 % by a power law, whereas the remaining 41 % could not be explained by any model (due to insufficient data points and extreme thresholds).

For several positive thresholds the k parameter is equal or close to zero, thus approaching an exponential distribution, whereas for other thresholds in the positive range, the generalized Pareto model passes with negative k, meaning a suppressed tail (Fig. 3).

4   Discussion

In this study we sought to systematically analyze scaling properties of human brain functional networks in the resting state, obtained from high-resolution fMRI data. We constructed networks of 10,000 nodes. Our analysis took into account actual weighted degree distributions from the data and we scanned through the full range of positive as well as negative correlation thresholds. For

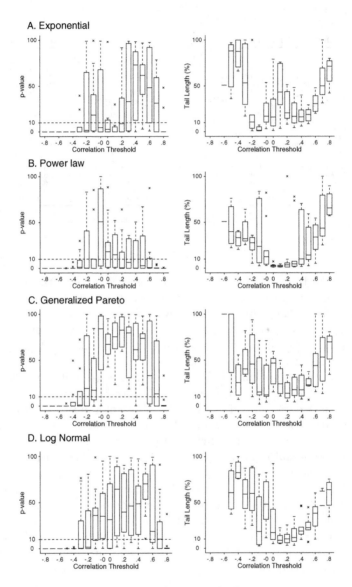

Fig. 2. Population averaged goodness-of-fit tests (left) and percentage of the tail of the distribution explained by the model (right) across different thresholds for each of the four distributions. Horizontal dashed lines in the boxplots indicate the acceptance criteria for a model to be considered plausible (*p*-value > 10 %). The central mark is the median, the edges of the boxes are the 25th and 75th percentiles. Asterisks correspond to outliers.

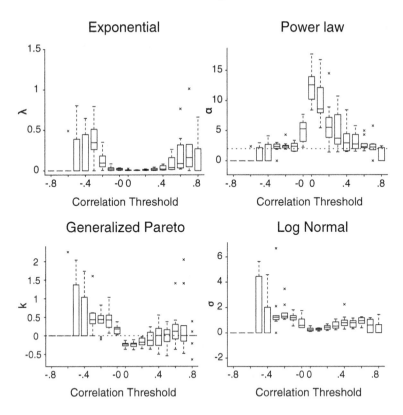

Fig. 3. Population averaged estimates of λ (top-left), α (top-right), k (bottom-left) and σ (bottom-right) model parameters for the four tested distributions across different thresholds.

model selection, we imposed a criterion of p-value > 0.1 and we conducted a log-likelihood ratio test among the different hypothesis.

We have shown that the degree distribution of the nodes does not follow a scale-free topology, as reported in [7]. The power law hypothesis is strongly rejected in the majority of the thresholds we examined. Indeed, it is the generalized Pareto distribution that is consistently preferable to the competing models for most of the thresholds.

These results suggest that after taking into account continuously weighted rather than binary networks, the dynamics of brain functional networks might not be governed by as many ultra-high degree hubs as a typical scale-free network might suggest. This bodes well for real brain networks when considering resilience to attacks, compared to their scale-free counterparts. For future work, we intend to test whether these distributions hold for different network resolutions and parcellations. Moreover, it would be interesting to see how these results compare to the "core-periphery" organization of brain structural networks [9,12], which shows a preference for a distributed core, rather than few ultra-high degree hubs.

Acknowledgments. The work has been supported by the European Research Council under the EUs *7th Framework Programme* (FP7/2007-2013)/ERC grant agreement no. 341196 to P. Verschure. Data were provided [in part] by the Human Connectome Project, WU-Minn Consortium (Principal Investigators: David Van Essen and Kamil Ugurbil; 1U54MH091657) funded by the 16 NIH Institutes and Centers that support the NIH Blueprint for Neuroscience Research; and by the McDonnell Center for Systems Neuroscience at Washington University.

References

1. Achard, S., Salvador, R., Whitcher, B., Suckling, J., Bullmore, E.: A resilient, low-frequency, small-world human brain functional network with highly connected association cortical hubs. J. Neurosci. Official J. Soc. Neurosci. **26**(1), 63–72 (2006)
2. Albert, R., Jeong, H., Barabási, A.L.: Error and attack tolerance of complex networks. Nature **406**(6794), 378–382 (2000)
3. Arsiwalla, X.D., Betella, A., Martínez, E., Omedas, P., Zucca, R., Verschure, P.: The dynamic connectome: a tool for large scale 3D reconstruction of brain activity in real time. In: Rekdalsbakken, W., Bye, R., Zhang, H., (eds.) 27th European Conference on Modeling and Simulation, ECMS, Alesund (Norway) (2013)
4. Arsiwalla, X.D., Dalmazzo, D., Zucca, R., Betella, A., Brandi, S., Martinez, E., Omedas, P., Verschure, P.: Connectomics to semantomics: addressing the brain's big data challenge. Procedia Comput. Sci. **53**, 48–55 (2015)
5. Arsiwalla, X.D., Zucca, R., Betella, A., Martinez, E., Dalmazzo, D., Omedas, P., Deco, G., Verschure, P.: Network dynamics with BrainX3: a large-scale simulation of the human brain network with real-time interaction. Front. Neuroinf. **9**(2) (2015)
6. Clauset, A., Shalizi, C., Newman, M.: Power-law distributions in empirical data. SIAM Rev. **51**(4), 661–703 (2009)
7. Eguíluz, V.M., Chialvo, D.R., Cecchi, G.A., Baliki, M., Apkarian, A.V.: Scale-free brain functional networks. Phys. Rev. Lett. **94**(1), 018102 (2005)
8. Fornito, A., Zalesky, A., Bullmore, E.T.: Network scaling effects in graph analytic studies of human resting-state fMRI data. Front. Syst. Neurosci. **4**, 22 (2010)
9. Harriger, L., Heuvel, M.P., Sporns, O.: Rich club organization of macaque cerebral cortex and its role in network communication. PloS One **7**(9), e46497 (2012)
10. Hayasaka, S., Laurienti, P.J.: Comparison of characteristics between region-and voxel-based network analyses in resting-state fMRI data. NeuroImage **50**(2), 499–508 (2010)
11. Heuvel, M.P., Stam, C.J., Boersma, M., Hulshoff Pol, H.E.: Small-world and scale-free organization of voxel-based resting-state functional connectivity in the human brain. NeuroImage **43**(3), 528–539 (2008)
12. Heuvel, M.P., Sporns, O.: Rich-club organization of the human connectome. J. Neurosci. **31**(44), 15775–15786 (2011)
13. Essen, D.C., Smith, S.M., Barch, D.M., Behrens, T.E.J., Yacoub, E., Ugurbil, K.: The WU-Minn human connectome project: an overview. NeuroImage **80**, 62–79 (2013)

Attractor Dynamics Driven by Interactivity in Boolean Recurrent Neural Networks

Jérémie Cabessa[1(✉)] and Alessandro E.P. Villa[2]

[1] Laboratory of Mathematical Economics (LEMMA),
University Panthéon-Assas – Paris 2, 4 Rue Blaise Desgoffe, 75006 Paris, France
jeremie.cabessa@u-pairs2.fr
[2] Neuroheuristic Research Group, Department of Information Systems,
University of Lausanne, 1015 Lausanne, Switzerland

Abstract. We study the attractor dynamics of a Boolean model of the basal ganglia-thalamocortical network as a function of its interactive synaptic connections and global threshold. We show that the regulation of the interactive feedback and global threshold are significantly involved in the maintenance and robustness of the attractor basin. These results support the hypothesis that, beyond mere structural architecture, global plasticity and interactivity play a crucial role in the computational and dynamical capabilities of biological neural networks.

1 Introduction

Experimental studies suggest that spatiotemporal patterns of discharges, i.e., ordered and precise interspike interval relationships [1–3], as well as specific attractor dynamics [4,5] are likely to be significantly involved in the processing and coding of information in the brain. The association between attractor dynamics and spatiotemporal patterns has been demonstrated in nonlinear dynamical systems [6] and in simulations of large scale neuronal networks [7], thus suggesting that spatiotemporal patterns might be considered as witnesses of underlying attractor dynamics – which itself would be a key feature of neural coding.

On the basis of these bioinspired considerations, we study the attractor dynamics of a Boolean model of the basal ganglia-thalamocortical network [8]. We investigate the richness of the attractor dynamics of this network as a function of its interactive synaptic connections – which are assumed to be significantly involved in the crucial exchange of information between the network and its environment – as well as of its global threshold – which represents a global notion of plasticity [9–14]. We show that the regulation of the interactive feedback and global threshold are significantly involved in the maintenance and robustness of optimal attractor potentialities. It is noteworthy that experimental evidence of a context-dependent modifiable central feedback to projection neurons has been reported in the invertebrate neural circuit [15].

© Springer International Publishing Switzerland 2016
A.E.P. Villa et al. (Eds.): ICANN 2016, Part I, LNCS 9886, pp. 115–122, 2016.
DOI: 10.1007/978-3-319-44778-0_14

2   Boolean Recurrent Neural Networks

It has early been observed that Boolean recurrent neural networks are computationally equivalent to finite state automata [16,17]. More precisely, recurrent
neural networks composed of McCulloch and Piits's cells [18] can simulate and
be simulated by finite state automata. The translation from a Boolean networks
to a corresponding finite automaton is illustrated in Fig. 1. The converse translation is not illustrated here.

Boolean Neural Network   Finite State Automaton

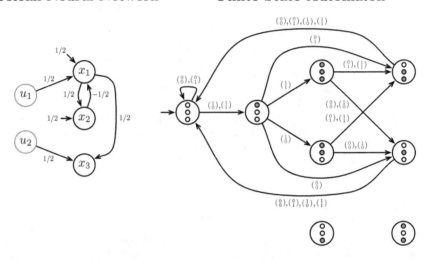

Fig. 1. Translation from a given Boolean neural network $\mathcal{N}$ to a corresponding finite
automaton $\mathcal{A}$. The nodes of $\mathcal{A}$ are the different states of $\mathcal{N}$ (represented as colored
triple dots that depict the three internal quiet or firing cells of $\mathcal{N}$). There is an edge
from node s to node s' labelled by x in $\mathcal{A}$ if and only if the network $\mathcal{N}$ moves from
state s to s' when receiving input x. (Color figure online)

According to the construction of Fig. 1, the possible *dynamics* of a given
Boolean network correspond precisely to the possible *paths* in the graph of its
associated automaton. Hence, the *attractors* of the Boolean network – i.e., the
cyclic dynamics – correspond exactly to the *cycles* of the automaton. Consequently, in order to compute the attractors of a Boolean network, it suffices
to construct its corresponding automaton and then list all the cycles of this
automaton. Note that in this context, whenever the dynamics of Boolean networks is falling into some *periodic attractor*, the activity of the network units is
necessarily characterized by some associated recurrent *spatiotemporal pattern of
discharges*, as illustrated in Fig. 2.

  This theoretical framework is illustrated by a simulation of a network formed
by interconnected thalamocortical modules of spiking units described elsewhere [19]. This model accounts for a first order dynamics of the membrane

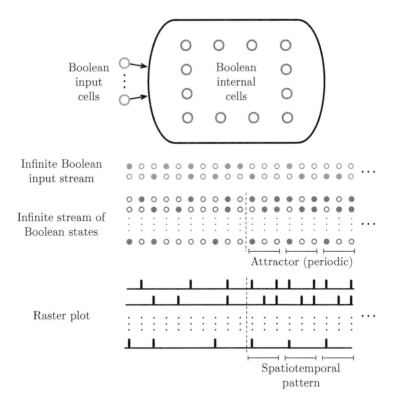

Fig. 2. In a Boolean neural networks, the attractor dynamics of the internal cells are the precise phenomenon that underly the emergence of spatiotemporal patterns of discharges. In fact, the raster plot of internal cells involved in some periodic attractor dynamics corresponds precisely to some spatiotemporal pattern of discharge.

potential characterized by a kinetic constant and for global excitability of the circuit. These parameters are controlled by the modulatory inputs that act differentially on the capacitance and resistance of the cell membrane. Monoamines and acetylcholine may regulate properties of voltage-sensitive ion channels [20] through the action of cellular second messengers. These mechanisms affect the shape of the postsynaptic potentials – i.e., the half-width of the decay – without modifying the membrane resistance which is related to the membrane potential. Modulatory projections from the brainstem may also affect the overall excitability of the thalamocortical network in relation to arousal, sleep-waking activity, and their role in modulation of sensory processes has been recognized long time ago [21, 22].

In the absence of background activity and noisy inputs, all the dynamics is deterministic, such that when an input pattern of activity is provided at the beginning of the simulation, the network activity stabilizes either to an extinction of the activity – no more units are firing – or to a cyclic pattern of activity – an attractor dynamics – which in turn induces a corresponding spatiotemporal

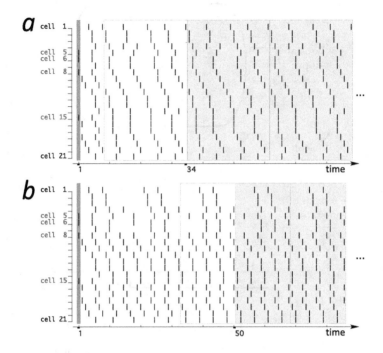

Fig. 3. Examples of raster displays showing repeating spatiotemporal patterns. The rows of the rasters correspond to each unit of a circuit composed of two coupled thalamocortical modules activation pattern. At time 1 the cells 5, 6, 8 and 25 were initially set active. The time constant of the membrane potential was fixed at 2.92 ms. Global excitability parameter was set at a lower level $ep = -31$ in panel (a) then in panel (b) where $ep = -29$. The spatiotemporal pattern started to repeat at time 34 with a cycle duration of 24 time steps and at time 50 with a cycle duration of 16 for panel (a) and panel (b), respectively.

pattern of discharges. The period of the attractor and the specificities of the associated spatiotemporal pattern may change greatly to tiny differences in the values of the two dynamical parameters for the same initial pattern of activation as illustrated by Fig. 3. Notice that with the same initial stimulation and same membrane dynamics, a change in the global excitability parameter may also lead to the extinction of the activity.

3   Boolean Model of the Basal Ganglia-Thalamocortical Network

We assume that the encoding of a large amount of the information treated by the basal ganglia-thalamocortical network is performed by recurrent patterns of activity circulating in the information transmitting system of this network.

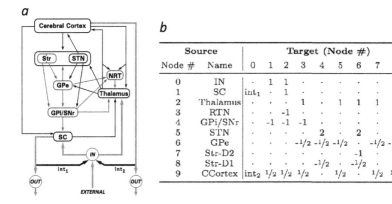

Source		Target (Node #)									
Node #	Name	0	1	2	3	4	5	6	7	8	9
0	IN	·	1	1	·	·	·	·	·	·	·
1	SC	int₁	·	1	·	·	·	·	·	·	·
2	Thalamus	·	·	·	1	·	1	1	1	1	1
3	RTN	·	·	-1	·	·	·	·	·	·	·
4	GPi/SNr	·	-1	-1	-1	·	·	·	·	·	·
5	STN	·	·	·	·	2	·	2	·	·	2
6	GPe	·	·	·	-1/2	-1/2	-1/2	·	-1/2	-1/2	·
7	Str-D2	·	·	·	·	·	·	-1	·	·	·
8	Str-D1	·	·	·	·	-1/2	·	-1/2	·	·	·
9	CCortex	int₂	1/2	1/2	1/2	·	1/2	·	1/2	1/2	·

Fig. 4. (a) Simple Boolean model of the basal ganglia-thalamocortical network and (b) its adjacency matrix. Each brain area is represented by a single node in the Boolean neural network model: superior colliculus (SC), Thalamus, thalamic reticular nucleus (NRT), Cerebral Cortex, the striatopallidal and the striatonigral components of the striatum (Str), the subthalamic nucleus (STN), the external part of the pallidum (GPe), and the output nuclei of the basal ganglia formed by the GABAergic projection neurons of the intermediate part of the pallidum and of the substantia nigra pars reticulata (GPi/SNR). We consider also the inputs (IN) from the ascending sensory pathway and the motor outputs (OUT). The excitatory pathways are labeled in blue and the inhibitory ones in orange. Part of the motor outputs are recurrently connected via the interactive connections int₁ and int₂. (Color figure online)

We extend our simplified model of the basal ganglia-thalamocortical network [8] in order to include *interactive connections*, enabling a feedback of information from the network activity to combine with the external inputs, see Fig. 4. We study the attractor dynamics of this network as a function of its interactive connections int_1 and int_2 and of its global excitability.

4   Results

We study the attractor dynamics of our simplified model of the basal ganglia-thalamocortical network, as a function of perturbations of its interactive connections (int_1 and int_2) and global threshold (θ). Overall, we notice that the regulation of the interactive feedback plays a crucial role in the maintenance of an optimal attractor-based level of complexity. There is always an optimal region for the interactive weights outside of which the number of attractors of the network significantly decreases. We also show that the network's attractor dynamics depends sensitively on the value of its global threshold. Small perturbations of the threshold significantly affect the attractor dynamics of the network.

More precisely, for each of the four threshold values $\theta = 0.4$, $\theta = 0.6$, $\theta = 0.8$ and $\theta = 1.0$, we preformed 1681 simulations to compute the number of basic attractors[1] of the network as a function of its two interactive weights int_1 and int_2,

---

[1] The basic attractors of a Boolean network are given by the basic cycles of its corresponding automaton, i.e., the cycles that do not visit the same vertex twice.

Number of basic attractors

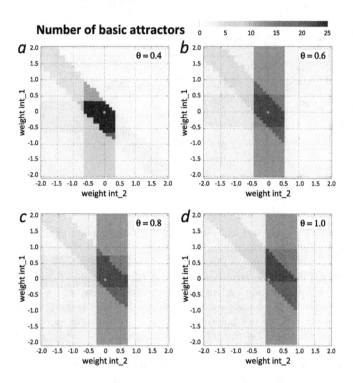

Fig. 5. Number of basic attractors of the network as a function of the interactive weights int_1 and int_2, and for different values of the global threshold θ of the cells. Four patterns of variation are observed and reported in the subfigures (a)–(d). The green point corresponds to no interactivity. (Color figure online)

where these latter are varying from -2 to 2 by steps of 0.1. The results are reported in Fig. 5. In each case, we notice the existence of an optimal region for the values of int_1 and int_2 where the number of attractors takes maximal values of 22 (in cases (b), (c), and (d)) or 25 (in case (a)). Around this optimal region, the number of attractors was much lower. This optimal region is 'continuous', in the sense of forming a well defined block without holes, as opposed to smaller discontinuous blocks that would be disseminated across the map. Hence, in the 'center' of this optimal region, the interactive weights int_1 and int_2 can vary in a relatively consequent neighborhood without compromising the attractor dynamics of the network.

Furthermore, we notice that the variation of the threshold θ affects significantly the attractors dynamics of the network. A higher excitability, i.e. a lower threshold ($\theta = 0.4$), favors the emergence of richer attractor dynamics in the optimal region (25 attractors in case (a) as opposed to 22 in the three other cases). However, this optimal region is surrounded by regions of lower complexities than in the other cases. Hence, an increase of the excitability (i.e. lowering of the threshold) acts as a "polarization" of the attractor dynamics: it increases the complexity of the optimal region and lowers the complexity of its neighbourhood.

5   Discussion

We have considered a simplified Boolean model of the basal ganglia-thalamocortical network, and provided new evidence of the effects that the global excitability and "interactivity" have on its dynamical properties. The interactivity is expresses in the form of a feedback informational loop, where the network's output together with the external environment produce a combined stream of information which is re-entered into the input layer of the network. This information can be assumed to represent precise contextual and explicit information recorded by the primary ascending (i.e. *lemniscal*) sensory channels via a thalamic relay [23]. The sensory information is also reaching modulatory centers in the brainstem and hypothalamus that may exert their modulatory influence by changing the global excitability of the network [24].

More generally, our results show that the interactive connections and global excitability of Boolean neural networks play a significant role in the maintenance and robustness of their attractor-based complexity. The networks are considered as dynamical systems operating in a range of control parameters. A global change in their excitability combined with selected interactively-generated input patterns will induce their dynamics to evolve into specific attractor dynamics, and in turn, into repeating spatiotemporal firing patterns. Those patterns should not be considered as high-order Morse codes, but rather as co-representations of contextual information, including a certain "central arousal" modulated by dopaminergic [25], cholinergic [26] and serotoninergic [27] pathways.

References

1. Abeles, M., Gerstein, G.L.: Detecting spatiotemporal firing patterns among simultaneously recorded single neurons. J. Neurophysiol. **60**(3), 909–924 (1988)
2. Villa, A.E.P., Abeles, M.: Evidence for spatiotemporal firing patterns within the auditory thalamus of the cat. Brain. Res. **509**(2), 325–327 (1990)
3. Villa, A.E.P., Fuster, J.M.: Temporal correlates of information processing during visual short-term memory. Neuroreport **3**, 113–116 (1992)
4. Celletti, A., Villa, A.E.P.: Determination of chaotic attractors in the rat brain. J. Stat. Phys. **84**(5), 1379–1385 (1996)
5. Villa, A.E.P., Tetko, I.V., Celletti, A., Riehle, A.: Chaotic dynamics in the primate motor cortex depend on motor preparation in a reaction-time task. Curr. Psychol. Cogn. **17**, 763–780 (1998)
6. Asai, Y., Villa, A.E.P.: Integration and transmission of distributed deterministic neural activity in feed-forward networks. Brain. Res. **1434**, 17–33 (2012)
7. Iglesias, J., Villa, A.E.P.: Recurrent spatiotemporal firing patterns in large spiking neural networks with ontogenetic and epigenetic processes. J. Physiol. Paris **104**(3–4), 137–146 (2010)
8. Cabessa, J., Villa, A.E.P.: An attractor-based complexity measurement for Boolean recurrent neural networks. PLoS ONE **9**(4), e94204 (2014)
9. McCormick, D.A., Bal, T.: Sleep and arousal: thalamocortical mechanisms. Annu. Rev. Neurosci. **20**, 185–215 (1997)

10. Terman, D., Rubin, J.E., Yew, A.C., Wilson, C.J.: Activity patterns in a model for the subthalamopallidal network of the basal ganglia. J. Neurosci. **22**(7), 2963–2976 (2002)
11. Silkis, I.: A hypothetical role of cortico-basal ganglia-thalamocortical loops in visual processing. Biosystems **89**(1–3), 227–235 (2007)
12. Spiga, S., Lintas, A., Diana, M.: Altered mesolimbic dopamine system in THC dependence. Current Neuropharmacol. **9**(1), 200–204 (2011)
13. Lintas, A.: Discharge properties of neurons recorded in the parvalbumin-positive (PV1) nucleus of the rat lateral hypothalamus. Neurosci. Lett. **571**, 29–33 (2014)
14. Guthrie, M., Leblois, A., Garenne, A., Boraud, T.: Interaction between cognitive and motor cortico-basal ganglia loops during decision making: a computational study. J. Neurophysiol. **109**(12), 3025–3040 (2013)
15. Blitz, D.M., Nusbaum, M.P.: Modulation of circuit feedback specifies motor circuit output. J. Neurosci. **32**(27), 9182–9193 (2012)
16. Kleene, S.C.: Representation of events in nerve nets and finite automata. In: Shannon, C., McCarthy, J. (eds.) Automata Studies, pp. 3–41. Princeton University Press, Princeton (1956)
17. Minsky, M.L.: Computation: Finite and Infinite Machines. Prentice-Hall Inc., Englewood Cliffs (1967)
18. McCulloch, W.S., Pitts, W.: A logical calculus of the ideas immanent in nervous activity. Bull. Math. Biophys. **5**, 115–133 (1943)
19. Villa, A.E.P., Tetko, I.V.: Spatio-temporal patterns of activity controlled by system parameters in a simulated thalamo-cortical neural network. In: Herrmann, H., Wolf, D., Poppel, E. (eds.) Supercomputing in Brain Research: From Tomography to Neural Networks, pp. 379–388. World Scientific, Singapore (1995)
20. Levitan, I.B.: Modulation of ion channels in neurons and other cells. Annu. Rev. Neurosci. **11**, 119–136 (1988)
21. Foote, S.L., Morrison, J.H.: Extrathalamic modulation of cortical function. Annu. Rev. Neurosci. **10**, 67–95 (1987)
22. McCormick, D.A., Pape, H.C.: Noradrenergic and serotonergic modulation of a hyperpolarization-activated cation current in thalamic relay neurones. J. Physiol. **431**, 319–342 (1990)
23. Kandel, E.R., Schwartz, J.H., Jessell, T.M., Siegelbaum, S.A., Hudspeth, A.J.: Principles of Neural Science, 5th edn. McGraw-Hill, New York (2012)
24. Saper, C.B., Lowell, B.B.: The hypothalamus. Curr. Biol. **24**(23), R1111–R1116 (2014)
25. Sesack, S.R., Grace, A.A.: Cortico-basal ganglia reward network: microcircuitry. Neuropsychopharmacology **35**(1), 27–47 (2010)
26. Villa, A.E.P., Lorenzana, V.M.B., Vantini, G.: Nerve growth factor modulates information processing in the auditory thalamus. Brain. Res. Bull. **39**(3), 139–147 (1996)
27. Lopez-Garcia, J.A.: Serotonergic modulation of spinal sensory circuits. Curr. Top. Med. Chem. **6**(18), 1987–1996 (2006)

Training Bidirectional Recurrent Neural Network Architectures with the Scaled Conjugate Gradient Algorithm

Michalis Agathocleous[1], Chris Christodoulou[1(✉)], Vasilis Promponas[2], Petros Kountouris[3], and Vassilis Vassiliades[1,4]

[1] Department of Computer Science, University of Cyprus,
P.O. Box 20537, 1678 Nicosia, Cyprus
{magath06,cchrist}@cs.ucy.ac.cy
[2] Dept. of Biological Sciences, University of Cyprus,
P.O. Box 20537, 1678 Nicosia, Cyprus
vprobon@ucy.ac.cy
[3] The Cyprus Institute of Neurology and Genetics, Nicosia, Cyprus
petrosk@cing.ac.cy
[4] Inria, Nancy - Grand Est, France
vassilis.vassiliades@inria.fr

Abstract. Predictions on sequential data, when both the upstream and downstream information is important, is a difficult and challenging task. The Bidirectional Recurrent Neural Network (BRNN) architecture has been designed to deal with this class of problems. In this paper, we present the development and implementation of the Scaled Conjugate Gradient (SCG) learning algorithm for BRNN architectures. The model has been tested on the Protein Secondary Structure Prediction (PSSP) and Transmembrane Protein Topology Prediction problems (TMPTP). Our method currently achieves preliminary results close to 73 % correct predictions for the PSSP problem and close to 79 % for the TMPTP problem, which are expected to increase with larger datasets, external rules, ensemble methods and filtering techniques. Importantly, the SCG algorithm is training the BRNN architecture approximately 3 times faster than the Backpropagation Through Time (BPTT) algorithm.

Keywords: Scaled Conjugate Gradient · Bidirectional Recurrent Neural Networks · Protein Secondary Structure Prediction · Transmembrane Protein Topology Prediction · Computational intelligence · Bioinformatics

1 Introduction

Even though a number of Machine Learning (ML) algorithms have been designed to process and make predictions on sequential data, the mining of such data types is still an open field of research due to its complexity and divergence [1]. Analysis and development of optimisation algorithms for specific ML techniques must

© Springer International Publishing Switzerland 2016
A.E.P. Villa et al. (Eds.): ICANN 2016, Part I, LNCS 9886, pp. 123–131, 2016.
DOI: 10.1007/978-3-319-44778-0_15

take into account (a) how to capture and exploit sequential correlations, (b) how to design appropriate loss functions, (c) how to identify long-distance interactions, and (d) how to make the optimisation algorithm fast [2]. One of the most successful classes of models which has been designed to deal with these questions is Recurrent Neural Networks (RNNs) [3]. The most common learning algorithm for such models is the Backpropagation Through Time (BPTT) [4,5], which is based on the gradient descent algorithm. Unfortunately, this kind of algorithms have a poor convergence rate [6]. Moreover, they depend on parameters which have to be specified by the user and are usually crucial for the performance of the algorithm. In order to eliminate these drawbacks, more efficient algorithms must be developed. One such algorithm is the Scaled Conjugate Gradient (SCG) [6], a second-order learning algorithm, that has been found to be superior to the conventional BPTT algorithm in terms of accuracy, convergence rate and the vanishing-gradient problem [7]. In addition, the original form of the algorithm [6] does not depend on any parameters.

Predictions on sequential data are particularly challenging when both the upstream and downstream information of a sequence is important for a specific element in the sequence. Application examples include problems from Bioinformatics such as Protein Secondary Structure Prediction (PSSP) [8–10] and other related problems (e.g., Transmembrane Protein Topology Prediction (TMPTP) [11]). In such sequence-based problems the events are dynamic and located downstream and upstream, i.e., left and right in the sequence. A ML model designed for such data must learn to make predictions based on both directions of a sequence. To predict these events, researchers utilise Bidirectional Recurrent Neural Network (BRNN) architectures [8]. The BRNN has proved to be a very efficient architecture for the PSSP problem with accuracy of approximately 76 % [8], while for the TMPTP problem to the best of our knowledge the BRNN architecture has not been used so far. The BRNN architectures are currently trained with an extension of the BPTT algorithm [5] with the error propagated in both directions of the BRNN. However, the SCG algorithm has not been developed for this architecture.

This paper introduces the mathematical analysis and development of the SCG learning algorithm for the BRNN architecture. The implemented model and learning algorithm is then tested on the PSSP and TMPTP problems.

2   Methodology

2.1   The BRNN Architecture

The BRNN architecture of Baldi et al. [8] consists of two RNNs and a Feed Forward Neural Network (FFNN). The novelty of this architecture is the contextual information contained in the two RNNs, the Forward RNN (FRNN) and the Backward RNN (BwRNN). The prediction at step t, for a segment in a sequence, is processed based on the information contained in a sliding window W_a. The FRNN iteratively processes the $(W_a - 1)/2$ residues located on the left side of the position t to compute the forward (upstream) context (F_t). Similarly, the BwRNN iteratively processes the ($W_a - 1)/2$ residues located on the right side of the position t to compute the backward (downstream) context (B_t). Hence, the two RNNs are used to implement F_t and B_t. These RNNs correlate each sequence separately and hold an internal temporary knowledge to form the network's internal memory [3].

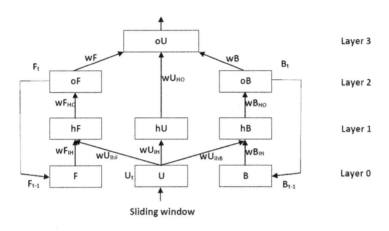

Fig. 1. The BRNN architecture

The BRNN architecture in Fig. 1 is inspired by the work of Baldi et al. [8]. Layer 0 in Fig. 1 is not an active layer, layers 1 and 2 have a hyperbolic tangent transfer function, while layer 3 is a softmax output layer which is calculated based on the result of Eq. 1. Box U stands for input nodes, F for the set of forward states and B for the set of backward states. The links between boxes oF and F and between boxes oB and B represent the recursive connections providing the information of the given number of states of current input U.

$$oU_i = softmax\left(\frac{1}{2\psi}\sum_{j=1}^{N_\phi} wF_{ij} \cdot f_{i,t} + \sum_{j=1}^{N_\beta} wB_{ij} \cdot b_{i,t} + \sum_{j=1}^{N_{hU}} wU_{ij} \cdot hU_{i,t}\right) \quad (1)$$

where ψ is the number of training patterns. N_ϕ, N_β and N_{hU} are the dimensions of oF, oB and hU layers, respectively. i stands for the position of a neuron in oU. wF_{ij}, wB_{ij} are the connection weights between layer 2 and 3, and wU_{ij} between layer 1 and 3. Finally, $f_{i,t}$, $b_{i,t}$ and $hU_{i,t}$ are the outputs of each neuron at time t of oF, oB and oU, respectively.

2.2 Development of the SCG Algorithm for BRNNs

As the Scaled Conjugate Gradient (SCG) learning algorithm [6] has not been previously developed for the BRNN architecture, we have mathematically analysed and developed the corresponding learning formulas and optimisation procedure. These formulas were based on an unfolded BRNN. Since stationarity is assumed, the connection weights do not change over time and the unfolding architecture of the BRNN is as indicated by the work of Baldi et al. [8]. We have used the straightforward cost function given by 2:

$$E = \frac{1}{2\psi} \sum_{p=1}^{\psi} \sum_{i=1}^{s} (\overline{y}_{p,i,t} - y_{p,i,t})^2 \tag{2}$$

where s the number of neurons in the output layer, $\overline{y}_{p,i,t}$ the target output and $y_{p,i,t}$ the system output for an input pattern p.

The partial derivatives with respect to the weights are hidden in the system output as usual. Consequently, the general formula of the partial derivative of E with respect to any weight in Fig. 1 can be written as below:

$$\frac{\partial E}{\partial w} = \frac{1}{\psi} \left(\frac{\partial E}{\partial y_{p,i,t}} \cdot \frac{\partial y_{p,i,t}}{\partial oU_t} \cdot \frac{\partial oU_t}{\partial w} \right) = \frac{1}{\psi} \left((\overline{y}_{p,i,t} - y_{p,i,t}) \cdot y_{p,i,t} \cdot (1 - y_{p,i,t}) \cdot \frac{\partial oU_t}{\partial w} \right) \tag{3}$$

Finally, based on Eq. 3, we have calculated the derivatives which are used in the SCG algorithm for training the weights of the BRNN architecture in Fig. 1. After the partial derivatives of the cost function of Eq. 2 with respect to individual weights were calculated, they were directly applied to the SCG algorithm in the work of Møller [6] and represent the formulas of updating weights in the unfolded version of the BRNN.

One of the most undesirable difficulties during the training of a RNN is the vanishing gradient problem. A mechanism introducing shortcut connections between the forward and backward states of the sequence was used (as in [8]), forming shorter paths along the sequence where gradients can be propagated. Therefore, the gradient information at each step t includes a strong signal from the whole sequence to encounter for the vanishing gradient problem and consequently avoid long range dependencies elimination.

Furthermore, we have introduced a couple of minor modifications on the SCG algorithm to increase the convergence rate and the ability of the algorithm to search for the best solution in a complicated error surface of such a network:

1. An **Adaptive Step Size Scaling Parameter** S_{cSS} was introduced at step 7 of the SCG algorithm (see [6]). We have modified the algorithm's update weight vector rule to Eq. 4:

$$w_{k+1} = w_k + S_{cSS} a_k p_k \tag{4}$$

where a_k is the step size and p_k is the search direction. During the first iterations this scalar is high, assuming that the algorithm has identified a direction to a minimum. Hence, we force the algorithm to use bigger step size in a specific direction to approach a minimum faster. The adaptive scaling parameter is exponentially decreasing as the algorithm approaches a minimum to avoid losing the lowest point of the curve. Furthermore, this parameter is redefined each time the SCG algorithm restarts. Empirically, the use of this parameter is mandatory for training a complicated BRNN architecture with the SCG algorithm.

2. Restart Algorithm Condition: The original SCG algorithm is restarted if the number of learning iterations surpasses the number of the network's parameters. However, this condition is successful only if the algorithm is used to optimize a quadratic function. Clearly, in the case of the BRNN architecture this condition fails because the error surface is more complicated than a quadratic function. Hence, we have chosen to restart the algorithm only if the training process develops slowly (improvement in training error $<10^{-7}$) and after the constant number of 20 iterations. Furthermore, our algorithm, before a restart, stores all the weight vectors and the respective training errors. Finally, after the algorithm reaches the final training iteration, it returns a trained model with the weight vector which was assigned to the lowest training error. Consequently, this version of the algorithm is widely exploring the respective error surface and is less likely to get stuck for a long time in a local minimum.

2.3 Application Domains and Data

High quality datasets for training and validation purposes are mandatory when constructing a prediction model. Therefore, we have chosen two well known bioinformatics problems which are suited to the BRNN architecture.

Protein Secondary Structure Prediction: The prediction of a protein's Secondary Structure (SS) from its Primary Structure (PS) is an important intermediate step to the identification of a protein's three-dimensional (3D) structure, which is crucial because it specifies the protein's functionality. Experimental methods for the determination of a protein's 3D structure are expensive, time consuming and frequently inefficient [8]. A protein is typically composed of 20 different amino acid types, which are chemically connected, folding into a 3D structure by forming short-, mid- and long-range interactions. When an experimentally determined 3D structure is available, each amino acid residue can be assigned to a SS class, usually under a commonly accepted scheme: helix (H), extended (E) and coil/loops (L). We use the CB513 [13], a non-redundant dataset, which has been heavily used as a PSSP benchmark dataset. Multiple sequence alignment (MSA) profiles have been shown to enhance machine learning-based PSSP, since they incorporate useful evolutionary information for the encoding of each position of a protein. More specifically, each protein sequence position is replaced by a 20-dimensional vector, which corresponds to the frequencies of 20 different amino acid types as calculated from a PSI-BLAST [12] search against the NCBI-NR (NCBI: http://www.ncbi.nlm.nih.gov/) database.

Transmembrane Protein Topology Prediction: Knowledge of the structure and topology of Transmembrane (TM) proteins is important since they are involved in a wide range of important biological processes and more than half of all drugs on the market target membrane proteins [11]. However, due to experimental difficulties, this class of proteins is under-represented in structural databases. Similarly to the PSSP problem, a TMPTP dataset consists of the proteins' PS and each amino acid can be assigned to a topology class: inside a cell (I), outsite a cell (O) and inside a cell's membrane (T). Such a dataset has been introduced by Nugent and Jones [11] which contained 131 sequences (TM131) with all available crystal structures, verifiable topology and N-terminal locations. As in the PSSP problem, MSA profiles have been used to represent a sequence's PS.

3   Results and Discussion

The developed SCG learning algorithm for BRNNs has been implemented and tested on both PSSP and TMPTP problems. To train the BRNNs, we have used the already mentioned CB513 and TM131 datasets. More specifically, the model's input vector was a sliding window on a protein's PS. The target output class was the SS class for PSSP and topology class for TMPTP which was assigned to the segment at the middle point of a sliding window.

A single BRNN has been trained each time. At this stage, we carried out multiple experiments to tune up our model and extract preliminary results, which are shown in Tables 1 and 2. One of the most important parameters with a big impact on the results is the sliding window size. Particularly, we have used 3 window size parameters. Parameter W_a stands for the sliding window size on the PS sequence. The first $(W_a - 1)/2$ residues of the sliding window are used as input to F_t and similarly the last $(W_a - 1)/2$ residues are used an input to B_t. The W_c window parameter represents the number of W_a residues which are located at the center of the window and are used as input to hU. Finally, the W_{fb} window parameter represents the number of residues that are used as input to F_t and B_t at each step. Each one of the 3 window size parameters is multiplied by 20 which is the length of each amino acid MSA representation. Furthermore, we had to tune up the parameters that determine the network's architecture. The parameter n is the length of the context vectors oF and oB. In addition, the parameter h_n is the number of hidden units in hU layer and similarly h_{fb} is the number of hidden units in hF and hB layers. We have also used the already mentioned adaptive step size scaling parameter $ScSS$. Finally, we have used the S_{fb} and S_{out}, which are the numbers of additional consecutive context vectors in the future and the past of F_t/B_T and O_t, respectively. In all experiments, the 2/3 of the datasets were used to train the model and the 1/3 for validation purposes. The performance of our model has been evaluated by the Q_3 metric, which corresponds to the percentage of the correctly predicted residues [14].

Firstly, we have trained the BRNN architecture on the PSSP problem. For the purpose of tuning up the network's parameters we have used a subset of CB513 dataset, which contained 150 randomly selected protein sequences. The results can be seen in Table 1. After we have tuned up the network architecture, we have noticed that in order to maximize the algorithm's performance the three windows W_a, W_{fb} and W_c must have values of 25, 3 and 3, respectively. Thus, shorter sliding window does not provide the network with enough information and longer sliding window cannot be captured by the network. As it can be seen from experiments 2 and 5 in Table 1, the correct tuning up of the sliding window parameter W_a can increase the algorithm's performance more than 3 %. Furthermore, we have noticed that the S_{cSS} parameter should be set to 100 to increase the convergence rate for this problem. As it can be seen from experiments 1, 3 and 5 in Table 1, this parameter can increase the performance of the algorithm near to 4 %. The final Q_3 metric has also increased by 2 % after we dropped the S_{fb} and S_{out} parameters from 3 to 2, as it can be seen from experiments 6 and 7 in Table 1. Finally, the best Q_3 result was **73.90 %** which has been achieved in 500 training iterations, the 1/3 of BPTT learning iterations.

Table 1. Experimental results using 1/3 of the CB513 subset as a test set (see text for description of the parameters)

A/A	W_a	W_{fb}	W_c	S_{cSS}	n	h_n	h_{fb}	S_{fb}	S_{out}	$Q_3(\%)$
1	25	3	3	10	11	11	11	2	2	69.64
2	31	3	3	100	11	11	11	2	2	70.26
3	25	3	3	1000	11	11	11	2	2	69.10
4	25	3	3	100	9	9	9	2	2	67.56
5	25	3	3	100	11	11	11	2	2	73.03
6	25	3	3	100	14	14	14	2	2	**73.90**
7	25	3	3	100	14	14	14	3	3	71.26

Similarly, we have used the TM131 dataset to train the model with the results shown in Table 2. The network needed for this problem was much bigger compared to the one used for the PSSP problem. Importantly, the W_{fb} window had to be always set to 1, as larger size windows reduced the algorithm's performance. Furthermore, the S_{cSS} parameter was set to 10 to increase more than 2 % the algorithm's Q_3 accuracy, as it can be seen from experiments 2 and 3 in Table 2. Surprisingly, the network cannot converge with any value more than 0 for the S_{out} parameter. The best Q_3 achieved was **78.85 %**. This Q_3 accuracy was achieved with no external rules, ensemble methods or filtering techniques, which will be used in our final methodology and we expect to increase the performance of our system. Consequently, our results are lower than the 89 % correct predictions of Nugent and Jones [11] on the same dataset. This observation shows that, at least with regards to the output layer, context networks seem to be less important compared to the PSSP problem. This fact was actually expected, since TM regions are on average much longer than SS elements in globular proteins.

The preliminary results on the PSSP and TMPTP problems have shown that a BRNN trained with our version of the SCG learning algorithm can capture patterns and make predictions on complicated sequences where the information in both upstream and downstream direction is important. Furthermore, the SCG

Table 2. Experimental results using 1/3 of the TM131 as a test set (see text for description of the parameters)

A/A	W_a	W_{fb}	W_c	S_{cSS}	n	h_n	h_{fb}	S_{fb}	S_{out}	$Q_3(\%)$
1	25	1	25	10	40	40	40	3	3	54.20
2	25	1	25	10	40	40	40	3	0	72.56
3	25	1	25	100	40	40	40	3	0	70.36
4	25	1	25	10	37	37	37	3	0	73.06
5	25	1	25	10	30	30	40	3	0	77.73
6	25	1	25	10	25	25	25	3	0	**78.85**
7	25	1	15	10	40	40	40	3	0	70.09

learning algorithm needs much less training iterations than the conventional BPTT learning algorithm. This is very important if we take into account the latest developments in the field which demand very big datasets and network architectures, which consequently increase exponentially the training time. In addition, many of these methods are used in ensemble methods (as in Baldi et al. [8]) where the training time is increased even further. Furthermore, our experiments have shown that in the absence of the S_{cSS} parameter, the SCG algorithm training the BRNN architecture could not converge (results not shown).

Importantly, our final methodology will be based on our previous work in [9,10]. Our current preliminary results, for the PSSP problem, are slightly lower than the 76 % Q3 accuracy of Baldi et al. [8], as no big datasets, external rules, ensemble methods or filtering techniques have yet been used, through which we expect (based on the results of our previous work [9,10]) to increase the final Q3 accuracy for both the PSSP and TMPTP problems. Moreover, we do not have in this paper a direct comparison with the results of Baldi et al. [8] because the dataset used is different. Consequently, the final results of training a BRNN with SCG on the PSSP and TMPTP problems and the direct comparison with similar methods will be presented at the conference.

References

1. Schuster, M., Paliwal, K.K.: IEEE Trans. Signal Proces. **45**, 2673–2681 (1997)
2. Dietterich, T.G.: Machine learning for sequential data: a review. In: Caelli, T.M., Amin, A., Duin, R.P.W., Kamel, M.S., de Ridder, D. (eds.) SSPR&SPR 2002. LNCS, vol. 2396, pp. 15–30. Springer, Heidelberg (2002)
3. Elman, J.L.: Cogn. Sci. **14**, 179–211 (1990)
4. Werbos, P.J.: Proc. IEEE **78**(10), 1550–1560 (1990)
5. Frasconi, P., Gori, M., Sperduti, A.: IEEE Trans. Neural Netw. **9**, 768–786 (1998)
6. Møller, M.F.: Neural Netw. **6**, 525–533 (1993)
7. Hochreiter, S., Schmidhuber, J.: Neural Comput. **9**, 1735–1780 (1997)

8. Baldi, P., Brunak, S., Frasconi, P., Soda, G., Pollastri, G.: Bioinformatics **15**, 937–946 (1999)
9. Kountouris, P., Agathocleous, M., Promponas, V., Christodoulou, G., Hadjicostas, S., Vassiliades, V., Christodoulou, C.: IEEE ACM Trans. Comput. Biol. Bioinform. **9**, 731–739 (2012)
10. Agathocleous, M., Christodoulou, G., Promponas, V., Christodoulou, C., Vassiliades, V., Antoniou, A.: Protein secondary structure prediction with Bidirectional recurrent neural nets: can weight updating for each residue enhance performance? In: Papadopoulos, H., Andreou, A.S., Bramer, M. (eds.) AIAI 2010. IFIP AICT, vol. 339, pp. 128–137. Springer, Heidelberg (2010)
11. Nugent, T., Jones, D.T.: BMC Bioinf. **10**, 159 (2009)
12. Altschul, S.F., Madden, T.L., Schäffer, A.A., Zhang, A., Zhang, Z., Miller, W., Lipman, D.J.: Nucleic Acids Res. **25**, 3389–3402 (1997)
13. Cuff, J.A., Barton, G.J.: Proteins **34**, 508–519 (1999)
14. Richards, F., Kundrot, C.: Proteins **3**, 71–84 (1988)

Learning Multiple Timescales in Recurrent Neural Networks

Tayfun Alpay$^{(\boxtimes)}$, Stefan Heinrich, and Stefan Wermter

Department of Informatics, Knowledge Technology, University of Hamburg,
Vogt-Kölln-Straße 30, 22527 Hamburg, Germany
{alpay,heinrich,wermter}@informatik.uni-hamburg.de
http://www.informatik.uni-hamburg.de/WTM/

Abstract. Recurrent Neural Networks (RNNs) are powerful architectures for sequence learning. Recent advances on the vanishing gradient problem have led to improved results and an increased research interest. Among recent proposals are architectural innovations that allow the emergence of multiple timescales during training. This paper explores a number of architectures for sequence generation and prediction tasks with long-term relationships. We compare the Simple Recurrent Network (SRN) and Long Short-Term Memory (LSTM) with the recently proposed Clockwork RNN (CWRNN), Structurally Constrained Recurrent Network (SCRN), and Recurrent Plausibility Network (RPN) with regard to their capabilities of learning multiple timescales. Our results show that partitioning hidden layers under distinct temporal constraints enables the learning of multiple timescales, which contributes to the understanding of the fundamental conditions that allow RNNs to self-organize to accurate temporal abstractions.

Keywords: Recurrent Neural Networks · Sequence learning · Multiple timescales · Leaky activation · Clocked activation

1 Introduction

Until recently RNNs were mainly of theoretical interest as their initially perceived shortcomings proved too severe to be used in complex applications. One deficiency that has been reported early on is the vanishing gradient problem [1]. When RNNs are trained with backpropagation, error signals over time vanish exponentially in RNNs. This has led to multiple highly specialized architectures such as the Long Short-Term Memory (LSTM [2]). Their success has sparked a renewed research interest in RNNs, which has led to a number of recently proposed RNN architectures, including those that try to improve control over the self-organization of temporal dynamics by learning on multiple timescales. However, as these novel approaches have not yet been rigorously compared, the fundamental principles that allow the capturing of dynamics on different timescales are still unknown.

© Springer International Publishing Switzerland 2016
A.E.P. Villa et al. (Eds.): ICANN 2016, Part I, LNCS 9886, pp. 132–139, 2016.
DOI: 10.1007/978-3-319-44778-0_16

In this paper, we therefore aim at contributing to the following research question: what are key concepts that allow RNNs to build long-term memory and learn on multiple timescales? We approach this question by investigating the Clockwork RNN (CWRNN [3]), which has been shown to allow emergence of multiple timescales by restricting update frequencies to temporal constraints. A different method with the same effect is the use of leakage and hysteresis parameters that constrain the amount of change within a system between time steps. The concept of leakage is most popularly used in the Echo State Network (ESN [4]) but has also been shown to improve the Simple Recurrent Network (SRN [5]). A related concept can be found in the Recurrent Plausibility Network (RPN [6]) which introduces a related hysteresis parameter φ to perform time-averaging. It also has shortcut connections, which provide shorter error propagation paths for the temporal context layers. Shortcuts have been shown to allow better training in very deep networks [7]. Both shortcuts and leaky units are used in the Structurally Constrained Recurrent Network (SCRN [8]) that additionally partitions its layer into modules, similarly to the CWRNN.

As the RPN, SCRN, and CWRNN share similar architectural concepts such as leakage, shortcuts, and partitioning the hidden layer into modules, their investigation is of particular interest for studying the effect of these concepts on the self-organization of the temporal dynamics. We evaluate these architectures on sequence generation and prediction tasks, using the SRN and the LSTM as a baseline. Even though the LSTM has no specific time scaling mechanism, it is included in the experiments due to its reported ability to capture long-term dependencies.

2   Recurrent Neural Networks

2.1   Recurrent Plausibility Network

The Recurrent Plausibility Network (RPN) was originally developed to learn and represent semantic relationships while disambiguating contextual relationships [9]. It is based on the state of an unfolded SRN during truncated BPTT (see Fig. 1(a)), i.e. each hidden layer $\mathbf{h}$ has its own set of m context layers $\mathbf{c}_k$ ($k \in \{1, ..., m\}$) which store past activations. The main difference to an unfolded SRN is the use of temporal shortcut connections for shorter context propagation paths, making vanishing or exploding gradients less likely (compare Fig. 1(b)). For time step t, the units of the hidden layer $\mathbf{h}$ are activated as follows:

$$\mathbf{h}^{(t)} = f_h \left(\mathbf{x}^{(t)} \, \mathbf{W}_{xh} + \sum_{k=1}^{m} \mathbf{c}_m^{(t-1)} \, \mathbf{W}_{mh} \right), \tag{1}$$

where the vector $\mathbf{c}$ denotes the context layers, that are activated by shifting their contents with $\mathbf{c}_{m-1}^{(t)} = \mathbf{c}_m^{(t-1)}$. The respective context activation for units in $\mathbf{c}_m$ is further constrained under the hysteresis parameter φ [10]:

$$\mathbf{c}_k^{(t)} = \begin{cases} (1 - \varphi_n) \cdot \mathbf{h}^{(t-1)} + \varphi \cdot \mathbf{c}_k^{(t-1)} & \text{iff } k = 1, \\ \mathbf{c}_{k-1}^{(t-1)} & \text{otherwise} \end{cases} \tag{2}$$

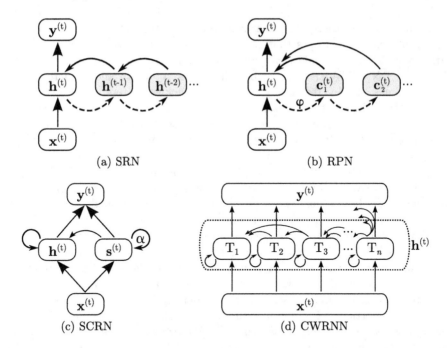

Fig. 1. Comparison of investigated RNN architectures. Figure (a) shows an SRN unfolded in time. The RPN (b) extends the SRN with its temporal shortcuts and the hysteresis φ. In case of a deep RPN, each vertical layer $\mathbf{h}_n^{(t)}$ can have its own hysteresis value φ_n. The SCRN (c) has an additional layer $\mathbf{s}^{(t)}$ that learns slower than in $\mathbf{h}^{(t)}$ due to its high leakage $\alpha = 0.95$. The modules T_k of the CWRNN (d) are sorted by increasing numbers from left to right and are only updated for $t \bmod T_i = 0$.

The hysteresis mechanism allows for a finer adjustment of context memory than in the SRN. Rather than accumulating past activations in a single feedback loop, the network is able to specifically learn the contribution between specific time frames due to the temporal shortcuts.

2.2   Structurally Constrained Recurrent Network

The Structurally Constrained Recurrent Network (SCRN) was recently proposed by Mikolov et al. [8]. The motivation behind the architecture is to achieve specialization of hidden layers by partitioning them into parallel "modules" that operate independently and under distinct temporal constraints. This theoretically allows to train on multiple timescales. While the left path in the SCRN equals a SRN with a regular hidden layer $\mathbf{h}^{(t)}$, the additional module $\mathbf{s}^{(t)}$ has units with different temporal characteristics (compare Fig. 1(c)). It is initialized with the recurrent identity matrix and its updates constrained by a leakage parameter $\alpha \in [0, 1]$. The authors set this leakage to 0.95, causing the states to change on a much slower scale than in $\mathbf{h}^{(t)}$. Similarly to the RPN, this architecture makes use of shortcut connections ($\mathbf{W}_{sh}$) that allow $\mathbf{h}^{(t)}$ to access long-term context which is learned in $\mathbf{s}^{(t)}$. The update rules of the SCRN are as follows:

$$\mathbf{s}^{(t)} = (1 - \alpha)\mathbf{W}_{xs}\ \mathbf{x}^{(t)} + \alpha\ \mathbf{s}^{(t-1)}, \tag{3}$$

$$\mathbf{h}^{(t)} = f_h(\mathbf{W}_{sh}\ \mathbf{s}^{(t)} + \mathbf{W}_{xh}\ \mathbf{x}^{(t)} + \mathbf{W}_{hh}\ \mathbf{h}^{(t-1)}), \tag{4}$$

$$\mathbf{y}^{(t)} = f_y(\mathbf{W}_{hy}\ \mathbf{h}^{(t)} + \mathbf{W}_{sy}\ \mathbf{s}^{(t)}), \tag{5}$$

where f_h and f_y are the respective activation functions for the hidden and output layers.

2.3   Clockwork Recurrent Neural Network

The discussed idea of partitioning the hidden layer into parallel modules with distinct temporal properties can also be found in the Clockwork Recurrent Neural Network (CWRNN). However, the main difference is that multiple timescales are not achieved by varying leakage but rather an external clock that determines *when* a module gets updated. This means that a module k is only updated if its clock period T_k satisfies the criterion $t \bmod T_k = 0$. Otherwise, the module is inactive in which case the previous activation $\mathbf{h}_k^{(t-1)}$ gets copied over:

$$\mathbf{h}_k^{(t)} = \begin{cases} f_h\left(\mathbf{x}^{(t)}\ \mathbf{W}_{xk} + \sum_{l=k}^{n}\mathbf{h}_l^{(t-1)}\ \mathbf{W}_{lk}\right) & \text{iff } t \bmod T_k = 0, \\ \mathbf{h}_k^{(t-1)} & \text{otherwise} \end{cases} \tag{6}$$

An additional constraint is that $T_l > T_k$ for $l < k$, i.e. the modules are ordered by increasing numbers from left to right (compare Fig. 1(d)). Therefore, modules on the left are updated more frequently than those on the right. Consequently, modules with greater periods (on the right) will self-organize slower and to long-term dependencies while those with small periods (on the left) change more often, focusing on short-term dependencies.

3   Experiments

All five architectures, the SRN, RPN, SCRN, CWRNN, and LSTM have been evaluated on two tasks; sequence generation of a sinusoid wave and sequence prediction of words created by embedded Reber grammar. They have been trained with RMSProp, which divides the current gradient by a sliding average of recent gradients [11]. Momentum was empirically set to 0.9 and the networks trained for a maximum number of 5000 epochs using early stopping. Weights were initialized using normalized initialization, sampling from $\mathcal{N}(0, 1/\sqrt{n+m})$ where n is the number of incoming and m the number of outgoing weights in the respective layer [12]. Linear and non-linear activation (tanh) were explored. The forget gate bias was initialized with a higher value of 2 to avoid initial forgetting [13]. All other hyperparameters were set empirically for each network and task. Each setup was run 100 times with different random initializations.

3.1 Sequence Generation

In the first task, the networks have to learn how to generate a target sequence. They receive no input while a single sequence is sequentially presented as the target. This sequence of length 256 is a composition of three different sine waves, normalized to $[-1, 1]$. A single output unit y_t encodes the respective sequence value at time step t. All networks were trained to minimize the mean squared error (MSE) with a learning rate of $\gamma = 10^{-4}$ and 64 hidden units. For the RPN, a context width $m = 5$ and $m = 15$ was explored with hysteresis values of $\varphi \in \{0.1, 0.2, 0.5\}$. Two variants of the SCRN were trained: (i) a constant leakage of $\alpha = 0.95$ and (ii) an adaptive leakage α_t that is trained as described in [8]. For the CWRNN, 8 equally sized modules with clock periods growing by the powers of 2 ($P_1 = \{1, 2, 4, 8, 16, 32, 64, 128\}$) are compared with a more coarse setup of 4 modules with the periods $P_2 = \{1, 4, 16, 64\}$.

The results for the best networks are depicted in Fig. 2. The CWRNN generates the most accurate sequences, which indicates an ability to capture the underlying subfrequencies, learning multiple timescales. It was also found that the investigated clock-timings P_1 (8 modules) and P_2 (4 modules) perform equally well. The SRN on the other hand merely captures the most dominant subfrequency of the sequence while the LSTM gives a sliding average. The SCRN always converges to the mean, being the only network which seems to be completely unable to learn this task. Similar to the SRN, the RPN is able to capture only one subfrequency. For the tested φ values, only 0.1 and 0.2 lead to convergence that is not located around the mean. There is also a slight difference that can be observed between these values: increasing φ from 0.1 to 0.2 causes an increasing phase shift, i.e. the prediction gets increasingly delayed over time. This effect can be explained by the fact that the temporal context, which is time-averaged by the hysteresis, will span a larger time window with growing hysteresis values.

3.2 Embedded Reber Grammar

In the second task, the networks are trained to sequentially predict the next symbol produced by Embedded Reber Grammar (ERG). The ERG is a well-known test for RNNs, since a SRN cannot be trained with BPTT to learn the grammar due to the presence of long-term dependencies. It is defined as follows:

$$
\begin{aligned}
S &\to \texttt{btRte} \mid \texttt{bpRpe} & A &\to \texttt{sA} \mid \texttt{x} & C &\to \texttt{xBD} \mid \texttt{s} \\
R &\to \texttt{btACe} \mid \texttt{bpBDe} & B &\to \texttt{tB} \mid \texttt{v} & D &\to \texttt{pC} \mid \texttt{v}
\end{aligned}
$$

We randomly generate two different sets with respective sequence lengths of 20 and 30. Both data sets consist of 250 sequences and are further split into 60 % training, 20 % test, and 20 % validation sets for cross validation. Each symbol is encoded with a feature vector of size 7 (1 unit per symbol), while softmax activation in the output layer yields the symbol probabilities. The minimized loss function is the Kullback-Leibler divergence [14]. For all networks, the number of hidden units was set to 15. For the SCRN, a learning rate of $\gamma = 0.01$ was

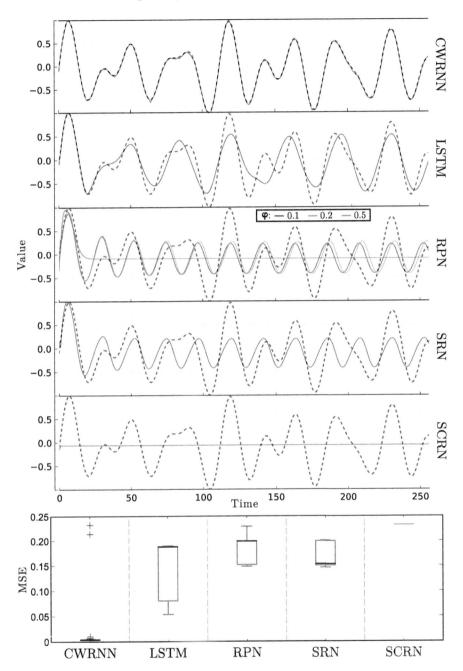

Fig. 2. Top: Sequences with the lowest MSE for the best trials. Generated sequences (solid lines) are plotted against the target sequence (dotted, red line). Bottom: MSE for each network. Boxes show 25 % and 75 % quartiles as well as the median (black line). The shown best trials were achieved with $\varphi = 0.2, m = 15$ for the RPN and $P_2 = \{1, 4, 16, 64\}$ for the CWRNN (P_1 produced nearly identical results). (Color figure online)

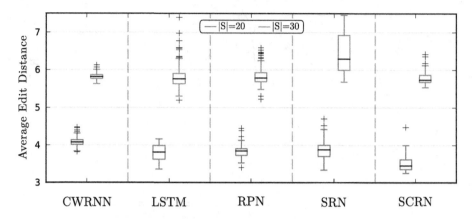

Fig. 3. Average edit distances (number of wrongly predicted symbols) for sequences of length $|S| = 20$ (left, blue) and $|S| = 30$ (right, green). Boxes show 25 % and 75 % quartiles as well as the median (black line). The best RPN trials were achieved with $\varphi = 0.2$. (Color figure online)

found to be optimal, whereas $\gamma = 10^{-4}$ worked best for the other architectures. The CWRNN's hidden layer was partitioned into 5 modules with the periods $P = \{1, 2, 4, 8, 12\}$. All other hyperparameters are set as in the first task.

The results for the best trials are depicted in Fig. 3. When trained with sequences of length 20, the SCRN with $\alpha = 0.95$ emerges as the best performing architecture, whereas the CWRNN seems to have the most difficulties. The LSTM shows an average accuracy, while the RPN seems to be less prone to bad initialization than the SRN. Especially for longer sequences, a large number of SRNs yield considerably more prediction errors than all other networks, which in turn share a similar overall performance.

4   Discussion

In this paper, we have explored various design concepts that allow emergence of multiple timescales and long-term memory in RNNs. Leaky and clocked activations have been investigated together with partitioning hidden layers into modules and using shortcut connections by comparing a number of architectures on the tasks of sequence generation and learning embedded Reber grammar.

Our results show that parallel hidden layers, which learn under different temporal constraints can lead to an emergence of multiple timescales in RNNs. Furthermore, shared weights in the form of shortcut connections (such as in the SCRN and CWRNN) allow units which self-organize to short-term context, to take long-term dependencies into account from specialized units that operating on a larger timescale. While the SCRN achieves this by means of leakage, the CWRNN utilizes clocked module activations. For the sequence generation task, the CWRNN was the only architecture to learn the decomposition of the trained sinusoid wave into all its subfrequencies. All other networks converged to the mean or a single subfrequency. This suggests that the CWRNN is able to store the entire sequence in the memory of the clocked modules, although it has half as much parameters as the SRN [3]. For the second task, the complete opposite can be observed; the SCRN is able to outperform all other networks for sequence lengths of 20 while the CWRNN has difficulties. Our findings suggest that the SCRN and RPN seem to work better for discrete, symbolic long-term decisions while the CWRNN is better at decomposing real-valued signals. Partitioning hidden layers with distinct temporal constraints has shown to be a viable method to capture different timescales. Future research should therefore concentrate on further exploring time scaling mechanisms on more challenging tasks such as sequence classification or language modeling.

References

1. Bengio, Y., Simard, P., Frasconi, P.: Learning long-term dependencies with gradient descent is difficult. IEEE Trans. Neural Netw. **5**(2), 157–166 (1994)
2. Hochreiter, S., Schmidhuber, J.: Long short-term memory. Neural Comput. **9**(8), 1735–1780 (1997)
3. Koutník, J., Greff, K., Gomez, F., Schmidhuber, J.: A clockwork RNN. In: Proceedings of ICML-2014, pp. 1863–1871 (2014)
4. Jaeger, H., Lukoševičius, M., Popovici, D., Siewert, U.: Optimization and applications of echo state networks with leaky-integrator neurons. Neural Netw. **20**(3), 335–352 (2007)
5. Bengio, Y., Boulanger-Lewandowski, N., Pascanu, R.: Advances in optimizing recurrent networks. In: Proceedings of ICASSP-2013, pp. 8624–8628 (2013)
6. Wermter, S., Panchev, C., Arevian, G.: Hybrid neural plausibility networks for news agents. In: Proceedings of AAAI-1999, pp. 93–98 (1999)
7. Pascanu, R., Gulcehre, C., Cho, K., Bengio, Y.: How to construct deep recurrent neural networks. ArXiv preprint arXiv:1312.6026v5 (2014)
8. Mikolov, T., Joulin, A., Chopra, S., Mathieu, M., Ranzato, M.: Learning longer memory in recurrent neural networks. ArXiv preprint arXiv:1412.7753v2 (2015)
9. Wermter, S.: Hybrid Connectionist Natural Language Processing. Chapman and Hall, Thompson International, London (1995)
10. Arevian, G., Panchev, C.: Robust text classification using a hysteresis-driven extended SRN. In: de Sá, J.M., Alexandre, L.A., Duch, W., Mandic, D.P. (eds.) ICANN 2007. LNCS, vol. 4669, pp. 425–434. Springer, Heidelberg (2007)
11. Graves, A.: Generating Sequences with recurrent neural networks. Arxiv preprint arXiv:1308.0850 (2013)
12. Glorot, X., Bengio, Y.: Understanding the difficulty of training deep feedforward neural networks. In: Proceedings of AISTATS-2010, pp. 249–256 (2010)
13. Jozefowicz, R., Zaremba, W., Sutskever, I.: An empirical exploration of recurrent network architectures. In: Proceedings of ICML-2015, pp. 2342–2350 (2015)
14. Kullback, S.: Information Theory and Statistics. Wiley, New York (1959)

Investigating Recurrent Neural Networks for Feature-Less Computational Drug Design

Alexander Dörr[✉], Sebastian Otte, and Andreas Zell

Cognitve Systems Group, University of Tuebingen,
Sand 1, 72076 Tübingen, Germany
alexander.doerr@uni-tuebingen.de

Abstract. This paper investigates Recurrent Neural Networks (RNNs) in the context of virtual High-Throughput Screening (vHTS). In the proposed approach, RNNs, particularly Bidirectional Dynamic Cortex Memories (BDCMs), are trained to derive the chemical activity of molecules directly from human readable strings (SMILES), uniquely describing entire molecular structures. Thereby, the so far obligatory procedure of computing task-specific fingerprint features is omitted completely. Moreover, it is shown that RNNs in principle are capable to incorporate contextual information even over entire sequences. They can not only gain information from this raw string representation, they are also able to produce comparably reliable predictions, i.e. yielding similar and partially even better AUC rates, as previously proposed state-of-the-art methods. Their performance is confirmed on different publicly available data sets. The research reveals a great potential of RNN-based methods in vHTS applications and opens novel perspectives in computational drug design.

Keywords: Recurrent Neural Networks · Bidirectional dynamic cortex memories · virtual High-Throughput Screening · Sequence learning

1 Introduction

Virtual screening refers to the computational processing of molecules in the field of pharmacy to predict their suitability as potential new drugs. To this end, machine learning methods are valuable tools in the process of ligand-based drug design. They can build models on the basis of existing libraries of molecular compounds with known effect on other macro-molecules in the human body. In general, a virtual screening problem can be described as a set of compounds that were already tested against a certain biological target, i.e. whether it is labeled as active or not. Compounds with unknown activity can be tested with said models to predict their fitness based on the similarity or consensus of their features with the ones the machine learning model regards as important. Virtual High-Throughput Screening (vHTS) is a well explored field, in which several machine

---

A. Dörr and S. Otte—Equal contribution

© Springer International Publishing Switzerland 2016
A.E.P. Villa et al. (Eds.): ICANN 2016, Part I, LNCS 9886, pp. 140–148, 2016.
DOI: 10.1007/978-3-319-44778-0_17

learning methods such as support vector machines [10] (SVMs), Bayesian learning [2], and Artificial Neural Networks (ANNs) [20] are frequently employed.

Particularly, SVMs perform very well on molecular 2D features presented as fingerprint bit vector, which encodes the presence or absence of a certain substructure in a compound. Popular representatives of these fingerprints are the connectivity fingerprints ECFP and FCFP. However, computing fingerprints generally causes a loss of information. Accordingly, selecting a particular fingerprint and finding a well suited parametrization requires domain-specific investigations to yield reliable results, which is usually the most crucial part in vHTS. Even though preliminary experiments showed that ANNs have difficulties to keep up with SVMs using the upper mentioned bit features (they tended to overfit), they have an important property, which is interesting regarding a more general methodology: they can implicitly compute their own features. At the base of the feature computation process in vHTS, molecules are given as encoded representations, which, on the one hand, carry the structure of the molecules but, on the other hand, provide a systematical processing, i.e., feature extraction. One such commonly used representation are SMILES strings [21]. SMILES strings convey the full 2D chemical information and thus allow unique descriptions of molecules. Their syntactical structure follows simple grammatical rules, making it easy to interpret them – they are even human readable. This language-like, essentially sequential representation is the starting point of our investigation.

In the last decade, *Recurrent Neural Networks* (RNNs), foremost Long Short Term Memories [11], have been shown to unfold impressive capabilities in the context of sequential pattern recognition. Since their upcoming, LSTMs were proven to be the first neural network architecture ever capable of learning intrinsic grammatical concepts, such as context free and context sensitive grammars [7], just from basic examples using simple gradient descent. Nowadays, LSTM-like methods are successfully applied even in one of the so far most ambitious sequence mapping applications, namely, automatic text translation [19]. Following these findings, the main contribution of this paper is to answer the question of whether RNNs are suitable for processing SMILES strings in vHTS scenarios directly without any previous task-specific feature computation. To the best of our knowledge, this has not been done yet. Indeed we show, that RNNs, in principle capable to incorporate contextual information even over entire sequences, can not only gain information from this "raw" string representation, they are also able to produce comparably reliable predictions, i.e. yielding similar AUC rates, as previously proposed state-of-the-art methods. Their performance is confirmed on different publicly available data sets. Thus, our research reveals a great potential of RNN-based methods in vHTS applications and opens novel perspectives to computational drug design.

2   Bidirectional Recurrent Neural Networks

In contrast to traditional RNNs, the before mentioned LSTM model [11], which can be seen as a differentiable memory cell, overcomes the problem of vanishing gradients. LSTMs are capable to handle even very long time lags up to 10 000 time steps. Due to this and other capabilities, e.g., precise timing, precise value reproduction, or counting, LSTMs unleash an impressive learning potential.

In this paper we used a special LSTM type called *Dynamic Cortex Memory* (DCM) [12], which provides a gate communication infrastructure. A DCM block is an LSTM block with *forget gate* [5] and *peep-hole connections* [6] but also consists of local self-recurrent connections of the gates (gate state) and connections from each gate to each other gate within one block (cortex) enabling the gates to share information and, thus, avoid redundant learning. For some problems DCMs were shown to converge faster during training and produce even better results than vanilla LSTMs [12,13].

Classical recurrent network architectures are considered as *unidirectional* – they compute in a temporal-causal way, since input sequences are presented to a network only in forward direction. Thereby, the input history is accumulated in a network's "past context". However, in some cases a past-context only is not sufficient enough to learn the problem satisfactorily. The information of *what-comes-next* provided by a "future context" might be helpful to recognize the local, possibly disturbed part of an input sequence. Obviously, such a future context violates causality, since it can only be entirely provided, if the input sequences are also entirely given at the point of computation. The concept of *Bidirectional Recurrent Neural Networks* (BRNNs) introduced in [16] incorporates recurrent computing with both past context and future context in the following manner. Consider an RNN with just a single recurrent hidden layer, which we refer to as forward hidden layer. Now, a second recurrent hidden layer – the backward hidden layer – is added and connected with the input layer as well as with the output layer but explicitly not with the forward hidden layer. The computation in a BRNN proceeds in three phases. First, a given input sequence is presented to the input layer regularly in forward direction. Only the forward hidden layer computes and all its activations for each time step are stored. Second, the input

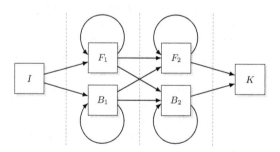

Fig. 1. Illustration of the bidirectional cross-architecture (xBRNN). Each arrow represents a full connection scheme. Like in one-layered bidirectional architectures, entire activation sequences are computed layer-wise. Differently, the forward context (provided by F_1) and backward context (provided by B_1) are already fused in both second hidden layers F_2 and B_2 and not in the output-layer. Afterwards again past-respective and future-respective activation sequences are computed separately by F_2 and B_2 respectively and then finally incorporated by the output layer K.

sequence is presented in backward direction. Now, only the backward hidden layer computes and all its activations are stored as well. Third, the output layer produces the output sequence by fusing the information coming from the past provided by the forward hidden layer and the information coming from the future provided by the backward hidden layer at each time step. The idea of bidirectional layers was later applied to LSTM networks analogously in [8]. In this paper we particularly focus on bidirectional DCMs (BDCMs) [13]. Moreover, it should be mentioned that the best results were achieved using a bidirectional cross-architecture (xBRNN) with two forward and two backward hidden layers as pointed out in Fig. 1. This architecture provides two-stage bidirectional sequence processing.

3 Experimental Results

In this study we used four data sets to compare the machine learning methods. The first data set was produced by Fontaine et al. [4] and consists of 435 factor Xa inhibitors, 156 low-active compounds as decoys and 279 highly active ones. Because of its plainness from the machine learning point of view, we used this data set as baseline to validate our experimental setup. The remaining three data sets originate from a study of Heikamp et al. [9] and were already used in a study of Dörr et al. [3]. They describe the molecular activity against three biological targets of the cytochrome P450 family. For our proof of concept, we only extracted the compounds that are active against one of the three targets or not active at all into the three separate data set CYP2C19 (152 actives), CYP2D6 (294 actives), and CYP3A4 (556 actives), with 2901 decoys each. Compounds with an erroneous SMILES representation were omitted.

For the SVM, we computed the wide-spread circular topological extended-connectivity fingerprint (ECFP) [15] with a bond diameter of 6 and a hashspace of 2^{20} bits with the Java library jCompoundMapper [10] and applied the Tanimoto kernel. We chose the range $\{0.1, 1, 10, 100, 1000\}$ for the regularization parameter C. The RNNs were given converted SMILES [21] strings with explicit hydrogens generated with CDK [17,18]. On all data sets we used a two layered BDCM cross-architecture in which each of the four hidden layers consisted of 10 DCM blocks, since it was identified as consistently well performing in preliminary experiments. The architecture had only one sigmoidal output neuron and the cross-entropy error was used as objective function for BPTT. The learning rate was set to 0.001 and the momentum rate to 0.8. For the RNN related experiments we used the JANNLab neural network framework [14].

3.1 String Representation for RNNs

A SMILES string is a human readable description of a molecule's composition and structure. The vocabulary of smiles describes the atom and bond types occurring in molecules, as well as their configuration via some grammar rules. Therefore, it is a language for molecular description and can be used to train

RNNs for structure-activity prediction. A benefit of SMILES is, that it offers a unique string for each molecule besides several generic ones. This allows for a setup of test sets with only unique strings, since each molecule has always the same unique SMILES expression. The training set can then be filled with additional generic strings for each molecule that effectively are synonyms. The RNN is presented with the consecutive symbols of a SMILES string transformed into an input pattern for each symbol. Table 1 describes our conversion of SMILES into RNN patterns. Figure 2 exemplarily shows the 2D image of an arbitrary molecule from the CYP2C19 data set and its translation. In some cases, multiple properties can apply simultaneously or context is directly assigned to the respective symbol in a string. For instance, a carbon atom contained in aromatic ring system results in the three properties carbon atom, aromatic atom, and ring membership. We tried to process the SMILES symbols as much as possible in the order given in each string. However, hydrogens atoms are initially counted, removed from the string, and directly assigned to the respective heavy atom they are attached to. This approach is similar to the ECFP fingerprint, that also assigns the number of attached hydrogens to heavy atoms. Square brackets also enclosing the formal charge are not treated as solitary symbol, but their properties are assigned to the associated atom.

Table 1. Conversion of SMILES symbols

Property	Symbol(s)	Conversion
Atom type	C, N, O, S,	Neuron for each chemical element in a data set
Bond type	$-, =, \#$	Neurons for the bond type (single, double, and triple)
Aromaticity	c, n, o, s,	Neuron for the aromaticity of atoms
Attached hydrogens	[H]	Neuron for the number of attached hydrogens
Atom charge	[N+]	Neuron for the pos./neg. charge of an atom (here: nitrogen)
Branching	(and)	Neurons for the start or closure of a branch in a molecule
Ring number	$1, ..., n$	2 neurons for the start and end of a cyclic structure
Ring membership	c1 [...] c1	Neuron for the membership of an atom in a cyclic structure (here: a carbon opens a ring and another closes it)

We applied a 5-fold cross-validation on each data set resulting in five distinct subsets. Four of those parts were used for training and the remaining fifth for testing. The cross-validation produced the same splits for SVM and RNN

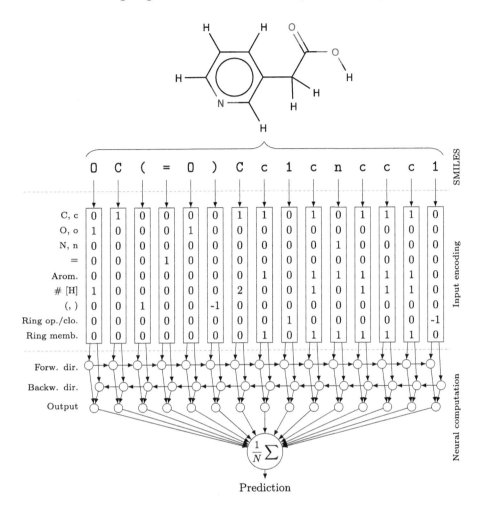

Fig. 2. 2D depiction of a representative molecule from the CYP2C19 data set and its computation with a bidirectional architecture. First, the hydrogens are removed from the original string ([H]OC(=O)C([H])([H])c1c([H])nc([H])c([H])c1[H]) and internally assigned to the respective heavy atoms. Then, each symbol is transformed into a vector representation, which can be fed into the network (there are particular input neurons for each possible symbol and related conditions). The transformed input sequence is presented in forward direction as well as in backward direction. The bidirectional contextual information is fused in the output layer of the neural network at each computation step. The overall prediction for a sequence is the mean output accumulated over the entire output sequence.

whereby the results are directly comparable. In drug discovery, getting an early enrichment of active compounds is considered to be important in order to save time and money. Hence, we used the area under the ROC curve (AUC) as performance metric. It shows how likely an active compound will be ranked higher than an inactive one.

3.2 Evaluation

The results of our virtual screening experiments can be seen in Table 2. We outlined the best AUC for each method on every fold and the overall AUC on each data set. Regarding the RNN two results are shown for each data set, whereas (u) denotes training based on unique strings only and (us) refers to training with a unique string and single synonym for each compound. The results of the vHTS on the Fontaine data set show that RNNs together with the proposed SMILES conversion are in general capable of learning the basic chemical properties to distinguish active compounds from decoys, since they perform comparably well. On the CYP2C19 data set the RNNs performed even better than the SVMs. Conclusively, it is considerable that training with synonyms can improve the results.

Table 2. Comparison of RNNs and SVMs on various data sets.

Data set	Method	Fold 1	Fold 2	Fold 3	Fold 4	Fold 5	Mean AUC
Fontaine	SVM	1.0	1.0	0.9994	0.9624	0.9858	0.9895
	RNN (u)	0.9941	0.9815	0.9815	0.9259	0.9525	0.9671
	RNN (us)	0.9935	0.9988	0.9665	0.9366	0.9414	0.9674
CYP2C19	SVM	0.7936	0.7717	0.8375	0.7650	0.7598	0.7855
	RNN (u)	0.8183	0.7274	0.818	0.7790	0.7429	0.7771
	RNN (us)	0.7916	0.8017	0.8291	0.7805	0.7582	0.7923
CYP2D6	SVM	0.9211	0.9103	0.8842	0.8601	0.8879	0.8927
	RNN (u)	0.8872	0.8958	0.8424	0.8624	0.8428	0.8661
	RNN (us)	0.8942	0.9001	0.8557	0.8661	0.8730	0.8778
CYP3A4	SVM	0.9219	0.9088	0.9222	0.9086	0.8870	0.9097
	RNN (u)	0.8281	0.8695	0.8496	0.8789	0.8521	0.8556
	RNN (us)	0.8357	0.8812	0.8596	0.8825	0.8551	0.8628

4   Conclusion

We showed that RNNs can successfully be trained with nothing but the information directly contained in SMILES strings without any parametrization like in other feature extraction methods. With this, a performance can be achieved in virtual high-throughput screening that is comparable to the frequently used combination of SVMs with connectivity fingerprints. It should be possible to further increase the performance by tweaking the RNN structure and the conversion of the SMILES strings. The toxicity and mutagenicity of molecular compounds can in some cases be decided with molecular similarity but often depends on certain patterns. In this case, our method should have an advantage in predicting such harmful properties of molecules.

It is also conceivable to transfer our setup to multi-target screening experiments, that were previously conducted with structured SVMs [1,3]. In this case, a machine learning method is present with the same features as for single target screening, but each molecular compound is associated with the labels for several biological targets at once. The task is then to predict the activity profile of each compound against all targets simultaneously.

References

1. Balfer, J., Heikamp, K., Laufer, S., Bajorath, J.: Modeling of compound profiling experiments using support vector machines. Chem. Biol. Drug Des. **84**(1), 75–85 (2014)
2. Bender, A., Mussa, H.Y., Glen, R.C., Reiling, S.: Molecular similarity searching using atom environments, information-based feature selection, and a naive bayesian classifier. J. Chem. Inf. Model. **44**(1), 170–178 (2004)
3. Dörr, A., Rosenbaum, L., Zell, A.: A ranking method for the concurrent learning of compounds with various activity profiles. J. Cheminf. **7**(1), 1–18 (2015)
4. Fontaine, F., Pastor, M., Zamora, I., Sanz, F.: Anchor-grind: filling the gap between standard 3D QSAR and the grid-independent descriptors. J. Med. Chem. **48**(7), 2687–2694 (2005)
5. Gers, F.A., Schmidhuber, J., Cummins, F.: Learning to forget: continual prediction with LSTM. Neural Comput. **12**, 2451–2471 (1999)
6. Gers, F.A., Schraudolph, N.N., Schmidhuber, J.: Learning precise timing with LSTM recurrent networks. J. Mach. Learn. Res. **3**, 115–143 (2002)
7. Gers, F., Schmidhuber, J.: LSTM recurrent networks learn simple context-free and context-sensitive languages. IEEE Trans. Neural Netw. **12**(6), 1333–1340 (2001)
8. Graves, A., Schmidhuber, J.: Framewise phoneme classification with bidirectional LSTM and other neural network architectures. Neural Netw. **18**(5–6), 602–610 (2005)
9. Heikamp, K., Bajorath, J.: Prediction of compounds with closely related activity profiles using weighted support vector machine linear combinations. J. Chem. Inf. Model. **53**(4), 791–801 (2013)
10. Hinselmann, G., Rosenbaum, L., Jahn, A., Fechner, N., Zell, A.: jCompoundMapper: an open source java library and command-line tool for chemical fingerprints. J. Cheminf. **3**(1), 3 (2011)
11. Hochreiter, S., Schmidhuber, J.: Long short-term memory. Neural Comput. **9**(8), 1735–1780 (1997)
12. Otte, S., Liwicki, M., Zell, A.: Dynamic cortex memory: enhancing recurrent neural networks for gradient-based sequence learning. In: Wermter, S., Weber, C., Duch, W., Honkela, T., Koprinkova-Hristova, P., Magg, S., Palm, G., Villa, A.E.P. (eds.) ICANN 2014. LNCS, vol. 8681, pp. 1–8. Springer, Heidelberg (2014)
13. Otte, S., Liwicki, M., Zell, A.: An analysis of dynamic cortex memory networks. In: International Joint Conference on Neural Networks (IJCNN), Killarney, Ireland, pp. 3338–3345, July 2015
14. Otte, S., Krechel, D., Liwicki, M.: JANNLab neural network framework for java. In: Poster Proceedings of the International Conference on Machine Learning and Data Mining (MLDM), pp. 39–46. ibai-publishing, New York, July 2013
15. Rogers, D., Hahn, M.: Extended-connectivity fingerprints. J. Chem. Inf. Model. **50**, 742–754 (2010)

16. Schuster, M., Paliwal, K.K.: Bidirectional recurrent neural networks. IEEE Trans. Signal Process. **45**(11), 2673–2681 (1997)
17. Steinbeck, C., Han, Y., Kuhn, S., Horlacher, O., Luttmann, E., Willighagen, E.: The chemistry development kit (CDK): an open-source java library for chemo-and bioinformatics. J. Chem. Inf. Model. **43**(2), 493–500 (2003)
18. Steinbeck, C., Hoppe, C., Kuhn, S., Floris, M., Guha, R., Willighagen, E.: Recent developments of the chemistry development kit (CDK)-an open-source java library for chemo-and bioinformatics. Curr. Pharm. Des. **12**(17), 2111–2120 (2006)
19. Sutskever, I., Vinyals, O., Le, Q.V.: Sequence to sequence learning with neural networks. In: Ghahramani, Z., Welling, M., Cortes, C., Lawrence, N.D., Weinberger, K.Q. (eds.) Advances in Neural Information Processing Systems, vol. 27, pp. 3104–3112. Curran Associates, Inc. (2014)
20. Swamidass, S.J., Azencott, C., Lin, T., Gramajo, H., Tsai, S., Baldi, P.: Influence relevance voting: an accurate and interpretable virtual high throughput screening method. J. Chem. Inf. Model. **49**(4), 756–766 (2009)
21. Weininger, D.: Smiles, a chemical language and information system. 1. introduction to methodology and encoding rules. J. Chem. Inf. Model. **28**(1), 31–36 (1988)

Inverse Recurrent Models – An Application Scenario for Many-Joint Robot Arm Control

Sebastian Otte[(⊠)], Adrian Zwiener, Richard Hanten, and Andreas Zell

Cognitve Systems Group, University of Tuebingen,
Sand 1, 72076 Tuebingen, Germany
sebastian.otte@uni-tuebingen.de

Abstract. This paper investigates inverse recurrent forward models for many-joint robot arm control. First, Recurrent Neural Networks (RNNs) are trained to predict arm poses. Due their recurrence the RNNs naturally match the repetitive character of computing kinematic forward chains. We demonstrate that the trained RNNs are well suited to gain inverse kinematics robustly and precisely using Back-Propagation Trough Time even for complex robot arms with up to 40 universal joints with 120 articulated degrees of freedom and under difficult conditions. The concept is additionally proven on a real robot arm. The presented results are promising and reveal a novel perspective to neural robotic control.

Keywords: Recurrent Neural Networks · Dynamic Cortex Memory · Neurorobotics · Inverse kinematics · Robot arm control

1 Introduction

Moving robotic arms requires typically forward as well as inverse kinematic control and planning. Planning trajectories of robotic arms in high dimensional configuration space is nontrivial. This planning process gets even more difficult under the objective to obtain feasible, smooth and collision free trajectories or if one includes orientation constraints, for example moving a cup of coffee without spilling. Consequently, in some cases planners fail to find a solution for given problem. State-of-the-art algorithms like *Rapid Exploring Random Trees* [5] or the *Covariant Hamiltonian Optimization Motion Planner* [12] need several hundred milliseconds to several seconds to plan trajectories, depending on the complexity of the planning task.

In this research we investigate *Recurrent Neural Networks (RNNs)*, particularly *Dynamic Cortex Memorys* (DCMs) [7,8], for computing inverse kinematics of robot arms, particularly with many joints. More concretely, we learned to estimate poses for given arm configurations with RNNs, which match the sequential nature of computing kinematic forward-chains. *Back-Propagation Through Time* (BPTT) is used to to generate the inverse mapping. We show that the presented approach can handle arms even with up to 120 articulated degrees of freedom

© Springer International Publishing Switzerland 2016
A.E.P. Villa et al. (Eds.): ICANN 2016, Part I, LNCS 9886, pp. 149–157, 2016.
DOI: 10.1007/978-3-319-44778-0_18

(DoF) and that it also works on real robot arms. Handling robot arms with many DoF have studied, e.g., by Rolf et al. in [9] in which the inverse kinematics of a bionic elephant trunk was learned, making use of known (explored) mappings from target space to configuration space.

2   Methodology

Our first step towards gaining inverse kinematics is to train a recurrent forward model. Particularly, the neural network must first learn to estimate end-effector poses based on configuration vectors, i.e. joint angles. Therefore, a set of configuration vector and pose pairs is required. When the mathematical forward model of the arm is known, samples can be computed directly. Otherwise, another feedback mechanism providing end-effector poses is required, for instance, a tracking system. The starting point is a general arm model with universal joints, each providing a yaw-pitch-roll rotation at once with three DoF. Note that this procedure can later be applied to realistic and more specific arms, which usually have only one DoF per joint. On the other hand, the configuration commands must not necessarily be angles, but can also be, for instance, muscular contraction forces, as used in octopus-arms [11].

2.1   Dynamic Cortex Memory Networks

A DCM [7,8] is in principle an LSTM with forget gate [2] and peephole connections [3], but additionally provides a communication infrastructure that enables the gates to share information. This infrastructure is established through two connection schemes. The first scheme is called cortex and connects each gate with every other gate. The second scheme equips each gate with a self-recurrent connection providing a local gate-state. In the original study [7] it was pointed out, that these two schemes used in combination lead to a synergy effect. In comparison with an LSTM block, a DCM block has nine additional connections that are all weighted and, hence, trainable.

Beyond the structural modification, DCMs are used exactly like LSTMs and are trained in the same manner. In this paper all recurrent networks are trained using gradient descent with momentum term, whereas the gradients are computed with *Back Propagation Through Time* (BPTT) [10]. The presented experiments were performed using the JANNLab neural network framework [6].

2.2   Learning the Forward Model

Let us consider an arm with n universal joints. The three angles for the j-th joint are given by a vector $\boldsymbol{\varphi}^{(j)} \in [-\pi, \pi]^3$. We refer to the entire sequence for all joints here as configuration state denoted by $\boldsymbol{\Phi}$. Let now M be the forward model of the robot arm, which maps a configuration state to the corresponding end-effector frame (denoted by N) relative to the base frame (denoted by 0)

$$\boldsymbol{\Phi} = \left(\boldsymbol{\varphi}^{(1)}, \dots, \boldsymbol{\varphi}^{(n)} \right) \overset{M}{\longmapsto} {}^0_N\mathbf{A} = \begin{bmatrix} {}^0_N\mathbf{R} & {}^0_N\mathbf{P} \\ \mathbf{0} & 1 \end{bmatrix}, \tag{1}$$

where $_N^0\mathbf{A} \in \mathbb{R}^{4\times4}$ can be decomposed into the rotation, i.e., the orientation of the end-effector, given by an orthonormal base $_N^0\mathbf{R} \in SO(3) \subset \mathbb{R}^{3\times3}$ and the translation, i.e., the position of end-effector, given by $_N^0\mathbf{p} \in \mathbb{R}^3$. It is important to mention that M also considers the lenghts of the segments and other possible offsets. They are, however, left out in the formulation, because they are constant and, moreover, the neural networks do not need them for learning the forward model. Preliminary experiments indicated that constant translations (joints off-sets etc.) can be deduced by the networks using trainable biases. Given such an observable model, our first objective is to train an RNN to become a neural approximation of M, able to produce pose estimates $_N^0\tilde{\mathbf{A}}$ for given configuration states. In the case of universal joints there are three variables per joint. At this point, the key aspect of the recurrent forward model comes into play: each joint transformation is considered as a "computing time-step" in the RNN. Accordingly, the RNN requires then only three input neurons, fully independently from the number of joints. The angle triples are presented to the network in a sequential manner. Due to this, the network is forced to use its recurrence to handle the repetitive character of computing chains of mostly very similar transformations. This forward computing procedure is illustrated in Fig. 1.

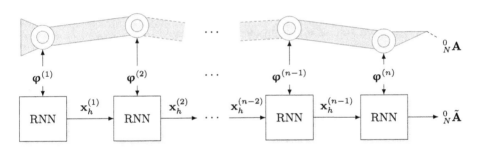

Fig. 1. The RNN based forward computation. The angle-triples of the joints are interpreted as a sequence. One computation step in the RNN is associated with a certain joint (3 rotations) and, implicitly, with its corresponding segment (translation). Thus, each hidden state $\mathbf{x}_h^{(j)}$ of the RNN at time step j is computed based on the associated angle triple $\boldsymbol{\varphi}^{(j)}$ and the previous hidden state $\mathbf{x}_h^{(j-1)}$ with $\mathbf{x}_h^{(0)} = \mathbf{0}$. The output of the RNN after n time steps is the pose estimate with regard to the given angles.

While the position can be represented directly using three output neurons, there are several options to represent the orientation. For this proof-of-concept we used a vector-based representation of the two base axes z and x, which worked significantly better than, e.g., 3 rotation angles. Thus, the orientation requires six output neurons such that the RNNs have overall nine linear output neurons, whereas we denote the final output vector (after n computing steps) of an RNN by $\mathbf{y} \in \mathbb{R}^9$ in which the first three components encode the position estimate $_N^0\tilde{\mathbf{p}}$ and the last six components encode the orientation estimate $_N^0\tilde{\mathbf{R}}$. In the long run, however, it could make sense to use a quaternion-based representation in combination with a special output layer providing normalized outputs directly.

2.3   Inverse Recurrent Model

During training of the forward model, the network learned to encode and decode
the kinematic behavior of the robot arm using an internal representation – a
recursive superimposition of sigmoidals – that is possibly a simplification of
the "real" kinematic relationships. To gain the inverse mapping, we utilize the
backward-pass of the network, namely, we back-propagate through time a change
in the output space. Note that a similar idea was used earlier for inverting feed-
forward networks in [4]. This allows us to yield a direction in the input space
in which the input must be adapted such that the output gets closer to the
desired output, i.e., the target pose. In an iterative process, starting from any
possible configuration state, when following the negative gradient through the
configuration space, we can obtain a possible solution for the inverse kinematics.
Let $\mathbf{\Phi}$ be the current configuration state from which we start computing the
inverse kinematic and let $_N^0\mathbf{\dot{A}}$ be the target pose. First, we perform a forward
pass with the RNN, yielding a pose estimate $_N^0\mathbf{\tilde{A}}$ with respect to $\mathbf{\Phi}$. Second, we
present the target pose $_N^0\mathbf{\dot{A}}$ as the desired output, like in a regular training step,
and perform the backward pass, which propagates the influence to the output
discrepancy (loss) $\mathcal{L}$ reversely in "time" though the recurrent network. Third,
we need to derive the influence of each input to $\mathcal{L}$. Since all $\delta_h^{(j)}$ are known we
can apply the chain rule as a step upon BPTT to yield

$$\frac{\partial \mathcal{L}}{\partial \varphi_i^{(j)}} = \sum_{h=1}^{H} \left[\frac{\partial net_h^{(j)}}{\partial \varphi_i^{(j)}} \frac{\partial \mathcal{L}}{\partial net_h^{(j)}} \right] \sum_{h=1}^{H} w_{ih} \delta_h^{(j)}. \tag{2}$$

This procedure of computing the input gradient joint-wise is illustrated in Fig. 2.
In LSTM-like networks the gradient can be kept more stable over time during
back-propagation, which plays obviously a major role for the proposed method,
particularly for arms with many joints, since traditional RNNs were not able to
learn the forward model precisely. Fourth, we update $\mathbf{\Phi}$ by simply applying the
rule

$$\mathbf{\Phi}(\tau + 1) \longleftarrow \mathbf{\Phi}(\tau) - \eta \nabla_{\mathbf{\Phi}(\tau)} \mathcal{L} + \mu \left[\mathbf{\Phi}(\tau) - \mathbf{\Phi}(\tau - 1) \right] \tag{3}$$

where τ denotes the current iteration step, $\eta \in \mathbb{R}$ is a gradient scale factor
(cf. learning rate in gradient descent learning). Note that large step size $\eta >$
0.5 may cause oscillations during this process. Optionally, we added the last
update step as momentum scaled with the rate $\mu \in \mathbb{R}$ (i.e., $\mu \approx 0.5$), which
results in a faster convergence. The entire procedure is repeated until the current
pose estimate is sufficiently close to $_N^0\mathbf{\dot{A}}$. The proposed method can be applied
offline, where a full solution is searched first and then the controller interpolates
towards it, or online, where the search process is (partially) synchronized with the
arm movement, whereas the motion-trajectory basically represents the gradient-
guided trajectory in configuration space.

A drawback of the approach is that the accuracy of potential solutions is limited to the accuracy of the neural forward model. However, this can be compensated if the "real" pose of the robot arm with respect to a given $\mathbf{\Phi}$ is accessible

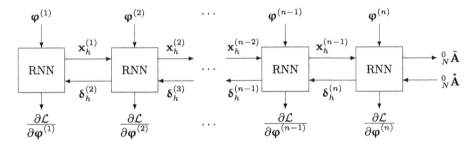

Fig. 2. Inverse computing using BPTT. After an input sequence (the current state of the arm) is presented, the discrepancy between the output and the desired pose is back-propagated through the network.

either via the exact mathematical forward model or another feedback provided. The idea is as follows: Instead of presenting the desired target, encoded as a vector $\mathbf{z} \in \mathbb{R}^9$ analogously to $\mathbf{y}$ in Sect. 2.2, we present a "modified" version $\tilde{\mathbf{z}}$. Let $\mathbf{u} \in \mathbb{R}^9$ be the true current pose, which encodes $_N^0\mathbf{p}$ in the same manner, we compute $\tilde{\mathbf{z}}$ with respect to a given $\mathbf{\Phi}$ through

$$\tilde{\mathbf{z}} = \begin{bmatrix} [y_i + \gamma_1(z_i - u_i)]_{1 \leq i \leq 3} \\ [y_j + \gamma_2(z_j - u_j)]_{4 \leq j \leq 9} \end{bmatrix}^\top, \tag{4}$$

where $\gamma_1, \gamma_2 \in [0, 1]$ are additional scaling factors weighting the influence of the position discrepancy and the orientation discrepancy respectively. The modification causes the networks to converge towards the real target pose.

3   Exerimental Results

The results presented in this section are based on four different simulated arms with 5, 10, 20, and 40 universal joints. The rotations along the segment axis z are restricted to angle range $[-\pi/4, +\pi/4,]$, whereas both orthogonal rotations (x, y) are restricted to the angle range $[-\pi/2, +\pi/2]$. A larger angle range for the z rotation caused problems during earlier experiments and we hence limited the range as stated above for the moment. To learn these arms $20,000$ random configurations and associated poses are used. To show that the approach also works on a real robot arm, we additionally included a CrustCrawler manipulator in our experiments. This is a light-weight, low budget manipulator with 9 Robotis Dynamixel servomotors, which we used in a four articulated DoF setup. For training also $20,000$ random poses were computed using the Trac-IK kinematic plugin [1] for ROS MoveIt[1]. Note, that only one parameter per computation step is required, whereby we do not have to distinguish the rotation axis – the correct association is ensured by the trained network – such that we can directly use the angles given in DH (Denavit-Hartenberg) notation. It should be mentioned

---

[1] ROS MoveIT see http://moveit.ros.org.

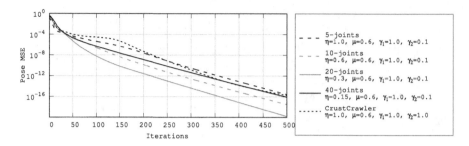

Fig. 3. Convergence (average MSE over 100 random samples) towards target poses for different arm models during 500 iterations.

that the position values in all experiments were normalized such that each arm has a unit-less length of 1.

The experiments are based on RNNs with two hidden layers, each consisting of 24 DCM blocks for the universal arms and 20 DCM block for the CrustCrawler, respectively. In both architectures each hidden block contains 3 inner cells and has variable biases for cells and gates. Further, each hidden layer is not recurrently connected to itself, but both hidden layers are mutually fully connected.

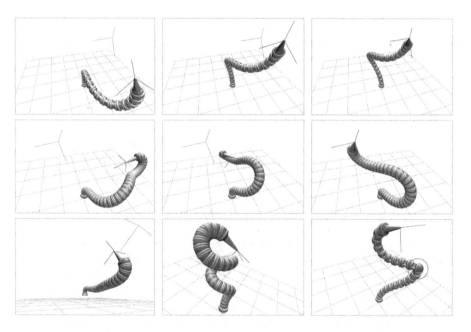

Fig. 4. The first two rows show the movement towards the target pose (blue) for a 20-joint arm (top) and a 40-joint arm (middle). In the bottom row it is shown that inverse kinematics can be produced even under difficult conditions (from left to right): Unreachable poses, heavily screwed, locked joints.(Color figure online)

This was the best architecture we discovered in preliminary investigations. During training, the learning rate was repeatedly decreased every 20 epochs (from 0.01 over $5 \cdot 10^{-3}$, 10^{-3}, $5 \cdot 10^{-4}$, 10^{-4}, $5 \cdot 10^{-5}$ to 10^{-5}) and the momentum rate was fixed to 0.95. However, with 10, 20, and 40 joints there was an issue concerning the covered angle ranges within the training samples. With increasing the number of joints, the learnable angle ranges descreased. We figured out that for those arms the forward model can be significantly improved, if the network is pretrained either on an arm with less joints or with limited angles. For these retraining procedures we performed similarly as described above but skipped the first two largest learning rates.

To analyze whether target poses can be reached reliably, we computed random configurations for which we then determined their corresponding poses using the known forward model. For the resulting poses we generated the inverse kinematics with the RNNs. Based on this configurations we computed again the pose using the forward model and finally compared both poses. Figure 3 shows the the average convergence of the pose error (MSE) over 100 random poses within 500 iterations on different arms.

As can be seen, on all arms the approach shows a relatively similar convergence behavior. Already after 50 iterations the end-effector poses are sufficiently close to the target poses. The results clearly indicate that for all arms, even for the one with 40 universal joints, precise solutions could be found consistently. Note that on the CrustCrawler for some random poses ($\approx 10\,\%$) the process got stuck in a local minimum. These cases were left out for computing the

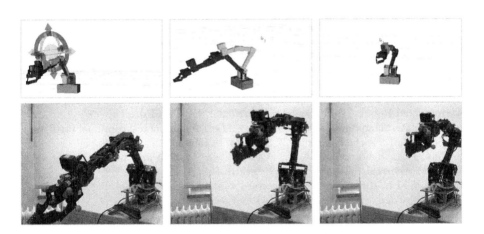

Fig. 5. In the top row the MoveIT rviz plug-in is displayed. The current configuration of the arm is rendered in black and the goal in orange. A movement of the marker changes the arm's goal pose. The kinematics solver is called and the goal configuration is rendered. In images from left to right the transition to the goal state is illustrated. Note that for this image series, we use one of MoveIT's planning algorithms for the real arm's trajectory generation in order to exclude self-collisions – nonetheless each particular call of the inverse kinematics is solved with the RNN.(Color figure online)

average curve. Figures 4 and 5 visually confirm the success of our approach, since the desired target poses are reached exactly. Figure 4 also demonstrates that good solutions can be found even under difficult conditions. If a target pose is unreachable the network drives the arm towards a close plausible pose. But also in the case when an arm is heavily screwed, the target can be reached robustly. Furthermore, entirely locked joints can also be easily compensated on the fly.

4   Conclusion

In this paper we introduced an approach for computing inverse kinematics of many-joint robot arms with inverse recurrent forward models. First, we learned to estimate poses for given arm configurations with RNNs. While the RNNs match the sequential nature of computing forward-chains, *Back-Propagation Through Time* (BPTT) is used to to generate the inverse mapping.

We verified our method on complex simulated 3D arms with multi-axis spherical joints. It was shown that the approach scales well, since we could effectively control arms with 5-joint, 10-joint, 20-joints, and even with 40-joints (the latter has 120 DoF). It is also shown that the approach can produce inverse kinematics precisely for a real robot arm. This research is to be regarded as a proof-of-concept and a first step towards a novel perspective on neural arm-control.

Acknowledgments. We would like to thank Martin V. Butz for helpful discussions concerning the method and its distinction to related approaches, Yann Berquin for constructive discussions, and Sebastian Buck for valuable technical support.

References

1. Beeson, P., Ames, B.: Trac-ik: an open-source library for improved solving of generic inverse kinematics. In: 2015 IEEE-RAS 15th International Conference on Humanoid Robots (Humanoids), pp. 928–935. IEEE (2015)
2. Gers, F.A., Schmidhuber, J., Cummins, F.: Learning to forget: continual prediction with LSTM. Neural Comput. **12**, 2451–2471 (1999)
3. Gers, F.A., Schraudolph, N.N., Schmidhuber, J.: Learning precise timing with LSTM recurrent networks. J. Mach. Learn. Res. **3**, 115–143 (2002)
4. Jordan, M.I., Rumelhart, D.E.: Forward models: supervised learning with a distal teacher. Cogn. Sci. **16**(3), 307–354 (1992)
5. Kuffner, J., LaValle, S.: RRT-connect: an efficient approach to single-query path planning. In: Proceedings of the 2000 IEEE International Conference on Robotics and Automation. ICRA 2000, vol. 2, pp. 995–1001 (2000)
6. Otte, S., Krechel, D., Liwicki, M.: JANNLab neural network framework for java. In: Poster Proceedings Conference MLDM 2013, pp. 39–46. ibai-publishing, New York (2013)
7. Otte, S., Liwicki, M., Zell, A.: Dynamic cortex memory: enhancing recurrent neural networks for gradient-based sequence learning. In: Wermter, S., Weber, C., Duch, W., Honkela, T., Koprinkova-Hristova, P., Magg, S., Palm, G., Villa, A.E.P. (eds.) ICANN 2014. LNCS, vol. 8681, pp. 1–8. Springer, Heidelberg (2014)

8. Otte, S., Liwicki, M., Zell, A.: An analysis of dynamic cortex memory networks. In: International Joint Conference on Neural Networks (IJCNN), pp. 3338–3345. Killarney, Ireland (2015)

9. Rolf, M., Steil, J.J.: Efficient exploratory learning of inverse kinematics on a bionic elephant trunk. IEEE Trans. Neural Networks Learn. Syst. **25**(6), 1147–1160 (2014)

10. Werbos, P.: Backpropagation through time: what it does and how to do it. Proc. IEEE **78**(10), 1550–1560 (1990)

11. Woolley, B.G., Stanley, K.O.: Evolving a single scalable controller for an octopus arm with a variable number of segments. In: Schaefer, R., Cotta, C., Kołodziej, J., Rudolph, G. (eds.) PPSN XI. LNCS, vol. 6239, pp. 270–279. Springer, Heidelberg (2010)

12. Zucker, M., Ratliff, N., Dragan, A., Pivtoraiko, M., Klingensmith, M., Dellin, C., Bagnell, J.A., Srinivasa, S.: CHOMP: covariant hamiltonian optimization for motion planning. Int. J. Robot. Res. **32**(9–10), 1164–1193 (2013)

Population Coding of Goal Directed Movements

Andreas G. Fleischer[⊠]

Department of Biology, Modelling Biological Systems, Informatikum,
University of Hamburg, Vogt-Kölln-Str. 30, 22527 Hamburg, Germany
fleischer@biokybernetik.uni-hamburg.de

Abstract. In order to intercept a moving target a motor schema causes the hand to aim ahead and to adapt to the target trajectory. During the performance of perception-action-cycles, a pre-programmed prototypical movement trajectory, a motor schema, may highly reduce the control load. From a modelling point of view, a neural network may allow the implementation of a motor schema interacting with feedback control in an iterative manner. A neural population net of the Wilson-Cowan type was allowing the generation of a moving bubble. This activation bubble runs down an eye-centered motor schema and causes a planar arm model to move towards the target. The bubble provides local integration and straightening of the trajectory during repetitive moves. The schema adapts to task demands by learning and serves as a forward controller.

Keywords: Population coding · Neural field · Recurrent nets · Attractor state · Convolution kernel · Motor control · Inverse dynamics · Schema theory

1 Introduction

Goal-directed hand movements are based on an anticipation of the outcome of a move within the context of the task. The initial conditions of a move differ widely, and a strategy is required to achieve robust movement control. A representation in terms of a generalized motor program has to be assumed concatenating motion primitives on the basis of the desired trajectory. This leads to a generalized program, a motor schema, allowing for size and position, and, especially, for effector independence. During goal-directed movements the motor schema of a perception-action sequence may be considered as a specific stabilizing entity. Thus, the system has to be protected against a prolonged search for an acceptable solution. This is the essence of the schema-theory. Similar to evolutionary algorithms, gained information has to be stored in terms of a motor schema and its stochastic variations may provide an increased effectiveness of the trajectory.

 With respect to motor schemata neural population coding in recurrent networks may provide a flexible attractor definition. An attractor is meant here to be one of the stable states of a complex system of non-linear differential equations. Complex patterns may emerge in such systems like spatial neural field

A.E.P. Villa et al. (Eds.): ICANN 2016, Part I, LNCS 9886, pp. 158–165, 2016.
DOI: 10.1007/978-3-319-44778-0_19

models [1,9] or reaction-diffusion equations [6,7] which show dynamic patterns similar to travelling waves. Temporal asymmetries in population coding may cause a shift of the activated part of the neural population [2].

2 Methods

2.1 Schema Generation

An attractor network (Fig. 1) of a neural population is constructed out of two layers of interacting neurons, one layer $u_e(\mathbf{z})$ consisting of excitatory neurons and one layer $u_i(\mathbf{z})$ of inhibitory neurons at corresponding positions $\mathbf{z} = [z_1, z_2]$.

$$\tau_e \frac{\partial u_e}{\partial t} = -u_e + h_e(w_{ee}[g_{ee} * u_e] - w_{ie}[g_{ie} * u_i] + I_e)$$
$$\tau_i \frac{\partial u_i}{\partial t} = -u_i + h_i(w_{ei}[g_{ei} * u_e] - w_{ii}[g_{ii} * u_i] + I_i) \tag{1}$$

Assuming two 2D-layers of interacting neurons (Fig. 1) Eq. (1) results. The four synaptic connection weight-functions between the neurons are defined by g_{ee}, g_{ei}, g_{ii} and g_{ie}. With respect to a given distance $|\mathbf{z} - \mathbf{z}'|$ the weights decay monotonically and have an isotropic Gaussian distribution of different width with short range excitation and long range inhibition. Changes of the activity in layer u_e and u_i depend on mutual interaction between the neurons. This is determined by the synaptic weights and the non-linear sigmoid activation function h_e and h_i of each neuron, respectively. The positive synaptic weights are indicated by w_{ee}, w_{ei}, w_{ii} and w_{ie}. This leads to a recurrent neural network of the Wilson-Cowan type [8] with $I_e(\mathbf{z}, t)$ and $I_i(\mathbf{z}, t)$ as input function and τ_e and τ_i as time constants. In terms of neural field theory this results in an integro-differential equation possibly eliciting static or dynamic patterns in a neuron population [4,5,8]. A point-like input pulse $I_e(\mathbf{z}, t)$ may result in a local asymptotically stable attractor state, i.e. a neural activity packet. This attractor state has been designated as a bubble [9]. It is hypothesized that such an activation bubble $B(\mathbf{z}, t)$ represents a fundamental structural component of a neural population. Equation (1) can be simplified mathematically by considering only a single layer u. This reads:

$$\tau \frac{\partial u(\mathbf{z}, t)}{\partial t} = -u(\mathbf{z}, t) + (w[g * h(u(\mathbf{z}, t))]) + I(\mathbf{z}, t). \tag{2}$$

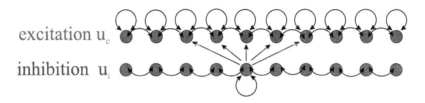

excitation u_e

inhibition u_i

Fig. 1. A simple neural network consists of two layers. One layer of excitatory neurons u_e and one layer of inhibitory neurons u_i. The neurons interact with each other.

A single two dimensional neural layer $u(\mathbf{z}, t)$ with sigmoid saturation curve is embedded in Eq. (2). The connection weight-function g includes excitation and inhibition by providing either a difference of two Gaussians, or, in order to simplify numerical computation, by providing a local excitation and a shunting inhibition as expressed in Eqs. (3) and (4).

$$\frac{\partial u(\mathbf{z}, t)}{\partial t} = f(u(\mathbf{z}, t)) + \mathbf{D}\,\Delta u(\mathbf{z}, t), \tag{3}$$

$$f(u) = -a\,u + \frac{1}{(b + d\,\bar{u})}\frac{u}{(c + e\,u^2)} + I(\mathbf{z}, t). \tag{4}$$

The diffusion of local excitation is determined by $\mathbf{D}\Delta u(\mathbf{z}, t)$, Eq. (3), Δ Laplacian. The function $f(u)$ in Eq. (4) is activated by excitation u. Factors a, b, c, d and e are constants. Inhibition of Eq. (2) is replaced by shunting inhibition, locally by u^2 and globally by $\bar{u}$, that is the average excitation of the neural layer. Compared with Eq. (2) Eqs. (3) and (4) are strictly simplified for numerical purposes and they result in a typical behaviour of non-linear neural field models. The border condition is of Dirichlet type with $u = 0$. Thus, a short point-like input pulse $I(\mathbf{z}, t)$ may generate a stable activation bubble $B(\mathbf{z}, t) > 0$ in the neural layer $u(\mathbf{z}, t)$. Diffusion will be considered as an isotropic or an anisotropic kernel function $g(\mathbf{z}, t)$ according to Eq. (5).

Modelling of the activation bubble $B(\mathbf{z}, t)$ is involved in a single two dimensional neural layer $u(\mathbf{z}, t)$ of 100×100 excitatory neurons according to Eq. (3). By choosing inhibition according to Eq. (4), a bistable state within neural layer $u(\mathbf{z}, t)$ is obtained which may result in an activation bubble [1,2,9]. A travelling bubble may be generated by choosing an anisotropic diffusion tensor, the *propagation tensor* $\mathbf{D} = d_{ij}(t) = [d_{11}(t)\ d_{12}(t),\ d_{21}(t)\ d_{22}(t)]$. For modelling purposes the time dependent anisotropic propagation tensor is computed by applying a kernel function $g(\mathbf{z}, t)$ (matrix 17×17) according Eq. (5) to neural layer $u(\mathbf{z}, t)$.

$$\begin{aligned}
h_1(z_1, t) &= d_{11}(z_1 - 8) \quad \text{for } (z_1 - 8) > 0 \quad \text{else } 0 \\
h_2(z_1, t) &= d_{12}(z_1 - 8) \quad \text{for } (z_1 - 8) <= 0 \quad \text{else } 0 \\
h_3(z_2, t) &= d_{21}(z_1 - 8) \quad \text{for } (z_1 - 8) > 0 \quad \text{else } 0 \\
h_4(z_2, t) &= d_{22}(z_1 - 8) \quad \text{for } (z_1 - 8) <= 0 \quad \text{else } 0 \\
g(\mathbf{z}, t) &= \exp(-0.05\,(h_1^2 + h_2^2 + h_3^2 + h_4^2))
\end{aligned} \tag{5}$$

$g(\mathbf{z}, t)$ represents a two-dimensional kernel function. $z_1, z_2 \in \{1..17\}$. The convolution of $[g * u](\mathbf{z}, t)$ is performed for every time step t of the simulation:

$$[g * u](\mathbf{z}, t) = \int_0^{\mathbf{z}} g((\mathbf{z} - \mathbf{z}'), t)\,u(\mathbf{z}', t)\,d\mathbf{z}' \tag{6}$$

A short local and sufficient excitation pulse $I(\mathbf{z}, t)$ may initiate a stable activation bubble $B(\mathbf{z}, t)$ at position $\mathbf{z}(t)$. If the excitation is too small the bubble will disappear. If there are more than one foci of excitation the winner takes all. If the propagation tensor $\mathbf{D}$ is isotropic, i.e. symmetric and positive definite, the position of the bubble is stable but not asmptotically stable. If $\mathbf{D}$ is anisotropic with different $d_{ij}(t) \in \mathbb{R}^+$ the activation bubble $B(\mathbf{z}, t)$ moves according to Eqs. (3) and (4) within the neural layer $u(\mathbf{z}, t)$.

2.2   Movement Dynamics

Considering a redundant human hand-arm system as an open kinematic chain one has to assume at least 6 degrees of freedom. Six angles $\mathbf{q}(t)$ describe the position of the hand or the position $\mathbf{x}(t)$ of an end-effector, i.e. the tip of a handheld stylus. To make the arm-system accessible to simpler theoretical considerations non-redundant planar arm movements with 2 degrees of freedom $\mathbf{q} = [q_1, q_2]^{\mathbf{T}}$, shoulder joint q_1 and elbow joint q_2, were chosen. Given the joint input torques $\tau(t) = [\tau_1(t), \tau_2(t)]^{\mathbf{T}}$, direct dynamics allows for the computation of the resulting joint positions, velocities, and accelerations $(\mathbf{q}, \dot{\mathbf{q}}, \ddot{\mathbf{q}})$, and the corresponding end-effector positions $(\mathbf{x}, \dot{\mathbf{x}}, \ddot{\mathbf{x}})$ with $\mathbf{x}(t) = [x_1(t), x_2(t)]^T$, respectively. Conversely, *inverse dynamics* maps kinematic data $(\mathbf{q}, \dot{\mathbf{q}}, \ddot{\mathbf{q}})$ to the required joint input torques $\tau(t) = [\tau_1(t), \tau_2(t)]^{\mathbf{T}}$. Thus, from a kinematic perspective start $\mathbf{x}_s$, end-effector position $\mathbf{x}(t)$, and desired position $\mathbf{x}_d(t)$ can be considered equivalent to $\mathbf{q}_s$, $\mathbf{q}(t)$, and $\mathbf{q}_d(t)$. Assuming $\mathrm{H}(\mathbf{q})$ to represent the inertia matrix, and $\mathrm{C}(\mathbf{q}, \dot{\mathbf{q}}) \dot{\mathbf{q}}$ the Coriolis and centrifugal forces, the dynamics of a planar hand-arm system with 2 degrees of freedom can be described as a set of the following system of coupled non-linear differential Eq. (7). This non-redundant system will be the basis of further simulations.

$$\mathrm{H}(\mathbf{q})\,\ddot{\mathbf{q}} + \mathrm{C}(\mathbf{q}, \dot{\mathbf{q}})\,\dot{\mathbf{q}} = \tau \tag{7}$$

3   Results

3.1   Trajectories of the Hand

The control task of hitting a moving target presented on a screen consists in moving the tip of a stylus on a digitizer board and a cursor, from a starting position $\mathbf{x}_s$ in the center of the screen, towards a desired target position $\mathbf{x}_d(t)$. The target moves on a circular path, 12 cm in diameter, with various velocities. The actual distance between $\mathbf{x}(t)$ and $\mathbf{x}_d(t)$ can be considered the control error $\mathbf{ew}(t)$ in the workspace, and the joint angles $\mathbf{q}(t)$ should change to reach the target position. Such goal directed hand movements require feedback control. It is applied by means of mapping control error $\mathbf{ew}(t)$ to joint input torques $\tau(t)$.

Experimental results were presented in [3]. Randomized initial target positions and their velocities were detected at the periphery of the eyes, and resulted in a saccade towards the target. While the eyes were following the target, the cursor was moved towards the target. The trajectories showed a stereotypical motor pattern (Fig. 2) which is assumed to be pre-programmed during the latency of the hand movement. The independent experimental variables velocity, direction, and visibility of the target had been investigated.

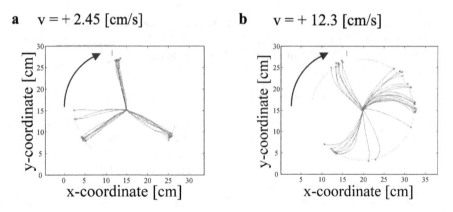

Fig. 2. Experimental sample trajectories towards clockwise moving targets. (a) v = +2.45 [cm/s], (b) v = +12.3 [cm/s].

3.2 Moving Bubble

Taking specific constraints into consideration a neural population [8,9] net may be formalized as reaction-diffusion equations [6,7]. Within a two-dimensional eye-centered neural layer a bubble $B(\mathbf{z},t)$ at position $\mathbf{z}$ may be generated. According to Eq. (5), choosing an anisotropic diffusion tensor $\mathbf{D}$ causes the bubble to move (Fig. 3).

Within the two-dimensional schema layer a motor schema $S(\mathbf{z}_S)$ at coordinates $\mathbf{z}_S$ represents a remembered engram of a recent neural activation sequence. Thus, the motor schema represents an activation sequence of given movement

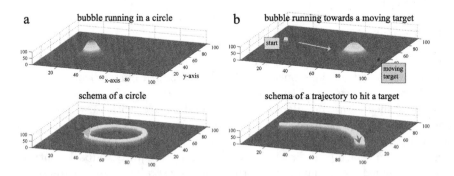

Fig. 3. Moving bubble. The isotropic synaptic weight function $g(\mathbf{z},t)$ represents the convolution kernel of the synaptic connection weight function within the excitatory neural layer. If instead an anisotropic weight function is chosen, the bubble moves. (a) The bubble is shown in the upper neural layer and the trajectory of following a circular schema is shown in the lower schema layer $S(\mathbf{z}_S)$. (b) The bubble is attracted to a moving target by choosing a corresponding anisotropic weight function which depends on target distance and direction.

directions and fits well into the concept of population coding. The interaction between activation bubble B($\mathbf{z}$,t) and motor schema S($\mathbf{z}_S$) results in a certain transition of the bubble position, a motion primitive. The bubble runs along the motor schema as if following the potential field of a gutter. This is caused by modifying the anisotropic characteristics of the propagation tensor $\mathbf{D}$ which determines the activity spread within the neural net. The mapping of the position of the activation bubble B($\mathbf{z}$,t) onto the angular positions of the arm is learned by means of a radial basis network.

3.3   Control and Schema Adaptation

A PID-controller with time-delay is insufficient to intercept a circular moving target at $\mathbf{x}_d(t)$ (Fig. 4). In order to reduce the control error the gain may be increased which inevitably leads to instability, i.e. a ringing effect of the end-effector position. It was the goal of the presented model considerations to overcome this problem. The schema learned represents a feed-forward model. It allows for generating a trajectory which aims ahead with respect to the target movement, and decreases systematically the final distance to the moving target by learning.

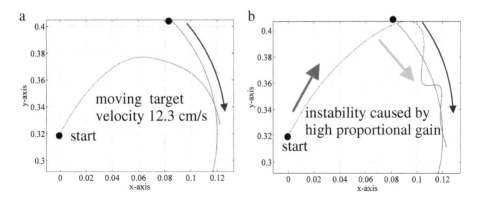

Fig. 4. Basic model considerations revealed that the moving target will not be reached by applying a PID-controller (a). Trying to increase the feedback gain leads inevitably to instability (b). This is mainly due to the mass of the arm, the delay-time (latency), and the required integrator.

The simulation presented is based on a first neural reference engram. This schema $S^0(\mathbf{z}_s)$ is modified by consecutive moves (Fig. 5). The bubble movement is determined by propagation tensor $\mathbf{D}$. This tensor is modified by both the motor schema and the visualized distance from and direction to the target. These different influences on the bubble movement result in a modified hand trajectory changing the preceding schema according to a given learning factor. If all influences on tensor $\mathbf{D}$ are balanced then an effective motor schema arises.

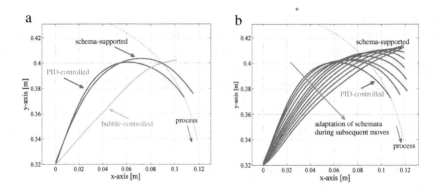

Fig. 5. (a) Three types of trajectory simulations are shown: Curve *PID-controlled* represents the basic trajectory, *bubble controlled:* only affected by distance from and direction towards the target, *schema supported:* motor control by a learned schema. (b) Training of new schemata. They are prepared in advance. The resulting trajectories are smoothed by the intrinsic properties of population dynamics and modified by feedback. Dependent on the outcome (error reduction), a new, more effective schema is adapted.

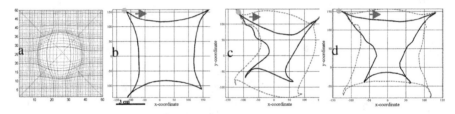

Fig. 6. Experimental sample recordings: (a) Topological distortion. (b) Copying of a cushion like figure, unperturbed. (c) 1st drawing under perturbed conditions, what the subject draws (solid line) and what the subject sees (dashed line). (d) 9th drawing under perturbed condition after having tested the topolgy 80 times with different figures.

The start of the learning sequence is based on an initial activation trace which is strictly generated by a PID-controlled hand movement towards the moving target. This reference trace represents the initial motor schema $S^0(\mathbf{z}_s)$, which is the basis for subsequent goal-directed movements. Next, new motor schemata $S^i(\mathbf{z}_s)$ at modified coordinates $\mathbf{z}_s$ are established which represent further learning steps under stochastic variations. Learning requires criteria for evaluation, i.e. final distance to target. If these criteria do not meet a given threshold the resulting motor schema is rejected, and the preceding motor schema remains unchanged. If the criterion meets the threshold, the current schema is improved.

3.4　Schema Perturbation

To differentiate between eye-centered motor schemata and generalized control strategies systematic perturbations are required. Subjects were asked to copy 9 alternating figures 10 times each from the left to the right side of a screen by means of a digitizer board and a stylus. 8 subjects were tested. The process of copying may be distorted by different topologies, i.e. what the subject draws is not what the subject sees. Figure 6 provides experimental sample recordings. However, the subjects were able to adapt even to complex topological distortions after various trials and may achieve reasonable results with respect to the original figure. A new schema was developed.

4 Discussion

A general problem of goal-directed motor behaviour is to overcome the complexity of a system comprising a large number of redundant degrees of freedom. An effective path through the state space has to be found. A motor schema reduces the complexity of the state space and provides the required constraints. The Gestalt of the schema is varied stochastically and explores the complex state space to find solutions for effective goal-directed movements. Even inverse solutions of redundant systems may be found. Dependent on the contextual conditions of the planned task specific schemata have to be activated for instance by associative recurrent networks of the Hopfield type. Perturbing a visually anticipated trajectory or the smooth course of a target causes an additional error to hit the target. Such perturbations may elicit a conflict. This will allow for testing to what extent the hypothesized motor schema prevails control strategies.

References

1. Bressloff, P.C., Coombes, S.: Neural 'bubble' dynamics revisited. Cogn. Comput. **5**, 281–294 (2013)
2. Cerda, M., Girau, B.: Asymmetry in neural fields: a spatiotemporal encoding mechanismen. Biol. Cybern. **107**, 161–178 (2013)
3. Fleischer, A.G.: Schema generation in recurrent neural nets for intercepting a moving target. Biol. Cybern. **102**, 451–473 (2010)
4. van Hemmen, J.L.: Continuum limit of discrete neuronal structures: is cortical tissue an "excitable" medium? Biol. Cybern. **91**, 347–358 (2004)
5. Malagarriga, D., Villa, A.E.P., García-Ojalvo, J., Pons, A.J.: Excitation/inhibition patterns in a system of coupled cortical columns. In: Wermter, S., Weber, C., Duch, W., Honkela, T., Koprinkova-Hristova, P., Magg, S., Palm, G., Villa, A.E.P. (eds.) ICANN 2014. LNCS, vol. 8681, pp. 651–658. Springer, Heidelberg (2014)
6. Meinhardt, H.: Models of Biological Pattern Formation. Academic Press, London (1982)
7. Murray, J.D.: Mathematical Biology I and II. Springer, Heidelberg (2004)
8. Wilson, H.R., Cowan, J.D.: A mathematical theory of the functional dynamics of cortical and thalamic nervous tissue. Kybernetik **13**, 55–80 (1973)
9. Taylor, J.G.: Neural 'bubble' dynamics in two dimensions: foundations. Biol. Cybern. **80**, 393–409 (1999)

Body Model Transition by Tool Grasping During Motor Babbling Using Deep Learning and RNN

Kuniyuki Takahashi[1,2(✉)], Hadi Tjandra[1], Tetsuya Ogata[3],
and Shigeki Sugano[1]

[1] Graduate School of Creative Science and Engineering,
Waseda University, Tokyo, Japan
takahashi@sugano.mech.waseda.ac.jp
[2] Japan and Research Fellow of Japan Society for the Promotion of Science
(JSPS Research Fellow), Tokyo, Japan
[3] Graduate School of Fundamental Science and Engineering,
Waseda University, Tokyo, Japan

Abstract. We propose a method of tool use considering the transition process of a body model from not grasping to grasping a tool using a single model. In our previous research, we proposed a tool-body assimilation model in which a robot autonomously learns tool functions using a deep neural network (DNN) and recurrent neural network (RNN) through experiences of motor babbling. However, the robot started its motion already holding the tools. In real-life situations, the robot would make decisions regarding *grasping* (handling) or *not grasping* (manipulating) a tool. To achieve this, the robot performs motor babbling without the tool pre-attached to the hand with the same motion twice, in which the robot handles the tool or manipulates without graping it. To evaluate the model, we have the robot generate motions with showing the initial and target states. As a result, the robot could generate the correct motions with grasping decisions.

Keywords: Grasping · Recurrent neural network · Deep neural network

1 Introduction

A robot with tool use skills would be useful in human society, as this would enable the robot to expand its capabilities in performing tasks. However, the modeling of robot tool use in its environment is challenging owing to the numerous possible ways to use tools and the easily changeable human environment. To address this issue, several approaches have been explored, such as model-based methods [4] and machine-learning-based methods [8].

With model-based methods, a robot estimates an assessment of objects from the overlapping situations and performs daily tasks such as cooking with a turner and putting a file into a folder [4]. Model-based methods assumes that all environmental information are known, and the tool model is pre-designed by a human.

© Springer International Publishing Switzerland 2016
A.E.P. Villa et al. (Eds.): ICANN 2016, Part I, LNCS 9886, pp. 166–174, 2016.
DOI: 10.1007/978-3-319-44778-0_20

Therefore, the robot knows where it should grasp and how to use the tools. This makes it difficult to use unknown tools in an unknown environment.

When modeling the tool and environment is difficult, machine-learning-based approaches can be employed for motion generation. In [8], a robot performed object-pulling task. The robot learned the relationship between the movement of tools and target object movement. Furthermore, the robot decided which tool should be used from the distance between the robot and the target object. The study by Tikhanoff et al. required pre-designed tool models and decision algorithms used mathematical equations.

In order to address these issues, in our previous research [7], we proposed a tool-body assimilation model in which the robot autonomously learns tool functions with a DNN and RNN through experiences acquired by motor babbling while holding several types of tools. Tool-body assimilation is the phenomenon where, when humans use a tool, they treat it as an extension of their own bodies [1]. Motor babbling is the motion process during the early days of human infants when they acquire their own body models as sensor-motor relationships [6]. However, the robot started its motion already holding tools. This means that the robot only has experiences in which it grasps tools. In real-life situations, the decision of *grasping* (handling) or *not grasping* (manipulation) a tool is necessary.

The objective of this study is to extend our tool-body assimilation model to perform both grasping and manipulating a tool without grasping it using a single model. To achieve this, the robot performs motor babbling without the tool in-hand performing the same motion twice, in which the robot grasps or manipulates the tool without grasping. The robot can thereby learn the experiences of both grasping and not grasping the tool.

The rest of this paper is organized as follows. Section 2 describes the method of body-model transition. Section 3 presents the experimental setup for the simulated robots. Section 4 presents the experiments by simulations. Section 5 concludes this paper with an outlook for our future work.

2   Body-Model Transition with Motor Babbling

In this section, we propose for body-model transition from not graping to grasping a tool during motor babbling. Figure 1 shows an overview of the model. The purpose of this model is to represent the state in which the robot handles the tools or manipulates the tool without grasping it using a single model. The model consists of three modules:

– Motor babbling module
– Image feature extraction module: DNN
– Body model module: the stochastic multiple timescale RNN (S-MTRNN)

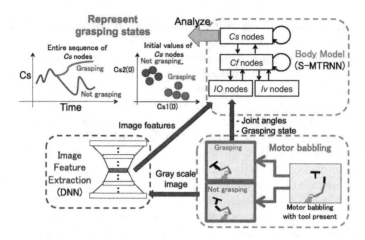

Fig. 1. The model for body-model transition from not graping to grasping the tool with motor babbling. This model consists of three modules: (1) motor babbling module, (2) image feature extraction module using a DNN, and (3) body model module using the S-MTRNN. The grasping state is represented in slow context nodes.

2.1   Motor Babbling Considering Tool Grasping Condition

The robot performs the motions of both handling and manipulating the tool by motor babbling. Then, the robot performs motor babbling without the tool in-hand at first with the same motion twice, during which if the robot hand and the tool are in contact, the robot either handles or manipulates the tool without grasping it (see the motor babbling module in Fig. 1). As a result, the robot has the experiences of both grasping and not grasping the tool. During motor babbling, sequences of joint angles, camera images, and grasping states (i.e., grasping and not graping) of the tool are obtained.

2.2   Image Feature Extraction Using DNN

DNNs such as auto-encoders have the ability to extract image features automatically unsupervised for large number of dimensions and numerous data. DNNs have recently drawn much attention as feature extraction tools for use with raw images in the robotics field [5,7]. Auto-encoders can almost completely restore original data from image features, as training is performed to give output values that are equal to the input values.

During auto-encoder training, Hessian-free optimization is applied as a 2nd-order optimization method based on Newton's method [2]. Details of the implementation are provided in study [2].

2.3   Body-Model Acquisition Using S-MTRNN

The robot learns the relationships between joint angles and sensors (i.e., image features and grasping states) to acquire its own body model through motor babbling using the S-MTRNN. The S-MTRNN has desirable characteristics for predicting the next state from the past history of neuron states, and predicts the variance as prediction accuracy [3] (Fig. 2). The S-MTRNN is composed of four types of neurons which have different time constants: input-output (IO) nodes, variance nodes (I_v), fast context (C_f) nodes, and slow context (C_s) nodes. The S-MTRNN calculates variance as an estimate of the prediction error of input-output (IO) nodes. The variance is calculated from the input signal without a teaching signal. The fast context nodes learn primitive movements from the data, whereas, the slow context nodes learn the sequence of the primitives of the data. The S-MTRNN can learn the dynamics of the data by combining these nodes. In addition, a motion sequence can be generated by searching the corresponding initial value of the (C_s) nodes. RNNs with context nodes can learn motion with branching data structures, as the motions are learned as different motions according to the initial values of the context in order to represent motion (see the region on representing grasping states in Fig. 1). In this study, during motor babbling, the robot performs the same motion with grasping and not grasping a tool. Even though the sequences of joint angles are the same between grasping and not grasping, image features and grasping states have different values between grasping and not graping the tool after contact between the robot hand and the tool. Therefore, the motion data will have a branched structure, and the slow context would diverge into different dynamics. For training the S-MTRNN, we use a maximization of likelihood using the gradient descent method. Details about of implementation are provided in [3].

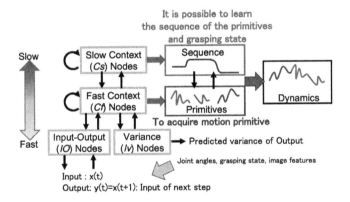

Fig. 2. Representation of the S-MTRNN which can predict the next state from the past history of neuron states, and predicts the variance as prediction accuracy with different time constants: input-output (IO) nodes, variance nodes (I_v), fast context (C_f) nodes, and slow context (C_s) nodes. The S-MTRNN calculates variance v as an estimate of the prediction error of input-output (IO) nodes.

3   Experimental Setup

3.1   Evaluation Using Simulated Robot Model

For evaluation, we used a simulated robot model based on the structure of the humanoid robot ACTROID implemented on the robotics simulator OpenHRP3 (see motor babbling in Fig. 1). The simulated robot has a seven-DOF right arm and camera. In this study, we use three DOFs of the right arm (the shoulder, elbow, and wrist). The range of joint angles is designed to refer humans. For the motion, the motor torque command to each joint is calculated by a proportional-derivative (PD) controller.

In this experiment, a T-shaped object-pulling task with the robot hand in the plane of the desk (two-dimensional movements) is used (see Fig. 1). This task is commonly used in tool-body assimilation studies with robots [7,8].

3.2   Procedure of Motor Babbling

To perform motor babbling, we set joint angles within their range of motion and the initial position of the T-shaped tool. Then, in a sequence, a random set of desired angles for each joint of the arm is given, and we record the joint angles, camera images, and grasping states for the duration of 6.0 s (30 steps) at the sampling intervals of 0.2 s. When the robot performed motor babbling, the robot handled or manipulated the T-shaped tool without grasping it in contact with it. The process was repeated 30 times for each (i.e., grasping and not grasping), comprising 60 instances in total, to generate random motions.

Image data were obtained as color images of 320×240 pixels; there were then converted to gray-scale images of 32×24 pixels. The values of the pixels were normalized to $[0.1, 0.9]$ for training of fully connected DNN auto-encoder. After training, two dimensions of image features were extracted (Table 1).

For acquisition of the body model, the S-MTRNN was trained with the recorded 60 sequences of motions data, including joint angles (3 dimensions), grasping states (1 dimension), and acquired image features (2 dimensions) (Table 2). The structure of the S-MTRNN is such that input-output (IO) and variance (I_v) nodes are only connected to the fast context nodes (C_f), the fast context (C_f) nodes are fully connected to all the nodes, and the slow context (C_s) nodes are only connected to the slow context (C_s) nodes and the fast context (C_f) nodes. To train the S-MTRNN, the values of joint angles and image features were normalized to $[-1.0, 1.0]$, and the grasping state were normalized to $[-0.6, 0.6]$: 0.6 corresponding to grasping the tool and -0.6 corresponding to not grasping the tool.

4   Experiments by Simulations

4.1   Representation of Grasping State by the Initial Values of the Slow Context Nodes

We analyze the internal representation of the body model using the initial values of the slow context nodes ($C_s(0)$). Figure 3 shows two out of 20 of $C_s(0)$

Table 1. Design of DNN

Number of input–output nodes	768
Number of hidden layers	9
Dimensions of hidden nodes	500-250-100-50-2-50-100-250-500
Number of teaching data	1800 ($60motions \times 30steps$)

Table 2. Design of S-MTRNN

Type of nodes	Node name	No. of nodes	Time constant
Input-output (IO)	Joint angles	3	1
	Grasping state	1	1
	Image features	2	1
Variance (I_v)	Variance	6	1
Fast context (C_f)	Fast context	40	5
Slow context (C_s)	Slow context	20	20

after the robot learned motor babbling motions. Figure 3 shows that the values with grasping and without grasping are clustered. The C_s1 represents the grasping state of the motion sequences. Therefore, we can say that the body model successfully acquired the grasping state.

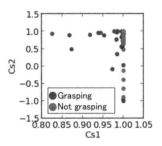

Fig. 3. Representation of the grasping states on two out of 20 of $C_s(0)$ after motor babbling motions. The C_s1 represents the grasping state of the motion sequences.

4.2   Motion Generation from the Initial States and Goal Images

We had the robot generate motion from the initial state (i.e., joint angles, grasping state, and image) and a target image, which were untrained data. The robot reproduced motion between initial state and final states. Figure 4(a) and (b) show the generated motion with handling and manipulating the tool without grasping, respectively. The graphs from above show the sequence of grasping states, variance of each input signal, and the slow context values. The circle plot in the figure of the initial grasping state is the given data used to generate motion, and the square plot of the final grasping state is the desired state, which is not given. The figures on the bottom in Fig. 4 are generated motion images.

In Fig. 4(a) and (b), the positions of the tool and postures of the robot's joint angles in the generated motion images are similar to the target image, respectively. From the results, it can be said that the robot has the ability to generate motion from an initial state and an untrained target image. The robot was capable of acquiring its body model as an inverse kinematics model because the robot could generate joint angles from the image. The grasping signal graph shows that the robot recognized the grasping state even though the grasping signal was not given during generation of the motion sequences. This results suggest that the robot could recognize the grasping state from the final image.

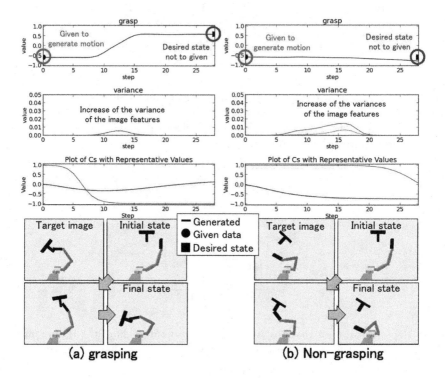

Fig. 4. Generated motions by recognition from the initial state (i.e., joint angles, grasping states, and images) and the goal state using untrained data. The robot reproduced the motion between the initial state and the finial state image. (a) shows the robot grasping the tool, and (b) shows the robot manipulating the tool without grasping it. The graphs, from the top, show the grasping state, variance of each input signal, and the values of the slow context plots, respectively. The figures at the bottom are generated motions from the initial state and the target image. (Color figure online)

At the moment of contact between the robot hand and the tool, an increase of the variances of the image features was observed. This was caused by the large differences in the tool state image features after contact was made. The image features before contact are the same between for sequences with and without grasping. This means that variance was increased at the point where prediction of the image became uncertain.

Through analysis of the slow context in Fig. 4, the changes in the values of two out of 20 of the slow context nodes were observed. Upon contact between the robot hand and the tool, when the robot grasped the tool, the values of the slow context node denoted by the green line show a decrease, while values of the slow context nodes shown by the blue line show a slight decrease followed by an increase. On the other hand, when the robot manipulated the tool without grasping it, the values of the slow context node shown by the blue line showed a decrease. The green line showed a decrease at the end of the sequence. The same result was observed in other motions, which suggests that some of the slow context nodes represent the grasping state.

5   Conclusion

The objective of this research was to express both handling a tool and manipulating a tool without grasping using a single model to extend our tool-body assimilation model. To do this, the robot learned the motion of motor babbling without a tool in-hand using the S-MTRNN. Upon contact between the robot's hand and the tool, the robot either grasped or manipulated the tool without grasping it. To evaluate our model, the robot T-shaped object-pulling task was performed. As a result, the robot generated motion from the initial and target images with decisions of grasping.

Acknowledgment. This work has been supported by JSPS Grant-in-Aid for Scientific Research 15J12683; the Program for Leading Graduate Schools, "Graduate Program for Embodiment Informatics" of the Ministry of Education, Culture, Sports, Science, and Technology; JSPS Grant-in-Aid for Scientific Research (S) (2522005); "Fundamental Study for Intelligent Machine to Coexist with Nature" Research Institute for Science and Engineering, Waseda University; MEXT Grant-in-Aid for Scientific Research (A) 15H01710; and MEXT Grant-in-Aid for Scientific Research on Innovative Areas "Constructive Developmental Science" (24119003)

References

1. Maravita, A., Iriki, A.: Tools for the body (schema). Trends Cogn. Sci. 8(2), 79–86 (2004)
2. Martens, J.: Deep learning via Hessian-free optimization. In: Proceedings of the 27th International Conference on Machine Learning (ICML 2010), pp. 735–742 (2010)
3. Murata, S., Yamashita, Y., Arie, H., Ogata, T., Sugano, S., Tani, J.: Learning to perceive the world as probabilistic or deterministic via interaction with others: a neuro-robotics experiment. IEEE Trans. Neural Netw. Learn. Syst. (2015)

4. Nagahama, K., Yamazaki, K., Okada, K., Inaba, M.: Manipulation of multiple objects in close proximity based on visual hierarchical relationships. In: IEEE International Conference on Robotics and Automation, pp. 1303–1310 (2013)
5. Noda, K., Arie, H., Suga, Y., Ogata, T.: Multimodal integration learning of robot behavior using deep neural networks. Robot. Auton. Syst. **62**(6), 721–736 (2014)
6. Sturm, J., Plagemann, C., Burgard, W.: Unsupervised body scheme learning through self-perception. In: IEEE International Conference on Robotics and Automation, pp. 3328–3333 (2008)
7. Takahashi, K., Ogata, T., Tjandra, H., Yamaguchi, Y., Sugano, S.: Tool-body assimilation model based on body babbling and neurodynamical system. Math. Prob. Eng. (2015)
8. Tikhanoff, V., Pattacini, U., Natale, L., Metta, G.: Exploring affordances and tool use on the iCub. In: IEEE-RAS International Conference on Humanoid Robots, pp. 130–137 (2013)

Centering Versus Scaling for Hubness Reduction

Roman Feldbauer$^{(\boxtimes)}$ and Arthur Flexer

Austrian Research Institute for Artificial Intelligence (OFAI),
Freyung 6/6/7, 1010 Vienna, Austria
{roman.feldbauer,arthur.flexer}@ofai.at

Abstract. Hubs and anti-hubs are points that appear very close or very far to many other data points due to a problem of measuring distances in high-dimensional spaces. Hubness is an aspect of the curse of dimensionality affecting many machine learning tasks. We present the first large scale empirical study to compare two competing hubness reduction techniques: scaling and centering. We show that scaling consistently reduces hubness and improves nearest neighbor classification, while centering shows rather mixed results. Support vector classification is mostly unaffected by centering-based hubness reduction.

Keywords: Hubness reduction · Curse of dimensionality · k-NN · SVM

1 Introduction and Related Work

Hubness is a general problem of learning in high-dimensional spaces and has been recognized as an aspect of the curse of dimensionality in machine learning literature [7,9]. Hub objects appear very close to many other data objects and anti-hubs very far from most other data objects. The effect has been shown to have a negative impact on classification [7], nearest neighbor based recommendation [2] and retrieval [10], outlier detection [6], clustering [8,12] and visualization [1].

Hubness is related to the phenomenon of concentration of distances, which is the fact that all points are at almost the same distance to each other for dimensionality approaching infinity [3]. Radovanović et al. [7] presented the argument that for any finite dimensionality, some points are expected to be closer to the center of all data than other points and are at the same time closer, on average, to all other points. Such points closer to the center have a high probability of being hubs, i.e. of appearing in nearest neighbor lists of many other points. Points which are further away from the center have a high probability of being anti-hubs, i.e. points that never appear in any nearest neighbor list.

In order to reduce hubness and its negative effects, we have proposed two unsupervised methods to re-scale high-dimensional distance spaces [9]: Local Scaling (LS) and Mutual Proximity (MP). Both methods aim at repairing asymmetric nearest neighbor relations. The asymmetric relations are a direct consequence of the presence of hubs. A hub y is the nearest neighbor of x, but the nearest neighbor of the hub y is another point a ($a \neq x$). This is because hubs are

© Springer International Publishing Switzerland 2016
A.E.P. Villa et al. (Eds.): ICANN 2016, Part I, LNCS 9886, pp. 175–183, 2016.
DOI: 10.1007/978-3-319-44778-0_21

by definition nearest neighbors to very many data points but only one data point can be the nearest neighbor to a hub. The principle of the scaling algorithms is to re-scale distances to enhance symmetry of nearest neighbors. A small distance between two objects should be returned only if their nearest neighbors concur. Application of LS and MP resulted in a decrease of hubness and an accuracy increase in k-nearest neighbor classification on thirty real world datasets including text, image and music data. The general influence of hubs and anti-hubs on classifiers beyond simple nearest neighbor approaches is so far largely unexplored, with the only result being that removal of certain hubs during support vector machine (SVM) training decreases classification rates [7].

A different approach to reduce hubness is to center the data either locally or globally [4,11]. Results so far are encouraging and comparable to those achieved with scaling. An advantage of global centering is that it computes centered data vectors whereas scaling and localized centering result in distance and similarity matrices, respectively, which can be a problem for many machine learning tasks. Since comparison of centering and scaling so far has only been conducted on seven datasets, all from the text domain, we present the first comprehensive empirical study of the two competing approaches on 28 diverse datasets. We also conduct a first analysis of the influence of centering on SVM classification.

2   Methods and Data

Before presenting our results in Sect. 3, we introduce all evaluation measures, methods and datasets used in this work.

2.1   Evaluation Measures

The following indices will be used to measure the performance achieved in original and re-scaled or centered data spaces.

Hubness (S^n): To characterize the strength of the hubness phenomenon in a dataset we use the hubness measure proposed by Radovanović et al. [7]. To compute hubness[1] we first define $O^n(x)$ as the n-occurrence of point x, that is, the number of times x occurs in the n-nearest neighbor lists of all other objects in the collection. Hubness S^n is then defined as the skewness of the distribution of n-occurrences O^n. A dataset having high hubness produces few hub objects with very high n-occurrence and many anti-hubs with n-occurrence of zero. This makes the distribution of n-occurrences skewed with positive skewness indicating high hubness. All our results are based on $n = 5$-occurences.

Nearest Neighbor Classification Accuracy (C^k): We report the k-nearest neighbor classification accuracy C^k using 5-fold cross-validation, where classification is performed via a majority vote among the k nearest neighbors, with the class of the nearest neighbor used for breaking ties. We use $k = 5$ for all

---

[1] Python scripts for hubness analysis are available at: https://github.com/OFAI

experiments. The classification accuracy measures to what degree the distance space reflects the class information, i.e. the semantic meaning of the data.

Support Vector Classification Accuracy: For selected datasets we perform support vector classification using nested cross-validation (CV), tuning the regularization parameter C for the linear kernel in the inner 3-fold CV, and reporting classification accuracy averaged over the outer 5-fold CV. All SVM calculations were performed with the scikit-learn package [13] for Python.

2.2   Reducing Hubness

We introduce four hubness reduction methods which either re-compute the whole distance matrix to so-called secondary distances (NICDM, MP, LCENT), or are applied to the data vectors directly (CENT).

NICDM: The non-iterative contextual dissimilarity measure [5] is a local scaling variant that transforms arbitrary distances according to:

$$\text{NICDM}(D_{x,y}) = D_{x,y} \frac{\mu_{geom}^2}{\sqrt{\mu_x\,\mu_y}}, \tag{1}$$

where μ_x (μ_y) denotes the average distance between object x (y) and its k nearest neighbors, and μ_{geom} denotes the geometric mean of all such average distances in the data. NICDM tends to make neighborhood relations more symmetric by including local distance statistics of both data points x and y in the scaling. We use NICDM with $k = 10$, as it returned the best and most stable results in previous studies [8].

Mutual Proximity (MP): MP reinterprets the original distance space so that two objects sharing similar nearest neighbors are more closely tied to each other, while two objects with dissimilar neighborhoods are repelled from each other [9]. This is done by transforming the distance of two objects into a mutual proximity in terms of their distribution of distances. We assume that distances $D_{x,i=1..N}$ from an object x to all other objects in a dataset follow a certain probability distribution, thus any distance $D_{x,y}$ can be reinterpreted as the probability of y being the nearest neighbor of x, given their distance $D_{x,y}$ and the probability distribution $P(X)$. MP is defined as the probability that y is the nearest neighbor of x given $P(X)$ and x is the nearest neighbor of y given $P(Y)$:

$$\text{MP}(D_{x,y}) = P(X > D_{x,y} \cap Y > D_{y,x}). \tag{2}$$

In this work we assume that distances $D_{x,i=1..N}$ follow a Gaussian distribution and that $P(X)$ and $P(Y)$ are statistically independent. Computing $1 - \text{MP}$ turns the respective similarities into distances.

Centering (CENT): Centering is a common preprocessing step in data analysis transforming vector data by subtracting the dataset centroid, thus shifting the origin to the latter. Suzuki et al. [11] use the method for hubness reduction in inner product similarity spaces, where the similarity of each sample to the centroid is equal to zero after centering. Since hubs are then no longer closer to the centroid than other samples, hubness might be reduced by centering. Since this holds only for inner product spaces, we replace Euclidean ℓ^2 norms with cosine distances to gain the same effect in case ℓ^2 is the original distance for the given dataset. This is also done in case of localized centering.

Localized Centering (LCENT): Localized centering tries to reduce hubness by considering *local affinity*, i.e. the average similarity of a sample x to its k nearest neighbors [4]. Similarities are calculated as

$$\text{Sim}(x,y)^{\text{LCENT}} = \text{Sim}(x,y) - \text{Sim}(x, c_\kappa(x))^\gamma \qquad (3)$$

where Sim denotes a similarity measure ($1 - D$, where D is a cosine distance) and $c(x)$ denotes the local centroid of x. We tune the parameters κ (neighborhood size) and γ (controls penalty) in nested cross-validation with a 3-fold inner loop in order to optimally reduce hubness.

2.3   Datasets

The four previously introduced hubness reduction methods are evaluated using 28 real-world datasets (Table 1), comprising data from biology, multimedia retrieval and general machine learning fields. All datasets have previously been used to evaluate NICDM and MP in [9] and are described further therein. Please note that we excluded two datasets from this previous study which use the symmetrized Kullback-Leibler divergence, since this is not a full metric and therefore not easy to combine with centering methods.

3   Results

We evaluate all centering and scaling methods on 28 datasets using the evaluation measures introduced in Sect. 2.1. Figure 1 shows the results of the evaluation, ordered by ascending hubness. Results are given as absolute decreases or increases in hubness and accuracy relative to the values obtained in original similarity spaces given in Table 1. Results are given in light blue (NICDM), blue (MP), light green (CENT) and green (LCENT) bars. For data sets based on Euclidean ℓ^2 norm, there is an additional black bar (COS) showing the decrease/increase due to switching to cosine distances alone. If cosine is already the original distance, this is marked with a small 'cos' instead of a black bar.

In accordance with the results from [9], we find that both scaling methods NICDM and MP consistently reduce hubness. For datasets of high hubness (defined as $S^{k=5} > 1.4$, from dataset 'corel1000' onwards) the reduction is more pronounced and leads to significant increases in classification accuracy (McNemar's test, marked with asterisks on right-hand side of Fig. 1). There are few significant changes among the low hubness datasets.

CENT reduces hubness and improves classification for all datasets, which are originally based on cosine distances ('c224a-web', 'reuters-transcribed', 'moviereviews', 'dexter', 'mini-newsgroups', 'c1ka-twitter'). Significant changes in other

Table 1. 28 real-world datasets are reported in terms of their name, number of classes (Cls.) and instances (N), dimensionality (d), original distance measure (Dist.) and classification accuracy ($C^{k=5}$). Datasets are ordered by ascending hubness ($S^{n=5}$).

Name	Cls.	N	d	Dist.	$C^{k=5}$	$S^{n=5}$
LibSVM fourclass (sc)	2	862	2	ℓ^2	1.0	0.15
UCI arcene	2	100	10000	ℓ^2	0.729	0.25
UCI liver-disorders (sc)	2	345	6	ℓ^2	0.594	0.38
LibSVM Australian	2	690	14	ℓ^2	0.677	0.44
UCI diabetes (sc)	2	768	8	ℓ^2	0.733	0.49
LibSVM heart	2	270	13	ℓ^2	0.815	0.50
KR ovarian-61902	2	253	15154	ℓ^2	0.917	0.66
LibSVM breast-cancer (sc)	2	683	10	ℓ^2	0.972	0.70
UCI mfeat-factors	10	2000	216	ℓ^2	0.946	0.79
LibSVM ger.num (sc)	2	1000	24	ℓ^2	0.711	0.81
LibSVM colon-cancer	2	62	2000	ℓ^2	0.740	0.81
KR amlall	2	72	7129	ℓ^2	0.830	0.82
UCI mfeat-karhunen	10	2000	64	ℓ^2	0.972	0.84
KR lungcancer	2	181	12533	ℓ^2	0.994	1.07
CP c224a-web	14	224	1244	cos	0.898	1.09
UCI mfeat-pixels	10	2000	240	ℓ^2	0.975	1.28
UCI duke (train)	2	38	7129	ℓ^2	0.582	1.37
Corel corel1000	10	1000	192	ℓ^2	0.671	1.45
UCI sonar (sc)	2	208	60	ℓ^2	0.513	1.54
UCI ionosphere (sc)	2	351	34	ℓ^2	0.875	1.56
UCI reuters-transcribed	10	201	2730	cos	0.478	1.61
PaBo movie-reviews	2	2000	10382	cos	0.696	4.07
UCI dexter	2	300	20000	cos	0.770	4.22
UCI gisette	2	6000	5000	ℓ^2	0.957	4.48
LibSVM splice (sc)	2	1000	60	ℓ^2	0.706	4.55
UCI mini-newsgroups	20	2000	8811	cos	0.672	5.14
UCI dorothea	2	800	100000	ℓ^2	0.891	12.93
CP c1ka-twitter	17	969	49820	cos	0.273	14.63

datasets appear to be either fully ('gisette', 'dorothea') or at least partially ('ionosphere', 'splice') caused by switching to cosine distances rather than centering, since results for COS are almost as high as those for CENT. In case of 'fourclass' both CENT and COS lead to considerable accuracy decreases. In two other cases CENT is beneficial for classification ('diabetes') or detrimental ('mfeat-factors'), with COS alone showing no effect.

We obtain very mixed results using LCENT. While the method performs equally in terms of hubness reduction and accuracy to scaling techniques for some datasets in high hubness regimes ('ionosphere', 'splice', 'dorothea', 'c1ka-twitter'), it increases hubness for some datasets and effectively decreases classification accuracy for 'fourclass', 'ovarian', 'mfeat-factors', 'mfeat-karhunen', 'mfeat-pixels' and 'mini-newsgroups'. Neither positive nor negative changes are strictly coupled to the original distance metric, and there is only a moderate correlation between changes in hubness and accuracy (Pearson's $r = -0.56$).

To sum up our results, whereas both scaling methods NICDM and MP consistently help against the negative effects of hubness, LCENT reaches the same performance only for some datasets, while at the same time having a higher computational cost due to tuning of two parameters. CENT on the other hand is computationally very efficient and effective for all cosine-based datasets.

Table 2. Classification accuracy for linear SVM. Results are given for the complete dataset (all). Additionally, they are partitioned into hubs (H), normal (N) and anti-hubs (A). Superscript C indicates centering. Significant changes between non-centered and centered data are marked with an asterisk ($\alpha = .05$). Three datasets do not contain hubs according to the $5 \times n$ criterion (N/A).

Name	all	H	N	A	all^C	H^C	N^C	A^C
c224a-web	0.929	N/A	0.934	0.885	0.906	N/A	0.914	0.846
Sonar	0.620	N/A	0.632	0.467	0.620	N/A	0.627	0.533
Reuters-transcribed	0.582	N/A	0.579	0.75	0.597	N/A	0.594	0.75
Movie-reviews	0.845	0.904	0.844	0.840	0.841*	0.885	0.842	0.826
Dexter	0.937	1.0	0.942	0.913	0.93	1.0	0.947	0.875
Gisette	0.972	0.948	0.975	0.950	0.973	0.948	0.976	0.950
Splice	0.793	0.931	0.805	0.751	0.794	0.931	0.805	0.754
Mini-newsgroups	0.954	1.0	0.949	0.970	0.956	0.976	0.952	0.974
c1ka-twitter	0.590	0.733	0.676	0.520	0.614	0.867	0.715	0.530

Centering and Support Vector Classification: Additionally, we investigated the effect of hubness on support vector machines. Among the introduced hubness reduction methods, only CENT returns vector data instead of distance matrices. We therefore restrict SVM analysis (i) to this technique and (ii) to datasets, which exhibit reduced hubness after centering (i.e. all cosine-based and three other datasets). In this section we refer to objects with an n-occurence greater than $5 \times n$ as 'hubs', to those with n-occurence of zero as 'anti-hubs' and to the remaining objects as 'normal' ($n = 5$). We perform support vector classification (linear kernel), tracking accuracies of hubs, normal points and anti-hubs before and after centering. Across all datasets (except 'gisette') and before and after centering, hub points show higher accuracy than normal and anti-hub points, which both seem to perform at a comparable level (Table 2). Using

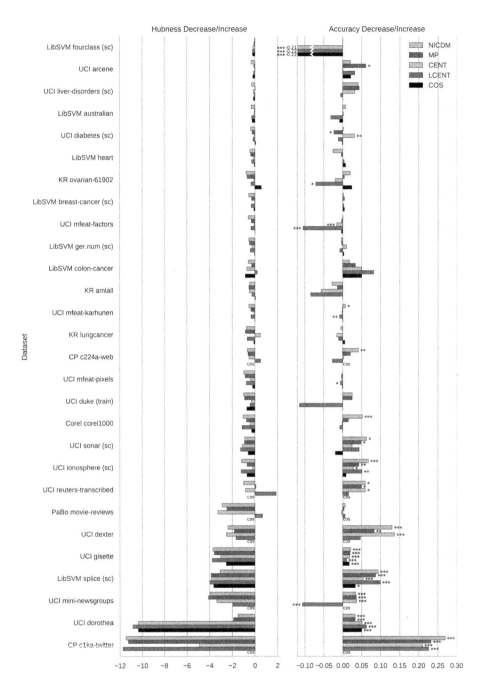

Fig. 1. Absolute decrease/increase in hubness (lower is better) and accuracy (higher is better) evaluated with $k = 5$. Significant changes are marked with asterisks: $^*\alpha = .05$, $^{**}\alpha = .01$, $^{***}\alpha = .001$. See Sect. 3 for more information. (Color figure online)

the same statistical testing procedure as above, we find no significant changes between centered and uncentered data except for the 'movie-reviews' dataset, for which we observe a minor decrease in accuracy. Centering appears to have no major impact on linear SVMs.

4 Conclusion

We have presented the first large-scale empirical study to compare scaling and centering techniques for hubness reduction. Scaling methods outperform centering methods in terms of reduced hubness and improved nearest neighbor classification in most datasets. They are effective for datasets from various domains, and for various distance measures. Centering performs equally well for cosine distances and has the advantage of being applicable to vector data. This is especially relevant for large datasets, for which operations on similarity matrices might be computationally intractable. Localized centering is effective only for few datasets. We find no evidence for improved support vector classification due to hubness reduction via centering.

Acknowledgments. This research is supported by the Austrian Science Fund (FWF): P27082, P27703.

References

1. Flexer, A.: Improving visualization of high-dimensional music similarity spaces. In: 16th ISMIR Conference (2015)
2. Flexer, A., Schnitzer, D., Schlüter, J.: A MIREX meta-analysis of hubness in audio music similarity. In: 13th ISMIR Conference (2012)
3. Francois, D., Wertz, V., Verleysen, M.: The concentration of fractional distances. IEEE Trans. Knowl. Data Eng. **19**, 873–886 (2007)
4. Hara, K., Suzuki, I., Shimbo, M., Kobayashi, K., Fukumizu, K., Radovanović, M.: Localized centering: reducing hubness in large-sample data hubness in high-dimensional data. In: 29th AAAI Conference on Artificial Intelligence, pp. 2645–2651 (2015)
5. Jegou, H., Harzallah, H., Schmid, C.: A contextual dissimilarity measure for accurate and efficient image search. In: Proceedings of the IEEE Computer Society Conference on Computer Vision and Pattern Recognition (2007)
6. Radovanović, M., Nanopoulos, A., Ivanović, M.: Reverse nearest neighbors in unsupervised distance-based outlier detection. IEEE Trans. Knowl. Data Eng. **27**(5), 1369–1382 (2015)
7. Radovanović, M., Nanopoulos, A., Ivanović, M.: Hubs in space: popular nearest neighbors in high-dimensional data. J. Mach. Learn. Res. **11**, 2487–2531 (2010)
8. Schnitzer, D., Flexer, A.: The unbalancing effect of hubs on K-medoids clustering in high-dimensional spaces. In: International Joint Conference on Neural Networks (2015)
9. Schnitzer, D., Flexer, A., Schedl, M., Widmer, G.: Local and global scaling reduce hubs in space. J. Mach. Learn. Res. **13**, 2871–2902 (2012)

10. Schnitzer, D., Flexer, A., Tomašev, N.: A case for hubness removal in high-dimensional multimedia retrieval. In: de Rijke, M., Kenter, T., de Vries, A.P., Zhai, C.X., de Jong, F., Radinsky, K., Hofmann, K. (eds.) ECIR 2014. LNCS, vol. 8416, pp. 687–692. Springer, Heidelberg (2014)
11. Suzuki, I., Hara, K., Shimbo, M., Saerens, M., Fukumizu, K.: Centering similarity measures to reduce hubs. In: Conference on Empirical Methods in Natural Language Processing (EMNLP 2013), pp. 613–623 (2013)
12. Tomašev, N., Radovanović, M., Mladenić, D., Ivanović, M.: The role of hubness in clustering high-dimensional data. IEEE Trans. Knowl. Data Eng. **26**(3), 739–751 (2014)
13. Pedregosa, F., Varoquaux, G., Gramfort, A., Michel, V., Thirion, B., Grisel, O., Blondel, M., Prettenhofer, P., Weiss, R., Dubourg, V., Vanderplas, J., Passos, A., Cournapeau, D., Brucher, M., Perrot, M., Duchesnay, E.: Scikit-learn: machine learning in Python. J. Mach. Learn. Res. **12**, 2825–2830 (2011)

High Integrated Information in Complex Networks Near Criticality

Xerxes D. Arsiwalla[1(✉)] and Paul F.M.J. Verschure[1,2]

[1] Synthetic Perceptive Emotive and Cognitive Systems (SPECS) Lab,
Center of Autonomous Systems and Neurorobotics,
Universitat Pompeu Fabra, Barcelona, Spain
x.d.arsiwalla@gmail.com

[2] Institució Catalana de Recerca i Estudis Avançats (ICREA), Barcelona, Spain

Abstract. Integrated information has recently been proposed as an information-theoretic measure of a network's dynamical complexity. It aims to capture the amount of information generated by a network as a whole over and above that generated by the sum of its parts when the network transitions from one dynamical state to another. Several formulations of this measure have been proposed, with numerical schemes for computing network complexity. In this paper, we approach the problem analytically. We compute the integrated information of weighted networks with stochastic dynamics. Our formulation makes use of the Kullback-Leibler divergence between the multi-variate distribution on the set of network states versus the corresponding factorized distribution over its parts. Using Gaussian distributions, we compute analytic results for several prototypical network topologies. Our findings show that operating near the edge of criticality is favorable for a high rate of information integration in complex dynamical networks. This observation is consistent across network topologies. We discuss the implication of these results for biological and communication networks.

Keywords: Network dynamics · Complexity measures · Information theory

1 Introduction

Integrated information, denoted as Φ, was first introduced in neuroscience as a complexity measure for neural networks, and by extension, as a possible correlate of consciousness itself [17]. It is defined as the quantity of information generated by a network as a whole, due to its causal dynamical interactions, and one that is over and above the information generated independently by the disjoint sum of its parts. As a complexity measure, Φ seeks to operationalize the intuition that complexity arises from simultaneous integration and differentiation of the network's structure and dynamics. Differentiation refers to specialized neuronal populations with distinct functionality. The complementary design principle, integration, results in distributed coordination among these populations, thus

A.E.P. Villa et al. (Eds.): ICANN 2016, Part I, LNCS 9886, pp. 184–191, 2016.
DOI: 10.1007/978-3-319-44778-0_22

enabling the emergence of coherent cognitive and behavioral states. The interplay of differentiation and integration in a network generates information that is highly diversified yet integrated, thus creating patterns of high complexity. Following initial proposals [15–17], several approaches have been developed to compute integrated information [3,4,6,8,12]. Some of these were constructed for networks with discrete/binary states, others for continuous state variables. In this paper, we will consider stochastic network dynamics with continuous state variables because this class of networks model many biological as well as communication systems that generate multivariate time-series signals. We want to study the precise analytic relationship between the information integrated by these networks and the couplings that parameterize their structure and dynamics. Our main finding is that tuning the dynamical operating point of a network towards the edge of criticality leads to a high rate of network information integration and that remains consistent across network topologies.

2   Methods

We consider complex networks with stochastic dynamics. The state of each node is given by a continuous random variable pertaining to a Gaussian distribution. For many realistic applications, Gaussian distributed variables are fairly reasonable abstractions. The state of the network $\mathbf{X_t}$ at time t is taken as a multivariate Gaussian variable with distribution $\mathbf{P_{X_t}}(\mathbf{x_t})$. $\mathbf{x_t}$ denotes an instantiation of $\mathbf{X_t}$ with components x_t^i (i going from 1 to n, n being the number of nodes). When the network makes a transition from an initial state $\mathbf{X_0}$ to a state $\mathbf{X_1}$ at time $t = 1$, observing the final state generates information about the system's initial state. The information generated equals the reduction in uncertainty regarding the initial state $\mathbf{X_0}$. This is given by the conditional entropy $\mathbf{H(X_0|X_1)}$. In order to extract that part of the information generated by the system as a whole, over and above that generated individually by its irreducible parts, one computes the relative conditional entropy given by the Kullback-Leibler divergence of the conditional distribution $\mathbf{P_{X_0|X_1=x'}}(\mathbf{x})$ of the system with respect to the joint conditional distributions $\prod_{k=1}^{n} \mathbf{P_{M_0^k|M_1^k=m'}}$ of its irreducible parts [3]. Denoting this as Φ, we have

$$\Phi(\mathbf{X_0} \rightarrow \mathbf{X_1} = \mathbf{x'}) = D_{KL}\left(\mathbf{P_{X_0|X_1=x'}} \middle\| \prod_{k=1}^{n} \mathbf{P_{M_0^k|M_1^k=m'}}\right) \qquad (1)$$

where state variables $\mathbf{X_0}$ and $\mathbf{X_1}$ can be decomposed as a direct sum $\mathbf{X_0} = \bigoplus_{k=1}^{n} \mathbf{M_0^k}$ and $\mathbf{X_1} = \bigoplus_{k=1}^{n} \mathbf{M_1^k}$ respectively. To have a measure that is independent of any particular instantiation of the final state $\mathbf{x'}$, we average Eq. (1) with respect to final states to obtain

$$\langle \Phi \rangle (\mathbf{X_0} \rightarrow \mathbf{X_1}) = -\mathbf{H(X_0|X_1)} + \sum_{k=1}^{n} \mathbf{H(M_0^k|M_1^k)} \qquad (2)$$

This is the definition of integrated information that we will use [3]. The state variable at each time $t = 0$ and $t = 1$ follows a multivariate Gaussian distribution $\mathbf{X_0} \sim \mathcal{N}(\bar{\mathbf{x}}_0, \mathbf{\Sigma}(\mathbf{X_0}))$ and $\mathbf{X_1} \sim \mathcal{N}(\bar{\mathbf{x}}_1, \mathbf{\Sigma}(\mathbf{X_1}))$ respectively. The generative model for this system is equivalent to a multi-variate auto-regressive process [7]

$$\mathbf{X_1} = \mathcal{A}\,\mathbf{X_0} + \mathbf{E_1} \tag{3}$$

where $\mathcal{A}$ is the weighted adjacency matrix of the network and E_1 is Gaussian noise. Taking the mean and covariance respectively on both sides of this equation, while holding the residual independent of the regression variables gives

$$\bar{\mathbf{x}}_1 = \mathcal{A}\,\bar{\mathbf{x}}_0 \qquad \mathbf{\Sigma}(\mathbf{X_1}) = \mathcal{A}\,\mathbf{\Sigma}(\mathbf{X_0})\,\mathcal{A}^{\mathbf{T}} + \mathbf{\Sigma}(\mathbf{E}) \tag{4}$$

In the absence of any external inputs, stationary solutions of a stochastic linear dynamical system as in Eq. (3) are fluctuations about the origin. Therefore, we can shift coordinates to set the means $\bar{\mathbf{x}}_0$ and consequently $\bar{\mathbf{x}}_1$ to the zero. The second equality in Eq. (4) is the discrete-time Lyapunov equation and its solution will give us the covariance matrix of the state variables. The conditional entropy for a multivariate Gaussian variable was computed in [8]

$$\mathbf{H}(\mathbf{X_0}|\mathbf{X_1}) = \frac{1}{2}n\log(2\pi e) - \frac{1}{2}\log\left[\det \mathbf{\Sigma}(\mathbf{X_0}|\mathbf{X_1})\right] \tag{5}$$

and depends on the conditional covariance matrix. Substituting in Eq. (2) yields

$$\langle \Phi \rangle (\mathbf{X_0} \to \mathbf{X_1}) = \frac{1}{2}\log\left[\frac{\prod_{k=1}^{n}\det \mathbf{\Sigma}(\mathbf{M_0^k}|\mathbf{M_1^k})}{\det \mathbf{\Sigma}(\mathbf{X_0}|\mathbf{X_1})}\right] \tag{6}$$

In order to compute the conditional covariance matrix we make use of the identity (proof of this identity for the Gaussian case was demonstrated in [7])

$$\mathbf{\Sigma}(\mathbf{X}|\mathbf{Y}) = \mathbf{\Sigma}(\mathbf{X}) - \mathbf{\Sigma}(\mathbf{X}, \mathbf{Y})\mathbf{\Sigma}(\mathbf{Y})^{-1}\mathbf{\Sigma}(\mathbf{X}, \mathbf{Y})^{\mathbf{T}} \tag{7}$$

Computing $\mathbf{\Sigma}(\mathbf{X_0}, \mathbf{X_1}) = \mathbf{\Sigma}(\mathbf{X_0})\,\mathcal{A}^{\mathbf{T}}$ and using the above identity, we get

$$\mathbf{\Sigma}(\mathbf{X_0}|\mathbf{X_1}) = \mathbf{\Sigma}(\mathbf{X_0}) - \mathbf{\Sigma}(\mathbf{X_0})\,\mathcal{A}^{\mathbf{T}}\,\mathbf{\Sigma}(\mathbf{X_1})^{-1}\mathcal{A}\,\mathbf{\Sigma}(\mathbf{X_0})^{\mathbf{T}} \tag{8}$$

$$\mathbf{\Sigma}(\mathbf{M_0^k}|\mathbf{M_1^k}) = \mathbf{\Sigma}(\mathbf{M_0^k}) - \mathbf{\Sigma}(\mathbf{M_0^k})\,\mathcal{A}^{\mathbf{T}}\big|_k\,\mathbf{\Sigma}(\mathbf{M_1^k})^{-1}\mathcal{A}\big|_k\,\mathbf{\Sigma}(\mathbf{M_0^k})^{\mathbf{T}} \tag{9}$$

the conditional covariance for the whole system and that for its parts respectively. The variable $\mathbf{M_0^k}$ refers to the state of the kth node at $t = 0$ and $\mathcal{A}\big|_k$ denotes the (trivial) restriction of the adjacency matrix to the kth node. Note, that for linear multi-variate systems, a unique fixed point always exists. We want to find stable stationary solutions of this system. In that regime, the multi-variate probability distribution of states approaches stationarity and the covariance matrix converges, such that $\mathbf{\Sigma}(\mathbf{X_1}) = \mathbf{\Sigma}(\mathbf{X_0})$ (here $t = 0$ and $t = 1$ refer to time-points after the system has converged to its fixed point). Then the discrete-time Lyapunov equations can be solved iteratively for the stable covariance matrix $\mathbf{\Sigma}(\mathbf{X_t})$.

For networks with symmetric adjacency matrix and independent Gaussian noise, the solution takes a particularly simple form

$$\Sigma(\mathbf{X_t}) = \left(1 - \mathcal{A}^2\right)^{-1} \Sigma(\mathbf{E}) \tag{10}$$

and for the parts, we have

$$\Sigma(\mathbf{M_0^k}) = \Sigma(\mathbf{X_0})\big|_{\mathbf{k}} \tag{11}$$

given by the restriction of the full covariance matrix on the kth component. Note that Eq. (11) is not the same as taking Eq. (10) on the restricted adjacency matrix as that would mean that the kth node has been explicitly severed from the rest of the network. In fact, Eq. (11) is the variance of the kth node while it is still part of the network and $\langle \Phi \rangle$ yields the amount of information that is still greater than that of the sum of these connected parts. Inserting Eqs. (8), (9), (10) and (11) into Eq. (6) yields $\langle \Phi \rangle$ as a function of network weights for symmetric networks[1].

3   Results

Using the mathematical tools described above, we now compute exact analytic solutions for $\langle \Phi \rangle$ for the 6 networks shown in Fig. 1 below. Each of these networks have 8 dimensional adjacency matrices with bi-directional weights (though our analysis does not depend on that and works as well with directed graphs). We want to determine the characteristics of $\langle \Phi \rangle$ as a function of network weights, which we keep as free parameters. However, in order to constrain the space of parameters, we shall set all weights to a single parameter, the global coupling strength g. This gives us $\langle \Phi \rangle$ as a function of g. The analytic results for each network labeled from A to F are shown in Eqs. (12), (13), (14), (15), (16) and (17) respectively. These are computed for a single time-step, when the dynamics of the system lies in the stable stationary regime.

$$\langle \Phi \rangle_A = \frac{1}{2} \log \frac{\left(1 - 43g^2\right)^8}{\left(1 - 50g^2 + 49g^4\right)^8} \tag{12}$$

$$\langle \Phi \rangle_B = \frac{1}{2} \log \frac{B_1 \cdot B_2 \cdot B_3 \cdot B_4 \cdot B_5}{\left(-1 + g^2\right)^4 \left(1 - 8g^2 + 4g^4\right)^6 \left(1 - 17g^2 + 72g^4 - 64g^6 + 16g^8\right)^8} \tag{13}$$

where

$$B_1 = \left(1 - 15g^2 + 56g^4 - 56g^6 + 16g^8\right)$$
$$B_2 = \left(1 - 15g^2 + 54g^4 - 54g^6 + 16g^8\right)$$
$$B_3 = \left(1 - 22g^2 + 159g^4 - 426g^6 + 336g^8 - 80g^{10}\right)^2$$
$$B_4 = \left(1 - 21g^2 + 147g^4 - 401g^6 + 374g^8 - 136g^{10} + 16g^{12}\right)^2$$
$$B_5 = \left(1 - 23g^2 + 183g^4 - 612g^6 + 835g^8 - 526g^{10} + 152g^{12} - 16g^{14}\right)^2$$

---

[1] For the case of asymmetric weights, the entries of the covariance matrix cannot be explicitly expressed as a matrix equation. However, they may still be solved by Jordan decomposition of both sides of the Lyapunov equation.

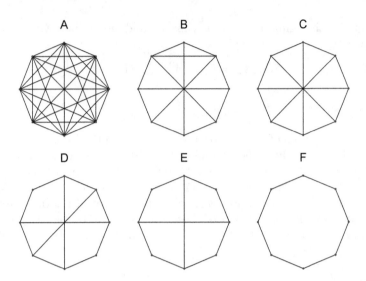

Fig. 1. Graphs of 6 networks, from the most densely connected (A) to the least (F).

$$\langle \Phi \rangle_C = \frac{1}{2} \log \frac{\left(1 - 13g^2 + 41g^4 - 17g^6\right)^8}{\left(1 - 16g^2 + 70g^4 - 64g^6 + 9g^8\right)^8} \tag{14}$$

$$\langle \Phi \rangle_D = \frac{1}{2} \log \frac{D_1 \cdot D_2 \cdot D_3}{\left(1 - 4g^2\right)^6 \left(-1 + g^2\right)^6 \left(1 - 6g^2 + g^4\right)^6 \left(1 - 10g^2 + 17g^4 - 4g^6\right)^8} \tag{15}$$

where

$$D_1 = \left(1 - 13g^2 + 49g^4 - 55g^6 + 10g^8\right)^2$$

$$D_2 = \left(1 - 13g^2 + 49g^4 - 61g^6 + 20g^8\right)^2$$

$$D_3 = \left(1 - 18g^2 + 115g^4 - 317g^6 + 368g^8 - 153g^{1}0 + 20g^{1}2\right)^4$$

$$\langle \Phi \rangle_E = \frac{1}{2} \log \frac{\left(1 - 2g^2\right)^8 \left(1 - 9g^2 + 18g^4\right)^4 \left(1 - 10g^2 + 25g^4 - 8g^6\right)^4}{\left(1 - 14g^2 + 65g^4 - 116g^6 + 64g^8\right)^8} \tag{16}$$

$$\langle \Phi \rangle_F = \frac{1}{2} \log \frac{\left(1 - 4g^2 + 2g^4\right)^8}{\left(1 - 6g^2 + 8g^4\right)^8} \tag{17}$$

In Fig. 2 we plot characteristic $\langle \Phi \rangle$ profiles for each network, based on the above solutions. This figure highlights a couple of interesting features about integrated information. First of all, irrespective of topology, all networks approach a pole at some value of g, near which, the integrated information of that network is extremely high. Further, we have checked that the location of the pole is precisely the critical point after which the largest eigenvalue of the network slips outside of the radius of stability. However, differences in network topologies do play a role in placing each network's $\langle \varPhi \rangle$ profile in distinct regions of the coupling phase space. Figure 2 shows an ordering of these profiles: the most densely packed networks lie towards the left end, while the least densely connected ones are more on the right.

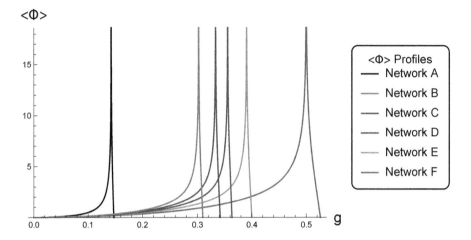

Fig. 2. $\langle \varPhi \rangle$ profiles showing an ordering, for the most densely connected network on the left to the least on the right.

4 Discussion

In this paper, we have developed a rigorous formulation of earlier ideas on information-theoretic complexity measures and applied it to explicitly compute the integrated information of networks with linear stochastic dynamics. We obtain exact analytic results for $\langle \varPhi \rangle$ as a function of the network's coupling parameter. We find poles in solutions of $\langle \varPhi \rangle$ at criticality, leading to high information integration near the edge of criticality. This implies that it is not only the network's topology that determines how much information it can integrate, but also its dynamical operating point. As a matter of fact, operating near the edge of criticality leads to a sharp increase in $\langle \varPhi \rangle$, irrespective of network topology. If $\langle \varPhi \rangle$ is taken as a proxy for a system's information processing capacity, it implies that operating near the edge of criticality is favorable for optimal information processing. This can be particularly beneficial in designing communication networks and also in understanding information processes in biological networks. In fact, recently it has been found that the resting-state dynamics of large-scale brain networks operates just at the edge of a bifurcation [11]. Indeed, from an information-theoretic perspective, it is interesting to check whether the reason why complex non-linear systems such as the brain might operate at the edge of criticality is because that is where optimal information processing may occur. Another interesting application of our formalism would be to investigate the integrated information associated to spontaneous activity of networks of cultured neurons. The work of [14] has shown that the emergence of coherent activity in neuronal cultures is driven by specifications of both, the network topology and dynamics. Our results in this paper have indeed emphasized the interplay of topology with dynamics. Therefore, as a next step, it might be reasonable to consider measures such as $\langle \Phi \rangle$ for quantifying collective phenomenon in controlled experimental settings.

More generally, information-based measures, like the one we have discussed above, may be useful as comparative measures of network information processing, which can then be related to the system's overall functions. For instance, it would be interesting to apply these measures to neurophysiologically-grounded network reconstructions of the brain such as those described in [1,2,5,9,10,13] in order to calibrate the informational complexity of brain networks in either the resting-state or during a task. As a measure of dynamical complexity, we see extensions of $\langle \Phi \rangle$ as clinically useful measures for quantifying network-level brain disorders, including those related to consciousness. More specifically, it can be used for assessing clinical levels of consciousness in patients with coma or in vegetative states compared to healthy controls. Just as metabolic activity serves as a measure of arousal in living tissue, in the same sense, with respect to information processes in systems biology, $\langle \Phi \rangle$ might be useful as a potential measure of awareness in cognitive agents. Furthermore, these measures may also be thought of as comparative tools for understanding differences in information processing between biological and non-biological systems. A classic question in this regard is how much does the human brain differ from the internet at the level of global information processing?

Acknowledgments. This work has been supported by the European Research Council's CDAC project: "The Role of Consciousness in Adaptive Behavior: A Combined Empirical, Computational and Robot based Approach" (ERC-2013-ADG 341196).

References

1. Arsiwalla, X.D., Betella, A., Martínez, E., Omedas, P., Zucca, R., Verschure, P.: The dynamic connectome: a tool for large scale 3d reconstruction of brain activity in real time. In: Rekdalsbakken, W., Bye, R., Zhang, H. (eds.) 27th European Conference on Modeling and Simulation (ECMS), Alesund, Norway (2013)
2. Arsiwalla, X.D., Dalmazzo, D., Zucca, R., Betella, A., Brandi, S., Martinez, E., Omedas, P., Verschure, P.: Connectomics to semantomics: addressing the brain's big data challenge. Procedia Comput. Sci. **53**, 48–55 (2015)
3. Arsiwalla, X.D., Verschure, P.: Computing information integration in brain networks. In: Wierzbicki, A., Brandes, U., Schweitzer, F., Pedreschi, D. (eds.) NetSci-X 2016. LNCS, vol. 9564, pp. 136–146. Springer, Heidelberg (2015). doi:10.1007/978-3-319-28361-6_11

4. Arsiwalla, X.D., Verschure, P.F.: Integrated information for large complex networks. In: The 2013 International Joint Conference on Neural Networks (IJCNN), pp. 1–7. IEEE (2013)
5. Arsiwalla, X.D., Zucca, R., Betella, A., Martinez, E., Dalmazzo, D., Omedas, P., Deco, G., Verschure, P.: Network dynamics with brainx3: a large-scale simulation of the human brain network with real-time interaction. Front. Neuroinf. 9(2) (2015). http://www.frontiersin.org/neuroinformatics/10.3389/fninf.2015.00002/abstract
6. Balduzzi, D., Tononi, G.: Integrated information in discrete dynamical systems: motivation and theoretical framework. PLoS Comput. Biol. 4(6), e1000091 (2008)
7. Barrett, A.B., Barnett, L., Seth, A.K.: Multivariate granger causality and generalized variance. Phys. Rev. E 81(4), 041907 (2010)
8. Barrett, A.B., Seth, A.K.: Practical measures of integrated information for time-series data. PLoS Comput. Biol. 7(1), e1001052 (2011)
9. Betella, A., Bueno, E.M., Kongsantad, W., Zucca, R., Arsiwalla, X.D., Omedas, P., Verschure, P.F.: Understanding large network datasets through embodied interaction in virtual reality. In: Proceedings of the 2014 Virtual Reality International Conference, p. 23. ACM (2014)
10. Betella, A., Cetnarski, R., Zucca, R., Arsiwalla, X.D., Martinez, E., Omedas, P., Mura, A., Verschure, P.: BrainX3: embodied exploration of neural data. In: Virtual Reality International Conference (VRIC 2014), Laval, France (2014)
11. Deco, G., Ponce-Alvarez, A., Mantini, D., Romani, G.L., Hagmann, P., Corbetta, M.: Resting-state functional connectivity emerges from structurally and dynamically shaped slow linear fluctuations. J. Neurosci. 33(27), 11239–11252 (2013)
12. Oizumi, M., Albantakis, L., Tononi, G.: From the phenomenology to the mechanisms of consciousness: integrated information theory 3.0. PLoS Comput. Biol. 10(5), e1003588 (2014)
13. Omedas, P., Betella, A., Zucca, R., Arsiwalla, X.D., Pacheco, D., Wagner, J., Lingenfelser, F., Andre, E., Mazzei, D., Lanatá, A., Tognetti, A., de Rossi, D., Grau, A., Goldhoorn, A., Guerra, E., Alquezar, R., Sanfeliu, A., Verschure, P.: XIM-engine: a software framework to support the development of interactive applications that uses conscious and unconscious reactions in immersive mixed reality. In: Proceedings of the 2014 Virtual Reality International Conference, VRIC 2014, p. 26. ACM (2014)
14. Orlandi, J.G., Soriano, J., Alvarez-Lacalle, E., Teller, S., Casademunt, J.: Noise focusing and the emergence of coherent activity in neuronal cultures. Nat. Phys. 9(9), 582–590 (2013)
15. Tononi, G.: An information integration theory of consciousness. BMC Neurosci. 5(1), 42 (2004)
16. Tononi, G., Sporns, O.: Measuring information integration. BMC Neurosci. 4(1), 31 (2003)
17. Tononi, G., Sporns, O., Edelman, G.M.: A measure for brain complexity: relating functional segregation and integration in the nervous system. Proc. Nat. Acad. Sci. 91(11), 5033–5037 (1994)

Comparison of Graph Node Distances
on Clustering Tasks

Felix Sommer[(✉)], François Fouss, and Marco Saerens

LSM and ICTEAM, Université catholique de Louvain,
Chaussée de Binche 151, 7000 Mons, Belgium
{felix.sommer,francois.fouss,marco.saerens}@ucLouvain.be

Abstract. This work presents recent developments in graph node distances and tests them empirically on social network databases of various sizes and types. We compare two versions of a distance-based kernel k-means algorithm with the well-established Louvain method. The first version is a classic kernel k-means approach, the second version additionally makes use of node weights with the Sum-over-Forests density index. Both kernel k-means algorithms employ a variety of classic and modern distances. We compare the results of all three algorithms using statistical measures and an overall rank-comparison to ascertain their capabilities in community detection. Results show that two recently introduced distances outperform the others, on our tested datasets.

Keywords: Clustering · Graph theory · Kernel k-means · Communtiy detection

1 Introduction

Clustering is a very common task in data analysis applications. It is widely used for many problems, for example, in social networks, biology, customer relationship management, advertising, etc. Grouping similar items together can lead to interesting and useful insights into data. Given today's computing power and availability of large amounts of data, these analyses become more and more important in a wide array of applications.

In clustering the k-means approach is very popular due to its relative simplicity, ease of implementation as well as low computational complexity. Distance-based clustering runs into limits, unfortunately, and therefore more elaborate methods, such as kernel k-means, were developed. Kernel k-kmeans in particular is used for clustering on graphs, which is commonly employed as a method for community detection, that is, finding similar nodes in a given graph and grouping them together. In this work we try to establish a first empirical comparison of two different kernel k-means approaches, and more importantly of the underlying kernels, distances, or dissimilarities. It is fundamental and important that a distance between nodes takes a graph's connectivity into account and thus far no analysis or comparison has been carried out to that effect.

© Springer International Publishing Switzerland 2016
A.E.P. Villa et al. (Eds.): ICANN 2016, Part I, LNCS 9886, pp. 192–201, 2016.
DOI: 10.1007/978-3-319-44778-0_23

Brief Related Work and Contributions. The distance between a graph's nodes is of particular importance in regard to clustering effectiveness. Existing popular distances have certain drawbacks. For example, the shortest-path distance does not convey information about the degree of connectivity between the nodes, which can lead to the problem that the presence of many indirect paths between nodes can suggest some kind of (non-existant) proximity between them. Similarly, with larger graphs the commute-time distance converges to a meaningless limit function (see [17,33,34]), which can lead to the so-called [33] "lost in space" effect and is related to the fact that a simple random walk mixes before hitting its target [17]. Recent developments lead to the following distances or dissimilarities in order to allow removing or alleviating these limitations.

Chebotarev introduced in [6] a new class of distances for graph nodes whose construction is based on the matrix forest theorem [7]. The distance reduces to the unweighted shortest-path and the commute-time distances (up to a scaling factor) at the limiting values of its parameter.

Von Luxburg et al. [33] proposed a corrected version of the commute-time distance, removing the undesirable terms. The main idea is to express the commute-time distance as a series of terms of decreasing significance and remove the two first terms that produce the "lost in space" effect (see also [13]).

The randomized shortest-path (RSP) [20,36] dissimilarity interpolates between the shortest-path distance and half the commute-time distance based on a pure random walk – the random walker therefore adopts a "randomized" strategy biased towards the paths with lowest cost (see [28] for details).

[14,20] equally proposed to base a distance on the computation of the Helmholtz free energy (FE), very similar to the RSP dissimilarity, that does not suffer from its drawbacks: it is a distance measure. Instead of cost, the random walker chooses a path that minimizes free energy.

The p-resistance distance [1,16] considers a graph as an electrical network, with edges having resistances. The distance between two nodes is then represented by the global resistance of the entire circuit between them. Despite its theoretically sound foundation, we do not test the p-resistance distance, as it lacks closed form expression and hence requires solving a minimization problem for each pair of nodes separately to obtain the distance, which is not feasible for networks of medium size.

However, up until now in-spite of their interesting theoretic bases, these distances have not been tested empirically, which is nevertheless an important step in their more widespread adoption and utilization. Therefore, in our work we: (i) analyze if and how an approach with weighted nodes, based on density, can improve clustering quality; (ii) compare these different distances for clustering tasks based on social network data, in order to identify a possible "best" distance; (iii) evaluate in what measure these distances compare to the sigmoid commute-time kernel k-means – a baseline which gives very good results already [35] – by solely changing the employed distance; (iv) finally, compare the kernel k-means clustering to the Louvain method [2], as the defacto standard and baseline in community detection.

2   Methodology

We test the following methods: (i) Kernel k-means, (ii) Weighted kernel k-means, (iii) Louvain method [2].

Kernel k-means is used as one of the testing algorithms. It is largely inspired by [4,19] and corresponds to a two-step iterative algorithm based on a distance, or dissimilarity, matrix instead of features. Given a meaningful, symmetric distance matrix Δ, containing the distances Δ_{ij}, the goal is to partition the nodes by minimizing the total *within-cluster sum of distances*. For details, see [13,35]. We denote this method with the label *km* followed by the employed kernel (see later).

Weighted Kernel k-means. The weighted kernel k-means algorithm is a modification of the kernel k-means algorithm mentioned in the previous paragraph. As such, it is again a two-step algorithm. In the first step each node is allocated to the closest node centroid–which we call prototype–according to the employed distance. For this variant, each node (each sample) is weighted by a local density measuring the Sum-over-Forests density index (see [30]). In the second step the prototypes are recomputed, again using the weighted distance and thus yielding new centroids for each cluster. These two steps represent the classical k-means approach of assigning nodes to centroids and then updating by calculating new centroids; they are repeated until convergence. For details on this version of the algorithm see [32]. We denote this method with the label *wkm* followed by the employed kernel (see later).

Louvain Method. The idea behind the Louvain method [2] is to first perform an *iterative local optimization* (see, e.g., [12]) for seeking local minimum of a specific criterion (step 1) – in our case, the modularity criterion [24–27]. Then, the second phase, called the *nodes aggregation* or *coarsening*, step whose purpose is to build a new agglomerated graph (step 2), is performed. These two steps are repeated until no further improvement of the employed criterion can be achieved. The details are described in the original work [2]. We denote this method with the label *LV*.

Experimental Methodology. For both kernel k-means approaches, we test six different kernels, which are covered in the following section. Each kernel is run with both k-means approaches. As such, we test a total of 13 different clustering methods.

Since the k-means approaches depend on a random initialization of the prototypes, we run 50 trials with different initializations and keep the partition showing the lowest *within-cluster sum-of-distances* among them. This procedure is repeated for 50 times and the results in the experiments section represent the mean of these 50 best trial results.

Prior to the experiments we optimize the parameters for each kernel on a special parameter tuning set. We test a very wide range of approximately 200 parameter values per kernel, including extremely small as well as extremely large values–within the limits of feasible values. Refer to Table 2 for the final parameter choices.

Additionally, as the weighted kernel k-means algorithm uses the Sum-over-Forests density index [30], its parameter θ has to be considered. Pretests [32] have shown that in certain scenarios results worsened given a large value of θ. Therefore, we fixed θ to a value of 1 for the comparison purposes of this work.

The Louvain method was used as a baseline comparison and determines the natural number of classes for each dataset by itself, it is thus not exactly comparable to the k-means algorithms which require the number of clusters.

All algorithms were implemented in Matlab.

3   Distances and Kernels

Let us consider a graph $G = (V, E)$ consisting of a set of n nodes or vertices V and a set of edges E. Each edge linking two nodes i and j is associated with a positive scalar $c_{ij} \geq 0$ representing the immediate cost of following this edge. The cost matrix $\mathbf{C}$ is the matrix containing the immediate costs c_{ij} as elements. Given an adjacency matrix $\mathbf{A}$, with its elements denoted a_{ij}, indicating the affinity between nodes i and j, instead of a cost matrix, we can compute the corresponding costs from the relation $c_{ij} = 1/a_{ij}$. From this matrix we can compute its Laplacian matrix $\mathbf{L} = \mathbf{D} - \mathbf{A}$, with the diagonal matrix $\mathbf{D} = \mathbf{Diag}(\mathbf{A}^\mathsf{T}\mathbf{e})$, that contains the column sums of $\mathbf{A}$. Here, $\mathbf{e}$ is a column vector full of ones and T signifies the transpose.

The remainder of this section briefly presents the distances and kernels used in our experiments. Please note that the distances and dissimilarities are transformed into a kernel $\mathbf{K}$ using the relationship $\mathbf{K} = -\frac{1}{2}\mathbf{H}\boldsymbol{\Delta}^{(2)}\mathbf{H}$, where $\boldsymbol{\Delta}^{(2)}$ is a square distance or dissimilarity matrix, and the centering matrix $\mathbf{H} = \mathbf{I} - \frac{\mathbf{E}}{n}$ (see [3]), where $\mathbf{E}$ is a matrix full of ones and n is the number of nodes. We omit details on the shortest-path (SP) distance, as these are readily available in the literature (see, e.g., [9]).

Randomized Shortest-Path (RSP) Dissimilarity. This aforementioned dissimilarity interpolates between the shortest-path distance (see, e.g., [20, 28, 37]) and half the commute-time distance based on a pure random walk. The random walker adopts a *randomized* strategy biased towards the paths with lowest cost ([20, 28], see also [13]). The randomized shortest-path cost corresponds to the *expected cost* over all paths connecting these two nodes. With the cost matrix $\mathbf{C}$, the transition probability matrix of the natural random walk $\mathbf{P} = \mathbf{D}^{-1}\mathbf{A}$, and the inverse temperature $\beta = 1/T$ parameter we can define the matrix $\mathbf{W} = \exp(-\beta\mathbf{C}) \circ \mathbf{P}$, where $\circ$ marks element-wise multiplication. Using this matrix we define the fundamental matrix of the killed, but non-absorbing Markov Chain $\mathbf{Z} = (\mathbf{I} - \mathbf{W})^{-1}$, and furthermore the matrix $\mathbf{S} = (\mathbf{Z}(\mathbf{C} \circ \mathbf{W})) \div \mathbf{Z}$, where $\div$ marks element-wise division. This step enables us to compute the expected cost of hitting walks as $\bar{\mathbf{C}} = \mathbf{S} - \mathbf{e}\mathbf{d}_\mathbf{S}^\mathsf{T}$. Recall, that $\mathbf{e}$ is a column vector of ones and here, $\mathbf{d_S}$ is a vector of the diagonal elements of $\mathbf{S}$. We can then symmetrize to obtain the dissimilarity matrix:

$$\boldsymbol{\Delta}^{\mathrm{RSP}} = (\bar{\mathbf{C}} + \bar{\mathbf{C}}^{\mathsf{T}})/2. \tag{1}$$

Free Energy (FE) Distance. This distance is based on the minimum Helmholtz free energy, which was called the potential distance in [14]. This minimization of free energy can be considered a variant of the randomized shortest-path dissimilarity (see previous section) [14,20]. We define the matrices $\mathbf{C}$, $\mathbf{W}$, $\mathbf{Z}$ and parameter β as we did for the randomized shortest-path above and compute the free energy between all pairs of nodes $\boldsymbol{\Phi} = \log(\mathbf{Z})/\beta$. Symmetrization then yields the free energy distance matrix [14,20]:

$$\boldsymbol{\Delta}^{\mathrm{FE}} = (\boldsymbol{\Phi} + \boldsymbol{\Phi}^{\mathsf{T}})/2. \tag{2}$$

Sigmoid Commute-Time (SCT) Similarity. This similarity has already proven useful in clustering applications [35,36]. It is obtained by applying a sigmoid transformation [29] on the commute-time kernel. The commute-time kernel without the sigmoid transformation does not work well as a distance measure between nodes in clustering [35], and is thus not included in our comparison. The kernel is based on the average commute time as the average number of steps a random walker takes, when starting in one node, going to another node and then back to the starting node. The aim of the sigmoid function is to normalize the range of similarities in a $[0,1]$ interval, in order to increase the contrast between the different clusters. We compute the kernel matrix using the Moore-Penrose pseudo-inverse $\mathbf{L}^+$ of the Laplacian matrix $\mathbf{L}$, with a normalizing factor σ, set to the standard deviation of the elements of $\mathbf{L}^+$, and α as a parameter (see also [13,35]):

$$\mathbf{K}_{\mathrm{SCT}} = \frac{1}{1 + \exp(-\alpha \mathbf{L}^+/\sigma)} \tag{3}$$

Corrected Commute-Time (CCT) Distance. For large graphs, the commute-time similarity tends to depend only on the degrees of the starting and ending nodes [33]. In order to alleviate this drawback, a correction term was proposed in [33] leading to the corrected commute-time distance. Using a matrix similar to the modularity matrix, we define $\mathbf{M} = \mathbf{D}^{-\frac{1}{2}}(\mathbf{A} - \frac{\mathbf{d}\mathbf{d}^{\mathsf{T}}}{\mathrm{vol}(G)})\mathbf{D}^{-\frac{1}{2}}$, where $\mathbf{d}$ is a vector of the diagonal elements of $\mathbf{D}$ and $\mathrm{vol}(G)$ is the volume of the graph, i.e., the sum of all elements of the adjacency matrix $\mathbf{A}$. We then derive the corrected commute-time kernel as follows ([33], see also [13]):

$$\mathbf{K}_{\mathrm{CCT}} = \mathbf{H}\mathbf{D}^{-\frac{1}{2}}\mathbf{M}(\mathbf{I} - \mathbf{M})^{-1}\mathbf{M}\mathbf{D}^{-\frac{1}{2}}\mathbf{H} \tag{4}$$

Logarithmic Forest (LF) Distance. Chebotarev introduced in [6] a new class of distances for graph nodes whose construction is based on the matrix forest theorem [5,7], and which reduces to the unweighted shortest-path and the commute-time distances (up to a scaling factor) at the limiting values of its parameter. Defining a new matrix $\mathbf{S}$ from the so-called regularized Laplacian kernel $\mathbf{K}_{RL} = (\mathbf{I} + \alpha\mathbf{L})^{-1}$ with $\alpha > 0$, such that $\mathbf{S} = (\alpha - 1)\log_\alpha \mathbf{K}_{RL}$ for $\alpha \neq 1$ and $\mathbf{S} = \ln \mathbf{K}_{RL}$ for $\alpha = 1$, the logarithmic forest distance matrix is defined as ([6], see also [13], recall, that $\mathbf{e}$ is a column vector of ones, and here $\mathbf{d_S}$ is a vector of the diagonal elements of $\mathbf{S}$):

$$\mathbf{\Delta}_{LF} = \mathbf{d_S}\mathbf{e}^\top + \mathbf{e}\mathbf{d_S^\top} - 2\mathbf{S}. \tag{5}$$

4   Experiments

Datasets. We investigate a total of 15 graphs, the smallest of which (Zachary's Karate club [38]) contains 34 nodes. The largest graph (a Newsgroup graph [23,35] with five classes) contains 999 nodes. We analyse a total of nine Newsgroup datasets. The remaining datasets are Football [15], political blogs [21], and three artificial Lancichinetti-Fortunato-Radicchi (LFR) graphs [22]. Table 1 shows some details on the datasets.

Evaluation Methods. To ascertain the algorithms' performance, we compute the adjusted rand index (ARI) [18], the normalized mutual information criterion (NMI) [8] as well as the classification rate. We compare the developed kernel k-means clustering methods to the Louvain method and amongst each other. This comparison is done using the raw numbers of the NMI given in Table 3. Furthermore, we perform two-by-two Wilcoxon signed-rank tests (see, e.g., [31]) and a multiple comparison test [11] based on a Friedman test [10], as shown in Fig. 1. The chart in this figure gives a graphical representation of the clustering methods ordered by their overall rank. Also, the statistical significance is indicated by the length and distance of the bars.

Results and Discussion. Based on our research questions we present and discuss the results. We omit the results from the classification rate and the ARI, as they show very similar behavior when compared to the NMI. (i) As can be seen from Table 3 as well as the multiple comparison test in Fig. 1, the weighted kernel k-means (wkm) does not manage to consistently improve on the results of the regular kernel k-means approach. It does perform better for some datasets, though. (ii) Comparing only kernels, irrespective of kernel weights, the RSP and FE-distance based kernels consistently

Table 1. Datasets

Name	Classes	Nodes	Edges
Football	12	115	613
LFR1	3	600	6142
LFR2	6	600	4807
LFR3	6	600	5233
News2cl1	2	400	33854
News2cl2	2	398	21480
News2cl3	2	399	36527
News3cl1	3	600	70591
News3cl2	3	598	68201
News3cl3	3	595	64169
News5cl1	5	998	176962
News5cl2	5	999	164452
News5cl3	5	997	155618
Polblogs	3	105	441
Zachary	2	34	78

Table 2. Algorithm overview

Name	Acronym		Equation	Parameter value
Corrected commute time	kmCCT	wkmCCT	Eq. (4)	$\alpha = 26$
Free energy	kmFE	wkmFE	Eq. (2)	$\theta = 0.1$
Logarithmic forest	kmLF	wkmLF	Eq. (5)	$\alpha = 1$
Randomized shortest-path	kmRSP	wkmRSP	Eq. (1)	$\theta = 0.03$
Sigmoid commute time	kmSCT	wkmSCT	Eq. (3)	$\alpha = 22$
Shortest-path	kmSP	wkmSP	See, e.g., [13]	–
Louvain	LV		See [2]	–

outperform the competition for the most part, but it is difficult to say that there is one "best" distance. The two-by-two Wilcoxon signed-rank tests comparing the NMI for the FE-distance to the four next competitors show that the FE-distance manages to outperform all but the RSP-distance to a statistically significant degree (kmSCT: $p < 2 \times 10^{-2}$; kmCCT: $p < 4 \times 10^{-3}$; kmLF: $p < 2 \times 10^{-3}$). However, it would seem that the performance strongly depends on the given dataset and varies depending on the dataset/kernel combination employed. Practically, all distances give better results than the SP-distance, which confirms that taking a graph's connectivity and further properties into account does indeed improve results for clustering tasks. (iii) In comparison to the SCT-distance based kernel, CCT most of the time improves on it slightly, whereas RSP and FE give clearly better results than both SCT and CCT. LF kernel-based clustering, however, shows equivalent performance as the SCT we deemed as a baseline for kernel k-means comparison. (iv) Both weighted and pure kernel k-means outperform the Louvain method on nearly all datasets and kernels. It is important to keep in mind, though, that unlike kernel k-means, the Louvain method derives the number of classes on its own.

Table 3. Normalized mutual information (NMI)

Dataset	kmCCT	kmFE	kmLF	kmRSP	kmSCT	kmSP	wkmCCT	wkmFE	wkmLF	wkmRSP	wkmSCT	wkmSP	LV
Football	0.7928	0.9061	0.9028	**0.9092**	0.8115	0.8575	0.7712	0.9057	0.9001	0.9083	0.8084	0.8515	0.6976
LFR1	**0.9904**	0.9811	0.8578	0.9830	0.9830	0.8899	0.9639	0.9671	0.7370	0.9904	0.9809	0.9263	0.9618
LFR2	1.0000	1.0000	0.9965	1.0000	1.0000	0.9856	1.0000	1.0000	0.9983	1.0000	1.0000	0.9656	0.8232
LFR3	0.9664	0.9932	0.9279	1.0000	0.9898	0.9886	0.9664	0.9832	0.9212	1.0000	0.9753	0.7800	0.8271
News2cl1	0.7944	0.8050	0.8381	0.7966	0.8174	0.6540	**0.8731**	0.7867	0.8157	0.7831	0.7965	0.6155	0.5734
News2cl2	0.5819	0.5909	0.5844	0.5797	0.5523	0.5159	0.5726	**0.6072**	0.5464	0.6037	0.5452	0.5461	0.4316
News2cl3	0.7577	0.8107	0.7482	0.7962	0.7857	**0.8592**	0.7460	0.8076	0.7427	0.8221	0.7544	0.8317	0.5859
News3cl1	0.7785	**0.7810**	0.7530	**0.7810**	0.7730	0.7426	0.7529	0.7306	0.7402	0.7365	0.7512	0.7087	0.6992
News3cl2	0.7616	**0.7968**	0.7585	0.7761	0.7282	0.6246	0.6933	0.7532	0.7362	0.7207	0.7096	0.5629	0.6612
News3cl3	0.7455	**0.7707**	0.7487	0.7300	0.7627	0.7203	0.6878	0.6719	0.6069	0.6766	0.7126	0.6457	0.6730
News5cl1	0.6701	0.6922	0.6143	**0.7078**	0.6658	0.6815	0.6456	0.6891	0.5722	0.6844	0.6519	0.6762	0.6840
News5cl2	0.6177	**0.6401**	0.5977	0.6243	0.6154	0.5970	0.5846	0.6227	0.5382	0.6144	0.5823	0.5831	0.6342
News5cl3	**0.6269**	0.6065	0.5729	0.5750	0.5712	0.4801	0.5766	0.5342	0.5122	0.5059	0.5078	0.4388	0.5717
Polblogs	0.5525	0.5813	0.5811	0.5815	0.5757	0.5605	0.5277	0.5809	0.5798	0.5815	0.5745	0.5531	**0.5975**
Zachary	1.0000	1.0000	1.0000	1.0000	1.0000	1.0000	1.0000	1.0000	1.0000	1.0000	1.0000	1.0000	0.9822

5   Conclusion and Further Work

This work presents a first empirical comparison of recent advances in graph distances. We compare six different graph kernels using two different clustering methods. The clustering performance depends on the dataset it is run on, but outperforms the Louvain method.

The results are strongly influenced by the choice of kernel, with the FE and RSP kernels showing an edge over the competition. The CCT

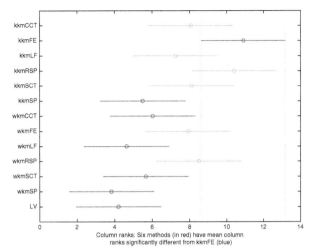

Fig. 1. Multiple comparison test on NMI

seems to provide a clear improvement over the SCT kernel. The SP kernel is clearly outperformed by the competition.

The weighted kernel k-means approach is almost always outperformed by the classic kernel k-means approach. Both methods underline the performance of the FE and RSP kernels.

Further work will be targeted towards (1) optimizing the individual distance parameters automatically based on the modularity criterion for each dataset, and (2) finding methods to estimate the number of clusters based on the modularity criterion for the kernel k-means algorithms.

Acknowledgements. We would like to thank our Master students Joëlle Van Damme and Augustin Collette for their valuable assistance in realizing this work. This work is supported in part by the FNRS through a PhD scholarship. This work was also partially supported by the Immediate and the Brufence projects funded by InnovIris (Brussels Region). We thank these institutions for giving us the opportunity to conduct both fundamental and applied research.

References

1. Bavaud, F., Guex, G.: Interpolating between random walks and shortest paths: a path functional approach. In: Aberer, K., Flache, A., Jager, W., Liu, L., Tang, J., Guéret, C. (eds.) SocInfo 2012. LNCS, vol. 7710, pp. 68–81. Springer, Heidelberg (2012)
2. Blondel, V.D., Guillaume, J.L., Lambiotte, R., Lefebvre, E.: Fast unfolding of communities in large networks. J. Stat. Mech. Theor. Exp. **2008**, P10008 (2008)
3. Borg, I., Groenen, P.: Modern Multidimensional Scaling. Springer, New York (1997)

4. Celeux, G., Diday, E., Govaert, G., Lechevallier, Y., Ralambondrainy, H.: Classification Automatique des Données. Dunod, Paris (1989)
5. Chebotarev, P., Shamis, E.: The matrix-forest theorem and measuring relations in small social groups. Autom. Remote Control **58**(9), 1505–1514 (1997)
6. Chebotarev, P.: A class of graph-geodetic distances generalizing the shortest-path and the resistance distances. Discrete Appl. Math. **159**(5), 295–302 (2011)
7. Chebotarev, P.: The graph bottleneck identity. Adv. Appl. Math. **47**(3), 403–413 (2011)
8. Collignon, A., Maes, F., Delaere, D., Vandermeulen, D., Suetens, P., Marchal, G.: Automated multi-modality image registration based on information theory. Inf. Process. Med. Imaging **3**, 263–274 (1995)
9. Cormen, T., Leiserson, C., Rivest, R., Stein, C.: Introduction to Algorithms, 3rd edn. The MIT Press, Cambridge (2009)
10. Daniel, W.: Applied Nonparametric Statistics. The Duxbury Advanced Series in Statistics and Decision Sciences. PWS-Kent Publications, Boston (1990)
11. Demšar, J.: Statistical comparisons of classifiers over multiple data sets. J. Mach. Learn. Res. **7**, 1–30 (2006)
12. Duda, R.O., Hart, P.E.: Pattern Classification and Scene Analysis. Wiley, New York (1973)
13. Fouss, F., Saerens, M., Shimbo, M.: Algorithms for Exploratory Link Analysis. Cambridge University Press (2016, to appear)
14. Françoisse, K., Kivimäki, I., Mantrach, A., Rossi, F., Saerens, M.: A bag-of-paths framework for network data analysis, pp. 1–36 (2013). arXiv:1302.6766
15. Girvan, M., Newman, M.E.J.: Community structure in social and biological networks. In: Proceedings of the National Academy of Sciences, vol. 99, pp. 7821–7826. National Academy of Sciences (2002)
16. Grady, L., Schwartz, E.: The graph analysis toolbox: image processing on arbitrary graphs. CAS/CNS Technical report Series (021) (2010)
17. Hashimoto, T., Sun, Y., Jaakkola, T.: From random walks to distances on unweighted graphs. In: Cortes, C., Lawrence, N.D., Lee, D.D., Sugiyama, M., Garnett, R. (eds.) Advances in Neural Information Processing Systems, vol. 28, pp. 3411–3419. Curran Associates, Inc. (2015)
18. Hubert, L., Arabie, P.: Comparing partitions. J. Classif. **2**(1), 193–218 (1985)
19. Kaufmann, L., Rousseeuw, P.: Finding Groups in Data: An Introduction to Cluster Analysis. Wiley, New York (1990)
20. Kivimäki, I., Lebichot, B., Saerens, M.: Developments in the theory of randomized shortest paths with a comparison of graph node distances. Physica A Stat. Mech. Appl. **393**, 600–616 (2014)
21. Krebs, V.: New political patterns (2008). http://www.orgnet.com/divided.html
22. Lancichinetti, A., Fortunato, S., Radicchi, F.: Benchmark graphs for testing community detection algorithms. Phys. Rev. E **78**(4), 46–110 (2008)
23. Lang, K.: 20 newsgroups dataset. http://bit.ly/lang-newsgroups
24. Newman, M.E.J.: Networks: An Introduction. Oxford University Press, New York (2010)
25. Newman, M.E.J.: Finding community structure in networks using the eigenvectors of matrices. Phys. Rev. E **74**(3), 036104 (2006)
26. Newman, M.E.J.: Modularity and community structure in networks. Proc. Natl. Acad. Sci. (USA) **103**, 8577–8582 (2006)
27. Newman, M.E.J., Girvan, M.: Finding and evaluating community structure in networks. Phys. Rev. E **69**, 026113 (2004)

28. Saerens, M., Achbany, Y., Fouss, F., Yen, L.: Randomized shortest-path problems: two related models. Neural Comput. **21**(8), 2363–2404 (2009)
29. Schölkopf, B., Smola, A.: Learning with Kernels. The MIT Press, Cambridge (2002)
30. Senelle, M., Garcia-Diez, S., Mantrach, A., Shimbo, M., Saerens, M., Fouss, F.: The sum-over-forests density index: identifying dense regions in a graph. IEEE Trans. Pattern Anal. Mach. Intell. **36**(6), 1268–1274 (2014). arXiv:1301.0725
31. Siegel, S.: Nonparametric Statistics for the Behavioral Sciences. McGraw-Hill, New York (1956)
32. Sommer, F., Fouss, F., Saerens, M.: Clustering using a Sum-Over-Forests weighted kernel k-means approach. LSM Working Paper 22 (2015)
33. von Luxburg, U., Radl, A., Hein, M.: Getting lost in space: large sample analysis of the commute distance. In: Proceedings of the 23th Neural Information Processing Systems Conference (NIPS 2010), pp. 2622–2630 (2010)
34. von Luxburg, U., Radl, A., Hein, M.: Hitting and commute times in large random neighborhood graphs. J. Mach. Learn. Res. **15**, 1751–1798 (2014)
35. Yen, L., Fouss, F., Decaestecker, C., Francq, P., Saerens, M.: Graph nodes clustering based on the commute-time Kernel. In: Zhou, Z.-H., Li, H., Yang, Q. (eds.) PAKDD 2007. LNCS (LNAI), vol. 4426, pp. 1037–1045. Springer, Heidelberg (2007)
36. Yen, L., Fouss, F., Decaestecker, C., Francq, P., Saerens, M.: Graph nodes clustering with the sigmoid commute-time kernel: a comprehensive study. Data Knowl. Eng. **68**(3), 338–361 (2008)
37. Yen, L., Mantrach, A., Shimbo, M., Saerens, M.: A family of dissimilarity measures between nodes generalizing both the shortest-path and the commute-time distances. In: Proceedings of the 14th SIGKDD International Conference on Knowledge Discovery and Data Mining (KDD 2008), pp. 785–793 (2008)
38. Zachary, W.W.: An information flow model for conflict and fission in small groups. J. Anthropol. Res. **33**, 452–473 (1977)

Higher Nervous Functions

Influence of Saliency and Social Impairments on the Development of Intention Recognition

Laura Cohen[⊠] and Aude Billard

Learning Algorithms and Systems Laboratory,
École Polytechnique Fédérale de Lausanne,
1015 Lausanne, Switzerland
laura.cohen@epfl.ch

Abstract. Among the symptoms of schizophrenia, deficits in the recognition of intention is one of the most studied. However, there is no cognitive model of intention recognition that takes into account both innate and environmental/developmental factors. This work proposes a developmental model of intention recognition based on a neural network. This model enables us to emulate different types of impairment. Particularly, the dopamine hypothesis of schizophrenia is simulated through an impairment of the visual saliency, and environmental influence of the behavior of the caregiver is evaluated.

Keywords: Intention recognition · Schizophrenia · Development · Neural networks

1 Introduction

Among the symptoms of schizophrenia, deficits in the recognition of others' intention is one of the most studied [1]. Literature related to this type of impairment is mainly focused on high-level cognitive processing, such as verbal theory of mind tasks. To achieve these high-level tasks, lower-level intention recognition (i.e. action level) is a prerequisite [2]. In the context of schizophrenia, there is no cognitive model of intention recognition that takes into account both innate and environmental/developmental factors, which constitutes an explanatory gap in our understanding of these effects and their interaction [3]. This work proposes a developmental model of intention recognition that is then exploited to emulate different types of impairment related to schizophrenia. In this paper, we focus on object-oriented actions. In this category of actions, the intention corresponds to the desired target object. Current models of intention recognition are mostly based on a comparator model [4–6]. This model exploits the fact that during the observation of an action, humans predict a sensory outcome based on an intention hypothesis. If the observed state at the next step fits to the prediction, the intention hypothesis is validated. This model can be criticized mainly on 2 aspects. First, this hypothesis is based on the motor component of the action. However, action monitoring and perception is mainly represented in

© Springer International Publishing Switzerland 2016
A.E.P. Villa et al. (Eds.): ICANN 2016, Part I, LNCS 9886, pp. 205–213, 2016.
DOI: 10.1007/978-3-319-44778-0_24

terms of their underlying goal [6]. Secondly, this model doesn't explain how the intention attribution capacity is learned through the development of the child. To overcome these limits, we propose a computational model of the development of this capacity through social interaction. To fit to the development of a human, the main issue is to avoid the need to give prior information in the model or in other words, to ground intentions into sensori-motor maps. This issue is known as the symbol grounding problem [7]. A solution to achieve this is to exploit sensori-motor contingencies that occur during interactions with social partners. In that context, we propose here to model the development of intention recognition through a sensori-motor architecture (PerAc) based on simple neural networks [8,9]. The simplicity of the networks guaranties a minimalistic solution for the development of complex abilities. We report on two experiments, (1) to validate our model comparatively to an infants study results and (2) to evaluate the effect of different types of impairment related to schizophrenia on the learning of intention recognition.

2   Experimental Protocol

In this paper, we argue that the intention recognition capacity can be developed by infants through simple interaction scenarios with a caregiver. To reproduce this interaction, a human participant plays the role of the caregiver and an avatar simulates the infant. The interaction starts with a learning phase during which the avatar generates random deictic gestures towards one of two objects. The caretaker takes the corresponding object to hand it to the avatar. During this phase, the model learns associations between its internal state and its visual perception. This learning is computed online. After learning, the model is able to reverse the process by predicting the intention based on the visual perception of the caretaker.

2.1   Model Validation

To validate our intention recognition model, we propose in a first experiment to reproduce the findings of a classical infant study. Infants' attribution of intentions to others' actions emerges in the first year of life. In an experiment proposed by Woodward et al., infants observe an actor performing objects-reaching actions [10,11]. Two objects are present in the scene. The first step is an habituation phase in which the actor reaches many times for the same object at the same position. Then, the objects' positions are reversed. If the actor reaches for the same goal in the new position (i.e. "new path" condition), the infants show less surprise than if the actor changed his goal but reaches to the same position (i.e. "new goal" condition). These conditions are illustrated on Fig. 1. The results show that infants from 3 to 9 months represent increasingly others' actions in terms of their goals (i.e. the target object) instead of their physical properties (i.e. the movements of the arm to grasp the goal-object). In this context, we reproduce the protocol of Woodward et al. with our architecture to show that

Fig. 1. Three different conditions exploited to test whether infants encode observed action in terms of the intention (i.e. the goal-object) or in terms of physical properties (i.e. the physical arm movement)

the encoding of the action in terms of goal and not in terms of path emerges from the proposed model. To simulate the habituation phase, the model learns only on one condition, i.e. the caretaker repeats the grabbing of the same object with the same hand, as shown on Fig. 1. The model is then tested on the other two conditions. The model is trained on 100 images of the caregiver, and tested on a database of 100 images for each test conditions. The process is repeated 10 times for each condition.

2.2   Model Impairment

In a second experiment, we propose to expose the model to different types of impairment. Recent studies emphasize the important role of developmental and social factors during childhood on the onset of schizophrenia [12]. Compared to previous models of intention recognition, our model has the capacity to simulate both developmental and innate impairments. In this experiment, these two aspects are explored.

(1) Schizophrenia has been related to a dysregulation of dopamine neurotransmission, as the effect of antipsychotic drugs is due to dopapamine D2 receptor blockade. Abnormal sub-cortical release of dopamine could lead to **aberrant salience assignment** to non-salient events [13]. The impairment of saliency is simulated by replacing some of the detected focus points on the input image by randomly extracted points. This method provides a metric to quantify the impairment of saliency in our system. This variable is noted N_{ip} (i.e. the number of impaired points).

(2) Convergent evidence supports an effect of **environmental risk factor** such as urban birth, prenatal stress, childhood trauma, migration and social isolation. Intention recognition learning requires a caretaker that mirrors the intention of the infant. It is a necessary condition to provide sensory-motor contingencies to the model. Based on these observations, we simulate the social environmental factors by variations of the number of images where the caretaker is acting accordingly to the intention of the avatar. We call

these coupled intentions a contingency. This variable is noted N_c (i.e. the number of contingencies). To extend the learning to more realistic contexts, we modify the protocol to learn to recognize two intentions (i.e. two goal-objects). The model is trained on 400 images of the caregiver, and tested on a database of 100 images per intention. The next section details the cognitive intention recognition architecture.

3   A Cognitive Model for Intention Recognition

To enable an online learning and to avoid the need to use prior information, the model of intention prediction is based on a PerAc (perception/action) architecture. The proposed architecture is shown on Fig. 2. The different modules of this architecture are detailed in the following sections.

3.1   Visual Perception

The visual system is based on the sequential exploration of P focus points extracted from the image perceived by the sensor. A gradient is extracted from the input image, that is convoluted with a difference of gaussian (DOG). The maxima of the resulting image correspond to the focus points (Fig. 3.1). To encode the orientation information, gradient patches are extracted around each focus points (Fig. 3.2). These patches are convoluted with g Gabor filters

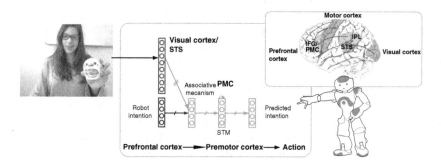

Fig. 2. Cognitive computational model for intention recognition.

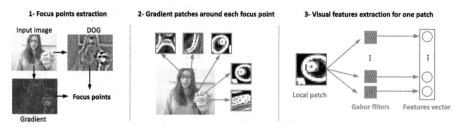

Fig. 3. Three steps for the extraction of visual features from an input image.

(Fig. 3.3). The final visual features vector v_p for a given focus point p corresponds to the concatenation of the means and standard deviations of a patch convoluted with each of the Gabor filters (i.e. $N = 2g$ features per focus point). The final features matrix V_i is the concatenation of all the v_p with $i = (1, ..., P)$. No prior constraint is given to this system, such as segmentation or object/body parts recognition. Thus, some focus points can be detected on the background or on irrelevant objects.

3.2 Visual Patterns Learning

The next step consists in learning meaningful visual patterns by recruiting new neurons when the visual information differs from previous visual features. Conversely, when the information is similar, it is average with the closest previously learned pattern. This approach is close to a Kohonen rule. This type of neural network is called Self Adaptive Winner (SAW). The synaptic weights' update rule is defined by the following equations:

$$F_j = s_j . H_{max(\lambda, \overline{s} + \sigma_s)}, \text{ where } \quad s_j = 1 - \frac{1}{N} \sum_{i=1}^{N} |W_{ij} - V_i| \tag{1}$$

$$\Delta W_{i,j} = \delta^k (a_j(t) I_i + \epsilon(V_i - W_{ij})(1 - F_j)) \tag{2}$$

where F_j is the activity of the neuron $j = (1, ..., m)$ in the group of visual features neurons F, $H_\theta(x)$ is the Heaviside function, λ is a vigilance value (i.e. a threshold of recognition), s_j is a measure of similarity between the previously learned patterns and the new visual information, $\overline{s}$ is the average of the similarity over j and σ_s its standard deviation, W the synaptic weight of the connection between the visual input V_i and the visual features F_j. The next step consists in the association of these visual patterns with intentions.

3.3 Intention Recognition Learning

All the detected focus points are learned by the previous group of neurons. Thus, non relevant patterns extracted on the background, or non relevant to the intention are also learned. To enable the model to reinforce specifically the visual pattern that are relevant to the caretaker's intention, an associative group of neuron is used. The synaptic weights $\omega_{i,j}$ are modified according to the following equation:

$$\Delta \omega_{i,j} = \epsilon F_i (I_j - \widehat{I}_j) \tag{3}$$

with ϵ a learning strength parameter, I_j the avatar's intention (object 1 or object 2), $\widehat{I}_j$ the predicted intention, j the index of the neuron corresponding to the intention $j = (1, 2)$. During the test phase, a short term memory (STM) layer is used to sum and filter the result over a short period of time, followed by a winner takes all to predict the intention.

4   Results

This section first presents the results of the model validation that reproduces the protocol of the infant studies experiment. In a second part, it shows the results obtained when the model is exposed to the impairments related to schizophrenia introduced in Sect. 2.2.

4.1   Results of the Model Validation

This first experiment reproduces the settings from the infant study presented in Sect. 2.1. The results in terms of percentage of recognition in all the different conditions are shown on Fig. 4a. It shows that the recognition rate in the new path condition is 1.77 times superior to the recognition rate in the new goal condition. This observation shows that after habituation, our model recognize preferentially the goal-object compared to the physical properties of the care-taker's movement. It is important to note that we did not use object recognition or positions of the hand and of the object. The focus points are all extracted in the same way and encode for both these properties. The preferential recognition of the goal-object compared to the path is thus emergent to our model. These results can be explained on a low level by the fact that the object is more salient than the arm of the caretaker. Thus, during the test phase, the model recognizes more easily the focus points that encode for the object which results in a higher activation of the visual neurons in the new path condition. To test this hypothesis, we plot the bar graph of the average number of activated visual neurons in each condition (Fig. 4b.). The results show a higher activation of the visual neurons in the new path condition which confirms this hypothesis.

4.2   Results of the Model Impairment

Impaired Saliency. We reproduced the described protocol with a variation of the $N_{ip} = \{1, ..., 10\}$. For each number of impaired points, the learning and testing phase is repeated 10 times. The average error rate for each number of impaired points is reported on Fig. 5a. When all the focus points are impaired (i.e. $N_{ip} = 10$), the error rate is close to random. Figure 5b shows the number of neurons recruited by the visual patterns learning module to encode the visual

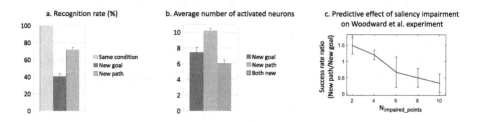

Fig. 4. Results obtained in the 3 conditions presented in Sect. 2.1.

information as presented in Sect. 3.2 [14]. The number of neurons increases as a function of N_{ip}. A randomly extracted saliency is thus more difficult to encode than a structured visual saliency.

Influence of the Caregiver. We reproduced the described protocol with a variation of the number of intention contingencies between the avatar and the caregiver. For each number of contingencies $N_c = \{20, 50, 80, 110\}$, the learning and testing phase is repeated 10 times. The average error rate for each number of contingencies is reported on Fig. 5c. Figure 5d shows the number of neurons recruited by the visual patterns learning module. The number of neurons increases as a function of N_c. A higher number of contingencies requires more neurons to encode all of the visual variations.

Interaction Effect. We evaluated whether there is an interaction effect between these two factors. In that purpose, we tested all the couples (N_c, N_{ip}). The results in terms of error rate is presented on Fig. 5e. It shows a negative interaction effect between these two factors. In presence of a strong impairment of saliency, there is no amelioration of the results when the number of contingencies is increased (i.e. a minimum error rate of 0.43). The number of contingencies can also be seen as different points on the developmental trajectory, as an infant will be exposed to more and more contingencies in the course of his development. In that sense, we show that an impaired saliency impacts all the developmental trajectory, with an increasing effect.

Predictive Influence of Saliency Impairment on Woodward's Experiment. Finally, we tested the effect of the saliency impairment on the Woodward et al. experiment protocol. We followed the same steps as in the model validation with increased impairment of saliency. We report on the ratio between the

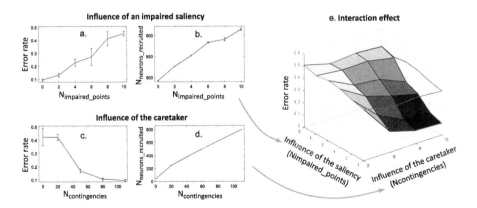

Fig. 5. Influence of an impaired saliency on the success of intention recognition and on the number of neurons recruited to learn the visual patterns

recognition rate in the new path condition and the recognition rate in the new goal condition as shown on Fig. 4c. This metric shows how much infants encode an observed action in terms of their goal-object as opposed to its physical properties. In that context, our model predicts a decreasing encoding of the observed action in terms of goal when the saliency is increasingly impaired.

5 Conclusion and Perspectives

Intention recognition is known to be impaired in schizophrenia. It is however not clear how to take into account in this deficit both innate/genetic factors and developmental trauma. In these paper, we have presented a developmental cognitive model of intention recognition. This model was validated by reproducing main findings of a seminal infant studies task [6,7], namely that infants encode observed actions in terms of its goal-object and not in terms of its physical properties. Our model was then exposed to different types of impairment related to schizophrenia (i.e. innate saliency impairment and environmental influence of the caretaker). The results show a negative interaction effect between these two factors. Moreover, the model predicts a weaker encoding of the goal-object compared to the physical hand movement in presence of a saliency impairment. The current model includes a bottom-up method for saliency detection. However, top-down signals are also important in directing attention [15]. A more realistic attention model is an interesting perspective to mimic more precisely the impairment of saliency in schizophrenia.

Acknowledgments. This work was supported by the European Project AlterEgo FP7 ICT 2.9-Cognitive Sciences and Robotics, grant number 600610.

References

1. Frith, C.D.: The Cognitive Neuropsychology of Schizophrenia. Psychology Press, New York (2015)
2. Blakemore, S.J., Decety, J.: From the perception of action to the understanding of intention. Nat. Rev. Neurosci. **2**(8), 561–567 (2001)
3. Harland, R., Morgan, C., Hutchinson, G.: Phenomenology, science and the anthropology of the self: a new model for the aetiology of psychosis. Br J. Psychiatry **185**, 361–362 (2004)
4. Oztop, E., Wolpert, D., Kawato, M.: Mental state inference using visual control parameters. Cogn. Brain Res. **22**, 129–151 (2005)
5. Cohen, L., Haliyo, S., Chetouani, M., Régnier, S.: Intention prediction approach to interact naturally with the microworld. In: AIM 2014, pp. 396–401 (2014)
6. Synofzik, M., Vosgerau, G., Newen, A.: Beyond the comparator model: a multifactorial two-step account of agency. Conscious Cogn. **17**(1), 219–239 (2008)
7. Harnad, S.: The symbol grounding problem. Phys. D **42**(1), 335–346 (1990)
8. Cohen, L., Abbassi, W., Chetouani, M., Boucenna, S.: Intention inference learning through the interaction with a caregiver. ICDL Epirob **2014**, 153–154 (2014)

9. Boucenna, S., Cohen, D., Meltzoff, A.N., Gaussier, P., Chetouani, M.: Robots learn to recognize individuals from imitative encounters with people and avatars. Sci. Rep., **6** (2016)

10. Woodward, A.L.: Infants selectively encode the goal object of an actor's reach. Cognition **69**(1), 1–34 (1998)

11. Sommerville, J.A., Woodward, A.L., Needham, A.: Action experience alters 3-month-old infants' perception of others' actions. Cognition **96**(1), B1–B11 (2005)

12. Howes, O.D., Murray, R.M.: Schizophrenia: an integrated sociodevelopmental-cognitive model. Lancet **383**, 1677–1687 (2014)

13. Meyer-Lindberg, A.: From maps to mechanisms through neuroimaging of schizophrenia. Nature **468**(7321), 194–202 (2010)

14. Boucenna, S., Anzalone, S., Tilmont, E., Cohen, D., Chetouani, M.: Learning of social signatures through imitation game between a robot and a human partner. IEEE Trans. Auton. Ment. Dev. **6**(3), 213–225 (2014)

15. Cutsuridis, V.: A cognitive model of saliency, attention, and picture scanning. Cogn. Comput. **1**(4), 292–299 (2009)

A System-Level Model of Noradrenergic Function

Maxime Carrere[1,2,3]($\boxtimes$) and Frédéric Alexandre[1,2,3]

[1] LaBRI, Université de Bordeaux, Bordeaux INP, CNRS, UMR 5800, Talence, France
{maxime.carrere,frederic.alexandre}@inria.fr
[2] Inria Bordeaux Sud-Ouest, 200 Avenue de la Vieille Tour, 33405 Talence, France
[3] IMN, Université de Bordeaux, CNRS, UMR 5293, Bordeaux, France

Abstract. Neuromodulation is an interesting way to display different modes of functioning in a complex network. The effect of Noradrenaline has often been related to the exploration/exploitation trade-off and implemented in models by modulation of the gain of activation function. In this paper, we show that this mechanism is not sufficient for system-level networks and propose another way to implement it, exploiting reported inhibition of a striatal region by Noradrenaline. We describe here the corresponding model and report its performances in a reversal task.

Keywords: Neuromodulation · Bio-inspiration · Decision making

1 Introduction

In neuromodulation, a principle of neural activation already observed in crustacea [5], a small set of neurons projects to most regions of the brain and can modify their functioning and learning modes by acting on the intrinsic properties of neurons and on the synaptic weights. Neuromodulators have been popularized in the modeling domain by a paper by Doya [7], proposing how different phases of reinforcement learning might be implemented by global signals representing such neuromodulators, where "dopamine signals the error in reward prediction, serotonin controls the time scale of reward prediction, noradrenaline controls the randomness in action selection, and acetylcholine controls the speed of memory update" (quoted from [7]).

Concerning dopamine [12] and acetylcholine [13], the role of these neuromodulators has been defined more precisely, relying on experimental data and on more precise or more biologically informed models. In this paper, we propose to revisit the role of noradrenaline (or norepinephrine, NE) and particularly of its effects on other brain regions. Whereas an excitatory attentional effect is generally reported for NE, we mention here a new inhibitory effect on a specific striatal region and explain why, in the brain and also in models, this additional effect is important for the global dynamics of the network. In the next sections, we introduce more precisely some information about noradrenaline and the way it is presently integrated in models, including data and results that will be important for our model that is subsequently presented together with simulation results.

A.E.P. Villa et al. (Eds.): ICANN 2016, Part I, LNCS 9886, pp. 214–221, 2016.
DOI: 10.1007/978-3-319-44778-0_25

2   The Noradrenergic System

NE originates mainly from the Locus Coeruleus (LC), a brainstem nucleus [4]. One acknowledged role of NE is to modify sensory processing in the thalamus and the cortex [15, 16], depending on the level of arousal and attention required by the external situation, proposed to be encoded by the tonic levels of NE [4]. At low level, the animal is at rest (sleeping or grooming). A highly salient stimulus (for example reliably announcing a reward) is going to increase tonic NE level and trigger phasic NE burst to precisely focus attentional processing on that stimulus and resist to distractors. The highest tonic levels of NE are observed when the conditions are no longer predictable (for example in unknown or changing environments) and require to explore among possible relevant stimuli to extract new contingencies [2].

This general view relating the level of NE to the level of arousal is consistent with its often mentioned implication in choosing between exploitation and exploration (with higher levels) of sensory criteria to select actions [2]. This is also consistent with the reported implication of NE during reversal [1] when a sensory criterion to predict a reward becomes suddenly invalid and requires to look for another predictive sensory criterion. This has been termed unexpected uncertainty in [17], in contrast to expected uncertainty, corresponding to the stochasticity of the criterion and encoded by another neuromodulator, acetylcholine, and requiring only patience and not reconsideration of the criterion.

Going deeper in the description of LC afferents and efferents can allow for a more precise interpretation of the role of NE, based on information available in LC to decide on the release of NE and the nature of NE actions in LC targets. Inputs to LC are of three kinds. Low level signals from peripheral centres give basic information about level of arousal from the sympathetic system and about salient sensory inputs from the oculomotor system [4]. More elaborated elements of information are sent by the central nucleus of the amygdala and the medial prefrontal cortex towards LC [16]. They are generally believed to contribute to evaluate the nature of the present situation, and correspond to information like reward history or response conflicts and errors [2]. Other noteworthy inputs to LC are from other neuromodulatory centres which reciprocally influence LC [16].

LC projects to most brain regions and more heavily to attentional structures like the parietal sensory cortex, where NE can enhance evoked activity [3]. Importantly, the basal ganglia is the only cerebral structure not receiving projections from LC, except for the shell region of the nucleus accumbens, where NE is reported to have an inhibitory effect [11].

3   Modeling the Role of Noradrenaline

In addition to [7, 17] other modeling papers have proposed to implement NE mechanisms. McClure and colleagues [10] propose that the level of NE is estimated by an evaluation function depending on the reward rate (corresponding to input of the orbitofrontal cortex to LC) and measures of response conflict (corresponding to input of the anterior cingulate cortex, ACC, to LC), computed from two windows of long term and short term history of activity.

The model by Aston Jones et al. [2] proposes a mechanism implementing the trade-off between exploration and exploitation, with the Drift Diffusion Model (DDM). This model can be applied for tasks with two choices with two units acting as accumulators, integrating over time possibly noisy signals favoring each choice and responding when the difference of levels exceeds a threshold. Interestingly, DDM has been originally proposed to reproduce reaction times and error rates in decision making processes but appears to explain well neuronal responses recorded during such processes. In the model, the value of the threshold is of course an important parameter, but also the gain of accumulator integration that can be modified to reach the threshold at different speeds. This simple model, which can be equivalently implemented with units in mutual inhibition, has been shown to be a good approximation of the optimal decision [6] but remains limited to two-alternative choices. It has also been shown to maximize the signal-to-noise ratio in the difference between the input signals and, when this ratio changes, [6] shows that the gain of the units (or their mutually inhibiting strength) must be modified accordingly.

It is proposed in [2] that, when tonic NE is released (in a situation identified as unexpected uncertainty), the gain of the sensory units will increase and this will facilitate random activation of sensory neurons and accordingly exploration. Nevertheless, we have observed some limitations, trying to apply DDM to act not only on a sensory layer of units representing candidate stimuli (as it is the case in [2,6]) but on the sensory part of a neural network learning to associate a representation of the value of stimuli to the best response, presented in [8] as an implementation of decision making in the brain.

In the [8] network, associations have been learned between sensory neurons and neurons triggering the actions. Even if by NE gain increase a new stimulus is more activated, associative weights might compensate and trigger the habitual action. To tell it differently, an excitatory noise in the sensory layer does not necessarily trigger motor exploration.

4   Our Model

We have mentioned above a biological fact that has not yet been exploited in models, the inhibitory effect of NE in the shell [11]. In fact, the shell is a striatal region known to participate in the evaluation of the value of stimuli in the orbitofontal cortex which can in turn activate motor responses toward stimuli. We can consequently explore another alternative of NE neuromodulation effect, where its action in the shell can inhibit previously learned sensorimotor associations.

Our model uses the DANA library for neuronal representation and computation [14]. It extends the model presented in [8] by studying the effect of exploration and tonic NE on it. All the code for the model and parameters are open-source and available online at https://github.com/carreremax/basal-ganglia-ne. We will only describe and discuss here changes made from the Guthrie model.

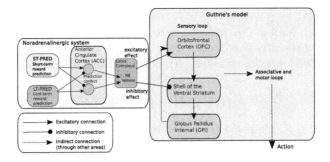

Fig. 1. Main features of our model compared to [8]. ST-PRED and LT-PRED are respectively short-term predictor and long-term predictor which predict reward arrival as the average reward from a long and short amount of trials. Each prediction inhibits the excitatory input of the other in ACC, resulting in ACC activation and NE release in LC only in case of discrepancy between the predictions, i.e. in case of unexpected uncertainty. NE release is then used to trigger exploration in [8], by facilitation of cortical excitation and inhibition of striatal inputs.

The level of NE is computed as the difference (or conflict) between a slow and a fast predictor as follows:

The noradrenaline system receives inputs from short and long-term reward predictors, as shown in Fig. 1. Short and long-term predictors are computed as the average reward on the respectively n_st_trials and n_lt_trials last trials.

$$lt\_prediction = \left(\sum\nolimits_{k \in n\_lt\_trials} reward_k\right)/n\_lt\_trials$$

$$st\_prediction = \left(\sum\nolimits_{k \in n\_st\_trials} reward_k\right)/n\_st\_trials$$

with $reward_k$ the reward received at trial k.

These rewards are respectively sent as inputs to two ACC units computing the conflict between the two predictions, ne_s and ne_l:

$$\frac{dU_{ne\_s}}{dt} = \tau * (-U_{ne\_s} + st\_prediction - lt\_prediction)$$

Similarly:

$$\frac{dU_{ne\_l}}{dt} = \tau * (-U_{ne\_l} + lt\_prediction - st\_prediction)$$

So the long-term prediction is inhibiting the ne_s, and the short-term one is inhibiting ne_l. The level of NE release, ne, is then taken as the sum of ne_s and ne_l activities. As a result, if both old and recent predictions are not predicting any reward, neither ne_s nor ne_l activities are strong, and then NE concentration is low. Symmetrically, if both systems are predicting rewards, the two predictions will inhibit the projections of each other, thus resulting in a low NE release. However, if only one system is predicting a reward, i.e. if the prediction following recent history is different from the prediction based on long history, the corresponding NE population will have a strong, non-inhibited activation, thus triggering a high level of NE release, corresponding to the fact that the reward contingency has recently changed.

Consistent with previous models, NE effect at the cortical level is an excitatory gain:

$$\frac{dV_{ctx}}{dt} = f(U_{ctx} * (1 + ne) * (1 + noise))$$

where V_{ctx} and U_{ctx} are respectively the firing rate and membrane potential of cortical neurons, f and $noise$ respectively the sigmoid function and activation noise used in [8]. NE inhibitory effect is an original mechanism added in our model, and impacts the output gain of projection from cortex to shell:

$$gain = g\_ctx\_cog\_str\_cog * ne\_modulation$$

with $g\_ctx\_cog\_str\_cog$ the constant gain between cortex and striatum in the sensory loop, and $ne\_modulation$ the modulatory effect of NE.

$$ne\_modulation = max(0.5, 1 - ne\_efficiency * ne)$$

NE modulatory effect is limited to halving excitatory projections from cortex to shell, consistent with the effect of NE observed in [11]. $ne\_efficiency$ is a constant set to 0.8, so that only maximum values of ne will provoke a minimum value of $ne\_modulation$.

Architectural parameters		
Parameter	Meaning	Value
$init\_critic$	Initial values of critic's predictions	0.25
α_critic	Learning rate of the critic	0.2
α_LTP	learning rate for long term potentiation	0.0001
α_LTD	learning rate for long term depression	0.00005
$g\_ctx\_cog\_str\_cog$	gain from cognitive cortex to cognitive striatum	1.2
$g\_ctx\_cog\_str\_ass$	gain from cognitive cortex to associative striatum	0.3
g_ne_exc	gain of excitatory projections in NE populations	1.0
g_ne_inh	gain of inhibitory projections in NE populations	-1.0
n_st_trials	Number of trials taken into account for the short-term predictor	3
n_lt_trials	Number of trials taken into account for the long-term predictor	30

Fig. 2. Description and values of the parameters added or modified compared to [8].

One of the main problems with unexpected uncertainty-based exploration is the learning rate of the model. If the learning speed of the network is too slow, the network will perform exploration, but will not be able to learn based on this exploration. At the opposite, if the learning is fast enough to learn from a few trials of exploration, it may converge too quickly, which can lead to sub-optimal choice or stability issues. To address this problem, we modified the learning rate of the critic module in the Guthrie's model, from previously 0.025 to 0.2, so that the critic could learn based on exploration, and we added critics' prediction as a sensory input of the network. Consequently, exploration helps the critic to learn insights of the values of alternative strategies, and such values are taken into account in the sensory loop, which in turn helps the network to choose the relevant alternative strategies, and learn from it.

5   Experiments

In order to analyze NE effects in the cortex and the shell, together with the switch between exploration and exploitation, we tested our model on reversal learning. At each trial, two sensory CS are simultaneously presented to the network, on two random positions during 2500 ms and the network has to perform an action toward one of the CS. As soon as the model performs an action, reward is distributed accordingly to the reward probability of the chosen CS. If no CS is selected after the 2500 ms of presentation, the network will not receive any reward. Then neural activities go down to their initial values, and we proceed to the next trial. The acquisition phase consists in 40 trials, in order to perform over-training and to allow habit formation. In each trial, one CS is systematically

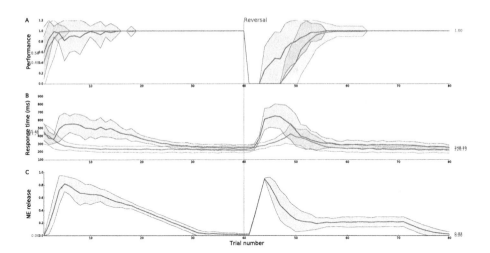

Fig. 3. Reversal experiments for our decision making model with NE effects (blue) or without NE effects (red). Each curve is the average of 100 experiments performed each time with a "naive" model. Surrounding shaded areas indicate the standard deviation for each curve. (A) Average performance by trials. Both NE and non-NE models are able to acquire CS values and to learn reversal. Exploration allows NE model to detect quicker the change in reward contingency, and to correctly perform faster than the non-NE one. (B) Average convergence time. During the first trials of reversal, exploration by inhibition of the striatum induces a larger response time for NE model. (C) Average release of NE. NE release is important at the beginning of exploration, and larger during the first trials of reversal. It correlates with unexpected uncertainty. (Color figure online)

rewarded while the other is not. During the reversal, which lasts for 40 trials, reward rates for each CS are switched, so the network has to detect the change in reward contingencies and to switch to the other CS.

In Fig. 3, we report the average performance and decision time on 100 reversal experiments with and without NE release. Each experiment is performed with a "naive" model. The model correctly learns to choose the best rewarded CS during the exploration and reversal phases. However, NE release allows to perform random exploration, and to gradually learn from this exploration, resulting in a faster convergence than networks without exploration (Fig. 3A). In addition NE release also increases the decision time of the model during the first trials of reversal (Fig. 3B). This is in accordance with [9] results, showing that animals with NE depletion respond with greater rapidity when perseverating. Figure 3C shows the release of noradrenaline during trials, which is indeed proportional to unexpected uncertainty, with a peak at the reversal onset.

6   Conclusion

In this paper, we have reported a model and associated experiments that illustrate the interest of neuromodulation, as a way to modulate existing networks, instead of complexifying their architecture. This is particularly the case for noradrenaline, and its confirmed role in the trade-off between exploration and exploitation. As illustrated in our experiments, NE-based exploration increases the convergence speed of a decision network in an unexpected situation, which is a decisive adaptive property for animals and other autonomous systems.

We have pointed out that another solution for NE-based exploration can be the inhibition of learnt rules rather than the excitation of the sensory gain, and have shown a biologically-inspired, neuronal implementation of it, using reported NE effect in the shell [11]. Its excitatory effect in the cortex, widely used in other models, is still present here. Yet, simulation of the model with only striatal NE (not reported here) still exhibits exploration, but with longer decision time. We hypothetize here that because the task does not require exploration of additional representation in the cortex, cortical NE is not necessary for exploration. If the task needs discovery and creation of adequate cortical representation, like for extra-dimensional shift, it would need cortical NE. Another prediction to be tested in both computational and experimental neuroscience is that inhibiting NE release in the shell should both impede exploration and decrease the decision time. These predictions are explored in ongoing work.

References

1. Aston-Jones, G., Rajkowski, J., Kubiak, P.: Conditioned responses of monkey locus coeruleus neurons anticipate acquisition of discriminative behavior in a vigilance task. Neuroscience **80**(3), 697–715 (1997)
2. Aston-Jones, G., Cohen, J.D.: An integrative theory of locus coeruleus-norepinephrine function: adaptive gain and optimal performance. Annu. Rev. Neurosci. **28**(1), 403–450 (2005)

3. Aston-Jones, G., Rajkowski, J., Cohen, J.: Role of locus coeruleus in attention and behavioral flexibility. Biol. Psychiatry **46**(9), 1309–1320 (1999)
4. Berridge, C.W., Waterhouse, B.D.: The locus coeruleus-noradrenergic system: modulation of behavioral state and state-dependent cognitive processes. Brain Res. Rev. **42**(1), 33–84 (2003)
5. Bouret, S., Sara, S.J.: Network reset: a simplified overarching theory of locus coeruleus noradrenaline function. Trends Neurosci. **28**(11), 574–582 (2005)
6. Brown, E., Gao, J., Holmes, P., Bogacz, R., Gilzenrat, M., Cohen, J.D.: Simple neural networks that optimize decisions. Int. J. Bifurcat. Chaos **15**(03), 803–826 (2005). http://dx.doi.org/10.1142/s0218127405012478
7. Doya, K.: Metalearning and neuromodulation. Neural Netw. **15**(4–6), 495–506 (2002). http://dx.doi.org/10.1016/s0893-6080(02)00044-8
8. Guthrie, M., Leblois, A., Garenne, A., Boraud, T.: Interaction between cognitive and motor cortico-basal ganglia loops during decision making: a computational study. J. Neurophysiol. **109**(12), 3025–3040 (2013)
9. Mason, S.T., Iversen, S.D.: An investigation of the role of corticalandcerebellar noradrenaline in associative motor learning in the rat. Brain Res. **134**(3), 513–527 (1977). http://dx.doi.org/10.1016/0006-8993(77)90826-5
10. McClure, S., Gilzenrat, M., Cohen, J.: An exploration-exploitationmodel based on norepinepherine and dopamine activity. In: Weiss, Y., Schölkopf, B.,Platt, J. (eds.) Advances in Neural Information Processing Systems, vol. 18, pp. 867–874. MIT Press (2006). http://www.csbmb.princeton.edu/~smcclure/pdf/MGC_NIPS.pdf
11. Nicola, S.M., Malenka, R.C.: Modulation of synaptic transmission bydopamine and norepinephrine in ventral but not dorsal striatum. J. Neurophysiol. **79**(4), 1768–1776 (1998). http://view.ncbi.nlm.nih.gov/pubmed/9535946
12. O'Reilly, R.C., Frank, M.J., Hazy, T.E., Watz, B.: PVLV: the primary value and learned value Pavlovian learning algorithm. Behav. Neurosci. **121**(1), 31–49 (2007). http://dx.doi.org/10.1037/0735-7044.121.1.31
13. Pauli, W.M., O'Reilly, R.C.: Attentional control of associative learning-a possible role of the central cholinergic system. Brain Res. **1202**, 43–53 (2008)
14. Rougier, N.P., Fix, J.: DANA: distributed (asynchronous) numerical and adaptive modelling framework. Netw. Comput. Neural Syst. **23**(4), 237–253 (2012)
15. Sadacca, B.F., Wikenheiser, A.M., Schoenbaum, G.: Toward a theoretical role for tonic norepinephrine in the orbitofrontal cortex in facilitating flexible learning. Neuroscience (2016)
16. Sara, S.J., Bouret, S.: Orienting and reorienting: the locus coeruleus mediates cognition through arousal. Neuron **76**(1), 130–141 (2012)
17. Yu, A.J., Dayan, P.: Uncertainty, neuromodulation, and attention. Neuron **46**(4), 681–692 (2005)

Phenomenological Model for the Adapatation of Shape-Selective Neurons in Area IT

Martin A. Giese[1]($\boxtimes$), Pradeep Kuravi[2], and Rufin Vogels[2]

[1] Section Compuational Sensomotorics,
Department of Cognitive Neurology, CIN&HIH,
University Clinic Tübingen,
Ottfried-Müller Street 25, 72076 Tübingen, Germany
martin.giese@uni-tuebingen.de
[2] Laboratory Neuro en Psychofysiologie, Department of Neuroscience, KU Leuven,
Campus Gasthuisberg, O&N 2, Herestraat 49, 3000 Leuven, Belgium

Abstract. Shape-selective neurons in inferotemporal cortex show adaptation if the same shape stimulus is shown repeatedly. Recent electrophysiological experiments have provided critical data that constrain possible underlying neural mechanisms. We propose a neural model that accounts in a unifying manner for a number of these critical observations. The reproduction of the experimental phenomenology seems to require a combination of input fatigue and firing rate fatigue mechanisms, and the adaptive processes need to be largely independent of the duration of the adapting stimulus. The proposed model realizes these constraints by combining a set of physiologically-inspired mechanisms.

Keywords: Object recognition · Adaptation · Inferotemporal cortex · Fatigue · Neural field

1 Introduction

Shape-selective neurons in inferotemporal cortex (area IT) show adaptation for repeated stimulus presentation [1]. This phenomenon has been of strong interest in neuroscience and functional imaging [2], since it might be contributing to high-level after-effects [3], might be related to the observation of repetition suppression effects in functional imaging [4], and efficient coding [5]. Various theories about the origin of adaptation effects have been proposed [6] and different models for such adaptation effects have been put developed [4,7–9]. However, the precise underlying neural processes remain largely unknown. Recent electrophysiological experiments provide strong constraints for the possible underlying neural mechanisms and their computational properties. Based on a collection of such experiments, we propose a neural model that accounts simultaneously for all of them, exploring a variety of possible neural adaptation mechanisms. We found that accounting for this data requires a combination of adaptation processes that act on different resolution levels in feature space (cf. specifically

© Springer International Publishing Switzerland 2016
A.E.P. Villa et al. (Eds.): ICANN 2016, Part I, LNCS 9886, pp. 222–229, 2016.
DOI: 10.1007/978-3-319-44778-0_26

Fig. 1D). Our solution combines *input fatigue* and *firing-rate fatigue* [10]. In addition, we assume that the relevant adaptation processes act largely independently of the duration of the adapting stimulus, while they are sensitive to the number of its repetitions. The proposed neural model combines a synaptic gain-control mechanism and a saturating firing-rate-dependent adaptation mechanism that shifts the threshold of the neurons in order to account for the data. We assume that the shape-selective neurons are recurrently connected and embedded in a neural field, resulting in a competition between different views and recognized shapes. Evidence from electrophysiology suggests an effective inhibitory interaction between shape-selective neurons in inferotemporal cortex [16].

In this paper, we describe the model and the assumed adaptation mechanisms. Then simulations of a set of critical experiments are presented, followed by a discussion.

2   Neural Model

Consistent with earlier work [11], we model IT neurons by radial basis function units that are selective for a learned shapes. We assume that these neurons are embedded within in a recurrent neural network, which can be approximated in the mean-field limit by a dynamic neural field that results in competition between neurons different recognized shapes and views. In other work similar models have been successfully exploited in order to account for electrophysiological results about object and action recognition (e.g. [11–13]). The recurrent network of shape-selective neurons is augmented by adaptation mechanisms. We have tested a variety of possible mechanisms and report here only a combination that accounts simultaneously for the critical data sets discussed below. In addition, the model contains a mechanism for spike-rate adaptation that is important to reproduce the signal shape of the post-stimulus time histograms (PSTHs) of IT neurons. The following sections give a more detailed description of the different model components.

2.1   Recurent Network (Field) of Shape-Selective Neurons

We assume that the individual shape-selective IT neurons obtain their input form a previous layer that encodes input features. We model this layer in an idealized way as two-dimensional neural field that represents input features with a well-defined metric for feature similarity. The dimensionality of this space could be chosen differently, as long as there is a defined similarity metric between the feature vectors. Let $v(\mathbf{y}, t)$ define the activity of the neurons in this input layer. We assume that this activity is always non-negative.

Consistent with electrophysiological data, we assume that the shape-selective IT neurons encode shapes in a view-specific manner, and we specify by the vector $\mathbf{x} = [\phi, \theta]$ the encoded shape and view. In our highly simplifying implementation we assumed a two-dimensional space for this representation, one dimension encoding view angle ϕ, and the other the location θ along a one-dimensional shape continuum. (The true dimensionality of shape spaces encoded in area IT is likely much higher.) The embedding of neurons in metric shape spaces simplifies the treatment of pattern similarity, which is a critical variable that was manipulated in the experiments. We assume that $u(\mathbf{x}, t)$ is the average activity of the neuron (ensembles) whose shape and view selectivity is given by the vector $\mathbf{x}$.

The shape-selective neurons are modeled by radial basis function (RBF) units that receive their inputs through a linear weight kernel $m(\mathbf{x}, \mathbf{y})$ from the input layer. This kernel specifies the strength of the synaptic connections from the input layer to the shape-selective IT neurons. We assume that, without adaptation, this kernel has a Gaussian characteristics, thus defining Gaussian RBFs. One of the assumed adaptation processes acts on the values of this weight kernel. This makes this kernel time-dependent.

The recurrent network of shape-selective neurons is modeled by a dynamic neural field of [14] that receives input from the input layer through the synaptic weight kernel m. The recurrent interactions in the field are specified by the interaction kernel w, resulting in the dynamical equation:

$$\tau \frac{\mathrm{d}}{\mathrm{d}t} u(\mathbf{x}, t) = -u(\mathbf{x}, t) + \int w(\mathbf{x} - \mathbf{x}') H(u(\mathbf{x}', t)) \, \mathrm{d}\mathbf{x}' - h$$
$$+ \underbrace{\int m(\mathbf{x}, \mathbf{y}, t) v(\mathbf{y}, t)) \, \mathrm{d}\mathbf{y} - F(a(\mathbf{x}, t)) + k_c c(\mathbf{x}, t)}_{s(\mathbf{x}, t)} \quad (1)$$

In this equation $H(x)$ is the Heaviside function, thus $H(x) = 1$ for $x > 0$ and $H(x) = 0$ otherwise. The positive constants τ ($= 60$ ms) and h define the time scale and the resting potential of the field.

2.2   Firing-Rate Fatigue Adaptation

The first adaptation mechanism is based on *firing rate fatigue*, i.e. an increase of the neuron thresholds after they have been continuously firing. This adaptation process is modeled by an adaptation variable $a(\mathbf{x}, t)$ that increases the effective threshold of the neurons. The dynamics of this variable is determined by a differential equation that is applied separately to each neuron (point in the neural field):

$$\tau_a \frac{\mathrm{d}}{\mathrm{d}t} a(\mathbf{x}, t) = -a(\mathbf{x}, t) + H(u(\mathbf{x}, t)) \quad (2)$$

The time constant τ_a of the adaptation process was chosen to be 1200 ms. The adaptation variable couples into the field dynamics through a saturating nonlinear function $F(a) = k_a \min(a, a_{\max})$, with $k_a > 0$ and $a_{\max} > 0$. This nonlinearity bounds the effect of this adaptation process for long adaptor durations, making adaptation largely independent from the duration of the adapting stimulus. (Such independence from adaptor duration has been observed in electrophysiological experiments; see Fig. 1C).

2.3 Input Fatigue Adaptation

A second adaptation process is acting on the synaptic strength of the input signals of the field, which is specified by the function m. An alternative interpretation is that this process captures adaptive changes in previous hierarchy layers of the shape recognition pathway. We assume that the strength of the synaptic connection between neurons at position $\mathbf{y}$ in the input layer and position $\mathbf{x}$ in the IT layer is decaying, when the input layer neuron has been activated. In addition, extensive simulation work shows that it has to be assumed that the main effect of the input fatigue adaptation emerges when the input signals decays after a sufficiently long activation period. A highly simplified mathematical model for this is a process that depends on the thresholded negative derivative of the input neuron activation. In our model we captured this by assuming a second adaptation variable b that follows the dynamical equation:

$$\tau_b \frac{\mathrm{d}}{\mathrm{d}t} b(\mathbf{y}, t) = -b(\mathbf{y}, t) + \left[-\frac{\partial}{\partial t} v(\mathbf{y}, t)) \right]_+ \tag{3}$$

Here $v(\mathbf{y}, t))$ signifies the activity of the input neuron at position $\mathbf{y}$ (with the linear threshold function $[a]_+ = \max(a, 0))$. As the time constant τ_b of this adaptation process we chose 1440 ms. Such transient signals that occur after longer periods of neuron activation might be generated, e.g., through post-inhibitory rebound activity of cortical interneurons that are suppressed by the activity of the shape-selective neurons.

We assume that the adaptation variable b modulates the strength of the synaptic input weights of the neurons by reducing their gain according to the relationship:

$$m(\mathbf{x}, \mathbf{y}, t) = m(\mathbf{x}, \mathbf{y}) \cdot \left(\frac{1}{b(\mathbf{y}, t)/c_b + 1} \right) \tag{4}$$

The function $m(\mathbf{x}, \mathbf{y})$ was chosen as two-dimensional gaussian filter kernel. The positive constant c_b determines a threshold level for the input fatigue adaptation process.

2.4 Spike Rate Adaptation

In order to reproduce the signal shape of the Peristimulus Time Histogram (PSTH) of typical IT neurons, we added another very fast transient process that models spike rate adaptation. This process acts on a much faster timescale than the other discussed adaptive processes. The effect of spike rate adaptation is that the neurons show a short overshoot of activity after stimulus onset that quickly decays. This phenomenon was modeled by adding a transient component to the effective input signal of the IT neurons that decays with a very fast time constant τ_c, which was about 9.6 ms. The spike rate adaptation is modeled by third adaptation state variable $c(\mathbf{x}, t)$ that obeys the dynamic equation

$$\tau_c \frac{\mathrm{d}}{\mathrm{d}t} c(\mathbf{x}, t) = -c(\mathbf{c}, t) + \left[\frac{\partial}{\partial t} s(\mathbf{x}, t)) \right]_+ , \tag{5}$$

where $s(\mathbf{x}, t)$ is the effective input signal of the IT neuron at position $\mathbf{x}$ in the neural field. (See also Eq. (1).) The spike rate adaptation process has only a small effect on the simulation results related to adaptation but is important to reproduce the shapes of the neural responses.

3 Simulation Results

The model provides a unifying account for several critical experiments that are discussed in the following in comparison with the simulation results.

Figure 1A shows a comparison between the PSTHs from a single stimulus repetition from a typical IT neuron [15] (right panel) in comparison with the simulation result (left panel). Due to the spike rate adaptation process, the model reproduces the signal overshoots after stimulus onset that is present for many IT neurons.

Figure 1B shows a simulation of the responses for many repetitions of the same shape stimulus, which is optimally stimulating the tested model neuron. The timing parameters match the ones by [1]. Consistent with the experiment the adaptation effect saturates largely after 5 stimulus repetitions. In the real experimental data there occurs a further slight decay that continues after more than 10 stimulus repetitions. Accounting for this effect would require an additional much slower process, which is not included in our model.

Figure 1C shows the simulation of an experiment (data not published) that varied the duration of an adaptor stimulus that stimulated the neuron maximally). For testing, stimuli with a fixed duration of 300 ms were shown after a fixed inter-stimulus interval. Quite unexpectedly, the duration of the adaptor stimulus had almost no influence on the observed adaptation effects for real IT neurons in the monkey (unpublished data). This experimental result is highly constraining for models, and it could not be reproduced by many model variants (including adaptation mechanisms depending on the tonic activity levels during adaptation, or dependent on the activity changes during stimulus onset - for both, firing-rate and input fatigue mechanisms).

Finally, Fig. 1D shows a simulation of another highly constraining experimental result by [10]. The neurons were stimulated with an effective stimulus (shape 1), that is a shape that elicited a maximum response in the neuron, and with an ineffective stimulus (shape 2), which elicited still a selective response, but a relatively weak one. Presented as an adaptor, obviously, the effective stimulus elicits a higher response than the ineffective stimulus, in the real data as well as for the model. If testing is done with an effective stimulus, evidently, the adaptation effect is larger for an effective adaptor stimulus than for an ineffective adaptor. An interesting situation emerges, however, when the model is tested with ineffective stimuli, and adapted with the effective or the ineffective stimulus. In this case, a statistical interaction occurs where the adaptation effect for an ineffective adaptor stimulus is larger than the one induced by an effective adaptor.

Consistent with the analysis in [10], simulations with different versions of the model confirm that this type of interaction cannot be obtained with models

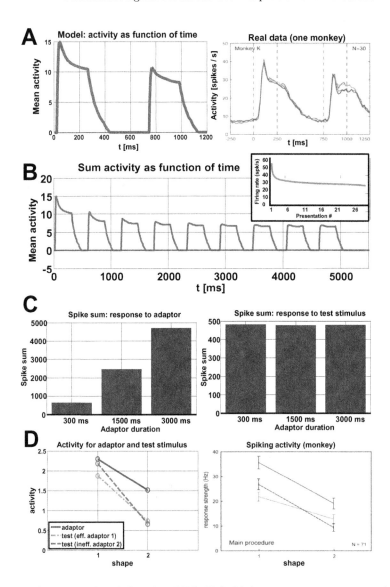

Fig. 1. Simulation results: **A** Simulated PSTH (left) (average activity over model neurons) in comparison with PSTH from typical IT neuron for single stimulus repetition [15]. **B** Simulated decay of stimulus responses for many repetitions of the same stimulus in comparison with real data (inset) from [1]. **C** Total responses strength (number of spikes integrated over time) for adaptor stimuli with different durations (300, 1500, and 1500 ms) (left). During the subsequent test stimuli with fixed duration (300 ms), the total response is almost identical (consistent with unpublished real data from monkey area IT). **D** Responses for adaptor stimulus (line) for effective and ineffective stimulus, and responses for test stimuli after adaptation either with an effective or an ineffective adaptor stimulus. Model responses (left) compared to corresponding physiological data from [10].

without an input fatigue mechanism that operates at a resolution level in feature space that is significantly higher than the width of the tuning curves in the neural field. For obtaining the strong adaptation effect for ineffective test stimuli the adaptation effects induced by the ineffective adaptor must remain highly local in the feature space.

For firing rate fatigue the localization of the induced adaptation effects is bounded by the spatial low-pass characteristics of the feed-forward kernel m and the lateral interaction kernel w. The width of the activation peak in the field determines the shape tuning, and thus the difference between the responses to the effective and the ineffective adaptor. Adapting a neuron with an ineffective stimulus will thus induce smaller activity than adaptation with an effective stimulus, resulting in a lower adaptation, which also remains visible when the neuron is tested with an inefficient stimulus. In contrast, if adaptation happens at the input or synaptic level, if one assumes that the tuning in the input level is highly localized in the $\mathbf{y}$ parameter-space, adaptation and testing with a inefficient stimulus leads to a strong adaptation effect since both, adaptation and test stimulus activate the same neurons in the input layer. At the same time, small adaptation emerges at the input level if adaptation and test stimulus are different, which explains the interaction effect. Detailed simulations show that both, input fatigue and firing rate fatigue are necessary to reproduce all results from [10] in Fig. 1D.

4   Conclusions

We have presented a phenomenological model that reproduces simultaneously a number of critical experimental results on adaptation effects in neurons in area IT. Testing different variations of the model, we found that an account for these results necessitates and input fatigue as well as a firing rate fatigue process. A second constraint from the data is the absence of an influence of the adaptor duration on the strength of the adaptation effect. In order to reproduce this result, we assumed a fast nonlinear saturation of the firing rate fatigue, and a dependence of the input fatigue on the decays of the synaptic input signals. With many other tested mechanisms, including models with transient-dependent firing-rate fatigue or saturating input fatigue mechanisms, we were not able to reproduce the data.

Since the model is qualitative and makes a number of ad hoc assumptions future work will have to verify the proposed mechanisms, ideally by deriving predictions from the model that can be tested physiologically by causal manipulations of proposed levels (e.g. input synapses or output firing rates). In addition, predictive simulations of new experiments will help to test the predictive power of the model. Also, different model component have to be linked closer to specific biophysical mechanisms and details, such as the postulated transient-dependent adaptation processes.

Acknowledgements. Thanks to L. Fedorov for helpful comments. Funded by EC FP7 ABC PITN-GA-011-290011, HBP FP7-604102; Koroibot FP7-611909, H2020 ICT-644727 CogImon; BMBF FKZ: 01GQ1002A, and DFG GZ: GI 305/4-1 + KA 1258/15-1.

References

1. Sawamura, H., Orban, G.A., Vogels, R.: Selectivity of neuronal adaptation does not match response selectivity: a single-cell study of the FMRI adaptation paradigm. Neuron **49**(2), 307–318 (2006)
2. Krekelberg, B., Boynton, G.M., van Wezel, R.J.A.: Adaptation: from single cells to BOLD signals. Trends Cogn. Sci. **12**(6), 230–236 (2006)
3. Leopold, D.A., O'Toole, A.J., Vetter, T., Blanz, V.: Prototype-referenced shape encoding revealed by high-level after effects. Nat. Neurosci. **4**(1), 89–94 (2006)
4. Grill-Spector, K., Henson, R., Martin, A.: Repetition and the brain: neural models of stimulus-specific effects. Trends Cogn. Sci. **10**(1), 14–23 (2006)
5. Wark, B., Lundstrom, B.N., Fairhall, A.: Sensory adaptation. Curr. Opin. Neurobiol. **17**(4), 423–429 (2007)
6. Vogels, R.: Sources of adaptation of inferior temporal cortical responses. Cortex **80**, 185–195 (2015). pii S0010-9452(15)00334-2
7. Sohal, V.S., Hasselmo, M.E.: A model for experience-dependentchanges in the responses of inferotemporal neurons. Network **11**(3), 169–190 (2000)
8. Friston, K.: A theory of cortical responses. Philos. Trans. R Soc. Lond. B Biol. Sci. **360**(1456), 815–836 (2005)
9. Wark, B., Fairhall, A., Rieke, F.: Timescales of inference in visual adaptation. Neuron **61**(5), 750–761 (2009)
10. De Baene, W., Vogels, R.: Effects of adaptation on the stimulus selectivity of macaque inferior temporal spiking activity and local field potentials. Cereb Cortex **20**(9), 2145–2165 (2010)
11. Riesenhuber, M., Poggio, T.: Hierarchical models of object recognition in cortex. Nat. Neurosci. **2**(11), 1019–1025 (1999)
12. Giese, M.A., Poggio, T.: Neural Mechanisms for the recognition of biological movements and action. Nat. Rev. Neurosci. **4**, 179–192 (2003)
13. Giese, M.A.: Skeleton model for the neurodynamics of visual action representations. In: Wermter, S., Weber, C., Duch, W., Honkela, T., Koprinkova-Hristova, P., Magg, S., Palm, G., Villa, A.E.P. (eds.) ICANN 2014. LNCS, vol. 8681, pp. 707–714. Springer, Heidelberg (2014)
14. Amari, S.: Dynamics of pattern formation in lateral inhibition type neural fields. Biol. Cybern. **27**, 77–87 (1977)
15. Kaliukhovich, D.A., Vogels, R.: Stimulus repetition probability does not affect repetition suppression in macaque inferior temporal cortex. Cereb Cortex **21**(7), 1547–1558 (2011)
16. Wang, Y., Fujita, I., Murayama, Y.: Neuronal mechanisms of selectivity for object features revealed by blocking inhibition in infrotemporal cortex. Nat. Neurosc. **3**(8), 807–813 (2000)

Deliberation-Aware Responder in Multi-proposer Ultimatum Game

Marko Ruman[✉], František Hůla, Miroslav Kárný, and Tatiana V. Guy

Department of Adaptive Systems, Institute of Information Theory and Automation,
Czech Academy of Sciences, P.O. Box 18, 182 08 Prague, Czech Republic
marko.ruman@gmail.com, hula.frantisek@gmail.com,
{school,guy}@utia.cas.cz

Abstract. The article studies deliberation aspects by modelling a responder in multi-proposers ultimatum game (UG). Compared to the classical UG, deliberative multi-proposers UG suggests that at each round the responder selects the proposer to play with. Any change of the proposer (compared to the previous round) is penalised. The simulation results show that though switching of proposers incurred non-negligible deliberation costs, the economic profit of the deliberation-aware responder was significantly higher in multi-proposer UG compared to the classical UG.

Keywords: Deliberation effort · Markov decision process · Ultimatum game

1 Introduction

The role of deliberation in decision making (DM) has been addressed in many ways. Examples can be found elsewhere, see, for instance, political sciences [4], economy [6], behavioral science [3]. The reason is simple: any decision made either by human or machine costs time, energy and possibly other resources, which are always limited. Importance of the proper balance between deliberation and quality of the resulting decision is repeatedly confirmed by a considerable effort devoted within different communities: computation costs in computer sciences [8,9]; transaction costs in financial sciences [7]; cooperation effort in social sciences [11], negotiation in multi-agent systems [10] and many others. Despite many promising results, see for instance recent work [5], the well-justified theoretical framework of deliberation is still missing.

The present article contributes to this problem by modelling a responder's DM in multi-proposers ultimatum game (UG) [2], introduces deliberation effort into reward function and optimises it. The simplicity of UG makes it a powerful test case providing a general insight into human DM, which can further serve to other

This work was partially supported by the Grant Agency of the Czech Republic under the project GA16-09848S.

A.E.P. Villa et al. (Eds.): ICANN 2016, Part I, LNCS 9886, pp. 230–237, 2016.
DOI: 10.1007/978-3-319-44778-0_27

fields. The basic model of UG consists of two players (*proposer* and *responder*) having different roles. The proposer's task is to share some known amount of money between him and the responder. The responder's role is to accept or reject the proposal. Acceptance leads to splitting the money according to the proposal, whereas rejection means none player gets anything.

Compare to [2], deliberative multi-proposers UG scenario suggests that at each round the responder selects the proposer to play with. However any change of the proposer (compare to the previous round) is penalised. The responder has no or little information about the proposers, thus the responder's optimal strategy should maximise economic profit while minimising deliberation cost under incomplete knowledge. It should be stressed that such modification of UG scenario makes a sense only for the studying either deliberation aspects or cooperative aspects of human DM. In the last case, repetitive selecting/non-selecting serves as a kind of the responder's feedback to a particular proposer and may influence future decision policy of the proposer.

Markov decision process (MDP) framework [1] has proven to be very useful for DM in stochastic environments. The paper considers modelling the responder's DM in the deliberation-aware multi-proposer multi-round UG experiment by MPD formalism and describes how *the responder's deliberation effort* can be respected and optimised.

The paper layout is as follows. Section 2 introduces necessary notations and formulates the problem. Section 3 introduces an optimal solution. Section 4 specialises the reward function of economic responder playing in multi-proposer UG. The experimental setup is described in Sect. 5. Section 6 summarises the main results and discusses open problems and possible solution ways.

2   Problem Formulation

The section introduces notations and a basic concept of Markov Decision Process (MDP) necessary to solve our problem. For more background on MDP, see [1].

2.1   Preliminaries

Throughout the paper, we use x_t to denote value of x at discrete time labelled by $t = 1, \ldots, t \in \mathbb{N}$. Bold capitals $\mathbf{X}$ denote a set of x-values; an abbreviation *pd* means probability density function, $p_t(x|y)$ is a conditional pd. $\chi(x,y)$ is a function defined on $\mathbb{R} \times \mathbb{R}$ as $\chi(x,y) = \begin{cases} 1 & x \neq y, \\ 0 & x = y. \end{cases}$

MDP provides us a mathematical framework for describing an *agent* (decision maker), which interacts with a *stochastic system* by taking appropriate actions to achieve her goal. The decisions about actions are made in the points of time referred as *decision epochs*. In each decision epoch, the agent's decisions are influenced only by a state of the stochastic system in a particular decision epoch, not by history of the system.

2.2 Markov Decision Process

Definition 1 (Markov Decision Process). Markov Decision Process *over the discrete finite set of* decision epochs $\boldsymbol{T} = \{1, 2, ..., N\}$, $N \in \mathbb{N}$ *is defined by a tuple* $\{\boldsymbol{T}, \boldsymbol{S}, \boldsymbol{A}, p, r\}$, *where:*

$\boldsymbol{S}$ *is a discrete, finite* state space $s \in \boldsymbol{S}$; $\boldsymbol{S} = \underset{t \in \boldsymbol{T}}{\cup} \boldsymbol{S}_t$, *where* $\boldsymbol{S}_t$ *is a set of possible states of the system at the decision epoch* $t \in \boldsymbol{T}$ *and* $s_t \in \boldsymbol{S}_t$ *is a state of the system at the decision epoch* $t \in \boldsymbol{T}$,

$\boldsymbol{A}$ *stands for a discrete, finite* action set; $\boldsymbol{A} = \underset{t \in \boldsymbol{T}}{\cup} \boldsymbol{A}_t$, *where* $\boldsymbol{A}_t$ *is a set of admissible actions in the decision epoch* $t \in \boldsymbol{T}$ *and* $a_t \in \boldsymbol{A}_t$ *denotes chosen action in the decision epoch* $t \in \boldsymbol{T}$,

p *represents a* transition probability function $p = p_t(s_t|s_{t-1}, a_t)$, *which is a non-negative function describing the probability that system reaches the state* s_t *after the action* a_t *is taken at the state* s_{t-1}; $\sum_{s_t \in S} p_t(s_t|s_{t-1}, a_t) = 1$, $\forall t \in$ $\boldsymbol{T}, \forall a_t \in \boldsymbol{A}, \forall s_{t-1} \in \boldsymbol{S}_{t-1}$,

r *stands for a* reward function $r = r_t(s_t, s_{t-1}, a_t)$, *which is used to quantify reaching of the agent's aim. The reward function* $r_t(s_t, s_{t-1}, a_t)$ *depends on the state* s_t *that the system occupies after action* a_t *is made.*

At the decision epoch t, an agent chooses an action a_t to be executed. As a result the system transits to a new state $s_t \in \boldsymbol{S}$ stochastically determined by $p_t(s_t|s_{t-1}, a_t)$. The agent gets a reward, which equals the value of reward function $r_t(s_t, s_{t-1}, a_t)$. The agent's goal is to find the optimal *DM policy*, which maximises the average reward received over time.

To avoid explicit dependence of the reward on the future state $s_t \in \boldsymbol{S}_t$ the *expected reward* is introduced as follows:

$$E_t[r_t(s_t, s_{t-1}, a_t)] = \sum_{a_t \in \boldsymbol{A}} \sum_{\substack{s_t \in \boldsymbol{S} \\ s_{t-1} \in \boldsymbol{S}}} r_t(s_t, s_{t-1}, a_t) p_t(s_t|s_{t-1}, a_t) p_t(a_t|s_{t-1}) p_t(s_{t-1})$$

(1)

In (1), $p_t(a_t|s_{t-1})$ is a *randomised decision rule* satisfying the condition $\sum_{a_t \in \boldsymbol{A}} p_t(a_t|s_{t-1}) = 1, \forall s_{t-1} \in \boldsymbol{S}_{t-1}, \forall t \in \boldsymbol{T}$.

Definition 2 (Stochastic policy). *A sequence of randomised decision rules* $\left\{ p_t(a_t|s_{t-1}) \middle| \sum_{a_t \in \boldsymbol{A}} p_t(a_t|s_{t-1}) = 1, \forall s_{t-1} \in \boldsymbol{S}_{t-1}, \forall t \in \boldsymbol{T} \right\}$ *forms the stochastic policy* $\pi_t \in \boldsymbol{\pi}$, *where* $p_t(a_t|s_{t-1})$ *is the probability of action* a_t *at the state* s_{t-1}.

To solve MDP (Definition 1) we need to find an optimal policy maximising the sum of expected rewards (1).

Definition 3. *The optimal solution to MDP is a policy π_t^{opt} that maximises the expected accumulated reward (1), $\pi_t^{opt} = \{p_\tau^{opt}(a_\tau|s_{\tau-1})\}_{\tau=1}^t \subset \boldsymbol{\pi}$.*

$$\max_{\{p_t(a_t|s_{t-1})\}_{t=1}^N} \sum_{t \in T} E_t[r_t(s_t, s_{t-1}, a_t)|s_{t-1}] =$$

$$\sum_{t \in T} \sum_{a_t \in A} \sum_{s_t, s_{t-1} \in S} r_t(s_t, s_{t-1}, a_t) p_t(s_t|s_{t-1}, a_t) p_t^{opt}(a_t|s_{t-1}) p_t(s_{t-1}) \quad (2)$$

2.3   Deliberation-Aware Multi-proposer Ultimatum Game

Compare to general formulation of UG [2], the considered *multi-proposer N-round UG* scenario assumes $n_P \in \mathbb{N}$ proposers and one responder. The goal is the same as in traditional UG, i.e. to maximise a total profit while sharing a fixed amount of money q. The main difference is that at the beginning of each round the responder chooses a proposer to play with. For choosing different proposer than that in the previous round, the responder is penalised by a so-called *deliberation penalty* $d \in \mathbb{N}$. Then, similarly to [2] the selected proposer offers a split $o_t \in \{1, 2, \ldots, q-1\}$ for the responder and $(q - o_t)$ for herself. If the responder accepts the offer, money split according to the proposal, otherwise none of the players get anything. Proposers not selected in this round play passive role.

Let us define a multi-proposer N-round UG via MDP (see Sect. 2.2) with proposers representing *stochastic environment* and the responder acting as *agent*. All proposers are part of the environment and have their policies fixed.

Definition 4. *Multi-proposer UG in MDP framework over a set of decision epochs (game rounds) $\boldsymbol{T}$ is defined as in Definition 1 and*

- $s_t = (o_t, P_t, D_t, Z_{R,t}, Z_{P,t}^1, Z_{P,t}^2, \ldots, Z_{P,t}^{n_P})$ *is environment state at $t \in \boldsymbol{T}$, where*
  $o_t \in \boldsymbol{O}$ *is an offer*
  $P_t \in \{P^1, \ldots, P^{n_P}\}$ *is the proposer chosen in the round $(t-1)$*
  $D_t \in \boldsymbol{D}$ *is the deliberation accumulated up to round t, $D_t = \sum_{\tau=1}^t d\chi(a_{1,\tau}, P_\tau)$*
  $Z_{R,t}$ *and $Z_{P,t}^i$ is an accumulated economic profit of the responder and proposer P^i, respectively*
- $a_t = (a_{1,t}, a_{2,t})$ *is a two-dimensional action, where $a_{1,t} \in \boldsymbol{A}_1 = \{1, 2, \ldots, n_P\}$ denotes the selection of a proposer to play with; $a_{2,t} \in \boldsymbol{A}_2 = \{1, 2\}$ stands for the acceptance ($a_{2,t} = 2$) or the rejection ($a_{2,t} = 1$) of the offer o_t, $\boldsymbol{A} = \boldsymbol{A}_1 \times \boldsymbol{A}_2$.*
- *The transition probabilities $p = p_t(s_t|s_{t-1}, a_1)$ and the reward function $r = r_t(s_t, s_{t-1}, a_t)$ are assumed to be known.*

The responder's accumulated *economic profit*, $Z_{R,t} \in \mathbf{Z}_R$, at the round t is:

$$Z_{R,t} = \sum_{\tau=1}^t o_\tau(a_{2,\tau} - 1), \quad (3)$$

and accumulated *economic profit of the ith proposer*, $Z_{P,t}^i \in \mathbf{Z}_P^i$, equals

$$Z_{P,t}^i = \sum_{\tau=1}^{t}(q - o_\tau)(a_{2,\tau} - 1)\chi(a_{1,\tau}, i), \ \forall i = 1, 2, ..., n_P. \tag{4}$$

The action $a_{2,t}$, see Definition 4, considers dependence on offer $o_t \in \mathbf{O}$. However action $a_{1,t}$ is made without this knowledge, thus

$$p_t(a_t|o_t, s_{t-1}) = p_t(a_{1,t}, a_{2,t}|o_t, s_{t-1}) = p_t(a_{1,t}|s_{t-1})p_t(a_{2,t}|o_t, a_{1,t}, s_{t-1}). \tag{5}$$

Thus, the optimal policy for MDP, given by Definition 4, is searched among sequences of functions $\left(p_t(a_{1,t}|s_{t-1}), p_t(a_{2,t}|o_t, a_{1,t}, s_{t-1})\right)_{t=1}^{N}$.

3   Optimal Solution

Let the state be decomposed as follows

$$s_t = (o_t, \bar{s}_t) \text{ where } \bar{s}_t = (P_t, D_t, Z_{R,t}, Z_{P,t}^1, Z_{P,t}^2, ..., Z_{P,t}^{n_P}) \ \bar{s}_t \in \bar{\mathbf{S}}. \tag{6}$$

Using (5) and (6), the conditional expected reward can be expressed as:

$$E_t[r_t(\bar{s}_t, o_t, s_{t-1}, a_{1,t}, a_{2,t})|s_{t-1}] =$$

$$\sum_{a_{1,t}\in\mathbf{A}_1} \sum_{a_{2,t}\in\mathbf{A}_2} \sum_{o_t\in\mathbf{O}} \left[\left(\sum_{\bar{s}_t\in\bar{\mathbf{S}}} r_t(\bar{s}_t, o_t, s_{t-1}, a_{1,t}, a_{2,t})p_t(\bar{s}_t|o_t, a_{1,t}, a_{2,t}, s_{t-1})\right)\right.$$

$$\left. p_t(a_{2,t}|o_t, a_{1,t}, s_{t-1})p_t(o_t|a_{1,t}, s_{t-1})p_t(a_{1,t}|s_{t-1})\right]. \tag{7}$$

Denoting the expression in round brackets in (7) by $\bar{r}_t(a_{2,t}, a_{1,t}, o_t, s_{t-1})$, the optimal decision rule $p_t^{opt}(a_{2,t}|o_t, a_{1,t}, s_{t-1})$ maximising (7) is given by

$$p_t^{opt}(a_{2,t}|o_t, a_{1,t}, s_{t-1}) = \chi(a_{2,t}, a_{2,t}^*(o_t, a_{1,t}, s_{t-1})), \text{ where} \tag{8}$$
$$a_{2,t}^*(o_t, a_{1,t}, s_{t-1}) \in \underset{a_{2,t}\in\mathbf{A}_2}{\operatorname{argmax}} \ \bar{r}_t(a_{2,t}, a_{1,t}, o_t, s_{t-1}) \ \forall(o_t, a_{1,t}) \in \mathbf{O} \times \mathbf{A}_1.$$

Now we have to maximize the remaining part of the expected reward (7):

$$\underset{p_t(a_{1,t}|s_{t-1})}{\max} \sum_{a_{1,t}\in\mathbf{A}_1} \left[\left(\sum_{a_{2,t}\in\mathbf{A}_2} \sum_{o_t\in\mathbf{O}} \bar{r}_t(a_{2,t}, a_{1,t}, o_t, s_{t-1})p_t^{opt}(a_{2,t}|o_t, a_{1,t}, s_{t-1})\right.\right.$$

$$\left.\left. p_t(o_t|a_{1,t}, s_{t-1})\right)p_t(a_{1,t}|s_{t-1})\right] \tag{9}$$

Similarly to the above let us denote:

$$\bar{\bar{r}}_t(a_{1,t}, s_{t-1}) = \sum_{a_{2,t}\in\mathbf{A}_2} \sum_{o_t\in\mathbf{O}} \bar{r}_t(a_{2,t}, a_{1,t}, o_t, s_{t-1})p_t^{opt}(a_{2,t}|o_t, a_{1,t}, s_{t-1})p_t(o_t|a_{1,t}, s_{t-1}). \tag{10}$$

Then the optimal decision rule $p_t^{opt}(a_{1,t}|s_{t-1})$ is

$$p_t^{opt}(a_{1,t}|s_{t-1}) = \chi(a_{1,t}, a_{1,t}^*(s_{t-1})), \text{ where} \tag{11}$$
$$a_{1,t}^*(s_{t-1}) \in \underset{a_{1,t}\in\mathbf{A}_1}{\operatorname{argmax}} \ \bar{\bar{r}}_t(a_{1,t}, s_{t-1}).$$

Theorem 1 (Optimal policy of the deliberation-aware responder). *A sequence of decision rules* $\left\{ (p_t^{opt}(a_{1,t}|s_{t-1}), p_t^{opt}(a_{2,t}|o_t, a_{1,t}, s_{t-1})) \right\}_{t=1}^{N}$ *maximising the reward (1) forms an optimal policy and is computed via modification of dynamic programming [12] starting with* $\varphi_N(s_N) = 0$, *where*

$$\varphi_{t-1}(s_{t-1}) = E_t[(r_t(\bar{s}_t, o_t, s_{t-1}, a_{1,t}^*, a_{2,t}^*) + \varphi_t(s_t))|s_{t-1}, a_{1,t}^*, a_{2,t}^*]$$

$$a_{1,t}^*(s_{t-1}) \in \underset{a_{1,t} \in A_1}{\operatorname{argmax}} \; E_t \left[\overline{\overline{r_t}}(a_{1,t}, s_{t-1}) + \varphi_t(s_t) \mid s_{t-1} \right] \tag{12}$$

$$a_{2,t}^*(o_t, a_{1,t}, s_{t-1}) \in \underset{a_{2,t} \in A_2}{\operatorname{argmax}} \; E_t \left[\overline{r_t}(a_{2,t}, a_{1,t}, o_t, s_{t-1}) + \varphi_t(s_t) \mid s_{t-1}, a_{1,t}^* \right]$$

Remark 1. Note that: (i) the actions $a_{1,t}$, $a_{2,t}$ and the offer o_t do not depend on the previous offer o_{t-1} explicitly; (ii) the action $a_{2,t}$ and the offer o_t do not depend on deliberation cost D_{t-1}; (iii) the action $a_{2,t}$ does not depend on the economic gains of proposers.

4   Decision Making of Economic Responder

This paper considers purely self-interested type of responder (so called *economic responder*), which behaves in accordance with Game Theory and accepts all offers as anything is better than nothing. The motivation of the *economic responder* is pure economic profit, thus her reward function in the round t equals:

$$r_t(s_t, s_{t-1}, a_t) = (Z_{R,t} - Z_{R,t-1}) - (D_t - D_{t-1}). \tag{13}$$

For simplicity of presentation let us assume that the transition probability functions of the proposers $p_t(o_t|Z_{R,t-1}, Z_{P,t-1}^{a_{1,t}}, a_{1,t})$, $\forall t \in \mathbf{T}$ are given.

The desired optimal strategy should maximize the expected reward (1) while respecting deliberation. Using (13) and Remark 1, the conditional expected reward of the economic responder reads:

$$E_t[r_t(s_t, s_{t-1}, a_{1,t}, a_{2,t})|s_{t-1}] = \sum_{\substack{a_{1,t} \in \mathbf{A}_1 \\ a_{2,t} \in \mathbf{A}_2}} \sum_{o_t \in \mathbf{O}} \left[[o_t(a_{2,t} - 1) - d_t\chi(a_{1,t}, a_{1,t-1})] \right.$$

$$\times \; p_t(a_{2,t}|o_t, a_{1,t}, Z_{R,t-1})p_t(o_t|Z_{R,t-1}, Z_{P,t-1}^{a_{1,t}}, a_{1,t})$$

$$\left. \times \; p_t(a_{1,t}|Z_{R,t-1}, D_{t-1}, Z_{P,t-1}^1, ..., Z_{P,t-1}^{n_P}) \right]. \tag{14}$$

With it, the optimal policy is given by Theorem 1.

5   Illustrative Example

The example considered a N-round UG as described in Sect. 2, with $N = 30$, $q = 30$, deliberation penalty $d = 5$ and number of proposers $n_P = 3$. The transition probabilities of respective proposers were considered independent of the economic profit. Before the simulation, the offers for all proposers were generated.

Table 1. Data obtained from the simulation of four games

No of game	$Z_R - D_R$	D_R	Z_R	Z_P^1	Z_P^2	Z_P^3	$\sum Z_P^i$
1	515	0	515	385	0	0	385
2	458	0	458	0	442	0	442
3	494	0	494	0	0	406	406
4	628	40	668	110	38	84	232

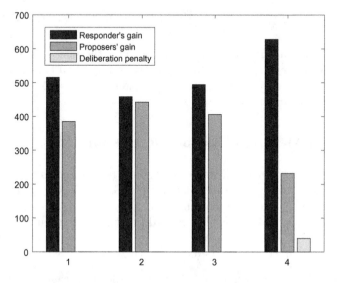

Fig. 1. Responder's overall profit (lowered by the deliberation penalty), economic gain of all proposers and deliberation penalty for each of 4 games

The probabilities of the offers are drawn from Gaussian distribution with $\sigma = 2$ and mean equal to the pre-generated offer. Then four games were played. Classical UG with each proposer and deliberative multi-proposer N-round UG. In the 4th game the responder played according to the optimal strategy found in Sect. 3. We analysed the result of the simulation by comparing the Responder gain in each game. The results are summarised in Table 1 (Z_R - Responder's profit, D_R - Deliberation cost, Z_P^i - Economic gain of the i-th proposer, $\sum Z_P^i$ - The total gain of all proposers) and Fig. 1.

6   Concluding Remarks

The paper examined the deliberation of the responder in multi-proposer Ultimatum Game. The responder behaviour was modelled by MDP and the deliberation cost was included into the responder's reward function and optimised so as economic profit. Comparison of the overall responder profit gained in the classical UG and in the deliberative multi-proposer UG was made. The results shown that though switching of proposers incurred non-negligible deliberation costs, the economic profit of the deliberation-aware responder was significantly higher in multi-proposer UG.

Many challenging aspects remain to be studied, in particular: (i) modelling other types of responders considering not only pure economic profit, but non-economic aspects (fairness); (ii) incorporating affective aspects of decision making, for example emotional state of the responder. Another direction is adding an adaptive feature, i.e. learning of the stochastic environment, i.e. learning the proposer model, see [13].

References

1. Puterman, M.L.: Markov Decision Processes. Wiley, New Jersey (1994)
2. Rubinstein, A.: Perfect equilibrum in a bargaining model. Econometrica **50**(1), 97–109 (1982). Wiley, 1994
3. Sulkin, T., Simon, A.F.: Habermas in the lab: a study of deliberation in an experimental setting. Polit. Psychol. **22**, 809–826 (2001)
4. Persson, M., Esaiasson, P., Gilljam, M.: The effects of direct voting, deliberation on legitimacy beliefs: an experimental study of small group decision making. Eur. Polit. Sci. Rev., 1–19 (2006)
5. Beara, A., Randa, D.G.: Intuition, deliberation, and the evolution of cooperation. PNAS **113**(4), 936–941 (2016)
6. Loewenstein, G., O'Donoghue, T.: Animal spirits: affective and deliberative processes in economic behavior (2004). http://papers.ssrn.com
7. Compte, O., Jehiel, P.: Bargaining over Randomly Generated Offers: A new perspective on multi-party bargaining. C.E.R.A.S.-E.N.P.C., C.N.R.S., France (2004)
8. Ortega, D.A., Braun, P.A.: Information, utility and bounded rationality. In: Schmidhuber, J., Thórisson, K.R., Looks, M. (eds.) AGI 2011. LNCS, vol. 6830, pp. 269–274. Springer, Heidelberg (2011)
9. Horvitz, E.J.: Reasoning about beliefs, actions under computational resource constraints (2013). arXiv:1304.2759
10. Dignum, F., Dignum, V., Prada, R., Jonker, C.M.: A conceptual architecture for social deliberation in multi-agent organizations. Multiagent Grid Syst. **11**(3), 147–166 (2015)
11. Gigerenzer, G.: Adaptative Thinking: Rationality in the Real World. Oxford University Press, Oxford (2000)
12. Bellman, R.: Dynamic programming. Princeton University Press, Princeton (1957)
13. F. Hůla, Ruman, M., Kárný, M.: Adaptive proposer for ultimatum game. In: Proceedings of ICANN 2016 (2016)

From Cognitive to Habit Behavior During Navigation, Through Cortical-Basal Ganglia Loops

Jean-Paul Banquet[✉], Souheïl Hanoune, Philippe Gaussier, and Mathias Quoy

Neurocybernetics Team,
ETIS UMR 8051 ENSEA - Universit de Cergy-Pontoise - CNRS, Cergy, France
jean-paul.banquet@upmc.fr, {souheil.hanoune,gaussier,quoy}@ensea.fr
http://www-etis.ensea.fr/

Abstract. The distinction between cognitive goal-oriented and SR habitual behavior has long been classical in Neuroscience. Nevertheless, the mechanisms of the two types of behaviors as well as their interactions are poorly understood, in spite of significant advances in the knowledge of their supporting structures, the cortico-striatal loops. A neural network (NN) model of the dynamics of these systems during a goal navigation paradigm is presented within the framework of reinforcement learning. The model supposing, the parallel interactive learning of cognitive and habitual strategies, replicates key experimental results related to the transition between them. The biological inspiration of the NN architecture provides insights on the nature of their interactions, and the conditions of their respective engagement in the control of behavior.

Keywords: Hippocampus · Entorhinal · Prefrontal · Parietal cortices · Limbic · Cognitive · Sensori-motor cortico-striatal loops · Goal-behavior · Habit

1 Introduction

Stimulus-response (S-R) and Cognitive opposed theories of behavior provide a useful framework for exploring their neural bases. Indeed, Cognitive Theory introduces the concepts of representation, and goal-oriented behavior, while the S-R paradigm includes habits as a result of an over-practice of the cognitive mode. Later on, these antagonistic views resolved into a multiple system account, under which the two control modes coexist as complementary. We propose a paradigm for representing and implementing cognitive and S-R habit strategies within the unitary coding frame of transition cells (TC) [1,2,7]. The asymmetrical learning dynamics prevailing in the two systems supposedly located in the cortico-basal ganglia loops, under the modulation of dopamine (DA) are supposed at the basis of the experimental and modeling results. Interrelated hypotheses inspired by experimental data are tested here. They suppose first a

© Springer International Publishing Switzerland 2016
A.E.P. Villa et al. (Eds.): ICANN 2016, Part I, LNCS 9886, pp. 238–247, 2016.
DOI: 10.1007/978-3-319-44778-0_28

parallel, interactive learning and implementation of the two control modes; secondly, a possible substitution of the two strategies after overtraining; third, the reactivation of the cognitive strategy after an alteration of a previously learned task or the adaptation to a novel one. Finally, beyond the competition between the two strategies, the possibility of a cooperation at an early learning stage is supposed, the cognitive strategy monitoring habit learning. After frontal-striatal loops discovery cortical-subcortical relationships are presented as segregated, parallel networks (limbic, associative-cognitive, sensory-motor), forming independent, functional channels. But recent evidence of "spiraling" connections between components of these loops, in particular between striatum compartments and midbrain DA systems suggests unidirectional, anterior-posterior interactions and integration, supposing oriented transfer of information and learning between devoted channels. The mathematical NN model approach provides for a precise mechanistic analysis of the dynamical processes and structural changes that support the two strategies. The mechanisms operating in navigation [6] could be generalized in a straightforward manner to general behavior [12].

2   Model and Biological Foundations

Cognitive goal-oriented and habitual SR behaviors both dedicated to goal-capture relate to reinforcement learning (RL). In instrumental conditioning or a more complex navigation task, the action first clearly oriented to goal capture, becomes through overtraining a SR habit independent of the goal value. Environmental states acting as action-contexts, acquire a cached value [5] originally associated with the corresponding actions and become capable to orient action choices. The main cortico-striatal loops are implicated in the transformation of motivation, related to vital drives or more general incentives, into sequences of actions and general behavior. The limbic loop identifies the goals; the cognitive loop planifies and controls the execution of adapted behaviors; and the sensory-motor loop implements the details of the motor programs. These loops function under the modulation of midbrain DA system which dynamically adapts the functional configuration of the cortico-subcortical circuits as a function of learning in particular. The mathematical NN model emulating these functions supposes the learning of a map implementing goal-oriented cognitive strategies corresponding to the associative-cognitive cortical-striatal loop; and a NN implementation of a Q-learning algorithm for learning a S-R habit strategy. Both systems receive similar hippocampal transition field inputs [1, 2, 7].

Transitions. Hippocampus (HS) fields CA3, CA1 and EC (entorhinal cortex) deep layers combine spatial and temporal (sequential) information into dynamical transition codes. Current direct EC input and preceding indirect DG (Dentate Gyrus) input upon respectively distal and proximal CA3 dendrites combine to form transitions in CA3-CA1. Thus, the CA3 processing stages access both present and previous input. Two successively activated place cells (PCs) recruit a cell (population) named Transition Cell [1,2]. CA3 and CA1 encode respectively the prediction of accessible places from the current position, and the actually selected transition [2,10]. Combination between allothetic visual inputs and idiothetic proprioceptive signals establishes a unique relationship between transition neural representation and the associated movement. The path integration starting from the last place and computed on the basis of odometric input and movement direction, associates a movement vector with every transition. The actions represented by the directions to take are encoded by neural fields. Path integration fields provide an unconditional input for movement selection.

Cognitive Map. In model-based RL, the state-action value estimation is based on transition and reward functions learned by the agent through past experience [5]. This function is performed here by the acquisition of a topological cognitive map representing the adjacency between places, and where goals have been localized. In the reactivated map, in working memory, the neuron synaptic weights are endowed with fast learning dynamics. Earlier models of navigation [2,4,7] activated a cognitive strategy when the agent could not directly perceive the goal or a cue for implementing a simpler heading vector strategy.

Building a Cognitive Map. The buildup of a cognitive map supposes a bottom-up process. Exploration of an environment establishes a temporal-topological relationship between two successively recognized places i, j, through a simple Hebbian modulation of the connections between corresponding nodes. Thus a graph of the spatial relationships between places is constructed by iteration of this process. Planning with this cognitive map supposes also learning a link between a specific place and the satisfaction of a drive, during exploration. A goal is defined as the location where a drive can be satisfied. Cells combining location and valence have been recorded in rat prelimbic-infralimbic (PL-IL) medial prefrontal cortex [11]. During exploitation, drive satisfaction reinforces a link between reward context (location) and the corresponding hypothalamic drive-neurons. Thereafter, the reactivation of a drive neuron, e.g. expressing a metabolic imbalance, induces the reactivation of the corresponding goal-related PC. Diffusion through the map of this activation constitutes a plausible solution to the path planning process, as a particular case of a top-down activation from hypothalamic drive neurons to the map storing sites, HS, prefrontal and/or posterior-parietal cortices in particular. Indeed, by a similar top-down process, the activation of PF goal cells modulates the activity of CA1 place cells, under the form of a secondary place field [11]. These weak top-down activations are still sufficient to bias the selection of competing inputs within the bottom-up stream. Functioning of such a planning process requires the activity X_i of cognitive map neurons to be a function of their topological distance (e.g. number of intermediate place cells) to the goal. A normalized weight value W_{max} lower than 1 fulfils this condition.

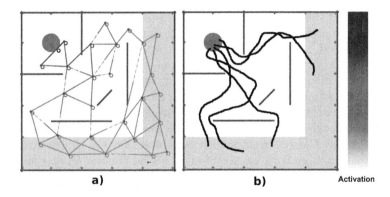

Fig. 1. Illustration of transitions and trajectories in the simulated environment. (a) Graph of all learned transitions by TQ-learning in the simulated environment, where the nodes represent place field location, and the links transitions between two place fields. Darker colors mean higher Q values for the corresponding transitions. (b) Trajectories taken by the agent during goal navigation using the cognitive map. The goal location is represented by a disk in the upper left corner of the environment. (Color figure online)

Implementation of the Cognitive Map. Different steps combine bottom-up and top-down processes: 1-the agent recognizes the place field corresponding to its current location; 2-the drive-modulated activation of the goal neuron diffuses within the graph-map inducing a differential activation of its nodes; 3-the agent moves in the direction maximizing the activity of the PC coding for the next subgoal, the most active node directly linked to its current location. 4-when the agent enters the place field corresponding to the subgoal, the process is reiterated until reaching the final goal. The feedback diffusion of activation and the feedforward computation selecting accessible transitions take place within the cortical cognitive map and the CA3-CA1 HS field, respectively. Implementing both in the same NN, the distance from the current position to the associated places and the distance to the goal would be confounded in the activation level of the single place cell layer.

$$X_i^C(t) = \begin{cases} f(max_j W_{ij}(t) \cdot X_j^C(t)) & \text{if } T(t) = 0, \ S(t) = 0 \\ X_i^{MEM}(t) & \text{otherwise} \end{cases} \tag{1}$$

$$\frac{dW_{ij}^{CC}(t)}{dt} = T(t) \cdot ((\gamma - W_{ij}^{CC}) \cdot X_i^C(t) \cdot X_j^C(t) - W_{ij}^{CC} \cdot (\lambda_1 \cdot X_j^C(t) + \lambda_2)) \tag{2}$$

$$\frac{dW_{ij}^{DC}(t)}{dt} = S(t) \cdot (X_i^C(t) \cdot X_j^D(t)), \text{ for i,j} = argmax_{k,l}(X_l^C(t) \cdot X_k^D(t)) \tag{3}$$

$X_k^C(t)$, a short-term working memory, describes the activation of the node k in the cognitive map; X_i^{MEM}: memory activity saving the two past transitions executed. $W_{ij}(t)$: connection weight between the i and j nodes in the cognitive map; f: threshold-linear output function; $T(t)$: binary signal (0 or 1) corresponding to a transition activation; $S(t)$: signal activated (0 or 1) when a goal is encountered.

Equations 2–3: learning in the recurrent connections of the neurons supporting the cognitive map. $T(t)$: as in Eq. 1, a binary signal (0 or 1) corresponding to a transition activation; in this equation, it controls recurrent connection learning W_{ij}^{CC}; γ is a parameter (smaller than 1), controlling the decremental diffusion of activation through the CM; λ_1 and λ_2: respectively, active and passive decay parameters on the CM recurrent connections, and thus the subtractive second term in Eq. 2 corresponds to memory weight decay. For the result simulations, $\lambda_1 = 0.01$, $\lambda_2 = 0.0001$ and $\gamma = 0.8$.

Equation 3 corresponds to connection learning between goal encoding node in the cognitive map and corresponding drive node. The $S(t)$ signal, as in Eq. 1, is activated when a reward is encountered; X_j^D: drive node, and X_i^C: CM node where reward is discovered. This signal controls the synaptic learning on W_{ij}^{DC}, between drive X_j^D and CM neurons X_i^C, with activities described in Eq. 1. The cognitive map can be conceived as a graph where nodes represent transitions, and edges the links between transitions. Each link has a value below 1. A previously learned transition can be forgotten if not reactivated, due to the active and passive decay parameters of the cognitive map [4]. Maps constitute fully-connected graphs. Any place on the map can be reached from any other through a given path. Such graphs contain a quasi-infinite number of trees according to starting and arrival point or goal. The pruning of the branches which are not or little practiced, along with the strengthening of the most practiced paths result in the specification of linear (not branching) trajectories, which constitute, according our hypothesis, the neural substrate of habit behaviors [14].

2.1   Transition-Q-learning

The state-action pair (s, a_1) leading to state s' of the classical Q-learning formalism can be represented by a transition ss' associated with action a_1. If the transition ss' is coded by a neuron (population) and the action a_1 by another one, then the strength of the link between the transition ss' and a_1 is equivalent to the Q-value Q_{s,a_1} in the classical formulation. In the Transition Q-learning algorithm (TQ-learning) (Eq. 4), the transition ss' is a substitute for the starting state s, the action a_1 and the resulting state s'. In the operation of the Transition Q-learning (TQ), the learned Q values for each predicted transitions are used to bias the activity of the transition cells (Fig. 2). A WTA competition allows selecting the optimal transition. The output of the competition is not a direct motor action but rather a sensory-motor transition. This transition then activates its corresponding action, which could range from elementary motor commands to more complex behaviors. The following equation represents the adaptation of the Q values, as a function of the previous ones and of the difference between expected and received reward, at each time step t.

$$Q_{ss'}(t) = (1 - \alpha)Q_{ss'}(t-1) + \alpha(r(t) + \gamma \max_{s''} Q_{s's''}(t) - Q_{ss'}(t-1)) \quad (4)$$

In order to accelerate the simulation computation, the above equation was modified by taking also the maximum between $r(t)$ and $\gamma \max_{s''} Q_{s's''}(t) - Q_{ss'}(t-1)$. The outputs of the cognitive and habit systems are compared through a WTA operation deciding which system takes the control of the motor execution.

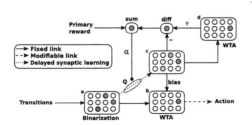

Fig. 2. NN implementation of the TQ learning equation: The different neural groups a-d represent the transition space, endowed with different functions. All the connections are one-to-one topology preserving, except one-to-all links between group a and c, for Q-value learning in their connection weights. The connections from c to b induce a modulation of the selected b transition as a function of its Q value. The upper path implements the update of the Q values as a function of the prediction error. The group d acts as a winner take all (equivalent to a max operation) and a storage group for the preceding $Q_{ss'}(t)$ values. The difference between the actual c signal and the max of the expected d signal modulated by γ is added to the primary reward. The modulation of this prediction error by α is used to update the weights of the connections between a and c.

3   Results

Experimental Paradigm. The environment is an open square with 20 perfectly identifiable visual landmarks equally spaced along the walls (Fig. 1). Obstacles are placed along southern and eastern walls, and around the goal, in the upper left corner. Exploration being based on random movements, the direction of the agent is periodically changed, through a Gaussian probability function (over 360°) centered on the current direction. A session supposes 200 to 300 successful captures of the goal, depending on the experimental group. A new starting point at each trial induces the learning of a new path, and thus a completion of the cognitive map [8,9].

Simulations. In absence of any control system, with a purely random behavior, the system reaches the goal after a very long delay, without learning across sessions (Fig. 3a). After initial inactivation of the habitual system, the cognitive system alone reaches floor performance after a very few trials (Fig. 3b), whereas early inactivation of the cognitive system, does not prevent learning, but the habit S-R system alone learns slowly (Fig. 3c). When the two systems operate together right from experiment onset (Fig. 3d and e), learning curve close to that of the cognitive system alone, suggests its dominance on behavior control at this stage. In contrast to these asymmetric results, a late inactivation of either one of the two systems does not affect significantly the performance, confirming the equal capability of the two systems to control behavior after overtraining. Nevertheless, habit system is significantly more performant that the cognitive system. This can suggest an early cooperation and a late competition.

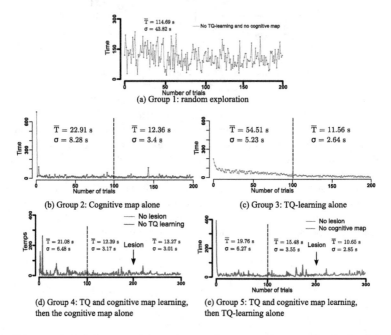

(a) Group 1: random exploration

(b) Group 2: Cognitive map alone

(c) Group 3: TQ-learning alone

(d) Group 4: TQ and cognitive map learning, then the cognitive map alone

(e) Group 5: TQ and cognitive map learning, then TQ-learning alone

Fig. 3. Time needed for reaching the goal versus the number of trials. After each completed trial, the agent is reset to a random position. Randdom exploration (a) induces no learning with poor performance. (b) and (c) representing early lesions of either the TQ-learning system or the cognitive system, demonstrate the fast learning of the CM alone, and the more progressive learning of the TQ-learning alone. Yet, the final performances (after 200 trials) are equivalent. The combination of the two strategies (d) and (e) (first 200 trials), display fast learning and high performance (hypothesis H1). Lesions of either TQ-learning or CM, after overlearning, does not hinder the perfomance (hypothesis H2), yet with a sligh advantage for the TQ-learning system alone. Enclosed in the figure is the mean time $\bar{T}$ over 10 agents necessary for reaching the goal; and standard deviation σ. Parameters are $\epsilon = 0.1$, $r = 1$, $\gamma = 0.8$, $\alpha = 0.5$.

3.1   Discussion

Biological Justification of the Model. Under different denominations (uncertainty, speed-accuracy trade-off...) the notion of competition between cognitive and habit modes of behavior is recognized. Conversely, the hypothesis emphasized here of a cooperation between them is less obvious. It supposes in particular that learning takes place in parallel within the cognitive and habit systems. Yet, a strong support in favor of such a cooperation can be found in the evolution of cortical afferents contribution to the activation of striatal neurons, in the limbic loop in particular, under DA modulation. During a novel task, the HS-subicular input (providing spatial-contextual information) plays a gating function in the activation of the originally hyperpolarized medium spiny neurons (MSN), the output neuron of striatum, by inducing an 'upstate' corresponding to a partially depolarized state, but still not sufficient to trigger spiking. Only the co-occurrence of a mPFC input can trigger a spike discharge. Symetrically, a mPFC input alone does not trigger discharge except for very strong ones. This permissive function of mPFC input can be considered as the hallmark of a cooperation between the two systems during learning, and more specifically of a supervision of habit learning by the mPFC-dependent cognitive mode. Repeated training in the same task reinforces the connection weights of the active populations between HS-subiculum and nucleus accumbens (NAC) MSNs, up to the point when subiculum neural population alone becomes capable to trigger firing of MSNs. The successful performance of the task ensures reinforcement through continuing phasic and tonic DA liberation which induces LTP in the subiculum-NAC connections through D1 receptor activation, and inhibition of the mPFC-NAC pathway through D2 receptor activation. This condition could correspond to the incremental learning of an habit, with the instauration of an S-R type of response, even though in the case of navigation S is in fact a whole context. This situation perdures until a change in task conditions or a novel task take over. In any case, the ensuing failure to capture the goal, and the lack of an expected reward trigger a cascade of neural events: absence of burst firing and phasic DA liberation in VTA neurons, inhibition of continuous DA firing and of tonic DA liberation in the same neurons, and finally desinhibition of mPFC-NAC pathway, through D2 receptor deactivation, characteristic of the takeover of the mPFC control on NAC neurons and the hallmark of flexibility and adaptive behavior.

Conditions of Engagement of the Control Modes. The different dynamics of the cortical and ganglio-basal NNs suggest the conditions of dominant engagement of each of the two systems. The fast build up of a spatial map in cortex, through the mediation of the HS system, and the corresponding strengthening of the connection weights on the 'tree' of the map leading to the goal ensures a dominance of the cognitive mode at task onset. All the more so since variability in starting positions favors the extensive exploration of the space and therefore the fast build up of the map, but slows down the incremental learning of an habit. Yet, noticeably this limited degree of variability in initial conditions does not prevent the instauration of the habit mode, in as far as these initial conditions can be merged into categories here corresponding to overlapping place fields. A temporal asymmetry must be noted in the engagement of the two control modes: to the incremental buid up of the habit mode corresponds a fast reinstatement of the cognitive mode consecutive to a failure in the goal capture. In any case, DA plays a crucial role in these changes through a dynamic modulation of the connectivity of afferent inputs to striatal neurons, thus modifying the functional organisation of these circuits. In the model, this DA modulation is represented through the reinforcing reward values $r(t) = +1$, 0 according to positive reinforcement, or failure triggering exploration. Importantly, the implementing motor system being common to cognitive and habit mode, a binary decision must be taken for the selection of the control mode implemented by a WTA between the outputs of the cognitive and habit systems. A weighted linear combination of the selections of each of the systems seems less plausible.

Insights from the Model in the Nature of the Interactions. The NN model provides also a mechanistic explanation on how the supervision of the habit learning by the cognitive system could take place. The fast learning of the cognitive map allows selecting specific transitions leading to the goal that are then imposed on both cognitive and habit systems. At the end of a trial, the robot is displaced to the starting area. If the starting point was never learned before, the exploration resumes on the basis of a random strategy. But as soon as a previously learned segment of a trajectory (transition) to the goal is crossed, the CM still remaining active, in particular the backpropagated activation of the current goal, the missing part of the path leading to the goal is step by step prospectively provided by the cognitive system according to the previously reinforced path. This near-optimal proposed path acts as an attractor for the habit system boosting habit learning which usually unfolds through random exploration of the task space, when performing alone. After overtraining, the system can take advantage of the two strategies, either favoring efficiency in stability condition, or favoring adaptability, during context or task change. A drop in tonic DA due to an absence of expected reward, triggers the transition from habit to cognitive mode, as previously mentioned.

Different Modalities of Habituation. Finally, the model suggests at least two possible kinds of habituation, plausibly consecutive during learning history. Overtraining in a map-based cognitive strategy first gives rise to an allothetic S-R habitual strategy, in which a complex stimulus, here the landmark configuration giving rise to a place field, can trigger a S-R type of response, but still in an allocentered reference frame. Yet, experimental evidence [13] points to a further learning stage in which the motor action reference frame is shifted from an allo- to an egocentered reference based on idiothetic proprioceptive stimuli, as in path integration. A simple 180° change in the starting box location in a cross-maze experiment allows to discriminate an external-cognitive referential which maintains the reward capture, from an ego-centered referential which fails capturing the goal. This shift of dominance of referential (external vs internal) could correspond to the takeover of the direct loop between sensori-motor cortex and DSL (dorsolateral striatum), previously performing under the supervision of the cognitive loop.

References

1. Banquet, J.P., Gaussier, P., Dreher, J.C., Joulain, C., Revel, A., Günther, W.: Space-time, order, and hierarchy in fronto-hippocampal system: a neural basis of personality. Adv. Psyc. **124**, 123–192 (1997). Amsterdam
2. Banquet, J.P., Gaussier, P., Quoy, M., Revel, A., Burnod, Y.: A hierarchy of associations in hippocampo-cortical systems. Neural Comput. **17**(6), 1339–1384 (2005)
3. Banquet, J.P., Gaussier, P., Quoy, M., Save, E., Sagolini, F., et al.: Representation-implementation trade-off in cortico-limbic ganglio-basal loops. In: Liljenström, H. (ed.) Advances in Cognitive Neurodynamics (IV). Springer, Netherlands (2015)
4. Cuperlier, N., Quoy, M., Gaussier, P.: Neurobiologically-inspired robot navigation-planning. Front. Neurorobot. **1**, 15 (2007)
5. Daw, N.D., Niv, Y., Dayan, P.: Uncertainty-based competition between prefrontal and dorsolateral striatal systems for behavioral control. Nat. Neurosci. **8**, 1704–1711 (2005)
6. Doll, L., Sheynikhovich, D., Girard, B., Chavarriaga, R., Guillot, A.: Path planning versus cue responding: a bio-inspired model of switching between navigation strategies. Biol. Cybern. **103**(4), 299–317 (2010)
7. Gaussier, P., Revel, A., Banquet, J.P., Babeau, V.: From view cells and place cells to cognitive map learning. Biol. Cyber **86**, 15 (2002)
8. Hanoune, S., Banquet, J.P., Quoy, M., Gaussier, P.: Cooperation of SR habit and cognitive learnings in goal-oriented navigation. In: SBDM 2014 Paris France, pp. 42–43 (2014)
9. Hanoune, S.: Vers un modèle biologiquement plausible de sélection de l'action pour un robot mobile. Thèse (2015)
10. Hirel, J., Gaussier, P., Quoy, M., Banquet, J.P., Save, E., Poucet, B.: The hippocampo-cortical loop: spatio-temporal learning and goal-oriented planning in navigation. Neural Netw. **43**, 8–21 (2013)
11. Hok, V., Lenck-Santini, P.P., Roux, S., Save, E., Poucet, B.: Goal-related activity in hippocampal place cells. J. Neurosci. **27**, 472–482 (2007)
12. Khamassi, M., Humphries, M.D.: Integrating cortico-limbic-basal ganglia architectures for learning model-based and model-free navigation strategies. Front. Behav. Neurosci. **6**(79), 1–19 (2012)
13. Packard, M.G., McGaugh, J.L.: Inactivation of hippocampus or caudate nucleus differentially affects expression of place and response learning. Neurobiol. Learn. Mem. **65**, 65–72 (1996)
14. Quoy, M., Laroque, P., Gaussier, P.: Learning and motivational couplings promote smarter behaviors of an animat in an unknown world. Robot. Auton. Syst. **38**(3), 149–156 (2002)

Fast and Slow Learning in a Neuro-Computational Model of Category Acquisition

Francesc Villagrasa[✉], Javier Baladron, and Fred H. Hamker

Artificial Intelligence, Chemnitz University of Technology,
Straße der Nationen 62, 09111 Chemnitz, Germany
vies@hrz.tu-chemnitz.de

Abstract. We present a neuro-computational model that, based on brain principles, succeeds in performing a category learning task. In particular, the network includes a fast learner (the basal ganglia) that via reinforcement learns to execute the task, and a slow learner (the prefrontal cortex) that can acquire abstract representations from the accumulation of experiences and ultimately pushes the task level performance to higher levels.

Keywords: Categorization · Basal ganglia · Fast-learner · Reinforcement learning · Prefrontal cortex · Slow-learner

1 Introduction

Categorization is the capacity to group items according to specific commonalities, in order to generalize or predict responses to new future stimuli and to build concepts that provide the world with meaning. Humans are especially good in this ability and therefore, we believe that to build a synthetic system capable of categorization we should look at mechanisms grounded in neuroscientific data.

The basal ganglia (BG) are a set of subcortical nuclei shown to be involved in a large number of categorization paradigms [1–5], especially those in which learning occurs via trial and error [6,7]. The BG are also associated with action selection [8], reinforcement learning [9] and it has been proposed to be involved in the training of cortico-cortical connections [10].

The prefrontal cortex (PFC) has also been shown to be involved in category tasks. It has been shown that neurons in this area can represent different categories [11–13]. Furthermore, the PFC plays a well-known role in executive functions [14].

We propose a novel principle of computation in which a fast-learner system (the BG) executes a category learning task via reinforcement learning while training a slower-learner system (the PFC) to acquire category information.

© Springer International Publishing Switzerland 2016
A.E.P. Villa et al. (Eds.): ICANN 2016, Part I, LNCS 9886, pp. 248–255, 2016.
DOI: 10.1007/978-3-319-44778-0_29

2   Methodology

2.1   Network Description

In our network, each nucleus of the BG and the PFC are represented by rate-coded neurons and their function arises from plastic synapses. Synaptic learning rules and neural activity are governed by differential equations which are solved by employing the Euler method with a time step of 1 ms. The network was built using the ANNarchy neural simulator [15] version 3.0.

We used a cortico-basalganglio-thalamic (CBGT) loop model based on preceding work [16] and connected it to the inferior temporal cortex (IT), the PFC and the premotor cortex (PM) (see Fig. 1). The IT represents stimuli information which is read by the Striatum (STR) and the subthalamic nucleus (STN), the two main input nuclei of the BG; the PM represents the different possible motor responses which can be initiated by the BG via the thalamus; and the PFC contains category information which will be acquired during the execution of the task. For further information about our BG model architecture consult [16].

In order to provide a sophisticated mechanism to learn categories, we have mainly introduced three connections linking the PFC with the thalamus and the IT. The IT is connected to the PFC with variable, excitatory synapses so that categories can be learned from the stimuli information. Each of the two thalamic neurons projects to a different PFC cell with fixed excitatory synapses, which allows the BG to transmit its action decision signal to the PFC, selecting one of the two PFC neurons to learn the current input pattern.

Finally, each PFC cell excites its afferent thalamic neuron back in order to bias the motor decision once enough information has been acquired. In particular, each PFC neuron is the only excitatory source of its corresponding thalamic neuron. Thus, when learning in the $IT \mapsto PFC$ connections still has not occurred, PFC provides both thalamic cells with the same input which is then just modulated or controlled by the inhibitory projections from the BG output. However, when category learning has been fully established in the PFC, the thalamic activity is completely biased by this knowledge. Then, a stimulus of a particular category will activate just one PFC cell and in doing so, just one of both thalamic cells will be activated by the PFC, impeding that BG can select the other thalamic neuron and consequently, it is now PFC which mainly rules thalamic activity and motor decision.

2.2   Experiment

We performed a numerical categorization experiment which consists of 400 trials in which learning took place. The model is taught to classify stimuli into one of two possible categories. Each trial starts with a rest period of 100 ms and is followed by 50 ms in which a randomly chosen stimulus is exposed. At the end of this period, the decision of the model is probabilistically evaluated via a

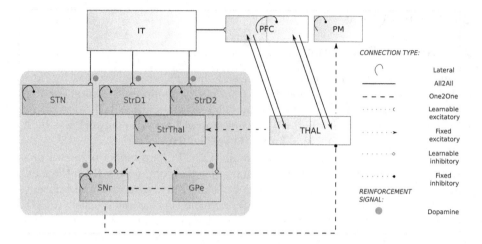

Fig. 1. Connections and connection types of the novel parts of the network. THAL: thalamus. PFC: prefrontal cortex. IT: inferior temporal cortex. PM: premotor cortex. The boxes inside the big shadow are the nuclei of the basal ganglia which correspond to the one introduced in [16]. One2One: each presynaptic population is only connected by its corresponding neuron of the postsynaptic population. All2all: every neuron in the presynaptic population is connected with every neuron in the postsynaptic population. $PFC \leftrightarrow THAL$ connections link half of the THAL neurons with half of the PFC neurons, constructing two loop structures.

soft-max rule depending on the activation of the PM and, if the model produces a correct response, reward is delivered for 500 ms.

Each stimulus or exemplar is defined by a 6×6 numerical matrix whose columns have one element set to one and the rest to zero, allowing for a total of 6^6 different exemplars. Category A represents all the stimuli whose first column has its first element set to one; the rest of exemplars belong to category B.

Each column of this matrix is considered as one of the stimuli's dimensions (color, shape, brightness, texture, size and orientation) and each row in the matrix as a value of each dimension (green, yellow, pink, red, purple and black for the color dimension), therefore category A encompasses all exemplars with green color and category B the rest of stimuli.

3   Results

We ran a set of 100 experiments with randomly initialized weights in the learnable connections and measured, among the trials of all experiments, the percentage of correct decisions (see Fig. 2). At the beginning, the model starts with a performance around 50 % which progressively increases until it reaches around 95 %, meaning that our model can successfully learn this category task.

The fast learning in the BG leads the STR cells to encode small sections of the stimuli (see Fig. 3c) and due to the high diversity of exposed exemplars,

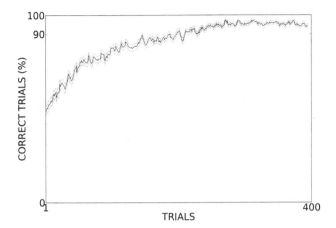

Fig. 2. Model performance in the 100 experiments per each of the 400 trials. The continuous line represents the average of successful trials and the two dotted lines indicate the corresponding standard error. To smooth the line plot, the average and the standard error are calculated from the data of the corresponding trial and the next 4 trials.

the input representation of most STR neurons strongly varies over time (see Fig. 3d). The slow learning in the PFC allows to eventually extract more generic and stable knowledge (see Fig. 3a and d).

In the exposed stimuli of each category, the IT neurons representing "color" are more probable to be active and thus more strongly encoded in PFC than the other IT cells. In the case of category A, the IT "green color" cell is always active and therefore, the PFC representations of category A eventually become selective just to this IT cell. In the case of category B, IT "color" neurons are just slightly more probable to be active than the rest of IT cells and thus, the PFC category B representations encode a broader range of IT neurons than just IT "color" cells. However, due to the random experiences in each experiment, the bias for encoding IT "color" cells can only be clearly observed in the average of the category B representations across all experiments (see Fig. 3b).

To compare both the STR and the PFC representations, we tested, at the end of each experiment, the capacity of both the PFC and the BG to correctly classify new, unseen, stimuli without the influence of the other while suppressing learning in the network. First, the effect of the PFC was tested by running 400 trials after removing the connections between the output nucleus of the BG and the thalamus. Then, the effect of the BG was tested by also running 400 trials after setting back the weights of the projections from the input neurons to the PFC to its initial conditions, thus removing any knowledge stored in them. The results of both are presented in Fig. 4.

Figure 4 shows that PFC can correctly classify around 99 % of the new stimuli while the BG, around the 68 %. This confirms that the slow learning system can acquire a better category representation. However, this is only possible due to the initial training performed by the BG.

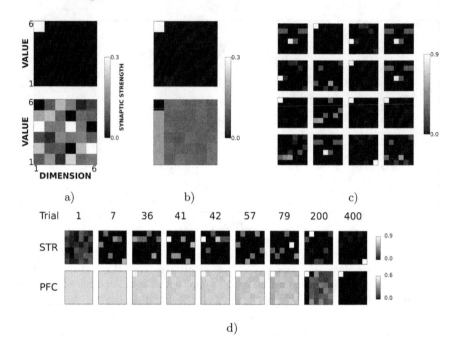

Fig. 3. "Receptive fields" of example PFC and STR cells at the end of the learning period. As illustrated in a), the x-axis, the y-axis and the grey scale of each subplot indicate the dimension of the input, the value of the input and the synaptic strength, respectively. (a) Two example PFC cells; one cell specializes in category A and the other in category B. (b) Mean across all experiments of the synaptic input representations in the two PFC cells. (c) Example of 16 STR neurons, which encode only small parts of stimuli information. (d) Evolution of the synaptic weights in one neuron of STR (first row) and one cell of PFC (second row) over time at nine different moments (trials).

4   Discussion

Our model succeeds in a category classification task and provides insight into the role of fast and slow learning in category acquisition. The high variability in the exposed stimuli impedes the input nuclei of the BG to clearly encode each category due to fast changes in the synaptic weights that force the neurons to extract only features of the most recent stimuli, while forgetting the rest. For this reason, the fast learning of the BG fails to produce a stable and complete category representation required for generalizing. However, it proves to be good enough to teach correct associations to the PFC.

Contrary to the stimuli specific knowledge acquired by the fast leaner, the slow learning in $IT \mapsto PFC$ projections allow them to gather a more general or broader amount of information. And because the fast leaning in BG produces a high enough number of correct associations, the BG train the PFC to more strongly encode those elements common in the stimuli of the corresponding

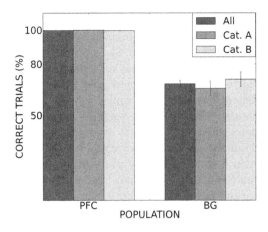

Fig. 4. Performance of the PFC and the BG alone in generalizing new stimuli. For each of both the PFC and the BG, there are three bars representing the percentage of trials correctly classified. Each bar disposes of an error bar indicating its standard error.

category, thus generating stable category representations that generalize across individual exemplars.

However, the slower learner would not be required if the number of stimuli were small enough. Hence, the fast learning could produce stable representations of the stimulus-response (SR) associations necessary to quickly achieve the highest performance [16–18]. Nevertheless, the task is no longer a category learning task but an SR learning task.

Although the fast learning system is not suitable for achieving the greatest scores in our task, it is appropriate for executing the initial trials, as it can reach a high performance in a small amount of time. Using a slow learner alone (without a fast learner) would take too much time to reach a high performance. Therefore, we believe that the brain requires a combination of both fast and slow learning for acquiring category representations while having a high task performance from the beginning.

Assigning fast and slow learning to BG and PFC respectively is in accordance with physiological considerations [19] built in a brain theory that proposes: first, a fast learning for extracting specific stimulus information, and a slow learning for identifying the commonalities among the elements of the same class [19]; and second, the BG to learn fast specific stimulus-motor associations while slowly teaching the PFC to learn categories [19–21]. Likewise, our model's function and architecture is in agreement with brain anatomy and neuroscience studies [22–24] which, for example, understand BG-cortex interaction via a cortico-basal ganglio-thalamic loop.

As in neuroscience, the machine learning community has been investigating the category recognition phenomenon. In particular, the state of the art of this field in machine learning belongs to deep neural networks with supervised learning (SL) which have won the latest contests and outperformed records in this domain [25,26]. However, learning to distinguish between entities just from the correct examples provided by a teacher (i.e. SL) works well if learning is done off-line. Category learning as discussed here relates more closely to reinforcement learning (RL), in which an agent pursues a goal by exploring and exploiting actions in its environment in order to maximize reward sensation [27].

Specifically, our model brings together both RL and categorization in such a way that fast RL learns useful actions while trains the slow learning to acquire category knowledge. Therefore, this model could be proposed as a novel deep networks' classifier, which could efficiently perform SR tasks, in case of a small number of stimuli, and categorization tasks, otherwise. Finally, further work should focus on adapting this model to more complex stimuli, for example, to learn to classify real objects by their shape.

Acknowledgments. This work has been funded by DFG HA2630/4-1 and in part by DFG HA2630/8-1.

References

1. Poldrack, R.A., Prabhakaran, V., Seger, C.A., Gabrieli, J.D.E.: Striatal activation during acquisition of a cognitive skill. Neuropsychology **13**, 564 (1999)
2. Poldrack, R.A., Clark, J., Pare-Blagoev, E.J., Shohamy, D., Moyano, J.C., Myers, C., Gluck, M.A.: Interactive memory systems in the human brain. Nature **414**, 546–550 (2001)
3. Nomura, E., Maddox, W.T., Filoteo, J.V., Ing, A.D., Gitelman, D.R., Parrish, T.B., Mesulam, M.M., Reber, P.J.: Neural correlates of rule-based and information-integration visual category learning. Cere. Cortex **17**, 37–43 (2007)
4. Seger, C.A., Cincotta, C.M.: The roles of the caudate nucleus in human classification learning. J. Neurosci. **11**, 2941–2951 (2005)
5. Zeithamova, D., Maddox, W.T., Schnyer, D.M.: Dissociable prototype learning systems: evidence from brain imaging and behavior. J. Neurosci. **28**, 13194–13201 (2008)
6. Merchant, H., Zainos, A., Hernández, A., Salinas, E., Romo, R.: Functional properties of primate putamen neurons during the categorization of tactile stimuli. J. Neurophysiol. **77**, 1132–1154 (1997)
7. Cincotta, C.M., Seger, C.A.: Dissociation between striatal regions while learning to categorize via feedback and via observation. J. Cognit. Neurosci. **19**, 249–265 (2007)
8. Humphries, M.D., Stewart, R.D., Gurney, K.N.: A physiologically plausible model of action selection and oscillatory activity in the basal ganglia. J. Neurosci. **26**, 12921–12942 (2006)
9. Grillner, S., Hellgren, J., Menard, A., Saitoh, K., Wikström, M.A.: Mechanisms for selection of basic motor programs-roles for the striatum and pallidum. Trends Neurosci. **28**, 364–370 (2005)
10. Hélie, S., Ell, S.W., Ashby, F.G.: Learning robust cortico-cortical associations with the basal ganglia: an integrative review. Cortex **64**, 123–135 (2015)
11. Freedman, D.J., Riesenhuber, M., Poggio, T., Miller, E.K.: A comparison of primate prefrontal and inferior temporal cortices during visual categorization. J. Neurosci. **23**, 5235–5246 (2003)

12. Freedman, D.J., Riesenhuber, M., Poggio, T., Miller, E.K.: Visual categorization and the primate prefrontal cortex: neurophysiology and behavior. J. Neurophysiol. **88**, 929–941 (2002)
13. Freedman, D.J., Riesenhuber, M., Poggio, T., Miller, E.K.: Categorical representation of visual stimuli in the primate prefrontal cortex. Science **291**, 312–316 (2001)
14. Miller, E.K., Cohen, J.D.: An integrative theory of prefrontal cortex function. Ann. Rev. Neurosci. **24**, 167–202 (2001)
15. Vitay, J., Dinkelbach, H., Hamker, F.H.: ANNarchy: a code generation approach to neural simulations on parallel hardware. Front. Neuroinf. **9**, 19 (2015)
16. Schroll, H., Vitay, J., Hamker, F.H.: Dysfunctional and compensatory synaptic plasticity in Parkinson's disease. Eur. J. Neurosci. **39**, 688–702 (2014)
17. Baladron, J., Hamker, F.H.: A spiking neural network based on the basal ganglia functional anatomy. Neural Netw. **67**, 1–13 (2015)
18. Packard, M.G., Knowlton, B.J.: Learning and memory functions of the basal ganglia. Ann. Rev. Neurosci. **25**, 563–593 (2002)
19. Seger, C.A., Miller, E.K.: Category learning in the brain. Ann. Rev. Neurosci. **33**, 203 (2010)
20. Antzoulatos, E.G., Miller, E.K.: Differences between neural activity in prefrontal cortex and striatum during learning of novel abstract categories. Neuron **71**, 243–249 (2011)
21. Miller, E.K., Buschman, T.J.: Rules through recursion: how interactions between the frontal cortex and basal ganglia may build abstract, complex rules from concrete, simple ones. In: Neuroscience of Rule-Guided Behavior, pp. 419–440 (2007)
22. Seger, C.A.: The basal ganglia in human learning. Neuroscientist **12**, 285–290 (2006)
23. Haber, S.N.: The primate basal ganglia: parallel and integrative networks. J. Chem. Neuroanat. **26**, 317–330 (2003)
24. McHaffie, J.G., Stanford, T.R., Stein, B.E., Coizet, V., Redgrave, P.: Subcortical loops through the basal ganglia. Trends Neurosci. **28**, 401–407 (2005)
25. Stallkamp, J., Schlipsing, M., Salmen, F., Igel, C.: Man vs. computer: benchmarking machine learning algorithms for traffic sign recognition. Neural Netw. **32**, 323–332 (2012)
26. Schmidhuber, J.: Deep learning in neural networks: an overview. Neural Netw. **61**, 85–117 (2015)
27. Sutton, R.S., Barto, A.G.: Reinforcement Learning: An Introduction. A Bradford Book, Cambridge (1998)

Realizing Medium Spiny Neurons with a Simple Neuron Model

Sami Utku Çelikok[1]([⊠]) and Neslihan Serap Şengör[2]

[1] Biomedical Engineering Department, Boğaziçi University,
34342 Bebek, Beşiktaş, Istanbul, Turkey
utku.celikok@boun.edu.tr
[2] Electronics and Telecommunication Department,
İstanbul Technical University, Istanbul, Turkey
sengorn@itu.edu.tr

Abstract. Striatal medium spiny neurons (MSNs) constitute input nuclei of the basal ganglia. Most well-known dichotomous of striatal MSNs stem from dopaminergic modulation of striatal processing. Dopamine modulates excitability in striatal MSNs with a complex underlying mechanism and lack of balance in this delicate system leads to pathologies such as Parkinson's disease. On the contrary, investigation of such a system requires simple, but yet comprehensive models that are capable of capturing complex behaviour of MSNs. We propose a reduced-computational but biologically plausible model that mimics the cell dynamics of striatal D_1- and D_2-type MSNs with different levels of dopamine using data from a recent study. Proposed computational model shows good matches to the MSN responses and captures some essential features of MSNs such as first spike latencies, dopamine modulated state transitions and enhanced response to depolarizing input during dopamine intervention.

Keywords: Dopamine · Electrophysiology · Medium spiny neurons · Simple model

1 Introduction

The striatum is a subcortical structure located in the human forebrain and one of the principal component of the basal ganglia, a group of nuclei that have a wide variety of functions but are best known for their role in cognitive functions and voluntary movement [1,2]. Realization of a specific inhibitory function, either during a cognitive task or action selection, depends on dopamine (DA) modulated activity of the medium spiny neurons (MSNs) within the striatum [3,4]. The striatum serves as the primary input to the basal ganglia system and is also shown to have a strong influence on basal ganglia output. In this sense, DA modulated striatal activity triggers the initiation of a decision on the sensory, limbic, or heteromodal information through multiple anatomical loops that process the information. Membrane excitability alterations by DA provide a

© Springer International Publishing Switzerland 2016
A.E.P. Villa et al. (Eds.): ICANN 2016, Part I, LNCS 9886, pp. 256–263, 2016.
DOI: 10.1007/978-3-319-44778-0_30

selection mechanism for cognitive and psychomotor functions, and a malfunction in the striatal circuitry and death of DA cells in the SNc are shown to be involved in several neuropsychiatric conditions including Parkinson's Disease (PD) and schizophrenia [5,6]. DA level in PD remains incapable of driving D_1 neurons to up state leading to excessive cortical inhibition. Schizophrenia causes excessive DA in the basal ganglia and low level of DA in the prefrontal cortex (PFC). This suggests a low-threshold for information update, causing attention to be easily altered; however, reduced activity in the PFC causes less maintenance of the representation [7].

One important way to enhance our understanding about the dynamics of MSNs is to employ mathematical/computational models to generate predictions. A wide variety of computational studies have been undertaken to investigate ion channel activities and electrophysiological properties of MSNs [8–10]. The model presented in [8] proposed a biologically realistic model that is capable of covering complex dynamics of MSNs and their modulation by DA. Their study established further differences between D_1- and D_2-type neurons and bistability of MSNs. Moreover, computational-models have provided valuable foresights about the deficits in striatal mechanism, and also drug medication [11,12]. Another relevant model suggested a unified role of phasic and tonic DA levels in PD on- and off-medication cases [11]. In [12], they discussed the DA modulation in basal ganglia network and also effect of drug medication. Additionally, some studies focused on DA modulated selection mechanism during cognitive and motor tasks by including cortico-striato-thalamocortical circuit [13,14]. In the light of these studies, study presented here aims to provide a simple computational model for use in large-scale striatum models. Construction of such a large-scale model should be simple, but yet still capable of capturing complex behaviour of MSNs. For this purpose, we extended Izhikevich's simple model of MSNs to mimic dopaminergic modulation of intrinsic ion channels. We aim to provide a novel set of mathematical model whose dynamics are modulated by intrinsic ion channel properties and extracellular dopamine level. D_1 and D_2-type receptor MSN models are tuned using data from a recent model and simulations revealed notable matches with the data in [15].

2   Medium Spiny Neurons

2.1   Physiology of MSNs

DA modulates excitability by interacting with a family of receptor subtypes and the assignment of these subtypes is based on the activated G protein type and whether it excites (D_1-type) or inhibits (D_2-type) adenylyl cyclase [16]. This leads to opposite effects of DA in modulating excitability of two classes of DA receptors. D_1 MSNs contain inward-rectifying K channel (KIR) that is active at hyperpolarized potentials. KIR current hyperpolarizes MSN to an unusually low membrane potential ($-85\,\mathrm{mV}$), mentioned in the introduction as the down-state [17]. A second underlying mechanism of the transition between up- and down-state is L-type Ca^{2+} channel that leads to increased discharge once the up-state had been achieved [18]. D_1 receptor activation has been shown to enhance L-type Ca^{2+} currents in MSNs where opposite effect is shown for D_2 receptors [19]. For our purpose, we concluded that for D_1 and for D_2 receptor activation may be mediated through differential modulation of L-type Ca^{2+} currents and through an increase in KIR currents. Studies also revealed a contrary DA modulation for MSNs as to enhanced/lowered state maintenance in response to depolarizing input for D_1/D_2 receptors. Such effect is interpreted as a result of changes in conductances from the baseline values [8,20]. An increase in conductance allows MSNs to have a stronger maintenance of the current state; stay in up-state or remain hyperpolarized at down-state.

2.2   Computational Models of MSNs

We fitted the proposed model to correctly match the input-output relation obtained in [15]. Considered study in [15], NEURON model of the MSNs established a dichotomy in excitability due to dendritic area properties; however, we take into consideration the electrophysiological properties of MSNs in terms of frequency-input curve (f-I curve) and spike generation characteristics. In [21], they built a computational model of basal ganglia, with a population-based model, realizing an action selection mechanism in terms of signal selection. Study concluded with a different interpretation of the basal ganglia architecture where the employment of various pathways are devoted to the selection and the control pathways. Presented study in [22] offers a multicompartment NEURON model of MSN in nucleus accumbens by taking all known ionic currents into account for these cells. They arrived at the conclusion that afferent NMDA/AMPA input ratio to MSNs may be a key reason underlying in the hysteresis of up- and down-state transitions and entrainment to oscillatory input. In addition, proposed model attributes a possible role to NMDA/AMPA ratio in schizophrenia and addiction due to lack/abundance of transition probabilities between states. Computational model proposed in [23] described a dynamical system accounting for DA modulation in terms of synchronized firing between MSNs and concluded with increased synchronization in D_1-type MSNs by the DA intervention. Differentiation of our model from other similar works is first its simplicity since we consider realization of dynamics by a simple neuron model. Second, proposed model is still capable of giving some foresights about DA modulation of ion channels even though it is simple.

3   A Computational Model of MSNs

Each individual neuron is modeled as a spiking point-like neuron of the threshold-firing type. We employed the simple model proposed by Izhikevich for spike generation [24]. It is given that v is the membrane potential, and u is the contribution of the dominant ion channel. Dynamics for the membrane potential of D_1 and D_2 MSNs and the recovery current are described by the following equations.

$$D_1 \rightarrow C\frac{dv(t)}{dt} = k[v(t) - v_r][v(t) - v_t] - u(t) + I(t) + \phi_1 g_{DA}(v(t) - E_{DA}), \quad (1)$$

$$D_2 \rightarrow C\frac{dv(t)}{dt} = k[v(t) - v_r][v(t) - v_t] - u(t) + I(t) + (1 - \phi_2)g_{DA}(v(t) - E_{DA}), \quad (2)$$

$$D_1 \text{ and } D_2 \rightarrow \frac{du(t)}{dt} = a(b[v(t) - v_r] - u(t)) \quad (3)$$

where C is the membrane capacitance, v_r, the resting membrane potential and v_t, the instantaneous threshold potential. $I(t)$ is the total DC current applied to the MSN at time t. We modeled contribution of dopamine sources by the parameters ϕ_1 (for D_1) and ϕ_2 (for D_2), normalized in the interval $[0, 1]$. Parameter a is the recovery time constant; k and b are obtained from frequency-current curve (f-I curve) by measuring the instantaneous firing-rate versus the synaptic current. As it can be followed from Eqs. 1–2, we extended the classical Izhikevich model by adding the contribution of the DA on the stability of up- and down-states; considering the contrary influence of different MSN subtypes. Stability of the state refers to the state where a MSN maintain the current up- or down-state and a transition between them is less likely to occur. In a D_1-type MSN, this effect is modeled by an increase in the DA conductance from the baseline that is proportional to the DA level [8]. However, DA level constitutes an opposite effect on D_2-type MSN. We describe an additional term for modeling such an effect on D_2 MSN in Eq. 2, differentiating the proposed model from [8]. We consider the following spike-generation conditions and reset of MSNs:

$$if \; v_{D1}/v_{D2} \geq v_{peak} \text{ then } \begin{cases} d_{D1} \leftarrow d_{D1}(1 - \phi_1 L) & , D_1 \text{ MSN reset} \\ v_{rD1} \leftarrow v_{rD1}(1 + \phi_1 K) & , D_1 \text{ MSN } " \\ v_{D1/2} \leftarrow c_{D1/2} & , D_1 \text{ and } D_2 \text{ MSN } " \\ u_{D1/2} \leftarrow u_{D1/2} + d_{D1/2} & , D_1 \text{ and } D_2 \text{ MSN } " \end{cases}$$
$$(4)$$

These extensions are inspired by [8]. Additional reset condition for parameter d allows MSN to enhance sensitivity to depolarizing input. Generation of a second spike becomes more likely to occur as L-type Ca^{2+} activation threshold reduces with the first spike. Another expansion involves parameter v_r that corresponds to enhancement of KIR current, hyperpolarising the membrane after depolarization. This modulation of the parameter results in decreased resting potential after depolarization, stabilizing down-state while avoiding subsequent spikes. Down-regulation of resting potential brings MSN closer to the reversal potential. We don't consider any extension of the reset condition for D_2 MSN. All derived parameters for D_1- and D_2-type receptors are given in Table 1.

Simulated neuron's firing behaviour is shown in Fig. 1. Model presents the MSN's characteristic delay to first spike after current injection and as input current increases, spike latency disappears [25]. We also observed that D_1 receptor stays hyperpolarized at around $-85\,mV$ without any stimulation and the level is higher for D_2 receptors [15]. Resting membrane potential for D_1 receptor is found at $-83\,mV$, and $-78\,mV$ for D_2 MSN. Up-state threshold for D_1 MSN

Table 1. MSNs parameters

Parameter	C	v_r	v_t	a	b	c	d	k	E_{DA}	g_{DA}	L	K
MSN D_1	50 μF	−75.9 mV	−33.8 mV	0.04	−8.0	−55	700	1.13	−68.4 mV	21.7 mS/cm^2	0.731	0.131
MSN D_2	50 μF	−77.0 mV	−44.1 mV	0.05	−15	−55	600	1.10	−68.0 mV	21.1 mS/cm^2	-	-

requires a membrane potential around −60 mV [15]. The rheobase current was significantly greater in D_1 MSN (D1 MSN: 270 pA; D2 MSN: 130 pA, compatible with [15]). We obtained a good fit to the f-I curve from simulations, shown in Fig. 2. As dichotomous between MSNs offered, D_2-type receptors are more excitable then the D_1 MSNs and has stronger response to depolarizing current. For both models, we obtained a linearity of MSN model's response to input. We also investigated the changes in bimodality and response of D_1-type receptor with the modulation of DA, and results are given in Fig. 3. In Fig. 3-A, we noted that increase in DA level doesn't allow MSN D_1 to response lower-injections but rather increases response during up-state and even causes burst of spikes. Figure 3-B shows that in the abundance of DA, slope of the f-I curve increases, and transition from down- to up-state is more abrupt but still found to be linear. We didn't obtain a left-shift in the f-I curve. Besides increasing firing response to injected current, spectrogram results also reveal an increase in power of D_1 activity in Fig. 3-C. DA-free simulations reveals a spread of power over different frequency values, specifically for low-level inputs in Fig. 2-A; however, DA intervention reveals most prominent frequency component more clearly, and also in a narrower frequency interval.

This may suggest that DA modulated increase in conductance in Eq. 1 ensures maintenance of up-state and allows a MSN to sustain this state during the DA intervention. Another prominent change was the repetitive spike generation of the D_1 MSN. DA increase lowers the activation threshold of L-type Ca^{2+} current, enabling a second or third spike to occur within a hundred milliseconds interval. Enhancement in hyperpolarizing KIR currents during depolarized state remains incapable of avoiding short-interval spikes.

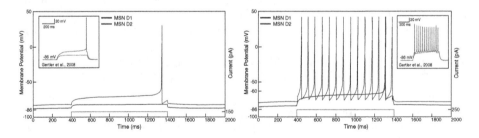

Fig. 1. Initial spike generation for D_1- and D_2-type receptors. As compitable with [15], activity of both receptor type presents spike latencies for the first spike and later spikes occur without such a delay with L-type Ca^{2+} current contribution.

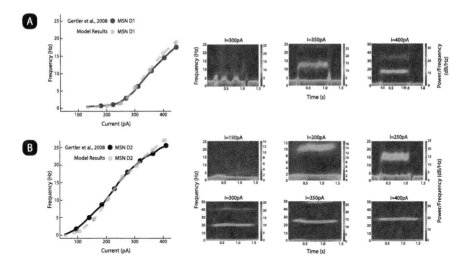

Fig. 2. Simulation results revealed a good fit to the considered study. (A) Left: f-I curve for modeled MSN D_1-type neuron with results from [15]. Right: spectrogram results for varying levels of DC input. (B) Left: f-I curve for modeled MSN D_2-type neuron with results from the multicompartment model in [15]. Right: spectrogram results for varying DC input. Both MSNs present a linear change in their response to depolarizing input. Rheobase current is higher for D_1-type neuron; D1 MSN: 270 pA; D2 MSN: 130 pA.

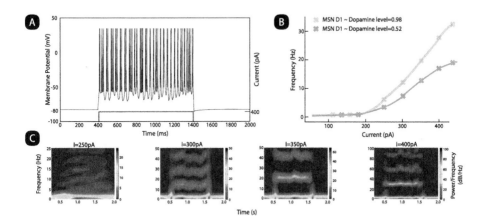

Fig. 3. D1 simple model predicts increase in the slope of the f-I curve with DA application and no change in rheobase current. (A) D_1 MSN response to DC current for 400 pA. (B) f-I curve comparison during DA free condition and DA modulated activity. (C) Spectrogram results for varying levels of input current.

4   Discussion

Proposed simple model is shown to be able to successfully present some important dynamics of striatal MSNs and excitability modulation by DA. It is also pointed out that DA modulation causes a strong response to same current injection while avoiding response to lower injections compared to the DA free trials, ensuring high signal to noise ratio. As proposed, D_1 dopamine receptor activation increases by augmenting L-type Ca^{2+} currents and DA ensures maintenance of the up-state. Results satisfied our aim which was to build a simple model that is capable of capturing electrophysiological dynamics of MSNs. Main contribution of the proposed model can be appreciated more specifically by the employment in a large scale model including the basal ganglia, the thalamus and the cerebral cortex. Recently, we have proposed a computational-model for the switching mechanism of the basal ganglia and integration of the proposed model into the design may allow us to have a deeper intuition about the underlying mechanism for action selection and working memory processes [26]. Such integration may enable us to investigate synchronization by DA modulation and deficits observed in PD. Lastly, this study puts support behind the usage of simple models in the investigation of complex brain mechanisms. Simplified model reveals notable fits to the corresponding study [15].

References

1. Cools, R., Ivry, R.B., D'Esposito, M.: The human striatum is necessary for responding to changes in stimulus relevance. J. Cogn. Neurosci. **18**, 1973–1983 (2006)
2. Gillies, A., Arbuthnott, G.W.: Computational models of the basal ganglia. Mov. Disord. **15**, 762–770 (2000)
3. Nieoullon, A.: Dopamine and the regulation of cognition and attention. Neurobiology **67**, 53–83 (2002)
4. Apicella, P., et al.: Neuronal activity in monkey striatum related to the expectation of predictable environmental events. J. Neurophysiol. **68**, 945–960 (1992)
5. Gerfen, C.R.: Molecular effects of dopamine on striatal projection pathways. Trends Neurosci. **23**, 64–70 (2000)
6. Keshavan, M.S., et al.: Psychosis proneness and ADHD in young relatives of schizophrenia patients. Schizophr. Res. **59**, 85–92 (2003)
7. Weiner, I., Joel, D.: Dopamine in schizophrenia: dysfunctional processing in basal ganglia-thalamocortical split circuits. In: Handbook of Experimental Pharmacology: Dopamine in the CNS, vol. 154, pp. 417–471 (2002)
8. Humphries, M.D., et al.: Capturing dopaminergic modulation and bimodal membrane behaviour of striatal medium spiny neurons in accurate, reduced models. Front. Comput. Neurosci **3**, e1001011 (2009)
9. Moyer, J.T., Wolf, J.A., Finkel, L.H.: Effects of dopaminergic modulation on the integrative properties of the ventral striatal medium spiny neuron. J. Neurophysiol. **98**, 3731–3748 (2007)
10. Gruber, A.J., Solla, S.A., Houk, J.C.: Dopamine induced bistability enhances signal processing in spiny neurons. In: Advances in Neural Information Processing Systems, vol. 15, pp. 165–172. MIT Press, Cambridge (2003)

11. Guthrie, M., Myers, C.E., Gluck, M.A.: A neurocomputational model of tonic and phasic dopamine in action selection: a comparison with cognitive deficits in Parkinson's disease. Behav. Brain Res. **200**, 48–59 (2009)

12. Frank, M.J., O'Reilly, R.C.: A mechanistic account of striatal dopamine function in human cognition: psychopharmacological studies with cabergoline and haloperidol. Behav. Neurosci. **120**, 497–517 (2006)

13. Navarro-Lopez, E.M., Celikok, U., Sengor, N.S.: Hybrid Systems Neuroscience. In: El Hady, A. (ed.) Closed-Loop Neuroscience. Academic Press (2016, in press)

14. Deco, G., Rolls, E.T.: Attention, short-term memory, and action selection: a unifying theory. Neurobiology **76**, 236–256 (2005)

15. Gertler, T.S., Chan, C.S., Surmeier, D.J.: Dichotomous anatomical properties of adult striatal medium spiny neurons. J. Neurosci. **28**, 10814–10824 (2008)

16. Nicola, S.M., Surmeier, J., Malenka, R.C.: Dopaminergic modulation of neuronal excitability in the striatum and nucleus accumbens. Annu. Rev. Neurosci. **23**, 185–215 (2000)

17. Nisenbaum, E.S., Wilson, C.J.: Potassium currents responsible for inward and outward rectification in rat neostriatal spiny projection neurons. J. neurosci. **15**, 4449–4463 (1995)

18. Lin, C.W., et al.: Characterization of cloned human dopamine D_1 receptor-mediated calcium release in 293 cells. Mol. Pharmacol. **47**, 131–139 (1995)

19. Seabrook, G.R., et al.: Pharmacology of high-threshold calcium currents in GH_4C_1 pituitary cells and their regulation by activation of human D_2 and D_4 dopamine receptors. Br. J. Pharmacol. **112**, 728–734 (1994)

20. Wilson, C.J., Kawaguchi, Y.: The origins of two-state spontaneous membrane potential fluctuations of neostriatal spiny neurons. J. Neurosci. **16**, 2397–2410 (1996)

21. Gurney, K., Prescott, T.J., Redgrave, P.: A computational model of action selection in the basal ganglia. I. A new functional anatomy. Biol. Cybern. **84**, 401–410 (2001)

22. Wolf, J.A., et al.: NMDA/AMPA ratio impacts state transitions and entrainment to oscillations in a computational model of the nucleus accumbens medium spiny projection neuron. J. Neurosci. **25**, 9080–9095 (2005)

23. Elibol, R., Sengor, N.S.: A computational model investigating the role of dopamine on synchronization of striatal medium spiny neurons. In: Medicine Technology Congress, pp. 147–150 (2014)

24. Izhikevich, E.M.: Dynamical Systems in Neuroscience. MIT Press, Cambridge (2007)

25. Mahon, S., et al.: Intrinsic properties of rat striatal output neurones and time-dependent facilitation of cortical inputs in vivo. J. Physiol. **527**, 345–354 (2000)

26. Celikok, U., Navarro-Lopez, E.M., Sengor, N.S.: A Computational Model Describing the Interplay of Basal Ganglia and Subcortical Background Oscillations during Working Memory Processes. arXiv preprint, arXiv:1601.07740 (2016)

Multi-item Working Memory Capacity: What Is the Role of the Stimulation Protocol?

Marta Balagué[1]([envelope]) and Laura Dempere-Marco[2]

[1] Universitat Pompeu Fabra, Barcelona, Spain
mbalaguees@yahoo.es
[2] University of Vic-Central University of Catalonia, Vic, Spain
laura.dempere@uvic.cat

Abstract. The dynamics of the stimulation protocol become relevant when investigating multi-item working memory (WM). In this work, we explore what is the effect of the stimulation protocol in the encoding and maintenance of multiple items in WM. To this end, we consider a biophysically-realistic attractor model of visual working memory endowed with synaptic facilitation. We show that such a mechanism plays a key role when sequential stimulation protocols are considered. On one hand, synaptic facilitation boosts WM capacity. On the other hand, it allows us to account for the experimentally reported recency effect (i.e. in sequential stimulation protocols, those items presented in the final positions of a sequence are more likely to be retained in WM). In this context, the time constant of the synaptic facilitation process has been found to play an important role in modulating such effects with large values leading to larger capacity limits. However, too large values lead to neuronal dynamics which are not compatible with the recency effect, thus constraining the range of values that the time constant may take.

Keywords: Working memory · Synaptic facilitation · Attractor networks

1 Introduction

Working memory (WM) is a cognitive function which is necessary to maintain and manipulate information that is not present physically through the senses. Its integrity is basic for higher cognitive functions, such as language, memory or reasoning. A hallmark property of WM is its limited capacity. Interestingly, several theories suggest a relation between WM and fluid intelligence (gF). Among the different factors involved in the WM construct, capacity is thought to play a key role in mediating the WM-gF relation [1].

Until recently, many studies supported the view that WM shows strict upper limits [2]. However, in the last few years, two competing theories have emerged which attempt to explain such capacity limits by not only paying attention to such absolute bounds but also to the accuracy with which the items are memorized. Fixed capacity models (or discrete-slot models) [3] claim that all

© Springer International Publishing Switzerland 2016
A.E.P. Villa et al. (Eds.): ICANN 2016, Part I, LNCS 9886, pp. 264–271, 2016.
DOI: 10.1007/978-3-319-44778-0_31

items are recalled with equal precision up to an upper limit (3–4 items in the case of visual WM) and no information is stored beyond this limit. In contrast, dynamic allocation models (or shared-resource models) [4] state that the limited resources are shared out between all of the items in the memory set although not necessarily equally. Although both models have been able to successfully account for psychophysical results, little neurophysiological evidence about the neural mechanisms underlying such predictions is available.

In fact, selectively enhanced activity throughout the delay period of delayed match-to-sample tasks has been traditionally regarded as a neural correlate of WM function [5]. Most neurophysiological studies have, nonetheless, been mostly concerned with the storage of single items in WM. Our reality is, however, more complex in that we simultaneoulsy receive many stimuli through the senses, and many of them must be kept in WM to understand the world around us. Although the neural mechanisms underlying the maintenance of multiple items in WM have not been clearly identified yet, several hypotheses have been considered, which include (1) sustained neural activation (e.g. [6–8]), (2) neural oscillations (e.g. [9]), or (3) patterns of synaptic strength [10].

Temporal Dynamics of Visual Stimuli and Multi-item WM Capacity Limits

It is clear that our perceptual reality is generally far from static. This is a consequence of the continuous influx of changing stimuli entering through our senses. While some of these stimuli appear simultaneously in the physical world, others appear asynchronously. In this work, we will focus on visual information processing and, in particular, on what is the impact of the temporal dynamics of visual stimuli on visual working memory (vWM). Of note, such temporal dimension has some important implications regarding not only *how many* of those items are maintained in vWM but also *which* of them are preferentially kept. In the remaining of the paper, *sequential stimulation* will refer to a serial display of the visual stimuli which are individually shown with a temporal separation between different items. Interestingly, several features specific to sequential stimulation protocols have been reported. In particular, both *primacy* and *recency* effects have been found (e.g. [11]). The primacy effect implies that items presented earlier during the stimulation protocol are recalled more often than those presented towards the middle of the sequence. In contrast, the recency effect establishes that those items which appear later in the sequence are also preferentially recalled when compared to the items which appear in the middle of the sequence. Multi-item WM and temporal dynamics are, thus, two concepts which are necessarily bound to each other. Yet, few systematic investigations about the role that the sequential stimulation protocol plays in establishing both the capacity limits of the WM system and the prevalence of an item as a consequence of its serial position have been conducted. Only recently, Kool et al. [12] have addressed this issue by assessing different dynamical aspects of vWM by means of sequential stimulation protocols.

In order to gain further insights into the neural mechanisms which give rise to a limited capacity WM system, we consider a biophysically-realistic attractor network with spiking neurons [13]. The spiking neural network considered in this study is based on the model proposed by Brunel and Wang [14] and is endowed with synaptic plasticity. Of particular interest to our study is the work by Edin et al. [6], in which a continuous attractor network is used to model visuospatial WM and the mechanisms underlying WM capacity are analyzed in depth. The authors show that there exists an upper boundary to the capacity limit arising from lateral inhibition in parietal cortex. Our model reproduces similar results while also accounting for the experimental results of a sequential test, inspired by Miller's distractor experiments and described in detail in [15].

It is worth noting that it is unclear how and whether the stimulation protocol modifies WM capacity. In this work, we tackle this question by means of a computational study. For simplicity, the level of accuracy with which a visual item is kept on visual memory has not been specifically addressed. Thus, we have considered that visual items are either kept in WM memory with sufficient precision for its reporting or not kept at all.

2   Materials and Methods

2.1   Computational Model

The model consists of a network structured into statistically homogeneous neural populations. In particular, the statistical properties of the synaptic currents and the connection strengths are identical for all the neurons within the same population. There is one population of inhibitory cells and one population of excitatory cells, which is partitioned into 10 subpopulations. Each of these populations selectively responds to a particular object. Each of these excitatory populations represents one short term memory by maintaining its activity during a delay period after a cue (λ_1, λ_2, ..., λ_{10}, of value $\lambda_i = 3.3125$ Hz/synapse) has been applied.

Recurrent connections between neurons from the same selective subpopulation are potentiated by a factor $\omega_+ > 1$ with respect to the baseline connectivity level, while connections between neurons from different selective subpopulations are weakened by a factor $0 < \omega_- < 1$. The strength of inhibitory-to-excitatory connections and inhibitory-to-inhibitory connections is denoted by the weight ω_{inh}. The synaptic connection strengths used in this study are: $\omega_+ = 2.3$, $\omega_- = 0.87$, $\omega_{inh} = 0.97$. The integrate-and-fire spiking network contained 1000 neurons (80 % excitatory and 20 % in the inhibitory pool). Each neuron in the network receives external Poisson inputs λ_{ext} from 800 external neurons at a rate of 3.05 Hz/synapse to simulate the effect of inputs coming from other brain areas.

The behavior of the neurons is modeled by means of the leaky integrate-and-fire (LIF) model, in which the membrane potential V(t) obeys the following differential equation:

$$C_m \frac{dV(t)}{dt} = -g_m \left(V(t) - V_L \right) - I_{syn}(t) \tag{1}$$

where C_m is the total membrane capacitance, g_L is the passive conductance, V_L is the resting potential, and $I_{syn}(t)$ is the synaptic current that charges the neuron. In this work, four families of synapses have been considered. The recurrent excitatory postsynaptic currents (EPSCs) have two components, which are mediated by AMPA and NMDA receptors. In contrast, only AMPA receptors mediate external EPSCs and GABA receptors mediate the inhibitory components. The total synaptic current is defined as follows:

$$I_{syn}(t) = I_{AMPA,ext}(t) + I_{AMPA,rec}(t) + I_{NMDA,rec}(t) + I_{GABA}(t) \qquad (2)$$

A full description of the model can be found in our original work [13].

2.2 Short-Term Facilitation and Stimulation Protocols

To the standard integrate-and-fire network [14], and following the model presented in [13], we added synaptic facilitation. Short-term synaptic facilitation has been implemented by using a phenomenological model of calcium-mediated transmission [10], which obeys the following equation:

$$\frac{du_j(t)}{dt} = \frac{U - u_j(t)}{\tau_F} + U\left(1 - u_j(t)\right) \sum_k \delta(t - t_j^k) \qquad (3)$$

In our model, the synaptic efficacy of the recurrent connections between all of the excitatory neurons is modulated by the utilization parameter u (the fraction of resources used) reflecting the calcium level. The value for the baseline utilization factor is U (0.15). The time constant of the decay of the synaptic facilitation is regulated by the parameter τ_F.

Since our focus in this study is on the temporal relationship between the stimuli, we have considered both simultaneous and sequential stimulation protocols. In both cases, each cue lasts for 1000 ms. In the sequential stimulation protocols, however, there is also an interstimulus period of 1000 ms between consecutive stimuli which is equivalent to that considered in [15]. In this work, we investigate the role that the time constant τ_F plays in terms of establishing an upper boundary for WM capacity but also how it crucially shapes the neurodynamical response of the system, which strongly depends on the stimulation protocol.

3 Results

3.1 Network Model Endowed with Short-Term Plasticity

In this section, we confront the predictions of our previously published model [13], which was validated only in the context of simultaneous stimulation protocols, with the results obtained when sequential stimulation protocols are considered. Figure 1A and B show how the number of items maintained in WM changes

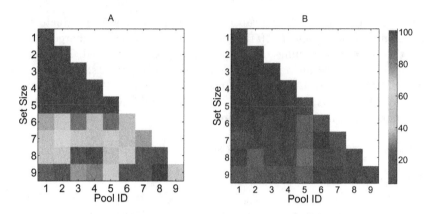

Fig. 1. Items maintained in visual WM. Histogram illustrating the percentage of trials in which different number of pools show high activity during 500 ms of the delay period 2 s after the last item of the memory set is displayed for simultaneous stimulation protocol (A) and sequential stimulation protocol (B) in 100 trials.

as a function of the number of items which have received suprathreshold stimulation. As can be seen, and in agreement with previous studies (e.g. [6,7]), the model predicts that the number of items that can be stored in WM reaches an upper boundary capacity value, which is around 5.

In order to further investigate the relevance of the stimulation protocol, we have focused on a particular case in which the number of items that are stimulated is above the capacity limit. This allows us to assess whether there is any dependence on *which* stimuli are maintained in WM as a function of the serial order. In all of the examples that we are showing next, 9 pools receive external stimulation as a consequence of the visual display of items to which the neuronal populations selectively respond. Interestingly, although there is no preference as to which items are kept in WM during the delay period in the simultaneous stimulation paradigm, Fig. 1B shows that, when the sequential stimulation paradigm is considered, those items which are seen last are less likely to be maintained in WM. A closer examination of Fig. 1B suggests that the reason for this happening is that such stimuli are less likely to be correctly encoded during the stimulation period. This is because of the competition between excitatory pools mediated by the inhibitory pool, whose activity increases when subsequent pools are stimulated during the experimental protocol and prevent the last pools from reaching a high firing rate during the stimulation (i.e. failure to encode the corresponding stimulus during the stimulation period). This is, however, at odds with the experimental observations suggesting a recency effect and indicates that this model, as it currently holds is not able to reproduce such findings.

3.2   Assessing the Role of τ_F

As discussed in [13], synaptic facilitation boosts WM capacity because of the effectively increased synaptic strengths of those pools to which the cues are applied, and then maintenance of this synaptic facilitation in just those pools when the cue is removed by the continuing neuronal firing in those pools. The time constant τ_F plays a critical role in establishing the dynamics of this mechanism. We have explored its role on the encoding and maintenance of items in WM.

In particular, Fig. 2A shows that WM capacity increases for increasing values of τ_F for sequential stimulation protocols. The same holds for simultaneous stimulation protocols (data not shown). Interestingly, as can be seen in Fig. 2B, there exists a value of τ_F between 1500 ms and 1000 ms below which the recency effect emerges. Thus, one should consider both WM capacity but also the emergence of the recency effect to establish an appropriate working regime for the network.

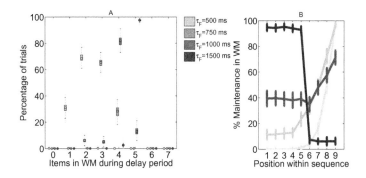

Fig. 2. Distribution of items in WM during the delay period. Results derived from computational simulations (100 blocks of 100 trials) when different values of τ_F (550 ms, 750 ms, 1000 ms, 1500 ms) are considered. Maintenance in WM is estimated by assuming that an item is held in memory when its associated selective pool shows a mean persistent activity $\nu > 20$ Hz during a period of 500 ms, 2 s after the last visual cue is removed. (A) Boxplot showing the number of items kept in WM during the delay period when 9 items are sequentially stimulated. An increasing number of items is kept in WM when τ_F increases. (B) Probability of maintaining an item in WM as a function of its serial order within the sequence. The likelihood that the last items in the sequence are kept in WM increases when τ_F decreases.

In order to understand the neurophysiological basis of the previous results, we have further investigated the dynamics of the utilization parameter u. Figure 3 reveals that the synaptic facilitation variable u_i associated which each pool i that is maintained in WM during the delay period not only reaches higher stationary values (denoted $u_{i\infty}$) but also more pools, among those which have received a cue during the stimulation period, reach such state characterized by a persistently

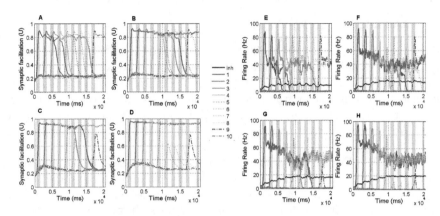

Fig. 3. Prediction of synaptic facilitation and firing rates. Simulations obtained from the network model. The stimulation period is depicted in pink whereas the delay period is depicted in gray. In these plots different values of τ_F have been considered. The panels on the left show the temporal evolution of the synaptic facilitation variable (u) for (A) τ_F=550 ms, (B) τ_F= 750 ms, (C) τ_F=1000 ms, (D)τ_F=1500 ms. The panels on the right represent the corresponding firing rates for (E)τ_F=550 ms, (F) τ_F=750 ms, (G) τ_F=1000 ms, (H)τ_F=1500 ms.

high firing rate when τ_F increases. Moreover, varying the time constant of the facilitation process also reverses the undesired effects regarding the sequential stimulation discussed in Fig. 1A and B (i.e. the last items were less likely to be successfully encoded). Interestingly, decreasing τ_F reduces WM capacity in a way that is compatible with reproducing the recency effect since the neuronal activity of the most recently stimulated pools is less likely to decay.

4   Conclusions and Discussion

In this work, we have investigated the importance that the stimulation protocol has on establishing WM capacity limits. In contrast to most computational studies, which only consider the behavior of the network during the steady state, we claim that it is most important to pay full attention to the encoding stage as well. We hereby recall the notion of effective WM (eWM [7]) as a construct which takes into account the important constraints imposed to the WM system during the encoding stage. This complete account provides both a general framework to investigate WM function and, importantly, a plausible explanation of the neuronal mechanisms yielding WM capacity limits.

In agreement with previous studies [13], we have found that synaptic facilitation boosts the WM capacity limit by effectively increasing the synaptic strengths one for those pools to which a cue is applied. Then, the synaptic facilitation is maintained by the continuing neuronal firing in only these same pools when the cue is removed. We suggest that short-term facilitation is a neurophysiological mechanism with a key role in establishing the WM capacity limits while also modulating the system response to the intrinsic dynamics of the experimental protocols. In particular, the time constant of the synaptic facilitation process τ_F has been found to play an important role in modulating WM with large values leading to larger capacity limits in both sequential and simultaneous stimulation protocols. However, too large values lead to neuronal dynamics which are not compatible with the recency effect reported in different experimental works (e.g. [11,12]), thus constraining the range of values that the time constant may take. In particular, it is within the range $\tau_F \in [750 - 1000]$ ms that 4–5 items are kept in WM and the system displays the recency effect.

References

1. Kane, M.J., Hambrick, D.Z., Conway, A.R.A.: Working memory capacity and fluid intelligence are strongly related constructs: comment on Ackerman, Beier, and Boyle. Psychol. Bull. **131**, 66–71 (2005)
2. Cowan, N.: The magical number 4 in short-term memory: a reconsideration of mental storage capacity. Behav. Brain Sci. **24**(1), 87–114 (2000)
3. Zhang, W., Luck, S.J.: Discrete fixed-resolution representations in visual working memory. Nature **453**, 233–235 (2008)
4. Bays, P.M., Husain, M.: Dynamic shifts of limited working memory resources in human vision. Science **321**(5890), 851–854 (2008)
5. Fuster, J.M., Alexander, G.: Neuron activity related to short-term memory. Science **173**(3997), 652–654 (1971)
6. Edin, F., Klingberg, T., Johansson, P., McNab, F., Tegnér, J., Compte, A.: Mechanisms for top-down control of working memory capacity. Proc. Natl. Acad. Sci. **106**(16), 6802–6807 (2009)
7. Dempere-Marco, L., Melcher, D.P., Deco, G.: Effective visual working memory capacity: an emergent effect from the neural dynamics in an attractor network **7**(10) (2012). doi:10.1371/journal.pone.0042719
8. Wimmer, K., Nykamp, D.Q., Constantinidis, C., Compte, A.: Bump attractor dynamics in prefrontal cortex explains behavioral precision in spatial working memory. Nature Neurosci. **17**, 431–439 (2014)
9. Lisman, J.E., Idiart, M.A.P.: Storage of 7 ± 2 short-term memories in oscillatory subcycles. Science **267**, 1512–1515 (1995)
10. Mongillo, G., Barak, O., Tsodyks, M.: Synaptic theory of working memory. Science **319**(5869), 1543–1546 (2008)
11. Hurlstone, M.J., Hitch, G.J., Baddeley, A.D.: Memory for serial order across domains: an overview of the literature and directions for future research. Psychol. Bull. **140**(2), 339–373 (2014)
12. Kool, W., Conway, A.R.A., Turk-Browne, N.B.: Sequential dynamics in visual short-term memory. Atten. Percept Psychophys. **76**, 1885–1901 (2014)
13. Rolls, E.T., Dempere-Marco, L., Deco, G.: Holding multiple items in short term memory: a neural mechanism. PLoS ONE **8**(4), e61078 (2013). doi:10.1371/journal.pone.0061078
14. Brunel, N., Wang, X.J.: Effects of neuromodulation in a cortical network model of object working memory dominated by recurrent inhibition. J. Comput. Neurosci. **11**(1), 63–85 (2001)
15. Amit, D.J., Bernacchia, A., Yakovlev, V.: Multiple-object working memory – a model for behavioral performance. Cereb. Cortex **13**, 435–443 (2003)

Plasticity in the Granular Layer Enhances Motor Learning in a Computational Model of the Cerebellum

Giovanni Maffei[1([⊠])], Ivan Herreros[1], Marti Sanchez-Fibla[1],
and Paul F.M.J. Verschure[1,2]

[1] SPECS Laboratory, Universitat Pompeu Fabra (UPF), Barcelona, Spain
{giovanni.maffei,ivan.herreros,marti.sanchez,paul.verschure}@upf.edu
[2] Instituciò Catalana de Recerca i Estudis Avançats (ICREA), Barcelona, Spain

Abstract. Learning mechanisms inspired by the animal cerebellum have shown promising achievements in artificial motor adaptation, mainly by focusing on the computation performed in the molecular layer. Other sites of cerebellar plasticity however are less explored whereas their understanding could contribute to improved computational solutions. In this study, we address the advantages of a form of plasticity found in the glomerulus, thought to control the temporal gating dynamics of the cerebellar pontine input. We explore this hypothesis from a system-level perspective within a simulated robotic rejection task, by implementing a model of the cerebellar microcircuit where adaptation of the input transformation dynamics, accounting for glomerular information processing, is controlled by a cost function. Our results suggest that glomerular adaptation (1) improves motor learning by adjusting input signal transformation properties towards an optimal configuration and shaping time and magnitude of the cerebellar output, and (2) contributes to fast readaptation during sudden plant perturbations. Finally, we discuss the implications of our results from a neuroscientific and articifical control perspective.

1 Introduction

Recent research in motor control has been focusing on understanding the type of computation performed by the cerebellum together with the adaptive capabilities that machines can gain by implementing a form of cerebellar adaptive feedforward control that overcomes the noise and delay of the sensory feedback [7–9,13,15]. A common algorithm used to study cerebellar functions [1,4] suggests that a single microcircuit would act as an analysis-synthesis adaptive filter performing a decomposition of its input into a set of bases characterized by different temporal profiles and accounting for the expansion of the signal carried by mossy fibers in the cerebellar granular layer. The output signal is then obtained by a weighted integration of the bases according to a teaching signal conveyed by the climbing fibers and accounting for plasticity in the molecular layer. Cerebellar in-vitro physiology however suggests that synaptic plasticity

A.E.P. Villa et al. (Eds.): ICANN 2016, Part I, LNCS 9886, pp. 272–279, 2016.
DOI: 10.1007/978-3-319-44778-0_32

found at the parallel fibers - Purkinje cell synapsis is not the only source of adaptation in the cerebellum. Adaptation in the glomerulus, at the input stage of the cerebellar microcircuit, is thought to modulate the characteristics of the input signal expansion [2,3] driven by the recursive excitatory-inhibitory non-linear dynamics introduced by the interplay between granule and Golgi cells, with significant effects on the temporal profile and amplitude of the transformation [10]. In a recent computational study [6], we supported this hypothesis by proposing a model of the cerebellar microcircuit where a fixed threshold applied to the cortical bases (accounting for glomerular non-linear response) achieved the temporal modulation of an acquired response according to the magnitude of the input signal (CS intensity effect). However a computational strategy for the active modulation of such threshold, and therefore accounting for input stage plasticity within the current model, is still missing. Here we propose a novel implementation of the cerebellar microcircuit based on [6] that interprets the adaptation in the glomerulus as a dynamic threshold applied to the excitatory and inhibitory components of the cortical bases. This is used to adjusts the non-linearity of the response to the input signal according to a cost function and to modulate the cerebellar output both at the input stage (basis functions expansion) and output stage (basis functions integration), improving its temporal resolution and fine-tuning its magnitude response to the input signal. We test the behavioral and computational advantages of the proposed model in a simulated robotic setup analogous to a human postural task [8,14], where an agent has to learn to anticipate the effects of a predictable disturbance by issuing an adaptive motor action. We design two sets of experiments involving trial-by-trial adaptation under constant disturbance and constant plant properties in one case, and constant disturbance and variable plant properties in the other, and compare the performance of the same control architecture under control condition (adaptation in the molecular layer only), and adaptive-input condition (adaptation in both granular and molecular layer). We suggest that input stage adaptation can lead to an enhanced decomposition of the input signal by converging to threshold values that shape the bases response profile in an optimal way according to the provided target signal and contributes to improved performance and learning speed. Finally, we discuss the implications of our results from a neuroscientific and robot-control perspective suggesting how the present results, coherent with physiological studies on cerebellar information processing, could possibly enhance the adaptation of artificial agents involved in real world tasks.

2   Methods

We implemented a trial-by-trial robotic postural task as a simulated cart-pole setup where an agent has to maintain a position of equilibrium ($90°$ with respect to the horizontal axis) by resisting an external disturbance (Fig. 1.D) of $4\,\mathrm{N}$ that displaces the pole from its fixed point. The goal of the agent is to learn to anticipate the disturbance by issuing an appropriate motor response useful to minimize

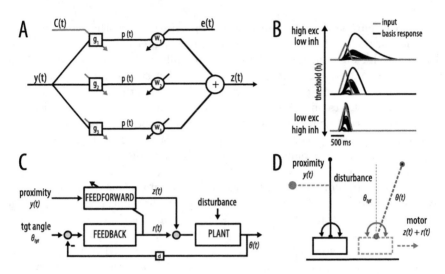

Fig. 1. A. Model of the cerebellum: input (y) is decomposed into bases (p) within the granular layer (g). Output (z) results form the weighted (w) sum of each component (p). C and E represent the teaching signals. **B.** Effect of threshold on bases response profile. **C.** Adaptive control architecture composed by reactive and adaptive layer. **D.** Postural task setup.

the error so that an initially reactive motor response is complemented with an anticipatory feedforward one acquired over trials by the cerebellar controller.

The agent is controlled by a layered architecture formed by a reactive and an adaptive component (Fig. 1.C). Within the reactive layer a feedback controller (PID) is in charge of stabilizing the angular position of the pendulum around its point of equilibrium by mapping the perceived delayed error (80 ms) into an appropriate motor output. Within the adaptive layer the cerebellar controller is in charge of learning to associate an initially neutral stimulus (the proximity signal to the disturbance) with a copy of the reactive motor response. After learning, such stimulus acquires a predictive value and triggers a learned anticipatory response that bypasses the error feedback and therefore precedes the reactive motor response. In order to achieve this, we use a learning algorithm [6] consistent with cerebellar physiology and anatomy [4] (Fig. 1.B), that expands an input $y(t)$ into a set of 100 bases (granular layer), where each basis is the results of a fast excitatory component (exc) subtracted by a slow inhibitory one (inh). Each component is obtained as a double convolution with two exponentials so that the response to a unitary pulse resembles an alpha function. The value obtained after the two convolutions is then thresholded and scaled. The final value of a basis function ($p(t)$) is computed by integrating exc and inh components and the output of a single adaptive module is obtained as a weighted linear combination the bases vector. Importantly, the threshold factor (h) is used to modulate the temporal and magnitude properties of a basis response to the input so that a low h^{exc} to the exc component coupled with a high h^{inh} of the *inh* component accounts for a fast rise - fast decay profile with lower amplitude and a a slow rise - slow decay with higher amplitude vice versa (Fig. 1.B).

The current implementation of the cerebellar microcircuit presents two forms of adaptation: (1) the weight (w) associated to each linearly integrated basis is individually updated according to a variation of the Widrow-Hoff rule such that:

$$\Delta w_j(t) = \beta e(t) p_j(t - \delta)$$

where β (=10) is the learning rate, δ accounts for feedback delay (= 80 ms) and e is the error at every time step, namely the difference between the reactive command and cerebellar output. (2) As main element of novelty, the thresholds h^{exc} and h^{inh} are adjusted dynamically. To achieve this we define a cost function C as:

$$C(\theta(t), \theta_{tgt}) = \int_0^t (\theta_{tgt} - \theta(t))^2$$

where t is a time step over the duration of a single trial, and θ_{tgt} and $\theta(t)$ are the target angle and the current angle position, respectively. We define this function under the assumption that an optimal configuration of the bases response can be found so that each component would more efficiently perform input expansion by better approximating the temporal and magnitude characteristics of the error signal and leading to a more effective integration of every component forming the output signal. Assuming that an optimal value for h^{exc} and h^{inh} can be jointly found by modulating the ratio of excitatory and inhibitory ranges across all the bases, we define an online update rule within the h parameter space to minimize C such as:

$$\Delta h(n) = \alpha(sign(\overline{C} - C(n - 1))sign(\overline{\Delta h} - \Delta h(n - 1)))$$

where $\Delta h(n)$ represents the change of threshold at trial n, α represents the learning rate (here fixed to 0.01) governing the magnitude of the change. $\overline{C}$ and $\overline{\Delta h}$ are the mean of the cost value and of the change in threshold values, respectively, for a number of previous trials. The change in threshold is then added to the parameters h^{exc} and h^{inh} with opposite signs computing the value for the next trial.In this way, we obtain a trial-by-trial modulation of the bases non-linear response that potentially spans from a combination of high excitatory - low inhibitory ranges to a combination of low excitatory - high inhibitory ranges.

3   Results

To test the effects of glomerular adaptation on motor learning we design two experimental procedures comparing adaptive-input condition (*AI* - adaptation in both granular and molecular layer) and control condition (*CT* - adaptation in molecular layer only). First, we asked whether the range of h^{exc} and h^{inh} could have an effect on the error minimization so that an optimal configuration, namely a balance between excitation and inhibition, can be found. If so, an online strategy for adaptation of such parameters should lead to convergence to optimal

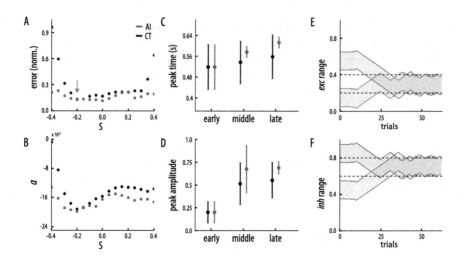

Fig. 2. A. Final error: s is the systematic change at every session where $s = 0$ corresponds to a range of 0.4–0.6 for both h^{exc} and h^{inh}. Normalization by session at trial 1. **B.** Learning speed: a denotes the slope of the regression function fit performed on the learning curve for each session. **C.** Mean response peak time for early (trial 0–23), middle (trial 24–46) and late (trial 47–70) stages. **D.** Mean response amplitude. **E. F.** Example of convergence for excitatory and inhibitory ranges respectively from different starting points. (Color figure online)

values appropriate for the task. To answer this question we instantiate a number of training sessions composed by 70 trials for each condition, where the initial h^{exc} and h^{inh} are both set to 0.4–0.6 and systematically updated every session by an increment step s of 0.05 in order to cover a full range of possible threshold configurations spanning from low excitatory range (0.0–0.2) coupled with high inhibitory one (0.8–1.0) and vice versa. In Fig. 2.A, a systematic change of h confirms, in CT, the presence of a global minimum error achieved with s of -0.2 (red arrow) corresponding to $h^{exc} = 0.2 - 0.4$ and $h^{exc} = 0.6 - 0.8$. This result suggests that, beside extreme initial conditions, the precise value of h is not critical for performance, as a relatively large range of parameter values converges to a similar error, nevertheless it supports faster learning for values closer to optimal (Fig. 2.B). As such, adaptation in the granular layer should guarantee optimal performance for every initial condition together with a faster learning curve. In (Fig. 2.A), a minimization of the error below 0.2 is achieved for almost every non-optimal initial value by progressively adapting the threshold parameters according to the trial-by-trial computed cost of the system (Fig. 2.E and F), while an improved learning speed is achieved, leading to faster convergence for every initial condition (Fig. 2.B). As expected, performance in the optimal range is highly comparable for both the control and the adaptive condition. Interestingly we show that the adaptation of the bases response influences both peak time and amplitude of the cerebellar output: an initial mean peak time of 0.52 s from cue signal onset detected at the early stages of learning for both conditions converges to a value of 0.62 s only in adaptive input condition (Fig. 2.C). In addition, initial mean peak amplitude of 0.25, equal for both conditions and expectedly low given the early stage of learning, converges to higher values (0.7) for the adaptive condition at the end of each session (Fig. 2.D).

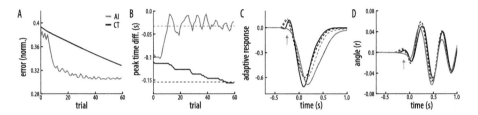

Fig. 3. A. Learning curve after plant perturbation (trial 0). **B.** Peak response time evolution after plant perturbation relative to disturbance peak time. **C.** Adaptive response after plant perturbation. **D.** Pendulum angle after plant perturbation. Dashed: mean trial 0–5; Solid: mean trial 55–60. (Color figure online)

In the second experiment, after the learning phase we introduce a sudden plant perturbation (i.e. lighter plant: cart weight at 0.2 kg) resulting in a decrease in the inertia (linear momentum) governing the motion of the agent. Shorter control latencies require less anticipation and make the previously acquired response inadequate (i.e. over-anticipation). The controller should therefore compensate for the self-introduced error or reduce anticipation. We test the system under AI and CL conditions, using h values found to be optimal (0.2–0.4 for h^{exc} and 0.6–0.8 for h^{inh}) in standard plant configuration. An increased error at early trials soon after the perturbation is due to over-anticipation, visible in the angular position of the pendulum (Fig. 3.D, red arrow) and adaptive motor response (Fig. 3.C, red arrow) before the delivery of the disturbance. Note that feedback control is also affected by shorter latencies and contributes to poorer performance. Error minimization however, can be appreciated in both conditions, even with different learning dynamics. In CL, a slower and constant reduction of the error reaches a minimum normalized value of 0.31 at trial 60. Differently, in AI, a sudden drop of the error can be appreciated at trial 10 (error at 0.33) followed by a progressive constant reduction till the end of the session (with a final value of 0.3) (Fig. 3.A). If this difference is due to the effect of the modulation of the glomerular signal transduction properties in re-adaptation a sudden change in the timings of the adaptive response which matches the evolution of the error should be visible in adaptive-input condition. This hypothesis is confirmed in (Fig. 3.B) where an initial similarity in the adaptive response time (relative to first disturbance peak) for the two conditions is broken by a suddenly delayed response in AI (starting at trial 5) that quickly moves and stabilizes around a relative peak time difference of −0.03 s (from trial 10 on), accounting for the shorter control time imposed by linear momentum. This shift in time eliminates the error generated by over-anticipation and produces an adaptive response more suitable for the properties of the new plant, and ultimately, useful for faster error minimization.

4   Discussion and Conclusions

We have shown that precise temporal dynamics can be shaped by glomerular modulation in a computational model of the cerebellum to: (1) achieve faster learning and improved performance by optimally shaping the bases response profile and (2) enhance the robustness of an already trained system under plant perturbation by adjusting the adaptive response peak latency to the new dynamics introduced by a lower system inertia. Our results are consistent with the modulation of the burst initiation delay and gain adaptation found at the mossy fiber granule cell synapses, where the active adjustment of the input threshold mimicked the effect of recurrent excitatory-inhibitory interplay among granule and Golgi cells [2]. Granular layer processing has been previously suggested to act as an automatic gain control mechanism maximizing the information transfer of the pontine input [12]. In contrast, our system level model suitable for robotic control, supports the hypothesis that the regulation of granule cells response initiation could implement an adaptive delay line affecting downstream activation of the cerebellar circuitry [3,10]. In addition, we proposed that adaptation could be driven by a mechanism of cost minimization as supported by recent physiological evidence showing a climbing fiber dependent modulation of the inhibition provided by Golgi cells onto the activation of granule cells [16]. Consistently with our model, such feature could serve as gating mechanism for the pontine input signal and result in an enhanced temporal coupling with the error signal conveyed by the same climbing fiber signal affecting Purkinje cell - parallel fiber synapsis. It has been suggested that multiple sites of cerebellar plasticity (i.e. parallel fiber - Purkinje cell synapsis, Purkinje cell - Deep Nucleus synapsis and Mossy fiber - deep nucleus synapsis) could account for the learning at different time scales shown in visuo-motor adaptation tasks [5]. Consistently in our model, a double form of plasticity provides a combination of fast reconfiguration of the bases profile with a slower adaptation of the weighted integration of these components, yielding enhanced re-adaptation of the adaptive control signals after sudden changes in the properties of the plant. Finally, this biomimetic feature could represent an advantage for humanoid robots postural control strategies during weight lifting tasks [11] where sudden changes in mass distribution severely affects stability and requires sophisticated adaptation. Future work should address the current limitations (i.e. the constant range width for both thresholds or the joint update of both excitatory and inhibitory thresholds) and explore more complex cost functions possibly resulting in an improved adaptation strategy with advantages for real-world control.

Acknowledgement. This work was supported by the European Commission's Horizon 2020 socSMC under agreement number: socSMC-641321H2020-FETPROACT-2014.

References

1. Albus, J.S.: A theory of cerebellar function. Math. Biosci. **10**(1–2), 25–61 (1971)
2. Crowley, J.J., Fioravante, D., Regehr, W.G.: Dynamics of fast and slow inhibition from cerebellar golgi cells allow flexible control of synaptic integration. Neuron **63**(6), 843–853 (2009)
3. De Schutter, E., Bjaalie, J.G.: Coding in the granular layer of the cerebellum. Prog. Brain Res. **130**, 279–296 (2001)
4. Dean, P., Porrill, J., Ekerot, C.F., Jörntell, H.: The cerebellar microcircuit as an adaptive filter: experimental and computational evidence. Nat. Rev. Neurosci. **11**(1), 30–43 (2010)
5. Garrido, J.A., Luque, N.R., D'Angelo, E., Ros, E.: Distributed cerebellar plasticity implements adaptable gain control in a manipulation task: a closed-loop robotic simulation. Front. Neural Circ. **7**, 159 (2013)
6. Herreros, I., Maffei, G., Brandi, S., Sanchez-Fibla, M., Verschure, P.: Speed generalization capabilities of a cerebellar model on a rapid navigation task. In: 2013 IEEE/RSJ International Conference on Intelligent Robots and Systems, pp. 363–368. IEEE (2013)
7. Herreros, I., Verschure, P.F.: Nucleo-olivary inhibition balances the interaction between the reactive and adaptive layers in motor control. Neural Netw. **47**, 64–71 (2013)
8. Maffei, G., Sanchez-fibla, M., Herreros, I., Paul, F.M.J.: Acquisition of synergistic motor responses through cerebellar learning in a robotic postural task. In: Biomimetic and Biohybrid Systems (2014)
9. Maffei, G., Santos-Pata, D., Marcos, E., Sánchez-Fibla, M., Verschure, P.: An embodied biologically constrained model of foraging: from classical and operant conditioning to adaptive real-world behavior in DAC-X. Neural Netw. **72**, 88–108 (2015)
10. Nieus, T.: LTP regulates burst initiation and frequency at mossy fiber-granule cell synapses of rat cerebellum: experimental observations and theoretical predictions. J. Neurophysiol. **95**(2), 686–699 (2005)
11. Nori, F., Traversaro, S., Eljaik, J., Romano, F., Del Prete, A., Pucci, D.: iCub whole-body control through force regulation on rigid non-coplanar contacts. Front. Robot. AI **2**, 6 (2015)
12. Schweighofer, N., Doya, K., Lay, F.: Unsupervised learning of granule cell sparse codes enhances cerebellar adaptive control. Neuroscience **103**(1), 35–50 (2001)
13. Shadmehr, R., Smith, M.A., Krakauer, J.W.: Error correction, sensory prediction, and adaptation in motor control. Ann. Rev. Neurosci. **33**, 89–108 (2010)
14. Timmann, D., Horak, F.B.: Perturbed step initiation in cerebellar subjects: 2. Modification of anticipatory postural adjustments. Exp. Brain Res. **141**(1), 110–120 (2010)
15. Wilson, E.D., Assaf, T., Pearson, M.J., Rossiter, J.M., Anderson, S.R., Porrill, J.: Bioinspired adaptive control for artificial muscles. In: Lepora, N.F., Mura, A., Krapp, H.G., Verschure, P.F.M.J., Prescott, T.J. (eds.) Living Machines 2013. LNCS, vol. 8064, pp. 311–322. Springer, Heidelberg (2013)
16. Xu, W., Edgley, S.A.: Climbing fibre-dependent changes in golgi cell responses to peripheral stimulation. J. Physiol. **586**(20), 4951–4959 (2008)

How Is Scene Recognition in a Convolutional Network Related to that in the Human Visual System?

Sugandha Sharma and Bryan Tripp[(⊠)]

Centre for Theoretical Neuroscience, University of Waterloo, Waterloo, Canada
{s72sharm,bptripp}@uwaterloo.ca

Abstract. This study is an analysis of scene recognition in a pre-trained convolutional network, to evaluate the information the network uses to distinguish scene categories. We are particularly interested in how the network is related to various areas in the human brain that are involved in different modes of scene recognition. Results of several experiments suggest that the convolutional network relies heavily on objects and fine features, similar to the lateral occipital complex (LOC) in the brain, but less on large-scale scene layout. This suggests that future scene-processing convolutional networks might be made more brain-like by adding parallel components that are more sensitive to arrangement of simple forms.

Keywords: Convolutional neural networks (CNNs) · Scene recognition · Human visual system

1 Introduction

It is remarkable that humans are able to perceive and interpret a complex scene in a fraction of a second, roughly the same time needed to identify a single object. When an image is briefly presented with less than 100 ms of exposure, observers usually perceive global scene information, e.g. whether the image was outdoor or indoor, well above chance. On the other hand, observers perceive details of objects with a couple of 100 ms more exposure time [2]. It has also been found that an exposure of 20–30 ms is enough for categorizing a scene as a natural or urban place [4]. However, it takes twice of that time to determine the basic level category of the scene, e.g. a mountain vs. a beach [3].

Studies in behavioral, computational and cognitive neuroscience suggest two complementary paths of scene perception in humans [7]. First, an object-centered approach, in which components of a scene are segmented and serve as scene descriptors (e.g., this is a street because there are buildings and cars). Second, a space-centered approach, in which spatial layout and global properties of the whole image or place act as the scene descriptors (e.g. this is a street because it is an outdoor, urban environment flanked with tall frontal vertical surfaces with squared patterned textures).

© Springer International Publishing Switzerland 2016
A.E.P. Villa et al. (Eds.): ICANN 2016, Part I, LNCS 9886, pp. 280–287, 2016.
DOI: 10.1007/978-3-319-44778-0_33

Several brain regions responsible for processing different scene properties have been identified, particularly the parahippocampal place area (PPA; a region of the collateral sulcus near the parahippocampal lingual boundary), the retrosplenial complex (RSC; located immediately behind the splenium of the corpus callosum), and the occipital place area (OPA; around the transverse occipital sulcus). PPA and RSC are most studied and respond preferentially to pictures depicting scenes, spaces and landmarks more than to pictures of faces or single movable objects [6].

While both PPA and RSC show selectivity to the spatial layout of the scene in various tasks, the responses of neither of them are modulated by the quantity of objects in the scene i.e., both regions are similarly active when viewing an empty room or a room with clutter [1].

The response of PPA is selective to different views of a panoramic scene, suggesting a view-specific representation in PPA. On the other hand, RSC seems to have a common representation of different views in a panorama, suggesting that RSC may hold a larger representation of the place beyond the current view [9]. However, scene representations in PPA have been found to be tolerant to severe transformations i.e., reflections about the vertical axis [7].

PPA and LOC represent scenes in an overlapping fashion. While PPA confuses scenes with similar spatial boundaries, regardless of the type of content, LOC confuses scenes with the same content, independent of their spatial layout [8]. LOC is not the only brain region involved in object processing, and thus multiple regions may represent different types of content and objects encountered in a scene [7].

Convolutional networks have many structural parallels with the visual cortex. Furthermore, they have recently begun to rival human performance in various vision tasks, including scene recognition as well as object recognition, stereoscopic depth estimation, etc. We would like to understand how similar the decision mechanisms of convolutional networks trained for scene recognition are to the corresponding mechanisms in the human cortex. As a first step, we analyze here the sensitivity of a scene-recognition network to certain input perturbations, to evaluate whether the network is more object-centred or space-centred.

2   Methods

We used the Places CNN [10], a network that has been previously trained for scene recognition on the Places205 dataset. The network has the same structure as [5]. It receives an image of a scene as input (e.g. the bedroom image in Fig. 1A). It has 205 outputs, corresponding to different scene categories. It is trained to output a high value for the category to which a given input image belongs (e.g. *bedroom*) and low values for other categories (e.g. *assembly line*, etc.).

2.1   Occlusion

We systematically occluded parts of the image in order to gauge how important different parts of the scene were for the network's prediction. To find which parts of an image were most important for the network, we slid a square occlusion window over an image. We set pixel values within the square to zero, passed the occluded image through the network, and recorded the output of the softmax output unit that corresponded to the correct category. In order to study the effect of objects of various sizes in the image, this procedure was repeated with squares of 9, 23, 39, 51, 87 and 113 pixels on a side. The full images had a fixed resolution of 227×227.

2.2   Blurring

We randomly selected 50 images from different categories in the Places205 test set and blurred them with a Gaussian filter of standard deviation varying between 0 and 13, in steps of 0.5. Thus there were 26 filtered images for each image in the original set of 50 images, leading to a total of 1300 images which were fed to the network. The output probabilities for correct predictions were normalized by dividing them by their maximum values across blur levels (typically the maximum occurred with zero blur). This was done to map the predictions for all the images to the same scale.

2.3   Spatial Boundaries

As discussed in Sect. 1, in the human visual system, PPA confuses scenes with similar spatial boundaries, regardless of the type of content, whereas the LOC makes the opposite errors, i.e. confusing scenes with the same content, independent of their spatial layout [7].

   We conducted an experiment to explore whether the network resembles either PPA, LOC or both of them in terms of the kind of mistakes it makes. First, two categories having similar spatial boundary were selected, 'forest path' and 'corridor'. Ten images of each of these categories were selected, and the average predicted probability (average of probability that it's a forest/corridor over 10 images) for both categories was recorded. Then two categories having similar content were selected, 'classroom' and 'conference room', and the average predicted probability for both categories was also recorded. All the images for this experiment were taken from a Google images search, i.e. not from the Places205 dataset.

2.4   Panoramic Scenes

As discussed in Sect. 1, PPA is selective for different views of a panoramic scene, while the response of RSC has a common representation of different views in a panorama [9]. Motivated by this, we conducted an experiment to see whether the response of the network was selective for different views in a panoramic scene. We collected 100 images from 12 different scene categories (images were obtained from a Google Images search), and split them up into left and right segments. These segments were then passed through the network and the correlation between the unit activations for the left and right segments were averaged over each layer and plotted as a function of layer number.

3 Results

3.1 Occlusion

Figure 1 shows heatmaps of occlusion effects over an image of a bedroom, for six different occlusion-window sizes. It is clear from the heatmaps that the bed is the most important object in the scene on which the model prediction is based. Moreover, occluding small parts of the bed has little impact on the model prediction, but occluding large areas has a large impact. This result was consistent with other experiments (not shown) in which we occluded various parts of the scene with unrelated pictures.

3.2 Blurring

Figure 2A visually shows the amount of blurring caused by the range of standard deviations used, on one of the sample images. Figure 2B shows the effect of

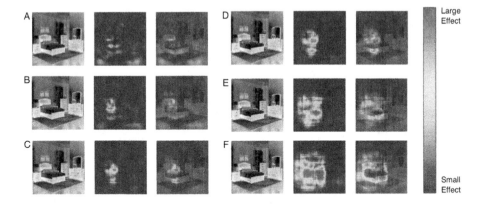

Fig. 1. Heatmaps of the effect of occlusion on the bedroom scene. The right image in each panel shows a heatmap superimposed on a black and white negative of the image. The image and the heatmap are also shown individually for clarity (left and centre; the left image is the same in each case). The red areas in the heatmap show the areas in the scene which are important for classification (the plotted values are the probabilities output by the *bedroom* node, with occlusion centred at the corresponding pixels; red is the lowest probability, or highest "effect" of occlusion). **A–F**: heat maps obtained by using occlusion windows of 9, 23, 39, 51, 87 and 113 pixels, respectively. (Color figure online)

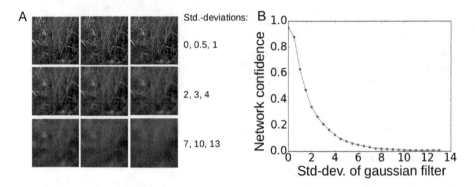

Fig. 2. Results of the blurring experiment. **A**: Effect of blurring on a sample image (shown for visual comparison). **B**: Effect of blurring on the confidence level of the network. The vertical axis shows the confidence level of the network normalized to lie within [0,1], averaged over 50 example images. The horizontal axis shows the standard deviation of the Gaussian filter used to blur the image (in pixels). (Color figure online)

blurring on the confidence level of the network (averaged over 50 randomly selected images). The confidence level of the model falls quickly with an increase in the standard deviation of the Gaussian filter. This shows that the model is not able to make predictions based on only the global features of the scenes, if it can't extract the local scene properties. This implies that the predictions of the network are based on local scene properties.

Table 1. Results from the spatial boundaries experiment. Integers indicate category indices (e.g. "Forest" is category 78).

	Forest [78] (Opponent: corridor)	Corridor [54] (Opponent: forest)	Classroom [44] (Opponent: conference room)	Conference room [51] (Opponent: classroom)
Categories predicted	[78, 78, 78, 78, 78, 78, 78, 79, 78, 78]	[54, 54, 54, 54, 54, 54, 54, 54, 54, 54]	[51, 44, 44, 44, 44, 44, 51, 44, 44, 51]	[51, 51, 51, 51, 51, 51, 51, 51, 51, 51]
Avg. probability	0.570 (grayscale: 0.562)	0.892 (grayscale: 0.929)	0.612 (grayscale: 0.606)	0.733 (grayscale: 0.581)
Avg. probability (opponent)	2.935e-05 (greyscale: 1.327e-04)	8.343e-06 (greyscale: 4.869e-06)	0.159 (greyscale: 0.115)	0.018 (greyscale: 0.025)
Top 5 probability	[(0.570, 'forest_path 78'), (0.288, 'forest_road 79'), (0.043, 'rainforest 149'), (0.0362, 'bamboo_forest 16'), (0.0129, 'tree_farm 186')]	[(0.892, 'corridor 54'), (0.033, 'locker_room 144'), (0.025, 'lobby 113'), (0.015, 'hospital 94'), '(0.007, 'jail_cell 105')]	[(0.6122, classroom 44'), (0.159, 'conference_room 51'), (0.0586, 'conference_center 50'), (0.0448, 'cafeteria 37'), (0.0375, 'auditorium 12')]	[(0.733, 'conference_room 51'), (0.064, 'Conference_center 50'), (0.029, 'banquet_hall 17'), (0.025, 'dinette/home 70'), (0.021, 'office 129')]

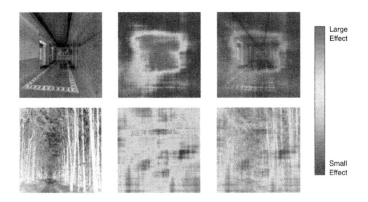

Fig. 3. Visualization of forest (bottom) and corridor (top) categories using a heatmap. The two rows show the negative of the scene on the left, heatmap in the middle and the heatmap superimposed on the scene on the right. The red areas are the most important for scene prediction. The important areas include distinguishing features of objects (e.g. tree trunks). (Color figure online)

3.3 Spatial Boundaries

We examined the extent to which the network confused scene categories with similar boundaries (specifically, forest paths and corridors) and categories with similar contents (classrooms and conference rooms).

The results are shown in Table 1. The network classified 3 of the 10 classrooms as conference rooms. However, it did not confuse forest paths and corridors. The average probability of the opponents is low for both forest and corridor, but higher for classroom and conference room. This suggests that the model confuses scenes with similar content but not the scenes with similar spatial boundaries. This was confirmed by looking at the top-5 predictions of the model. For example, for the 'forest' category, all top-5 predictions contained trees, but spatial boundaries varied (e.g. forest path vs. tree farm). Figures 3 and 4 also show the heatmaps for the four categories chosen in this experiment. The heatmaps suggest that the network is using objects to make its predictions. For example, in the classroom tables and chairs are important.

To test the extent to which colour differences accounted for the lack of confusion between forest paths and corridors, we repeated the tests with greyscale images. The results were similar to those with colour images (Table 1).

3.4 Panoramic Scenes

Figure 5 shows the correlations between the unit activations of the left and right segments of the panoramic scenes averaged over the units in each layer, over 100 different images. As expected, the average correlation is low for the input layers and increases for higher level layers.

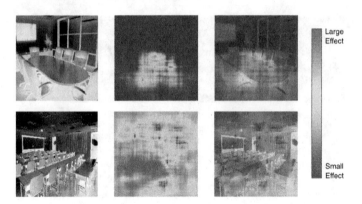

Fig. 4. Visualization of classroom (bottom) and conference room (top) categories using a heatmap. The two images show the negative of the scene on the left, heatmap in the middle and the heatmap superimposed on the scene on the right. The red areas are the most important for scene prediction. (Color figure online)

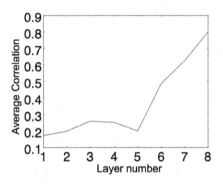

Fig. 5. Average correlation for left and right segments plotted as a function of layer number. Correlations were calculated between the activations of each unit in response to left and right parts of the panoramic images. The correlations of all units within a layer were then averaged to compute the average correlation for each layer. The later layers respond similarly to different views of each scene, similar to RSC.

4   Discussion

Our experiments suggest that the network is more object-centered (reliant on objects or local scene properties for its predictions) than space-centered (reliant on global scene properties). Its performance is impaired by occlusion of specific objects. It is sensitive to small amounts of blur (whereas humans can categorize scenes using very low spatial frequencies). This suggests that it is not able to make accurate predictions based only on the global scene properties, if it can't extract the local scene properties. Additionally, the network confuses scenes with similar content (objects, e.g. chairs etc.), but it does not confuse scenes with similar spatial boundaries but different textures. This further emphasizes the importance of objects in a scene for accurate predictions, and suggests the relative insignificance of spatial layout for distinguishing different scenes. It would be worthwhile in future work to more specifically compare the effects of the same image manipulations on human and network performance.

It may be possible to make convolutional networks for scene recognition more robust, or at least more similar to the human visual system, by adding parallel components that are specifically trained to encourage space-centered representations. One possible approach would be to train such a parallel network on blurred images. The parallel networks might then complement each other in a way that is similar to the multiple scene processing regions in the human brain.

Acknowledgments. Supported by CFI & OIT infrastructure funds, the Canada Research Chairs program, NSERC Discovery grants 261453 and 296878, ONR grant N000141310419, AFOSR grant FA8655-13-1-3084 and OGS.

References

1. Epstein, R., Kanwisher, N.: A cortical representation of the local visual environment. Nature **392**(6676), 598–601 (1998)
2. Fei-Fei, L., Iyer, A., Koch, C., Perona, P.: What do we perceive in a glance of a real-world scene? J. Vis. **7**(1), 10–10 (2007)
3. Greene, M.R., Oliva, A.: The briefest of glances: the time course of natural scene understanding. Psychol. Sci. **20**(4), 464–472 (2009)
4. Greene, M.R., Oliva, A.: Recognition of natural scenes from global properties: seeing the forest without representing the trees. Cogn. Psychol. **58**(2), 137–176 (2009)
5. Krizhevsky, A., Sutskever, I., Hinton, G.E.: Imagenet classification with deep convolutional neural networks. Adv. Neural Inf. Process. Syst. **25**, 1097–1105 (2012)
6. MacEvoy, S.P., Epstein, R.A.: Constructing scenes from objects in human occipitotemporal cortex. Nature Neurosci. **14**(10), 1323–1329 (2011)
7. Oliva, A.: Scene perception. In: Werner, J.S., Chalupa, L.M. (eds.) The New Visual Neurosciences, pp. 725–732. MIT Press, Cambridge (2014)
8. Park, S., Brady, T.F., Greene, M.R., Oliva, A.: Disentangling scene content from spatial boundary: complementary roles for the parahippocampal place area and lateral occipital complex in representing real-world scenes. J. Neurosci. **31**(4), 1333–1340 (2011)
9. Park, S., Chun, M.M.: Different roles of the parahippocampal place area (PPA) and retrosplenial cortex (RSC) in panoramic scene perception. Neuroimage **47**(4), 1747–1756 (2009)
10. Zhou, B., Lapedriza, A., Xiao, J., Torralba, A., Oliva, A.: Learning deep features for scene recognition using places database. Adv. Neural Inf. Process. Syst. **27**, 487–495 (2014)

Hybrid Trajectory Decoding from ECoG Signals for Asynchronous BCIs

Marie-Caroline Schaeffer and Tetiana Aksenova[(✉)]

CEA/LETI/CLINATEC, 17 Rue des Martyrs, 38054 Grenoble Cedex 9, France
tetiana.aksenova@cea.fr

Abstract. Brain-Computer Interfaces (BCIs) are systems which convert brain neural activity into commands for external devices. BCI users generally alternate between No Control (NC) and Intentional Control (IC) periods. Numerous motor-related BCI decoders focus on the prediction of continuously-valued limb trajectories from neural signals. Although NC/IC discrimination is crucial for clinical BCIs, continuous decoders rarely support NC periods. Integration of NC support in continuous decoders is investigated in the present article. Two discrete/continuous hybrid decoders are compared for the task of asynchronous wrist position decoding from ElectroCorticoGraphic (ECoG) signals in monkeys. One static and one dynamic decoder, namely a Switching Linear (SL) decoder and a Switching Kalman Filter (SKF), are evaluated on high dimensional time-frequency-space ECoG signal representations. The SL decoder was found to outperform the SKF for both NC/IC class detection and trajectory modeling.

Keywords: Asynchronous BCIs · Switching linear models · Switching Kalman filter

1 Introduction

Brain-Computer Interface (BCI) systems permit severely motor-impaired patients to use their brain activity to control external devices such as a cursor on a screen, upper limb orthoses or protheses etc. [9]. Several steps are usually necessary to translate users neuronal activity into effector commands. First step consists in invasive or noninvasive brain activity acquisition. Invasive BCIs are generally more efficient than noninvasive ones [9]. Neurons' Single Unit Activity (SUA), Multi Unit Activity (MUA) and ElectroCorticoGraphic (ECoG) signals are the main signals acquired by invasive methods. SUA/MUAs are recorded by microelectrode arrays directly implanted in the cortex. They are spatially highly resolved, but biocompatibility issues result from the microelectrode array's implantation [10]. ECoG signals are acquired by arrays implanted on the cortex surface. ECoG signals offer a trade-off between biocompatibility and signal quality [10]. Pre-clinical and clinical studies have confirmed the

© Springer International Publishing Switzerland 2016
A.E.P. Villa et al. (Eds.): ICANN 2016, Part I, LNCS 9886, pp. 288–296, 2016.
DOI: 10.1007/978-3-319-44778-0_34

potential of ECoG for long-term and accurate BCI systems [3,19]. Signal acquisition is followed by feature extraction. Characteristics related to user intentions are extracted from brain signals [10]. A decoder is then used to estimate the user's intention from the brain features. Different decoding strategies have been explored to provide continuous control over a neuroprosthesis or orthesis position in time. SUA/MUA-based BCIs generally rely on the decoding of the continuously-valued kinetics or kinematics of the intended movement. Best strategy for ECoG decoding is still unclear. Several studies exploited the difference in patterns generated by various motor imageries (e.g., [19]) to discriminate between a few available directions. Promising decoding results using regression approaches were reported recently [3,14]. The latter approach is expected to be more intuitive for users [14].

The BCI system developed at Clinatec aims at providing quadraplegic users with control over a 4-limb exoskeleton [5]. The wireless 64-channel ECoG WIMAGINE implant [12] was developed for stable and chronic signal acquisition. A set of decoding algorithms based on a high dimensional time-frequency-space representation of ECoG neural activity was proposed [4]. After encouraging preclinical studies, the next step consists in bringing Clinatec's BCI system to practical application in a clinical setting. Despite several proofs of concept in laboratory environments, clinical application of BCI systems for neuroprosthesis or orthesis control is a challenging task [9]. Asynchronicity of control is one of the objectives which remain to be addressed. Most BCI studies are conducted using cue-paced control paradigms. Control over the BCI system is only periodically available to the user, namely between exterior cues [11]. Asynchronous BCI decoders are continuously available to users, who alternate between No Control (NC) periods and Intentional Control (IC) periods [11]. NC support is highly desirable for clinical applications. Solutions for NC support have initially been studied for binary decoders (Brain-Switches). Integration of NC/IC class detection in continuous decoding approaches was considered for both SUA/MUA and ECoG signal (e.g., [2,17]). Hybrid discrete/continuous decoders use a class detector to bring out NC and IC periods. Continuous movement models are applied when appropriate. The movement decoder associated to NC periods issues the NC neutral value. In the majority of studies [6,17,18], class and movement decoders are independent. They are generally combined using a Winner-Takes-All strategy: the movement model corresponding to the most likely class at a given time is applied on input data. Another approach which embeds state detection inside the continuous decoder was proposed in [15]. Namely, a Switching Kalman Filter (SKF) was used for a simulated task of EEG-based asynchronous wheelchair control. The use of a SKF has also been reported for the task of 2D wrist position decoding from SUA signals in monkeys, but latent classes were not associated to NC and IC periods [22]. Both static and dynamic linear movement models were used by hybrid decoders. Wiener filters were combined with LDA class detector in SUA signals [16], and were mixed with logistic regression [2] or linear classification [6,21] in ECoG signals. Kalman filters and variants were gated by LDA in SUA signals [17] or Bayes classifier in ECoG signals [18].

In this paper, the performance of one static and one dynamic hybrid decoder was evaluated for the task of asynchronous wrist position decoding from high dimensional representations of ECoG data in monkeys. The Switching Linear (SL) decoder was developed as a particular case of supervised Mixtures of Experts (ME). The SL decoder computes the Bayes estimator of the target value by gating the movement model predictions according to estimated class probabilities. This permits to overcome the major drawback of the Winner-Takes-All strategy, namely abrupt model transitions. The Switching Kalman Filter (SKF) was chosen as a dynamic hybrid decoder with embedded class detection. The SL decoder was found to outperform to SKF approach for both trajectory and NC/IC class estimation.

2   Methods

2.1   Switching Linear Decoder

The SL decoder combined an NC/IC class decoder and movement models using the framework of MEs [20]. Let $\boldsymbol{x}^t \in \mathbb{R}^m$ be the explanatory variable, and $\boldsymbol{y}^t \in \mathbb{R}^n$ be the continuous response variable. Samples are indexed by $t \in \mathbb{N}$. Let $z^t \in \{0,1\}$ represent the class variable: $z^t = 0$ if sample t belongs to class "NC", and $z^t = 1$ if sample t belongs to class "IC". The Bayes estimate $\widehat{y}^t = E(\boldsymbol{y}^t|\boldsymbol{x}^t)$ of target variable $\boldsymbol{y}^t$ is computed via the decomposition of conditional expectation [20]:

$$E(\boldsymbol{y}^t|\boldsymbol{x}^t) = \sum_{k=0}^{1} E(\boldsymbol{y}^t, z^t = k|\boldsymbol{x}^t) = \sum_{k=0}^{1} P(z^t = k|\boldsymbol{x}^t) \, E(\boldsymbol{y}^t|\boldsymbol{x}^t, z^t = k) \ . \quad (1)$$

The posterior class probabilities $P(z^t = k|\boldsymbol{x}^t), k \in \{0,1\}$ are issued by the class decoder. The conditional expectations $E(\boldsymbol{y}^t|\boldsymbol{x}^t, z^t = k)$ correspond to the movement estimated by the NC or IC movement models ($z^t = 0, z^t = 1$ respectively). The NC model issues the NC neutral value. Various discrete and continuous models can be combined by this hybrid structure. Typically used in MEs [20], logistic regression was applied in this article to model the input-dependent mixing coefficients $P(z^t = k|\boldsymbol{x}^t)$. This classification method determines the probability of the outcome $z^t = k$ on the basis of a linear combination (score) of the observed features $\boldsymbol{x}^t \in \mathbb{R}^m$. Estimation of trajectory expectation $E(\boldsymbol{y}^t|\boldsymbol{x}^t, z^t = 1)$ was performed using a noise Gaussian probability density associated to a linear model. Prior to application, Maximum Likelihood estimation of the class and movement model parameters $\boldsymbol{\Theta} = \{\boldsymbol{\Theta}^e, \ \boldsymbol{\Theta}^g\}$ was performed using a training data set $\{\mathbf{X}, \mathbf{Y}, \boldsymbol{z}\} = \{\boldsymbol{x}^t, \boldsymbol{y}^t, z^t\}_{t=1}^{T}$. Because the sequence $\boldsymbol{z} = \{z^t\}_{t=1}^{T}$ is known, the typical Expectation-Maximization ME training is simplified.

2.2   Switching Kalman Filter

The SKF model (also referred to as Switching Dynamic Linear Model) considers a continuous state variable $\tilde{\boldsymbol{y}}^t \in \mathbb{R}^{\tilde{n}}$, a switching latent variable $z^t \in \{0,1\}$ and an explanatory variable $\boldsymbol{x}^t \in \mathbb{R}^m$ [13]:

$$z^{t+1} = \mathbf{Z}z^t , \tag{2}$$

$$\tilde{\boldsymbol{y}}^{t+1} = \mathbf{A}_{z^t}\tilde{\boldsymbol{y}}^t + \boldsymbol{w}_{z^t}^t , \tag{3}$$

$$\boldsymbol{x}^t = \mathbf{C}_{z^t}\tilde{\boldsymbol{y}}^t + \boldsymbol{v}_{z^t}^t . \tag{4}$$

The SKF model is composed by switching transition Eq. (2), response variable transition (3) and emission (4) equations. By contrast to the SL decoder, the continuous response (state) variable $\tilde{\boldsymbol{y}}^t \in \mathbb{R}^{\tilde{n}}$ is composed by the trajectory coordinates and derivatives (velocity, acceleration etc.). $\mathbf{Z}$ is the switching transition matrix. As expressed by (2), variable z^t is assumed to be generated by a first-order Markov process. $\mathbf{A}_k \in \mathbb{R}^{n \times n}$ and $\mathbf{C}_k \in \mathbb{R}^{m \times n}$ are the transition and emission matrices. $\boldsymbol{w}_{z^t}^t \in \mathbb{R}^n$ and $\boldsymbol{v}_{z^t}^t \in \mathbb{R}^m$ are the transition and observation noises with Gaussian distributions $P(\boldsymbol{w}^t| z^t = k) \sim \mathcal{N}(0, \boldsymbol{\Gamma}_k)$ and $P(\boldsymbol{v}^t| z^t = k) \sim \mathcal{N}(0, \boldsymbol{\Sigma}_k)$. The transition and emission parameters are conditioned on z^t. Supervised Maximum-Likelihood estimation of SKF parameters $\boldsymbol{\Theta} = \{\mathbf{Z}, \mathbf{A}_k, \mathbf{C}_k, \boldsymbol{\Gamma}_k, \boldsymbol{\Sigma}_k\}$ was performed using a training data set $\{\mathbf{X}, \mathbf{Y}, z\} = \{\boldsymbol{x}^t, \boldsymbol{y}^t, z^t\}_{t=1}^T$. The traditional unsupervised Expectation-Maximization training presented in [13] was reduced to a single M-step with known $(z^t)_1^T$. Estimate $\hat{\boldsymbol{y}}^t = E(\boldsymbol{y}^t|\boldsymbol{x}^{1:t})$, $\boldsymbol{x}^{1:t} = (\boldsymbol{x}^i)_{i=1}^t$ is iteratively computed by the SKF. Inference formula can be found in [13].

2.3 Application

Data Set and Feature Extraction. Decoders were evaluated on a publicly available ECoG dataset (http://neurotycho.org/food-tracking-task) [3]. The cortical activity of 2 Non-Human Primates (Monkeys A and K) was recorded by a subdural ECoG array (32-channel and 64-channel arrays for Monkeys A and K respectively) during a 3D food reaching task. ECoG signals were acquired at a sampling rate of 1 kHz. A motion tracking system tracked monkeys' wrist coordinates. The dataset consists in 5 sessions acquired with Monkey A and of 3 sessions acquired with Monkey K. Session duration is 17.7±2.0 min. Full description of the experimental set-up can be found in [3].

Time-frequency features were extracted for each channel from Δt-long ECoG sliding epochs ($\Delta t = 1$ s, sliding step 100 ms) following [4]. A Complex Continuous Wavelet Transform (CCWT) was applied on the ECoG epochs (Morlet wavelet). Frequency content was analyzed between 1 and 250 Hz. Sampling of this frequency domain was achieved via 38 daughter wavelets chosen with a logarithmic scale. Average logarithm of the CCWT's absolute value was computed in 100ms windows. Following [14], low frequency components were estimated using a Savitzky-Golay filter and added to the CCWT-based frequency features. Finally, ECoG epoch $[t - \Delta t]$ was described by the temporal-frequency-spatial feature vector $\boldsymbol{x}^t$: $\boldsymbol{x}^t \in \mathbb{R}^m$, where $m = 32 \times 10 \times (38+1)$, $m = 64 \times 10 \times (38+1)$ for Monkeys A and K respectively. Wrist position $\boldsymbol{y}^t \in \mathbb{R}^3$ was issued by the motion tracking system. Velocity $\dot{\boldsymbol{y}}^t \in \mathbb{R}^3$ was derived from position using a central-difference approximation. NC and IC periods were labelled on the basis of monkeys' tracked wrist movements: $z^t = 0$ (NC) when monkey's wrist speed was close to zero, and $z^t = 1$ (IC) otherwise.

Decoder Implementation and Training

Switching Linear Decoder. Dimensionality reduction was carried out before feeding neural features to the logit class decoder. Neural feature vector $x^t \in \mathbb{R}^m$ was projected onto the low dimensional latent subspace issued by a PLS regression between x^t and z^t [7]. Dimension of the latent subspace was chosen by 6-fold cross-validation. Maximum Likelihood estimation of the logit model parameters was performed using Iteratively Reweighted Least Squares [1]. Movement model parameters were identified using PLS regression on IC samples $\{\mathbf{X}_{IC}, \mathbf{Y}_{IC}\} = \{x^t, y^t\}_{t \in [1,T] s.t. z^t=1}$ of the training data set. The optimal number of PLS factors was estimated by 6-fold cross-validation. Neutral NC position was estimated as $\bar{y}_{NC} = \frac{1}{card(z^t=0)} \sum_{t \in [1,T] s.t. z^t=0} y^t$. PLS regression was chosen because of its ability to extract relevant information from high dimensional explanatory variables, in particular when the explanatory variable's dimension is higher than the number of training samples.

Switching Kalman Filter. The SKF state variable (i.e., response variable) was composed of the monkey's wrist position and velocity $[y^t \ \dot{y}^t]$, as it was reported as optimal for ECoG decoding [14]. Similarly to the SL class decoder, dimensionality reduction was carried out to reduce the SKF computational cost. PLS regression between x^t and $[y^t \ \dot{y}^t]$ was used to identify the low-dimensional subspace. Subspace dimension was chosen by 6-fold cross-validation.

Performance Indicators. Assessment of class detection accuracy relied on the confusion matrix. It gathers the number of NC samples which are correctly (True Negatives, TN) or wrongly (False Positives, FP) labelled, and the number of IC samples which are correctly (True Positives, TP) or wrongly (False Negatives, FN) labelled by the decoder [11]. The True Positive Rate $TPR = TP/(TP+FN)$ and False Positive Rate $FPR = FP/(FP + TN)$ were used to monitor the performance of asynchronous NC/IC decoding.

Trajectory decoding accuracy is assessed via the Pearsons Correlation Coefficient $PCC(y, \hat{y}) = cov(y, \hat{y})/(\sigma_y \sigma_{\hat{y}})$ and the Normalized Root-Mean-Squared Error $NRMSE = \|y - \hat{y}\|_2 / \|y - \bar{y}\|_2$, where y and $\hat{y}$ are observed and estimated trajectories, $\|.\|_2$ is the l_2-norm and $\bar{y}$ is the average value. The Normalized Mean Absolute Error $NMAE = \|y - \hat{y}\|_1 / \|y - \bar{y}\|_1$, and the Normalized Mean Absolute Differential Error $NMADE = \|\dot{y} - \hat{\dot{y}}\|_1 / \|\dot{y} - \bar{\dot{y}}\|_1$, where $\|.\|_1$ is the l_1-norm, were additionally computed. The NMAE issues a measure of the l_1-error between y and $\hat{y}$, and is less sensitive to outliers than the NRMSE. The NMADE was used to measure the smoothness of the decoded trajectory.

Table 1. Overall decoding performance

Axis	Method	PCC	NRMSE	NMAE	NMADE
y_1	SL	0.52	0.88	0.90	1.40
	SKF	0.43	1.07	1.22	1.86
y_2	SL	0.76	0.66	0.76	1.28
	SKF	0.67	0.80	0.98	1.62
y_3	SL	0.85	0.51	0.38	1.41
	SKF	0.75	0.71	0.73	1.75

3 Results

Both the SL decoder and the SKF were applied to decode wrist trajectories
$y^t \in \mathbb{R}^3$ from ECoG features $x^t \in \mathbb{R}^m$. Decoders were trained on the first 70 %
of each session, and were tested and compared on the remaining 30 %. Table 1
shows the overall decoding performance of the SL and SKF approaches. The SL
decoder significantly (significance level $\alpha = 0.05$) outperformed the SKF decoder
for overall trajectory decoding. The PCC, NRMSE, NMAE and NMADE criteria
were in average improved by 17 %, 21 %, 31 % and 21 % (p = 0.00, p = 0.00, p
= 0.00 and p = 0.00, respectively).

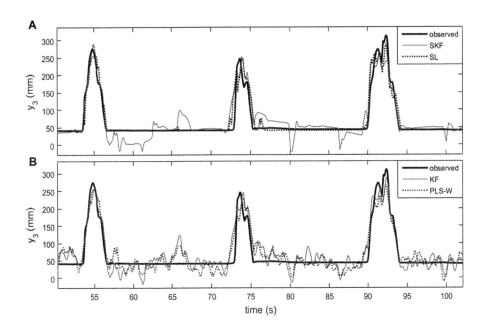

Fig. 1. Example of hybrid (A) and generic (B) trajectory decoding

The SL-based class detection (median FPR = 5.7 %, TPR = 90.6 %) significantly outperformed the SKF-based detection (median FPR = 20.4 %, TPR = 84.9 %) (p = 0.02 and p = 0.03 respectively). Figure 1A presents an example of hybrid SL- and SKF-based trajectory decoding.

4 Discussion

Kalman Filter (KF) dynamic modeling is one of the most popular approaches for limb kinematic decoding from SUA/MUA signals in BCI studies. Limb trajectory decoding from ECoG signals is mainly performed using linear regression approaches. PLS family decoders were reported as an efficient tool by several teams [2–4]. Motivation of the present study was to evaluate these two major approaches in the framework of ECoG-based hybrid decoder supporting NC periods. Importance of hybrid decoders is illustrated by the comparison between Figs. 1A and B, where generic, non-hybrid decoders (PLS-based Wiener filter, PLS-W and KF) were applied. In our study the SL PLS-based decoder significantly outperformed the SKF for all performance indicators. Reasons for this could be the Kalman filter sensitivity to outliers. ECoG data are known to be liable to artifact corruption (e.g., [4]). The SKF is considered as efficient tool for smooth trajectory decoding [8]. Interestingly, the SKF model failed to improve the NMADE criterion which reflects trajectory smoothness. It can be explained by lower performance of SKF for class decoding. Erroneous switches may degrade smoothness while the KF itself provides smooth solutions. Admissible number of FP and FN depends on the application and command rate, but a general consensus states that FP occurrences must be as rare as possible for a viable BCI clinical application. Low class decoding accuracy of SKF could limit its practical application. It should be noticed that sample misclassification does not necessarily result in trajectory jumps, because of probabilistic gating in both the SL decoder and the SKF. Additional studies are required to explore decoder performance during online BCI experiments. Closed-loop performance can be significantly different from open-loop decoding performance [8].

Acknowledgments. This work was supported in part by grants from the French National Research Agency (ANR-Carnot Institute), Fondation Motrice, Fondation Nanosciences, Fondation de l'Avenir, and Fondation Philanthropique Edmond J. Safra. The authors are grateful to all members of the CEA-LETI-CLINATEC, and especially to A. Eliseyev, M. Janvier, G. Charvet, C. Mestais and Prof. A.-L. Benabid.

References

1. Bishop, C.: Pattern Recognition and Machine Learning (Information Science and Statistics), 1st edn. Springer, New York (2007). corr. 2nd printing edn
2. Bundy, D.T., Pahwa, M., Szrama, N., Leuthardt, E.C.: Decoding three-dimensional reaching movements using electrocorticographic signals in humans. J. Neural. Eng. **13**, 026021 (2016)

3. Chao, Z.C., Nagasaka, Y., Fujii, N.: Long-term asynchronous decoding of arm motion using electrocorticographic signals in monkey. Front. Neuroeng. **3**, 3 (2010)
4. Eliseyev, A., Aksenova, T.: Stable and artifact-resistant decoding of 3D hand trajectories from ECoG signals using the generalized additive model. J. Neural. Eng. **11**, 066005 (2014)
5. Eliseyev, A., Mestais, C., Charvet, G., Sauter, F., Abroug, N., Arizumi, N., Moriniere, B.: CLINATEC BCI platform based on the ECoG-recording implant WIMAGINE and the innovative signal-processing: preclinical results. In: 2014 36th Annual International Conference of the IEEE Engineering in Medicine and Biology Society (EMBC), pp. 1222–1225 (2014)
6. Flamary, R., Rakotomamonjy, A.: Decoding finger movements from ECoG signals using switching linear models. arXiv preprint (2011). arXiv:1106.3395
7. Höskuldsson, A.: PLS regression methods. J. Chemometr. **2**, 211–228 (1998)
8. Koyama, S., Chase, S.M., Whitford, A.S., Velliste, M., Schwartz, A.B., Kass, R.E.: Comparison of brain-computer interface decoding algorithms in open-loop and closed-loop control. J. Comput. Neurosci. **29**, 73–87 (2010)
9. Lebedev, M.A., Nicolelis, M.A.L.: Brain-machine interfaces: past, present and future. TRENDS Neurosci. **29**, 536–546 (2006)
10. Leuthardt, E.C., Schalk, G., Moran, D., Ojemann, J.G.: The emerging world of motor neuroprosthetics: a neurosurgical perspective. Neurosurgery **59**, 1–14 (2006)
11. Mason, S.G., Kronegg, J., Huggins, J., Fatourechi, M., Schlögl, A.: Evaluating the performance of self-paced brain computer interface technology. Neil Squire Society, Vancouver, BC, Canada, Technical report (2006)
12. Mestais, C.S., Charvet, G., Sauter-Starace, F., Foerster, M., Ratel, D., Benabid, A.L.: WIMAGINE: wireless 64-channel ECoG recording implant for long term clinical applications. IEEE Trans. Neural Syst. Rehabil. Eng. **23**, 10–21 (2015)
13. Murphy, K.P.: Switching kalman filters. Technical report (1998)
14. Pistohl, T., Ball, T., Schulze-Bonhage, A., Aertsen, A., Mehring, C.: Prediction of arm movement trajectories from ECoG-recordings in humans. J. Neurosci. Meth. **167**, 105–114 (2008)
15. Srinivasan, L., Eden, U.T., Mitter, S.K., Brown, E.N.: General-purpose filter design for neural prosthetic devices. J. Neurophysiol. **98**, 2456–2475 (2007)
16. Suway, S.B., Tien, R.N., Jeffries, S.M., Zohny, Z., Clanton, S.T., McMorland, A.J., Velliste, M.: Resting state detection for gating movement of a neural prosthesis. In: 6th International IEEE EMBS Conference on Neural Engineering (NER), pp. 665–668 (2013)
17. Velliste, M., Kennedy, S.D., Schwartz, A.B., Whitford, A.S., Sohn, J.W., McMorland, A.J.: Motor cortical correlates of arm resting in the context of a reaching task and implications for prosthetic control. J. Neurosci. **34**, 6011–6022 (2014)
18. Wang, P.T., Puttock, E.J., King, C.E., Schombs, A., Lin, J.J., Sazgar, M., Chui, L.A.: State and trajectory decoding of upper extremity movements from electrocorticogram. In: 6th International IEEE EMBS Conference on Neural Engineering (NER), pp. 969–972 (2013)
19. Wang, W., Collinger, J.L., Degenhart, A.D., Tyler-Kabara, E.C., Schwartz, A.B., Moran, D.W., Kelly, J.W.: An electrocorticographic brain interface in an individual with tetraplegia. PloS One **8**, e55344 (2013)
20. Waterhouse, S.R.: Classification and regression using mixtures of experts. Ph.D. thesis (1998)

21. Williams, J.J., Rouse, A.G., Thongpang, S., Williams, J.C., Moran, D.W.: Differentiating closed-loop cortical intention from rest: building an asynchronous electrocorticographic BCI. J. Neural. Eng. **10**, 046001 (2013)
22. Wu, W., Black, M.J., Mumford, D., Gao, Y., Bienenstock, E., Donoghue, J.P.: Modeling and decoding motor cortical activity using a switching Kalman filter. IEEE Trans. Biomed. Eng. **51**, 933–942 (2004)

Dimensionality Reduction Effect Analysis of EEG Signals in Cross-Correlation Classifiers Performance

Jefferson Tales Oliva$^{(\boxtimes)}$ and João Luís Garcia Rosa

Bioinspired Computing Laboratory, Institute of Mathematics and Computer Science,
University of São Paulo, São Carlos, São Paulo 13566–590, Brazil
jeffersonoliva@usp.br, joaoluis@icmc.usp.br

Abstract. In this paper, it is reported a study conducted to verify whether the dimensionality reduction of electroencephalogram (EEG) segments can affect the application performance of machine learning (ML) methods. An experimental evaluation was performed in a set of 200 EEG segments, in which the piecewise aggregate approximation (PAA) method was applied for 25 %, 50 %, and 75 % settings of the original EEG segment length, generating three databases. Afterwards, cross-correlation (CC) method was applied in these databases in order to extract features. Subsequently, classifiers were built using J48, 1NN, and BP-MLP algorithms. These classifiers were evaluated by confusion matrix method. The evaluation found that the reduction of EEG segment length can increase or maintain performance of ML methods, compared to classifiers built from EEG segments with original length in order to differentiate normal signals from seizures.

Keywords: Electroencephalogram · Piecewise aggregate approximation · Cross-correlation · Machine learning

1 Introduction

According to the World Health Organization (WHO)[1], mental and neurological disorders affect approximately 700 million people in the world, corresponding to 13 % of the global burden of disease [24]. Epilepsy, for example, is the fourth most common neurological disorder, less incident only than migraine, stroke, and Alzheimer's disease [19]. Epileptic seizures are brief occurrences of signals and/or symptoms resulting from disturbances in the brain electrical activity [7]. This disease can be diagnosed by electroencephalography, whose records are called electroencephalograms (EEG), which is an important tool for detecting epileptiform discharges and diagnosing this illness [1].

J. T. Oliva would like to thank the Brazilian funding agency Coordenação de Aperfeiçoamento de Pessoal de Nível Superior (CAPES) for financial support.

[1] http://www.who.int.

© Springer International Publishing Switzerland 2016
A.E.P. Villa et al. (Eds.): ICANN 2016, Part I, LNCS 9886, pp. 297–305, 2016.
DOI: 10.1007/978-3-319-44778-0_35

EEG and other examinations are stored in medical databases to maintain the patients' clinical history in order to be reused by experts in decision-making processes for diagnosis of illnesses and accomplishment of future procedures [15].

However, the large amount of information makes its manual analysis an unfeasible task. Also, rigorous training of experts for EEG analysis is required due to the fact that this examination can contain patterns that are difficult to be identified. In this context, data mining supported by machine learning (ML) methods can be applied for building predictive classifiers from implicit knowledge existing in the data to support these tasks [23].

In order to use ML methods, the data should be represented in an appropriate format, *e.g.*, attribute-value table. To do so, several feature extraction methods are described in the literature, such as the cross-correlation (CC) [5], which uses an arbitrary EEG signal as reference for its correlation with other EEG signals.

The CC method was applied and evaluated in other works that use ML techniques. In [11], CC and other feature extraction methods with ML techniques, such as decision trees, naive Bayes, and support vector machines (SVM) are performed in order to classify EEG signals as healthy or epileptic. In [6], CC and artificial neural networks (ANN) are used for heart beat categorization. In [20], CC and logistic regression are applied aiming to identify tasks of motor imagery tasks. In [22], CC and SVM are applied for emotion recognition based on EEG signals.

Although these works have reached good results, the computational cost for extracting features is directly proportional to the EEG length, *i.e.*, their processing can be highly costly for large EEG databases.

To the best of our knowledge, no study has been conducted to evaluate whether the reduction of EEG segment length by a preprocessing technique can affect the application performance of CC and ML methods in the classifier building. In [21], for example, the dimensionality reduction method called particle swarm optimization [12] is applied in order to investigate the impact of the selection of multiple electrodes and EEG features in a brain computer interface application. In [9], a dimensionality reduction algorithm, based on spatio-spectral decomposition [14], is proposed and applied in order to analyze brain oscillations.

In this sense, this work verifies whether the reduction of EEG segment dimension by a preprocessing technique (Sect. 2.2) can affect the performance of classifiers built using CC and ML methods.

2   Materials and Methods

2.1   EEG Dataset

The Bern-Barcelona EEG database[2] [3] was used for the experimental evaluation. This database is publicly available and organized into five sets, where each set contains 100 single-channel EEG segments with 23.6 s. Accordingly, a

---

[2] http://epileptologie-bonn.de/cms/front_content.php?idcat=193\&lang=3.

128-channel amplifier system using common average referencing[3] was applied to sample these segments, at a sampling rate of 173.61 Hz and 12-bit resolution, from different subjects. Also, these signals were band-pass filtered at 0.53–40 Hz and the international 10–20 system was used for electrode placement. The subject descriptions for each set are the following: (A) non-epileptic subjects with eyes open, (B) non-epileptic subjects with eyes closed, (C) hippocampal formation of the opposite brain hemisphere from epileptic patients, (D) epileptogenic zone from patients diagnosed with epilepsy, and (E) seizure activity from epileptic patients.

In this paper, only the sets A (normal) and E (abnormal), totalling 200 EEG segments, were considered in the experimental evaluation. Figure 1 shows a sample for an epileptic (abnormal) EEG example.

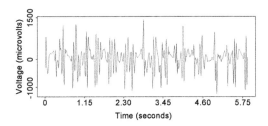

Fig. 1. Epileptic EEG segment sample.

2.2   Preprocessing

This step is performed to solve potential problems related to data, such as: noise, presence of outliers, missing values, oversize, among others [4]. In this work, the preprocessing is focused on dimensionality reduction of time series (TS). To do so, the piecewise aggregate approximation (PAA) method was used.

The PAA method (Eq. 1) reduces the dimensionality of a TS with size n to an equivalent TS (TS') with size n', $n' < n$. This is achieved by division of TS into equal-sized segments, in which the arithmetic mean of each segment is calculated [13].

$$TS'(i) = \frac{n'}{n} * \sum_{j=\frac{n}{n'}*i}^{\frac{n}{n'}*(i+1)-1} TS(j) \qquad (1)$$

2.3   Feature Extraction

Feature extraction is an essential task for medical data representation and it influences the classification performance [11]. In this work, we extracted features

---

[3] Average of all potentials generated by electrodes.

based in a mathematical operation named cross-correlation (CC) [5], which is used to measure the extent of similarity between two signals [16].

CC between signals X and Y can be calculated by Eq. 2, where n is the signal length and Φ is the time shift parameter, $\Phi = \{-n+1, ..., -1, 0, 1, ..., n-1\}$.

$$CC(X, Y, \Phi) = \begin{cases} \sum_{i=0}^{n-\Phi-1} X_{i+\Phi} * Y_i & \Phi \geq 0 \\ \\ CC(X, Y, -\Phi) & \Phi < 0 \end{cases} \tag{2}$$

In this sense, the application of CC method generates cross-correlogram (CCo) with length $2*n-1$, where the j-th CCo value is the CC measured using the j-th time shift. Figure 2 shows examples of two CCo, one resulted from a healthy and an epileptic EEG segments, and the other between two epileptic EEG segments.

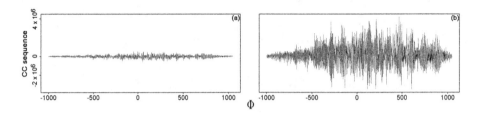

Fig. 2. CCo examples for: an epileptic and a healthy EEG segments (a) and two epileptic EEG segments (b).

In this sense, the following features can be measured from CCo [5]: peak value, which is the maximum value; instant value, that is the value of CCo at any particular instant associated with peak value; centroid, the geometric center of the CCo; equivalent width, the wave width from the peak; and mean square abscissa, which is the spread of CCo amplitude on the centroid. To do so, initially, an arbitrary EEG segment is selected as reference, decreasing by 1 the instance number. Subsequently, this EEG is used with all other EEG segments to generate CCo [11].

2.4   Building Classifiers

In this step, classifiers were built using ML methods: (1) decision tree (DT), (2) nearest-neighbor (NN), and (3) artificial neural network (ANN).

Method (1) builds classifiers using a divide-and-conquer paradigm. The DT data structure is hierarchically organized, whose classes are represented by a set of rules, which are derived from the tree. For classification of new examples, the classifiers are traversed from its root to verify values of features and to label the analyzed example [17].

Method (2) classifies a new example by calculating its similarity to examples of training set, whose classes were previously defined by experts. In the NN method, the similarity is computed by distance measurements, such as Euclidean distance. This method is based in memory and it does not build a classifier, *i.e.*, the classifier is the training set itself [2].

Method (3) builds mathematical classifiers inspired by the biological neural structure and it is generally abstracted as an interconnected neuron system, whose computational capacity is achieved by learning and generalization. ANN training is commonly performed by using the error correction approach [10].

In this work, the DT and NN methods were applied because their abstractions can be understandable by professionals without computational expertise and ANN technique was performed due to its high generalization ability.

2.5   Classifier Evaluation

In this step, classifiers are evaluated according to their efficiency to predict classes of new examples. This step may be conducted using the confusion matrix (CM) method, which is used to evaluate relationships between two or more nominal variables, was applied. In the CM, the following measures can be calculated [8]: positive predictive value (PPV), negative predictive value (NPV), sensitivity (Sen), and specificity (Spe).

In this paper, evaluation methods were applied in classifiers, separately, according to databases generated by PAA method and the original database. Also, the classifiers were evaluated separately according to ML techniques.

In this sense, Java[4] language with NetBeans[5] development environment was used to build a tool for preprocessing and feature extraction of EEG segments. The WEKA tool[6] was used to build and to evaluate the classifiers. This tool contains several ML algorithms, such as J48 (based on C4.5 algorithm) [18] used to build DT, 1NN (1-nearest-neighbor) [2] applied to perform NN method, and BP-MLP (backpropagation based on multilayer perceptron) [10] used to build ANN.

3   Results and Discussion

In this work, we evaluated whether the application of the PAA method in EEG segments before feature extraction based on CCo can influence the performance of ML methods. To do so, an experimental evaluation was conducted in a set of 200 EEG segments, being 100 healthy (normal) and 100 epileptic (abnormal).

Posteriorly, the PAA technique was performed in the EEG segments set using the following settings: 25 % (EEG25), 50 % (EEG50), and 75 % (EEG75) of the original length for each EEG segment. In this sense, 200 EEG segments were generated for each setting. So, considering the original EEG segment set (EEG100), four EEG sets were used.

---

[4] http://www.oracle.com/technetwork/java/index.html.

[5] https://netbeans.org/.

[6] http://www.cs.waikato.ac.nz/ml/weka/.

Subsequently, the first abnormal EEG from each set was selected as reference for CCo building and its respective feature extraction. Each remaining EEG segment was represented by a set of five features. It is important to emphasize that the same EEG signal from the EEG100 set used as a reference was used in its reduced form in the databases generated by PAA method. Thus, four datasets were constructed using CC method. The CCo can be understandable by professionals without computational expertise because it can be displayed through charts, as shown in Fig. 2, in which it is possible to observe graphically the correlation between different signals.

Afterwards, the J48, 1NN, and BP-MLP algorithms were applied in each dataset to build classifiers. In this way, 12 classifiers were built. Unlike related work [6,11,20,22], this paper compares the performance among these algorithms to differentiate EEG segments between abnormal and normal classes. Also, J48 and 1NN methods were used in this work due to their low computational cost. The BP-MLP method was performed due to its high adaptability with non-linear problems.

The classifiers were evaluated according to their predictive accuracy using the CM method. In resulting matrices, precision measures such as PPV, NPV, Sen, and Spe were extracted. Table 1 presents four precision measures for each built CM.

Based on Table 1, classifiers built using the J48 algorithm obtained the highest values for parameters PPV, NPV, sensibility, and specificity considering their respective datasets.

For each ML method, the J48 built classifier using the EEG25 dataset obtained the highest values for PPV, NPV, and specificity parameters, determining that this classifier was more accurate to classify normal EEG segments and was more likely to rightly categorize abnormal and normal EEG than the other J48 classifiers. However, all J48 classifiers obtained the same value for the sensibility parameter, which reached 97.98 %, finding that J48 classifiers achieved the same accuracy to classify abnormal EEG segments.

The 1NN trained classifier using the EEG25 dataset obtained the highest value for PPV, NPV, and specificity parameters, evidencing that this classifier was more accurate to classify healthy EEG segments and it was more likely to rightly categorize epileptic and healthy EEG than the other 1NN classifiers. Nonetheless, all 1NN classifiers reached the same value for the sensibility parameter, which was measured as 90.91 %, evidencing that 1NN classifiers achieved the same accuracy to classify epileptic EEG segments.

The BP-MLP classifier, built using the EEG75 dataset, obtained the highest value for PPV, NPV, and sensibility parameters, finding that this classifier was more accurate to classify abnormal EEG segments and was more likely to rightly categorize abnormal and normal EEG than other BP-MLP classifiers. However, all BP-MLP classifiers obtained the same value for the specificity parameter, which was measured as 90.00 %, finding that BP-MLP classifiers achieved the same accuracy to classify normal EEG segments.

Table 1. Measures calculated in each CM.

Dataset	Algorithm	PPV	NPV	Sen	Spe
EEG25	J48	100.00 %	98.04 %	97.98 %	100.00 %
	1NN	93.75 %	91.26 %	90.91 %	94.00 %
	BP-MLP	89.58 %	87.38 %	86.87 %	90.00 %
EEG50	J48	98.98 %	98.02 %	97.98 %	99.00 %
	1NN	92.78 %	91.18 %	90.91 %	93.00 %
	BP-MLP	89.58 %	87.38 %	86.87 %	90.00 %
EEG75	J48	97.98 %	98.00 %	97.98 %	98.00 %
	1NN	92.78 %	91.18 %	90.91 %	93.00 %
	BP-MLP	89.69 %	88.24 %	87.88 %	90.00 %
EEG100	J48	98.98 %	98.02 %	97.98 %	99.00 %
	1NN	92.78 %	91.18 %	90.91 %	93.00 %
	BP-MLP	89.58 %	87.38 %	86.87 %	90.00 %

4   Conclusion

In this work, the PAA method was applied in three settings (25 %, 50 %, and 75 % of the original length for each EEG segment), generating EEG25, EEG50, and EEG75 databases. Thus, these sets and the original database were used in order to extract features based on cross-correlogram (CCo) and to build 12 classifiers using the J48, 1NN, and BP-MLP algorithms.

The evaluation found that J48 classifiers performed better and was more likely to classify EEG segments in each database. Also, considering only the evaluation of each algorithm, J48 and 1NN classifiers generated by EEG25 dataset reached the highest value for positive predictive value (PPV), negative predictive value (NPV), and specificity (Spe) parameters. However, all J48 and 1NN classifiers obtained the same value for sensitivity (Sen) parameter. The BP-MLP built by EEG75 dataset reached the highest value for PPV, NPV, and Sen. Therefore, all BP-MLP classifiers obtained the same value for Spe.

In this sense, with the evaluation using CC method, it was found that the reduction of EEG segment length can increase or maintain performance of ML methods, compared to classifiers built from EEG segments with original length to differentiate normal EEG signals from seizures. Thus, the computational cost of feature extraction based on CCo can be reduced without significant loss of accuracy in building classifiers, considering widely different EEG signals.

Future studies include using other approaches for evaluation of the classifiers generated in this work, feature extraction based on CCo using other EEG databases, expansion of the EEG representation by using other feature extraction methods, and development of an approach to select an EEG as reference.

References

1. Adeli, H., Zhou, Z., Dadmehr, N.: Analysis of EEG records in an epileptic patient using wavelet transform. J. Neurosci. Meth. **123**(1), 69–87 (2003)
2. Alpaydin, E.: Introduction to Machine Learning. MIT press, Cambridge (2014)
3. Andrzejak, R.G., Lehnertz, K., Mormann, F., Rieke, C., David, P., Elger, C.E.: Indications of nonlinear deterministic and finite-dimensional structures in time series of brain electrical activity: dependence on recording region and brain state. Phys. Rev. E **64**(6), 061907 (2001)
4. Castro, N.C.: Time series motif discovery. Ph.D. thesis, Universidade do Minho, Braga, Portugal (2012)
5. Chandaka, S., Chatterjee, A., Munshi, S.: Cross-correlation aided support vector machine classifier for classification of EEG signals. Expert Syst. Appl. **36**(2), 1329–1336 (2009)
6. Dutta, S., Chatterjee, A., Munshi, S.: Identification of ECG beats from cross-spectrum information aided learning vector quantization. Measurement **44**(10), 2020–2027 (2011)
7. Fisher, R.S., Boas, W.E., Blume, W., Elger, C., Genton, P., Lee, P., Engel, J.: Epileptic seizures and epilepsy: definitions proposed by the international league against epilepsy (ILAE) and the international bureau for epilepsy (IBE). Epilepsia **46**(4), 470–472 (2005)
8. Fredman, D., Pisani, R., Ourvers, R.: Statistics. Norton, New York (1988)
9. Haufe, S., Nikulin, S.D.V.V.: Dimensionality reduction for the analysis of brain oscillations. NeuroImage **101**, 583–597 (2014)
10. Haykin, S.: Neural Networks and Learning Machines. Pearson Education, Upper Saddle River (2009)
11. Iscan, Z., Dokur, Z., Demiralp, T.: Classification of electroencephalogram signals with combined time and frequency features. Expert Syst. Appl. **38**(8), 10499–10505 (2011)
12. Kenndy, J., Eberhart, R.C.: Particle swarm optimization. In: Proceedings of ICNN, pp. 1942–1948, Perth, Australia (1995)
13. Keogh, E., Chakrabarti, K., Pazzani, M., Mehrotra, S.: Dimensionality reduction for fast similarity search in large time series databases. Knowl. Inf. Syst. **3**(3), 263–286 (2001)
14. Nikulin, V.V., Nolte, G., Curio, G.: A novel method for reliable and fast extraction of neuronal EEG/MEG oscillations on the basis of spatio-spectral decomposition. NeuroImage **55**(4), 1528–1535 (2011)
15. Oliva, J.T.: Automating the process of mapping medical reports to structured database (in Portuguese). Master thesis, Western Paraná State University, Foz do Iguaçu, Brazil (2014)
16. Proakis, J.G., Manolakis, D.K.: Digital Signal Processing: Principles, Algorithms, and Application. Prentice Hall, Saddle River (2006)
17. Quinlan, J.R.: Simplifying decision trees. Int. J. Man. Mach. Stud. **27**(3), 221–234 (1987)
18. Quinlan, J.R.: C4.5: Programs for Machine Learning. Elsevier, San Francisco (2014)
19. Shafer, P.O., Sirven, J.I.: Epilepsy statistics (2015). http://www.epilepsy.com/learn/epilepsy-statistics
20. Siuly, Li, Y., Wen, P.: Identification of motor imagery tasks through CC–LR algorithm in brain computer interface. Int. J. Bioinform. Res. Appl. **9**(2), 156–172 (2013)

21. Tang, J., Bian, W., Yu, N., Zhang, Y.: Intelligent processing techniques for semantic-based image and video retrieval. Neurocomputing **119**, 319–331 (2013)
22. Vijayan, A.E., Sen, D., Sudheer, A.P.: EEG-based emotion recognition using statistical measures and auto-regressive modeling. In: Proceedings of CICT. pp. 587–591, Ghaziabad, India (2015)
23. Witten, I., Frank, E., Hall, M.A.: Machine Learning: Practical Machine Learning Tools and Techniques. Morgan Kaufmann, San Francisco (2011)
24. World Health Organization: Draft comprehensive mental health action plan 2013–2020 (2013). http://apps.who.int/gb/ebwha/pdf_files/EB132/B132_8-en.pdf

EEG-driven RNN Classification for Prognosis of Neurodegeneration in At-Risk Patients

Giulio Ruffini[✉], David Ibañez, Marta Castellano, Stephen Dunne, and Aureli Soria-Frisch

Starlab Barcelona/Neuroelectrics, Avda. Tibidabo 47 bis, 08035 Barcelona, Spain
{giulio.ruffini,david.ibanez,stephen.dunne,
aureli.soria-Frisch}@starlab-int.com
http://starlab-int.com
http://neuroelectrics.com

Abstract. REM Behavior Disorder (RBD) is a serious risk factor for neurodegenerative diseases such as Parkinson's disease (PD). We describe here a recurrent neural network (RNN) for classification of EEG data collected from RBD patients and healthy controls (HC) forming a balanced cohort of 118 subjects in which 50 % of the RBD patients eventually developed either PD or Lewy Body Dementia (LBD). In earlier work [1,2], we implemented support vector machine classifiers (SVMs) using EEG mean spectral features to predict the course of disease in the dual HC vs. PD problem with an accuracy of 85 %. Although largely successful, this approach did not attempt to exploit the non-linear dynamic characteristics of EEG signals, which are believed to contain useful information. Here we describe an Echo State Network (ESN) classifier capable of processing the dynamic features of EEG power at different spectral bands. The inputs to the classifier are the time series of 1 second-averaged EEG power at several selected frequencies and channels. The performance of the ESN reaches 85 % test-set accuracy in the HC vs. PD problem using the same subset of channels and bands we selected in our prior work on this problem using SVMs.

Keywords: Echo state networks · RNNs · EEG · Parkinson's disease · Reservoir computing

1 Introduction

The human brain can be modeled as a highly dimensional complex dynamical system in which electrochemical communication and computation play a central role. Electroencephalographic (EEG) and magnetoencephalographic (MEG) signals contain rich information associated with these processes. To a large extent, progress in the analysis of such signals has been driven by the study of classical

This work partly supported by the Michael J. Fox Foundation within the project "Discovery of EEG biomarkers for Parkinson Disease and Lewy Body Dementia using advanced Machine Learning techniques".

© Springer International Publishing Switzerland 2016
A.E.P. Villa et al. (Eds.): ICANN 2016, Part I, LNCS 9886, pp. 306–313, 2016.
DOI: 10.1007/978-3-319-44778-0_36

temporal and spectral features in electrode space, which has proven useful to study the human brain in health and disease. For example, the "slowing down" of EEG is known to characterize neurodegenerative diseases [3, 4]. However, brain activity measurements exhibit non-linear dynamics and non-stationarity across temporal scales that cannot be addressed well by classical, linear approaches. The complexity of these signals calls for the use of novel tools capable of exploiting such features and representing rich spatio-temporal hierarchical structures. Interestingly, deep learning techniques in particular and neural networks in general are bio-inspired by the brain—the same biological system generating the electric signals we aim to decode. They should be well suited for the task.

Here we explore a particular class of recurrent neural networks (RNNs) called Echo State Networks (ESNs) that combine the power of RNNs for classification of temporal patterns and ease of training. RNNs and, in particular, ESNs implement non-linear dynamics with memory and seem ideally poised for the classification of complex time series data. The main concept in ESNs and related types of so-called "reservoir computation" systems is to have data inputs drive a semi-randomly connected, large, fixed recurrent neural network (the "reservoir") where each node/neuron in the reservoir is activated in a non-linear fashion— see Fig. 2. The interior nodes with random weights constitute what is called the "dynamic reservoir" (DR) of the ESN. The motivation for keeping interior connection weights random but fixed (not to be learned) is, on the one hand, to allow for high dimensional feature mapping of the inputs (in a sense much like a kernel method) while, on the other, to avoid the complex problem of training recurrent neural network architectures (such as the vanishing of training error gradients [5]). An important feature of ESNs is that only the output weights (and various hyperparameters) are trained [7, 8]. Although we explore ESN architectures here, other relevant RNN options include long-short term memory networks (LSTMs) [6].

2   The Dataset

The data in this study consisted of resting-state EEG collected from awake patients using 14 scalp electrodes [4]. The recording protocol consisted of conditions with periods of "eyes open" of variable duration ($\sim$2 min) followed by periods of "eyes closed" in which patients were not asked to perform any particular task. EEG signals were digitized with 16 bit resolution at a sampling rate of 256 S/s. The amplification device implemented hardware band pass filtering between 0.3 and 100 Hz and notch filtering at 60 Hz to minimize the influence of power line noise. All recordings were referenced to linked ears. The dataset includes a total of 59 patients diagnosed of REM (random eye movement sleep) Behavioral Disorder (RBD) and 53 healthy controls without sleep complaints in which RBD was excluded. EEG data was collected in every patient at baseline, i.e., when they were still RBD. After 1–10 years of clinical follow-up, 14 patients developed Parkinson disease (PD), 14 Lewy body dementia (LBD) and the remaining 31 remained idiopathic. The data was collected by the

Hopital du Sacre-Coeur, Montrèal [4]. Our classification efforts here focus on the HC *vs.* PD dual problem involving the available 14 PD converters and 14 HCs randomly selected for each classification train/test cycle. Each data snipped per subject contains information of power in 10 bands, 14 elecrtrodes and about 200 samples.

EEG feature time series to feed the ESN (typically five channel-band signal streams—see Fig. 1) were extracted after manual quality control and artifact correction of the data. Only eyes-closed sequences were considered for further analysis. Here we computed essentially a spectrogram per subject to extract temporal series of power for each electrode and band. In particular, we used a set of features selected in prior work for average power SVM classification [1] which include the combination of delta and theta band power from frontal and temporal channels. While we explored the use of 4 s and 1 s spectrogram windowing, the latter provided superior performance. As we discuss below, we hypothesize that this improvement reflects a better capture of relevant signal dynamics which can be used by the ESN. Our present study aimed to explore whether there is useful dynamic information on the EEG power data time series from subjects. We did not carry out an exhaustive test of the performance of classifiers using multiple feature and channel combinations, which is left for future work.

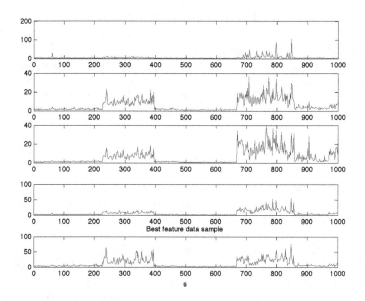

Fig. 1. Example of ESN input data. Five streams of EEG power time series at different bands and scalp channels. From top to bottom: Delta-T4 power, Theta-F8 power, Theta-T4 power, Theta-F7 and Theta-F4 power (horizontal units are samples corresponding to 1 s window power averages sliding every 0.5 s).

3 Echo State Network Description

Following [7,8] we have designed ESNs driven by multi-channel temporally-varying power data as inputs, and providing as desired output the class label (after mapping it to a square like signal taking values in $\{-0.5, 0.5\}$, see Fig. 3). The ESN node dynamics are captured by the state variable $x \in \mathbb{R}^D$, and driven by inputs $u \in \mathbb{R}^{N_{in}}$. Evolution is described iteratively by

$$x(n+1) = \alpha_{leak}\, f(W^{in}[u(n+1);1] + Wx(n) + W^{back}y(n) + noise)$$
$$+(1 - \alpha_{leak})\, x(n) \tag{1}$$

and

$$y(n) = f(W^{out}[u(n); x(n); 1]), \tag{2}$$

with $f(x) = \tanh x$ (point by point hyperbolic tangent) [7,8]—see Fig. 2. The internal weight matrices are initialized semi-randomly using a sparsity criterion and an important parameter—called α_W here and usually known as the *spectral radius*—that determines the damping of the system. We explored ranges of $\alpha_W = 0.5$ to 2. We note that while it is normally stated that values less than one are required for a stable ESN, greater values applicable in some cases when the ESN inputs are non-zero [9]. W^{out} is computed using regularized least squares to ensure a match of output with the target signal in the training phase.

Overall, the parameters in our implementation of the ESN model are:

- D: DR dimension/the number of internal nodes. In our problem, the best performances were obtained with reservoirs with 3000 nodes (the maximum we tested).
- Sparsity threshold S: enforces sparsity in the W matrix when it is first created using a random uniform distribution in the range ± 1. Values with absolute value below the threshold are set to 0.

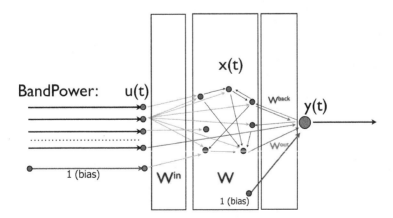

Fig. 2. ESN model displaying input, internal and output nodes and bias terms.

- α_W: spectral radius. Used to map the thresholded random $W \rightarrow \alpha_W W/S(W)$, where $S(A)$ denotes the spectral radius of a matrix A. Defines the "gain" of the DR.
- α_{in}: sets the scale of random input connections W_{in} to the range of $\pm\frac{1}{2}\alpha_{in}$.
- α_{back}: sets the scale of random connections of the feedback teacher signal W_{back} to the range of $\pm\frac{1}{2}\alpha_{back}$.
- α_{leak}: leaking rate of the neurons, useful for time smoothing of the dynamics.
- λ: Tickhonov parameter for regularization of the inverse problem of the output weights W_{out} (in the sense of modifying least squares cost to $F(w) = \frac{1}{\sigma}||Aw - y||^2 + \lambda||w||^2$).
- Input Channels and bands: The selection of N_{input} input time series.
- Initial conditions of the nodes of the ESN: $x(t_0)$.
- Training noise level: *noise*

Different parameter configurations have been tested, with emphasis on the relevance of spectral radius, DR size, the role of feedback teacher signal W_{back} and the initial conditions of the nodes of the ESN $x(t_0)$. In particular, three scenarios are discussed here after the ESN has been trained to assess the stability of the network following the analysis in [7]:

- Teaching signal (output for feedback) 'on' for the whole duration of ESN run (see Fig. 3 first row). All other parameters of the ESN are kept constant, including the initial conditions of the nodes of the ESN.
- Teaching signal 'on' for a short interval, then turned off and provided by the ESN output (see Fig. 3 second row). All other parameters of the ESN are kept constant, including the initial conditions of the nodes of the ESN.
- ESN provides its own feedback all the time (see Fig. 3 third row). All other parameters of the ESN are kept constant, except the initial conditions of the nodes of the ESN.

4   Classification Performance Assessment

In order to map out the classification performance of the ESN for different parameter sets, we implemented a set of algorithms in Matlab (run on a MacBook Pro laptop) as described by the following pseudocode:

```
FOR each parameter set:
        REPEAT M times (runs):
                A- Create (random, balanced) training and test sets
                B- Find a good DR (W_out matrix) with respect to the
                   training set (see below)
                C- Evaluate its performance on training and test set
        END
        Compute mean performances over the M runs, save
END
Provide a map of the saved mean performances in parameter space
```

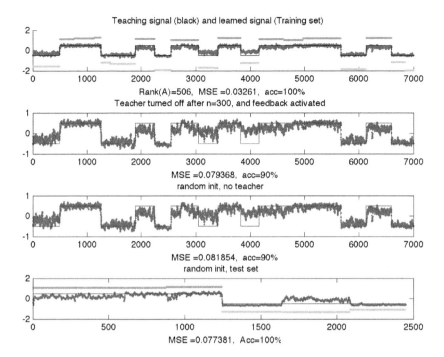

Fig. 3. Sample pot of the match of ESN output to desired target with accuracy for the trained signal (first three plots in sequence: ESN with teacher forcing, ESN with teacher forcing discontinued after N = 300, and ESN with no teacher forcing at any time) and for the test set signal in the last row. The cyan and green lines denote the rescaled subject ID (cyan is HC, green PD). The horizontal axis denotes sample. (Color figure online)

For each run, 10 % of the BandPower data of the PD and HC groups (subject-wise) was left out as a test set (step A above). Cycles of 50 iterations of *leave-10 %-out* train/test were carried out to obtain an estimation of the classification performance for each set of parameters. Typically, classification accuracy in the training set was near 95–100 % across all parameter configurations.

To select a good ESN DR (i.e., the W_{out} matrices) using the *training data* (step B above), the following steps were employed:

1. The DR network is initialized with random weights for all weight matrices (except output connections W_{out}).
2. In the parameter configuration where the feedback teacher signal W_{back} is on, the network is "forced" with the desired *teacher* signal (with values of $W_{back} = \pm 0.5$), and the associate state dynamics saved. Otherwise, the state dynamics of the network with no feedback are saved.
3. The best output connections W_{out} are found in the optimized, Tikhonov regularized least squares sense by comparing the output dynamics with the desired teacher signal. This provides the following quality metrics: the (L2)

mean squared error (MSE) of output to teacher, and an accuracy metric. The accuracy per subject is measured by finding which teacher signal the output is closest to in the L2 sense.

4. Once the W_{out} are computed, a second run is then carried out to extract the training MSE and accuracy.
5. The above process is repeated N times or until good training set accuracy is provided, to find a good W_{out} matrix set based on the prior step. The best W_{out} and its corresponding parameter set are saved, and the ESN classifier is thus fully defined.

Finally, the performance of the ESN classification is estimated the test set with the selected W_{out} and its corresponding parameter set on the *testing data* (step C above).

5   Discussion

A first observation is that—as proposed in [8]—our best results were obtained with large dynamic reservoirs ($D = 3000$) with least-squares regularization, with accuracies reaching an 85 % average on the test set. In addition, spectral radii larger than one were effective as well—with good results with $\alpha_W \sim 2$—and feedback did not seem to play an important role in the problem.

These early results are promising, as is the fact that the match of ESN outputs to target was excellent on training set and often on test sets (see Fig. 3 bottom row for an example of 100 % classification performance on the test set). However, from this alone it does not follow that the ESN was actually exploiting dynamical features in the data streams (which is what we wished to demonstrate). One simple way to test if this is happening is to reshuffle the data time-wise (within each subject) to see if classification accuracy is affected. We indeed found that classification performance degraded if the data was reshuffled in time (85/55 % train/test accuracy). While suggestive, however, this may simply highlight the fact that ESNs require some "smooth" input dynamics to emulate data streams at all.

A better test to check for the used amount of information in the dynamics as opposed to mean amplitude is to normalize each input stream—independently per channel and per subject—to unit standard deviation. This is rather extreme—it would make any spectral power based classification impossible. We found that this did indeed cause a degradation of performance both for training and test sets, but not as much as temporal reshuffling (with train/test accuracy up to 95/65 %). Thus, although mean power amplitude information is used by the network, we conclude that the ESN is also using dynamic information in the inputs. Along these lines, it is especially interesting to note that we also saw an improvement in performance using 1 s vs. 4 s sliding windowed data (about 10 %), with accuracy consistently in the range 80–85 %. This result is rather interesting in itself and suggests we could get additional classification performance by fusing ESN classifiers with SVM-spectral ones.

Finally, we note that in this particular study we did not carry out an exhaustive search in the feature space of channels and bands, but relied on the best performing features found in prior SVM classification studies which were blind to dynamically encoded information. More tests exploring the feature space and different feature combinations should therefore be carried out even if the search is restricted to bandpower signals (not the only choice with EEG data). Future work should also explore the role of dynamic reservoir architecture, which with large dimensions ought to be studied as a complex network [10].

Acknowledgments. This work has been partially funded by The Michael J. Fox Foundation for Parkinsons Research under Rapid Response Innovation Awards 2013. The data was collected by Jacques Montplaisir's team at the Center for Advanced Research in Sleep Medicine affiliated to the University of Montrèal, Hopital du Sacre-Coeur, Montrèal and provided within the scope of the aforementioned project.

References

1. Soria-Frisch, A., Marin, J., Ibañez, D., Dunne, S., Grau, C., Ruffini, G., Rodrigues-Brazète, J., Postuma, R., Gagnon, J.-F., Montplaisir, J., Pascual-Leone, A.: Machine learning for a Parkinsons prognosis and diagnosis system based on EEG. In: Proceedings of the International Pharmaco-EEG Society Meeting, IPEG 2014, Leipzig, Germany (2014)
2. Soria-Frisch, A., Marin, J., Ibañez, D., Dunne, S., Grau, C., Ruffini, G., Rodrigues-Brazète, J., Postuma, R., Gagnon, J.-F., Montplaisir, J., Pascual-Leone, A.: Evaluation of EEG biomarkers for Parkinson disease and other Lewy body diseases based on the use of machine learning techniques (in prep)
3. Fantini, M.L., Gagnon, J.F., Petit, D., Rompr, S., Dcary, A., Carrier, J., Montplaisir, J.: Slowing of electroencephalogram in rapid eye movement sleep behavior disorder. Ann. Neurol. **53**(6), 774–780 (2003)
4. Rodrigues Brazète, J., Gagnon, J.F., Postuma, R.B., Bertrand, J.A., Petit, D., Montplaisir, J.: Electroencephalogram slowing predicts neurodegeneration in rapid eye movement sleep behavior disorder. Neurobiol. Aging, pp. 74–81 (2016). doi:10. 1016/j.neurobiolaging.2015.10.007.
5. Bengio, Y., Simard, P., Frasconi, P.: IEEE Trans. Neur. Netw. **5**(2), 157–166 (1994)
6. Hochreiter, S., Schmidhuber, J.: Long short-term memory. Neural Comput. **9**(8), 1735–1780 (1997)
7. Jaeger, H.: The "echo state" approach to analysing and training recurrent neural networks, GMD Report 148, German National Research Center for Information Technology (2001). Fourth revision, July 2013. http://minds.jacobs-university.de/ sites/default/files/uploads/papers/EchoStatesTechRep.pdf
8. Lukoševičius, M.: A practical guide to applying echo state networks. In: Montavon, G., Orr, G.B., Müller, K.-R. (eds.) Neural Networks: Tricks of the Trade, 2nd edn. LNCS, vol. 7700, pp. 659–686. Springer, Heidelberg (2012)
9. Yildiz, I.B., Jaeger, H., Kiebel, S.J.: Re-visiting the echo state property. Neural Netw. **35**, 1–9 (2012). ISSN 0893–6080
10. Albert, R., Barabasi, A.-L.: Statistical mechanics of complex networks. Rev. Mod. Phys. **74**, 47–97 (2002)

Competition Between Cortical Ensembles Explains Pitch-Related Dynamics of Auditory Evoked Fields

Alejandro Tabas[1]([✉]), André Rupp[2], and Emili Balaguer-Ballester[1,3]

[1] Faculty of Science and Technology, Bournemouth University, BH12 5BB Poole, UK
atabas@bournemout.ac.uk
[2] Biomagnetism Section, Im Neuenheimer Feld 400, 69120 Heidelberg, Germany
[3] Bernstein Center for Computational Neuroscience,
Heidelberg/mannheim, Germany

Abstract. The latency of the N100m transient component of the magnetic auditory evoked fields presents a widely reported correlation with perceived pitch. These observations have been robustly reproduced in the literature for a number of different stimuli, indicating that the neural generator of the N100m has an important role in cortical pitch processing. In this work, we introduce a realistic cortical model of pitch perception revealing, for the first time to our knowledge, the mechanisms responsible for the observed relationship between the N100m and the perceived pitch. The model describes the N100m deflection as a transient state in cortical dynamics that starts with the incoming of a new subcortical input, holds during a winner-takes-all ensemble competition, and ends when the cortical dynamics reach equilibrium. This model qualitatively predicted the latency of the N100m of three families of stimuli.

Keywords: Cortical dynamics · Auditory evoked fields · N100m · Pitch perception · Perceptual integration · Multi-attractor systems

1 Introduction

Auditory evoked fields (AEFs) observed in MEG experiments systematically present a transient deflection known as the N100m, elicited around 100 ms after tone onset in the antero-lateral Heschl's Gyrus. The exact N100m's latency is correlated with the perceived pitch of a wide range of stimuli [5,7,8], suggesting that the cortical source of the transient component has an important role on the processing of pitch in auditory cortex [9]. However, the biophysical substrate of the relationship between pitch decoding and the N100 morphology remains an enigma.

Existing models of pitch, focused on perceptual phenomena, do not explain the mechanisms generating cortical evoked fields during pitch processing in biophysical detail (e.g. [1,6]). Cortical models of the evoked fields, like the Dynamic Causal Models [3], often assume an unrealistic cortical input (e.g. white noise)

© Springer International Publishing Switzerland 2016
A.E.P. Villa et al. (Eds.): ICANN 2016, Part I, LNCS 9886, pp. 314–321, 2016.
DOI: 10.1007/978-3-319-44778-0_37

and are thus unable to reproduce stimulus-driven properties of the AEF. In this work, and for the first time to our knowledge, we introduce a model of interacting neural ensembles describing how stimulus-dependent cortical pitch processing gives rise to the observed human neuromagnetic responses. Specifically, we focus on the N100m transient dynamics and its peak latency. Our conclusion is that the N100m reflects a decoding process occurring in the onset of the stimuli, that can be described as a competition between neural ensembles sensitive to different pitch values.

2 The Model

Subcortical input was simulated using a realistic model of the peripheral auditory system generating realistic auditory nerve spike trains [14] followed by a *delay-and-multiply* processing carried out by chopper neurons in cochlear nucleus and coincidence detector units in the inferior colliculus [6]. The spike trains generated by the peripheral system, represented by the probability of spiking $p(t)$, are phase-locked to the waveform of the stimulus, thus preserving all the periodicities of the sound. Chopper neurons systematically delay input spike trains by $\{\delta t_n\}_1^N$, whilst coincidence detector units spike for such specific delays of the auditory nerve fibres. The final subcortical output $A_n(t)$ represents a leaky-integration of the coincidence detectors output as follows:

$$\tau_n^{sc} \dot{A}_n(t) = -A_n(t) + p(t)p(t - \Delta t) \tag{1}$$

Lag-dependent time constants τ_n^{sc} were taken from the literature [11].

The formulation in Eq. 1 yields a series of $N = 300$ channels characterised by the chopper delays δt_n. Channel n activates when the stimulus' waveform presents a periodicity with frequency $f_0 = 1/\delta t_n$. Channels corresponding to lower harmonics of the peridocities of the stimulus (i.e. channels characterised by delays $\delta t_n = 1/kf$ with $k = 1, 2, \dots$) are also coactivated after the delay-and-multiply process. Figure 1 shows the subcortical inputs elicited by three different tonal stimuli with the same pitch ($f_0 = 250$ Hz, $\delta = 4$ ms).

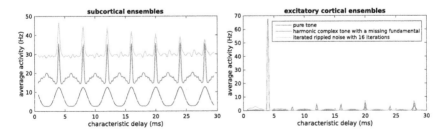

Fig. 1. (Left) Average of the subcortical input generated by the model for a pure tone, a harmonic complex tone, and an iterated rippled noise. All stimuli have the same $f_0 = 250$ Hz. (Right) Average cortical output for the same stimuli. Plots show the activity per ensemble averaged at 100–200 ms after onset.

The cortical model consists of a series of $N = 300$ cortical microcolumns described as sets of two neural ensembles: one excitatory H_n^e and one inhibitory H_n^i (see Fig. 2). An excitatory ensemble in one of such blocks n receives realistic input from the nth subcortical channel. A large activation in a column is typically associated with a fundamental pitch of δt_n [1].

Excitatory ensembles connect to both excitatory and inhibitory ensembles of adjacent blocks; whereas inhibitory ensembles connect globally with other inhibitory and excitatory populations. Crucially, inhibitory-to-excitatory connections are stronger when they link a population encoding the period δt_n with a population encoding any of its lower harmonics $k\delta t_n$ (see full connectivity matrices in Fig. 2); in agreement with reported data on cortical connectivity in mammals [10]. This setting facilitates the inhibition of low harmonics elicited during the peripheral processing as will be discussed next.

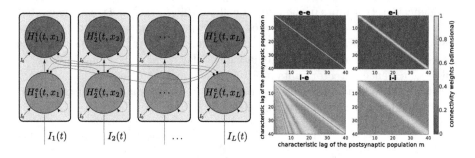

Fig. 2. (Left) Basic schematics of the model. Each block represents a cortical micro-column. Each column consist of excitatory pyramidal neurons (blue) and inhibitory interneurons (red). (Right) Connectivity weights between the ensembles of the model. Excitatory-to-excitatory (e-e), excitatory-to-inhibitory (e-i), inhibitory-to-excitatory (i-e) and inhibitory-to-inhibitory (i-i) connectivity matrices. Note that, although the excitation is local, inhibition is induced globally. (Color figure online)

Ensembles are modelled using a neural rate model with a mean-field approximation, where empirically shaped transference functions $\phi^{e,i}(I)$ are [13]:

$$\tau^{\mathrm{pop}}(t)\, \dot{H}_n^{e,i}(t) = -H_n^{e,i} + \phi^{e,i}(I_n^{e,i}(t)) \tag{2}$$

with

$$\phi^{e,i}(I) = \frac{a^{e,i}I - b^{e,i}}{1 - e^{-d^{e,i}(a^{e,i}I - b^{e,i})}} \tag{3}$$

Excitatory connections consist of NMDA- and AMPA-driven synapses. Inhibitory connections are only of the GABA$_A$ type. AMPA and GABA synapses were modelled using leaky integrators with instantaneous rising times [2]:

$$\dot{S}_n^j(t) = -\frac{S_n^j(t)}{\tau_j} + H_n^{e,i}(t), \quad j = \mathrm{AMPA}, \mathrm{GABA} \tag{4}$$

NMDA dynamics were modelled considering slow rising times [2]:

$$\dot{S}_n^{\text{NMDA}}(t) = -\frac{S_n^{\text{NMDA}}(t)}{\tau_{\text{NMDA}}} + \gamma(1 - S_{\text{NMDA}}(t))H_n^{e,i}(t) \tag{5}$$

Additive synaptic noise was introduced in the form of white noise in the gating variables S_n^j. Subcortical input was driven by NMDA and AMPA dynamics according to Eqs. 4 and 5, using the ensemble firing rates of the coincidence detectors $A_n(t)$ as gate triggers. Thus, the total synaptic input for the excitatory populations can be written as follows:

$$\begin{aligned}
I_n^e(t) = &\ J^{\text{NMDA,th}}\, S_n^{\text{NMDA,th}}(t) + J^{\text{AMPA,th}}\, S_n^{\text{AMPA,th}}(t) \\
&+ \sum_k C_{n,k}^{\text{ee}} \left(J^{\text{NMDA}}\, S_k^{\text{NMDA}}(t) + J^{\text{AMPA}}\, S_k^{\text{AMPA}}(t) \right) \\
&- \sum_k C_{n,k}^{\text{ie}}\, J^{\text{GABA}}\, S_k^{\text{GABA}}(t)
\end{aligned} \tag{6}$$

In Eq. 6, the first two terms correspond to the subcortical input, the third term accounts for cortical excitatory input, and the last term accounts for cortical inhibitory inputs. The conductivities $J^{\text{NMDA,th}}$, $J^{\text{AMPA,th}}$, J^{NMDA}, J^{AMPA}, and J^{GABA} were taken from the literature [13] and slightly tuned within the biophysical range to match the experimental observations.

Synaptic inputs for the inhbitory populations follow a similar pattern:

$$\begin{aligned}
I_n^i(t) = &\ \sum_k C_{n,k}^{\text{ei}} \left(J^{\text{NMDA}}\, S_k^{\text{NMDA}}(t) + J^{\text{AMPA}}\, S_k^{\text{AMPA}}(t) \right) \\
&- \sum_k C_{n,k}^{\text{ii}}\, J^{\text{GABA}}\, S_k^{\text{GABA}}(t)
\end{aligned} \tag{7}$$

The connectivity matrices used in Eqs. 6 and 7 ($\mathbf{C}^{\text{ee}}, \mathbf{C}^{\text{ei}}, \mathbf{C}^{\text{ie}}$, and $\mathbf{C}^{\text{ii}}$) are depicted in Fig. 2. The connectivity patterns were designed ad-hoc, always following biophysical constraints defined in the literature [10].

Neural adaptation in cortex was modelled as an effective negative input current $B_n^{e,i}(t)$ in the neural ensembles $H_n^{e,i}$ [4]. Adaptation effective currents followed leaky-integrator-like dynamics:

$$\tau_{\text{adapt}}\dot{B}_n^{e,i}(t) = -B_n^{e,i}(t) + \theta_{\text{adapt}}H_n^{e,i}(t) \tag{8}$$

Adaptation parameters were identical in both excitatory and inhibitory ensembles. τ_{adapt} was chosen from the literature [4] and $\theta_{\text{adapt}} \ll 1$ such that the effect of adaptation is only noticeable under high firing rate regimes.

3 Results

The model was tested using three families of stimuli typically eliciting N100m auditory cortex responses highly correlated with pitch: pure tones (PT), harmonic complex tones (HCT), and iterated rippled noises (IRN, consisting on the aggregation of iteratively lagged copies of a white noise with a fixed delay δt). HCTs typically evoke the pitch of the fundamental frequency f_0 of the harmonic mixture, even if f_0 itself is not present in the tone (phenomenon known as *virtual pitch* [6]). IRNs evoke a pitch equivalent to the inverse of the delay $1/\delta t$.

We considered a variable number of harmonics in the HCT (with and without missing fundamental) and IRNs of 8, 16 and 32 iterations; for a range of pitch values between 200 Hz and 1000 Hz for all stimulus types. After an unstable transient response of around 100–150 ms, the activity in the cortical ensembles systematically converged to a unimodal distribution centred on the population corresponding to the perceived fundamental (see Figs. 1 and 3), fully in line with predictions of abstract pitch perception models from the literature [1] (Fig. 3).

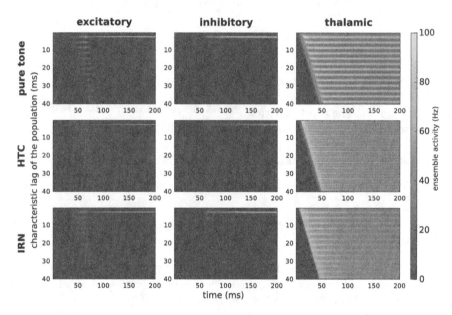

Fig. 3. Time evolution of the activity of the ensembles for three different stimuli with the same pitch ($f = 333$ Hz). From left to right, plots show the temporal evolution of the $N = 300$ ensembles (y-axis) in each of the different groups: excitatory populations $H^e(t)$, inhibitory populations $H^i(t)$, and subcortical populations $A(t)$. From top to bottom, each row shows results for: a pure tone, a harmonic complex tone with 10 harmonics, and an iterated rippled noise with 32 iterations.

Simulations were performed using the same parameters for all stimuli, with the only exception of the conductivity of the connection between subcortical and excitatory cortical ensembles J_{thal}, which was tuned for each of the three families of stimuli in order to compensate the large differences between the average activity elicited in the subcortical patterns (see Fig. 1).

Auditory evoked fields were predicted by the activity dynamics of the excitatory pyramidal ensembles in the cortical model. Auditory evoked fields are typically represented using equivalent dipoles that model neural activity in a localised cortical area. Dipoles in auditory cortex are usually fitted using band-passed MEG fields averaged along a few hundreds of trials. In order to predict the elicited fields, we assumed that all microcolumns in our model present the same orientation. Then, the total dipolar moment elicited by the cortical model is proportional to the aggregated activity across populations $m(t) = \sum_n H_n^e(t + \Delta t)$, where Δt accounts for the time elapsed from tone onset until the signal first arrives in primary auditory cortex ($\Delta t \simeq 30$–50 ms). To account for the trial to trial variability of the model, we further averaged the predicted dipole moment across 10 runs $M(t) = \langle m(t) \rangle_{\text{runs}}$.

An example of the simulated fields is shown in Fig. 4 for several stimuli. The resulting waveform components can be related with the evoked fields observed in MEG auditory experiments: the first large negative transient predicts the N100m component, whilst the sustained model response shows a good agreement with the sustained field.

In order to assess quantitatively the relation between the N100m and the model's output, we computed the latency of the component for pure tones and HCTs and compared them with available results in the literature [5,7,8]. Results are shown in Fig. 4. Good agreements between the model's response and the experimental data were generally observed in the range $f_0 \sim 150$–2000 Hz. Specifically, latency predictions over 1000 Hz where all quite similar, consistently with experimental observations.

Stimuli presenting fundamental or effective frequencies under $f_0 = 150$ Hz yielded an overly late predicted N100m. This is due to intrinsic limitations of the peripheral model, that does not present cochlear channels solving frequencies under $f = 125$ Hz [14]. Stimuli with $f_0 > 2000$ Hz failed to yield satisfactory perceptual outputs, as a reflection of the limit for phase-locking in the peripheral auditory system [14].

4 Discussion and Conclusions

We introduced a biophysical model of cortical responses related to pitch processing. The model accounts for the pitch-related components of auditory evoked fields for the first time to our knowledge, and quantitatively explains the observed N100m transient neural response in a range of stimuli as a transient instability in the neural dynamics underlying pitch processing. The instability period begins at the cortical input onset i.e. when cortical ensembles start to integrate the subcortical activation patterns. Pyramidal neurons encoding the perceived pitch and lower harmonics become increasingly active, propagating forward activity to the inhibitory ensembles; whose feedback reduce the activation of excitatory ensembles encoding lower harmonics. Thus, the aggregated activity in the excitatory neurons shows a transient component that begins with the subcortical input onset, peaks when the inhibitory/excitatory input is balanced, and stabilises when the population encoding the perceived pitch is the more active one;

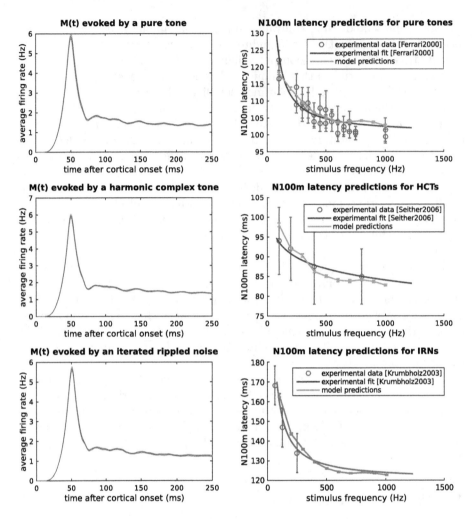

Fig. 4. Simulations of the auditory evoked fields evoked by pure tones, harmonic complex tones, and iterated rippled noises. In the left column, we show an example of the $M(t)$ for each of the families of stimuli with a pitch of 500 Hz (blue shades represent the standard deviation). In the right column, we show the derived predictions of the N100m latency and the observed experimental data for a range of fundamental frequencies.

accounting for the perceived pitch. A balanced excitation and inhibition setting such as the one shown in this model has been found to underlie cognitive flexibility [12].

Importantly, we found that the latency of the N100m component directly stems from the time required by the model to achieve equilibrium after stimulus' onset. High-pitched sounds typically have a larger amount of lower harmonics represented in cortex than low-pitched ones, and thus they elicit bottom-up activation in more excitatory ensembles; which induce top-down inhibitory activity in a larger amount of inhibitory populations. Namely, high pitched sounds trigger top-down inhibition faster, thus explaining the observed dependency on pitch of the N100m's latency.

Conclusion. This study shows that N100m morphology associated with pitch perception can be explained by transient dynamics of a winner-takes-all competition among balanced, excitatory and inhibitory populations, tonotopically distributed in cortex. In conclusion, we suggest that these characteristics provide a specific mechanism which enables alHG ensembles to process pitch.

References

1. Balaguer-Ballester, E., Clark, N.R., Coath, M., Krumbholz, K., Denham, S.L.: Understanding pitch perception as a hierarchical process with top-down modulation. PLoS Comput. Biol. **5**(3), e1000301 (2009)
2. Brunel, N., Wang, X.J.: Effects of neuromodulation in a cortical network model of object working memory dominated by recurrent inhibition. J. Comput. Neurosci. **11**(1), 63–85 (2001)
3. Daunizeau, J., David, O., Stephan, K.E.: Dynamic causal modelling: a critical review of the biophysical and statistical foundations. NeuroImage **58**(2), 312–322 (2011)
4. Gerstner, W., Kistler, W.M., Naud, R., Paninski, L.: Neuronal Dynamics: From Single Neurons to Networks and Models of Cognition, 1st edn. Cambridge University Press, Cambridge (2014)
5. Krumbholz, K., Patterson, R., Seither-Preisler, A., Lammertmann, C., Lütkenhöner, B.: Neuromagnetic evidence for a pitch processing center in Heschl's gyrus. Cereb. Cortex **13**(7), 765–772 (2003)
6. Meddis, R., OMard, L.P.: Virtual pitch in a computational physiological model. J. Acoust. Soc. Am. **120**(6), 3861 (2006)
7. Roberts, T.P.L., Ferrari, P., Stufflebeam, S.M., Poeppel, D.: Latency of the auditory evoked neuromagnetic field components. J. Clin. Neurophysiol. **17**(2), 114–129 (2000)
8. Seither-Preisler, A., Patterson, R., Krumbholz, K., Seither, S., Lütkenhöner, B.: Evidence of pitch processing in the N100m component of the auditory evoked field. Hear. Res. **213**(1–2), 88–98 (2006)
9. Tabas, A., Siebert, A., Supek, S., Pressnitzer, D., Balaguer-Ballester, E., Rupp, A.: Insights on the neuromagnetic representation of temporal asymmetry in human auditory cortex. Plos One **11**(4), e0153947 (2016)
10. Wang, X.: The harmonic organization of auditory cortex. Front. Syst. Neurosci. **7**, 114 (2013)
11. Wiegrebe, L.: Searching for the time constant of neural pitch extraction. J. Acoust. Soc. Am. **109**(3), 1082–1091 (2001)
12. Wimmer, K., Compte, A., Roxin, A., Peixoto, D., Renart, A., de la Rocha, J.: Sensory integration dynamics in a hierarchical network explains choice probabilities in cortical area MT. Nature Commun. **6**, 6177 (2015)
13. Wong, K.F., Wang, X.J.: A recurrent network mechanism of time integration in perceptual decisions. J. Neurosci. **26**(4), 1314–1328 (2006)
14. Zilany, M.S.A., Bruce, I.C., Carney, L.H.: Updated parameters and expanded simulation options for a model of the auditory periphery. J. Acoust. Soc. Am. **135**, 283–286 (2014)

Dynamics of Reward Based Decision Making: A Computational Study

Bhargav Teja Nallapu[1,2(✉)] and Nicolas P. Rougier[2,3,4]

[1] International Institute of Information Technology (I.I.I.T), Hyderabad, India
bhargav.rrv@gmail.com
[2] INRIA, Bordeaux Sud-Ouest, Talence, France
[3] IMN, CNRS, University of Bordeaux, UMR 5293, IMN, Bordeaux, France
[4] University of Bordeaux, CNRS UMR 5800, Labri, IPB, Talence, France

Abstract. We consider a biologically plausible model of the basal ganglia that is able to learn a probabilistic two armed bandit task using reinforcement learning. This model is able to choose the best option and to reach optimal performances after only a few trials. However, we show in this study that the influence of exogenous factors such as stimuli salience and/or timing seems to prevail over optimal decision making, hence questioning the very definition of action-selection. What are the ecological conditions for optimal action selection?

Keywords: Decision making · Neural dynamics · Basal ganglia · Optimal behavior

1 Introduction

Basal ganglia are known to be involved in decision making and action selection based on reinforcement learning and a number of models have been designed to give account on such action selection [2,3,10]. We have been studying a specific computational model of the basal ganglia that has been introduced in [4] and replicated in [13]. This model has been used to explain, to some extent, decision making in primates on a two armed bandit task. One of the questions we attempt to address in this study is to what extent the physical properties of the stimulus such as the visual salience or other characteristics affect the decision and lead to a suboptimal choice. For example (and quite obviously), a stimulus is very likely to be selected, if it is presented before the other stimuli and this selection will be made irrespectively of the potential reward associated with this stimulus. Moreover, there may be other factors such as stimulus salience or population size that may also disrupt the optimal performance. This led us to do a systematic study of the influence of such exogenous factors to understand what are the ecological conditions for optimal decision making.

© Springer International Publishing Switzerland 2016
A.E.P. Villa et al. (Eds.): ICANN 2016, Part I, LNCS 9886, pp. 322–329, 2016.
DOI: 10.1007/978-3-319-44778-0_38

2   Methods

2.1   Task

The task that has been used to demonstrate action selection in the model is a probabilistic learning task that is described in [8]. Four target shapes are associated with different reward probabilities (see Fig. 1). A trial is a time period in which any two of the four possible shapes are presented at two random positions (out of the four possible positions - up, right, down and left). The model is allowed to settle for the first 500 ms of the trial and then two random cues are presented. By the end of trial period, a choice is made and the reward is given according to the reward probability associated with the chosen shape.

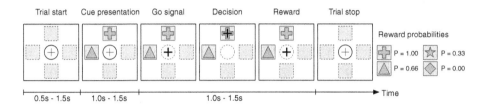

Fig. 1. The two armed bandit task as described in [4,8].

A trial is considered to be successful if a decision is made by the model, irrespective of the reward received. In a single independent trial, the cognitive decision (shape of the cue) and motor decision (position of the cue) are independent of each other. At any decision-making level of the model, each of the four cue shapes and each of the four motor movement directions is represented by one unit (neuron) each. Thus in a given trial, when two cue shapes are presented at two different positions, two cognitive, two motor and two associative (in cortex and striatum, see Fig. 2) neurons are activated. The task is run for a session, a number of trials, while at the end of each trial, the model learns the reward associated to its selection. (see *Learning*).

2.2   Model

In [5], authors demonstrated an action selection mechanism in the cortico-basal ganglia loops based on a competition between the positive feedback, direct pathway through the striatum and the negative feedback, hyperdirect pathway through the subthalamic nucleus. In [4], authors investigated further how multiple level action selection could be performed by the basal ganglia, and the model has been extended in a manner consistent with known anatomy and electrophysiology of the basal ganglia in the monkey (see Fig. 2). This model allows a bidirectional information flow between loops such that during early trials,

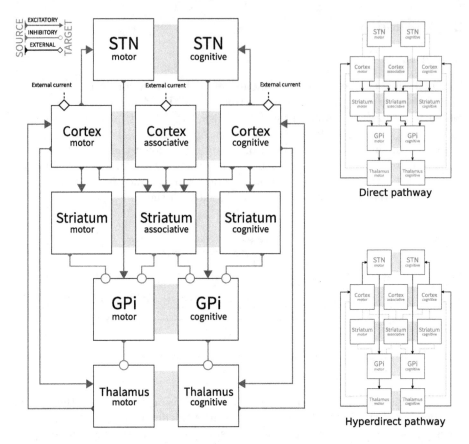

Fig. 2. Architecture of the basal ganglia model which is organised around three parallel loops: cognitive, associative and motor. Only the direct and hyperdirect pathways have been modelled.

a direction can be selected randomly, irrespective of the cue positions. However, after repeated trials, the model is able to consistently make the cognitive decision before the motor decision in each trial (see Fig. 3) and most frequently the motor decision, biased by the cognitive decision, towards the position of the more rewarding cue shape.

Learning. Learning has been derived from a simple actor-critic algorithm [12] that shapes the gain between the cognitive cortex and the cognitive striatum. According to the amount of reward received at the end of each trial (0 or 1), the model learns to estimate the value of chosen stimulus and then the cognitive pathway is biased in favor of the stimulus with the highest value.

Neuronal Dynamics. This model uses the same, simple neuronal rate model as in [4,5] to focus on the network dynamics. Within each structure, each neuron (in each channel of any loop) is modeled as a single rate coded neuron with the equation:

$$\tau \frac{dm}{dt} = -m + I_s + I_{Ext} - T \tag{1}$$

decay time constant of the synaptic input τ, negative values of activation, m and threshold of the neuron T are set to respective constant values as per the model in [4]. I_{Ext} is an external input representing the sensory visual salience of the cue, which is unchanged throughout the process of learning.

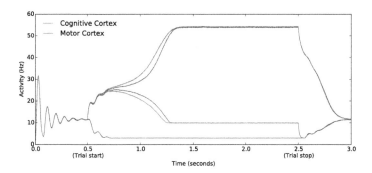

Fig. 3. Time course of a decision in the motor cortex (blue curves) and cognitive cortex (red curve) before learning. At trial start ($t = 500$ ms), there is a first bifurcation between stimuli that are actually presented and those who are not. The second bifurcation around $t = 750$ ms is the actual decision of the model. (Color figure online)

3   Results

In all the following cases, we consider 4 stimuli A, B, C, D respectively associated with reward probability of 1.0, 0.66, 0.33 and 0.0. Learning is performed over 120 trials until the model reaches a performance of 0.90, meaning it chooses the best stimulus 90 % of the time. We then stopped learning in the model and simulated a scenario where one stimulus is presented first and the other follows after a certain *delay*. Another scenario involved presenting one stimulus with more *salience* than the other. In both the scenarios, the intent was to emphasize the advantage (earlier presentation or higher salience) to the lesser rewarding stimulus and see if that leads the model to a suboptimal decision. We presented the model with various scenarios involving different *delays* and *saliences*. (see Fig. 4).

3.1   Influence of Delay

We first tested the influence of a small delay (between 0 ms and 60 ms) between the presentation of the two stimuli. The worst stimulus, that is the one associated with the lesser probability of reward, is presented first and after the delay,

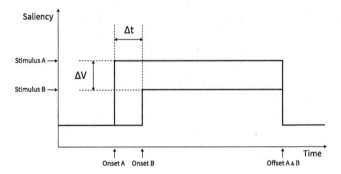

Fig. 4. Two stimuli A & B can differ in salience (ΔV) and/or in timing (Δt). ΔV is expressed as the relative ratio between the less salient and the most salient stimuli ($\Delta V = (V_A - V_B)/V_B$. Δt is expressed as the delay separating the two stimuli onsets ($\Delta t = t_A - t_B$).

the second (better rewarding) stimulus is presented. We have been testing systematically all combinations of stimuli (A/B, A/C, A/D, B/C, B/D, C/D) and averaged the mean performance over 25 trials (see Fig. 5). As expected, the performance decreased with the increase in delay and the crossing (i.e. performance is random) happens around 35 ms for all combinations but the last one (C/D) that happens very early, around 20 ms. This specific case can be explained by the poor estimation of the value of C and D during learning because those stimuli are almost never chosen (most of the time, they are presented with a better stimuli).

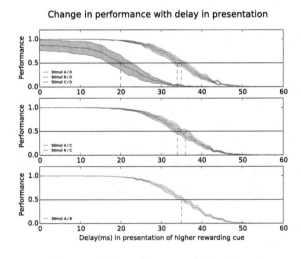

Fig. 5. Performance of the model as a function of the delay between the worst and the best stimuli. All combinations have been tested and mean performance has been averaged over 25 trials.

3.2   Influence of Salience

We tested the influence of salience by presenting simultaneously the two stimuli but the worst stimulus, i.e., the one associated with a lesser probability of reward, has been made virtually stronger than the other. The model, having learned the rewarding probabilities, is expected to select the higher rewarding stimulus irrespective of the salience. However, the increased salience of the lesser rewarding stimulus affects the model and leads it to take a bad decision (see Fig. 6). As the salience of the lesser rewarding stimulus increases, a consistent decrease in the performance of model is observed. Interestingly, the threshold percentage of salience difference after which the performance of the model decreases, is a characteristic of the difference in the reward probabilities of both the stimuli presented. Quite visibly (Fig. 6), it takes higher salience difference for a lesser rewarding stimulus to be chosen against the best rewarding one (in this case, A) whereas a lesser increase in salience seems to be sufficient to compromise the decisions involving lesser rewarding stimuli, like B.

In various neuropsychological studies on humans, like in [7,9], it has been emphasized that the visual saliency of stimuli influences the choices over the learned preferences and visual working memory. Interestingly, in [7] where at an exposure time of 1500 ms, which is quite similar to that of the model discussed here, the influence of visual saliency was particularly evident when there were no strong preferences among the options. This observation is supported by the early performance decline of the model discussed here, when presented with two closely rewarding stimuli (Stimuli C/D in Fig. 6).

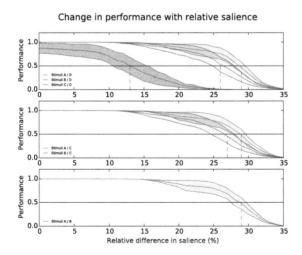

Fig. 6. Performance of the model as a function of the delay between the worst and the best stimuli. All combinations have been tested and mean performance has been averaged over 25 trials. Decrease in performance of the model when the lesser rewarding stimulus is presented with stronger salience than the higher rewarding stimulus.

3.3   Joint Influence of Delay and Salience

We further tested the model and studied the joint influence of delay and salience by make the worst stimulus to be presented earlier and with a stronger salience. As shown in Fig. 7, this dramatically degrades the performance and the domain of optimal performance is even more restricted compared to original results.

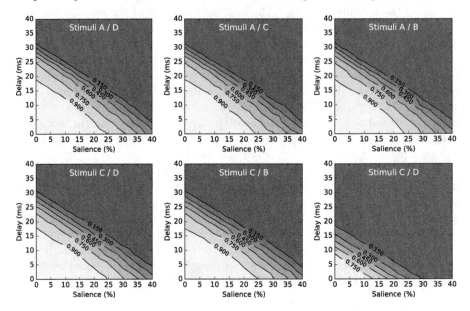

Fig. 7. Joint influence of delay and salience on the performance of the model. The two effects appears to linearly sum up and the domain of optimal performance is even more restricted.

4   Conclusion

These early results tend to question the very notion of optimal action selection as defined in a number of theoretical works. The action may be considered optimal provided the two options are presented simultaneously and with an equivalent representation. In the reinforcement learning paradigm, such consideration does not hold much relevance. However, from a more behavioral and embodied perspective, we think this is an important dimension to consider because an animal is scarcely confronted by a set of perfectly equivalent options (but their associated value). One may come first or one may just appear more "obvious" (i.e. more salient). In such a case, the inner dynamics of the model may lead to a suboptimal choice as it is the case using the model from [4]. Although we did not perform the study presented here on primates yet, the results from the model assert the need for a closer look at the way we perceive decision making paradigms. The question is to know to what extent some dedicated brain mechanisms are able to cope with these problems. For example, concerning the time delay, a *stop* signal, as it has been reported in [11], may represent a potential mechanism to be able to solve the problem for small delays ($< 200\,\text{ms}$).

For the salience difference however, and to the best of our knowledge, there is no such *dedicated* mechanism. In [6], a stimulus-reward association study on macaque monkeys, spike recordings showed significant reward dependence in their responses to the visual cues. In [1], rewards were shown to teach visual selective attention maximizing the positive outcomes. However both the studies do not identify the underlying mechanisms that caused the observations on the effect of salience. This study hence suggests that measuring experimentally performance using different salience levels could bring useful insights into decision making.

Acknowledgements. The authors would like to acknowledge the funds received from Centre Franco-Indien pour la Promotion de la Recherche Avance (CEFIPRA) under the project DST-INRIA 2013-02/Basal Ganglia.

References

1. Chelazzi, L., Perlato, A., Santandrea, E., Della Libera, C.: Rewards teach visual selective attention. Vision. Res. **85**, 58–72 (2013)
2. Gurney, K., Prescott, T.J., Redgrave, P.: A computational model of action selection in the basal ganglia. I. A new functional anatomy. Biol. Cybern. **84**(6), 401–410 (2001)
3. Gurney, K., Prescott, T.J., Redgrave, P.: A computational model of action selection in the basal ganglia. II. Analysis and simulation of behaviour. Biol. Cybern. **84**(6), 411–423 (2001)
4. Guthrie, M., Leblois, A., Garenne, A., Boraud, T.: Interaction between cognitive and motor cortico-basal ganglia loops during decision making: a computational study. J. Neurophysiol. **109**(12), 3025–3040 (2013)
5. Leblois, A., Boraud, T., Meissner, W., Bergman, H., Hansel, D.: Competition between feedback loops underlies normal and pathological dynamics in the basal ganglia. J. Neurosci. **26**, 3567–3583 (2006)
6. Mogami, T., Tanaka, K.: Reward association affects neuronal responses to visual stimuli in macaque te and perirhinal cortices. J. Neurosci. **26**(25), 6761–6770 (2006)
7. Mormann, M.M., Navalpakkam, V., Koch, C., Rangel, A.: Relative visual saliency differences induce sizable bias in consumer choice. J. Consum. Psychol. **22**(1), 67–74 (2012)
8. Pasquereau, B., Nadjar, A., Arkadir, D., Bezard, E., Goillandeau, M., Bioulac, B., Gross, C.E., Boraud, T.: Shaping of motor responses by incentive values through the basal ganglia. J. Neurosci. **27**(5), 1176–1183 (2007)
9. Pooresmaeili, A., Bach, D.R., Dolan, R.J.: The effect of visual salience on memory-based choices. J. Neurophysiol. **111**(3), 481–487 (2014)
10. Redgrave, P., Prescott, T.J., Gurney, K.: The basal ganglia: a vertebrate solution to the selection problem? Neuroscience **89**(4), 1009–1023 (1999)
11. Schmidt, R., Leventhal, D.K., Mallet, N., Chen, F., Berke, J.D.: Canceling actions involves a race between basal ganglia pathways. Nat. Neurosci. **16**(8), 1118–1124 (2013)
12. Sutton, R., Barto, A.: Reinforcement Learning: An Introduction. MIT Press, Cambridge (1998)
13. Topalidou, M., Rougier, N.: [re] interaction between cognitive and motor cortico-basal ganglia loops during decision making: a computational study. ReScience 1(1) (2015)

Adaptive Proposer for Ultimatum Game

František Hůla[✉], Marko Ruman, and Miroslav Kárný

Department of Adaptive Systems, Institute of Information Theory and Automation, Czech Academy of Sciences, POB 18, 182 08 Prague 8, The Czech Republic
hula.frantisek@gmail.com, marko.ruman@gmail.com, school@utia.cas.cz
http://www.utia.cz/AS

Abstract. Ultimate Game serves for extensive studies of various aspects of human decision making. The current paper contribute to them by designing proposer optimising its policy using Markov-decision-process (MDP) framework combined with recursive Bayesian learning of responder's model. Its foreseen use: (i) standardises experimental conditions for studying rationality and emotion-influenced decision making of human responders; (ii) replaces the classical game-theoretical design of the players' policies by an adaptive MDP, which is more realistic with respect to the knowledge available to individual players and decreases player's deliberation effort; (iii) reveals the need for approximate learning and dynamic programming inevitable for coping with the curse of dimensionality; (iv) demonstrates the influence of the fairness attitude of the proposer on the game course; (v) prepares the test case for inspecting exploration-exploitation dichotomy.

Keywords: Games · Markov decision process · Bayesian learning

1 Introduction

Since ancient times people trade with each other. Modern man cannot imagine life without exchange of goods, services, information etc. It is something like the cornerstone of our civilization. This human activity divides people to proposers of some merit and responders who either accept or refuse it. Both of them can often bargain but a price tag in the store represents a sort of ultimatum: if we buy the product we agree with the seller's price without any direct negotiation. This motivates investigations of human behaviour connected with the bargaining and trading. They concern economical, game-theoretical, social, cultural and emotional aspects and they often use standardised "laboratory" variants of the discussed interaction. Ultimatum Game (UG) is a prominent test case [18].

UG considers a fixed number of rounds of the two-player game. A fixed amount of money is split in each round. The proposer offers a part of this amount and the responder either accepts the offer and money are split accordingly or refuses it and both get nothing. Seemingly, the game should have a definite

This research was supported by Grant Agency of the Czech Republic, No 13-13502S.

A.E.P. Villa et al. (Eds.): ICANN 2016, Part I, LNCS 9886, pp. 330–338, 2016.
DOI: 10.1007/978-3-319-44778-0_39

course: the proposer offers the smallest possible positive amount and the responder accepts it. No such behaviour is observed in reality as people judge the game not only according to monetary profit. Typically, they try to earn at least as their opponent, they care about self-fairness [8,20] influenced by culture, sex, etc. [5]. An important influence of emotions are also studied [7].

While an appropriate model of self-fairness leads to surprisingly accurate predictions of responders' behaviours [9], to get a statistically significant quantification of emotional influences has been found quite hard. The hypothesis that an actively optimising proposer could make this influence more pronounced has led to the design of the standardised active proposer described here. Theory of Markov decision processes (MDP) [17] was selected as the basis of such a design. This choice avoiding the standard game-theoretical formulation [22] is motivated by the inherent trap of the dimensionality curse [3] of the Bayesian games [10].

The use of MDP supposes knowledge of responder's model, which is in realistic scenarios unknown and, moreover, it is very individual in the targeted emotion-oriented studies. This calls for a combination of MDP with a permanent learning of this model, i.e. for adaptive MDP. The inherent small amount of available data singles out recursive Bayesian learning in the closed decision loop as the (only) appropriate methodology [16]. Even then, approximations of recursive learning like [11] and dynamic programming [21] are needed. This text makes just the preparatory steps towards the complete solution. It recalls MDP, the dynamic programming as the optimisation tool and the recursive Bayesian learning, Sect. 2. UG is formulated in MDP terms for various types of proposers, Sect. 3. A numerical illustration is in Sect. 4. Section 5 adds remarks.

2   Mathematical Background

This section is based on [3,9,16,17]. It introduces the adopted notions, recalls the used mathematical tools, and makes the paper relatively self-containing.

2.1   General Formulation and Solution of Markov Decision Process

The considered system consists of *decision maker* (DM), and *responder*. They interact in discrete time (*decision epochs*) $t \in \mathbf{T} = \{1, 2, \ldots, |\mathbf{t}|\}$, $|\mathbf{t}| < \infty$. DM chooses a discrete-valued *action* (an irreversible decision) $a_t \in \mathbf{A} = \{1, 2, \ldots, |\mathbf{a}|\}$, $|\mathbf{a}| < \infty$, in each epoch $t \in \mathbf{T}$. Consequently, the closed decision loop transits from a discrete-valued *state* $s_{t-1} \in \mathbf{S} = \{1, 2, \ldots, |\mathbf{s}|\}$, $|\mathbf{s}| < \infty$ to the state $s_t \in \mathbf{S}$. The use of *regression pair* $\psi_t = (a_t, s_{t-1}) \in \mathbf{\Psi} = (\mathbf{A}, \mathbf{S})$, $t \in \mathbf{T}$, simplifies the presentation. With it, the random transition is described by *transition probabilities*[1] $\left(p(s_t|\psi_t) \right)_{t \in \mathbf{T}} \in \mathbf{P} = \left\{ p(s_t|\psi_t) \geq 0 \ \middle| \ \sum_{s_t \in \mathbf{S}} p(s_t|\psi_t) = 1, \ \forall \psi_t \in \mathbf{\Psi} \right\}$. After the transition, the DM receives a real-valued *reward* $r(s_t, \psi_t) \in \mathbf{R} = \left\{ r(s_t, \psi_t) \ \middle| \ s_t \in \mathbf{S}, \ \psi_t \in \mathbf{\Psi}, \ t \in \mathbf{T} \right\}$. The DM cannot use the state s_t for choosing the action $a_t \in \mathbf{A}$ and thus it can at most maximise *aggregate expected reward*

---

[1] All functions with time-dependent arguments generally depend on time.

$$\sum_{t \in \mathbf{T}} \mathsf{E}[r(s_t, \psi_t)] = \sum_{t \in \mathbf{T}} \sum_{s_t \in \mathbf{S}, \psi_t \in \mathbf{\Psi}} r(s_t, \psi_t) p(s_t, \psi_t) \tag{1}$$

$$= \sum_{t \in \mathbf{T}} \sum_{\substack{s_t \in \mathbf{S}, a_t \in \mathbf{A} \\ s_{t-1} \in \mathbf{S}}} r(s_t, \psi_t) p(s_t | \psi_t) p(a_t | s_{t-1}) p(s_{t-1}).$$

The last equality in (1) follows from the chain rule [17]. It expresses the probability $p(s_t, \psi_t)$ as the product of the given *transition probability* $p(s_t|\psi_t) \in \mathbf{P}$, of the optional *decision rules* $(p(a_t|s_{t-1}))_{t \in \mathbf{T}} \in \mathbf{\Pi} = \left\{ p(a_t|s_{t-1}) \middle| s_{t-1} \in \mathbf{S}, a_t \in \mathbf{A} \right\}$ forming the *decision policy* and of the *state probability* $p(s_t) \in \mathbf{PS}$, where

$$\mathbf{PS} = \left\{ p(s_t) \middle| p(s_t) = \sum_{\psi_t \in \mathbf{\Psi}} p(s_t|\psi_t) p_t(a_t|s_{t-1}) p_t(s_{t-1}), \ s_t \in \mathbf{S}, t \in \mathbf{T} \right\}. \tag{2}$$

The state probability $p(s_t)$ is influenced by the "policy prefix" $(p(a_\tau|s_{\tau-1}))_{\tau \le t}$ and the probability $p(s_0)$ of the initial state $s_0 \in \mathbf{S}$. Often, $p(s_0) = \delta(s_0, \tilde{s}_0)$ with *Kronecker* δ equal to 1 for equal arguments and 0 otherwise. It concentrates $p(s_0)$ on a given $\tilde{s}_0 \in \mathbf{S}$.

Thus, the optimising DM maximises the aggregate expected reward (1) over *decision policies* $\mathbf{\Pi}$. For known $\mathbf{R}$, $\mathbf{P}$ and $\tilde{s}_0$, DM takes as the *optimal policy*

$$(p_{opt}(a_t|s_{t-1}))_{t \in \mathbf{T}} \in \underset{(p(a_t|s_{t-1}))_{t \in \mathbf{T}} \in \mathbf{\Pi}}{\mathrm{Arg\,max}} \sum_{t \in \mathbf{T}} \mathsf{E}[r(s_t, \psi_t)]. \tag{3}$$

Definition 1 (Optimal MDP). *The given 7-tuple* $\{\mathbf{T}, \mathbf{A}, \mathbf{S}, \mathbf{PS}, \mathbf{P}, \mathbf{R}, \mathbf{\Pi}\}$ *together with the maximisation (3) is referred as Markov decision process (MDP).*

Theorem 1 (Dynamic Programming, proof e.g. in [17]). *The policy* $(p_{opt}(a_t|s_{t-1}))_{t \in \mathbf{T}} \in \mathbf{\Pi}$ *maximising the aggregate expected reward (3) consists of the deterministic decision rules* $p_{opt}(a_t|s_{t-1}) = \delta(a_t, a_t^\star(s_{t-1}))$, *where*

$$a_t^\star(s_{t-1}) \in \mathrm{Arg\,max}_{a \in \mathbf{A}} \mathsf{E}[r(s_t, a, s_{t-1}) + \varphi_t(s_t)|a, s_{t-1}] \text{ with value function}$$

$$\varphi_t(s_t) = \sum_{s_{t+1} \in \mathbf{S}} [r(s_{t+1}, a_{t+1}^\star(s_t), s_t) + \varphi_{t+1}(s_{t+1})] p(s_{t+1}|a_{t+1}^\star(s_t), s_t).$$

The backward recursion starts with $\varphi_{|t|}(s_{|t|}) = 0, \forall s_{|t|} \in \mathbf{S}$.

2.2 Bayesian Learning of Transition Probabilities

The unrealistic assumption that the transition probabilities from the set $\mathbf{P}$ are given, see Definition 1, is removed via Bayesian recursive learning [16] recalled here. It relates the state $s_t \in \mathbf{S}$ to the action $a_t \in \mathbf{A}$ and observed states $s_\tau \in \mathbf{S}$, $\tau < t$, by transition probability parameterised by its unknown values Θ

$$p(s_t|a_t,\ldots,a_1,s_{t-1},\ldots,s_0,\Theta) = p(s_t|\psi_t,\Theta) = \prod_{s \in \mathbf{S}} \prod_{\psi \in \mathbf{\Psi}} \Theta_{s|\psi}^{\delta(s,s_t)\delta(\psi,\psi_t)}, \text{where}$$

$$\Theta \in \mathbf{\Theta} = \left\{ \Theta_{s|\psi} \geq 0 \,\middle|\, s \in \mathbf{S}, \psi \in \mathbf{\Psi}, \sum_{s \in \mathbf{S}} \Theta_{s|\psi} = 1, \forall \psi \in \mathbf{\Psi} \right\}. \tag{4}$$

It provides the transition probabilities as predictors

$$p(s_t|\psi_t,\ldots,\psi_1) = \int_\Theta p(s_t|\psi_t,\Theta)p(\Theta|s_{t-1},\psi_{t-1},\ldots,\psi_1)\mathrm{d}\Theta, \tag{5}$$

where the posterior probability density $p(\Theta|s_{t-1},\psi_{t-1},\ldots,\psi_1)$ has the support Θ and is given by the observed condition $s_{t-1},\psi_{t-1},\ldots,\psi_1$. Bayes' rule [4,16] evolves it

$$p(\Theta|s_t,\psi_t,\ldots,\psi_1) = \frac{p(s_t|\psi_t,\Theta)p(\Theta|s_{t-1},\psi_{t-1},\ldots,\psi_1)}{p(s_t|a_t,\psi_{t-1},\ldots,\psi_1)}. \tag{6}$$

An optional prior probability density $p(\Theta) = p(\Theta|\psi_1,\psi_0)$ initiates (6).

Importantly, the learning (5), (6) is valid for any policy for which the parameter $\Theta \in \mathbf{\Theta}$ is unknown, i.e. which meets *natural conditions of control* [16]

$$p(a_t|\psi_{t-1},\ldots,\psi_1,\Theta) = p(a_t|\psi_{t-1},\ldots,\psi_1). \tag{7}$$

The learning is correct in loops closed by any (say human) policy meeting (7).

The product forms of the model (4) and of Bayes' rule (6) imply Dirichlet's form of the posterior probability density, [12], which uses Euler's gamma Γ [1],

$$p(\Theta|\psi_t,\ldots,\psi_1) = p(\Theta|V_t) =, \prod_{\psi \in \mathbf{\Psi}} \Gamma\left(\sum_{\tilde{s} \in \mathbf{S}} V_{t;\tilde{s}|\psi}\right) \frac{\prod_{s \in \mathbf{S}} \Theta_{s|\psi}^{V_{t;s|\psi}-1}}{\Gamma(V_{t;s|\psi})}, \text{ where}$$

$$V_{t;s|\psi} = V_{t-1;s|\psi} + \delta(s,s_t)\delta(\psi,\psi_t), \text{form } occurence \; array, \; s \in \mathbf{S}, \psi \in \mathbf{\Psi}. \tag{8}$$

The initial occurrence array $V_0 = (V_{0;s|\psi} > 0)_{s \in \mathbf{S}, \psi \in \mathbf{\Psi}}$ describes the used conjugated (Dirichlet form preserving) prior probability density $p(\Theta)$. The gained predictive probability resembles the frequentist estimate $\hat{\Theta} \in \mathbf{\Theta}$ of $\Theta \in \mathbf{\Theta}$

$$p(s_t = s|\psi_t = \psi, V_{t-1}) = \frac{V_{t-1;s|\psi}}{\sum_{\tilde{s} \in \mathbf{S}} V_{t-1;\tilde{s}|\psi}} = \hat{\Theta}_{t-1;s|\psi}, \; s \in \mathbf{S}, \; \psi \in \mathbf{\Psi}. \tag{9}$$

3 Ultimatum Game as Adaptive MDP

According to UG rules, $|\mathbf{t}|$ (tens) rounds are played. Possible actions $a_t \in \mathbf{A}$ of the proposer P (DM supported here) in the round $t \in \mathbf{T}$ are the offered splits of $q = |\mathbf{a}| + 1$ (often monetary) units. The responder R generates the *observed response* $o_t \in \mathbf{O} = \{1,2\} = \{$reject the offer, accept the offer$\}$. The profits of the proposer $Z_{t;P}$ and responder $Z_{t;R}$ accumulated after tth round are

$$Z_{t;P} = \sum_{\tau=1}^{t}(q-a_\tau)(o_\tau - 1) \in \mathbf{Z}_{t;P}, \ Z_{t;R} = \sum_{\tau=1}^{t} a_\tau(o_\tau - 1) \in \mathbf{Z}_{t;R}. \qquad (10)$$

The profits (10) determine the observable (non-minimal) state s_t of the game

$$s_t = (Z_{t;P}, Z_{t;R}) \in \mathbf{S} = (\mathbf{Z}_{t;P}, \mathbf{Z}_{t;R}), \ t \in \mathbf{T}. \qquad (11)$$

It has a finite amount of values and starts with zero profits $s_0 = (0,0)$.

Altogether, UG rules directly specify sets of epochs $\mathbf{T}$, actions $\mathbf{A}$, and state probabilities $\mathbf{PS}$, cf. (2), in the 7-tuple delimiting MDP, see Definition 1. The peculiarities of the use of adaptive MDP by the proposer thus reduce to those connected with transition probabilities $\mathbf{P}$, rewards $\mathbf{R}$ and with the curse of dimensionality connected with the policy space $\mathbf{\Pi}$. They are discussed below.

3.1   Transition Probabilities

Bayesian learning, Sect. 2.2, formally provides the needed transition probabilities in $\mathbf{P}$ under acceptable assumption that the responder does not vary them abruptly during the game course. The lack of learning data, consequence of the dimensionality curse [3], is, however, serious obstacle. Indeed, the sufficient statistics V_t (8) has $|\mathbf{o}| \times |\mathbf{\Psi}| = |\mathbf{o}| \times |\mathbf{a}| \times |\mathbf{s}|$ entries. In a typical case $|\mathbf{o}| = 2$, $|\mathbf{a}| = 9$ and reduced $|\mathbf{s}| = 10$, it needs 180 values to be populated by data, which requires unrealistic hundreds' game rounds. The ways out are as follows.

Reduction of the State Space: The size of V is determined by the richness of the state space $\mathbf{S}$. The UG rules imply that the two-dimensional s_t (11) stays in $(s_{t-1}, s_{t-1} + [a_t, q - a_t])$, i.e. many transitions are impossible. The above example, respecting this fact, indicates the need for additional countermeasures.

Use of Population Based Priors: It is possible to obtain a reliable description of responders' population and convert it into the prior occurrence array $V_{0;s|\psi} = v_{0;\psi}\hat{\Theta}_{0;s|\psi}$, $s \in \mathbf{S}$, $\psi \in \mathbf{\Psi}$ (9). V_0 is modified by at most $|\mathbf{t}|$ data records specific for the individual responder in the individual game. Thus, the choice of the *prior weight* $v_{0;\psi} > 0$ is critical. Due to data sparsity, a few observations of a specific s, ψ within tens of rounds are expected. Thus, $v_{0;\psi} \leq |\mathbf{t}|$ is recommendable.

Assuming ψ-independent prior weight $v_0 = v_{0;\psi}$, its hierarchical Bayesian learning [4] becomes feasible. Hypotheses h : proper $v_0 = v_{0;h} =$ a value in $(0,1)$, $h \in \mathbf{H} = \{1, 2, \ldots, |\mathbf{h}|\}$ with a small $|\mathbf{h}|$ are formulated. For each h, the predictor (9), becomes h dependent $p(s_t = s|\psi_t = \psi, V_{t-1;h})$ via h-dependent array $V_{0;h} = v_{0;h}\hat{\Theta}$. Then, Bayes' rule is directly applicable. The h-independent predictor (transition probability) becomes mixture of predictors within respective hypotheses with weights being their posterior probabilities, see [4,16].

This Bayesian averaging is of a direct relevance for the motivating studies of influence of emotions on decision making. It suffices to collect descriptions of sub-populations differing by observed or stimulated emotional states and compare hypotheses about suitability of the transition probabilities learnt with prior parameter probability densities reflecting these sub-populations.

Choice of the Model Structure: The above Bayesian treatment of the finite amount of compound hypotheses can also serve for the desirable reduction of the parametric-model structure. For instance, experimental evidence strongly indicates, e.g. [9], that the proposer action decisively influences responder's response. Thus, the hypothesis that $p(s_t|a_t, s_{t-1}) = p(s_t - s_{t-1}|a_t)$ can be and should be compared to the general form of $p(s_t|a_t, s_{t-1})$. It fits to attempts to use more parsimonious parametrisation like special mixtures in [11] are.

3.2   Rewards

The reward $r(s_t, \psi_t) \in \mathbf{R}$, used in the design of the optimal policy (3) reflects attitude of the proposer to inter-relation of its profit and responder's profit. The sole action values play no role unless they are connected with DM's deliberation effort as in [19]. Then, rewards studied in [9] from responder's view-point, are worth considering.

Economic Proposer: It is interested in its own profit only, paying no attention to co-player. Its reward is $r(s_t, \psi_t) = Z_{t;P} - Z_{t-1;P}$. It is taken as economically rational DM but almost nobody acts in the way optimal for this reward.

Self-interested Proposer: It partially maximises its profit but also watches the responder's profit not to let the responder to win too much. Such attitude was modelled by $r(s_t, \psi_t) = wZ_{t;P} - (1 - w)Z_{t;R}$, with the weight $w \in [0, 1]$ controlling self-fairness level. This reward quite successfully models human responders when the weight w is recursively personalised [9,14]. The weight is conjectured to depend on the player's personality and emotions. The preliminary results confirm this [2], but statistically convincing results are unavailable. The adaptive proposer's discussed here is expected to help in this respect.

Fair Responder: It jointly maximises profits of both players by using $r(s_t, \psi_t) = wZ_{t;P} - (1 - w)\mathrm{abs}(Z_{t;P} - Z_{t;R})$, with the weight $w \in [0, 1]$ balancing own profit with the difference of both profits. No human responder's policy has indicated adoption of such a reward [9]. But the performed experiments limited to greedy (one-stage-ahead) optimisation and the adoption of proposer's view point make us to inspect this variant.

3.3   Policy

The last item to be commented is the set of policies $\mathbf{\Pi}$ within which (approximate) optimum is searched. The described adaptive design extremely increases the extent of the state space as the sufficient statistics V_t (8) is a part of the (information) state. It is obvious as the value function in dynamic programming, Proposition 1, depends on it. This reflects that the selected actions influence not only rewards but also future statistics. The optimal policy is to properly balance the dual – exploitation and exploration – features optimal actions [6]. At present, we are giving it up and use certainty equivalent policies, which perform dynamic programming with the newest parameter estimate $\hat{\Theta}$ taken as known transition probabilities. If need be, the known divergence danger [15] can be overcome by randomising the proposed policy. Foreseen ways are out of our scope.

4   Illustrative Experiments

The limited extent of the paper prevents us to report properly on performed experiments. The illustrative one split $q = |\mathbf{a}| + 1 = 10$, in each of $|\mathbf{t}| = 10$ rounds. The self-fair proposer used the reward $0.5Z_{t;P} - 0.5Z_{t;P}$ and the responder used a fixed randomised decision rule given by the probability $p(o_t = 2 = accept|\psi_t) = p(o_t = 2 = accept|a_t)$, $a_t \in \mathbf{A} = \{1, \ldots, 9\}$. The proposer assumed the same structure but the values $\Theta_{o=2|a}$, $a \in \mathbf{A}$, were recursively estimated, see Sect. 2.2, and used in designing certainty-equivalent strategy found by dynamic programming, Theorem 1. Samples of experiments running with different weights of the prior estimate v_0 are in Fig. 1, where also the used responder's description is visible.

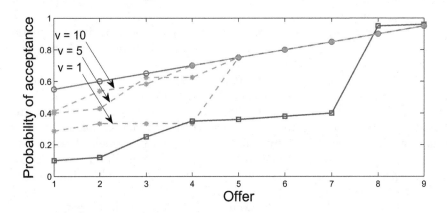

Fig. 1. Final estimates of acceptance probability for possible offers (actions $a \in \mathbf{A}$) are displayed for several weights $\mathrm{v} = v_0$ of the prior occurrence array $V_0 = v_0\hat{\Theta}_0$ and are marked by dots connected with violet dashed lines for distinguishing of each game. The simulated values $\Theta_{o=2|a}$, $a \in \mathbf{A}$ are marked by squares and the prior values $\hat{\Theta}_{o=2|a}$, $a \in \mathbf{A}$ are marked by circles. Both of them are connected with blue and red line respectively. (Color figure online)

The results are just illustrative and correspond with the expected behaviour: too high weight v_0 makes a significant correction of the prior estimate by a few available data impossible.

5   Conclusion

The paper contributes to a wider research oriented towards influence of personal characteristics, emotional states and available deliberation resources on decision making. Unreported experiments with the proposed optimising adaptive proposer indicate that it can serve to this purpose. On its own, it reveals general problems related to curse of dimensionality and offers test-bed for a further development of techniques fighting with it. Addressing of exploitation-exploration dichotomy is the nearest foreseen problem. In this respect, different types of proposers behaved differently: the economic and self-fair ones, unlike the fair one, exhibited tendency to select a narrow range of actions and as such they are more prone to divergence from optimum. The use of randomised strategies resulting from fully probabilistic design of decision policies [13] seems to be the proper direction.

References

1. Abramowitz, M., Stegun, I.A.: Handbook of Mathematical Functions. Dover Publications, New York (1972)
2. Avanesyan, G.: Decision making in ultimatum game. Master's thesis. University of Economics, Prague (2014)
3. Bellman, R.E.: Adaptive Control Processes. Princeton University Press, Princeton (1961)
4. Berger, J.O.: Statistical Decision Theory and Bayesian Analysis. Springer, New York (1985)
5. Boyd, R.: Cross-cultural Ultimatum Game Research Group - Rob Boyd, Joe Henrich problem. Unpublished article
6. Feldbaum, A.A.: Theory of dual control. Autom. Remote Control **21**(9), 874–880 (1960)
7. Fiori, M., Lintas, A., Mesrobian, S., Villa, A.E.P.: Effect of emotion and personality on deviation from purely rational decision-making. In: Guy, T.V., Kárný, M., Wolpert, D.H. (eds.) Decision Making and Imperfection, vol. 474, pp. 129–169. Springer, Berlin (2013)
8. Güth, W.: On ultimatum bargaining experiments: a personal review. J. Econ. Behav. Org. **27**(3), 329–344 (1995)
9. Guy, T.V., Kárný, M., Lintas, A., Villa, A.E.P.: Theoretical models of decision-making in the ultimatum game: fairness vs. reason. In: Wang, R., Pan, X. (eds.) Advances in Cognitive Neurodynamics (V). Advances in Cognitive Neurodynamics. Springer, Singapore (2015)
10. Harsanyi, J.C.: Games with incomplete information played by Bayesian players I-III. Manage. Sci. **50**(12), 1804–1817 (2004). Supplement
11. Kárný, M.: Recursive estimation of high-order Markov chains: approximation by finite mixtures. Inf. Sci. **326**, 188–201 (2016)
12. Kárný, M., Böhm, J., Guy, T.V., Jirsa, L., Nagy, I., Nedoma, P., Tesař, L.: Optimized Bayesian Dynamic Advising: Theory and Algorithms. Springer, London (2006)
13. Kárný, M., Kroupa, T.: Axiomatisation of fully probabilistic design. Inf. Sci. **186**(1), 105–113 (2012)
14. Knejflová, Z., Avanesyan, G., Guy, T.V., Kárný, M.: What lies beneath players' non-rationality in ultimatum game? In: Guy, T.V., Kárný, M. (eds.) Proceedings of the 3rd International Workshop on Scalable Decision Making, ECML/PKDD 2013 (2013)

15. Kumar, P.R.: A survey on some results in stochastic adaptive control. SIAM J. Control Appl. **23**, 399–409 (1985)
16. Peterka, V.: Bayesian approach to system identification. In: Eykhoff, P. (ed.) Trends and Progress in System Identification, pp. 239–304. Pergamon Press, Oxford (1981)
17. Puterman, M.L.: Markov Decision Processes. Wiley, New York (1994)
18. Rubinstein, A.: Perfect equilibrium in a bargaining model. Econometrica **50**(1), 97–109 (1982)
19. Ruman, M., Hůla, F., Kárný, M., Guy, T.V.: Deliberation-aware responder in multi-proposer ultimatum game. In: Proceedings of ICANN 2016 (2016)
20. Sanfey, A.G., Rilling, J.K., Aronson, J.A., Nystrom, L.E., Cohen, J.D.: The neural basis of economic decision-making in the ultimatum game. Science **300**(5626), 1755–1758 (2003)
21. Si, J., Barto, A.G., Powell, W.B., Wunsch, D. (eds.): Handbook of Learning and Approximate Dynamic Programming. Wiley-IEEE Press, Danvers (2004)
22. von Neumann, J., Morgenstern, O.: Theory of Games and Economic Behavior. Princeton University Press, New York (1944)

Dynamical Linking of Positive and Negative Sentences to Goal-Oriented Robot Behavior by Hierarchical RNN

Tatsuro Yamada[1], Shingo Murata[2], Hiroaki Arie[2], and Tetsuya Ogata[1]([✉])

[1] Department of Intermedia Art and Science, Waseda University, Tokyo, Japan
ogata@waseda.jp
[2] Department of Modern Mechanical Engineering, Waseda University, Tokyo, Japan

Abstract. Meanings of language expressions are constructed not only from words grounded in real-world matters, but also from words such as "not" that participate in the construction by working as logical operators. This study proposes a connectionist method for learning and internally representing functions that deal with both of these word groups, and grounding sentences constructed from them in corresponding behaviors just by experiencing raw sequential data of an imposed task. In the experiment, a robot implemented with a recurrent neural network is required to ground imperative positive and negative sentences given as a sequence of words in corresponding goal-oriented behavior. Analysis of the internal representations reveals that the network fulfilled the requirement by extracting XOR problems implicitly included in the target sequences and solving them by learning to represent the logical operations in its nonlinear dynamics in a self-organizing manner.

Keywords: Symbol grounding · Recurrent neural network · Human–robot interaction · Logical operation

1 Introduction

Previous studies have conducted experiments on integrative learning between language expressions and robot behavior by means of feed-forward or recurrent neural networks (RNN) [1–5] with the aim of understanding of symbol-grounding structures [6] and robot applications. To appropriately respond to a human's instructions, robots must be able to link instructions to goal-oriented behavior by integrating their meanings with environmental situations and the robot's current posture. In conventional experiments, tasks imposed on the robot are designed so that each word in an imperative sentence corresponds to a matter in the real or simulated world, such as a target object (noun) or a feature element of motion (verb, adverb). Analyses have shown that various forms of internal representations involved in different types of elements can be self-organized by learning. In especial, Sugita and Tani [2] and Arie et al. [3] demonstrated that representations corresponding to nouns and verbs are topologically embedded as different components in the feature space binding language and robot behavior.

© Springer International Publishing Switzerland 2016
A.E.P. Villa et al. (Eds.): ICANN 2016, Part I, LNCS 9886, pp. 339–346, 2016.
DOI: 10.1007/978-3-319-44778-0_40

They interpreted this kind of self-organized structure as a possible representation or appearance of "compositionality" in the connectionist scheme. Compositionality means that the whole meaning of a sentence is combinatorially constituted by meanings of words as reusable parts.

Formal semantics based on the principle of compositionality (also referred to as Frege's principle) also models language as follows: the meaning of a phrase or a sentence is given as a function of the meanings of its parts [7]. Here, in accordance with such a formulation of formal semantics, even words that do not correspond to matters in the world directly, but instead add to the meaning of a sentence by working as a logical operator such as "*not*," can be handled in a unified way. For example, "close the door" and "do not open the door" can indicate the same behavior. This type of words has not been dealt with in previous studies of integrative learning between language and behavior by connectionist models. It is beneficial if the robots can acquire functions that process both words directly grounded on the world and those working as logical operators instead of being grounded on the world, and link the constituted meanings to appropriate goal-oriented behavior. This study shows that by implementing a hierarchical RNN that stacks multiple context layers given different time constants [8], these requirements can be realized by learning just from experiences of sequential data of an imposed task. We also analyze the self-organized internal representations of these functions in order to understand the grounding structure in detail.

2   Task Design

As a task that simply but clearly includes the aforementioned requirements, we use the flag up/down game (hereinafter, the flag game), a popular children's game in Japan (Fig. 1). The following briefly describes the flag game:

1. The experimenter makes the robot grasp red and green flags, one in the left hand and the other in the right, at random.
2. The experimenter gives the robot an imperative sentence. The sentence consists of a combination of objective ["red", "green"]–verb ["(lift) up", "(lift) down"]–truth value ["true", "false"]. Thus, there are eight possible sentences. Note that the words are given in this order because Japanese is an SOV language. "True" and "false" respectively correspond to "do" and "don't", thus work as logical operators.
3. The robot generates a goal-oriented behavior corresponding to the imperative. As an example, consider the case where the robot grasps the red flag in its left arm, and the green in its right. If the robot receives the sentence "red up true," it must choose the goal-oriented behavior LEFT-UP. In the case of "green down false," the robot must choose the behavior RIGHT-UP. In this rule, there are four possible goal-oriented behaviors (LEFT-UP, LEFT-DOWN, RIGHT-UP, RIGHT-DOWN). Furthermore, even when the same goal-oriented behavior is required, the actual motion generated by the robot varies according to its current posture (shown as arrows in Fig. 1; note that there are cases where the robot should not move its arms).
4. Repeat the above many times over.

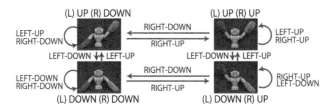

Fig. 1. Overview of the flag game. Imperative sentences are given as three-word sentences in the form objective ["red", "green"]–verb ["(lift) up", "(lift) down"]–truth value ["true", "false"]. The flags can be exchanged. The robot must choose and generate one of four goal-oriented behaviors (LEFT-UP, LEFT-DOWN, RIGHT-UP, RIGHT-DOWN). The actual movements that materialize goal-oriented behaviors from each posture follow the arrows in this figure. (Color figure online)

The requirements imposed on the robot in this game are analyzed as follows:

Requirement 1–Integration with environmental information. Which of the LEFT or RIGHT arm is indicated by the color words "red" or "green" depends on with which arm the robot holds the flag.

Requirement 2–Integration with robot state. The actual motion to be generated depends on the robot's current posture, even in cases where the robot is commanded to execute the same goal-oriented behavior.

Requirement 3–Logical operation. "Up true" and "down false" indicate the same meaning UP. Similarly, "down true" and "up false" both mean DOWN.

Requirements 1 and 2 belong to categories dealt with in previous studies, namely the learning of relations between goal-oriented behavior determined by the target object or joint movements and sentences consisting of words directly corresponding to those elements. The novelty of this study is its demonstration that an RNN can fulfill these requirements, in particular Requirement 3, the processing of logical operators. More precisely, the robot must solve an XOR problem consisting of pairs of up/down and true/false, and choose either UP or DOWN as appropriate behavior.

3   Proposed Method

3.1   Training Method

We train an RNN just to predict the subsequent state of the sequential data that represent the actual temporal flow of the flag game (Fig. 2). By constructing the target sequence not as separated sets of imperative sentence and responding behavior, but just as a continuous series of alternating instructions and responses, the RNN self-organizes the internal dynamics that allow the robot to interactively respond to human's instructions just in the RNN's unceasing forward calculation without an external phase switching signal. This training method was presented in our previous study [9]. An extension in method from [9] to solve the aforementioned problems is described in Sect. 3.2.

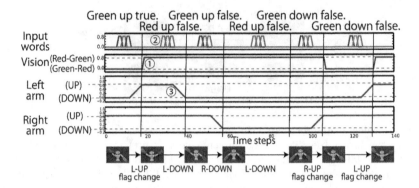

Fig. 2. The training sequence representing the temporal flows of the flag-game task. (1) The flag order is exchanged at random. (2) A human gives an imperative sentence. (3) The robot responds to the instruction by generating appropriate behavior. (Color figure online)

3.2 Hierarchical RNN

We employ hierarchical RNN stacking of two context layers given different activity speeds (Fig. 3). The internal state of the ith node in the context layer at time-step $t(u_{t,i})$ is calculated as

$$u_{t,i} = \left(1 - \frac{1}{\tau_i}\right) u_{t-1,i} + \frac{1}{\tau_i}\left(\boldsymbol{w}_i^{\mathrm{T}}[\boldsymbol{x}_t; \boldsymbol{c}_{t-1}] + b_i\right), \tag{1}$$

where $\boldsymbol{x}_t$, $\boldsymbol{c}_t$ are the external input vector and the output vector of the context layer at time step t, respectively, and $\boldsymbol{w}_i$, b_i are the connection weight vectors to the ith node and bias term of the node optimized in the learning process. The activity speed of a neuron is determined by the time constant τ_i. A neuron assigned the small time constant can change its state drastically. In contrast, neurons assigned the larger time constant can retain longer short-term memory. The context layer was hierarchically separated. The time constant of neurons whose index is in the range 0 to 99 (bottom layer) is 2, and the neurons from 100 to 129 (the top layer) is 15. Here, the top layer is not directly connected with the input and output layers. The information is exchanged only through the bottom layer. It is expected that after learning, the top layer engages in maintaining the robot's current posture stably while the bottom layer flexibly receives positive and negative imperatives and integrates them with externally input visual information. Eventually, the RNN integrates the information encoded in both layers and generates appropriate goal-oriented behavior.

4 Experiment

4.1 Training Data

Target data representing the flag game were collected on a computer without a real robot as a sequence of nine-dimensional vectors consisting of six elements for

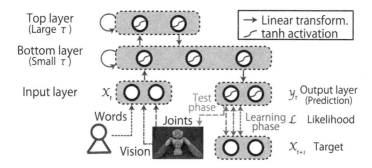

Fig. 3. A hierarchical RNN stacking of two context layers given different time constants. In the learning phase, the RNN is trained to predict the subsequent external states of multimodal sequential data. In the test phase, the RNN also predicts subsequent external states, and the outputs on joint nodes are fed into the next inputs.

words ("red", "green", "up", "down", "true", "false"), an element for vision, and two elements for the arm joints (Fig. 2). The learning was iteratively advanced by a gradient method using back-propagation through time algorithm [10]. The number of iteration was set to 30,000.

4.2   Task Performance

After learning, we evaluated the performance of executing the game. In the test phase, instructions and visual information were given externally. In contrast, the joint nodes of the input layer received previous output values of the output layer (Fig. 3). Conducting forward calculation in this condition, we can interpret the generated sequence of joints as the robot's autonomous behavior. In this condition, the robot actually performs the flag game online by generating correct goal-oriented behaviors responding to human instructions. Every after motion generation, the errors between the output value and correct one of both joint nodes were within 0.006 (the correct values are UP: 0.6, DOWN: 0.0).

4.3   Internal Representations in the Bottom Layer

Next, we visualized the internal states of both context layers during a test by principal component analysis (PCA) to investigate how the RNN internally represent the execution of the game. First, we visualized the internal states of the bottom layer after giving each of eight imperative sentences to the robot with both arms down (see Fig. 4(a), where both cases according to the flag order are included). Different components representing pairs of "true"/"false", "up"/"down" and "red"/"green" can be seen in the PC1, 2, and 5 directions. Here, the representation corresponding to "red"/"green" is reversed in accordance with the flag order. In other words, PC5 represents the LEFT/RIGHT pair that is achieved by integrating an objective (color word) with visual information according to the flag order (Requirement 1).

Subsequently, we again gave the RNN eight instructions to analyze how the logical operation, our prime concern, was realized. Here, the flag order is fixed as the red in left hand and the green in the right (Fig. 4(b)). In the directions of PC1–3, similarly, representations corresponding to the "true"/"false", "red"/"green", and "up"/"down" pairs can be seen. Here, the RNN must solve the XOR problem consisting of "up"/"down" and "true"/"false" to map to UP or DOWN. Indeed, in the PC4 direction, the representation corresponding to the UP/DOWN pair is achieved. This component seems to have been acquired by nonlinearly transforming the input sequence of words, that is, "up"/"down" followed by "true"/"false". Thus, the RNN has extracted the XOR problem implicitly included in the target sequential data, and learned to represent the logical operation to ground the instructions on correct goal-oriented behavior in its nonlinear dynamics of forward calculation (Requirement 3).

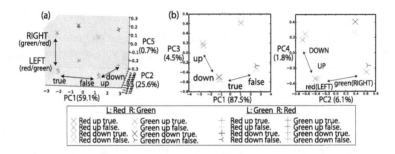

Fig. 4. Internal states after giving each of eight imperative sentences to the robot with both arms down; (a) includes both flag orders, and (b) fixes the order as red in the left hand and green in the right. (a) In the PC5 direction, the representation of LEFT/RIGHT pair gained by integrating an objective with visual input can be seen (Requirement 1). (b) In the PC4 direction, the activation corresponding to UP/DOWN pair gained by solving the XOR problem consisting of "up"/"down" and "true"/"false" pairs can be seen. (Color figure online)

4.4 Internal Representations in the Top Layer

Finally, we analyzed the internal representations in the top layer. Figure 5(a) shows the internal states just after giving each of the eight instructions to the robot waiting at four different postures. The plots are differently colored according to the given instruction and shaped according to the robot's current posture. In contrast to the bottom layer, the arm posture is dominantly represented. Differences of the activations corresponding to given instructions can hardly be seen. Moreover, analyzing the whole time development of internal states in the top layer during game execution revealed that the generation of goal-oriented behavior was represented as transitions among self-organized fixed-point attractors corresponding to four postures (Fig. 5(b)).

Taken together, the RNN integrates the given words with visual information and also flexibly processes logical operators in the bottom layer, which has faster response. At the same time, the robot stably maintains its posture by the slower response of the top layer. Eventually, after receiving an instruction, it newly integrates the information represented by both layers and generates the correct motion to achieve the appropriate goal-oriented behavior by converging to one of the fixed-point attractors (Requirement 2).

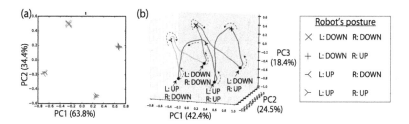

Fig. 5. (a) Internal states after giving each of eight imperative sentences to the robot waiting at four different postures. (b) Time development of the internal state in the top layer during the test. Indicated black dots are fixed-point attractor corresponding to the four postures. In this case, the arm posture changed in the order of DOWN-DOWN, DOWN-UP, UP-UP, UP-DOWN. When an instruction is input to the RNN, the internal state is activated in the PC3 direction (each shaped plot means a time point just after receiving an instruction), and immediately, the state converges to another fixed-point while the correct motion is generated in the output layer. (Color figure online)

5   Conclusion

This study realized integrative learning that grounds positive and negative sentences in goal-oriented robot behavior by hierarchical RNN. The RNN integrated the given words with visual information and also flexibly processed logical operators, thanks to the nonlinear forward dynamics of the bottom layer with fast response, and stably maintained the robot's posture through the slow response of the top layer. By integrating the representations in both layers correctly, the RNN generated the appropriate goal-oriented behavior. The analysis of the time development revealed that the sustainable execution of the game was represented as the transitions among the fixed-point attractors. These functions and representations were achieved just by learning from the sequential data of the imposed task in a self-organizing manner. Future work will investigate whether this framework can be applied to deal with tasks that requires more complicated grounding and logical operations. Because in the current experiment, the RNN experienced all the possible patterns in the learning phase, the generalization ability should also be evaluated.

Acknowledgments. This work was supported by a Grant-in-Aid for Scientific Research on Innovative Areas "Constructive Developmental Science" (24119003), CREST, JST, and a Grant-in-Aid for Young Scientists (B) (26870649).

References

1. Cangelosi, A.: The sensorimotor bases of linguistic structure: experiments with grounded adaptive agents. In: Schaal, S., et al. (eds.) Proceedings of the Eighth International Conference on the Simulation of Adaptive Behaviour: From Animals to Animats, vol. 8, pp. 487–496. MIT Press, Cambridge (2004)
2. Sugita, Y., Tani, J.: Learning semantic combinatoriality from the interaction between linguistic and behavioral processes. Adapt. Behav. **13**(1), 33–52 (2005)
3. Arie, H., Endo, T., Jeong, S., Lee, M., Sugano, S., Tani, J.: Integrative learning between language and action: a neuro-robotics experiment. In: Diamantaras, K., Duch, W., Iliadis, L.S. (eds.) ICANN 2010, Part II. LNCS, vol. 6353, pp. 256–265. Springer, Heidelberg (2010)
4. Tuci, E., Ferrauto, T., Zeschel, A., Massera, G., Nolfi, S.: An experiment on behavior generalization and the emergence of linguistic compositionality in evolving robots. IEEE Trans. Auton. Ment. Dev. **3**(2), 176–189 (2011)
5. Stramandinoli, F., Marocco, D., Cangelosi, A.: The grounding of higher order concepts in action and language: a cognitive robotics model. Neural Netw. **32**, 165–173 (2012)
6. Harnad, S.: The symbol grounding problem. Physica D **42**(1–3), 335–346 (1990)
7. Partee, B.H.: Compositionality in Formal Semantics. Blackwell Publishers, Oxford (2004). Selected papers by Barbara H. Partee
8. Yamashita, Y., Tani, J.: Emergence of functional hierarchy in a multiple timescale neural network model: a humanoid robot experiment. PLoS computational biology **4**(11), e1000220 (2008)
9. Yamada, T., Murata, S., Arie, H., Ogata, T.: Attractor representations of language-behavior structure in a recurrent neural network for human-robot interaction. In: 2015 IEEE/RSJ International Conference on Intelligent Robots and Systems (IROS2015), pp. 4179–4184 (2015)
10. Rumelhart, D.E., Hinton, G.E., Williams, R.J.: Learning internal representations by error propagation. In: Parallel Distributed Processing: Explorations in the Microstructure of Cognition, pp. 318–362. MIT Press, Cambridge (1986)

Neuronal Hardware

Real-Time FPGA Simulation of Surrogate Models of Large Spiking Networks

Murphy Berzish, Chris Eliasmith, and Bryan Tripp$^{(\boxtimes)}$

Centre for Theoretical Neuroscience, University of Waterloo, Waterloo, Canada
bptripp@uwaterloo.ca

Abstract. Models of neural systems often use idealized inputs and outputs, but there is also much to learn by forcing a neural model to interact with a complex simulated or physical environment. Unfortunately, sophisticated interactions require models of large neural systems, which are difficult to run in real time. We have prototyped a system that can simulate efficient surrogate models of a wide range of neural circuits in real time, with a field programmable gate array (FPGA). The scale of the simulations is increased by avoiding simulation of individual neurons, and instead simulating approximations of the collective activity of groups of neurons. The system can approximate roughly a million spiking neurons in a wide range of configurations.

Keywords: FPGA · Neural Engineering Framework · Neuromorphic engineering

1 Introduction

Large-scale neural models have recently become central to several large research investments. For instance, the Human Brain Project (HBP) has a central goal of developing a human-scale neural simulation in the next 10 years. Similarly, the Brain Initiative in the US is making a heavy investment in both computational and experimental neuroscience. Both projects have identified massive increases in computational performance as a critical for achieving their goals.

One approach to large-scale neural simulations is to employ standard supercomputers. Another is to build specialized "neuromorphic" hardware [3,12]. Compared to supercomputer simulations, neuromorphic simulations generally have less biological detail, but are faster and more power-efficient. However, neither of these solutions are currently available to the majority of researchers.

We recently showed that the activity of a neural population model can often be closely approximated by a much simpler surrogate model [14]. The surrogate model consists of feedback dynamics in a space of latent variables that account for correlated population activity, and a model of spike-related fluctuations in synaptic current. Here, we employ this approach to roughly approximate large neural systems with modest hardware.

We present a prototype implementation of this approach for field-programmable gate arrays (FPGAs). We simulate compressed surrogate models

© Springer International Publishing Switzerland 2016
A.E.P. Villa et al. (Eds.): ICANN 2016, Part I, LNCS 9886, pp. 349–356, 2016.
DOI: 10.1007/978-3-319-44778-0_41

of roughly a million neurons with arbitrary connectivity, in real time, on a single off-the-shelf chip. We describe general considerations for implementing these models on FPGAs, key design elements of the hardware prototype, and preliminary simulation results from the hardware.

There have been other attempts to build neuromorphic systems on FPGAs [2,11,15]. The present approach is distinct in simulating simplified models of groups of neurons, rather than individual neurons, increasing scale at the expense of fidelity. Large scale simulation is important because even the simplest behaviours in mammals involve many millions of neurons.

2   Methods

Our surrogate modelling approach builds on the Neural Engineering Framework [5]. We briefly describe this framework below, and then describe the surrogate modelling approach, with particular considerations for FPGA hardware.

2.1   The Neural Engineering Framework

The Neural Engineering Framework (NEF) is method for constructing biologically realistic neural models [5]. The NEF is a general-purpose approach to implementing high-level algorithms using spiking neurons [6]. Importantly, the high-level description is expressed in terms of vectors and functions on those vectors (including differential equations). Several overviews of the NEF are available [8]. Here we outline the NEF's three main principles.

Principle 1 - Representation. Groups of neurons are taken to represent vectors, and connections between groups of neurons compute functions on those vectors. The first NEF principle shows how the activity of a group of neurons can be said to represent a vector. The NEF identifies the preferred stimulus for a neuron with a "preferred direction vector" associated with each neuron [9]. That vector determines the neuron's tuning curve, which can be written for any neuron i as:

$$\delta_i(\mathbf{x}) = G_i[\alpha_i \mathbf{e}_i \mathbf{x} + J_i^{bias}] \tag{1}$$

where δ_i is the spiking output of the neuron, G_i is the neuron model, α_i is a randomly chosen gain term, $\mathbf{x}$ is the input space driving the neuron, $\mathbf{e}_i$ is the preferred direction vector, and J_i^{bias} is a randomly chosen fixed background current.

Given an "encoding" of this type, we can define a *decoding* operation, to characterize the information processing characteristics of the neural population. A biologically plausible, continuous, and time-varying measure of the neuron's response is generated by the reception of a spike at a synapse, which can be written:

$$a_i(\mathbf{x}) = \sum_j h_i(t) * \delta_i(t - t_j(\mathbf{x}))$$

where $h_i(t)$ is the synaptic response (e.g., a decaying exponential with a time constant, τ_{PSC}, whose temporal properties are determined by the neurotransmitter type at the synapse), '*' is the convolution operator, and $\delta_i(t - t_j(\mathbf{x}))$ is the spike train produced by neuron i, with spike times indexed by j.

Having defined this continuous variable, we can specify a decoding operation for estimating the input $\mathbf{x}$:

$$\hat{\mathbf{x}} = \sum_i^N a_i(\mathbf{x})\mathbf{d}_i \tag{2}$$

where N is the number of neurons in the group, $\mathbf{d}_i$ are the linear decoders, and $\hat{\mathbf{x}}$ is the estimate of the original $\mathbf{x}$ value that produced the neural activity (1). We can use least-squares optimization to find these decoders:

$$\arg\min_{\mathbf{d}_i} \int [\mathbf{x} - \sum_i^N a_i(\mathbf{x})\mathbf{d}_i]^2 d\mathbf{x} \tag{3}$$

where the integral is over all $\mathbf{x}$ values.

Note that employing linear decoding allows us to directly compute connection weights. For example, if a connection between neural groups is meant to compute the identity function $\mathbf{y} = \mathbf{x}$, the connections between individual neurons are given by

$$\omega_{ji} = \alpha_j \mathbf{e}_j^T \mathbf{d}_i \tag{4}$$

where i indexes the neurons in group A and j indexes the neurons in B, and T indicates the transpose.

Principle 2 - Transformation. Connections between groups of neurons can also approximate arbitrary functions: $\mathbf{y} = f(\mathbf{x})$. In the NEF this is accomplished by finding decoders $\mathbf{d}_i^f$ that produce the approximation $\hat{f}(\mathbf{x}) \approx f(\mathbf{x})$. This requires the same optimization as in (3), substituting $\mathbf{d}_i^f$ for $\mathbf{d}_i$.

The connection weights can then be computed using (4). In general, the neural connection weights needed to approximate the function $\mathbf{y} = \mathbf{L}f(\mathbf{x})$ are:

$$\omega_{ji} = \alpha_j \mathbf{e}_j^T \mathbf{L}\mathbf{d}_i^f \tag{5}$$

Principle 3 - Dynamics. The first two principles can be used to build neural implementations of any feedforward function of $\mathbf{x}$. The NEF also provides a method for computing functions of the form

$$\frac{d\mathbf{x}}{dt} = f(\mathbf{x}, \mathbf{u}) \tag{6}$$

where $\mathbf{u}$ is the input from some other population.

The NEF exploits the fact that the post-synaptic current induced by a spike is well-approximated by $h(t) = u(t)e^{-t/\tau}$, where $u(t)$ is the step function and τ is the time constant of the neurotransmitter used. This time constant varies throughout the brain, e.g., from 2–5 ms (AMPA; [10]) up to ∼100 ms (NMDA; [13]). Explicitly identifying this aspect of the neural response demonstrates that any connection actually computes $\mathbf{y}(t) = f(\mathbf{x}(t)) * h(t)$.

Given a neural population representing $\mathbf{x}$, an input $\mathbf{u}(t)$, and a connection from $\mathbf{x}$ back to itself computing $g(\mathbf{x}(t))$, we can show

$$\frac{d\mathbf{x}}{dt} = \frac{g(\mathbf{x}(t)) - \mathbf{x}(t)}{\tau} + \frac{\mathbf{u}(t)}{\tau}. \tag{7}$$

Thus, if we desire the dynamics

$$\frac{d\mathbf{x}}{dt} = f(\mathbf{x}(t)) + \mathbf{u}(t), \tag{8}$$

we introduce a feedback connection that uses the previous two NEF principles to find connection weights that compute $g(\mathbf{x}(t)) = \tau f(\mathbf{x}) + \mathbf{x}$ and we scale the input $\mathbf{u}(t)$ by τ.

Our exploitation of the inherent first-order low-pass filter found in synaptic connections allows for the implementation of a very wide variety of systems, including linear and nonlinear oscillators, integrators, and arbitrary attractor networks [4]. In short, the NEF approach allows for the construction of neural models that correspond to a very large family of functions, including those typically employed by modern control theory and dynamic systems theory. The NEF was recently used to build the large-scale Spaun model [7].

2.2   Surrogate Population Models

As described in the previous section, the NEF allows construction of neural models that optimally approximate idealized dynamics (Eq. 8), within constraints that are grounded in physiology (these include sensitivity to spike-related fluctuations, saturation of spike rates, etc.). One implication of this approach is that the idealized dynamics serve as a rough approximation of the neural model. NEF simulators allow direct simulation of the idealized dynamics as an aid to debugging. We call such simulations "direct mode" simulations, as opposed to "default mode" spiking simulations.

Beginning with the idealized dynamic model (Eq. 8), we showed recently [14] that the dynamics of the full spiking model can often be largely recovered via efficient approximations of the difference $\hat{\mathbf{f}}(\mathbf{x}) - \mathbf{f}(\mathbf{x})$. This difference consists of static distortion components that can be approximated by interpolation, and spike-related fluctuating components that can be approximated with an auto-regressive moving average (ARMA). We refer to this new type of simulation as "population mode" simulation, because it models population-level dynamics. In practice, we actually model $\hat{\mathbf{f}}(\mathbf{x})$ directly, rather than $\hat{\mathbf{f}}(\mathbf{x}) - \mathbf{f}(\mathbf{x})$.

3   Surrogate Models on FPGAs

The ARMA components of the surrogate models are suitable for FPGA simulation. However, interpolation of the static distortions is a performance bottleneck.

The bottleneck arises due to a mismatch between processing capacity and on-chip memory. The hardware can simulate a population much faster than real time, so we multiplex simulation of many populations in the same hardware component (a "population unit"). However, on-chip memory is insufficient to store the model parameters of all these populations. For this reason, the population parameters must be stored in off-chip RAM and loaded for each population, each simulation step. We therefore sought to approximate $\hat{\mathbf{f}}(\mathbf{x})$ using as few unique parameters per population as possible.

The functions that a population can approximate well belong to the space of the first few principal components (PCs) of the population's tuning curves $a_i(\mathbf{x})$ [6]. For this reason, static population output can be approximated efficiently by linear regression with these first few principal components. This requires only as many coefficients as there are important principal components. The advantage (vs. direct interpolation of outputs) is greatest with multidimensional populations. Accuracy depends on regularization of the decoders (Eq. 2), in that stronger regularization reduces contributions from minor PCs.

Parameter distributions are often shared by several populations. Moreover, we find empirically (Fig. 1) that the principal components of populations with quite diverse parameter distributions are often quite similar. Our approach is therefore to group populations by clustering their principal components, and use the cluster-averaged principal components as basis functions for regression of each required $\hat{\mathbf{f}}(\mathbf{x})$. With this approach, it is necessary to load only a small number of unique regression parameters per population.

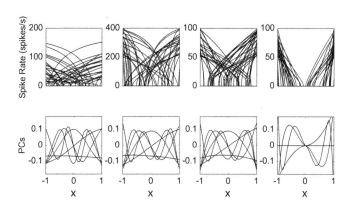

Fig. 1. Tuning curves of four different example populations and their principal components. Each column corresponds to a population of spiking LIF neurons with different parameters. The top panels are 50 tuning curves drawn from populations of 1000 neurons. The bottom panels are the first six principal components of each population. Despite differences between the three leftmost populations, their principal components are nearly the same. As a counter-example, the population on the right has very different principal components (due to a very distinct intercept distribution) so it should go in a different cluster.

3.1 Hardware Prototype

A block diagram of a prototype hardware platform is shown in Fig. 2. The design connects fourteen population units, 7 for 1D populations, and 7 for 2D populations (D is the dimension of $\mathbf{x}$; Eq. 1). Each population unit consists of a fixed bank of principal components, an encoder unit, and a decoder unit. The encoder and decoder units perform the encoding and decoding operations described in Sect. 2.1. Both are implemented as circular buffers containing parameters for each population. The encoder unit is also responsible for saving the states of low-pass filters that model synaptic dynamics. The principal components are implemented as interpolating lookup tables with a 12-bit fixed-point representation, and are the same across every population on the same population unit. Both 1D and 2D principal component tables have been implemented with linear and bilinear interpolation. An additional decoder is used to scale pseudo-random Gaussian noise. The interconnect is designed around an all-to-all shared bus architecture that allows any encoder unit to read decoded values from any population unit, or from any external input source. At the end of each timestep, outputs from each population are written to RAM buffers and can be read by encoders in the following timestep. The population units are otherwise independent from each other and use internal RAM buffers to save and load the state of each population as it is time-multiplexed on and off the hardware.

As the simulation time for one population is on the microsecond scale, we time-multiplex 1024 populations on each population unit and run a maximum of 14×1024 population models in real-time simulation, at a rate of 1000 updates per second. In software simulations, 1D populations often have about 10 to 100 neurons, and 2D populations often have 100 to 1000 neurons, so we consider this system to model an approximation of roughly 0.8 to 8 million neurons.

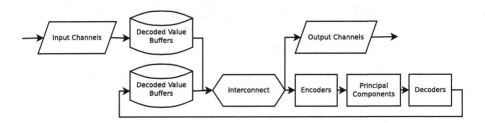

Fig. 2. Block diagram of the hardware design. Of note, concurrent access to the interconnect is coordinated via distinct fixed delays for each encoder unit.

We extended the Nengo neural simulator [1] with a custom backend that translates neural models to FPGA configuration data. The backend determines which PCs can be clustered onto the same population units with the smallest absolute error. It transmits the model parameters to the hardware, and controls the simulation in real time, transferring external input values to the board and reading population outputs.

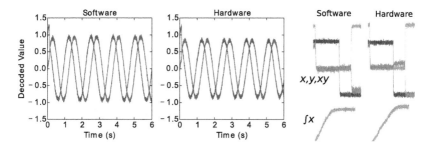

Fig. 3. The left plot shows a software simulation of an NEF spiking recurrent network that implements a van der Pol nonlinear oscillator. The two plotted values correspond to the two state variables of the system, decoded from filtered spike trains. The centre plot is a hardware simulation of the same recurrent network. The plotted values are decoded from principal components of the population, with a model of spike noise. The recurrent connection in hardware is also a function decoded from principal components, with added noise. On the right are two additional examples: a product decoded from a 2D population, and an integrator recurrent network.

4   Results

We ran simulations on a Xilinx VC707 development board. The design used a large fraction of the device resources, including 44 % of its 37080 Kb of block RAM and 61 % of its 2800 customizable DSP operator slices. The design was estimated to use at most 5.675 W of power.

As a demonstration of the hardware, we simulated a neural model consisting of 4096 recurrent networks that approximate van der Pol oscillators. Output from an example population simulated in software (with spiking neurons) is shown in Fig. 3 (left). Output from the same population simulated in our hardware is also shown in Fig. 3 (centre). The oscillator requires a brief non-zero "startup" initial input in order to begin oscillating. Once this input disappears, at 0.1 s, both dimensions of the decoded output can be seen to oscillate.

5   Discussion

We have described the design and prototype of a new approach to large-scale, real-time neural model simulation using off-the-shelf hardware. This approach allows us to approximately simulate NEF networks of about a million neurons in real time on a single chip. This approach appears promising for three kinds of applications. First, it allows power-efficient real-time simulation of fairly large neural systems. Second, it is well-suited for embedding sophisticated network models in robots. Third, interconnection of multiple FPGAs would potentially allow very large real-time simulations, although such a system would scale sub-linearly, depending on the communication required between devices.

Although population mode does not simulate individual neurons, approximations of network dynamics are often quite close [14]. Some of the missing details are undoubtedly important. However scale is also important. As well, our approach could be used as part of a multi-scale approach, with a small detailed network embedded in an approximate simulation of a larger system.

A more specific limitation of our prototype is that we have only implemented principal component lookup tables of one and two dimensions. The system can simulate populations that encode higher-dimensional vectors, but only if the decoded functions are either linear, or nonlinear only in groups of one or two dimensions. More generally, we emphasize that our implementation is a proof of concept, and that further development and validation is needed.

Acknowledgments. Funded by Discovery Grants (261453 and 296878) and a USRA from NSERC, Canada. The VC707 was donated by RTDS Technologies.

References

1. Bekolay, T., et al.: Nengo: a Python tool for building large-scale functional brain models. Front. Neuroinformatics **7**(48), 1–13 (2014)
2. Cassidy, A., et al.: Design of a one million neuron single fpga neuromorphic system for real-time multimodal scene analysis. In: 2011 45th Annual Conference on Information Sciences and Systems (CISS), pp. 1–6. IEEE (2011)
3. Choudhary, S., et al.: Silicon neurons that compute. In: International Conference on Artificial Neural Networks, pp. 121–128 (2012)
4. Eliasmith, C.: A unified approach to building and controlling spiking attractor networks. Neural Comput. **17**(6), 1276–1314 (2005)
5. Eliasmith, C., Anderson, C.H.: Developing and appl a toolkit from a general neurocomputational framework. Neurocomputing **26**, 1013–1018 (1999)
6. Eliasmith, C., Anderson, C.H.: Neural Engineering: Computation, Representation and Dynamics in Neurobiological Systems. MIT Press, Cambridge (2003)
7. Eliasmith, C., Stewart, T.C., Choo, X., Bekolay, T., DeWolf, T., Tang, C., Rasmussen, D.: A large-scale model of the functioning brain. Science **338**(6111), 1202–1205 (2012)
8. Eliasmith, C., et al.: A large-scale model of the functioning brain. Science **338**, 1202–1205 (2012)
9. Georgopoulos, A., et al.: Mental rotation of the neuronal population vector. Science **243**, 234–236 (1989)
10. Jonas, P., et al.: Quantal components of unitary EPSCs at the mossy fibre synapse on CA3 pyramidal cells of rat hippo. J. Physio. **472**(1), 615–663 (1993)
11. Li, J., et al.: An FPGA-based silicon neuronal network with selectable excitability silicon neurons. Front. Neuroscience **6**(183), 1 (2012)
12. Merolla, P., et al.: Artificial brains: a million spiking-neuron IC with a scalable communication network and interface. Science **345**(6197), 668–673 (2014)
13. Sah, P., et al.: Properties of excitatory postsynaptic currents recorded in vitro from rat hippocampal interneurones. J. Physio. **430**(1), 605–616 (1990)
14. Tripp, B.P.: Surrogate population models for large-scale neural simulations. Neural Comput. **27**(6), 1186–1222 (2015)
15. Wang, R., et al.: An FPGA implementation of a polychronous spiking neural network with delay adaptation. Front. Neuroscience **7**(14), 1 (2013)

Randomly Spiking Dynamic Neural Fields Driven by a Shared Random Flow

Benoît Chappet de Vangel$^{(\boxtimes)}$ and Bernard Girau

Université de Lorraine, Nancy, France
bdevangel@gmail.com

Abstract. Dynamic Neural Fields (DNF) is a well studied mean field model introduced by Amari. It is commonly used for high level bio-inspired cognitive architecture modeling or as a module for autonomous bio-inspired robotics. In a previous work we studied the feasibility of a purely cellular hardware implementation of this model in a digital substratum. We introduced the randomly spiking dynamic neural fields which successfully reproduced the DNF model's behavior with local and decentralized computations implemented on FPGA. The lateral synaptic weights are computed with a random propagation of binary information generated with a cellular array of pseudo random number cellular automata. More than half of the area utilization was dedicated to the random numbers generation. In this paper we investigate two ways of reducing the surface of random number generators while keeping a cellular architecture.

1 Introduction

In the quest for more robust and reliable computing, cellular computing is regarded as a promising candidate as it is based on massively parallel computations [1]. In cellular computing, behavior emerges from the interactions of simple cells. This emergence is an interesting property to study as it can be robust to perturbations such as bad signal-to-noise ratio or hardware faults.

Dynamic neural fields (DNF) (also called continuous attractor neural networks [2]) is a simple model capturing the behavior of cortical neural populations with the help of one single differential equation [3]. It is used by computational neuroscientists for high level cortical modeling but it has many interesting properties which can be used in other computational approaches for memory [4], tracking [5], selection [6], classification [7] and clustering [8]. It can also be combined with more plastic neural models to allow a variety of learning mechanisms and adaptation [9].

If we consider the discrete version of this differential equation, we can see that all these powerful properties emerge from the interactions of simple computing cells (we will call them neurons). DNFs have indeed the robustness of bio-inspired emergent systems. For instance in [6] an emergent property is studied (visual attention) and it is shown to be robust to noise or distracters in the visual field.

© Springer International Publishing Switzerland 2016
A.E.P. Villa et al. (Eds.): ICANN 2016, Part I, LNCS 9886, pp. 357–364, 2016.
DOI: 10.1007/978-3-319-44778-0_42

We are studying the digital hardware implementation of this model and taking advantage of its robustness to improve the scalability. In [10] we introduced a spiking version of the DNF model, which diminishes the inter-neuron communication bandwidth requirements (and which happened to improve the tracking ability and robustness with respect to the initial analog model). In [11] we introduced a way to change the connectivity requirements from all-to-all connectivity to local von Neumann connectivity using a random propagation of spikes with a grid of cellular automata-based pseudo random number generators (CAPRNG). We called this model RSDNF for randomly spiking dynamic neural fields.

Through these works, we reached the main goal of designing a purely cellular and scalable implementation of a hardware compliant version of DNFs, while maintaining (and sometimes improving) its well-known behavioral properties. Nevertheless, the RSDNF model scalability is not competitive compared to a more centralized approach in term of implementation area [12].

The goal of this paper is to propose a way to reduce the area dedicated to the pseudo-random number generators in our cellular version of DNFs, so as to simultaneously reach the goal of a decentralized and scalable implementation of DNFs.

2   Spiking Dynamic Neural Fields

Dynamic neural fields is a model inspired from the neural population behavior of cortical columns. Its simplicity comes from the fact that the neurons are considered as a homogeneous continuum and that both excitatory and inhibitory neural connections share a common function to compute the lateral synaptic weights.

The DNF model can be described as follows:

$$\tau \frac{\partial u}{\partial t}(x,t) = -u(x,t) + \sum_{y} w(||x-y||)f(u(y,t)) + I(x,t) + h \qquad (1)$$

where f is an activation function (generally a sigmoid or a step function), I is the afferent input and h is the resting potential. $w(||x-y||)$ is the lateral weights function. It is a difference of Gaussian (sometime called Mexican hat function) which only depends on the distance d between x and y: $w(d) = A_e \exp[\frac{-d^2}{2\sigma_e^2}] - A_i \exp[\frac{-d^2}{2\sigma_i^2}]$.

We use a discretized version of this differential equation using a simple Euler forward method for time and using a resolution R for space (if not stated the space is two-dimensional with each dimension discretized in $R = 49$ points which gives $R^2 = 2401$ simulated neurons).

A spiking version of the DNFs has been proposed in [10], which helps reducing the inter-neuron communication bandwidth requirements as only one bit can represent the activity and the high state is less frequent in a spiking neuron than in a rate-coded neuron with an step activation function. We will use this version, that can be described in a time-discretized way as follows:

$$u(x, t + dt) = u(x, t) + \frac{dt}{\tau}(-u(x, t) + I(x, t) + h) + I^{syn}(x, t). \quad (2)$$

The lateral influence is computed by instantaneously applying the synaptic weight (w) to each received spike:

$$I^{syn}(x, t) = \sum_y w(||x - y||)f(u(y, t)). \quad (3)$$

Finally the neurons emit a spike when their potential reaches a threshold θ, viz. $f(x) = 1$ if $x \geq \theta$ else 0. If a spike is fired, the potential is reset: $u(x, t) = h$. Thus neurons exchange simple binary information, instead of several bits to code for neural potentials in the initial DNF model.

3   RSDNF: Cellular Hardware Implementation of DNFs

In his seminal paper [3], Amari gave general rules to choose a lateral weights function. It has to be positive in the center (local cooperation) and then negative (global competition). Consequently we proposed in [11] to replace the traditional Mexican hat function by a difference of exponential which has the same global properties but is much easier to reproduce with a cellular random diffusion.

To approximate the difference of exponential lateral weights function we subdivide each spike in N excitatory sub-spikes and N inhibitory sub-spikes. Thus a sub-spike will be one bit of information, randomly transmitted from neuron to neuron giving information on the lateral feeding. These sub-spikes are routed on a network of routers on two separate layers (excitatory and inhibitory). The transmission of each sub-spike by a router depends on a Bernoulli trial with a probability p_e for the excitatory layer and p_i for the inhibitory layer. Consequently the average number of sub-spikes received by a neuron at a distance d from the emitting neuron will be p_e^d excitatory sub-spikes and p_i^d inhibitory sub-spikes. We then compute the asymptotical lateral synaptic weights with

$$w(d) = Nk_e p_e^d - Nk_i p_i^d \quad (4)$$

where k_e and k_i are constants of the model. In [11] we proved that despite the difference between the asymptotical weights and the weights effectively induced by the random transmission of N sub-spikes with $N \simeq 10$, the behavior of this RSDNF model is similar to the one of the spiking DNF model.

3.1   Spike Routing

The routing layers ensure a XY broadcast of every sub-spike so that every neuron receives a propagated sub-spike at most once. It means that there are 4 directional routers per neuron on each layer. Two horizontal routers (east ans west) propagate the sub-spikes in their direction while two vertical routers (north and south) propagate the sub-spikes in their direction and towards horizontal directions (see Fig. 1a). Overall there are 8 routers per neuron: 4 for the excitatory layer routing and 4 for the inhibitory layer routing.

The sub-spike routing is performed during the spike diffusion period which can last more or less iterations depending on N and the number of activated neurons P. The horizontal routers have more inputs than outputs. Consequently they need to store the exceeding sub-spikes in a local buffer. Because of these buffers the worst case scenario (every sub-spike is transmitted according to an always positive Bernoulli trial) for the diffusion period is $t_d = NP + 2R$.

3.2 Random Number Generation with CAPRNG

This design requires many random numbers (we need 8 random numbers by neuron and by spike propagation iteration). Therefore we use a very compact distributed pseudo random number generation method that follows a cellular strategy as presented in [13]. High quality pseudo-random numbers are generated on a 8-periodic synchronous heterogeneous cellular automaton. The update rule is a combination of XOR and AND gates and is different for every cell. This method is more advantageous than using linear-feed-back registers when the quantity of needed pseudo random numbers (PRN) is important. Its compactness results in the ability to produce one random bit per clock cycle per utilized LUT in the FPGA.

In [11] it was shown that the minimum required precision to compute Bernoulli trials is 8 bits for excitatory and inhibitory routers, which leads to a total of $64R^2$ CAPRNG cells. Despite the compactness of the CAPRNGs, the cost of the random number generation is almost half of the total implementation area of the RSDNF model.

4 Random Numbers Generation Optimisation

We propose two ways to optimize the area cost of the random numbers generation.

(a) *Random number sharing.* Every router of the same neuron will share the same 8 bits of a random number. We can thus divide the size of the CAPRNG by 8. Since the different routers of a single neuron are not involved in the propagation of a same sub-spike, the behavior of the model is expected to be maintained despite the induced correlations.

(b) *Random bit pre-computation and propagation.* A random bit resulting from one Bernoulli trial is precomputed and loaded on a dedicated flip-flop of every router. Then the random bits are propagated at every step of the spike diffusion along a shared flow throughout the map of neurons.

Random number sharing show good experimental results (see Sect. 5) and are not developed more in this paper, since it is not the most area-optimizing method. The random bit propagation is more challenging but the area gains are more important than with the random number sharing as it does not require any look-up-table for the hardware implementation.

4.1   Bit Propagation Scheme

The main challenge for designing the bit transmission from router to router is to minimize the random correlation during the spike propagation while maintaining a von Neumann neighborhood (the architecture has to remain cellular).

We propose the propagation described in Fig. 1b. The motivations is to decorrelate the random bits propagation from the spike propagation as much as possible with two means: (1) the propagation of the random bits is not on the same axis as the propagation of spikes (2) the direction of propagation is inverted from row to row and from column to column.

This propagation graph will then be connected differently on the border of the cell array. We will distinguish two types of wrapping connection.

(1) Short propagation. The bits are propagated on a row (for instance) and the last router is connected to the first one. The random bits will thus be propagated in a cyclic way with a period of R (see Fig. 1c).

(2) Long propagation. Here the connection on the border is different as the last router will be connected to the first one of a different row. Consequently the random bits are propagated over every two rows. Even row to even row and odd row to odd row. The period is $R^2/2$ (see Fig. 1d).

As the periodicity of the random bit flows might be too small, we introduce a "open" version of each wrapping method. An "open" version will have one PRNG on every propagation path in order to introduce clean random numbers and avoid long term bias. Thus we introduce $4R$ PRNG for the short propagation and 8 PRNG for the long propagation.

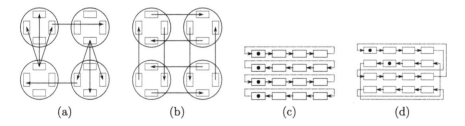

(a)   (b)   (c)   (d)

Fig. 1. Connectivity between routers. Only one connection by router direction is shown for clarity. (a) the XY broadcast for the sub-spikes. (b) connection graph of the random bits. The connection is inverted from row to row and from column to column. (c) and (d) short and long propagation of random bits over a full map of $4 \times 4 (R = 4)$ neurons. The dashed arrow represent wrapped connections. A black circle represent the PRNG emplacement in "open" version. Only one router is represented (north router) the other routers connectivity is symmetric.

4.2   Random Diffusion Analysis

To analyze this propagation scheme, we first study the behavior of one diffusion layer (the transmission probability on this layer is $p = 0.93$).

On Fig. 2 the normalized root mean square error (NRMSE) at the end of one propagation phase is displayed. The NRMSE is computed between the number of received sub-spikes per neuron and the expected (asymptotical) number $E(x, y)$ computed as a convolution:

$$E(x, y) = N \sum_{x'=0}^{R} \sum_{y'=0}^{R} A(x', y') p^{|x-x'|+|y-y'|} \tag{5}$$

where $A(x, y) = 1$ if there is an activation (neuron at position (x, y) emits N sub-spikes). Note that the random bits are *not* reinitialized between propagation phase.

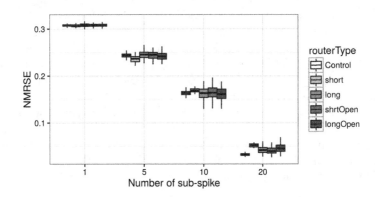

Fig. 2. NRMSE for different random bit propagation. The propagation was computed over an array of resolution $R = 49$ and repeated 100 times. A patch of 10 spikes was set at the center of the grid, and the diffusion lasted for $10N + 2R$ to ensure a full propagation even in the worst case scenario. The probability of each sub-spike transmission is 0.93.

The variances being different we use the pairwise Welch t-test [14] to compare the mean of each distribution. The short propagation is different from both the control (initial RSDNF) and the other propagation methods The other propagation methods have the same mean as the control except when $N = 20$ where their mean is slightly higher. As we generally try to use as few sub-spikes as possible to reduce the execution time we can conclude that the proposed optimization methods are good except for the short propagation.

5   Experimental Results

The validation of the different candidate methods is performed with a DNF simulation on a control scenario. The scenario tests the ability of the neural field activity to follow a rotating target in the input map (I). We then asses the quality of the tracking by computing the mean of the error over 30 s of

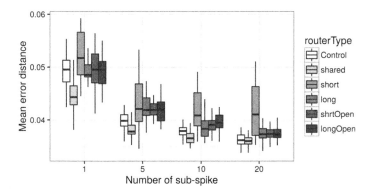

Fig. 3. Mean error distance for the control scenario with different number of sub-spike and different random numbers generation. Mean of 50 repetitions.

simulation, with a discrete time step of $0.1\,$s. The error is computed at every step as the distance between the barycentre of the neural activity and the center of the rotating target. The simulation results are given on Fig. 3.

Tests show that from $N = 3$ to $N = 20$, every architecture behaves quite differently from the control RSDNF, except for the shared method which results in the same mean as the control when $N = 20$ (p-value of 0.5). The short propagation is statistically worse than the other propagation methods when N reaches 10. This is because it is getting more and more biased with the number of computations, hence when diffusion needs a lot of time the bias completely disturbs the behavior. Adding one random number generator per cycle ("open" version) is enough to fix the behavior. However the three other propagation methods are equivalent thus supporting the results of the previous section. We will choose the long propagation scheme as it is the less expensive for the implementation area.

6   Conclusion

As expected the area reduction is significant with the precomputed random bits. It uses a similar number of flip-flops as the shared CAPRNG version (9800 against 9984 with $R = 35$), but there is no look-up-table required when 7804 is required for the shared version. For comparison the original RSDNF version needed 79872 FF and 62432 LUT. Once again the robustness of the DNF emergent computation allows aggressive optimization of the area of the FPGA implementation.

The model's robustness to noise allows a noisy inter neuron communication as long as the mean is similar to what is expected. We have shown that if the mean of the inter-spike communication is too far from the expected one, the model's behavior becomes faulty as it is the case with the short random bit propagation method.

Note that it might be possible to improve the random bit diffusion graph to have even less correlations with a more extensive research on all possible schemes of connectivity, or by extending the neighborhood to 8 neighbors. It would maybe slightly improve the behavior of the model when the spike sub-division N rises, but the hardware area utilization would not change.

References

1. Sipper, M.: The emergence of cellular computing. IEEE Comput. **32**(7), 18–26 (1999)
2. Si, W., Hamaguchi, K., Amari, S.: Dynamics and computation of continuous attractors. Neural Comput. **20**(4), 994–1025 (2008)
3. Amari, S.: Dynamics of pattern formation in lateral-inhibition type neural fields. Biol. Cybern. **27**, 77–87 (1977). doi:10.1007/BF00337259
4. Ferreira, F., Erlhagen, W., Bicho, E.: Multi-bump solutions in a neural field model with external inputs. Physica D Nonlinear Phenom. **326**, 32–51 (2016)
5. Mi, Y., Fung, C.C.A., Wong, K.Y.M., Wu, S.: Spike frequency adaptation implements anticipative tracking in continuous attractor neural networks. In: Advances in Neural Information Processing Systems, pp. 505–513 (2014)
6. Rougier, N.P., Vitay, J.: Emergence of attention within a neural population. Neural Netw. **19**(5), 573–581 (2006)
7. Cerda, M., Girau, B.: Bio-inspired visual sequences classification. In: From Brains to Systems - Brain-Inspired Cognitive Systems (2010)
8. Jin, D., Peng, J., Li, B.: A new clustering approach on the basis of dynamical neural field. Neural Comput. **23**(8), 2032–2057 (2011)
9. Rougier, N.P., Detorakis, G.I.: Self-organizing dynamic neural fields. In: Yamaguchi, Y. (ed.) Advances in Cognitive Neurodynamics (III), pp. 281–288. Springer, Heidelberg (2013)
10. Vazquez, R.A., Girau, B., Quinton, J.: Visual attention using spiking neural maps. In: The 2011 International Joint Conference on Neural Networks (IJCNN), pp. 2164–2171, 31 July–5 August 2011
11. de Vangel, B.C., Torres-Huitzil, C., Girau, B.: Randomly spiking dynamic neural fields. ACM J. Emerg. Technol. Comput. Syst. **11**(4), 1–26 (2015)
12. de Vangel, B.C., Torres-Huitzil, C., Girau, B.: Spiking dynamic neural fields architectures on FPGA. In: 2014 International Conference on ReConFigurable Computing and FPGAs (ReConFig), pp. 1–6, December 2014
13. Vlassopoulos, N., Girau, B.: A metric for evolving 2-D cellular automata as pseudo-random number generators. J. Cell. Automata **9**, 139–152 (2014)
14. Welch, B.L.: The generalization of student's problem when several different population variances are involved. Biometrika **34**(1/2), 28–35 (1947)

Synfire Chain Emulation by Means of Flexible SNN Modeling on a SIMD Multicore Architecture

Mireya Zapata$^{(\boxtimes)}$ and Jordi Madrenas

Department of Electronics Engineering, Universitat Politècnica de Catalunya,
Jordi Girona, 1-3, edif. C4, 08034 Barcelona, Catalunya, Spain
{mireya.zapata,jordi.madrenas}@upc.edu

Abstract. The implementation of a synfire chain (SFC) application that performs synchronous alignment mapped on a hardware multiprocessor architecture (SNAVA) is reported. This demonstrates a flexible SNN modeling capability of the architecture. The neural algorithm is executed by means of a digital Spiking Neural Network (SNN) emulator, using single instruction multiple data (SIMD) processing. The flexibility and capability of SNAVA to solve complex nonlinear algorithm was verified using time slot emulation on a customized neural topology. The SFC application has been implemented on an FPGA Kintex 7 using a network of 200 neurons with 7500 synaptic connections.

Keywords: SNN emulation · FPGA · AER · Time slot processing · Real time · Massive parallelism

1 Introduction

Over the last years, the interest to characterize and simulate in real-time structural and functional neural activities have increased with the ultimate goal of imitating brain capabilities. A better comprehension of brain functionality yields in new bio-inspired applications with intelligent behavior such as vision, speech recognition, robotics, real-time neuromorphic chips, or signal processing.

Several research works are aimed at SNN (Spiking Neural Network) hardware implementations using different approaches like mixed signal chips [1], ASIC with standard processor [2], Graphic Processor Units, FPGAs [3], supercomputers, and any other combinations.

Among SNN hardware simulators, we consider only the ones with emulation capability, i.e. that allow real-time operation. Many emulators support a huge number of neurons, however, this is at a price of fixed and simplified neural algorithm, reduced number of synapses per neuron, and limited or lacking plasticity or even with fixed synaptic weights.

Most of the emulators based on multiprocessors or GPUs, support neural and synaptic algorithm programming. Their Processing Element (PE) is a general-purpose complex processor, which lacks specialization on SNN emulation.

© Springer International Publishing Switzerland 2016
A.E.P. Villa et al. (Eds.): ICANN 2016, Part I, LNCS 9886, pp. 365–373, 2016.
DOI: 10.1007/978-3-319-44778-0_43

For instance, [2] uses a set of ARM processors along with other peripherals obtaining high flexibility and programmability features with a significant power consumption and resource overhead. In case of [4], it can implement up to 250,000 neurons, however, it is restricted to a single neuron model i.e. Izhikevich.

Our contribution is based on a multi-model SNN multiprocessor architecture called SNAVA constituted by a 2D array of specialized processing elements (PE) working with Single Instruction Multiple Data (SIMD) computing strategy [5]. SNAVA is a scalable and compact architecture that has been prototyped on FPGAs. It is able to emulate any spiking neural algorithm programmed through a customized set of instructions. Besides, it offers flexibility for specifying full synaptic connectivity and allows configuration of neuronal and synaptic para-meters.

These features allow emulation of complex neural algorithms, which will be illustrated by means of a Synfire Chain (SFC) application example. In this appli-cation, neurons execute an enhanced Leaky Integrate-and Fire (LIF) algorithm. The synaptic topology is composed of interconnected layers of several neuronal cells where synchronization within layers can be achieved by propagating pre-synaptic inputs through the feed-forward network [7].

For the sake of completeness, in Sect. 2, the SNAVA architecture is briefly introduced and the SFC application is presented in Sect. 3. In Sect. 4 the exper-imental results are reported, follow by conclusion in Sect. 5.

2   SNAVA Multi-processor System

SNAVA is a multi-chip digital platform, scalable, reconfigurable, real-time, SNN emulator, working with time-slot computational approach based on FPGA [5]. Such architecture allows the implementation of any particular spiking neu-ron model applying parallel processing using Single Instruction Multiple Data (SIMD) computing strategy. Besides, as clock driven method is used, neurons are updated simultaneously at a fixed time rate.

Figure 1 shows the SNAVA general block diagram, which contains the main modules of the architecture, namely:

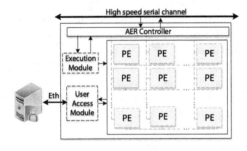

Fig. 1. Symplified SNAVA block diagram.

– *Multi-processor Array:* This array is composed off specialized neural Processing Elements (PE) along with block RAM and other elements. They process data to mimic the synaptic and neuronal biological dynamics. PEs process neuron algorithms in parallel and synapses sequentially, being able to perform arithmetic, boolean, logical and SNN-customized operations. The default resolution for synapse and neural parameters is 16-bit. Furthermore, each PE is capable of emulating neural dynamics of more than one neuron using digital multiplexing (virtualization) while exhibiting real time operation.
– *User Access Module:* Monitor buffers are implemented on each PE in order to transmit the calculated neural parameters to a PC visual interface.
– *Execution Module:* It is responsible for the system control flow, which is performed in two phases: Execution Phase and Distribution Phase. In the Execution Phase, the neural and synapse dynamics are processed and calculated. The Distribution Phase carries out the spike distributions between neurons in the neural network.
– *AER Controller:* The spike distributions between neurons are conducted by a packet-based synchronous AER scheme. It is implemented with high-speed point to point serial links in a ring topology pipeline fashion for multi-chip SNN interconnection. The fast speed channel usage limits the time of spike distributions to values that allow real-time operation [6].

3   The SynFire Chain (SFC) Application Example

Empirical studies of structural and functional brain architecture have demonstrated a highly modular anatomical structure. These neural modules are formed by interconnected layers of neuronal cells associated with cognitive process. According to anatomical and physiological considerations, the synchronization within layers of neurons can be achieved by propagating pre-synaptic inputs through feed-forward excitatory layers of neurons [7]. This network known as Synfire Chain (SFC), has been used for characterizing brain modules, and building low-level sensory systems, i.e. vision, olfactory or tactile sensors.

The basic configuration consists of a group of layers where all neurons in a layer are connected unidirectionally to that of the successive tier. For a group of random input spikes, a stable propagation is obtained, if synchronization between spikes at each layer is enhanced as they pass down the network. Unstable behavior results in low spike synchrony, which eventually vanishes.

3.1   Design Parameters of the SFC

The computation of the neural model in the SFC behaves according to the LIF model reported in [7]. In this network, the neurons are evolve as a function of three state variables in Eq. (1) with excitatory synapses only. The membrane potential denoted by $V(t)$ is calculated depending on the membrane recovery variables $x(t)$ and $y(t)$. These state variables are involved in the activation of K+ ionic currents and inactivation of Na+ ionic currents. In addition, a stochastic term ζ_i is used to emulate background activity through a noise signal acting on $y(t)$.

$$\tau_{mem}\frac{dV}{dt} = x(t) - (V(t) - V_{rest}).$$

$$\tau_{rft}\frac{dx}{dt} = -x(t) + y(t). \tag{1}$$

$$\tau_{rft}\frac{dy}{dt} = -y(t) + \tau_{rft} \cdot 25.27 \; mV + \zeta_i.$$

When a pre-synaptic neuron fires a spike, the synaptic model performs equally for all the synapses by adding the same synaptic weight (11 mV) to the synaptic current $y(t)$ after a spike. The neural parameter values used in this model are presented in Table 1.

Table 1. Neural algorithm parameters.

Name	Description	Value
V_{Th}	Threshold potential	$-55\,$mV
V_{rest}	Resting potential	$-70\,$mV
τ_{mem}	Membrane time constant	$10\,$ms
τ_{rft}	Relative refractoriness	$15\,$ms
T_{ref}	Absolute refractoriness	$1\,$ms

The SFC emulated network consists of 3 layers, each consisting of 50 neurons, as shown in Fig. 2. The input layer is generated by 50 neurons which work as Spike Generators (SG). This layer fires 50 spikes at Gaussian distributed times centered at 14 ms with a standard deviation of 1.2 ms.

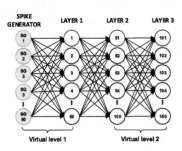

Fig. 2. SFC neural topology

The network size was set according to SNAVA architecture and verified through BRIAN simulator 2.0 [8]. The software simulations were performed using a time step of $\Delta t = 0.1$ ms. This value is taken into account for implementing the neuronal algorithm into SNAVA.

3.2 SFC Mapping and Programming Description

This section describe the procedure of mapping a SFC on SNAVA according to the topological and dynamic neuron specifications simulated with BRIAN. For this application, we use a single board with a 10×10-PE array and two virtualization levels, i.e. two neurons per PE. The SGs and the first neural layer were configured in virtual level 1, and the layers 2 and 3 in level 2 (Fig. 2).

Each synaptic connection is defined by an 18-bit address that identifies the presynaptic neuron connected to it. It consists of a 4-bit row and a 4-bit column location into the SNAVA array, a 3-bit virtual level, and a 7-bit chip identifier address.

In this case, 200 neurons and 7500 synaptic connections are employed to define the SFC topology in SNAVA. These connections are mapped on a text file assigning every neuron to a PE.

The neural algorithm is written with a simple assembler code using custom instructions detailed in [5]. The code is processed concurrently for all neurons. The main program structure (Fig. 3) employs two loops to execute the neural algorithm. The SYNAPTIC_LOOP reads the pre-synaptic spikes sequentially. This subroutine compute the synaptic weights and sending these values to a monitor buffer. In the NEURAL_LOOP the following subroutines are processed:

– GENERATOR_SPIKES: They carry out the task of generating the spike input activity for the SG neurons.
– NEURAL_ALGORITH: The logical and arithmetic computation is perform to solve Eq. (1) using Euler approximation.
– SPIKE_UPDATE: Once the membrane voltage value is obtained, if $V(t) > V_{Th}$, a spike is generated.

Besides, instruction STOREB is used to send the neural algorithm values to a monitor buffer for external parameter display. STOREPS records the post-synaptic spikes to be distributed throughout the neural network during execution of SPKDIS.

3.3 SFC Implementation

With the defined network topology (topology.txt) and neural dynamic (algorithm.asm) input files, a File Generator tool developed for SNAVA architecture (Fig. 4), translates: the neural parameter initialization, network topology and neural dynamic algorithm description to output files used for simulating and implementing the SFC into SNAVA.

The synthesis of the SNAVA RTL source files, along with the SFC topology (cfg_synap.vhd) is performed using Vivado Design Suite Xilinx tool. Full simulation has been tested in QuestaSim.

The USER INTERFACE utilizes a Ethernet link to send a binary file with the SFC neural algorithm (cfg_snn.bin) to the Kintex 7 FPGA board and, receive the data from the SNAVA monitor buffer to be analysed and displayed.

```
define synapses 100
define neuron_virtualization  2
    MAIN:
      SYNAPTIC_LOOP:
          LOADSP
          GOTO SYNAP_WEIGHT
          GOTO SYNAP_SAVE
      ENDL
      NEURAL_LOOP:
          GOTO GENERATOR_SPIKES
          GOTO NEURAL_ALGORITH
          GOTO SPIKE_UPDATE
          STOREB
          STOREPS
      ENDL
    SPKDIS
    GOTO MAIN
end.
```

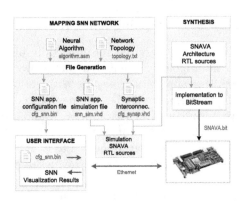

Fig. 3. SFC assembly main code program

Fig. 4. SNAVA flow chart

4   Experimental Results

In this section, SNAVA accuracy is analyzed by comparison with the results of the BRIAN simulator. In both cases, the synaptic noise was removed, and the same spikes input activity were applied for having the same conditions. SNAVA like BRIAN uses the time step of 0.1 ms for calculating the three differential equations of Eq. (1). According to the variation of the state variables, different binary scaling was applied to a range of $(-32767\ +32767)$ using fixed point representation. The precision used for each variable corresponds to 4-bits for $x(t)$ and $y(t)$, and 7-bit for $v(t)$.

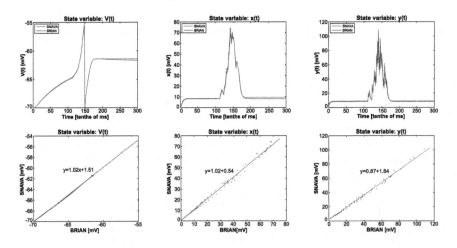

Fig. 5. Neural algorithm state variable in neuron 10

In Fig. 5 are shown the matching between BRIAN and the SNAVA outputs along with the corresponding dispersion diagram for characterizing the error. The linear equations for the state variables $v(t), x(t)$ and $y(t)$ express the variation between the hardware and the simulation data in each case. The obtained relative error are $V = 0.15\%$ $x = 8.33\%$, $y = 8.76\%$.

The main source of error are due to the quantification of data. Higher errors presented in the variables x(y) and y(t) are derived from the smallest precision used compared to that used in the variable v(t). Furthermore, these variations do not affect the LIF algorithm behavior significantly and conversely, using fixed point representation reduce the complexity and the number of operations needed to complete the arithmetic calculations. As a result, a trade-off between optimization and accuracy is obtained.

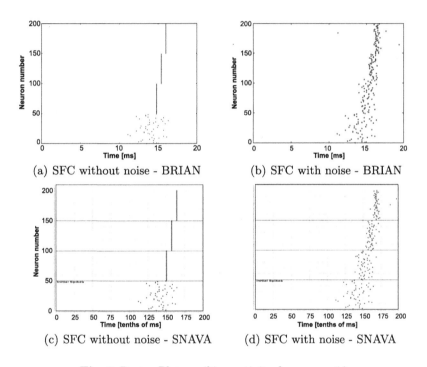

(a) SFC without noise - BRIAN   (b) SFC with noise - BRIAN

(c) SFC without noise - SNAVA   (d) SFC with noise - SNAVA

Fig. 6. Raster Plot - spiking activity for neuron 10

Figures 6(a) and (c) show the SFC Raster Plot response without noise in order to compare the firing accuracy time in each layer from SNAVA and BRIAN. SNAVA exhibits a time accuracy of $t + 0.4$ ms from BRIAN.

Figures 6(b) and (d) show the SFC response with synaptic noise ζ_i added to the neural algorithm to emulate background activity in the brain. It can be seen that incoming spikes are synchronized as they are transmitted through each layer. This behavior represents a stable SFC operation. The differences between

BRIAN and SNAVA raster plots are due to the noise function used in each case is different and not deterministic.

As it can be seen, the SNAVA hardware implementation response follow the same trend as simulated in BRIAN. Consequently, high similarity between the hardware and software implementations of the analyzed three neural state variables is observed. Finally, with these results, the functionality and operability of SNAVA are demonstrated to solve complex differential equations and non-linear functions.

5 Conclusions

In this work, we demonstrated that SNAVA architecture is capable of emulating complex neural dynamics in real time. In order to accomplish this target, we presented the implementation of a SFC application, its characterization according to the SNAVA resources, implementation steps, and test to verify the functionality and accuracy of the hardware architecture.

As a result, SNAVA has proved to be flexible enough to be adapted to the needs of multi model SNN emulation, being capable to reproduce in real-time complex neural dynamics.

Finally, the SFC application demonstrates the ability of SNAVA to implement an enhanced LIF algorithm and solve non-linear functions by means of approximations without incurring to computationally expensive operations in exchange for resolution. As future work, the approximation errors can be overcome by extending the precision of the required variables, which is supported by the programmable SNAVA architecture, with some cost of execution time trade-off.

Acknowledgments. This work was supported in part by the Spanish Ministry of Science and Innovation under Project TEC2015-67278-R, and European Social Fund (ESF). Mireya Zapata holds a scholarship from National Secretary of High Education, Science, Technology, and Innovation (SENACYT) of Ecuador.

References

1. Carrillo, S., et al.: Scalable hierarchical network on chip architecture for spiking neural network hardware implementations. IEEE Trans. Parallel Distrib. Syst. **24**(12), 2451–2461 (2012)
2. Khan, M., et al.: SpiNNaker: mapping neural networks onto a massively-parallel chip multiprocessor. In: International Joint Conference on Neural Networks (2008)
3. Moore, S., et al.: Bluehive a field programmable custom computing machine for extreme-scale real-time neural network simulation. In: IEEE 20th Annual International Symposium Field-Programmable Custom Computing Machines (FCCM) (2012)
4. Nageswaran, J.M., et al.: A configurable simulation environment for the efficient simulation of large-scale spiking neural networks on graphics processors. Neural Netw. **22**(5–6), 791–800 (2009)

5. Sanchez, G.: Spiking neural network emulation based on configurable devices. Doctoral dissertation, Universitat Politecnica de Catalunya (2014)
6. Dorta, T., et al.: AER-SRT: scalable spike distribution by means of synchronous serial ring topology address event representation. Neurocomputing **171**, 1684–1690 (2015)
7. Diesmann, M., et al.: Stable propagation of synchronous spiking in cortical neural networks. Nature **402**, 529–533 (1999)
8. Brette, R., Goodman, D.: Brian documentation realease 1.4.2 (2016)

Towards Adjustable Signal Generation with Photonic Reservoir Computers

Piotr Antonik[1]($\boxtimes$), Michiel Hermans[1], Marc Haelterman[2], and Serge Massar[1]

[1] Laboratoire d'Information Quantique, Université Libre de Bruxelles,
50 Avenue F. D. Roosevelt, CP 225, 1050 Brussels, Belgium
pantonik@ulb.ac.be
[2] Service OPERA-Photonique, Université Libre de Bruxelles,
50 Avenue F. D. Roosevelt, CP 194/5, 1050 Brussels, Belgium

Abstract. Reservoir Computing is a bio-inspired computing paradigm for processing time dependent signals. We have recently reported the first opto-electronic reservoir computer trained online by an FPGA chip. This setup makes it in principle possible to feed the output signal back into the reservoir, which in turn allows to tackle complex prediction tasks in hardware. In present work, we investigate numerically the performance of an offline-trained opto-electronic reservoir computer with output feedback on four signal generation tasks. We report very good results and show the potential of such setup to be used as a high-speed analog control system.

Keywords: Reservoir Computing · FPGA · Pattern generation · Numerical results · Opto-electronic systems

1 Introduction

Reservoir Computing (RC) is a set of methods for designing and training artificial recurrent neural networks [11,14]. A typical reservoir is a randomly connected fixed network, with random coupling coefficients between the input signal and the nodes. This reduces the training process to solving a system of linear equations [7,13]. The RC algorithm has been successfully applied to channel equalisation [6,16,20], phoneme recognition [18] and won an international competition on prediction of future evolution of financial time series [1].

Reservoir Computing is very well suited for analog implementations: various electronic [4,8], opto-electronic [12,15,16] and all-optical [5,6,19,20] implementations have been reported since 2012. We have recently reported the first online-trained opto-electronic reservoir computer [2]. The key feature of this implementation is the FPGA chip, programmed to generate the input sequence, train the reservoir computer using the simple gradient descent algorithm, and compute the reservoir output signal in real time.

This setup offers the possibility to tackle prediction tasks in hardware by feeding the output signal back into the reservoir. We have shown numerically

© Springer International Publishing Switzerland 2016
A.E.P. Villa et al. (Eds.): ICANN 2016, Part I, LNCS 9886, pp. 374–381, 2016.
DOI: 10.1007/978-3-319-44778-0_44

that such a system could perform well on pattern generation and Mackey-Glass chaotic time series prediction tasks [3]. In this work we improve the experimental setup and focus on the pattern generation task [9], with several additional tasks that have been investigated in the RC community. We adapt the use of the FPGA chip to train the neural network offline for higher precision and more control of the process. The performance of the setup is tested in simulations on four signal generation tasks: simple pattern generation [3], frequency generation, multi-pattern generation [17] and tunable frequency generation [21]. These tasks have various applications in motion generation, robot control and data storage [17]. Solving them in hardware can allow opto-electronic reservoir computers to be applied in fast control applications, for example high-speed robot control [9]. The promising results we report here thus pave the way towards experimental investigations we are planning to carry out in the upcoming months.

2   Reservoir Computing

A general reservoir computer is described in [13]. In our implementation, depicted in Fig. 1, we use a sine function $f = \sin(x)$ and a ring topology to simplify the interconnection matrix, so that only the first neighbour nodes are connected [12,16]. The evolution equations are given by

$$x_0(n+1) = \sin\left(\alpha x_N(n-1) + \beta M_0 u(n)\right), \tag{1a}$$
$$x_i(n+1) = \sin\left(\alpha x_{i-1}(n) + \beta M_i u(n)\right), \tag{1b}$$

where $x_i(n)$, $i = 0, \ldots, N-1$ are the internal variables, evolving in discrete time $n \in \mathbb{Z}$, α and β parameters are used to adjust the feedback and the input signals, respectively, $u(n)$ is a time multiplexed input signal, and M_i is the input mask, drawn from a uniform distribution over the interval $[-1, +1]$ [6,16]. The reservoir computer produces an output signal

$$y(n) = \sum_{i=0}^{N} w_i x_i(n), \tag{2}$$

where $x_N = 1$ is a constant neuron used to adjust the bias of the output signal and w_i are the readout weights, trained offline [4–6,12,15,16,19] in order to minimise the Mean Square Error (MSE) between the output signal $y(n)$ and the target signal $d(n)$.

During the training phase, the reservoir computer receives a periodic training sequence as input $u(n)$ and is trained to predict the next value of the sequence from the current one. During the test phase, the reservoir input $u(n)$ is switched from the training sequence to the reservoir output signal $y(n)$, and the system is left running autonomously. In that case, the dynamics of the systems is described by the following equations

$$x_0(n+1) = \sin\left(\alpha x_N(n-1) + \beta M_0 y(n)\right), \tag{3a}$$
$$x_i(n+1) = \sin\left(\alpha x_{i-1}(n) + \beta M_i y(n)\right). \tag{3b}$$

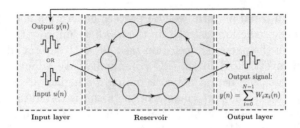

Fig. 1. Schematic representation of our reservoir computer with output feedback. The recurrent neural network with N nodes denoted $x_i(n)$ in ring-like topology (in brown) is driven by either a time multiplexed input signal $u(n)$, or its own output signal $y(n)$, given by a linear combination of the readout weights w_i with the reservoir states $x_i(n)$. (Color figure online)

3 Signal Generation Tasks

Pattern Generation. A pattern is a short sequence of randomly chosen real numbers (here within the interval $[-0.5, 0.5]$) that is repeated periodically to form an infinite time series [3]. The aim is to obtain a stable pattern generator, that reproduces precisely the pattern and doesn't deviate to another periodic behaviour. To evaluate the performance of the generator, we compute the MSE between the reservoir output signal and the target pattern signal during the training phase and the autonomous run.

Frequency Generation. The system is trained to generate a sine wave given by

$$u(n) = \sin(\nu n), \tag{4}$$

where ν is a relative frequency and n is the discrete time. The physical frequency f of the sine wave depends on the experimental roundtrip time T (see Sect. 4) as follows

$$f = \frac{\nu}{2\pi T}. \tag{5}$$

This task allows to measure the bandwidth of the system and investigate different timescales within the neural network.

Multi-pattern Generation. This tasks adds another dimension to the simple pattern generation. The network is trained to generate several different patterns and a second input signal $u_2(n)$ is introduced to select the pattern to generate. Equations (3) thus become

$$x_0(n+1) = \sin(\alpha x_N(n-1) + \beta M_0 y(n) + \beta_2 M_0' u_2(n)), \tag{6a}$$

$$x_i(n+1) = \sin(\alpha x_{i-1}(n) + \beta M_i y(n) + \beta_2 M_i' u_2(n)), \tag{6b}$$

where β_2 is a second input gain and M_i' is a second input mask. Both input masks are generated randomly, and both input gains are optimised independently.

During the autonomous run, the second input signal $u_2(n)$ is regularly changed in order to test the performance of the system on all patterns.

Tunable Frequency Generation. Here the frequency generator is upgraded with a second input signal to tune its frequency. The network is trained to generate several sine waves with different frequencies, given by

$$u(n) = \sin\left(\bar{\nu}(n)n\right), \tag{7}$$

where $\bar{\nu}(n)$ is a time-dependent user-defined frequency, that is fed into the system through the second input $u_2(n) = \bar{\nu}(n)$. The physical output frequency f can be computed using Eq. (5). Testing of the performance is similar to the multi-pattern generation task.

4   Numerical Simulations

Figure 2 depicts the experimental setup [2], which is the basis for numerical simulations presented here. The opto-electronic reservoir, a replica of previously reported works [2,16], is driven by a Xilinx ML605 evaluation board, powered by a Virtex 6 FPGA chip and paired with a 4DSP FMC-151 daughter card, used for signal acquisition and generation. The FPGA is programmed to record the reservoir states $x_i(n)$ and send them to the personal computer, running Matlab, through an Ethernet connection. The readout weights w_i are uploaded on the chip for real-time computation of the reservoir output signal $y(n)$ during the autonomous run.

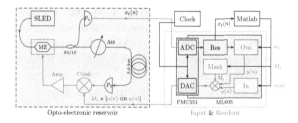

Fig. 2. (a) Schematic representation of the simulated setup, based on the experimental system [2,16]. Optical and electronic components of the opto-electronic reservoir are shown in red and green, respectively. It contains an incoherent light source (SLED), a Mach-Zehnder intensity modulator (MZ), a 90/10 beam splitter, an optical attenuator (Att), a 9.6 km fibre spool, two photodiodes (P_r and P_f), a resistive combiner (Comb) and an amplifier (Amp). The FPGA board acquires the reservoir states $x_i(n)$ and generates analog input and output signals to the reservoir. A personal computer, running Matlab, computes the readout weights w_i. (Color figure online)

The experiment roundtrip time is defined by the length of the delay loop. We are planning to use 9.6 km of fiber in order to obtain a delay of $T = 32\,\mu$s.

This would allow sampling the entire loop 8000 times at 250 MS/s (maximum sampling frequency of the FMC-151 Analog-to-Digital Converter) and thus fit up to 1000 neurons into the reservoir, with at least 8 samples per neuron.

All numerical experiments were performed in Matlab, on a standard personal computer. The simulations account for major aspects of the experimental setup and allow to scan the most influential parameters, such as input gains β and β_2, feedback gain α and reservoir size N.

5   Results

Pattern Generation. As we have shown previously [3], this task works well with online learning even on small reservoirs: a 51-neuron network is capable of generating patterns up to 51-element long, where 51 is expected to be a fundamental limit because it is the upper bound on the linear memory of the network [10]. We obtained the same results with offline training here, and found optimal gain parameters. The system works best with a very low input gain $\beta = 0.001$ and high feedback gain $\alpha = 0.9$. The system was trained over $5k$ inputs and then left running autonomously for $50k$ timesteps. We obtained training errors ranging from 10^{-25} (for short patterns with $L = 10$) to 10^{-12} (for long patterns, $L = 51$), and autonomous errors ranging from 10^{-22} to 10^{-8}, respectively.

Frequency Generation. Frequency generation requires a different method for computing the error during the autonomous run, that would focus on the frequency of the generated signal. For this reason we used the Fast Fourier Transform (FFT) algorithm to compute the frequency of the reservoir output signal and compare it to the frequency of the target signal.

We used a slightly larger reservoir with $N = 100$ and trained it over $1k$ input samples. We tried increasing the reservoir size up to $N = 1000$ and the training length up to $10k$ samples without noticeable improvements. The output frequency was measured after an autonomous run of $20k$ timesteps.

With optimal gain parameters $\alpha = 0.9$ and $\beta = 0.1$, we were able to generate relative frequencies within $\nu \in [0.06, 3.14]$ with MSE of order of 10^{-7} and Full Width at Half Maximum (FWHM) of the FFT of about 10^{-3}. The upper limit is given by half of the sampling rate of the system and corresponds to the Nyquist frequency. As for the lower limit, we couldn't obtain stable output signal with frequency lower than 0.06 for most random input mask. The roundtrip time $T = 32\,\mu s$ of the experimental setup gives a sampling frequency of 31.2 kHz. Using Eq. (5), this sets the bandwidth of the generator to 300 Hz–15.6 kHz.

Multi-pattern Generation. This task is significantly more complex than the simple pattern generation, as the network needs to learn to switch between several different patterns. Good performance thus requires a large reservoir and a carefully chosen training sequence which contains all possible transitions between the patterns. We also noted that results depend on the shape of the input mask. Figure 3 shows an example of simulation with 3 different patterns.

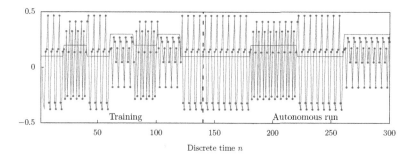

Fig. 3. Example of simulation result for the multi-pattern generation task. The reservoir output signal (blue dots) is almost identical to the target signal (green curve). The second input signal $u_2(n)$, shown in red, switches between 3 values, as the system is trained to generate three short patterns. The training sequence contains all transitions between different patterns. The autonomous run continues beyond the scope of the figure. (Color figure online)

For this task the reservoir size was increased to $N = 800$ neurons. We were able to generate up to 4 different patterns of length 10, with training error of 2×10^{-7}, and 4×10^{-4} for the autonomous run. The system was trained over 850 inputs and then ran autonomously for 4250 timesteps. All transitions occured synchronously, that is, from the last element of a pattern to the first element of another. We also tried generating shorter patterns and could store 8 patterns of length 5, with training and autonomous run errors of 2×10^{-6} and 4×10^{-4}, respectively. This required much longer simulations, with $5.6k$ inputs for the training and $28k$ timesteps for the autonomous run.

Tunable Frequency Generation. Similar to multi-pattern generation, this task requires a large reservoir capable of containing many smaller clusters oscillating at different frequencies (see [21] for a more in-depth overview). The reservoir computer was trained to generate different sine waves given by Eq. (7), FFT algorithm was used to evaluate the performance.

We used a large reservoir with $N = 1000$ neurons and the following parameters: $\alpha = 0.7$, $\beta = 0.03$ and $\beta_2 = 0.9$. The network was trained over $6.6k$ samples and was taught to generate 40 frequencies equally spaced between 0.1 and 1.1. Each frequency was learned for 10 periods, to ensure smooth transitions. For the autonomous run, we investigated different scenarios. At first, we decreased the frequency back to 0.1 and then increased it to 1.1 again. This was done by large steps of 0.05 every $5k$ timesteps to test the stability of the generator. The system produces very good results, with frequency MSE of 1.5×10^{-6}. As another test case, the second input signal $u_2(n)$ was first decreased to 0.6, and then followed a random walk. The reservoir computer generated the desired frequencies very well, with frequency MSE of 1.4×10^{-6}. The FWHM of the FFT for these two cases is about 0.005. Faster control modulation, with $u_2(n)$ changing every 200 timesteps, results in higher frequency MSE (1.2×10^{-3}, with FFT

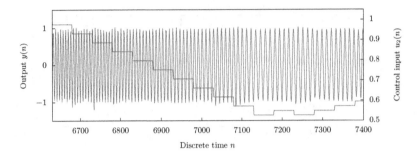

Fig. 4. Example of autonomous run for the tunable frequency generation task. The control signal, shown in red, is decreased down to 0.6 every 50 timesteps, and then follows a random walk, that continues beyond the scope of the figure. Although u_2 switches asynchronously, the RC shifts smoothly from one frequency to another. (Color figure online)

FWHM of order of 0.1), but still the RC follows the desired frequency reasonably well. Figure 4 shows an example of simulation with fast modulation (every 50 timesteps).

6   Conclusion

We investigated numerically how an opto-electronic reservoir computer with output feedback performs on various signal generation tasks. We evaluated optimal gain parameters, reservoir sizes and elaborated specific training sequences for each tasks. We obtained very good results, showing that the upcoming experimental setup could in principle be employed as a fast analog control system. Coupled with the recently implemented online learning [2] this system could possibly be used as an analog "brain" for high-speed self-learning robots.

Acknowledgements. We acknowledge financial support by Interuniversity Attraction Poles program of the Belgian Science Policy Office under grant IAP P7-35 "photonics@be", by the Fonds de la Recherche Scientifique FRS-FNRS and by the Action de la Recherche Concertée of the Académie Universitaire Wallonie-Bruxelles under grant AUWB-2012-12/17-ULB9.

References

1. The 2006, 07 forecasting competition for neural networks & computational intelligence (2006). http://www.neural-forecasting-competition.com/NN3/. Accessed 21 Feb 2014
2. Antonik, P., Duport, F., Smerieri, A., Hermans, M., Haelterman, M., Massar, S.: Online training of an opto-electronic reservoir computer. In: Arik, S., Huang, T., Lai, W.K., Liu, Q. (eds.) ICONIP 2015. LNCS, vol. 9490, pp. 233–240. Springer, Heidelberg (2015). doi:10.1007/978-3-319-26535-3_27

3. Antonik, P., Hermans, M., Duport, F., Haelterman, M., Massar, S.: Towards pattern generation and chaotic series prediction with photonic reservoir computers. In: SPIE's 2016 Laser Technology and Industrial Laser Conference, vol. 9732 (2016)
4. Appeltant, L., Soriano, M.C., Van der Sande, G., Danckaert, J., Massar, S., Dambre, J., Schrauwen, B., Mirasso, C.R., Fischer, I.: Information processing using a single dynamical node as complex system. Nat. Commun. **2**, 468 (2011)
5. Brunner, D., Soriano, M.C., Mirasso, C.R., Fischer, I.: Parallel photonic information processing at gigabyte per second data rates using transient states. Nat. Commun. **4**, 1364 (2012)
6. Duport, F., Schneider, B., Smerieri, A., Haelterman, M., Massar, S.: All-optical reservoir computing. Opt. Express **20**, 22783–22795 (2012)
7. Hammer, B., Schrauwen, B., Steil, J.J.: Recent advances in efficient learning of recurrent networks. In: Proceedings of the European Symposium on Artificial Neural Networks, pp. 213–216, Bruges, Belgium, April 2009
8. Haynes, N.D., Soriano, M.C., Rosin, D.P., Fischer, I., Gauthier, D.J.: Reservoir computing with a single time-delay autonomous Boolean node. Phys. Rev. E **91**(2), 020801 (2015)
9. Ijspeert, A.J.: Central pattern generators for locomotion control in animals and robots: a review. Neural Netw. **21**(4), 642–653 (2008)
10. Jaeger, H.: Short term memory in echo state networks. Technical GMD report 152 (2001)
11. Jaeger, H., Haas, H.: Harnessing nonlinearity: predicting chaotic systems and saving energy in wireless communication. Science **304**, 78–80 (2004)
12. Larger, L., Soriano, M., Brunner, D., Appeltant, L., Gutiérrez, J.M., Pesquera, L., Mirasso, C.R., Fischer, I.: Photonic information processing beyond turing: an optoelectronic implementation of reservoir computing. Opt. Express **20**, 3241–3249 (2012)
13. Lukoševičius, M., Jaeger, H.: Reservoir computing approaches to recurrent neural network training. Comp. Sci. Rev. **3**, 127–149 (2009)
14. Maass, W., Natschläger, T., Markram, H.: Real-time computing without stable states: a new framework for neural computation based on perturbations. Neural Comput. **14**, 2531–2560 (2002)
15. Martinenghi, R., Rybalko, S., Jacquot, M., Chembo, Y.K., Larger, L.: Photonic nonlinear transient computing with multiple-delay wavelength dynamics. Phys. Rev. Let. **108**, 244101 (2012)
16. Paquot, Y., Duport, F., Smerieri, A., Dambre, J., Schrauwen, B., Haelterman, M., Massar, S.: Optoelectronic reservoir computing. Sci. Rep. **2**, 287 (2012)
17. Sussillo, D., Abbott, L.: Generating coherent patterns of activity from chaotic neural networks. Neuron **63**(4), 544–557 (2009)
18. Triefenbach, F., Jalalvand, A., Schrauwen, B., Martens, J.P.: Phoneme recognition with large hierarchical reservoirs. Adv. Neural Inf. Process. Syst. **23**, 2307–2315 (2010)
19. Vandoorne, K., Mechet, P., Van Vaerenbergh, T., Fiers, M., Morthier, G., Verstraeten, D., Schrauwen, B., Dambre, J., Bienstman, P.: Experimental demonstration of reservoir computing on a silicon photonics chip. Nat. Commun. **5**, 3541 (2014)
20. Vinckier, Q., Duport, F., Smerieri, A., Vandoorne, K., Bienstman, P., Haelterman, M., Massar, S.: High-performance photonic reservoir computer based on a coherently driven passive cavity. Optica **2**(5), 438–446 (2015)
21. Wyffels, F., Li, J., Waegeman, T., Schrauwen, B., Jaeger, H.: Frequency modulation of large oscillatory neural networks. Biol. Cybern. **108**(2), 145–157 (2014)

Hierarchical Networks-on-Chip Interconnect for Astrocyte-Neuron Network Hardware

Junxiu Liu[✉], Jim Harkin, Liam McDaid, and George Martin

School of Computing and Intelligent Systems,
University of Ulster, Magee Campus,
Derry BT48 7JL, Northern Ireland, UK
{j.liu1,jg.harkin,lj.mcdaid,martin-g11}@ulster.ac.uk

Abstract. Scalable hardware interconnect is a significant research challenge for neuromorphic systems in particular, this becomes more pronounced when we seek to realise the integration of neurons with astrocytes cells. This paper presents a novel interactive architecture for the astrocyte-neuron network (ANN) hardware systems, and the novel Hierarchical Astrocyte Network Architecture (HANA) using networks-on-chip (NoC) for the efficient information exchange between astrocyte cells. The proposed HANA incorporates a two-level NoC packet transmission mechanism to increase the information exchange rate between astrocyte cells and to provide a NoC traffic balance for local and global astrocyte networks. Experimental results demonstrate that the proposed HANA approach can provide efficient information exchange rates for the ANN, while the hardware synthesis results using 90 nm CMOS technology show that it has a low area overhead which maintains scalability.

Keywords: Astrocyte-neuron network · Networks-on-chip · Interconnect · Self-repair · FPGAs

1 Introduction

Recent publications have highlighted that astrocytes (a sub-type of glial cells in the central nervous system) continually exchange information with multiple synapses and consequently play a crucial role in brain re-wiring by regulating synaptic formation/elimination, synaptic morphology and structural plasticity [1, 2]. The authors have developed a computational model in software [3] and hardware [4] which captures this behaviour and have demonstrated how astrocytes cells merged within spiking neurons in an astrocyte-neuron network can perform distributed and fine grained self-repair under the presence of faults. In the ANN, there are large volumes of interconnected neurons and astrocytes and they have different communication patterns, e.g. high speed temporal spike event for the neuron network, low speed numerical inositol trisphosphate (IP_3) information exchange for astrocyte network. The ANN can be viewed as a two-tiered network comprised of a neuron and astrocyte network. Therefore for large ANN hardware implementations, the traditional hardware architectures and topologies are not suitable for the interconnections, and a new interconnection strategy should be explored

© Springer International Publishing Switzerland 2016
A.E.P. Villa et al. (Eds.): ICANN 2016, Part I, LNCS 9886, pp. 382–390, 2016.
DOI: 10.1007/978-3-319-44778-0_45

which exploits this network hierarchy. This paper presents a novel interactive architecture for ANN and a hierarchical astrocyte network architecture (HANA) for the information exchange between the astrocyte cells, which addresses the interconnection challenge in ANN hardware. Section 2 introduces the ANN briefly and Sect. 3 presents the proposed ANN hardware interactive architecture. Section 4 reports on experimental results and scalability performance analysis, while Sect. 5 provides a summary.

2   Spiking Astrocyte-Neuron Networks

Recent research showed that synapses exchange signals between neurons and astrocytes, namely the tripartite synapse [5]. In a tripartite synapse, when an action potential axon arrives, the glutamate is released across the cleft and binds to receptors on the post-synaptic dendrite. This causes a depolarization of the post-synaptic neurons and allows the influx of calcium (Ca^{2+}) into the dendrite causing endocannabinoids to be synthesized and subsequently released from the dendrite. The 2-arachidonyl glycerol (2-AG), a type of endocannabinoid, binds directly to type 1 Cannabinoid Receptors (CB1Rs) on the pre-synaptic terminal. This results in a decrease in transmission probability (PR). In the meantime, the 2-AG binds to CB1Rs on an astrocyte which enwraps the synapse increasing IP_3 levels and triggering the intracellular release of Ca^{2+}. This results in the astrocytic release of glutamate which binds to pre-synaptic group I metabotropic Glutamate Receptors. Such signalling results in an increase of synaptic transmission PR. This process describes the signal exchange between a single astrocyte cell and synapses. Additionally, astrocyte cells are also connected together and exchange information between each other, which facilitate a global self-repairing capability in the astrocyte-neuron networks [3]. In this approach, the boundary conditions in the approach of [6] are used for linking the astrocyte cells. Each astrocyte cell is connected to the nearest neighbour using molecular gap junctions which facilitate astrocyte to astrocyte communications over long distances using calcium waves. The propagating calcium pulses are elicited following the gap-junction transfer of inositol trisphosphate (IP_3) second messenger molecules [6]. A linear diffusion gap junction model, $J_{i \to j} = F\Delta_{ij}IP_3$, is considered to describe the exchange of IP_3 between any two astrocyte [6], where $\Delta_{ij}IP_3 = IP_3^i - IP_3^j, i, j \in [1, m]$, and the coupling strength (or permeability) F depends on the number of gap junction channels and their unitary permeability. For further details on the astrocyte cell and neuron, synapse models please refer to our previous work [3].

3   Hierarchical Astrocyte Network Architecture

This section presents the proposed hierarchical astrocyte network architecture. The interactive architecture for the ANN is described first; then the information exchange and communication strategies for the astrocyte networks are presented in detail.

(1) Spiking astrocyte-neuron interactive architecture. In our previous work [7], a hierarchical NoC architecture (H-NoC) was designed for the spiking neural networks (SNN) hardware implementations. The H-NoC implemented the connections for

clusters of neurons and synapses using NoC strategies. It has three hierarchical levels, namely *neuron, tile* and *cluster* facilities. The *neuron facility* is at the bottom level, which connects a number of neuron together (e.g. 10 in [7]). The *neuron facilities* are connected to a *tile facility* (second layer) via tile router. Several *tile facilities* are connected by a cluster router which compose a *cluster facility* (i.e. top layer). However, the H-NoC strategy only focused on addressing interconnection for spiking neurons in an SNN. As discussed in previous sections, the astrocytes communicate with synapses/neurons, and more importantly with other astrocytes as well. Therefore, this paper extends our previous research [7], and focuses on the interactive architecture for the ANN, especially the interconnection requirements for the astrocyte networks.

Figure 1 illustrates HANA for the astrocyte networks and its connection to the H-NoC. In order to establish the interconnection between the neuron cells and the astrocyte cell, a dedicated connection is created, e.g. the astrocyte cell *A1* communicates with neuron cells via the node router of H-NoC in the bottom right of Fig. 1. Using this connection, the astrocyte cell can communicate with a group of neurons via the H-NoC (10 neurons in this approach as in biology it varies between 6–8 per astrocyte cell). In addition to the connection with neurons, HANA creates the interconnections for the astrocyte networks. It has two layers – *astrocyte cells* and *astrocyte tile facilities*. This HANA approach exploits locality between *astrocyte cells*, by allocating a group of *m astrocyte cells* (e.g. 10 in this approach) together, which is located at the bottom of the hierarchy. In each *astrocyte cell* group, the *astrocyte cells* are connected to an *astrocyte cell router* using the NoC star topology. This topology is employed for the hardware interconnection between the local astrocyte cells as cells communicate with one another. The *astrocyte cell router* is then connected to a higher level router (i.e. the *astrocyte tile router*) to comprise an *astrocyte tile facility*. The *astrocyte tile facilities* are connected by a two dimensional mesh topology which provides the communication for the astrocyte cells in different *astrocyte cell* groups. Therefore, HANA is a two-layer interconnection topology, i.e. the *astrocyte cell* group for the local astrocyte connectivity, and the *astrocyte tile facility* for global astrocyte connectivity. As a result, one *astrocyte tile facility* includes 10 *astrocyte cells*, and each *astrocyte cell* communicates with 10 *neuron cells*; therefore one *astrocyte tile facility* can accommodate 10 *astrocyte cells* and 100 *neuron cells*. If more *astrocyte tile facilities* are required, the *astrocyte tile facilities* can be easily replicated by forming a grid of *astrocyte tiles* using the regular mesh topology layout.

(2) HANA for the astrocyte networks. HANA uses a uniform NoC packet layout for both local and global communications. The packet layout is defined in Table 1 where a packet consists of four fields, i.e. header, astrocyte tile router address, astrocyte cell address, and payload. The header field defines the packet communication pattern, e.g. for the local or global astrocytes, as defined in the bottom half of Table 1. The tile router/astrocyte cell address fields provide the address information of the astrocyte tile router and astrocyte cell respectively. The payload of the packet contains the astrocyte exchange information (e.g. IP_3) between the astrocyte cells. According to the astrocyte cell model and parameters, the range of IP_3 is from 0 to ~2 microMolar [3], therefore an unsigned fixed-point data type with a total 16-bit (2-bit integer length and 14-bit fraction length) is used to represent the IP_3 value.

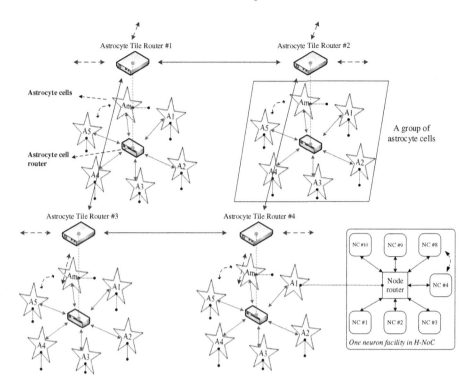

Fig. 1. HANA: Hardware interconnectivity for astrocyte networks and its interface with H-NoC.

Table 1. Packet layout definition

Packet layout				
Header	Tile router address		Astrocyte cell address	Payload
	X	Y		
4-bit	4-bit	4-bit	4-bit	16-bit
Header definition				
Header	0001	Communication inside the astrocyte tile facility (intra-facility)		
	0010	Communication between the astrocyte tile facilities (inter-facility)		
	....	Reserved		

Figure 1 illustrates that the two key components for interconnectivity are the astrocyte cell router and astrocyte tile router, i.e. the former provides the local connections for the astrocyte cells inside a tile facility, and the latter creates the global communications between the tile facilities. Figure 2 details the astrocyte cell router and includes the input/output ports (from/to the astrocyte cells and tile router) and a controller ($m = 10$). The controller consists of an arbiter, a routing module, and a scheduler. The arbiter controls the data reading from multiple input ports. A round-robin arbitration policy [8] is employed to give a fair access to the astrocyte cells and tile router. The routing module makes the routing decisions based on the traffic statuses from the local astrocyte cells and tile router. The scheduler forwards the received packets to the destination ports based on the routing decision from the routing module.

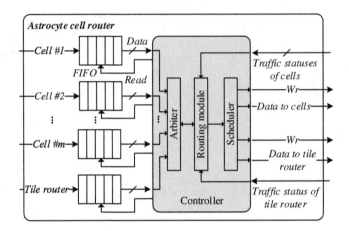

Fig. 2. Astrocyte cell router

The working flow of the astrocyte cell router is given by Fig. 3. After reset, the astrocyte cell router is in state S1, i.e. checks the data request from the first input channel. If there is no data request, it checks the next input port (state S6). If there is a data request in S1, it changes to S2 i.e. saves the packet and makes the routing. For the local transmission, the cell router checks the traffic statuses of local cells (S3). If they can receive the packet, the cell router forwards the received packet to the local cells (S5). If the packet is for the global transmission in S2, the traffic status of the tile router is checked (S4). The packet is forwarded to the tile router (S5) if the traffic status of tile router is not congested. After, it forwards the received packet in S5 and the cell router checks the next input port (S6 and S1) and repeats the same process. This working flow allows the prompt packet transmissions for the astrocyte cell routers, and also achieves a low hardware area overhead which is given in next section.

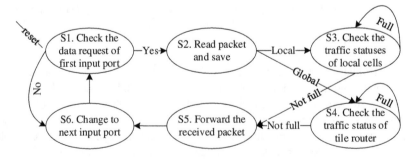

Fig. 3. Working flow of the astrocyte cell router.

The top layer in HANA is the astrocyte tile router which connects the astrocyte tile facilities together. The adaptive NoC routing strategy from our previous work [7] is utilised in the astrocyte tile router. This router has four ports to facilitate north, east, south and west inter-tile router connectivity, and a fifth network interface (NI) port. The NI port provides the connections between the astrocyte tile router and local astrocyte cell router. The astrocyte tile router employs an adaptive arbitration policy module combing the fairness of the round-robin and the priority schedule scheme of first-come-first-server approach [7]. This improves the router throughput according to the traffic behaviour presented across the astrocyte network.

4   Experimental Results

This section presents the test bench setup and the IP_3 exchange rate analysis for the local and global astrocyte cells in the proposed HANA. The astrocyte tile facilities were implemented on a Xilinx Virtex-7 XC7VX485T-2FFG1761C FPGA device running at 200 MHz, and real-time performances were verified. The output signals from the hardware astrocyte cells in [4] were used as stimulus for evaluating HANA. A single astrocyte facility is also synthesized using Synopsys Design Compiler based on a SAED 90-nm CMOS technology in order to analyse the area utilization.

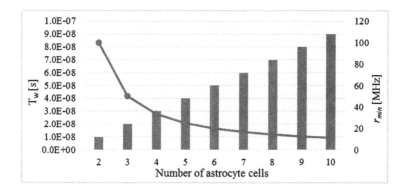

Fig. 4.   Maximum packet transmission waiting time T_w (bars) and minimum IP_3 exchange rate r_{min} (line) inside an astrocyte tile facility.

Inside an astrocyte tile facility, the maximum packet transmission waiting time (T_w) and minimum IP_3 exchange rate (r_{min}) express a measure of how rapid the astrocyte cells can exchange information with each other, e.g. communication throughput. As the astrocyte tile facility employs a star topology for interconnection and all the astrocyte cells share a single astrocyte cell router, each cell has to wait for permission to transmit (exchange) data if multiple astrocyte cells have packet transmission requests. T_w denotes the maximum packet transmission waiting time in a tile, and the r_{min} denotes the minimum IP_3 exchange rate. Figure 4 presents performance data based on these two metrics for a single astrocyte tile facility. In this work $m = 10$ which matches our previous computational model of the astrocyte network [3]. Figure 4 shows that when the number of astrocyte cell (m) increase, T_w increases from 10 ns (i.e. 2 clock cycles latency when $m = 2$) to 90 ns ($m = 10$) as expected, i.e. T_w scales linearly with m which maintains the system scalability. In the meantime, r_{min} decreases from 100 MHz to 11 MHz. In biological astrocyte cells typically exchange information at a frequency of 10 Hz [6]. Therefore, from a hardware point of view, if a higher IP_3 exchange rate can be achieved, the platform can be used as an accelerator for astrocyte network models. Alternatively, the number of astrocyte cells (m) that can be accommodated within an astrocyte tile facility can be further increased, and the information exchange on the biological-scale can also be met.

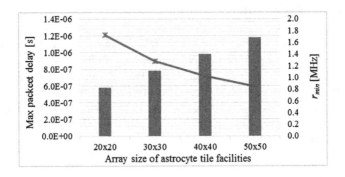

Fig. 5. Maximum packet delay σ (bars) and minimum IP_3 exchange rate r_{min} (line) for different array sizes of astrocyte tile facilities.

To demonstrate that HANA is scalable, four different large scale systems based on the astrocyte tile facilities were evaluated including 2-D mesh sizes of 20×20, 30×30, 40×40 and 50×50, respectively. In this experiment, m is ten, thus they can accommodate 4 K, 9 K, 16 K, 25 K astrocyte cells, and communicate with 40 K, 9 K, 160 K, 250 K neurons. Figure 5 shows the maximum packet delay (σ) and minimum IP_3 exchange rate (r_{min}) under different array sizes. As the array size increases, the maximum packet delay increases from 580 ns (20×20) to 1,180 ns (50×50) and the minimum IP_3 exchange rate decreases from 1.7 MHz to 0.8 MHz. The proposed HANA achieves a high IP_3 exchange rate, which is significantly greater (4 orders of magnitude faster) than the biological exchange rate (i.e. ~10 Hz). The speedup of this exchange rate is critical for large scale implementations and therefore demonstrates the key performance benefit of using NoCs as proposed in HANA.

The hardware resource of the HANA compared with other existing approaches is shown in Table 2. Note that the same node degree of mesh and star topologies (i.e. degree = 4) is used Table 2 to give a fair comparison of the hardware area utilizations. It shows that for the 2D mesh topology, the astrocyte tile router achieves a relatively low area utilization (only 0.156 mm^2) using Synopsys Design Compiler based on a SAED 90 nm CMOS in comparison with other approaches (e.g. 0.182 mm^2 [9], 0.267 mm^2 [10]). The approach of [8] has a lower area as the packet size is much smaller however the HANA astrocyte cell router has a very low area utilization, ~50 % of the

NoC router in [8], ~10 % of the CG/FG routers [10]. Table 2 highlights that compared to other approaches, the HANA interconnection NoC strategy has a relatively low area utilization which maintains the scalability of astrocyte networks in hardware.

Table 2. Hardware area utilizations of different approaches

The approach		Topology	Area overhead (mm²)	
			Router	Device technology
[8]		2D Mesh	0.056	90 nm CMOS
[9]		2D Mesh	0.182	SAED 90 nm
CG router [10]		2D Mesh	0.237	SAED 90 nm
FG router [10]		2D Mesh	0.267	SAED 90 nm
HANA	Astrocyte cell router	Star	0.024	SAED 90 nm
	Astrocyte tile router	2D Mesh	0.156	SAED 90 nm

5 Conclusion

An interactive architecture for hardware ANN was proposed in this paper. It employs the H-NoC [7] for the spiking neuron connections and uses the proposed HANA NoC interconnection strategy for the astrocyte network communication. The presented HANA is a hierarchical architecture using a two-level network of NoC routers that enables scalable communications in hardware between tiles of astrocyte cells. The experimental results demonstrate that HANA offers a high speed IP_3 exchange rate, and achieves a low area overhead which maintains system scalability.

References

1. Clarke, L.E., Barres, B.A.: Emerging roles of astrocytes in neural circuit development. Nat. Rev. Neurosci. **14**, 311–321 (2013)
2. Stevens, B.: Neuron-astrocyte signaling in the development and plasticity of neural circuits. Neurosignals **16**, 278–288 (2008)
3. Naeem, M., McDaid, L.J., Harkin, J., Wade, J.J., Marsland, J.: On the role of astroglial syncytia in self-repairing spiking neural networks. IEEE Trans. Neural Netw. Learn. Syst. **26**, 2370–2380 (2015)
4. Liu, J., Harkin, J., Maguire, L., McDaid, L., Wade, J., McElholm, M.: Self-repairing hardware with astrocyte-neuron networks. In: IEEE International Symposium on Circuits and Systems (ISCAS), pp. 1–4 (2016)
5. Araque, A., Parpura, V., Sanzgiri, R.P., Haydon, P.G.: Tripartite synapses: glia, the unacknowledged partner. Trends Neurosci. **22**, 208–215 (1999)
6. Goldberg, M., De Pittà, M., Volman, V., Berry, H., Ben-Jacob, E.: Nonlinear gap junctions enable long-distance propagation of pulsating calcium waves in astrocyte networks. PLoS Comput. Biol. **6**, 1–14 (2010)

7. Carrillo, S., Harkin, J., McDaid, L.J., et al.: Scalable hierarchical network-on-chip architecture for spiking neural network hardware implementations. IEEE Trans. Parallel Distrib. Syst. **24**, 2451–2461 (2013)
8. Carrillo, S., Harkin, J., McDaid, L.J., et al.: Advancing interconnect density for spiking neural network hardware implementations using traffic-aware adaptive network-on-chip routers. Neural Netw. **33**, 42–57 (2012)
9. Liu, J., Harkin, J., Li, Y., Maguire, L.: Online traffic-aware fault detection for NoC. J. Parallel Distrib. Comput. **74**, 1984–1993 (2014)
10. Liu, J., Harkin, J., Li, Y., Maguire, L.P.: Fault tolerant networks-on-chip routing with coarse and fine-grained look-ahead. IEEE Trans. Comput. Aided Des. Integr. Circ. Syst. **35**, 260–273 (2016)

Restricted Boltzmann Machines Without Random Number Generators for Efficient Digital Hardware Implementation

Sansei Hori[✉], Takashi Morie, and Hakaru Tamukoh

Graduate School of Life Science and Systems Engineering,
Kyushu Institute of Technology,
2-4 Hibikino, Wakamatsu-ku, Kitakyushu 808-0196, Japan
hori-sansei@edu.brain.kyutech.ac.jp

Abstract. Restricted Boltzmann machines (RBMs) have actively been studied in the field of deep neural networks. RBMs are stochastic artificial neural networks that can learn a probability distribution of input datasets. However, they require considerable computational resources, long processing times and high power consumption due to huge number of random number generation to obtain stochastic behavior. Therefore, dedicated hardware implementation of RBMs is desired for consumer applications with low-power devices. To realize hardware implementation of RBMs in a massively parallel manner, each unit must include random number generators (RNGs), which occupy huge hardware resources. In this paper, we propose a hardware-oriented RBM algorithm that does not require RNGs. In the proposed method, as a random number, we employ underflow bits obtained from the calculation process of the firing probability. We have developed a software implementation of fixed-point RBMs to evaluate the proposed method. Experimental results show that a 16-bit fixed-point RBM can be trained by the proposed method, and the underflow bits can be used as random numbers in RBM training.

Keywords: Restricted Boltzmann machines · Deep learning · Random number generators · Digital hardware · FPGA

1 Introduction

Deep learning (DL) [4] has actively been studied in the field of neural networks. It is learning methods for multilayer neural networks to obtain high-level features of input datasets [7,8]. A lot of architectures of deep neural networks (DNNs) have been proposed to realize DL, and restricted Boltzmann machines (RBMs) are one of DNNs [2]. This model operates stochastically and can learn a probability distribution of input datasets. However, training an RBM on software systems using CPU and GPU requires considerable computational resources, a long processing time and high power consumption.

Recently, hardware implementations of RBMs, which improve the processing speed and power efficiency, have been reported [5,6,9–11]. These architectures

© Springer International Publishing Switzerland 2016
A.E.P. Villa et al. (Eds.): ICANN 2016, Part I, LNCS 9886, pp. 391–398, 2016.
DOI: 10.1007/978-3-319-44778-0_46

introduce random number generators (RNGs) to determine an unit state based on a firing probability. To realize hardware implementation of an RBM in a massively parallel manner, each unit should have an RNG which occupies considerable hardware resources.

This paper proposes a new hardware-oriented RBM algorithm for an efficient field programmable gate array (FPGA) implementation. The proposed algorithm can be implemented without RNGs. In the proposed method, we employ underflow bits obtained from the calculation process of the firing probability in each unit as a random number. Using the proposed method, we can implement an RBM on an FPGA with small hardware resources because RNGs can be replaced by the underflow bits. In order to evaluate the proposed method, we have developed a software implementation of fixed-point RBMs and clarified the relationship between the bit width and learning results of the RBM. Experimental results show that the fixed-point RBM with 8-bit integer and 8-bit fractional parts can be trained by the proposed method and the underflow bits can be used as random numbers in the training phase of the RBM.

2   Restricted Boltzmann Machines

The structure of an RBM is shown in Fig. 1. It consists of a visible and a hidden layer, which have N and M units, respectively ($v_1, v_2 \ldots v_N$ and $h_1 \ldots h_M$). This network operates stochastically, and each unit state is determined by the firing probability, which is calculated from the states of units in the other layer.

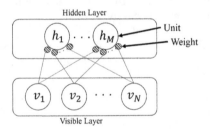

Fig. 1. Structure of an RBM.

2.1   Learning Algorithm of RBMs

In RBMs, each unit has the firing probability:

$$p(h_j = 1|\boldsymbol{v}, \boldsymbol{\theta}) = \sigma\left(b_j + \sum_i w_{ij}p(v_i)\right), \tag{1}$$

$$p(v_i = 1|\boldsymbol{h}, \boldsymbol{\theta}) = \sigma\left(a_i + \sum_j w_{ij}h_j\right), \tag{2}$$

where v_i and h_j represent the states of visible and hidden units, respectively, w_{ij} is the weight between the i- and j-th units, a_i and b_j are the biases of visible and hidden units, respectively, $\boldsymbol{\theta}$ is a set of network parameters, and σ is the sigmoidal function.

A processing flow of the learning phase of an RBM is as follows.

1. Set training data to the visible units, and give the distribution probability of the data, $p(v_i)$.
2. Calculate $p(h_j = 1|\boldsymbol{v}, \boldsymbol{\theta})$ by Eq. (1).
3. Update the hidden unit states (if $p(h_j = 1|\boldsymbol{v}, \boldsymbol{\theta}) > r$, then $h_j = 1$, where r is a random number).
4. Calculate $p(v_i = 1|\boldsymbol{h}, \boldsymbol{\theta})$ by Eq. (2).
5. Update the parameters.

This flow is called CD-1 learning. In CD-k learning, steps 2 to 4 are repeated k times. The detailed algorithm is shown in [3].

In step 3, random numbers are required to determine the hidden unit state h_j. To implement RBMs on an FPGA, we need RNGs to obtain random numbers.

3   Hardware-Oriented RBM

In this section, we propose an RBM implementation method that can save the hardware resources and evaluate the learning accuracy of RBMs in a fixed-point binary number environment.

3.1   Fixed-Point RBM

We have developed a software RBM using fixed-point binary numbers to validate the proposed method. Generally, software implementations use floating-point numbers. On the other hand, digital hardware implementations use fixed-point binary numbers. Although digital hardware can obviously process floating-point numbers, this requires large hardware resources, and therefore it is a disadvantage of the implementation of large-scaled RBMs.

3.2   Fixed-Point RBM Using Underflow Bits as Random Numbers

We propose a new method to generate random numbers for hardware RBMs. Hardware RBMs require RNGs to determine the state of each unit from the firing probability. Generally, we use Linear Feedback Shift Registers (LFSRs) to generate random numbers in digital hardware, but they require large hardware resources. In contrast, the proposed method does not use RNGs but uses underflow bits obtained from the RBM learning process as random numbers.

We use a 16-bit fixed-point number for a firing probability and a weight, as shown in Fig. 2. We assume that the visible layer consists of 1,024 visible units. In the calculation process of the firing probability of hidden units based on Eq. (1), the bit width is changed as follows:

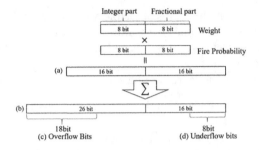

Fig. 2. Proposed method: (a) result of multiplication, (b) result of summation, (c) overflow bits, and (d) underflow bits.

1. Multiply w_{ij} and the firing probability $p(v_i)$. The result has a 16-bit integer and a 16-bit fractional parts, as shown in Fig. 2(a).
2. Sum up all values of $w_{ij}p(v_i)$. As a result of summation, the number of carry bits is equal to $\log_2 1,024$. Therefore, the result of summing operation has a 26-bit integer part, as shown in Fig. 2(b).
3. Cut off the resultant value in the integer and fractional parts to hold the initial bit width. In this operation, 18 overflow bits in the integer and 8 underflow bits in the fractional part are generated, as shown in Figs. 2(c) and (d). We employ these underflow bits instead of random numbers generated by LFSRs.

4 Experimental Results

In the experiments to validate our proposed method, we converted from floating-point variables to fixed-point variables in a software implementation of RBMs, and evaluated learning results by observing cross-entropy errors calculated as follows:

$$CE = \mathbf{v}\ln\{\sigma\left(\mathbf{h}\cdot\mathbf{w} + \mathbf{b}\right)\} + (1 - \mathbf{v})\ln\{1 - \sigma\left(\mathbf{h}\cdot\mathbf{w} + \mathbf{b}\right)\}, \qquad (3)$$

where $\mathbf{v}$ and $\mathbf{h}$ represent the states of visible and hidden units, respectively, $\mathbf{w}$ is the weights, $\mathbf{b}$ is the hidden unit bias, and σ is the sigmoid function.

In the experiments, we used three images extracted from Standard Image Data BAse (SIDBA) [1] for training the RBM, as shown in Fig. 3. The image size was 32×32 pixels. The parameters of the RBM network were set as follows; the number of visible units was 1024, the number of hidden units was 16, the initial learning rate was 0.01, the initial temperature was 10. The number of epoch executed for training was 800.

4.1 Bit Width of Fixed-Point RBM

We evaluated the relationship between the bit width and the learning results of the fixed-point RBM by changing the bit width of fixed-point numbers expressing

Fig. 3. Training images extracted from SIDBA.

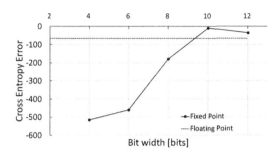

Fig. 4. Cross-entropy error in each bit width.

firing probabilities, biases, weights and all temporary values. Figure 4 shows the results of cross-entropy errors in each bit width. In this experiment, we used 4- to 12-bit fractional parts. The integer part was fixed at an 8-bit width, and a sign bit was added.

From the experiments, better learning results were obtained as the longer fractional part bit width was used. However, the results in 12 bits were slightly worse than those for 10 bits. In addition, the maximum cross-entropy error was -65.82 when we performed the same experiment with floating-point variables. Therefore, it is concluded that the bit width of the fractional part required for successful learning is 10 bits, and even an 8-bit width is often sufficient. In other words, if we use a more than 8-bit width, fixed-point RBMs can have nearly the same performance as RBMs using floating-point variables.

4.2   Evaluation of Randomness of Data of Underflow Bits

We evaluated randomness of the overflow and underflow bits. Since the overflow bits showed no randomness, we evaluated randomness of the underflow bits.

Figure 5 shows a histogram of underflow bits in the fractional part. It shows that the underflow bits appear in the entire range of values like the white noise, which suggests that the underflow bits in the fractional part meet one of the requirements for random numbers, and they could be used as random number generators instead of LFSRs.

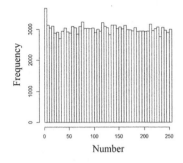

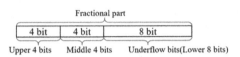

Fig. 5. Histogram of underow bits in the learning process.

Fig. 6. Fractional part structure.

4.3   Learning in RBMs Without RNGs

We measured cross-entropy errors for learning in the fixed-point RBM using underflow bits. In this experiment, we used CD-5 learning. In the first phase of CD-5, the underflow bits are not generated at step 2 described in Sect. 2.1 because the input images (training data) are binary images. In other words, the firing probability of visible units, $p(v)$, is set to 0 or 1 in the binary images at the first step of CD-5, and thus, the multiplication of w and $p(v)$ generates no underflow bits. However, in the second to fifth phases of CD-5, underflow bits are generated as mentioned in Sect. 3. Thus, we trained the RBM in the following four cases to evaluate the proposed method.

Method 1. Use random numbers generated by a software function in all learning phases.
Method 2. Use random numbers generated by a software function only in the first phase of CD-5.
Method 3. Use the upper 4 bits and middle 4 bits (Fig. 6) in the fraction part in the first phase.
Method 4. Use the middle 4 bits (Fig. 6) in the fraction part in the first phase.

It is noted that, in Methods 2 to 4, each RBM used the underflow bits (lower 8 bits) in the second to fifth phases of CD-5. Experimental results are shown in Fig. 7, and Table 1 shows maximum cross-entropy errors. In Method 3, the maximum cross-entropy error was close to that in Method 1. From these results, the fixed-point RBM can be trained by the proposed method, and the underflow bits can be used as random numbers in the training phase of the RBM.

4.4   Experimental Result with 12 Images

The previous experimental results show that the Method 3 is the best in the proposed method. Therefore, to assess feasibility of the proposed method, we measured cross-entropy errors of Methods 1 and 3 using 12 images from SIDBA.

Table 1. Maximum cross-entropy error in each method.

Method no.	Cross-entropy error
Method 1 (Using software RNGs)	−193.66
Method 2 (Using software RNGs & underflow bits)	−282.73
Method 3 (Using upper and middle 4 bits & underflow bits)	−149.05
Method 4 (Using middle 4 bits & underflow bits)	−253.07

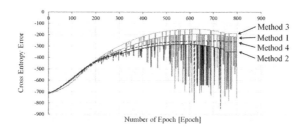

Fig. 7. Cross-entropy error in each method.

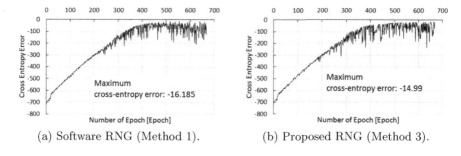

(a) Software RNG (Method 1).   (b) Proposed RNG (Method 3).

Fig. 8. Cross-entropy error with 12 images.

In this experiment, parameters of a fixed-point RBM were set as follows; the number of hidden units was 64, the learning rate was 0.1, the number of epochs were 668 and other parameters were identical with previous experiments.

Figure 8(a) and (b) show learning results of Methods 1 and 3, respectively. From these results, we confirmed that the underflow bits can be used as random numbers to train the fixed-point RBM.

5   Conclusion

In this paper, we proposed a hardware-oriented RBM without RNGs for efficient digital hardware implementation. In proposed method, underflow bits obtained from the calculation process of the RBM are used as random numbers. By using the proposed method, hardware resources for RNGs can be saved when RBMs are implemented on an FPGA, which leads to reduce the hardware size and power consumption.

In the future, we will implement the proposed method on an FPGA and evaluate hardware properties such as hardware size and power consumption. We will then develop a hardware DNNs and evaluate the effectiveness of the proposed method.

Acknowledgement. This research was supported by JSPS KAKENHI Grant Numbers 26330279, 15K12110 and 15H01706.

References

1. Standard image data base. http://vision.kuee.kyoto-u.ac.jp/IUE/IMAGE_DATABASE/STD_IMAGES/
2. Fischer, A., Igel, C.: An introduction to restricted Boltzmann machines. In: Alvarez, L., Mejail, M., Gomez, L., Jacobo, J. (eds.) CIARP 2012. LNCS, vol. 7441, pp. 14–36. Springer, Heidelberg (2012)
3. Hinton, G.E.: A practical guide to training restricted boltzmann machines. Technical report UTML TR 2010–003, Department of Computer Science, University of Tronto (2010)
4. Hinton, G.E., Osindero, S., Teh, Y.W.: A fast learning algorithm for deep belief nets. Neural Comput. **18**(7), 1527–1554 (2006)
5. Kim, S.K., McAfee, L.C., McMahon, P.L., Olukotun, K.: A highly scalable restricted boltzmann machine FPGA implementation. In: International Conference on Field Programmable Logic and Applications, pp. 367–372 (2009)
6. Kim, S.K., McMahon, P.L., Olukotun, K.: A large-scale architecture for restricted boltzmann machines. In: 18th IEEE Annual International Symposium on Field-Programmable Custom Computing Machines, pp. 201–208 (2010)
7. Krizhevsky, A., Sutskever, I., Hinton, G.E.: Imagenet classification with deep convolutional neural networks. In: Pereira, F., Burges, C.J.C., Bottou, L., Weinberger, K.Q. (eds.) Advances in Neural Information Processing Systems, vol. 25, pp. 1097–1105. Curran Associates, Inc. (2012)
8. Le, Q., Ranzato, M., Monga, R., Devin, M., Chen, K., Corrado, G., Dean, J., Ng, A.: Building high-level features using large scale unsupervised learning. In: International Conference in Machine Learning, pp. 8595–8598 (2012)
9. Ly, D.L., Chow, P.: High-performance reconfigurable hardware architecture for restricted Boltzmann machines. IEEE Trans. Neural Netw. **21**(11), 1780–1792 (2010)
10. Park, S., Bong, K., Shin, D., Lee, J., Choi, S., Yoo, H.J.: A 1.93 TOPS/W scalable deep learning/inference processor with tetra-parallel mimd architecture for big-data applications. In: IEEE International Solid - State Circuits Conference - (ISSCC), pp. 80–82 (2015)
11. Ueyoshi, K., Asai, T., Motomura, M.: Scalable and highly parallel architecture for restricted boltzmann machines. In: 2015 RISP International Workshop on Nonlinear Circuits, Communications and Signal Processing, pp. 369–372 (2015)

Compact Associative Memory for AER Spike Decoding in FPGA-Based Evolvable SNN Emulation

Mireya Zapata$^{(\boxtimes)}$ and Jordi Madrenas

Department of Electronics Engineering, Universitat Politècnica de Catalunya,
Jordi Girona, 1-3, edif. C4, 08034 Barcelona, Catalunya, Spain
{mireya.zapata,jordi.madrenas}@upc.edu

Abstract. A spike decoding scheme for Address Event Representation (AER)-based transmission in Spiking Neural Network (SNN) emulators is introduced. The proposed scheme is a modified associative memory based on an efficient use of BRAM, supporting connectivity upgrade in real-time for hardware implementations of evolutionary networks. After analysing the different options and selecting the most efficient one, a prototype example based on FPGA is provided together with a novel hashing technique to demonstrate a compact on-chip solution for implementing inter-chip connectivity in SNN.

Keywords: Associative memory · SNN · AER · Digital neuromorphic systems · Evolvable connections

1 Introduction

Brain-inspired computing has drawn enormous interest as a computer paradigm to yield applications that demand intelligent behavior. However, neuron interconnectivity involves a massive wiring problem due to high fan in/out in the neural cells [1]. Interconnectivity modelling is a bottleneck in terms of throughput and resource consuming for hardware emulation of the brain. Neuron have been mapped using content address memory (CAM), where data is matched to the content. However, CAM is highly resource consuming and, alternatives like hash coding (exact match association) can also be used for implementing this association using search functions. For large-scale networks, the number of connections that can be modelled is limited by routing resources.

SNN architectures based on FPGAs like Vogelstein [2] and Cassidy [3] employ off-chip SDRAM for mapping presynaptic and postsynaptic neuron address, increasing the size and density of their routing tables and the memory traffic. SpiNNaker [4] implements synaptic connectivity, applying multiplexing techniques and 1024×32 CAM along with lookup RAM for routing purposes. These approaches are costly in area and power consumption. Furthermore, NoC based

© Springer International Publishing Switzerland 2016
A.E.P. Villa et al. (Eds.): ICANN 2016, Part I, LNCS 9886, pp. 399–407, 2016.
DOI: 10.1007/978-3-319-44778-0_47

architectures require a large amount of distributed memory on chip for holding synaptic connectivity trading higher flexibility against energy efficiency. It means a resource-demanding problem for compact embedded applications.

Our contribution to SNN emulation (real time operation hardware) is based on a Multi-Chip SNN architecture (MCS) (Fig. 1) in a ring topology. In our approach, we propose to use distributed Associative Memories (AM) implemented with on-chip block RAMs (BRAMs), along with a novel hashing technique for routing sparse connections. Thus, each AM just needs to infer the associated post-synaptic neuron synapse from the incoming pre-synaptic spiking neuron address generated in a different cluster or chip. Distributed BRAMs of modern FPGAs can be advantageously used to operate as local AMs as well. Furthermore, using BRAM allows for real-time connection modification, enabling evolvable networks. Besides, AM matches an input value to predefined data with low latency.

The proposed Distributed AM with a specific hierarchical configuration to reduce area overhead deduced from Sect. 3 along with a novel hashing technique with a numeric mapping example is presented in Sect. 4. In Sect. 5 conclusions are reported.

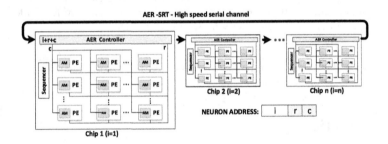

Fig. 1. Generic SIMD multiprocessor architecture

2 Multichip SNN Architecture

The MCS based on Xilinx Kintex 7 XC7K325T, is a general purpose computing platform for SNN, capable of implementing any neural algorithm according to user needs with programmable synapses connectivity. Each chip contains a 2D array of specific-purpose Processing Elements (PEs) with Single-Instruction Multiple Data parallel processing. Each PE is in charge of emulating several neurons and manage the local and global neural connectivity. In [5], the operability of this system it has been proven experimentally with the implementation of Leaky Integrate and Fire, Izhikevich [6] and Iglesias y Villa [7] neural algorithms.

Spike communication between neurons in the same chip and across the chips is through a custom packet-based AER protocol [8]. AER reduces interconnects by time multiplexing the spikes, taking into account the low rate of biological SNNs and simplifies spike transmission by encoding the pre-synaptic neuron address; however, spike decoding at reception becomes challenging due to the long source neuron address.

3   Associative Memory Implementation

In our MCS prototype, it is possible to map up to 131 synapse connections/PE. In order to emulate a hierarchical neural topology, 100 local and 31 global connections were defined. Local ones are on-chip locally distributed, so there is no need for AER transmission. Global ones receive spikes from long-distance interconnects and take advantage of the AER bus. These are the ones that need to be decoded by means of the AM.

From now on, we concentrate only on global synapses. Currently, we consider as input data to the AER controller the pre-synaptic neuron address of 18-bit length, composed of ID, row and column. ID (i) corresponds to the chip where the pre-synaptic spike is generated, while rows (r) and columns (c), indicate the pre-synaptic neuron position on the chip array using 4-bit wide each.

A 31-bit synapse register (S_j) stores the AM output data. It contains the synaptic match positions corresponding to the specific neuron. For the spike decoding purpose, the AM does not have to output the matching register address but the matching bit itself. AM can be implemented using register banks, combinational logic or standard RAM/ROM memory.

3.1   Register-Based (RB) Associative Memory Scheme

At first approximation, the network topology can be stored in a register bank, where the pre-synaptic neuron address has to be compared with all registers to detect any match, that is further stored into the post-synaptic register S_j.

Despite in general associative memories multi-match is necessary, for our distributed spike decoding application single match detection is enough. This is because normally single connection between a given pre-synaptic neuron and the post-synaptic neuron is needed. Furthermore, if parallel connections were needed, this issue can be normally circumvented by multiplying the synapse strength of the single connection by a factor. The required bits for this single match approach are:

$$\#bit_{RB} = (i + r + c) \cdot s. \tag{1}$$

where i, r, c are the chip ID, row, column of the pre-synaptic neuron address and s corresponds to post-synaptic register number of bits. This approach is compact in bit number, but registers draw important resources from an FPGA and bit area is much less compact than RAM bits.

3.2   Combinational Logic Implementation (CLI)

Assuming the associative memory register contents are constant, synthesis to combinational logic can be committed. Depending on the specific connectivity, this may lead to a compact approach, so it has been used in previous implementations; however, its main drawback is that, once synthesized, the interconnect pattern remains fixed, and any change implies resynthesizing and reprogramming the device. This is, in the best case, a tedious and inconvenient task. Furthermore, the area occupancy is data-dependent, which is highly inconvenient for the floor-plan definition.

3.3   Memory-Based Direct Implementation (DI)

This is the most straightforward method for AM implementation using FPGA BRAMs. The source neuron address $(i + r + c)$, is fully decoded by connecting it to the BRAM address input. The BRAM output data is one-hot encoded, so it directly contains the information that is transferred to the spike register S_j. The memory required for this implementation is:

$$\#bit_{DI} = 2^{i+r+c} \cdot s. \tag{2}$$

This address decoding produces inefficient memory usage from the bit number point of view, compared to the optimal RB implementation (1), as the exponential factor of 2 indicates in (2). In particular, for an s-bit synapse register, the memory efficiency η_1 is:

$$\eta_1 = \frac{\#bit_{RB}}{\#bit_{DI}} = \frac{i+r+c}{2^{i+r+c}}. \tag{3}$$

Even for a small number of addresses, most of the memory rows will be unused, so efficiency is very low.

3.4   Output Data Encoding (ODE) Memory Implementation

From the previous consideration, one obvious way to compact the memory is to binary encode in $log_2 s$ bits the one-hot s output data bits. This reduces the memory size to:

$$\#bits_{ODE} = 2^{i+r+c} \cdot log_2 s. \tag{4}$$

A limitation of ODE is that a pre-synaptic neuron can excite only a single synapse of the post-synaptic neuron. As discussed before, this is not an issue in our case. A side effect is the reduction of one count in the number of synaptic bits, because unmatched input data need to be encoded somewhat. We arbitrarily assign to that data the 0 code. Row occupancy is almost the same but efficiency improves as the data field is reduced; however, the exponential factor remains unchanged, so it is still quite low. The ODE requires also an output data decoder.

$$\eta_2 = \frac{(i+r+c)(s-1)}{2^{i+r+c} \cdot log_2 s}. \tag{5}$$

3.5 Input and Output Data Encoding (IODE) Memory Scheme

Taking into account that only a few registers contain association data, we can compress the input data information by means of translation memories. This encoding technique can also be considered as a kind of hashing [9]. Since at most s chip ID numbers will produce spike, we can encode those chips with $log_2 s$ bits. The sum of rows and columns $(r + c)$ can be recorded in a similar way.

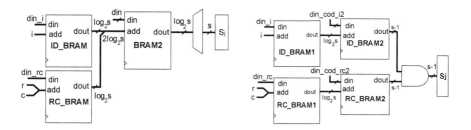

Fig. 2. IODE scheme.   **Fig. 3.** IDE-ODA scheme.

In Fig. 2 the diagram for this approach is shown. Two BRAMs perform the input data encoding, compressing the $i + r + c$ bits in $2 \cdot log_2 s$ bits. The required RAM number of bits becomes:

$$\#bits_{IODE} = (2^i + 2^{r+c} + s^2) \cdot log_2 s. \tag{6}$$

The exponential factor of (4) has been significantly reduced, being divided into three terms, two of them exponential but with reduced exponents in practice. We assign the 0 code arbitrarily to unmatched i and $r+c$. Thus, as in ODE one code is lost, and the number of possible synapses is reduced to $s - 1$. Efficiency is clearly improved:

$$\eta_3 = \frac{(i + r + c)(s - 1)}{(2^i + 2^{r+c} + s^2) \cdot log_2 s}. \tag{7}$$

3.6 Input Data Encoding, Output Data ANDed (IDE-ODA) Memory Scheme

Additional improvement from the previous encoding can be obtained by splitting the output BRAM2 from IODE, in ID_BRAM2 and RC_BRAM2, which detect matches separately for chip ID and row+column (Fig. 3). In this case, it is not possible to keep the output data encoded, because multi-hit may happen for both chip ID and/or row+column. The reason is because a given chip may contain more than one pre-synaptic neurons connected to a post-synaptic neuron. Analogously, several neurons from different chips located at the same r+c position may be connected to the same post-synaptic neuron. Thus, the outputs from both BRAM2s need to be ANDed to obtain the valid data. Therefore, expanding the output data back to one-hot becomes necessary. The number of bits required in this architecture becomes:

$$\#bits_{IDE\_ODA} = (2^i + 2^{r+c}) \cdot log_2 s + 2s \cdot (s - 1). \tag{8}$$

If the dominant terms in (8) are the exponential ones, no significant improvement is produced, but when the terms are comparable, efficiency is improved. Furthermore, there is no need of output decoder.

$$\eta_4 = \frac{(i + r + c)(s - 1)}{(2^i + 2^{r+c}) \cdot log_2 s + 2s \cdot (s - 1)}. \tag{9}$$

4   Application Example and Results

In this section, a numerical example and an application based on our MCS is presented. For the defined approaches, numerical results for our implementation ($i = 7$, $r = c = 4$, $s = 32$) are shown in Table 1.

Table 1. Comparison of analyzed schemes

AM implementation	η (%)	LUT6s	FF/RAM (bits)	Total consumed BRAM
RB	1	384	576	-
Combin. Logic	-	[a]	-	-
DI	0.006	-	8192k	8352k
ODE	0.04	31	1280k	1440k
IODE	4.84	31	11.25k	54k
IDE-ODA	6.65	31[b]	8.19k	54k

[a]Data dependent
[b]LUT4

In the MCS FPGA mapping, LUTs are the limiting resource because PEs demand mostly these. On the other hand, almost fully availability of BRAMs is possible in SIMD multiprocessing applications such as ours. So, even if the register implementation could eventually be more compact, from the FPGA resource balance point of view, it is much more convenient to map the AM into BRAMs.

Thus, discarding the Register-Based, and the Combinational Logic solutions, that does not allow dynamic connections, the best scheme is the IDE-ODA, closely followed by IODE. IDE-ODA scheme only requires 8.19 kbit per PE, and its efficiency is 1000 times better than DI and slightly better than IODE scheme. When mapped on the FPGA the number of BRAMs is the same for IODE and IDE-ODA because of quantization.

Table 2. Spike encoding

ID (10-bit)	r+c (8-bit)	Synaptic position
48h	93h	15
48h	47h	5
1ch	**52h**	**7**
1ch	79h	20
1ch	80h	1
33h	43h	2
33h	51h	4
5fh	52h	3
5fh	72h	9
5fh	80h	10

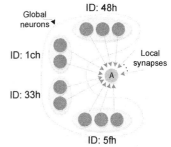

Fig. 4. Global synaptic connections for neuron A

It may seem that 6.65 % efficiency is a low number; however, a BRAM bit is much more compact than a register bit. Also, notice the improvement compared to DI and ODE. Furthermore, as mentioned before, in the multiprocessing array registers are much scarcer than BRAMs, so using BRAMs balances the resource usage of the architecture. Finally, 54 kbit per PE is totally achievable in modern FPGAs, which would not be the case for ODE scheme, for instance.

An example of the mapping technique used in the IDE-ODE configuration for implementing global spiking connectivity is now discussed. As shown in Fig. 4, a post-synaptic neuron A is connected to 10 global neurons located in 4 different chips. Table 2 shows the codes of ID, r+c and synapse, highlighting in bold the numeric example that follows. The 4 keys rules to detect the pairwise synaptic connection between the pre and postsynaptic neurons are the following:

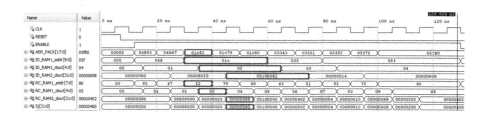

Fig. 5. IDE-ODA simulated waveforms. (Color figure online)

ID_BRAM1: Same index for the neurons that share same ID. *RC_BRAM1*: Same index for the neuron that share same r+c independently of ID value. *ID_BRAM2*: Bit set in the corresponding synaptic position that share same ID index. *RC_BRAM2*: Bit set in the respective synaptic position that share same r+c index.

The AND operation between the two 32-bit output vectors from ID_BRAM2 and RC_BRAM2, generate a one-hot register S_j which represents the presynaptic spike received by the neuron A. The encoding used in this example is shown in the simulated waveform of Fig. 5. Notice that BRAMs output are one clock cycle delay in each case. The red mark points to the case of the neuron address 0x1c52, where the obtained S_j register (00000080h) indicates that a spike has been received on the seventh synaptic connection.

5   Conclusions

Six different implementations of AMs for spike decoding have been analysed. Resource analysis has been performed and IDE-ODA memory scheme along with a hashing technique to reduce memory occupancy. It has been found as the most compact solution in terms of area for a reasonably efficient implementation of sparse connectivity. Correct operation has been demonstrated with a mapping simulation example. The IDE-ODA presented in this work allows a flexible and dynamic synaptic connectivity employing an effective use of resource in advanced FPGAs by balancing memory (BRAM) and logic resources, without incurring to off-chip additional RAM memory and controllers. Furthermore, the number of cycles used to search data is always constant; it does not depend on the BRAM size or the number of stored synaptic addresses obtaining an effective and fast retrieval data.

However, this alternative is limited by the encoding post-synaptic address length which determines the BRAMs size. Furthermore, the consuming resources in BRAMs implementation on FPGA depends on its primitives. In a BRAM, increasing width word is more logic costly rather than increasing length address. As a consequence the MSC scalability is imposed by number of bits used for encoding spike events and the available resources.

Finally, the applicability on multi-chip architectures like ours, can be found as a convenient solution for building structural brain networks that go from inter-neuronal to inter-regional connectivity. Hardware emulation of genetic algorithms for supervised learning and evolutionary neural applications are possible with dynamic connectivity. Inter-chip fault tolerance communication can be easily carried out, providing the advantage of complete availability to the network.

Acknowledgments. Work supported in part by the Spanish Ministry of Science and Innovation under Project TEC2015-67278-R, and European Social Fund (ESF). Mireya Zapata holds a scholarship from National Secretary of High Education Science Technology and Innovation (SENACYT) of the Ecuadorian government.

References

1. Cattell, R., et al.: Challenges for Brain Emulation: Why is Building a Brain so Difficult? (2002)
2. Vogelstein, R.J., et al.: Dynamically reconfigurable silicon array of spiking neurons with conductance-based synapses. IEEE Trans. Neural Netw. **18**, 253–265 (2007)

3. Cassidy, A., Andreou, A., et al.: Design of a one millon neuron single FPGA neuro-morphic system for real time multimodal scene analysis. In: Information Sciences and Systems (2011)
4. Khan, M.M., Lester, D.R., Plana, L.A., Rast, A., Jin, X., Painkras, E., Furber, S.B.: SpiNNaker: mapping neural networks onto a massively-parallel chip multiproces-sor. In: Proceedings of the International Joint Conference on Neural Networks (2008)
5. Sanchez, G.: Spiking Neural Network emulation based on configurable devices. Doctoral dissertation, Universitat Politecnica de Catalunya (2014)
6. Izhikevich, E.M.: Polychronization: computation with spikes. Neural Comput. **18**, 245–282 (2006)
7. Iglesias, J., et al.: Dynamics of pruning in simulated large-scale spiking neural networks. Biosystems **79**, 11–20 (2005)
8. Dorta, T., Zapata, M., Madrenas, J., Sánchezb, G.: AER-SRT: scalable spike dis-tribution by means of synchronous serial ring topology address event representatio. Neurocomputing **171**, 1684–1690 (2015)
9. Dhawan, U., DeHon, A.: Area-efficient near-associative memories on FPGAs. In: ACM/SIGDA International Symposium on Field Programmable Gate Arrays, pp. 191–200 (2013)

Learning Foundations

Combining Spatial and Parametric Working Memory in a Dynamic Neural Field Model

Weronika Wojtak[1,3], Stephen Coombes[2], Estela Bicho[1],
and Wolfram Erlhagen[3(✉)]

[1] Research Centre Algoritmi, University of Minho, Guimarães, Portugal
{w.wojtak,estela.bicho}@dei.uminho.pt
[2] School of Mathematical Sciences, Centre for Mathematical Medicine and Biology,
University of Nottingham, Nottingham, UK
stephen.coombes@nottingham.ac.uk
[3] Research Centre for Mathematics, University of Minho, Guimarães, Portugal
wolfram.erlhagen@math.uminho.pt

Abstract. We present a novel dynamic neural field model consisting of two coupled fields of Amari-type which supports the existence of localized activity patterns or "bumps" with a continuum of amplitudes. Bump solutions have been used in the past to model spatial working memory. We apply the model to explain input-specific persistent activity that increases monotonically with the time integral of the input (parametric working memory). In numerical simulations of a multi-item memory task, we show that the model robustly memorizes the strength and/or duration of inputs. Moreover, and important for adaptive behavior in dynamic environments, the memory strength can be changed at any time by new behaviorally relevant information. A direct comparison of model behaviors shows that the 2-field model does not suffer the problems of the classical Amari model when the inputs are presented sequentially as opposed to simultaneously.

1 Introduction

A hallmark of higher brain function is the capacity to bridge gaps between sensation and action by maintaining goal-relevant information that is needed to perform a given task. Persistent neural activity which is commonly observed in prefrontal and association cortices is thought to represent a neural substrate for the accumulation and storage of information across time [11]. Neurophysiological studies of persistent activity have frequently used a delayed response task in which the animal is required to remember a transient sensory stimulus (e.g., spatial location or frequency) across a short period to guide a rewarded response [15]. To serve a working memory function, the internally sustained activity must be stimulus-selective so that the content of the memory can be decoded by downstream neural circuits. Neural discharge that varies according

W. Wojtak—The work received financial support from the EU-FP7 ITN project NETT: Neural Engineering Transformative Technologies (no. 289146).

© Springer International Publishing Switzerland 2016
A.E.P. Villa et al. (Eds.): ICANN 2016, Part I, LNCS 9886, pp. 411–418, 2016.
DOI: 10.1007/978-3-319-44778-0_48

to the value of continuous sensory or motor variables can be broadly classified in two distinct but not mutually exclusive coding schemes. Summation coding reflects the idea that parameter values are represented by a monotonic variation in neural firing rate [12]. Place coding assumes a smooth bell-shaped tuning curve of individual neurons with a peak at a preferred value. At the population level, a specific parameter value is represented by a localized activity pattern in parametric space [5]. Depending on the specific coding scheme, stimulus-dependent persistent activity of neural populations has been classified as parametric or spatial working memory, respectively [15]. While theoretical and experimental work has focused mainly on distinguishing both coding schemes based on optimality principles (e.g., accuracy of memorized sensory information), a more behavior-oriented perspective suggests that combining both types of memory representations might be advantageous for motor functions [13]. Imagine for instance a delayed response task in which the subject has to memorize the location of several stimuli, which, however, may differ in luminance contrast or the level of spatial attention directed to them. The memory strength of each item should reflect this additional information to bias, for instance, saccadic eye movements towards more salient stimulus locations.

In this paper, we present a novel dynamic field model that allows one to represent and memorize the integral of previous inputs in a robust manner. The framework of dynamic neural fields has been widely used in the past to model spatial working memory of continuous variables like position [2,7,10,14]. The memory mechanism is based on the idea that a localized pattern of excitation (or "bump"), which is initially triggered by a brief input, can be sustained through strong recurrent excitatory and inhibitory connections within a neural population tuned to the continuous dimension. Since their level of abstraction favors analytical treatment [4], dynamic field models are also utilized for the development of new technical solutions inspired by neural processing principles [6]. The two specific challenges we address in the present study are motivated by applications of a multi-item working memory [16]. The first question is concerned with the impact on the memory representation when multiple sensory events are presented sequentially as opposed to simultaneously. Since any existing bump in the field changes the initial condition for subsequent stimuli, it is not clear whether a stable multi-bump solution evolves in response to a series of sensory events even if the solution exists when the stimuli are presented simultaneously. The second question is more directly related to the suggested advantage of a combined spatial and parametric memory representation. Does the field dynamics support a simple monotonic relationship between the bump amplitude and the strength and/or duration of external stimuli [3]. In a similar vein, given a changing visual environment, can the internal representation be updated in the face of new input directed to a specific memory item ("retro-cuing" [8]). To answer these questions, we directly compare in numerical simulations the behavior of the classical Amari model [1] with the behavior of a new model consisting of two reciprocally coupled fields.

2   Model Details

The dynamics of the field model proposed and analyzed by Amari is governed by the following nonlinear integro-differential equation on a one-dimensional, spatially extended domain:

$$\frac{\partial u(x,t)}{\partial t} = -u(x,t) + \int_{-\infty}^{\infty} w(|x-y|)f(u(y,t)-h)\mathrm{d}y + S(x,t), \qquad (1)$$

where $u(x,t)$ represents the activity at time t of a neuron at field position x. In spatial working memory applications, neuron x is assumed to be tuned to a continuous parameter (e.g., target direction). The function $w(|x-y|)$ denotes the distance-dependent strength of connections to neighboring neurons y. $S(x,t)$ represents a time-dependent localized input centered at site x, and $f(u-h)$ defines a firing rate function with threshold $h > 0$ [1].

To simplify the analysis of pattern formation in his field model, Amari assumed $f(u)$ to be the Heaviside step function. In the present study, we use a smooth sigmoidal function with steepness parameter β, which approximates the Heaviside function for $\beta \to \infty$:

$$f(x) = \frac{1}{1 + e^{-\beta(x-h)}}. \qquad (2)$$

Our novel model consists of two coupled fields, $u(x,t)$ and $v(x,t)$, governed by the two integro-differential equations

$$\frac{\partial u(x,t)}{\partial t} = -u(x,t) + v(x,t) + \int_{-\infty}^{\infty} w(|x-y|)f(u(y,t)-h)\mathrm{d}y + S(x,t), \quad (3a)$$

$$\frac{\partial v(x,t)}{\partial t} = -v(x,t) + u(x,t) - \int_{-\infty}^{\infty} w(|x-y|)f(u(y,t)-h)\mathrm{d}y. \qquad (3b)$$

Note that the neurons in field v are driven by the summed activity from neurons in field u, but project their activity back locally only. For the coupling function $w(x)$, we follow Amari's original work and chose a Mexican-hat connectivity given by the difference of two Gaussian functions with a constant global inhibition:

$$w(x) = A_{ex}e^{\left(-x^2/2\sigma_{ex}^2\right)} - A_{in}e^{\left(-x^2/2\sigma_{in}^2\right)} - g_{in}, \qquad (4)$$

where $A_{ex} > A_{in} > 0$ and $\sigma_{in} > \sigma_{ex} > 0$ and $g_{in} > 0$.

Since the same coupling function is applied to the field v with a negative sign, the shape of the synaptic strengths represents an inverted Mexican-hat, that is, inhibition dominates at shorter and excitation at longer distances.

To numerically approximate solutions of the continuum field models, we apply a forward Euler method with a sufficiently fine discretization mesh to Eqs. (1) and (3). We assume a finite domain Ω of length $L = 120$, which we discretize by dividing it into N equal intervals of size $\Delta_x = 0.005$. The chosen time interval $T = 60$ is divided into M equal steps of size $\Delta_t = 0.01$.

To compute the spatial convolution, we used the convolution theorem, stating that convolution in one domain equals point-wise multiplication in the other domain. The Fourier transform and the inverse Fourier transform were performed using MATLAB's in-built functions `fft` and `ifft`, respectively.

3   Results

In the following numerical examples, we consider an input distribution given by the sum of three equally spaced Gaussian functions

$$S_{nb}(x) = \sum_{j=1}^{n} S_{s_j} e^{\left(-(x-x_{c_j})^2/2\sigma_s^2\right)} - S_i, \tag{5}$$

centered at positions $x_{c_j} \in \{-40, 0, 40\}$. The parameter $S_i > 0$ has been introduced to define a finite width of the positive input range. We use the same set of parameter values for both models to allow a direct comparison of results. These values are $\sigma_s = 1.5$ and $S_i = 1$ for the input, $A_{ex} = 10$, $A_{in} = 3$, $\sigma_{ex} = 2$, $\sigma_{in} = 3.5$ and $g_{in} = 1$ for the coupling function given by (4), and $\beta = 1000$ for the firing rate function given by (2). The strength S_{s_j} and duration d_{s_j} of the inputs are adjusted in the different examples as indicated in the figure captions.

Figure 1 shows the evolution of a 3-bump solution in response to the three inputs applied simultaneously at time $t = 1$. The steady states of the field activity after cessation of the inputs indicate that both models support, in principle, the existence of multiple bumps, and thus, a multi-item working memory. However, the models behave quite differently when the same inputs are presented sequentially. As shown in the Fig. 2, the Amari model evolves a single bump whereas the 2-field model again converges to the 3-bump solution. In the Amari case, the steady state excitation pattern in response to the first input (which occupies the permitted total excitation length explained by the theory [1]) creates additional surround inhibition, which ultimately suppresses the initial excitation caused by the subsequent inputs. This is not the case for the 2-field model since the increased lateral inhibition in the u-field is compensated by positive feedback from the neurons in the v-field.

The results depicted in Fig. 3 demonstrate that in the Amari model, the relative timing of the inputs and their relative strength play a crucial role in a multi-item memory formation. If the temporal delay between inputs is sufficiently short so that excitation patterns triggered by previous inputs have not yet fully evolved, a multi-bump pattern may emerge (first row). Also, increasingly stronger inputs may compensate for the additional inhibition caused by existing bumps (second row). Importantly, since the bump shape is completely determined by the recurrent interactions, the input strength is not reflected in the bump amplitude. The 2-field model, on the other hand, shows a monotonic relationship as required by a parametric working memory that encodes analog parameters like for instance stimulus contrast in the firing rate (Fig. 4, left). The dependency of bump amplitude on input strength is nearly linear for a

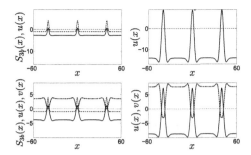

Fig. 1. Left: snapshot of the evolution of a 3-bump solutions at a time when the input distribution $S_{3b}(x)$ (dashed line) is still present. Right: steady state solutions at time $t = 60$. Top: activity $u(x)$ (solid line) of the Amari model. Bottom: activities $u(x)$ (solid line) and $v(x)$ (dashed-dotted line) of the 2-field model. Input parameters are $S_{s_j} = 5$ and $d_{s_j} = 1$.

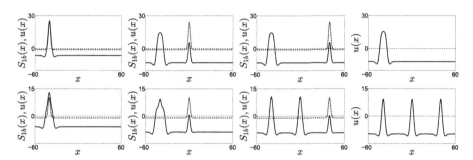

Fig. 2. Simulation of the field models with a sequence of three transient inputs $S_{1b}(x)$ (dashed line). Top: activity $u(x)$ of the Amari model with inputs given by (5) with $S_{s_j} = 25$ and $d_{s_j} = 1$. Bottom: activity $u(x)$ of the 2-field model with inputs given by (5) with $S_{s_j} = 11$ and $d_{s_j} = 1$. The inputs were applied at times $t_1 = 1$ (first column), $t_2 = 17$ (second column) and $t_3 = 33$ (third column). The forth column shows the steady state solutions at time $t = 60$.

very steep firing rate function, and becomes progressively more nonlinear with decreasing β (right). The variation in the steepness of $f(u)$ over a relatively large parameter range shows that the encoding mechanism does not crucially depend on the fine tuning of parameters affecting the recurrent interactions. For a neural integrator to work properly, not only stimulus strength but also stimulus duration should matter. In the simulation presented in the Fig. 5, we study the influence of stimulus duration on the pattern formation. For the Amari model, as well as an increase of input strength also a prolonged input duration may overcome the additional inhibition caused by an already existing bump (left panel, compare with the simulation in Fig. 2). The 2-field model shows the same monotonic dependency of bump amplitude on duration (right panel) as for input strength (Fig. 4). In line with continuously changing task demands in dynamic environments, converging experimental evidence indicate that top-down signals

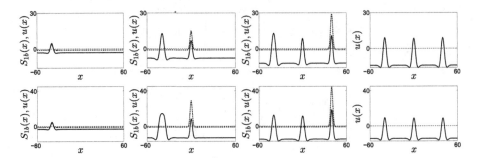

Fig. 3. Simulation of the Amari model with a sequence of three transient inputs $S_{1b}(x)$ (dashed line). In the first row, the inputs were applied at times $t_1 = 1$ (first column), $t_2 = 2$ (second column) and $t_3 = 3$ (third column). In the second row, the inputs were applied at times $t_1 = 1$ (first column), $t_2 = 17$ (second column) and $t_3 = 33$ (third column). Input parameters are $S_{s_j} \in \{5, 16, 30\}$ (first row) and $S_{s_j} \in \{5, 30, 45\}$ (second row) and stimulus duration $d_{s_j} = 1$. The fourth column shows the steady state solutions at time $t = 60$.

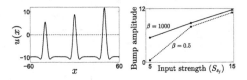

Fig. 4. Left: Steady state solution of the 2-field model with a firing rate function given by (2) with steepness parameter $\beta = 1000$. A sequence of three inputs with different strengths $S_{s_j} \in \{5, 10, 15\}$ and equal duration $d_{s_j} = 1$ was applied. Right: bump amplitude as a function of the input strength for two steepness parameter values, $\beta = 1000$ and $\beta = 0.5$.

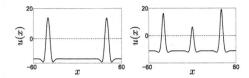

Fig. 5. Steady state solutions of the Amari model (left) and the 2-field model (right) triggered by a sequence of three inputs of different durations $d_{s_j} \in \{2.5, 1, 3\}$. The inputs are given by (5) with $S_{s_j} = 25$ (left) and $S_{s_j} = 11$ (right), applied at times $t_j \in \{1, 17, 33\}$.

can prioritize items in working memory even after encoding [8]. For the working memory model this means that the bump amplitude should adapt to changing evidence at any time during the maintenance phase. Figure 6 shows this ability in a model simulation in which a steady state activity pattern consisting of three bumps of equal strength (left) is updated by new inputs arriving at later times (right).

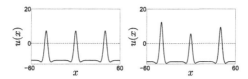

Fig. 6. Left: steady state solution of the 2-field model in response to a sequence of three inputs of equal strength $S_{s_j} = 10$ presented at times $t_j \in \{1, 2, 3\}$. Right: steady state solution of the 2-field model after the presentation of additional inputs at position $x_{c_4} = -40$ (with strength $S_{s_4} = 10$) and at position $x_{c_5} = 40$ (with strength $S_{s_5} = 5$). The inputs were applied for a duration $d_{s_j} = 1$ at times $t_4 = 20$ and $t_5 = 22$, respectively.

4 Discussion

In this paper we have incorporated a second population into Amari's one-population neural field model of lateral inhibition type. The second population integrates the activity from the first population with an inverted Mexican-hat connectivity function and projects it's activity back locally. We have shown in numerical simulations that the novel field model is able to explain input-selective persistent activity that increases monotonically with the time integral of the input. Since the sustained activity is spatially localized, the model combines the defining features of spatial and parametric working memory [15]. Moreover, the model supports a robust temporal integration of behaviorally relevant information over longer timescales.

Carroll and colleagues [3] have recently proposed a field model that also supports a continuum of possible bump amplitudes. Their model consists of separate excitatory and inhibitory populations that are intra- and interconnected with distance-dependent connectivity functions. However, the parameters of the network and the firing rate function (necessarily of piecewise linear shape) must be tuned precisely (see also [9]). In particular, the recurrent excitation must be inversely proportional to the slope of the nonlinearity to show a monotonic dependency of the bump amplitude on input strength. In contrast, the evidence of the present numerical study strongly suggests that the 2-field model is structurally stable to changes in model parameters. The lateral inhibition-type coupling function of the Amari model is known to support stable bumps over a whole range of parameter values [1,4], and significant changes in the shape of the firing rate function do not disturb parametric working memory (Fig. 4).

Motivated by specific challenges in modeling multi-item memory with dynamic fields, we have also directly compared the behavior of the full 2-field model with the behavior of the u-population alone (Amari model). The results show that the feedback from the second population is necessary to ensure a robust formation of a multi-bump solution independent of whether the inputs are presented simultaneously or sequentially.

In future work, we plan to complement the numerical analysis of the novel field model with a more rigorous analysis of bump stability and the dependence of bump amplitude on the integral of the input.

References

1. Amari, S.: Dynamics of pattern formation in lateral-inhibition type neural fields. Biol. Cybern. **27**(2), 77–87 (1977)
2. Camperi, M., Wang, X.-J.: A model of visuospatial working memory in prefrontal cortex: recurrent network and cellular bistability. J. Comput. Neurosci. **5**(4), 383–405 (1998)
3. Carroll, S., Krešimir, J., Kilpatrick, Z.P.: Encoding certainty in bump attractors. J. Comput. Neurosci. **37**(1), 29–48 (2014)
4. Coombes, S.: Waves, bumps, and patterns in neural field theories. Biol. Cybern. **93**(2), 91–108 (2005)
5. Erlhagen, W., Bastian, A., Jancke, D., Riehle, A., Schöner, G.: The distribution of neuronal population activation (DPA) as a tool to study interaction and integration in cortical representations. J. Neurosci. Meth. **94**(1), 53–66 (1999)
6. Erlhagen, W., Bicho, E.: The dynamic neural field approach to cognitive robotics. J. Neural Eng. **3**, 36–54 (2006)
7. Ferreira, F., Erlhagen, W., Bicho, E.: Multi-bump solutions in a neural field model with external inputs. Physica D **326**, 32–51 (2016)
8. Griffin, I.C., Nobre, A.C.: Orienting attention to locations in internal representations. J. Cogn. Neurosci. **15**(8), 1176–1194 (2003)
9. Koulakov, A.A., Raghavachari, S., Kepecs, A., Lisman, J.E.: Model for a robust neural integrator. Nat. Neurosci. **5**(8), 775–782 (2002)
10. Laing, C.R., Troy, W.C., Gutkin, B., Ermentrout, G.B.: Multiple bumps in a neuronal model of working memory. SIAM J. Appl. Math. **63**(1), 62–97 (2002)
11. Miller, E.K.: The prefontral cortex and cognitive control. Nat. Rev. Neurosci. **1**(1), 59–65 (2000)
12. Romo, R., Brody, C.D., Hernández, A., Lemus, L.: Neuronal correlates of parametric working memory in the prefrontal cortex. Nature **399**(6735), 470–473 (1999)
13. Salinas, E.: How behavioral constraints may determine optimal sensory representations. PLoS Biol. **4**(12), e387 (2006)
14. Schutte, A.R., Spencer, J.P., Schöner, G.: Testing the dynamic field theory: working memory for locations becomes more spatially precise over development. Child Dev. **74**(5), 1393–1417 (2003)
15. Wang, X.-J.: Synaptic reverberation underlying mnemonic persistent activity. Trends Neurosci. **24**(8), 455–463 (2001)
16. Wojtak, W., Ferreira, F., Erlhagen, W., Bicho, E.: Learning joint representations for order and timing of perceptual-motor sequences: a dynamic neural field approach. In: 2015 International Joint Conference on Neural Networks (IJCNN), pp. 3082–3088. IEEE (2015)

C4.5 or Naive Bayes: A Discriminative Model Selection Approach

Lungan Zhang[1], Liangxiao Jiang[1(✉)], and Chaoqun Li[2]

[1] Department of Computer Science, China University of Geosciences,
Wuhan 430074, Hubei, China
ljiang@cug.edu.cn
[2] Department of Mathematics, China University of Geosciences,
Wuhan 430074, Hubei, China

Abstract. C4.5 and naive Bayes (NB) are two of the top 10 data mining algorithms thanks to their simplicity, effectiveness, and efficiency. It is well known that NB performs very well on some domains, and poorly on others that involve correlated features. C4.5, on the other hand, typically works better than NB on such domains. To integrate their advantages and avoid their disadvantages, many approaches, such as model insertion and model combination, are proposed. The model insertion approach such as NBTree inserts NB into each leaf of the built decision tree. The model combination approach such as C4.5-NB builds C4.5 and NB on a training dataset independently and then combines their prediction results for an unseen instance. In this paper, we focus on a new view and propose a discriminative model selection approach. For detail, at the training time, C4.5 and NB are built on a training dataset independently, and the most reliable one is recorded for each training instance. At the test time, for each test instance, we firstly find its nearest neighbor and then choose the most reliable model for its nearest neighbor to predict its class label. We simply denote the proposed algorithm as C4.5‖NB. C4.5‖NB retains the interpretability of C4.5 and NB, but significantly outperforms C4.5, NB, NBTree, and C4.5-NB.

Keywords: Model selection · C4.5 · naive Bayes · The nearest neighbor

1 Introduction and Related Work

Classification is one of the fundamental problems in data mining, in which a learner attempts to construct a classifier from a given set of training instances with class labels. Given an unseen instance x, represented by an attribute vector $< a_1, a_2, \cdots, a_m >$, the constructed probability-based classifier classifies x into the class $\hat{c}(x)$ with the maximum class membership probability $\hat{P}(c|x)$:

$$\hat{c}(x) = \arg\max_{c \in C} \hat{P}(c|x) \tag{1}$$

where C is a set of all possible values of class c, $\hat{P}(c|x)$ is the estimated class membership probability of x, and $\hat{c}(x)$ is the estimated class value of x.

© Springer International Publishing Switzerland 2016
A.E.P. Villa et al. (Eds.): ICANN 2016, Part I, LNCS 9886, pp. 419–426, 2016.
DOI: 10.1007/978-3-319-44778-0_49

Naive Bayes (NB) is a typical probability-based classifier, which uses Eq. 2 to estimate its class membership probabilities.

$$\hat{P}(c|x) = \frac{\hat{P}(c) \prod_{j=1}^{m} \hat{P}(a_j|c)}{\sum_c \hat{P}(c) \prod_{j=1}^{m} \hat{P}(a_j|c)}, \tag{2}$$

where the prior probability $\hat{P}(c)$ with Laplace smoothing is defined using Eq. 3, and the conditional probability $\hat{P}(a_j|c)$ with Laplace smoothing is defined using Eq. 4.

$$\hat{P}(c) = \frac{\sum_{i=1}^{n} \delta(c_i, c) + 1}{n + n_c}, \tag{3}$$

$$\hat{P}(a_j|c) = \frac{\sum_{i=1}^{n} \delta(a_{ij}, a_j)\delta(c_i, c) + 1}{\sum_{i=1}^{n} \delta(c_i, c) + n_j}, \tag{4}$$

where n is the number of training instances, n_c is the number of classes, c_i is the class label of the ith training instance, n_j is the number of values of the jth attribute, a_{ij} is the jth attribute value of the ith training instance, a_j is the jth attribute value of the test instance, and $\delta(\bullet)$ is a binary function, which is one if its two parameters are identical and zero otherwise.

Because of its easiness to construct and interpret, along with its good performance, it is widely used to address classification problems and has been one of the top 10 algorithms in data mining [1]. However, it is well known that NB performs poorly on the domains that involve correlated features [2] and its classification performance does not scale up as well as decision trees in some large databases [3].

C4.5 [4] is another top 10 algorithm in data mining [1] due to its simplicity, effectiveness, efficiency, and interpretability. However, the splitting process of C4.5 easily suffers from the fragmentation problem. That is, when the partitioning process continues, there is no enough instances on a leaf node, which has been proved to produce poor performance of class probability estimation. In order to alleviate this problem, Eq. 5 with Laplace smoothing [5] is used to estimate its class membership probabilities.

$$\hat{P}(c|x) = \frac{\sum_{i=1}^{k} \delta(c_i, c) + 1}{k + n_c} \tag{5}$$

where k is the number of training instances in the leaf node that x falls into.

It can be seen that NB performs very well on some domains, and poorly on others that involve correlated features. C4.5, on the other hand, typically works better than NB on such domains. To integrate their advantages and avoid their disadvantages, many approaches, such as model insertion and model combination, are proposed. The model insertion approach such as NBTree [3] inserts NB into each leaf of the built decision tree. The model combination approach such as C4.5-NB [6] builds C4.5 and NB on a training dataset independently and then combines their prediction results for an unseen instance.

In this paper, we focus on a new view and propose a discriminative model selection approach. For detail, at the training time, C4.5 and NB are built on a training dataset independently, and the most reliable one is recorded for each training instance. At the test time, for each test instance, we firstly find its nearest neighbor and then choose the most reliable model for its nearest neighbor to predict its class label. We simply denote the proposed algorithm as C4.5‖NB. C4.5‖NB retains the interpretability of C4.5 and NB, but significantly outperforms C4.5, NB, NBTree, and C4.5-NB.

The rest of this paper is organized as follows. In Sect. 2, we propose a discriminative model selection approach. In Sect. 3, we describe experimental methodology and results in detail. Finally, we draw conclusions and outline the main directions for our future work.

2   A Discriminative Model Selection Approach

In this section, we focus on a new view and propose a discriminative model selection approach. Now, let us introduce our proposed approach. At the training time, we build multiple classification models and compare their reliability for each training instance. For example, we build two classification models M1 and M2, e.g., C4.5 and NB, on a training dataset. For each training instance x, $\hat{P}_1(c|x)$ and $\hat{P}_2(c|x)$ are the class membership probabilities that the instance x belongs to each possible class c estimated by M1 and M2, respectively. Then Eqs. 6 and 7 are used to predict the class of the instance x respectively, here $\hat{c}_1(x)$ and $\hat{c}_2(x)$ denote the class value of the instance x predicted by M1 and M2, respectively.

$$\hat{c}_1(x) = \arg\max_{c \in C} \hat{P}_1(c|x) \tag{6}$$

$$\hat{c}_2(x) = \arg\max_{c \in C} \hat{P}_2(c|x) \tag{7}$$

Then, for each training instance x, how to compare the reliability of two models? Let $c(x)$ be the true class label of x and $flags(x)$ be a mark variable which indicates which model is more reliable for x. When $flags(x) = 1$, it means that the first model M1 is more reliable than M2. When $flags(x) = 2$, it means that the second model M2 is more reliable than M1. We decide the reliability of two models by comparing $c(x)$ with $\hat{c}_1(x)$ and $\hat{c}_2(x)$. There are four possible cases: the first one is that $\hat{c}_1(x) = c(x)$ and $\hat{c}_2(x) \neq c(x)$. Obviously, in this case, the first model is more reliable for the instance x and thus $flags(x) = 1$. The second one is that $\hat{c}_2(x) = c(x)$ and $\hat{c}_1(x) \neq c(x)$. In this case, the second model is more reliable for the instance x and thus $flags(x) = 2$. The third one is that both $\hat{c}_1(x)$ and $\hat{c}_2(x)$ are equal or not equal to $c(x)$, but $\hat{P}_1(c(x)|x) \geq \hat{P}_2(c(x)|x)$. In this case, we think that the first model is more reliable for the instance x and thus $flags(x) = 1$. The fourth one is that both $\hat{c}_1(x)$ and $\hat{c}_2(x)$ are equal or not equal to $c(x)$, but $\hat{P}_1(c(x)|x) < \hat{P}_2(c(x)|x)$. In this case, we think that the second model is more reliable for the instance x and thus $flags(x) = 2$.

After above training stage, two classification models have been built, and the mark array $flags$ that records the more reliable model for each training instance has been learned. At the test time, how to predict the class value of a test instance? We borrow the idea from the k-Nearest Neighbor (kNN) algorithm, which is also one of the top 10 data mining algorithms [1]. The kNN algorithm firstly finds k nearest neighbors of a test instance from the whole training instances and then classifies the test instance as the majority class of its k nearest neighbors. The kNN algorithm is in fact a local learning algorithm, and it builds different local target functions for different test instances. When the target function is very complex, the local learning technique always shows good performance. When $k = 1$, the resulting algorithm is called the 1-Nearest Neighbor (1NN) algorithm. Motivated by the 1NN algorithm, we firstly find the nearest neighbor of a test instance from the whole training instances and then choose the more reliable model of its nearest neighbor to predict its class label. That is to say, if the mark variable of its nearest neighbor is equal to 1, we use the first model to predict its class label. Otherwise, we use the second model to predict its class label.

Based on above process, our proposed approach can be divided into a training algorithm and a testing algorithm, which are described as **Algorithms** 1 and 2, respectively.

Algorithm 1. Discriminative Model Selection-Training (TD)

Input: TD-a training dataset
Output: $M1$-the first built model; $M2$-the second built model; $flags$-the learnt mark array that records the more reliable model for each training instance
1: Build $M1$ using TD
2: Build $M2$ using TD
3: **for** each training instance x **do**
4:     Use $M1$ to estimate $\hat{P}_1(c(x)|x)$
5:     Use $M2$ to estimate $\hat{P}_2(c(x)|x)$
6:     Use $M1$ to predict $\hat{c}_1(x)$
7:     Use $M2$ to predict $\hat{c}_2(x)$
8:     //Tackle the following four cases discriminatively:
9:     **if** $\hat{c}_1(x) = c(x)$ and $\hat{c}_2(x) \neq c(x)$ **then**
10:        $flags(x) = 1$
11:     **else if** $\hat{c}_2(x) = c(x)$ and $\hat{c}_1(x) \neq c(x)$ **then**
12:        $flags(x) = 2$
13:     **else if** $\hat{P}_1(c(x)|x) \geq \hat{P}_2(c(x)|x)$ **then**
14:        $flags(x) = 1$
15:     **else**
16:        $flags(x) = 2$
17:     **end if**
18: **end for**
19: Return $M1$, $M2$, and $flags$

It can be seen that our proposed approach is a meta learning approach. When we choose different base classifiers, we will get different classifiers. In this paper, we choose C4.5 and NB as two base classifiers, respectively. We simply denote the resulting algorithm as C4.5∥NB. In real-world applications, we can choose any two classifiers that can output class membership probabilities to construct a discriminative model selection algorithm in the manner above. Traditional machine learning algorithms usually train a single model to predict the class labels of all test instances. Different from those algorithms, our proposed approach chooses

---

Algorithm 2. Discriminative Model Selection-Testing $(M1, M2, flags, TD, y)$

Input: $M1$-the first built model; $M2$-the second built model; $flags$-the learnt mark array; TD-a training dataset; y-a test instance
Output: $\hat{c}(y)$-the predicted class label of y
1: Find the nearest neighbor x of y from TD
2: //Tackle the following two cases discriminatively:
3: **if** $flags(x)=1$ **then**
4:    Use $M1$ to predict $\hat{c_1}(y)$
5:    $\hat{c}(y) = \hat{c_1}(y)$
6: **else**
7:    Use $M2$ to predict $\hat{c_2}(y)$
8:    $\hat{c}(y) = \hat{c_2}(y)$
9: **end if**
10: Return $\hat{c}(y)$

---

different learning models to predict the class labels for different test instances, and the selected model is the more reliable one for a specific test instance. This is the reason why our proposed approach can always improve the classification performance compared to its competitors. The detailed experimental results in Sect. 3 validate the effectiveness of our proposed approach.

3 Experiments and Results

In this section, we design a group of experiments to validate the classification performance of our proposed algorithm C4.5‖NB. We compare it to its competitors including C4.5, NB, 1NN, NBTree, and C4.5-NB in terms of classification accuracy. We apply the existing implementations of NB, C4.5, 1NN and NBTree in the WEKA platform [7] and implement our proposed algorithm C4.5‖NB and its competitor C4.5-NB in the WEKA platform. Note that, we use Laplace smoothing [5] in C4.5 to estimate its class membership probabilities.

We ran our experiments on 36 UCI data sets [8] published on the main web site of the WEKA platform [7], which represent a wide range of domains and data characteristics. In our experiments, the classification accuracy of each algorithm on each dataset is obtained via 10 runs of 10-fold cross-validation. Runs with the various algorithms are carried out on the same training sets and evaluated on the same test sets. In particular, the cross-validation folds are the same for all experiments on each dataset. Table 1 shows the detailed classification accuracy of each algorithm on each dataset. Besides, averages are summarized at the bottom of the table. The average (arithmetic mean) across all datasets provides a gross indication of relative performance in addition to other statistics.

Then, we take advantage of KEEL Data-Mining Software Tool [9] to complete the Wilcoxon signed-ranks test [10] for comparing each pair of algorithms. The Wilcoxon signed-ranks test is a non-parametric statistical test, which ranks the differences in performances of two classifiers for each dataset, ignoring the signs, and compares the ranks for positive and negative differences. Table 2 shows the detailed ranks computed by the Wilcoxon test. In Table 2, each number below the diagonal is the sum of ranks for these datasets on which the algorithm in the row outperforms the algorithm in the corresponding column (the sum of ranks for positive differences, denoted by R^+), and each number above the diagonal

Table 1. The detailed comparison results in terms of classification accuracy (%).

Dataset	NB	C4.5	1NN	NBTree	C4.5-NB	C4.5‖NB
Anneal	86.59 ± 3.31	98.57 ± 1.04	99.13 ± 1.06	98.50 ± 1.30	98.78 ± 0.99	98.81 ± 1.03
Anneal.ORIG	75.03 ± 4.45	92.35 ± 2.53	95.45 ± 2.21	97.13 ± 2.10	94.00 ± 2.95	95.10 ± 2.00
Audiology	72.64 ± 6.10	77.26 ± 7.47	75.29 ± 7.44	76.82 ± 7.38	76.32 ± 6.49	78.56 ± 6.56
Autos	57.41 ± 10.77	81.77 ± 8.78	74.55 ± 9.40	77.82 ± 9.63	81.56 ± 8.78	79.29 ± 8.38
Balance-scale	90.53 ± 1.67	77.82 ± 3.42	78.16 ± 4.98	75.96 ± 5.16	78.41 ± 3.19	81.44 ± 3.56
Breast-cancer	72.70 ± 7.74	74.28 ± 6.05	68.58 ± 7.52	70.99 ± 7.94	71.66 ± 6.73	73.57 ± 6.81
Breast-cancer	96.07 ± 2.18	95.01 ± 2.73	95.45 ± 2.52	96.37 ± 2.15	95.77 ± 2.28	96.37 ± 2.16
Colic	78.70 ± 6.20	85.16 ± 5.91	79.11 ± 6.51	81.11 ± 6.50	83.35 ± 5.41	81.96 ± 5.79
Colic.ORIG	66.18 ± 7.93	66.31 ± 1.23	65.18 ± 7.93	68.94 ± 8.00	66.08 ± 6.91	72.19 ± 7.93
Credit-rating	77.86 ± 4.18	85.57 ± 3.96	81.57 ± 4.57	85.42 ± 4.06	84.12 ± 4.28	82.57 ± 4.75
German-credit	75.16 ± 3.48	71.25 ± 3.17	71.88 ± 3.68	74.64 ± 3.89	72.44 ± 3.47	73.18 ± 3.52
Pima-diabetes	75.75 ± 5.32	74.49 ± 5.27	70.62 ± 4.67	74.96 ± 5.09	75.79 ± 5.12	75.10 ± 4.92
Glass	49.45 ± 9.50	67.63 ± 9.31	69.95 ± 8.43	69.84 ± 9.81	68.61 ± 9.26	68.55 ± 9.66
Heart-c	83.34 ± 7.20	76.94 ± 6.59	76.06 ± 6.84	80.03 ± 6.92	80.11 ± 7.00	82.09 ± 7.27
Heart-h	83.95 ± 6.27	80.22 ± 7.95	78.33 ± 7.54	81.50 ± 6.53	84.06 ± 6.65	83.38 ± 6.95
Heart-statlog	83.59 ± 5.98	78.15 ± 7.42	76.15 ± 8.46	80.93 ± 7.19	80.26 ± 7.14	81.78 ± 6.84
Hepatitis	83.81 ± 9.70	79.22 ± 9.57	81.40 ± 8.55	81.30 ± 9.20	80.98 ± 10.74	80.15 ± 9.80
Hypothyroid	95.30 ± 0.73	99.54 ± 0.36	91.52 ± 1.16	99.59 ± 0.36	99.52 ± 0.38	99.02 ± 0.49
Ionosphere	82.17 ± 6.14	89.74 ± 4.38	87.10 ± 5.12	90.03 ± 4.72	90.63 ± 4.17	93.05 ± 3.76
Iris	95.53 ± 5.02	94.73 ± 5.30	95.40 ± 4.80	93.47 ± 5.19	95.53 ± 5.02	95.33 ± 4.69
kr-vs-kp	87.79 ± 1.91	99.44 ± 0.37	90.61 ± 1.65	97.81 ± 2.05	99.44 ± 0.37	99.05 ± 0.50
Labor	93.57 ± 10.27	78.60 ± 16.58	84.30 ± 16.24	91.63 ± 13.03	89.30 ± 12.70	91.77 ± 11.21
Letter	64.07 ± 0.91	88.03 ± 0.71	95.99 ± 0.41	86.77 ± 0.77	88.31 ± 0.71	88.16 ± 0.65
Lymphography	83.13 ± 8.89	75.84 ± 11.05	81.54 ± 8.48	81.90 ± 9.78	78.46 ± 9.70	82.31 ± 8.37
Mushroom	95.76 ± 0.73	100.00 ± 0.00	100.00 ± 0.00	100.00 ± 0.00	100.00 ± 0.00	100.00 ± 0.02
Primary-tumor	49.71 ± 6.46	41.39 ± 6.94	34.64 ± 7.07	47.50 ± 6.49	45.49 ± 6.71	48.30 ± 6.67
Segment	80.17 ± 2.12	96.79 ± 1.29	97.15 ± 1.11	95.23 ± 1.43	96.36 ± 1.29	96.15 ± 1.28
Sick	92.75 ± 1.36	98.72 ± 0.55	96.10 ± 0.92	97.88 ± 0.71	98.45 ± 0.62	98.49 ± 0.68
Sonar	67.71 ± 8.66	73.61 ± 9.34	86.17 ± 8.45	77.11 ± 0.33	74.49 ± 9.52	78.91 ± 9.20
Soybean	92.94 ± 2.92	91.78 ± 3.19	90.17 ± 3.29	92.87 ± 3.07	93.54 ± 2.70	93.16 ± 2.95
Splice	95.41 ± 1.18	94.03 ± 1.30	75.97 ± 2.07	95.40 ± 1.18	95.83 ± 1.00	95.76 ± 1.11
Vehicle	44.68 ± 4.59	72.28 ± 4.32	69.59 ± 3.77	70.98 ± 4.72	72.41 ± 4.49	72.73 ± 4.06
Vote	90.02 ± 3.91	96.57 ± 2.56	92.23 ± 3.95	95.03 ± 3.29	96.32 ± 2.72	93.17 ± 3.56
Vowel	62.90 ± 4.38	80.20 ± 4.36	99.05 ± 1.04	92.35 ± 3.02	80.78 ± 4.39	85.14 ± 3.85
Waveform	80.01 ± 1.45	75.25 ± 1.90	73.41 ± 1.82	79.84 ± 2.18	76.44 ± 1.79	79.79 ± 1.67
Zoo	94.97 ± 5.86	92.61 ± 7.33	96.55 ± 5.34	94.73 ± 6.72	95.48 ± 6.11	96.93 ± 4.61
Average	79.37	83.37	82.62	84.79	84.42	85.31

is the sum of ranks for these datasets on which the algorithm in the column is worse than the algorithm in the corresponding row (the sum of ranks for negative differences, denoted by R^-). According to the table of exact critical values for the Wilcoxon test, for a confidence level of $\alpha = 0.05$ and $N = 36$ data sets, we speak of two classifiers as being "significantly different" if the smaller of R^+ and R^- is equal or less than 208 and thus we reject the null-hypothesis. Table 3 summarizes the comparison results of the Wilcoxon test. In Table 3, • indicates that the algorithm in the row significantly outperforms the algorithm in the corresponding column.

Table 2. Ranks computed by the Wilcoxon test.

Algorithm	NB	C4.5	1NN	NBTree	C4.5-NB	C4.5‖NB
NB	-	214.0	287.0	165.0	162.0	128.5
C4.5	452.0	-	412.5	210.5	144.5	124.5
1NN	379.0	253.5	-	157.5	173.5	139.0
NBTree	501.0	455.5	508.5	-	343.5	190.0
C4.5-NB	504.0	521.5	492.5	322.5	-	207.5
C4.5‖NB	537.5	541.5	527.0	476.0	458.5	-

Table 3. Summary of the Wilcoxon test.

Algorithm	NB	C4.5	1NN	NBTree	C4.5-NB	C4.5‖NB
NB	-					
C4.5		-				
1NN			-			
NBTree	●		●	-		
C4.5-NB	●	●	●		-	
C4.5‖NB	●	●	●	●	●	-

From these experimental results, we can see that our discriminative model selection algorithm C4.5‖NB significantly outperforms its competitors: C4.5, NB, 1NN, NBTree, and C4.5-NB. Now, we summarize some highlights briefly as follows:

1. Our C4.5‖NB significantly outperforms three single models. C4.5‖NB outperforms NB with $R^+ = 537.5$ and $R^- = 128.5$, C4.5 with $R^+ = 541.5$ and $R^- = 124.5$, and 1NN with $R^+ = 527.0$ and $R^- = 139.0$. The smallers of each pair of R^+ and R^- are all much less than 208, and thus the differences between C4.5‖NB and NB, C4.5, and 1NN are all significant. Additionally, the averaged classification accuracy of C4.5‖NB (85.31 %) is also much higher than those of NB (79.37 %), C4.5 (83.37 %), and 1NN (82.62 %).
2. Our C4.5‖NB is markedly better than other two hybrid models. C4.5‖NB outperforms NBTree with $R^+ = 476.0$ and $R^- = 190.0$, and C4.5-NB with $R^+ = 458.5$ and $R^- = 207.5$. The smallers of each pair of R^+ and R^- are all less than 208, and thus the differences between C4.5‖NB and NBTree and C4.5-NB are all significant. Additionally, the averaged classification accuracy of C4.5‖NB (85.31 %) is also higher than those of NBTree (84.79 %) and C4.5-NB (84.42 %).
3. Seen from above comparison results, our C4.5‖NB is overall the best one among all these algorithms used to compare. That is to say, our proposed discriminative model selection approach is effective, and is even better than the existing model insertion and model combination approaches.

4   Conclusions and Future Work

C4.5 and naive Bayes (NB) are two of the top 10 data mining algorithms thanks to their simplicity, effectiveness, and efficiency. To integrate their advantages and avoid their disadvantages, many approaches, such as model insertion and model combination, are proposed. However, all these approaches always try to train a single model to predict all test instances' class labels. In this paper, we focus on a new view and propose a discriminative model selection approach. Our proposed approach discriminatively chooses different single models (C4.5 or NB) for different test instances. We simply denote the proposed algorithm as C4.5‖NB. C4.5‖NB retains the interpretability of C4.5 and NB, but significantly outperforms its competitors: C4.5, NB, 1NN, NBTree, and C4.5-NB.

Future work has two primary points. The first point is that, our current version only builds two models (C4.5 and NB) using a training dataset. In fact, our approach can be extended to build more models at the training time. This is a main research direction for our future work. In addition, our current version requires that the selected base classifiers can output class membership probabilities, and thus how to adapt it to decision bound-based classifiers is another research direction for our future work.

Acknowledgments. This work was partially supported by the National Natural Science Foundation of China (61203287), the Program for New Century Excellent Talents in University (NCET-12-0953), and the Chenguang Program of Science and Technology of Wuhan (2015070404010202).

References

1. Wu, X., Kumar, V., Quinlan, J.R.: Top 10 algorithms in data mining. Knowl. Inf. Syst. **14**(1), 1–37 (2008)
2. Ratanamahatana, C.A., Gunopulos, D.: Feature selection for the naive bayesian classifier using decision trees. Appl. Artif. Intell. **17**, 475–487 (2003)
3. Kohavi, R.: Scaling up the accuracy of naive-bayes classifiers: a decision-tree hybrid. In: Proceedings of the Second International Conference on Knowledge Discovery and Data Mining, pp. 202–207. ACM (1996)
4. Quinlan, J.R.: C4.5: Programs for Machine Learning, 1st edn. Morgan Kaufmann, San Mateo (1993)
5. Provost, F., Domingos, P.: Tree induction for probability-based ranking. Mach. Learn. **52**, 199–215 (2003)
6. Jiang, L., Li, C.: Scaling up the accuracy of decision-tree classifiers: a naive-Bayes combination. J. Comput. **6**(7), 1325–1331 (2011)
7. Witten, I.H., Frank, E., Hall, M.A., Mining, D.: Practical Machine Learning Tools and Techniques, 3rd edn. Morgan Kaufmann, Burlington (2011)
8. Frank, A., Asuncion, A.: UCI machine learning repository. Department of Information and Computer Science, University of California, Irvine (2010)
9. Alcalá-Fdez, J., Fernandez, A., Luengo, J., Derrac, J., García, S., Sánchez, L., Herrera, F.: Keel data-mining software tool: data set repository, integration of algorithms and experimental analysis framework. J. Multiple-Valued Logic Soft Comput. **17**(2–3), 255–287 (2011)
10. Demsar, J.: Statistical comparisons of classifiers over multiple data sets. J. Mach. Learn. Res. **7**, 1–30 (2006)

Adaptive Natural Gradient Learning Algorithms for Unnormalized Statistical Models

Ryo Karakida[1]([⊠]), Masato Okada[1,2], and Shun-ichi Amari[2]

[1] The University of Tokyo, 5-1-5 Kashiwanoha, Kashiwa, Chiba 277-8561, Japan
karakida@mns.k.u-tokyo.ac.jp, okada@k.u-tokyo.ac.jp
[2] RIKEN Brain Science Institute, 2-1 Hirosawa, Wako, Saitama 351-0198, Japan
amari@brain.riken.jp

Abstract. The natural gradient is a powerful method to improve the transient dynamics of learning by utilizing the geometric structure of the parameter space. Many natural gradient methods have been developed for maximum likelihood learning, which is based on Kullback-Leibler (KL) divergence and its Fisher metric. However, they require the computation of the normalization constant and are not applicable to statistical models with an analytically intractable normalization constant. In this study, we extend the natural gradient framework to divergences for the unnormalized statistical models: score matching and ratio matching. In addition, we derive novel adaptive natural gradient algorithms that do not require computationally demanding inversion of the metric and show their effectiveness in some numerical experiments. In particular, experimental results in a multi-layer neural network model demonstrate that the proposed method can escape from the plateau phenomena much faster than the conventional stochastic gradient descent method.

Keywords: Natural gradient · Score matching · Ratio matching · Unnormalized statistical model · Multi-layer neural network

1   Introduction

The natural gradient method was invented to accelerate the steepest gradient descent learning by using underlying Riemannian parameter space [1,2]. Many natural gradient methods have been developed with regards to Kullback-Leibler (KL) divergence and its Riemannian metric, Fisher information matrix, and succeeded in practical applications. In particular, for training multi-layer perceptrons, the natural gradient has been superior to other methods such as second-order optimization because it can avoid or alleviate the plateau phenomena [3,4]. However, the natural gradient methods based on KL divergence are hard to apply to models with an analytically intractable normalization constant. The computation of the normalization constant requires some approximation of the object function or computationally demanding sampling approaches such as Markov chain Monte Carlo method.

© Springer International Publishing Switzerland 2016
A.E.P. Villa et al. (Eds.): ICANN 2016, Part I, LNCS 9886, pp. 427–434, 2016.
DOI: 10.1007/978-3-319-44778-0_50

To avoid computing the normalization constant, alternative divergences have been developed such as score matching [5] and ratio matching [6]. For training unnormalized models with continuous random variables, score matching has been successfully applied to various practical applications such as signal processing [5] and representation learning for visual and acoustic data [7]. We can also train single-layer neural network models [8,9] or two-layer ones including the analytically intractable normalization constants [7]. For training those with binary random variables, ratio matching was also invented as an extension of the score matching [6]. The object functions of score matching and ratio matching are usually optimized by the conventional steepest gradient decent algorithm. If we can extend the natural gradient framework to score matching or ratio matching divergences, it will improve the transient dynamics of the learning.

In this study, we first derive the Riemannian metric of score matching and propose its natural gradient learning. In particular, we propose adaptive natural gradient algorithms that do not require computationally demanding inversion of the metric. Moreover, we also derive the metric and adaptive algorithms for the ratio matching. In numerical experiments, we show that the proposed adaptive algorithms can converge faster than the conventional steepest gradient descent. In particular, experimental results in a multi-layer neural network model demonstrated that it can escape from the plateau region much faster than the conventional one.

2   Score Matching and Its Natural Gradient

The score matching measures a difference between two probability distributions $q(\mathbf{x})$ and $p(\mathbf{x})$ by the squared distance between derivatives of the log-density,

$$D_{SM}[q:p] = \int d\mathbf{x} q(\mathbf{x}) \sum_i |\partial_i \log q(\mathbf{x}) - \partial_i \log p(\mathbf{x})|^2, \tag{1}$$

where we denote the derivative with respect to the i-th random variable as a partial derivative symbol $\partial_i = \frac{\partial}{\partial x_i}$. This derivative makes it possible to avoid computing the normalization constant. In this paper, we refer to this objective function (1) as score matching (SM) divergence. Its Riemannian metric and natural gradient are derived as below.

2.1   Riemannian Metric of Score Matching

As is known in information geometry, we can derive the Riemannian structure from any divergence [2,10]. Let us consider a parametric probability distribution $p(\mathbf{x}; \boldsymbol{\xi})$. When we estimate the parameter $\boldsymbol{\xi}$ with a divergence $D[q:p]$, its parameter space has the Riemannian metric matrix G defined by $D[p(\mathbf{x}; \boldsymbol{\xi}) : p(\mathbf{x}; \boldsymbol{\xi} + d\boldsymbol{\xi})] = \sum_{i,j} G_{ij} d\xi_i d\xi_j$. The metric matrix G can be obtained by the second derivative, i.e., $G_{ij} = \frac{\partial^2}{\partial \xi'_i \partial \xi'_j} D[p(\mathbf{x}; \boldsymbol{\xi}) : p(\mathbf{x}; \boldsymbol{\xi}')]\big|_{\boldsymbol{\xi}'=\boldsymbol{\xi}}$.

When we consider the SM divergence, we can derive its metric as the following positive semi-definite matrix,

$$G = \sum_i < \nabla \partial_i \log p(\mathbf{x}; \boldsymbol{\xi}) \nabla \partial_i \log p(\mathbf{x}; \boldsymbol{\xi})^T >_{p(\mathbf{x};\boldsymbol{\xi})}, \tag{2}$$

where we denote the derivative with regard to a parameter vector $\boldsymbol{\xi}$ as $\nabla = \frac{\partial}{\partial \boldsymbol{\xi}}$ and the average over a probability distribution p as $< \cdot >_p$. Note that, when we consider KL divergence, $D_{KL}[q : p] = \int d\mathbf{x} q(\mathbf{x}) \log \frac{q(\mathbf{x})}{p(\mathbf{x})}$, its metric becomes the Fisher information matrix, i.e., $G = < \nabla \log p(\mathbf{x}; \boldsymbol{\xi}) \nabla \log p(\mathbf{x}; \boldsymbol{\xi})^T >_{p(\mathbf{x};\boldsymbol{\xi})}$. In contrast to the Fisher metric, which is composed of the derivatives of the log likelihood, the score matching metric is composed of those differentiated with respect to ∂_i.

2.2   Adaptive Natural Gradient of Score Matching

Taking the Riemannian structure of an objective function into consideration, one can find the steepest direction of parameter space by natural gradient learning [1,2]. The natural gradient update is written as

$$\boldsymbol{\xi}_{t+1} = \boldsymbol{\xi}_t - \eta_t G_t^{-1} \nabla L_t, \tag{3}$$

where $\boldsymbol{\xi}_t$ is the parameter at time step t and η_t is a learning rate that may depend on t. In the case of score matching, the objective function L_t is defined by $L_t = D_{SM}[q(\mathbf{x}) : p(\mathbf{x}; \boldsymbol{\xi}_t)]$, where we denote an input data distribution as $q(\mathbf{x})$ and a model distribution with learning parameter $\boldsymbol{\xi}$ as $p(\mathbf{x}; \boldsymbol{\xi})$. After straightforward calculation, this objective function can be transformed into $L_t = < l(\mathbf{x}; \boldsymbol{\xi}_t) >_{q(\mathbf{x})} + const.$ with $l(\mathbf{x}; \boldsymbol{\xi}) = \sum_i \left\{ \frac{1}{2} (\partial_i \log p(\mathbf{x}; \boldsymbol{\xi}))^2 + \partial_i^2 \log p(\mathbf{x}; \boldsymbol{\xi}) \right\}$ [5]. In this study, we compute the natural gradient in the form of online learning algorithm where $L_t = l(\mathbf{x}_t; \boldsymbol{\xi}_t)$, and where each data sample $\mathbf{x}_t$ is independently generated from $q(\mathbf{x})$.

The inversion of metric (2) at time step t defined by G_t^{-1} is approximately obtained as below. In general, the exact analytical calculation of metric (2) may be intractable, because it requires the average over the unnormalized statistical model, i.e., $< \cdot >_{p(\mathbf{x};\boldsymbol{\xi}_t)}$. Here, let us approximate the average over $p(\mathbf{x}; \boldsymbol{\xi}_t)$ by empirical expectation,

$$G \sim \sum_i < \nabla f_i(\mathbf{x}; \boldsymbol{\xi}) \nabla f_i(\mathbf{x}; \boldsymbol{\xi})^T >_{q(\mathbf{x})}, \tag{4}$$

where we define a score function by $f_i(\mathbf{x}; \boldsymbol{\xi}) = \partial_i \log p(\mathbf{x}; \boldsymbol{\xi})$. If the input data is generated by a true model distribution $q(\mathbf{x}) = p(\mathbf{x}; \boldsymbol{\xi}^*)$ and the learning parameter $\boldsymbol{\xi}_t$ converges to the true value $\boldsymbol{\xi}^*$, the approximated metric over the input data is asymptotically equivalent to the exact metric.

In addition, we introduce an adaptive method to calculate the inversion of empirical metric (4), because the inversion of the matrix demands much computational time in practice. Similar to the derivation of the adaptive natural gradient on KL divergence [3], we consider the online update of the metric,

$$G_{t+1} = (1 - \varepsilon_t)G_t + \varepsilon_t \sum_i \nabla f_i(\mathbf{x}_t; \boldsymbol{\xi}_t) \nabla f_i(\mathbf{x}_t; \boldsymbol{\xi}_t)^T. \tag{5}$$

When a learning rate ε_t is small enough, we may approximate the inversion G_{t+1}^{-1} by using an approximation formula $(A + \varepsilon B)^{-1} \sim A^{-1} - \varepsilon A^{-1} B A^{-1}$ and obtain the adaptive update rule of the inverted metric,

$$G_{t+1}^{-1} = (1 + \varepsilon_t)G_t^{-1} - \varepsilon_t G_t^{-1} \sum_i \nabla f_i(\mathbf{x}_t; \boldsymbol{\xi}_t) \nabla f_i(\mathbf{x}_t; \boldsymbol{\xi}_t)^T G_t^{-1}. \tag{6}$$

Note that, when there are N input dimensions x_j $(j = 1, ..., N)$ and K parameter dimensions ξ_j $(j = 1, ..., K)$, the computational complexity at every update step becomes $O(NK^2)$.

In this paper, we also propose another adaptive algorithm with less computational complexity than (6). The ordinary online update of the metric (5) is composed from the summation over all the score functions f_i $(i = 1, ..., N)$. In contrast, we may asynchronously update the contribution of each score function as follows:

$$G_{t+1} = (1 - \varepsilon_t)G_t + \varepsilon_t \nabla f_{i(t)}(\mathbf{x}_t; \boldsymbol{\xi}_t) \nabla f_{i(t)}(\mathbf{x}_t; \boldsymbol{\xi}_t)^T, \tag{7}$$

where the index number $i(t)$ is randomly chosen from $\{1, 2, ..., N\}$ at every time step t. The inversion of (7) leads to

$$G_{t+1}^{-1} = (1 + \varepsilon_t)G_t^{-1} - \varepsilon_t G_t^{-1} \nabla f_{i(t)}(\mathbf{x}_t; \boldsymbol{\xi}_t) \nabla f_{i(t)}(\mathbf{x}_t; \boldsymbol{\xi}_t)^T G_t^{-1}. \tag{8}$$

Let us refer to update rule (6) as an adaptive natural gradient (ANG) learning algorithm and (8) as an asynchronous adaptive natural gradient (A-ANG) learning algorithm. The computational complexity $O(NK^2)$ in ANG learning is reduced to $O(K^2)$ in A-ANG learning. Numerical experiments in Sect. 4 demonstrate that A-ANG learning can converge faster than ANG learning.

3   Ratio Matching and Its Natural Gradient

Our framework to derive the adaptive natural gradient learning algorithms for score matching in Sect. 2 is also applicable to the case of ratio matching. In ratio matching, the score function is changed from the derivative of the log-density to a nonlinear function of the density ratio [6]. The objective function of ratio matching is given by

$$D_{RM}[q : p] = \sum_{\mathbf{x}} q(\mathbf{x}) \sum_i |g\left(q(\mathbf{x})/q(\bar{\mathbf{x}}_i)\right) - g\left(p(\mathbf{x})/p(\bar{\mathbf{x}}_i)\right)|^2. \tag{9}$$

We define the nonlinear function $g(x) = 1/(1+x)$ that represents a vector in which the i-th element of $\mathbf{x}$ has been flipped as $\bar{\mathbf{x}}_i$. Numerical experiments in neural network models such as Boltzmann machine [6] and restricted Boltzmann machine [11] have demonstrated that ratio matching can perform comparably to or better than maximum likelihood estimation.

In a process similar to that in the score matching, we can derive the following Riemannian metric of the ratio matching:

$$G = \sum_i \left\langle \nabla g \left(\frac{p(\mathbf{x}; \boldsymbol{\xi})}{p(\bar{\mathbf{x}}_i; \boldsymbol{\xi})} \right) \nabla g \left(\frac{p(\mathbf{x}; \boldsymbol{\xi})}{p(\bar{\mathbf{x}}_i; \boldsymbol{\xi})} \right)^T \right\rangle_{p(\mathbf{x}; \boldsymbol{\xi})}. \tag{10}$$

For update rule (3), the objective function of ratio matching is given $L_t = D_{RM}[q(\mathbf{x}) : p(\mathbf{x}; \boldsymbol{\xi}_t)]$. After straightforward calculation, one can transform this object function into $L_t = < l(\mathbf{x}; \boldsymbol{\xi}_t) >_{q(\mathbf{x})} + \quad const.$ with $l(\mathbf{x}; \boldsymbol{\xi}) = \sum_i g^2(p(\mathbf{x})/p(\bar{\mathbf{x}}_i))$ [6]. For the inversion of the metric in ratio matching, we can use ANG algorithm (6) and A-ANG algorithm (8) by substituting the score function $f_i(\mathbf{x}; \boldsymbol{\xi}) = g(p(\mathbf{x}; \boldsymbol{\xi})/p(\bar{\mathbf{x}}_i; \boldsymbol{\xi}))$.

4   Numerical Experiments

4.1   Restricted Boltzmann Machine

To confirm the performance of the proposed methods, we first conducted numerical experiments in the restricted Boltzmann machine (RBM) [11]. The model distribution of RBM is defined by $\log p(\mathbf{x}; W, \mathbf{b}, \mathbf{c}) = \sum_i \log(1 + \exp(\sum_j W_{ij}x_j + c_i)) + \mathbf{b}^T\mathbf{x} - \log Z$ with binary visible variable $\mathbf{x} = \{0, 1\}^N$ and model parameters

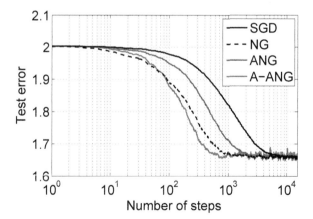

Fig. 1. Transient dynamics of ratio matching learning in RBM model: the conventional stochastic gradient descent (SGD) method, the proposed adaptive natural gradients (ANG and A-ANG), and natural gradient with exact metric (NG) are shown. Test error means the object function on test data samples.

$W \in \mathbb{R}^{N \times N}$, $\mathbf{b} \in \mathbb{R}^N$ and $\mathbf{c} \in \mathbb{R}^N$. The normalization constant Z is analytically intractable and requires the summation over 2^N states. We artificially generated 5,000 input data samples from a RBM with fixed parameters and trained another RBM by using ratio matching.

Figure 1 shows the averaged transient dynamics over 10 randomly chosen initial conditions. We set $N = 8$ and learning rates $\eta_t = 0.001$ and $\varepsilon_t = 0.5/t$. The proposed methods converged faster than the conventional stochastic gradient descent (SGD) algorithm. The update rule of SGD was given by $\boldsymbol{\xi}_{t+1} = \boldsymbol{\xi}_t - \eta_t \nabla L_t$. In the sense of the number of steps, the A-ANG learning (red line) converged much faster than ANG learning (blue line) and as fast as the exact natural gradient learning (dashed line). Note that the metric of the exact natural gradient learning, $\sum_i < \nabla f_i \nabla f_i^T >_p$, requires the summation over 2^N states at every time step. In the sense of CPU processing time, the exact natural gradient learning and A-ANG learning took the longest and shortest times to converge, respectively, among the four learning algorithms shown in Fig. 1. Therefore, we can conclude that A-ANG learning is the most efficient way to train the RBM.

We also conducted similar experiments in the score matching learning of Gaussian-Bernoulli RBM [8] by using the proposed adaptive natural gradient methods. In this case, we also confirmed that the A-ANG learning converges much faster than SGD learning.

4.2   Multi-layer Neural Network Model

Next, we trained the energy-based model of a two-layer neural network for natural stimuli proposed by Köster and Hyvärinen [7]. This model is defined by $\log p(\mathbf{x}; W, V) = \sum_h F(\mathbf{v}_h^T G(W\mathbf{x})) - \log Z(W, V)$, where the nonlinear activation functions are given by $F(u) = -\sqrt{u+1}$ and element-wise square $G(\mathbf{u}) = \mathbf{u}^2$. We denote an N-dimensional random variable as $\mathbf{x} \in \mathbb{R}^N$, an $N \times N$ weight matrix between the input and the first hidden layers as W, an $N \times N$ non-negative

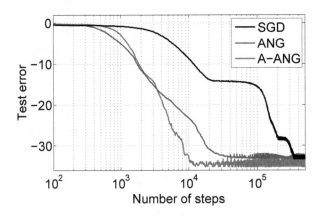

Fig. 2. Transient dynamics of score matching learning in a two-layer neural network model: Test error means the object function on test data samples.

Table 1. Averaged performance of each learning algorithm over 10 randomly chosen initial conditions.

	SGD	ANG	A-ANG
Test error (ave. $\pm$ std)	-33.21 ± 2.25	-32.14 ± 3.58	-33.84 ± 2.50
The number of steps for test error < -28	2.16×10^5	1.93×10^4	1.09×10^4
Processing time (relative to SGD)	1.0	0.34	0.18

weight matrix between the first and second hidden layers as V, and the rows of V as $\mathbf{v}_h^T$. This model trained with score matching learns responses similarly to simple cells and complex cells in the sensory cortex [7]. Note that since the normalization constant $Z(W, V)$ is given by an intractable integral, this model is difficult to train by maximum likelihood learning and its natural gradient with a Fisher metric.

In this study, we set $N = 8$ and trained the model in an unsupervised manner with 5,000 samples of eight-dimensional data artificially generated by the Independent Subspace Analysis (ISA) model [7]. We set the data vector $\mathbf{x}$ to be composed from four subspace vectors $\mathbf{s}_i \in \mathbb{R}^2$ ($i = 1, 2, 3, 4$), that is, $\mathbf{x} = A[\mathbf{s}_1\ \mathbf{s}_2\ \mathbf{s}_3\ \mathbf{s}_4]^T$, where each $\mathbf{s}_i$ is independently generated by a product between a uniform random variable and a two-dimensional random Gaussian variable, and A is a random mixing matrix. The learning rates were set to $\eta_t = 5 \times 10^{-5}$ and $\varepsilon_t = 0.5/t$. To preserve non-negativity constraint $V_{ij} \geq 0$ and make the learning trajectory more stable, we transformed the variables V_{ij} to $V_{ij} = U_{ij}^2$ ($U_{ij} \in \mathbb{R}$) without loss of generality.

As shown in Fig. 2, we found that the proposed methods converge much faster than the SGD learning. Similar to the experiments in RBMs, A-ANG learning converged faster than ANG learning. More interestingly, we revealed that ANG and A-ANG avoid the plateau caused by the singularity of the parameter space, where the transient dynamics of SGD learning become very slow. The similar superiority of the natural gradient methods to SGD has also been reported in training multi-layer perceptrons based on KL divergence and Fisher metric [4].

Table 1 lists the averaged performances of learning algorithms over ten runs with different initial values of W and V. ANG and A-ANG learning achieved the test error comparable to that of SGD learning. Until the test error became small enough, A-ANG was about 20 times faster than SGD in terms of the number of steps and more than five times faster in terms of processing time.

5 Conclusion

We have proposed novel adaptive natural gradient algorithms for score matching and ratio matching and demonstrated in numerical experiments that they accelerate the convergence of learning. In particular, we showed that they can escape from the plateau in the training of the multi-layer model. In general, nonlinear activation in multi-layer models or nonlinear transformation in hierarchical models causes the intractable normalization constant. In such models, our natural gradient methods are expected to be helpful to avoid the plateau and accelerate the convergence of learning.

In this study, we confirmed the effectiveness of our adaptive natural gradient methods in the models with a relatively small number of parameters. Deep networks with many more parameters have recently been developed, and even our adaptive method may require much computational time and memory space. Fortunately, we expect that implementations suited to large scale problems [12] such as the block diagonal approximation of the Fisher metric [13], metric-free optimization with conjugate gradients [14], or the method exploiting the structure of the metric on exponential family models [15] will also be applicable to the natural gradient with the score matching metric and ratio matching metric.

Acknowledgments. This work was supported by a Grant-in-Aid for JSPS Fellows (No. 14J08282) from the Japan Society for the Promotion of Science (JSPS).

References

1. Amari, S.-I.: Natural gradient works efficiently in learning. Neural Comput. **10**(2), 251–276 (1998)
2. Amari, S.-I.: Information Geometry and Its Applications. Springer, Japan (2016)
3. Amari, S.-I., Park, H., Fukumizu, K.: Adaptive method of realizing natural gradient learning for multilayer perceptrons. Neural Comput. **12**(6), 1399–1409 (2000)
4. Park, H., Amari, S.-I., Fukumizu, K.: Adaptive natural gradient learning algorithms for various stochastic models. Neural Netw. **13**(7), 755–764 (2000)
5. Hyvärinen, A.: Estimation of non-normalized statistical models by score matching. J. Mach. Learn. Res. 695–709 (2005)
6. Hyvärinen, A.: Some extensions of score matching. Comput. Stat. Data Anal. **51**(5), 2499–2512 (2007)
7. Köster, U., Hyvärinen, A.: A two-layer model of natural stimuli estimated with score matching. Neural Comput. **22**(9), 2308–2333 (2010)
8. Swersky, K., Ranzato, M., Buchman, D., Marlin, B.M., Freitas, N.D.: On autoencoders and score matching for energy based models. In: International Conference on Machine Learning, pp. 1201–1208 (2011)
9. Vincent, P.: A connection between score matching and denoising autoencoders. Neural Comput. **23**(7), 1661–1674 (2011)
10. Eguchi, S.: Second order efficiency of minimum contrast estimators in a curved exponential family. Ann. Stat. **11**(3), 793–803 (1983)
11. Marlin, B.M., Swersky, K., Chen, B., Freitas, N.D.: Inductive principles for restricted Boltzmann machine learning. In: International Conference on Artificial Intelligence and Statistics, pp. 509–516 (2010)
12. Pascanu, R., Bengio, Y.: Revisiting natural gradient for deep networks. arXiv preprint, arXiv:1301.3584 (2013)
13. Roux, N.L., Manzagol, P.-A., Bengio, Y.: Topmoumoute online natural gradient algorithm. In: Advances in Neural Information Processing Systems, pp. 849–856 (2008)
14. Desjardins, G., Pascanu, R., Courville, A., Bengio, Y.: Metric-free natural gradient for joint-training of boltzmann machines, arXiv preprint, arXiv:1301.3545 (2013)
15. Grosse, R., Salakhudinov, R.: Scaling up natural gradient by sparsely factorizing the inverse fisher matrix. In: International Conference on Machine Learning, pp. 2304–2313 (2015)

Octonion-Valued Neural Networks

Călin-Adrian Popa[✉]

Department of Computer and Software Engineering,
Polytechnic University Timişoara, Blvd. V. Pârvan, No. 2,
300223 Timişoara, Romania
calin.popa@cs.upt.ro

Abstract. Neural networks with values in multidimensional domains have been intensively studied over the last few years. This paper introduces octonion-valued neural networks, for which the inputs, outputs, weights and biases are all octonions. They represent a generalization of the complex- and quaternion-valued neural networks, that do not fall into the category of Clifford-valued neural networks, because, unlike Clifford algebras, the octonion algebra is not associative. The full deduction of the gradient descent algorithm for training octonion-valued feedforward neural networks is presented. Testing of the proposed network is done using two synthetic function approximation problems and a time series prediction application.

Keywords: Complex-valued neural networks · Gradient descent · Octonion-valued neural networks

1 Introduction

In the last few years, there has been an increasing interest in the study of neural networks with values in multidimensional domains. The most popular form of multidimensional neural networks are complex-valued neural networks, which were first introduced in the 1970's (see, for example, [19]), but have received more attention in the 1990's and in the past decade, because of their numerous applications, starting from those in complex-valued signal processing and continuing with applications in telecommunications and image processing (see, for example, [7,9]).

Neural networks defined on the 4-dimensional quaternion algebra gained more interest in the last few years. Quaternion-valued neural networks were also first introduced in the 1990's, in the beginning as a generalization of the complex-valued neural networks, see [1,2,10]. Later, quaternion-valued neural networks were applied to chaotic time series prediction, the 4-bit parity problem, and, recently, to quaternion-valued signal processing. Another emerging application field for these networks is 3-dimensional and color image processing, because three dimensional objects and color pixels can be represented using quaternions.

© Springer International Publishing Switzerland 2016
A.E.P. Villa et al. (Eds.): ICANN 2016, Part I, LNCS 9886, pp. 435–443, 2016.
DOI: 10.1007/978-3-319-44778-0_51

The complex and quaternion algebras are all special cases of Clifford algebras, which have dimension 2^n, $n \geq 1$. Also called geometric algebras, they have numerous applications in physics and engineering, which made them appealing for use in the field of neural networks, also. Clifford-valued neural networks were defined in [12,13], and later discussed, for example, in [3].

A generalization of the complex and quaternion numbers, the 8-dimensional octonions are not a type of Clifford algebra, because Clifford algebras are associative, whereas the octonion algebra is not. Octonions have numerous applications in physics and geometry (see [4,11]), and they have been successfully used in signal processing over the last few years (see [17]). These considerations in mind, we considered a promising idea to define neural networks with octonion values.

Octonion-valued neural networks might have interesting applications in signal processing and all other areas related to higher-dimensional objects, but they might also perform better on some n-dimensional problems than the solutions available at this time, where $n \leq 8$.

The remainder of this paper is organized as follows: Sect. 2 gives the full deduction of the gradient descent algorithm for training an octonion-valued neural network. The experimental results of three applications of the proposed algorithm are shown and discussed in Sect. 3. Section 4 is dedicated to presenting the conclusions of the study.

2   Octonion-Valued Neural Networks

An octonion is a number defined by 8 real numbers and 8 octonion units: $x = \sum_{a=0}^{7}[x]_a e_a$, where $[x]_a$ represent the real numbers, and e_a represent the octonion units, $0 \leq a \leq 7$. The addition of octonions is defined by: $x + y = \sum_{a=0}^{7}([x]_a + [y]_a)e_a$, and the multiplication is given by the multiplication of the unit octonions given in the following table:

$\times$	e_0	e_1	e_2	e_3	e_4	e_5	e_6	e_7
e_0	e_0	e_1	e_2	e_3	e_4	e_5	e_6	e_7
e_1	e_1	$-e_0$	e_3	$-e_2$	e_5	$-e_4$	$-e_7$	e_6
e_2	e_2	$-e_3$	$-e_0$	e_1	e_6	e_7	$-e_4$	$-e_5$
e_3	e_3	e_2	$-e_1$	$-e_0$	e_7	$-e_6$	e_5	$-e_4$
e_4	e_4	$-e_5$	$-e_6$	$-e_7$	$-e_0$	e_1	e_2	e_3
e_5	e_5	e_4	$-e_7$	e_6	$-e_1$	$-e_0$	$-e_3$	e_2
e_6	e_6	e_7	e_4	$-e_5$	$-e_2$	e_3	$-e_0$	$-e_1$
e_7	e_7	$-e_6$	e_5	e_4	$-e_3$	$-e_2$	e_1	$-e_0$

Octonions form a non-associative real algebra denoted by $\mathbb{O}$. The conjugate of an octonion x is defined by $\bar{x} = [x]_0 e_0 - \sum_{a=1}^{7}[x]_a e_a$. The norm of an octonion can be defined as $|x| = \sqrt{x\bar{x}} = \sqrt{\sum_{a=0}^{7}[x]_a^2}$, and the inverse of an octonion as $x^{-1} = \frac{\bar{x}}{|x|^2}$. Thus, the octonions are a normed division algebra, unlike the 8-dimensional Clifford algebras, which are associative algebras, but not division algebras. In fact, the complex, quaternion, and octonion algebras are the only three division algebras that can be defined over the reals.

In what follows, we will define feedforward neural networks for which the inputs, outputs, weights, and biases are all from $\mathbb{O}$, which means that they are octonions. Let's assume we have a fully connected feedforward neural network with values from $\mathbb{O}$, with L layers, where 1 is the input layer, L is the output layer, and the layers denoted by $\{2, \ldots, L-1\}$ are hidden layers. The error function $E : \mathbb{O}^N \to \mathbb{R}$ for such a network is

$$E(\mathbf{w}) = \frac{1}{2} \sum_{i=1}^{c} (y_i^L - t_i)\overline{(y_i^L - t_i)}, \tag{1}$$

where $\overline{y}$ is the conjugate of the octonion y. $\mathbf{y}^L = (y_i^L)_{1 \leq i \leq c} \in \mathbb{O}^c$ represents the vector of outputs of the network, $\mathbf{t} = (t_i)_{1 \leq i \leq c} \in \mathbb{O}^c$ represents the vector of targets of the network, and $\mathbf{w} \in \mathbb{O}^N$ represents the vector of the N weights and biases of the network, all being vectors whose components are octonions.

If we denote by $w_{jk}^l \in \mathbb{O}$ the weight connecting neuron j from layer l with neuron k from layer $l-1$, for all $l \in \{2, \ldots, L\}$, we can define the update step of weight w_{jk}^l in epoch t as being $\Delta w_{jk}^l(t) = w_{jk}^l(t+1) - w_{jk}^l(t)$. With this notation, the gradient descent method has the following update rule for the weight $w_{jk}^l \in \mathbb{O}$: $\Delta w_{jk}^l(t) = -\varepsilon \left(\sum_{a=0}^{7} \frac{\partial E}{\partial [w_{jk}^l]_a}(t) e_a \right)$, where ε is a real number representing the learning rate, and we denoted by $\frac{\partial E}{\partial [w_{jk}^l]_a}(t)$ the partial derivative of the error function E with respect to each element $[w_{jk}^l]_a$ of the octonion $w_{jk}^l \in \mathbb{O}$, where $0 \leq a \leq 7$. Thus, we need to compute the partial derivatives $\frac{\partial E}{\partial [w_{jk}^l]_a}(t)$. For this, we will make the following notations

$$s_j^l = \sum_k w_{jk}^l x_k^{l-1}, \tag{2}$$

$$y_j^l = G^l(s_j^l), \tag{3}$$

where Eq. (2) shows that the multiplication from the real-valued case is replaced by the octonion multiplication, G^l represents the activation function for the layer $l \in \{2, \ldots, L\}$, $\mathbf{x}^1 = (x_k^1)_{1 \leq k \leq d} \in \mathbb{O}^d$ is the vector of inputs of the network, and we have that $x_k^l := y_k^l$, $\forall l \in \{2, \ldots, L-1\}$, $\forall k$, because x_k^1 are the inputs, y_k^L are the outputs, and $y_k^l = x_k^l$ are the outputs of layer l, which are also inputs to layer $l+1$. The activation function is considered to be defined element-wise. For instance, for the octonion $x = \sum_{a=0}^{7} [x]_a e_a$, an example of activation function is the element-wise hyperbolic tangent function defined by $G \left(\sum_{a=0}^{7} [x]_a e_a \right) = \sum_{a=0}^{7} (\tanh[x]_a) e_a$.

We will first compute the update rule for the weights between layer $L-1$ and output layer L, i.e. $\Delta w_{jk}^L(t) = -\varepsilon \left(\sum_{a=0}^{7} \frac{\partial E}{\partial [w_{jk}^L]_a} e_a \right)$. Using the chain rule, we can write $\forall 0 \leq a \leq 7$:

$$\frac{\partial E}{\partial [w_{jk}^L]_a} = \sum_{b=0}^{7} \frac{\partial E}{\partial [s_j^L]_b} \frac{\partial [s_j^L]_b}{\partial [w_{jk}^L]_a}. \tag{4}$$

To compute $\frac{\partial [s_j^L]_b}{\partial [w_{jk}^L]_a}$, we need an explicit formula for $[s_j^L]_b$, which can be easily deduced from (2): $[s_j^L]_b = \left[\sum_k w_{jk}^L x_k^{L-1} \right]_b$, $\forall 0 \le b \le 7$. Now, we can easily see that

$$\frac{\partial [s_j^L]_b}{\partial [w_{jk}^L]_a} = \frac{\partial \left[\sum_k w_{jk}^L x_k^{L-1} \right]_b}{\partial [w_{jk}^L]_a} = \frac{\partial [w_{jk}^L x_k^{L-1}]_b}{\partial [w_{jk}^L]_a}. \tag{5}$$

Using the fact that $w_{jk}^L x_k^{L-1} = \sum_{0 \le c,d \le 7} [w_{jk}^L]_c [x_k^{L-1}]_d e_c e_d$, Eq. (5) can be written as

$$\frac{\partial [s_j^L]_b}{\partial [w_{jk}^L]_a} = \frac{\partial \left[\sum_{0 \le c,d \le 7} [w_{jk}^L]_c [x_k^{L-1}]_d e_c e_d \right]_b}{\partial [w_{jk}^L]_a} = \frac{\partial \left(\sum_{\substack{0 \le c,d \le 7 \\ \kappa_{c,d} e_c e_d = e_b}} \kappa_{c,d} [w_{jk}^L]_c [x_k^{L-1}]_d \right)}{\partial [w_{jk}^L]_a}$$

$$= \kappa_{a,d} [x_k^{L-1}]_d, \; \kappa_{a,d} e_a e_d = e_b, \; \kappa_{a,d} \in \{\pm 1\}.$$

So, relation (4) can be written in the form

$$\frac{\partial E}{\partial [w_{jk}^L]_a} = \sum_{\substack{0 \le b \le 7 \\ \kappa_{a,d} e_a e_d = e_b}} \frac{\partial E}{\partial [s_j^L]_b} \kappa_{a,d} [x_k^{L-1}]_d. \tag{6}$$

Next, by denoting $\delta_j^L := \frac{\partial E}{\partial s_j^L}$, we have from the chain rule that $[\delta_j^L]_b = \frac{\partial E}{\partial [s_j^L]_b} = \sum_{0 \le e \le 7} \frac{\partial E}{\partial [y_j^L]_e} \frac{\partial [y_j^L]_e}{\partial [s_j^L]_b}$, $\forall 0 \le b \le 7$. Taking into account notation (3), and the expression of the error function given in (1), we have that

$$[\delta_j^L]_b = \sum_{0 \le e \le 7} ([y_j^L]_e - [t_j]_e) \frac{\partial [G^L(s_j^L)]_e}{\partial [s_j^L]_b} = ([y_j^L]_b - [t_j]_b) \frac{\partial [G^L(s_j^L)]_b}{\partial [s_j^L]_b},$$

$\forall 0 \le b \le 7$, because $[G^L(s_j^L)]_e$ depends upon $[s_j^L]_b$ only for $e = b$, which means that $\frac{\partial [G^L(s_j^L)]_e}{\partial [s_j^L]_b} = 0$, $\forall e \ne b$. If we denote by $\odot$ the element-wise multiplication of two octonions, the above relation gives

$$\delta_j^L = (y_j^L - t_j) \odot \frac{\partial G^L(s_j^L)}{\partial s_j^L}, \tag{7}$$

where $\frac{\partial G^L(s_j^L)}{\partial s_j^L}$ represents the octonion of element-wise derivatives of the activation function G^L. For instance, if $x = \sum_{a=0}^{7} [x]_a e_a \in \mathbb{O}$, then $\frac{\partial G(x)}{\partial x} = \sum_{a=0}^{7} \left(\text{sech}^2 [x]_a \right) e_a$, with the function G defined as in the above example.

Finally, from (6), we get the expression for the desired update rule in the form: $\Delta w_{jk}^L(t) = -\varepsilon \delta_j^L x_k^{L-1}$, where the octonion $\delta_j^L \in \mathbb{O}$ is given by relation (7).

Now, we will compute the update rule for an arbitrary weight w_{jk}^l, where $l \in \{2, \ldots, L-1\}$. First, we can write that $\Delta w_{jk}^l(t) = -\varepsilon \left(\sum_{a=0}^7 \frac{\partial E}{\partial [w_{jk}^l]_a} e_a \right)$, and then, from the chain rule, we have that

$$\frac{\partial E}{\partial [w_{jk}^l]_a} = \sum_{0 \leq b \leq 7} \frac{\partial E}{\partial [s_j^l]_b} \frac{\partial [s_j^l]_b}{\partial [w_{jk}^l]_a}. \tag{8}$$

$\forall 0 \leq a \leq 7$. Applying the chain rule again, we obtain that

$$\frac{\partial E}{\partial [s_j^l]_b} = \sum_r \sum_{0 \leq c \leq 7} \frac{\partial E}{\partial [s_r^{l+1}]_c} \frac{\partial [s_r^{l+1}]_c}{\partial [s_j^l]_b}, \tag{9}$$

$\forall 0 \leq b \leq 7$, where the sum is taken over all neurons r in layer $l+1$ to which neuron j from layer l sends connections. Next, we can write that $\frac{\partial [s_r^{l+1}]_c}{\partial [s_j^l]_b} = \sum_{0 \leq d \leq 7} \frac{\partial [s_r^{l+1}]_c}{\partial [y_j^l]_d} \frac{\partial [y_j^l]_d}{\partial [s_j^l]_b}$, $\forall 0 \leq b, c \leq 7$. Again from (2), we can compute

$$\frac{\partial [s_r^{l+1}]_c}{\partial [y_j^l]_d} = \frac{\partial \left[\sum_j w_{rj}^{l+1} y_j^l \right]_c}{\partial [y_j^l]_d} = \frac{\partial [w_{rj}^{l+1} y_j^l]_c}{\partial [y_j^l]_d}. \tag{10}$$

From $w_{rj}^{l+1} y_j^l = \sum_{0 \leq e, f \leq 7} [w_{rj}^{l+1}]_e [y_j^l]_f e_e e_f$, Eq. (10) can be written as

$$\frac{\partial [s_r^{l+1}]_c}{\partial [y_j^l]_d} = \frac{\partial \left[\sum_{0 \leq e, f \leq 7} [w_{rj}^{l+1}]_e [y_j^l]_f e_e e_f \right]_c}{\partial [y_j^l]_d} = \frac{\partial (\sum_{\substack{0 \leq e, f \leq 7 \\ \kappa_{e,f} e_e e_f = e_c}} \kappa_{e,f} [w_{rj}^{l+1}]_e [y_j^l]_f)}{\partial [y_j^l]_d}$$

$$= \kappa_{e,d} [w_{rj}^{l+1}]_e, \ \kappa_{e,d} e_e e_d = e_c, \ \kappa_{e,d} \in \{\pm 1\},$$

and then

$$\frac{\partial [s_r^{l+1}]_c}{\partial [s_j^l]_b} = \sum_{0 \leq d \leq 7} \kappa_{e,d} [w_{rj}^{l+1}]_e \frac{\partial [G^l(s_j^l)]_d}{\partial [s_j^l]_b} = \kappa_{e,b} [w_{rj}^{l+1}]_e \frac{\partial [G^l(s_j^l)]_b}{\partial [s_j^l]_b}, \ \kappa_{e,b} e_e e_b = e_c,$$

$\forall 0 \leq b, c \leq 7$, where again we took into account the fact that $\frac{\partial [G^l(s_j^l)]_d}{\partial [s_j^l]_b} = 0$, $\forall d \neq b$. Now, returning to Eq. (9), and putting it all together, we have that

$$\frac{\partial E}{\partial [s_j^l]_b} = \sum_r \sum_{\substack{0 \leq c \leq 7 \\ \kappa_{e,b} e_e e_b = e_c}} \frac{\partial E}{\partial [s_r^{l+1}]_c} \kappa_{e,b} [w_{rj}^{l+1}]_e \frac{\partial [G^l(s_j^l)]_b}{\partial [s_j^l]_b} = \sum_r \left(\sum_{\substack{0 \leq c \leq 7 \\ \kappa_{e,b} e_e e_b = e_c}} \frac{\partial E}{\partial [s_r^{l+1}]_c} \right.$$

$$\left. \cdot \kappa_{e,b} [w_{rj}^{l+1}]_e \frac{\partial [G^l(s_j^l)]_b}{\partial [s_j^l]_b} \right) = \sum_r [\overline{w_{rj}^{l+1}} \delta_r^{l+1}]_b \frac{\partial [G^l(s_j^l)]_b}{\partial [s_j^l]_b},$$

$\forall 0 \leq b \leq 7$. By denoting $\delta_j^l := \frac{\partial E}{\partial s_j^l}$, we can write the above relation in the form

$$\delta_j^l = \left(\sum_r \overline{w_{rj}^{l+1}} \delta_r^{l+1} \right) \odot \frac{\partial G^l(s_j^l)}{\partial s_j^l}. \tag{11}$$

Finally, taking into account the fact that $\frac{\partial [s_j^l]_b}{\partial [w_{jk}^l]_a} = \kappa_{a,d}[x_k^{l-1}]_d$, $\kappa_{a,d}e_a e_d = e_b$, relation (8) becomes $\frac{\partial E}{\partial [w_{jk}^l]_a} = \sum_{\substack{0 \leq b \leq 7 \\ \kappa_{a,d}\overline{e}_a \overline{e}_d = e_b}} \frac{\partial E}{\partial [s_j^l]_b} \kappa_{a,d}[x_k^{l-1}]_d = [\delta_j^l \overline{x_k^{l-1}}]_a$, $\forall 0 \leq a \leq 7$. Thus, the update rule for the weight w_{jk}^l can be written in octonion form in the following way: $\Delta w_{jk}^l(t) = -\varepsilon \delta_j^l \overline{x_k^{l-1}}$, which is similar to the formula we obtained for the layer L.

To summarize, we have the following formula for the update rule of the weight w_{jk}^l:

$$\Delta w_{jk}^l(t) = -\varepsilon \delta_j^l \overline{x_k^{l-1}}, \ \forall l \in \{2, \ldots, L\},$$

where

$$\delta_j^l = \begin{cases} \left(\sum_r \overline{w_{rj}^{l+1}} \delta_r^{l+1} \right) \odot \frac{\partial G^l(s_j^l)}{\partial s_j^l}, & l \leq L-1 \\ (y_j^l - t_j) \odot \frac{\partial G^l(s_j^l)}{\partial s_j^l}, & l = L \end{cases}.$$

3   Experimental Results

3.1   Synthetic Function Approximation Problem I

The first function we will test the proposed algorithm on is the simple quadratic function $f_1(o_1, o_2) = \frac{1}{6}(o_1^2 + o_2^2)$. This function was used to test the performance of different complex-valued neural network architectures and learning algorithms, for example in [14, 16, 18], and so we decided to test the octonion-valued algorithms on it, also.

For training of the octonion-valued neural network, we generated 1500 octonion training samples with random elements between 0 and 1. The testing set contained 500 samples generated in the same way. The network had 15 neurons on a single hidden layer. The activation function for the hidden layer was the element-wise hyperbolic tangent function given by $G^2 \left(\sum_{a=0}^7 [x]_a e_a \right) = \sum_{a=0}^7 (\tanh[x]_a) e_a$, and for the output layer, the activation function was the identity function: $G^3(S) = S$.

The experiment showed that the neural network converges, and the mean squared error (MSE) for the training set was 0.000733 and for the test set was 0.000651. Training was done for 5000 epochs. Although the result is not spectacular, we must take into account the fact that each octonion is formed of 8 real numbers.

3.2 Synthetic Function Approximation Problem II

A more complicated example, which involves four input variables and the reciprocal of one of the variables, is given by the following function: $f_2(o_1, o_2, o_3, o_4) = \frac{1}{1.5}\left(o_3 + 10o_1o_4 + \frac{o_2^2}{o_1}\right)$, which was used as a benchmark in [15, 16] for complex-valued neural networks, so we used it for octonion-valued neural networks, also. The training and testing sets were randomly generated octonions with elements between 0 and 1, 1500 for the training set, and 500 for the test set. The activation functions were the same as the ones above. The architecture had 15 neurons on a single hidden layer, and the network was trained for 5000 epochs.

In this experiment, the training and testing MSE had similar values, and equal approximately with 0.0071. The performance is worse than the one obtained in the previous experiment, but in this case, the function was more complicated. These results give reasons for hope that in the future these networks can be optimized to perform better on octonion-valued function approximation problems.

3.3 Linear Time Series Prediction

A possible application of octonion-valued neural networks is in signal processing. A known benchmark proposed in [8], and used in [5, 6, 20] for complex-valued neural networks, is the prediction of the white noise $n(k)$, passed through the stable autoregressive filter given by $y(k) = 1.79y(k-1) - 1.85y(k-2) + 1.27y(k-3) - 0.41y(k-4) + n(k)$. In the octonion setting, the octonion-valued white noise $n(k)$ is given by $n(k) = \sum_{a=0}^{7}[n(k)]_a e_a$, where $[n(k)]_a \sim \mathcal{N}(0, 1)$, $\forall 0 \le a \le 7$.

The tap input of the filter was 4, so the networks had 4 inputs, 4 hidden neurons on a single hidden layer, and one output. The activation function for the hidden layer was the element-wise hyperbolic tangent function and for the output layer was the identity. Training was done for 5000 epochs with 2500 training samples.

We use a measure of performance called *prediction gain*, defined by $R_p = 10\log_{10}\frac{\sigma_x^2}{\sigma_e^2}$, where σ_x^2 represents the variance of the input signal and σ_e^2 represents the variance of the prediction error. The prediction gain is given in dB. It is obvious that, because of the way it is defined, a bigger prediction gain means better performance. The network obtained a prediction gain of 0.485.

4 Conclusions

The full deduction of the gradient descent algorithm for training octonion-valued feedforward neural networks was presented. Octonion-valued neural networks are a generalization of the complex- and quaternion-valued neural networks, that do not fall under the category of Clifford-valued neural networks. Because the octonions are not a Clifford algebra, but are a division algebra, we considered a promising subject to study neural networks with values in this algebra, also.

Two synthetic function approximation problems, and a linear time series prediction application were used to test the octonion-valued gradient descent algorithm. The performance of the networks in terms of training and testing mean squared error and prediction gain, although not spectacular, was promising, leaving place for future developments in the topic of octonion-valued neural networks.

The present work represents another step done towards a more general framework for neural networks, which could benefit not only from increasing the number of hidden layers and making the architecture ever more complicated, but also from increasing the dimensionality of the data that is being handled by the network.

References

1. Arena, P., Fortuna, L., Muscato, G., Xibilia, M.: Multilayer perceptrons to approximate quaternion valued functions. Neural Netw. **10**(2), 335–342 (1997)
2. Arena, P., Fortuna, L., Occhipinti, L., Xibilia, M.: Neural networks for quaternion-valued function approximation. In: International Symposium on Circuits and Systems (ISCAS), vol. 6, pp. 307–310. IEEE (1994)
3. Buchholz, S., Sommer, G.: On clifford neurons and clifford multi-layer perceptrons. Neural Netw. **21**(7), 925–935 (2008)
4. Dray, T., Manogue, C.: The Geometry of the Octonions. World Scientific (2015)
5. Goh, S., Mandic, D.: A complex-valued rtrl algorithm for recurrent neural networks. Neural Comput. **16**(12), 2699–2713 (2004)
6. Goh, S., Mandic, D.: An augmented crtrl for complex-valued recurrent neural networks. Neural Netw. **20**(10), 1061–1066 (2007)
7. Hirose, A.: Complex-Valued Neural Networks, Studies in Computational Intelligence, vol. 400. Springer, Heidelberg (2012)
8. Mandic, D., Chambers, J.: Recurrent Neural Networks for Prediction: Learning Algorithms, Architectures and Stability. Wiley, New York (2001)
9. Mandic, D., Goh, S.: Complex Valued Nonlinear Adaptive Filters Noncircularity, Widely Linear and Neural Models. Wiley, New York (2009)
10. Nitta, T.: A quaternary version of the back-propagation algorithm. In: International Conference on Neural Networks, pp. 2753–2756. No. 5, IEEE (1995)
11. Okubo, S.: Introduction to Octonion and Other Non-Associative Algebras in Physics. Cambridge University Press, Cambridge (1995)
12. Pearson, J., Bisset, D.: Back propagation in a clifford algebra. In:International Conference on Artificial Neural Networks, vol. 2, pp. 413–416 (1992)
13. Pearson, J., Bisset, D.: Neural networks in the clifford domain. In: International Conference on Neural Networks, vol. 3, pp. 1465–1469. IEEE (1994)
14. Savitha, R., Suresh, S., Sundararajan, N.: A fully complex-valued radial basis function network and its learning algorithm. Int. J. Neural Syst. **19**(4), 253–267 (2009)
15. Savitha, R., Suresh, S., Sundararajan, N.: A meta-cognitive learning algorithm for a fully complex-valued relaxation network. Neural Netw. **32**, 209–218 (2012)
16. Savitha, R., Suresh, S., Sundararajan, N., Saratchandran, P.: A new learning algorithm with logarithmic performance index for complex-valued neural networks. Neurocomputing **72**(16–18), 3771–3781 (2009)

17. Snopek, K.M.: Quaternions and octonions in signal processing - fundamentals and some new results. Przeglad Telekomunikacyjny + Wiadomosci Telekomunikacyjne **6**, 618–622 (2015)
18. Suresh, S., Savitha, R., Sundararajan, N.: A sequential learning algorithm for complex-valued self-regulating resource allocation network-csran. IEEE Trans. Neural Netw. **22**(7), 1061–1072 (2011)
19. Widrow, B., McCool, J., Ball, M.: The complex LMS algorithm. Proc. IEEE **63**(4), 719–720 (1975)
20. Xia, Y., Jelfs, B., Van Hulle, M., Principe, J., Mandic, D.: An augmented echo state network for nonlinear adaptive filtering of complex noncircular signals. IEEE Trans. Neural Netw. **22**(1), 74–83 (2011)

Reducing Redundancy with Unit Merging for Self-constructive Normalized Gaussian Networks

Jana Backhus[1(✉)], Ichigaku Takigawa[1,2], Hideyuki Imai[1], Mineichi Kudo[1], and Masanori Sugimoto[1]

[1] Department of Computer Science and Information Technology,
Graduate School of Information Science and Technology, Hokkaido University,
Kita 14 Nishi 9, Kita-ku, Sapporo 060-0814, Japan
`jana@main.ist.hokudai.ac.jp`
[2] JST PRESTO, 4-1-8 Honcho, Kawaguchi, Saitama 332-0012, Japan

Abstract. In this paper, a Normalized Gaussian Network (NGnet) is introduced for online sequential learning that uses unit manipulation mechanisms to build the network model self-constructively. Several unit manipulation mechanisms have been proposed for online learning of an NGnet. However, unit redundancy still exists in the network model. We propose a merge mechanism for such redundant units, and change its overlap calculation in order to improve the identification accuracy of redundant units. The effectiveness of the proposed approach is demonstrated in a function approximation task with balanced and imbalanced data distributions. It succeeded in reducing the model complexity around 11 % on average while keeping or even improving learning performance.

Keywords: Normalized Gaussian Networks · Self-constructive model adaptation · Redundancy reduction

1 Introduction

In applications where data samples are received sequentially, incremental learning schemes have to be applied to train neural networks. In truly sequential learning schemes [10], only one data sample is observed at any time and directly discarded after learning. So, no prior knowledge is available on the number of training data or the data distribution. Furthermore, training data is often not independent and identically distributed (i.i.d.) in real world applications. This can be a problem since neural network models are generally changed in favor of newly arriving training data. If the data distribution is not i.i.d., then networks are prone to forget already learned information. When this phenomenon is not wanted, it is called negative or in severe cases catastrophic interference.

Normalized Gaussian networks (NGnet) are feed-forward three layer neural networks that are related to Radial Basis Function (RBF) networks. They have localized learning behavior by partitioning the input space with local units.

© Springer International Publishing Switzerland 2016
A.E.P. Villa et al. (Eds.): ICANN 2016, Part I, LNCS 9886, pp. 444–452, 2016.
DOI: 10.1007/978-3-319-44778-0_52

Then, only a few units are updated for a newly received data sample. Local model networks are often applied to sequential learning schemes, because their model structure eases the effects of negative interference. NGnets differ from RBF networks in the normalization of the Gaussian activation function. The normalization switches the traditional roles of weights and activities in the hidden layer, and NGnets therefore exhibit better generalization properties [1].

An online learning approach has been proposed for the NGnet's parameter estimation by Celaya and Agostini [2] that provides robust learning performance even for non i.i.d. data. While this learning approach considers only network parameter estimation, network model selection is yet another problem. One solution is self-constructive model adaptation that builds a network model from scratch during learning. This avoids the selection of an initial model complexity. For the NGnet, unit manipulation mechanisms have been proposed [9], including unit production, deletion and splitting. We can adapt these mechanisms and apply it self-constructively to the used method. However, none of these mechanisms considers unit redundancy. Redundancy refers to two local units approximating a similar partition of the input-output-space. In this paper, we propose a merge manipulation mechanism in order to reduce redundancies by merging similar units. In addition, we revise the overlap calculation for the output space to improve the identification accuracy of redundant units. The effectiveness of the proposed method is demonstrated in a function approximation task with balanced and imbalanced data distributions. The newly added merge mechanism reduces the model complexity around 11 % on average while keeping or even improving learning performance in test cases where up to 95 % of the sample data are concentrated in a small sub-region of the whole input space.

2 Normalized Gaussian Network

The Normalized Gaussian network (NGnet) is a universal function approximator that was first proposed by Moody and Darken [7]. The NGnet approximates a mapping $f : \mathbb{R}^N \to \mathbb{R}^D$ from an N-dimensional input space to a D-dimensional output space, where an input vector x is transformed to an output vector y with

$$y = \sum_{i=1}^{M} N_i(x) \tilde{W}_i \tilde{x}. \qquad (1)$$

Here, M is the number of units, $\tilde{x}$ is an $(N+1)$-dimensional input vector with $\tilde{x}' \equiv (x', 1)$, and $\tilde{W}_i$ is a $D \times (N+1)$-dimensional linear regression matrix. Normalized Gaussian functions are used as activation functions, and $N_i(x)$ is the normalized output of the i-th multivariate Gaussian probability density function (pdf). The model then softly partitions the input space into local units i.

A stochastic interpretation of the NGnet has been first proposed by Xu et al. [11]. The model parameters are then estimated by maximum likelihood learning based on the log-likelihood of the observed in- and output data (x, y).

The Expectation-Maximization (EM) algorithm is used for parameter estimation, and an offline approach has been proposed by Xu et al. that was later adapted to an online EM-algorithm by Sato and Ishii [9]. Celaya and Agostini [2] have further improved the approach to achieve robust learning performance in regard to negative interference.

For the online EM-algorithm, the stochastic model is defined by a probability distribution $P(x, y, i|\theta)$, where $\theta \equiv \{\mu_i, \Sigma_i, \sigma_i^2, \tilde{W}_i | i = 1, ..., M\}$ is the set of model parameters that have to be estimated. Here, μ_i and Σ_i are the center and covariance matrix of the i-th Gaussian pdf, and $\sigma_i^2(t)$ is an output variance for the i-th unit. The parameters are updated incrementally for every time step t:

$$\mu_i(t) = \langle\langle x \rangle\rangle_i(t) / \langle\langle 1 \rangle\rangle_i(t) \tag{2}$$

$$\Sigma_i^{-1}(t) = [\langle\langle xx' \rangle\rangle_i(t) / \langle\langle 1 \rangle\rangle_i(t) - \mu_i(t)\mu_i'(t)]^{-1} \tag{3}$$

$$\tilde{W}_i(t) = \langle\langle y\tilde{x}' \rangle\rangle_i(t)[\langle\langle \tilde{x}\tilde{x}' \rangle\rangle_i(t)]^{-1} \tag{4}$$

$$\sigma_i^2(t) = \frac{[\langle\langle |y|^2 \rangle\rangle_i(t) - Tr(\tilde{W}_i(t)\langle\langle \tilde{x}y' \rangle\rangle_i(t))]}{D\langle\langle 1 \rangle\rangle_i(t)} \tag{5}$$

These parameter updates include a symbol $\langle\langle \cdot \rangle\rangle_i$ that denotes a weighted accumulator and is defined by the following step-wise equation

$$\langle\langle f(x, y) \rangle\rangle_i(t) = \Lambda_i(t)\langle\langle f(x, y) \rangle\rangle_i(t - 1) + \Omega_i(t)f(x(t), y(t)). \tag{6}$$

Here, $\Lambda_i(t)$ is a forgetting factor determining how much old training results are forgotten at time t; $\Omega_i(t)$ is an update factor influencing how much each unit i learns about the newly received data sample $(x(t), y(t))$. Celaya and Agostini have proposed a new update approach with localized forgetting [2]. This approach ensures that only as much old information is forgotten as new information is received for a unit i. The forgetting factor is set to $\Lambda_i(t) = \lambda(t)^{P_i(t)}$, and the update factor is $\Omega_i(t) = \frac{1-\lambda(t)^{P_i(t)}}{1-\lambda(t)}$. The factors include a posterior probability $P_i(t) \equiv P(i|x(t), y(t), \theta) = \frac{P(x,y,i|\theta)}{\sum_{j=1}^{M} P(x,y,j|\theta)}$ functioning as a weight and a discount factor $\lambda(t)$. The discount factor $\lambda(t)$ has to be chosen so that $\lambda \to 1$ when $t \to \infty$ for fulfilling the Robbins-Monro condition for convergence of stochastic approximations. $\lambda(t)$ plays an important role in discarding the effect of old learning results that were employed to an earlier inaccurate estimator.

3   Network Model Selection

In the following, we discuss network model selection, another problem that arises especially for the application of NGnets to sequential learning problems. It is difficult to choose an accurate network model complexity and initialization of model parameters without incorporating domain knowledge. Learning results can be highly dependent on a good initialization, but an accurate model selection by hand needs excessive trial-and-error studies. One solution is a dynamic adaptation of the network model during learning. This avoids the need of setting the model complexity in advance. Model adaptation is executed with some methods to increase or reduce model complexity. These methods can also be applied self-constructively to build the model from scratch during learning which has the advantage that the initialization problem is avoided. Several works for RBF networks have proposed self-constructive unit adaptation, Platt's Resource Allocating Network (RAN) [8] as well as its extensions (RANEKF [5], MRAN [6]) and the GGAP-RBF network that has been proposed by Huang et al. [4].

3.1   Unit Manipulation Mechanisms

Some unit manipulation mechanisms have been introduced for the NGnet [9] and are adapted in this paper to use with the localized forgetting approach proposed by Celaya and Agostini [2]. Previously, dynamic model selection was not considered for the localized forgetting approach. The adapted unit manipulation mechanisms include a produce, delete and split mechanism. In addition, we propose a merge mechanism to reduce redundancy of units and further improve model compactness.

Produce. $P(x(t), y(t)|\theta(t-1))$ is the probability that indicates how properly the current model parameters $\theta(t-1)$ can estimate the newly received data sample $(x(t), y(t))$. When the probability is smaller than a certain threshold $T_{Produce}$, a new unit is created according to the produce mechanism in [9].

Delete. A weighted accumulator of one $\langle\!\langle 1 \rangle\!\rangle_i(t)$ indicates how much the i-th unit has been in charge of the observed data until the current time step t. When the delete mechanism has been first proposed in [9], it was assumed that $\langle\!\langle 1 \rangle\!\rangle_i(t)$ is a weighted mean scaled between zero and one. In the applied local forgetting approach, $\langle\!\langle 1 \rangle\!\rangle_i(t)$ is however a weighted sum which is not scaled and therefore cannot be used directly as a reference. We introduce a local unit update counter c_{update} as a normalizer to overcome this problem. The update counter is incremented by one at every time step where the unit's update is numerically important. In other words, when the update factor is $\Omega_i(t) > 10^{-16}$, c_{update} is incremented. A unit is deleted if $\langle\!\langle 1 \rangle\!\rangle_i(t)/c_{update} < T_{Delete}$ with delete threshold T_{Delete}.

Split. The output variance of a unit i, $\sigma_i^2(t)$, represents the accumulated squared error between the unit's predictions and the real outputs. High variance values are related to the unit being in charge of a too large partition of the input space, and splitting such units can improve learning performance. Our split decision compares $\sigma_i^2(t)$ to the output variances of the other units using a local evaluation where only output variances of some nearest neighbors are considered. When the unit's output variance is considerably bigger than the biggest variance of its neighbors, the unit is split according to the split mechanism in [9].

Merge. In the following, we introduce the main contribution of this paper, a merge manipulation mechanism, that is an important addition to reduce redundancy in the network model. Redundancy means here that two network units overlap so much that they are approximating almost the same partition of the input-output-space. For finding possible merge candidates, the grade of overlap between units has to be evaluated over the input and output space. Similar to a merge approach discussed in [3], we use the Bhattacharyya Coefficient (BC) to measure the overlap between two multivariate Gaussian distributions $G_1(\mu_1, \Sigma_1)$ and $G_2(\mu_2, \Sigma_2)$. In case of Gaussian distributions, a closed form solution for the BC exists as stated below

$$d_B(G_1, G_2) = \frac{1}{8} \cdot (\mu_1 - \mu_2)' \Sigma^{-1} (\mu_1 - \mu_2) + \frac{1}{2} \cdot log \frac{|\Sigma|}{\sqrt{|\Sigma_1| \cdot |\Sigma_2|}} \tag{7}$$

$$BC(G_1, G_2) = \exp\left(-d_B(G_1, G_2)\right) \tag{8}$$

Here, d_B is the Bhattacharyya distance and $\Sigma = (\Sigma_1 + \Sigma_2)/2$. For a similarity $S(i, j)$ between two units i and j, we have to calculate the overlap of the units's input and output pdfs. Suppose, the input pdf of a unit i is $G_i^{input}(\mu_i, \Sigma_i)$ and the output pdf is $G_i^{output}(\tilde{W}_i \tilde{x}, \sigma_i^2 I)$. The similarity $S(i, j)$ is then calculated by

$$S(i, j) = BC(G_i^{input}, G_j^{input}) \cdot BC(G_i^{output}, G_j^{output}). \tag{9}$$

If $S(i, j) > T_{Merge}$ with a threshold T_{Merge}, then the units are possible merge candidates. The flow of the merge mechanism is described in the following:

1. Calculate the similarity $S(i, j)$ for all pairs $\{i, j\}$.
2. Choose the pair $\{i_{max}, j_{max}\}$ with maximal similarity.
3. If $S(i_{max}, j_{max}) > T_{Merge}$ then merge units into one and go to step 1.
4. Otherwise, stop routine.

The merge mechanism is computationally heavy, especially when the network model complexity M is high. Furthermore, it is unnecessary to apply merge at every time step t, because merge candidates are not found that frequently. Intervals of a few hundred time steps are sufficient. Yet, a new problem arises when applying merge in intervals, because the calculation of the output BC depends on input x for the output center $\tilde{W}_i \tilde{x}$. A calculation of similarities using current input $x(t)$, in the form $\tilde{x}'(t) \equiv (x(t), 1)'$, is therefore inappropriate since the calculated similarities depend on and change with $x(t)$. Preliminary experiments showed that this can lead to an underestimation of similarity, for example when $x(t)$ and the units are in different parts of the input space. A possible alternative would be to use the weighted sum $\langle\!\langle \tilde{x} \rangle\!\rangle_i'(t) \equiv (\langle\!\langle x \rangle\!\rangle_i(t), \langle\!\langle 1 \rangle\!\rangle_i(t))'$, however preliminary experiments showed that this approach is overestimating the similarity between the output distributions. Especially the first term of d_B becomes very small due to the output center. Therefore, we revise the overlap calculation to avoid the inclusion of input x in the output center for the BC calculation.

We use a multivariate theorem applicable to Gaussian distributions to conduct an affine transformation of the output distribution. According to the theorem, a distribution $U \sim N(\mu, \Sigma)$ can be linearly transformed with a vector

c and a matrix D to a distribution $V \sim N(c + D\mu_U, D\Sigma_U D')$. Here, we want to transform the output distribution $y \sim N(\tilde{W}_i \tilde{x}, \sigma_i^2 I)$ so that input x is not included in the center of the output distribution. For convenience, we consider the transformation of the transpose $y' \sim N(\tilde{x}'\tilde{W}_i', \sigma_i^2 I)$ instead. $\tilde{W}_i$ is defined in (4), and the transpose is

$$\tilde{W}_i' = (\langle\!\langle y\tilde{x}'\rangle\!\rangle_i(t)[\langle\!\langle \tilde{x}\tilde{x}'\rangle\!\rangle_i(t)]^{-1})' = [\langle\!\langle \tilde{x}\tilde{x}'\rangle\!\rangle_i(t)]^{-1}\langle\!\langle \tilde{x}y'\rangle\!\rangle_i(t). \tag{10}$$

We then use $U = y'$, $\mu_U = \tilde{x}'\tilde{W}_i'$, $\Sigma_U = \sigma^2 I$, $V = \tilde{W}_i'$, $D = [\langle\!\langle \tilde{x}\tilde{x}'\rangle\!\rangle_i(t)]^{-1}\langle\!\langle \tilde{x}\rangle\!\rangle_i(t)$ and $c = 0$ to transform U to V.

$$\mu_V = [\langle\!\langle \tilde{x}\tilde{x}'\rangle\!\rangle_i(t)]^{-1}\langle\!\langle \tilde{x}\rangle\!\rangle_i(t)\langle\!\langle \tilde{x}'\rangle\!\rangle_i(t)\tilde{W}_i' = \tilde{W}_i' \tag{11}$$

$$\Sigma_V = [\langle\!\langle \tilde{x}\tilde{x}'\rangle\!\rangle_i(t)]^{-1}\langle\!\langle \tilde{x}\rangle\!\rangle_i(t)\sigma_i^2 I([\langle\!\langle \tilde{x}\tilde{x}'\rangle\!\rangle_i(t)]^{-1}\langle\!\langle \tilde{x}\rangle\!\rangle_i(t))' = \sigma_i^2[\langle\!\langle \tilde{x}\tilde{x}'\rangle\!\rangle_i(t)]^{-1} \tag{12}$$

So, V becomes $\tilde{W}_i' \sim N(\tilde{W}_i', \sigma_i^2[\langle\!\langle \tilde{x}\tilde{x}'\rangle\!\rangle_i(t)]^{-1})$, and input x is excluded from the output center. But $\tilde{W}_i'$ is a $(N+1) \times D$-dimensional matrix, and the left term of (7) becomes a $D \times D$-dimensional matrix dependent on the output dimension D. Therefore, we update (7) to

$$d_B(G_1, G_2) = \frac{1}{8D} \cdot Tr\left((\mu_1 - \mu_2)'\Sigma^{-1}(\mu_1 - \mu_2)\right) + \frac{1}{2} \cdot log\frac{|\Sigma|}{\sqrt{|\Sigma_1| \cdot |\Sigma_2|}}, \tag{13}$$

where Tr is the trace of the matrix.

Finally, we need to merge units when the similarity between them is higher than a threshold T_{Merge}. Again, we consider the Gaussian distributions for the input and output space and merge their center and covariances in the same matter. A new center μ_{new} and covariance Σ_{new} are calculated by

$$\mu_{new} = \omega_1\mu_1 + \omega_2\mu_2, \tag{14}$$

$$\Sigma_{new} = \sum_{i=1}^{2} \omega_i\left(\Sigma_i + (\mu_i - \mu_{new})(\mu_i - \mu_{new})'\right), \tag{15}$$

where $\omega_{1,2} = \frac{\langle\!\langle 1\rangle\!\rangle_{1,2}(t)}{\langle\!\langle 1\rangle\!\rangle_1(t)+\langle\!\langle 1\rangle\!\rangle_2(t)}$ is functioning as a weight.

4   Experiments

In order to evaluate the effectiveness of the proposed method, we compare an NGnet with merge manipulation to an NGnet without merging. We consider a commonly used function approximation task [2,9,10] to test the learning performance of the NGnets. The function has the input dimension $N = 2$, output dimension $D = 1$, and is defined by:

$$g(x_1, x_2) = \max\{e^{-10x_1^2}, e^{-50x_2^2}, 1.25e^{-5(x_1^2+x_2^2)}\}. \tag{16}$$

Also, a normally distributed random noise $\epsilon(t) \sim N(0, 0.01)$ is added to the function output $g(x(t))$, with input vector $x(t) = (x_1(t), x_2(t))$.

Then, $y(t) = g(x(t)) + \epsilon(t)$ is obtained as the noisy sample output. Four tests are conducted, one with a balanced and three with imbalanced data distributions, each applying 10,000 training data samples. For the *Balanced* test case, the training data are i.i.d for $(-1 \leq x_1, x_2 \leq 1)$. For the imbalanced test cases, non-identically distributed data are used. This means that a certain percentage of the data samples are extracted from a sub-region of the input domain with $(0 \leq x_1, x_2 \leq 0.25)$, and the remaining data are i.i.d in $(-1 \leq x_1, x_2 \leq 1)$. We have named the imbalanced test cases *ImbXX %* in our results, and three different percentages are tested with 50 %, 75 %, and 95 % of the data sampled in the sub-region. Imbalanced data distributions are applied to test the robustness of the proposed method in environments prone to negative interference. For all test cases, merge is applied after every 1,000 updates and its threshold is set to $T_{Merge} = 0.7$. The other manipulation thresholds are set to $T_{Produce} = 0.1$ and $T_{Delete} = 0.001$. The discount factor $\lambda(t)$ is updated with $\lambda(t) = 1 - \frac{0.99}{0.01t+50}$, depending on time step t.

Table 1. Experimental results

Test case	Without merge			With merge		
	RMSE	Net. size	Time (min.)	RMSE	Net. size	Time (min.)
Balanced	0.0464	53.12	0.22	0.0423	50.04	0.21
Imb50 %	0.0491	58.2	0.32	0.0475	52.66	0.27
Imb75 %	0.0565	60.96	0.35	0.0562	53.26	0.30
Imb95 %	0.0954	70.26	0.36	0.0959	59.18	0.32

The experiments are simulated on an Intel Xeon E5-2650@2 GHz, RAM 64 GB, Win7 x64 machine. Learning performance is evaluated with the Root Mean Square Error (RMSE) and the same test data set (1,000 samples) for all test cases. Obtained results are presented in Table 1 as an average over 50 test runs. Overall, merging results in a performance improvement while network model complexity is visibly reduced. Although, merge manipulation adds some extra computations, an NGnet with merging results in shorter computation times because of the reduced model complexity, and the average computation time per test run decreases in all cases. Even for the imbalanced test cases, the merge approach performs better overall despite the approximation task being more difficult. An exception is *Imb95 %*, here performance decreases slightly when merge is applied. We think, the decrease in performance is related to the cooperation of the model units when calculating an output for a received input vector. Due to the unit's cooperation, existing units need to readjust their parameters after a change in model complexity [10] to cope with the changing relationships between them. An additional merge mechanism leads to further changes of model complexity during learning. In case of imbalanced data distributions, higher sample frequencies in the sub-region lead to more overlapping units, implying more merges and resulting in more parameter readjustments. The opportunities for readjustments are however little in rarely sampled regions which may result in decreasing learning performance when additional unit manipulations by merging take place. Yet, it is worth noting that *Imb95 %* is an extreme case where 95 % of the data are sampled in the sub-region that consists only of 1.56 % of the input space. Still, performance barely decreases while model complexity is reduced largely to 84 % of the non-merge size. Overall, the performance of merge is robust and the cooperative nature of the model has almost no negative impact on the performance even in extreme cases.

5   Conclusion

In this paper, we have proposed a way of unit merging for a self-constructive NGnet in order to reduce redundancies in the network model. In addition, we have changed the overlap calculation for the output space to select redundant units more accurately. We have demonstrated the effectiveness of the proposed method for a function approximation tasks with balanced and imbalanced training data distributions. Compacter models are created with the additional merge mechanism while in most cases improving learning performance. We have considered test cases where up to 95 % of the data were sampled in a very small sub-region of the input space and model complexity was reduced around 11 % on average. Even for a strongly imbalanced data distribution, the proposed method succeeded in largely reducing the model complexity while keeping a good learning performance.

Possible future work includes the application of the proposed method to real world systems and the automation of the unit manipulation threshold parameter selection.

References

1. Bugmann, G.: Normalized Gaussian radial basis function networks. Neurocomputing **20**(1–3), 97–110 (1998)
2. Celaya, E., Agostini, A.: On-line EM with weight-based forgetting. Neural Comput. **27**(5), 1142–1157 (2015)
3. Hennig, C.: Methods for merging Gaussian mixture components. Adv. Data Anal. Classif. **4**(1), 3–34 (2010)
4. Huang, G.-B., Saratchandran, P., Sundararajan, N.: A generalized growing and pruning RBF (GGAP-RBF) neural network for function approximation. IEEE Trans. Neural Netw. **16**(1), 57–67 (2005)
5. Kadirkamanathan, V., Niranjan, M.: A function estimation approach to sequential learning with neural networks. Neural Comput. **5**(6), 954–975 (1993)
6. Lu, Y., Sundararajan, N., Saratchandran, P.: A sequential learning scheme for function approximation using minimal radial basis function neural networks. Neural Comput. **9**(2), 461–478 (1997)
7. Moody, J., Darken, C.J.: Fast learning in networks of locally-tuned processing units. Neural Comput. **1**(2), 281–294 (1989)

8. Platt, J.: A resource-allocating network for function interpolation. Neural Comput. **3**(2), 213–225 (1991)
9. Sato, M., Ishii, S.: On-line EM algorithm for the normalized Gaussian network. Neural Comput. **12**(2), 407–432 (2000)
10. Schaal, S., Atkeson, C.G.: Constructive incremental learning from only local information. Neural Comput. **10**(8), 2047–2084 (1998)
11. Xu, L., Jordan, M., Hinton, G.: An alternative model for mixtures of experts. In: Cowan, J.D., Tesauro, G., Alspector, J. (eds.) Advances in Neural Information Processing Systems, vol. 7, pp. 633–640. MIT Press, Cambridge (1995)

Learning to Enumerate

Patrick Jörger[1,2]([✉]), Yukino Baba[1], and Hisashi Kashima[1]

[1] Kyoto University, Kyoto, Japan
ufdee@student.kit.edu
[2] Karlsruhe Institute of Technology, Karlsruhe, Germany

Abstract. The Learning to Enumerate problem is a new variant of the typical active learning problem. Our objective is to find data that satisfies arbitrary but fixed conditions, without using any prelabeled training data. The key aspect here is to query as few as possible non-target data. While typical active learning techniques try to keep the number of queried labels low they give no regards to the class these instances belong to. Since the aim of this problem is different from the common active learning problem, we started with applying uncertainty sampling as a base technique and evaluated the performance of three different base learner on 19 public datasets from the UCI Machine Learning Repository.

Keywords: Active learning · Learning to enumerate · Exploration vs. exploitation · Epsilon-greedy

1 Introduction

The pervasiveness of sensors, the popularity of the web and the existence of big data repositories make it very easy to collect huge amounts of data. For that reason we have a need to analyze big data and machine learning is a promising approach that is already successfully applied. Yet in contrast with the ease of data collection, collecting annotations (such as the ground truth labels used in supervised learning) requires human input and is therefore quite costly and not scaleable. There is much effort done to reduce such annotation costs, especially active learning research tries to cut down the number of needed annotations by intelligently selecting examples to train good predictors.

Sometimes we want to find data satisfying some particular conditions and our goal is to find such data from among the whole dataset. One scenario might be to find high risk patients among a big group of people. Without existing labeled data to train a predictive model, we have to construct a training set, while finding existing high risk patients under the constraint of a limited number of checkups we can perform [3]. Another scenario could be constructing a knowledge database with implicit knowledge not covered in the documents used as a source and must be annotated by human experts. Among the high number of possible implicit knowledge we want to choose only that which is true, but because we are just constructing the knowledge database, there is no or not much data we can use

© Springer International Publishing Switzerland 2016
A.E.P. Villa et al. (Eds.): ICANN 2016, Part I, LNCS 9886, pp. 453–460, 2016.
DOI: 10.1007/978-3-319-44778-0_53

to train a predictor [4]. So the problem is to reduce the number of annotations, building a knowledge database and training a good predictive model at the same time.

The existing active learning approaches are not designed to address this problem directly, so we call this problem "learning to enumerate" and investigate approaches, mainly based on active learning, to deal with it.

In the previously mentioned work [3] they used the same approach as in this paper but limited their experiments to a Logistic Regression model with uncertainty heuristic. Their results showed for $\epsilon = 0.8$ the best and most stable performance, yet they did not attempt to broaden their experiment to other datasets. For the "dataset construction problem" [4] they do not use a ϵ-greedy like strategy but randomly sample a batch of instances and perform a scoring on them, selecting only the best few. This corresponds to the $\epsilon = 0$ case in our paper. Their experiments showed that training on a pure positive dataset results in worse performance than training on a mixed one, which indicates an $\epsilon > 0$ might be better, because it takes in some well chosen negative instances.

In this paper we use a simple ϵ-greedy like strategy testing different base learners and heuristic functions on 19 small and medium-sized, public datasets accessible through the UCI Machine Learning Repository. The best results in our experiments were shown by a RandomForest base learner with a EXPLOITATION-ONLY ($\epsilon = 0$) strategy, but the difference in performance compared to other configurations is only minimal.

2   Problem Definition

Let us assume we have an Oracle $\mathcal{O}$, that always gives us the correct label to a queried instance, and call our data set X. In each round T we choose an instance $x_T \in X$ with $x_T \neq x_t \forall t \in \{1, .., T-1\}$ and query the Oracle for the label $y_T = \mathcal{O}(x_T)$. Our objective is to find all $\tilde{X} \subseteq X$ so that $x \in \tilde{X}, \mathcal{O}(x) = y_{\text{target\_class}}$ with the least amount of rounds.

3   Approaches

If we had an extensive, labeled dataset to train our model, the best strategy would be to solely rely on its predictions to identify all instances of the target class. However, for this problem we do not have any labeled data, so we are forced to construct our training set from scratch. Yet, only selecting instances which are useful for improving our model does not necessarily comply with our goal to gather all target class instances with as few queries as possible. This is a typical exploitation vs. exploration dilemma that has been studied extensively in Reinforcement Learning. Although there are more sophisticated strategies we decided to start out by using a simple, fixed ϵ-greedy strategy [5] in our approach, where, with probability ϵ, we either explore new helpful instances with some active learning heuristic or, with probability $1 - \epsilon$, exploit the prediction of our current model to find the instance with the highest likelihood of being part of the target class (see Algorithm 1 FULLUPDATE).

We also tested a slightly different version of this approach, only adding those examples to the training set that have been selected by the heuristic (see Algorithm 1 SELECTIVEUPDATE). On one side this change was aimed to decrease the bias of the training set leaning too much towards the target class and improving the quality of the training set by not adding instances the base learner is already confident about. On the other side, this all happens at the expense of having less training data.

In active learning there are different basic heuristics we decided to use. These are uncertainty sampling, that uses the entropy function to compute the informativeness of each instance, and disagreement-based active learning with different disagreement measures. Disagreement-based active learning uses a committee of hypotheses to select those instances the committee can not agree on, hence this approach is called Query-by-Committee. The disagreement measure we applied are (hard) vote entropy and soft vote entropy, which can be seen as a committee-based generalization of uncertainty sampling, as well as the Kullback-Leibler divergence. The Kullback-Leibler divergence measures the difference between two probability distributions and in this case it is used to quantify disagreement as the average divergence of each committee members prediction from that of the consensus [2].

Algorithm 1. ϵ-active strategy

---

input: dataset X, ϵ, heuristic $\mathcal{H}$, Oracle $\mathcal{O}$

$X_{\text{train}} = \{\}$
$X_{unlabeled} = X$
Train model $\mathcal{M}$ on X_{train}
while *target class not completely separated* **do**
    if *With probability ϵ* **then**
        $x_T \leftarrow \mathcal{H}(X_{\text{unlabeled}})$
        Query $\mathcal{O}$ for the true label y_T of x_T
        Add (x_T, y_T) to X_{train} (ONLY SELECTIVEUPDATE)
    else
        Compute target class probability p_i for each instance $x_i \in X_{\text{unlabeled}}$
        using $\mathcal{M}$
        $x_T \leftarrow$ instance x_i with highest p_i
        Query $\mathcal{O}$ for the true label y_T of x_T
    end
    Remove x_T from $X_{\text{unlabeled}}$
    Add (x_T, y_T) to X_{train} (ONLY FULLUPDATE)
    Retrain $\mathcal{M}$
end

---

4   Evaluation

We compare the two algorithms with different configurations for ϵ and heuristic functions in terms of positive coverage rate under budget constraints. A configuration is then declared superior when it shows a better positive coverage rate over the complete budget and we call it a tie if there is either no difference or one method performs better for cost rate < 0.5 and another for cost rate > 0.5.

4.1   Experimental Setting

For our experiments we choose datasets to cover a variety of different criteria. The size ranges between 168 instances for the smallest and 8124 instances for the biggest dataset. The number of attributes lies between six and 168, with the majority being in the 10 to 40 attributes interval. Since the target class ratio of the dataset could have a strong impact on the performance, we also included datasets with 8 % and 79 % target class instances. We reduced any dataset with more than two classes into a binary dataset, merging all classes not being the target class into one.

The main objective of this paper is, to check the applicability of basic active learning techniques compared to a straight forward EXPLOITATION-ONLY approach. Therefore we choose following five epsilon values $\{0, 0.2, 0.5, 0.8, 1\}$ to get an idea about which side tends to be more profitable: exploitation or exploration.

The basic active learning techniques we tested are uncertainty sampling and disagreement-based active learning. We implemented Query-by-Committee with three disagreement measures: vote entropy, soft vote entropy and Kullback-Leibler (KL) divergence [2]. In order to compare and understand the general impact of those heuristic functions, random sampling was added as a base line heuristic.

In our experiments, we use RandomForest (RF), Stochastic Gradient Descent Training with LogisticRegression loss (LR) and SGD Training with the modified huber loss (HL) as different base learners to evaluate the impact of different kind of models on this problem. We choose those models for different reasons. RandomForest performs well in the general case but is especially suited for categorical input features, LR trains a linear model that may converge faster and handle a small training set better and HL trains a linear model that is more robust towards possible outliers in the dataset. As for the implementation, we used the scikit-learn framework [1]. Since we aim towards a most general investigation, we choose the hyper parameters according to the general recommandation made in the scikit-learn user guide [6]. With no initial training data, optimizing hyper parameters has to happen in the course of exploration, which would introduce new problems about expending the few training data on a cross-validation set and finding the right point to split and update the datasets.

All in all we ran 6 experiments with the following configurations for each our algorithms: For each model we run experiments with varying epsilon and fixed KL-heuristic as well as with fixed ϵ at 0.2 and varying heuristics. We choose the KL-heuristic for the varying epsilon configurations because it performed best in the initial experiments and ϵ was fixed at 0.2 for the same reasons. For each dataset we averaged across 20 iterations to compute a reliable result.

We started every experiment with a training set of one randomly sampled instance from each class. This is a implementation constraint to ensure that our model can output a probability for each class.

4.2 Comparing the Two Algorithms

In this section we compare both our algorithms with their best performing ϵ. For ϵ-ACTIVE-FULL this is $\epsilon = 0$ and for ϵ-ACTIVE-SEL it is $\epsilon = 0.2$. ϵ-ACTIVE-FULL outperforms ϵ-ACTIVE-SEL on 18 datasets and ties on the last using RF model and using LR and HL models it shows in 15 out of 19 cases better results, while going head to head on the last 4 datasets (see Table 1). This shows us that even though we may add redundant instances to our training set and shift the class balance heavily towards the target class, more low-quality training instances are more useful than few with higher quality. The class imbalance seems be mostly dealt with in the training of the model, so it holds no advantage to restrict the addition of instances based on confidence.

4.3 Comparing Different Epsilons

Figure 1 shows that for ϵ-ACTIVE-FULL the EXPLOITATION-ONLY ($\epsilon = 0$) strategy works best on this dataset. This holds true for most datasets and for all the other datasets EXPLOITATION-ONLY is at least tied with the best competitor. Even though the EXPLOITATION-ONLY strategy is always one of the best choice independent of the base learner, what changes with the base learner is the amount of datasets, where EXPLOITATION-ONLY is tied for best strategy with other ϵ values. From Table 1 you can see that the combination of RF and $\epsilon = 0$ is superior for on all datasets, while with the LR and HL model $\epsilon = 0$ is only distinguishable superior for 10 out of 19 datasets (not in Table 1).

ϵ-ACTIVE-SEL shows the same results with the difference that for ϵ-ACTIVE-SEL $\epsilon = 0.2$ is the best strategy, whereas $\epsilon = 0$ performs much worse than for ϵ-ACTIVE-FULL. This is to be expected since ϵ-ACTIVE-FULL enables $\epsilon = 0$ to add new instances to the training set after each iteration, which does not happen in ϵ-ACTIVE-SEL, where instances are only added if they were selected by the heuristic. There is also a clear trend that bigger epsilon perform gradually worse than smaller ones. While for ϵ-ACTIVE-FULL it is clear that $\epsilon = 0$ is the best option, for ϵ-ACTIVE-SEL the best epsilon value might still be in the interval of $[0, 0.2]$.

4.4 Comparing Different Heuristic Functions

We tested every base learner with fixed $\epsilon = 0.2$ for different heuristic functions. The results differ slightly between algorithms and base learners. For ϵ-ACTIVE-FULL with RandomForest uncertainty sampling, hard vote entropy and soft vote

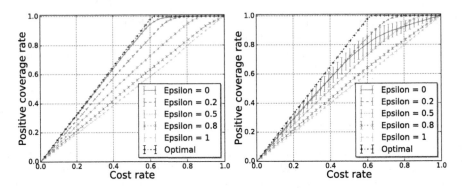

Fig. 1. RandomForest model (left: ε-ACTIVE-FULL, right: ε-ACTIVE-SEL) on the congressional voting records dataset with varying ε. For ε-ACTIVE-FULL the performance drops the higher ε gets. The same holds still true for ε-ACTIVE-SEL with the exception of ε = 0, which shows a typical good start performance that gets worse due to the constant training set. Optimal depicts the case where only target class instances are queried.

entropy proofed to be the best heuristics in 15 cases and in 4 cases random sampling outperformed all other heuristics.

In ε-ACTIVE-SEL with LR there was no heuristic that clearly performed the best. KL-heuristic was best on five datasets the same number as uncertainty sampling. Hard vote entropy, soft vote entropy and random sampling were best on two datasets each and on five data there was no distinct winner. In conclusion it is to say that which heuristic to choose strongly depends on the base learner, but the performance difference to the other heuristics is often only a small one.

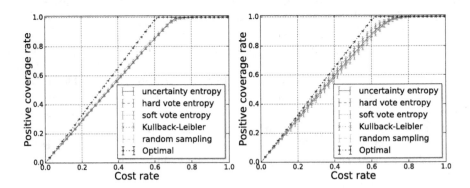

Fig. 2. Results on the congressional voting records dataset using a RandomForest model for ε-ACTIVE-FULL (LEFT) and a logistic regression model for ε-ACTIVE-SEL (RIGHT). For ε-ACTIVE-FULL random sampling (DASHED LINE WITH TRIANGLE UP MARKER) performs sometimes better than the other heuristics, while in ε-ACTIVE-SEL uncertainty sampling or KL-heuristic are in general a bit ahead.

Table 1. This table summarizes the results from our experiments. The last column states which class was selected as target class. We use following abbreviations: Full = FullUpdate, Sel = SelectiveUpdate, RF = RandomForest, LR = LogisticRegression, r = random sampling, u = uncertainty sampling, h = hard vote entropy, s = soft vote entropy, kl = Kullback-Leibler, all = all variants performed the same.

Dataset name	ϵ		Algorithm	Learner		Heuristic		Target class
	Full	Sel		Full	Sel	Full	Sel	
Annealing	0	0.2	Full	RF	RF	all	s	5
Chess (K-R vs. K-P)	0	0.2	Full	RF	LR	r	kl	won
CongressionalVotingRecords	0	0.2	Full	RF	LR	r	kl	democrat
Forest type mapping	0	0.2	Full	RF	LR	u/h/s	all	h
Horse Colic	0	0.2	Full	RF	LR	u/h/s	all	1 (outcome)
Indian Liver Patient Dataset	0	0.2	Full	RF	RF	u/h/s	all	2
Ionosphere	0	0.2	Full/Sel	RF	LR	r	u/h	g
Mammographic Mass	0	0.2	Full	RF/LR	LR	u/h/s	r	1
Mushroom	0	0.2	Full	RF/LR	LR	r	r	e
Musk (Version 2)	0	0.2	Full	RF	LR	u/h/s	u/s	1
Pima Indians Diabetes	0	0.2	Full/Sel	RF	LR	u/h/s	kl	1
Qualitative_Bankruptcy	0	0.2	Full/Sel	LR	LR	u/h/s	h	B
SPECT Heart	0	0.2	Full/Sel	RF/LR	LR	u/h/s	u	1
Statlog (German Credit Data)	0	0.2	Full	RF	all	u/h/s	kl	2
Statlog (Heart)	0	0.2	Full	RF	RF	u/h/s	kl	2
Urban Land Cover	0	0.2	Full	RF	LR	u/h/s	u	1
Red Wine Quality	0	0.2	Full	RF	LR	u/h/s	all	7
White Wine Quality	0	0.2	Full	RF	LR	u/h/s	u	7
Yeast	0	0.2	Full	RF	LR	u/h/s	all	CYT

4.5 Comparing Different Base Learners

For the reasons explained in Sect. 4.1 we included different base learner in our experiments. We use the best known ϵ for each algorithm, that is 0 for ϵ-ACTIVE-FULL and 0.2 for ϵ-ACTIVE-SEL. There is a big difference in the results between the two algorithms: For ϵ-ACTIVE-FULL RF is the best model in 18 cases and LR beats RF only on one datset and ties on three (compare Table 1 column: learner/Full). HL always performs worse than the other two.

In ϵ-ACTIVE-SEL LR shows the better general performance. In 14 cases it is superior to RF and only on 4 datasets RF is better than LR. HL ties on 8 datasets with LR but is never better.

These results suggest that RF works better with more training data even though they might be redundant or low quality. ϵ-ACTIVE-SEL seems to have not enough training set instances for RF to converge to the same level as LR. The results also show that for ϵ-ACTIVE-FULL RF is still better than LR even in the beginning, when the number of instances is still low. Again this suggest that LR seems to have problems handling the lower quality training set compared to RF.

5   Conclusion

To sum it all up, based on our results we can state the following: The configuration that performed the best is a RandomForest model, with a EXPLOITATION-ONLY strategy, adding every selected instance to the training set. We could not identify any pattern regarding class bias, number of attributes or total number of instances, that influenced certain configurations in any consistent way. Hence the classify and retrain approach beats the simple ϵ-*greedy* approach, yet the results also show that for many not so simple datasets, where we got a bad performance in general, there is still a lot of room to improve.

In this paper we only began working on this problem, for future work there is still lot unclear. One possible question is to explore even more base learner or let the base learner gradually tune their hyper parameters to better adapt to the data. Another direction would be adapting more sophisticated state-of-the-art active learning techniques, like some contextual bandit approaches, that have already proved to be superior on the more typical active learning problems.

Acknowledgments. This research was supported by the Landesstiftung Baden-Württemberg (Baden-Württemberg-STIPENDIUM) and by MEXT Grant-in-Aid for Scientific Research on Innovative Areas.

References

1. Pedregosa, F., Varoquaux, G., Gramfort, A., Michel, V., Thirion, B., Grisel, O., Blondel, M., Prettenhofer, P., Weiss, R., Dubourg, V., Vanderplas, J., Passos, A., Cournapeau, D., Brucher, M., Perrot, M., Duchesnay, E.: Scikit-learn: machine learning in Python. J. Mach. Learn. Res. **12**, 2825–2830 (2011)
2. Settles, B.: Active Learning. Synth. Lect. Artif. Intell. Mach. Learn. **6**, 1–114 (2012). Morgan & Claypool Publishers
3. Baba, Y., Kashima, H., Nohara, Y., Kai, E., Ghosh, P., Islam, R., Ahmed, A., Kuruda, M., Inoue, S., Hiramatsu, T., Kimura, M., Shimizu, S., Kobayashi, K., Tsuda, K., Sugiyama, M., Blondel, M., Ueda, N., Kitsuregawa, M., Nakashima, N.: Predictive approaches for low-cost preventive medicine program in developing countries. In: Proceedings of the 21st ACM SIGKDD International Conference on Knowledge Discovery and Data Mining, pp. 1681–1690. ACM (2015)
4. Kajino, H., Kishimoto, A., Botea, A., Daly, E., Kotoulas, S.: Active learning for multi-relational data construction. In: Proceedings of the 24th International Conference on World Wide Web, pp. 560–569. ACM (2015)
5. Auer, P., Cesa-Bianchi, N., Fischer, P.: Finite-time analysis of the multiarmed bandit problem. Mach. Learn. **47**(2–3), 235–256 (2002). Springer
6. Scikit-Learn User Guide. http://scikit-learn.org/stable/user_guide.html
7. UC Irvine Machine Learning Repository. https://archive.ics.uci.edu/ml/index.html

Pattern Based on Temporal Inference

Zeineb Neji[(✉)], Marieme Ellouze, and Lamia Hadrich Belguith

Miracl Laboratory, Computer Department, Faculty of Economics
and Management, University of Sfax, Sfax, Tunisia
zeineb.neji@gmail.com, mariem.ellouze@planet.tn,
l.belguith@fsegs.rnu.tn

Abstract. Inference approaches in Arabic question answering are in their first steps if we compare them with other languages. Evidently, any user is interested in obtaining a specific and precise answer to a specific question. Therefore, the challenge of developing a system capable of obtaining a relevant and concise answer is obviously of great benefit. This paper deals with answering questions about temporal information involving several forms of inference.

We have implemented this approach in a question answering system called IQAS: Inference Question Answering System for handling temporal inference.

Keywords: Question answering system · Temporal inference · Several forms of inference

1 Introduction

Advances in Natural Language Processing (NLP), Information Retrieval techniques (IR) and Information Extraction (IE), have given Question/answering systems (QA) a strong boost. QA have started incorporating NLP techniques to parse natural language documents, extract entities, resolve anaphora, and other language ambiguities [1]. In order to develop question answering capabilities, we believe that a large corpus of questions and answers that are based on temporal information should be discovered. In this paper, we focus on the task of question answering in Arabic by thinking of an approach which can improve the performance of traditional Arabic question answering systems for handling temporal inference. Obviously, any user is interested in obtaining a specific and precise answer to a specific question [2]. Therefore, the challenge of developing a system capable of obtaining a relevant and concise answer is obviously of great benefit. The challenge becomes huge when we try to automatically process a complex natural language such Arabic.

In this paper, we propose a new approach dealing with the recognition and processing of temporal information for Question Answering (QA).

The remaining of this paper is organized as follow. In the next section, we give a short overview of QA systems with a special attention to the QA systems based on complex questions. After that, we describe our proposed approach and its different steps. Finally, we conclude this work and make suggestions for future researches.

© Springer International Publishing Switzerland 2016
A.E.P. Villa et al. (Eds.): ICANN 2016, Part I, LNCS 9886, pp. 461–467, 2016.
DOI: 10.1007/978-3-319-44778-0_54

2 Related Works

In this section, we present the earlier works related to question answering in Arabic. Despite extensive research in Arabic, the criteria represent a challenge to the automatic language processing systems [3]. In the last decade, the volume of Arabic textual data has started growing on the Web. Question-Answering systems represent a good solution for textual information retrieval and knowledge sharing and discovery. This is reason why a large number of QA systems has been developed and extensively studied recently.

Those approaches deal only with non-complex questions where the answers are selected from their corresponding short and simple texts. The challenge becomes greater when we try to create capabilities of processing complex questions and finding their answers from a collection of texts. An important component of this effort deals with the recognition and processing of temporal information for Question Answering (QA).

When asking a question that refers directly or indirectly to a temporal expression, the answer is expected to validate the temporal constraints. To achieve such functionality, QA systems need first, to deal with relations between temporal expressions and events mentioned in the question and, second, to rely on temporal inference to justify the answer. Whenever the answer to a question needs to be justified, if temporal expressions are involved, the justification must contain some form of temporal inference [9]. For example, the expected answer type of question Q1 is a Date:

Q1: متى تقلد المنصف المرزوقي رئاسة الجمهورية التونسية؟

Q1: When Moncef Marzouki has held the presidency of the Republic of Tunisia?

The expected answer type is an argument of the first event Evt1=تقلد / held the presidency which has two more arguments: المنصف المرزوقي/Moncef Marzouki and الجمهورية التونسية / Republic of Tunisia.

The answer to Q1: 2011 ديسمبر 12 / 12 December 2011, extracted from the context:

> P1: The doctor was elected as the interim President of Tunisia on 12 December 2011 by the Constituent Assembly of Tunisia with 153 votes for, 3 against, and 44 blank votes.

> P1 : انتخب الدكتور رئيساً مؤقتاً لتونس في 12 ديسمبر 2011 بواسطة المجلس الوطني التأسيسي بعد حصوله علي أغلبية 153 صوتاً مقابل ثلاثة أصوات معارضة وامتناع اثنين و 44 بطاقة بيضاء.

In the paragraph P1, the event Evt2=انتخب/ elected which has as arguments الدكتور/ the doctor and تونس/ Tunisia. The event Evt1 differs from the event Evt2, but they are related. To justify the answer, these relations must be recognized into the temporal inference. In fact, it is through this example that we illustrate the importance of temporal inference to determine the full content.

In this paper, we present a Question Answering (QA) methodology to handle temporal inference by combining all these forms of inference.

3 Proposed Approach

The proposed approach involves three main modules (Fig. 1), namely: (1) question processing for interpreting the question, its temporal requirements and selecting candidate answers, (2) document processing, which includes indexation based on temporal information, finally (3) answer processing, where we start with the temporal inference before getting the answer.

3.1 Question Processing

The objective of this process is to understand the asked question, for which analytical operations are performed for the representation and classification of the questions.

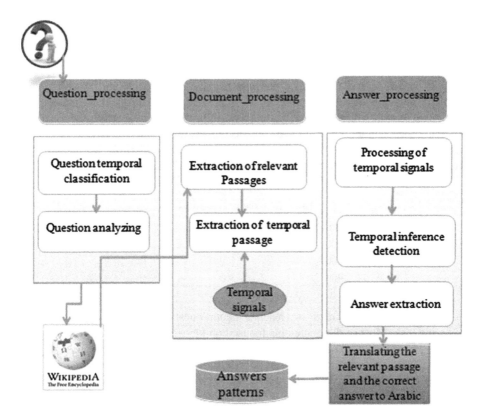

Fig. 1. Proposed approach

The first step of **question processing** is based on the classification of the questions referring to the temporal information extracted from the question. We have used the list of questions produced in TERQAS Workshop[1].

Some of the question classes are listed in Fig. 2. This classification is based on the ways questions signal their time or event dependence and on how straightforward it is to determine the time at which information needs to be understood from a question so that will be possible to provide a suitable answer.

The classes of questions in Table 1, are characterized by the presence of a date and temporal signals, e.g. "since", "after" and in some of them, we need to decompose the question to a temporal relation between events, indicated by a temporal signal.

Table 1. Classes of temporal questions

Question class	Example
Time-Related	**When** was Moncef Marzouki president of Tunisia?
	How long did the Tunisian revolution last?
Event-Related	**What** must happen before the {Christmas} feast can begin in Poland?
Temporal-Order	Did John Sununu resign **before** or **after** George Bush's ratings began to fall?
Entity-Related	How old was Mondela **when** he died?

We have experimented in a **first time** this classification using a set of 100 temporal questions and a set 100 associated answers extracted from temporal passages. The obtained results are very encouraging: **80 %** of the temporal information selected from the suitable answer which contains the temporal information already expected from the question classification, **13 %** to the unexpected answers (not correspond with the classification) and **7 %** to the unfounded answers. In **second time**, we expand the number of questions; the results are shown in Table 2.

Table 2. Experiment results

Number of questions	Suitable answers
100	80
200	172
400	365

Some attempts were made to reach a better question analysis in the question answering task. Most of these attempts focused on keyword extraction from the user's question [4] made some query formulation and extracted the expected answer type, question focus, and important question keywords. To perform a better question analysis, the research of [5] analyzed questions by eliminating stop words, extracting

---

[1] TERQAS was an ARDA Workshop focusing on Temporal and Event Recognition for Question Answering Systems. www.cs.brandeis.edu/_jamesp/arda/time/readings.html.

named entities and classified the questions into Name, Date, Quantity, and Definition questions according to the question word used.

The research of [6] made some query formulation and extracted the expected answer type, question focus, and important question keywords. The question focus is the main noun phrase of the question that the user wants to ask about. For example, if the user's query is "What is the capital of Tunisia?" then the question focus is "Tunisia" and the keyword "capital" and the expected answer type is a named entity for a location.

In our proposal, the step of analyzing the question is based on the elimination of stop words, extraction of the name entities and on the question classification.

3.2 Document Processing

Extraction of the Relevant Document. QA systems benefit from keywords to quickly and easily find the relevant passages. All the documents are indexed with all these forms of information that enable the retrieval of the candidate's text passages.

Extraction of the Relevant Passage. Passages that do not contain time stamps or do not comply with the temporal relations that are searched are filtered out. Event recognition and classification as well as temporal expressions have been pointed out to be very important for our approach. TimeML [7] is a corpus annotated with: (a) time expressions; (b) events and (c) links between them. These annotations enable several forms of temporal inference [8–10]. The temporal information processing includes extracting events (TimeML EVENT tag), temporal expressions (TimeML TIMEX) and identifying temporal relations (TimeML TLINK tag).

The step of temporal passage retrieval has allowed only passages that contained at least one absolute or relative time expression. It also captures the event temporal orderings of the predicates and their relations to the answer structures.

3.3 Answer Processing

This module is responsible for selecting the response based on the relevant fragments of the documents. To be able to answer time-related questions, a question answering system has to know when specific events took place. For this purpose, temporal information can be associated with extracted facts from text documents [11, 12].

Temporal Inference. Either time expressions or events are related but are sometimes ambiguous. For example, the question Q: "how long did the Tunisian revolution last?" is classified to ask about a Time-Related, due to the presence of the question stem "how long".

```
The Jasmine Revolution   began on 18 December 2010 and led to the oust-
ing of longtime president Zine El Abidine Ben Ali finally in 14 January
2011. Following the events, a state of emergency was declared.
```

The answer that is inferred from this paragraph is "18 December 2010–14 January 2011".

In Q, the event of the "Tunisian revolution" can be paraphrased by the "The Jasmine Revolution" expressed in the first sentence of the paragraph. The same mining is referred to the underlined expression "The events".

The first reference *(The Jasmine Revolution began on 18 December 2010)* indicates a relation of **INITIATION** between the event *"The Jasmine Revolution"* and the fully specified temporal expression *"18 December 2010"* strengthened by the adverb *"began"*. The second reference has an aspectual relation of **TERMINATION**, which is strengthened by the adverb *"finally"*.

The final inference enables the recognition of duration of an event when a time expression is identified for its initiation and for its termination. The correct answer is 27 days. The Automatic Translation provided by Wikipedia allows us to have by a simple and a quick projection to translate the pertinent passage and the right answer already found to Arabic. Such answers are important in Arabic QA system as they can be used to provide an answer from a document collection. We therefore decided to investigate the potential of those answers by acquiring patterns automatically.

4   Answers Patterns

It has been noted in several QA systems that certain types of answer are expressed using regular forms [13, 14]. For example, for temporal question like BIRTHDATEs (with questions like "When was X born?"/؟متى ولد فلان), typical answers are:

```
Mozart was born in 1756.
  Gandhi (1869-1948)
These examples suggest
pattern like
  <NAME> was born in <BIRTHDATE>
  <NAME> <BIRTHDATE>-
```

```
ولد موزارت في سنة 1756
غاندي (1948- 1869)
These examples suggest pattern like
<إسم> ولد في سنة <تاريخ ميلاد>
-<إسم><تاريخ ميلاد>
```

When formulated as regular expressions, they can be used to locate the correct answer. Patterns are then automatically extracted from the returned documents and standardized to be then applied to find answers to new questions from a document collection. The precision of the patterns is calculated by cross-checking the patterns across various examples of the same type. This step will help to eliminate dubious patterns.

5   Conclusion

One of the most crucial problems in any Natural Language Processing (NLP) task is the representation of time. This includes applications such as Information Retrieval techniques (IR), Information Extraction (IE) and Question/answering systems (QA). This paper deals with temporal information involving several forms of inference in Arabic language. We introduced a methodology to compute temporal inference for QA that enables us to enhance the recognition of the exact answers to a variety of questions about time. We have argued that answering questions about temporal information requires several different forms of inferences, including inferences that derive from relations between events and their arguments.

References

1. Vicedo, J., Ferrandez, A.: Importance of pronominal anaphora resolution in question answering systems. In: Proceedings of the 38th Annual Conference of the Association for Computational Linguistics (ACL 2000), pp. 555–562 (2000)
2. Benajiba, Y.: Arabic named entity recognition. Ph.D. dissertation, Polytechnical University of Valencia, Spain (2009)
3. Ezzeldin, A.M., Shaheen, M.: A survey of Arabic question answering: challenges, tasks, approaches, tools, and future trends. In: The 13th International Arab Conference on Information Technology, ACIT 2012 (2012)
4. Hammo, B., Abu-Salem, H., Lytinen, S.: QARAB: a QA system to support the Arabic language. In: Proceedings of the Workshop on Computational Approaches to Semitic Languages, Philadelphia, pp. 55–65 (2002)
5. Harabagiu, S., Bejan, C.A.: Question answering based on temporal inference. In: Proceedings of the AAAI-2005 Workshop on Inference for Textual Question Answering (2005)
6. Ingria, B., Pustejovsky, J.: TimeML: A Formal Specification Language for Events and Temporal Expressions (2002). http://www.cs.brandeis.edu/~jamesp/arda/time/
7. Rosso, P., Benajiba, Y., Lyhyaoui, A.: Towards an Arabic question answering system. In: Proceedings of 4th Conference on Scientific Research Outlook Technology Development in the Arab World, SROIV, Damascus, Syria, pp. 11–14 (2006)
8. Harabagiu, S., Bejan, C.: An answer bank for temporal inference. In: Proceedings of LREC (2006)
9. Boguraev, B., Ando, R.K.: TimeML-compliant text analysis for temporal reasoning. In: Proceedings of the Nineteenth International Joint Conference on Artificial Intelligence (IJCAI 2005) (2005)
10. Harabagiu, S.M., Moldovan, D.I., Pasca, M., Mihalcea, R., Surdeanu, M., Bunescu, R.C., Girju, R., Rus, V., Morarescu, P.: The role of Lexico-Semantic Feedback in Open-Domain Textual Question-Answering. In: Proceedings of 39th Annual Meeting of the Association for Computational Linguistics (ACL 2001), pp. 274–281 (2001)
11. Harabagiu, S., Bejan, C.A.: Question answering based on temporal inference. In: Proceedings of the AAAI-2005 Workshop on Inference for Textual Question Answering (2005)
12. Pasca, M.: Towards temporal web search. In: Proceedings of the 2008 ACM Symposium on Applied Computing (SAC 2008), pp. 1117–1121 (2008)
13. Lee, G.G., Seo, J., Lee, S., Jung, H., Cho, B.-H., Lee, C., Kwak, B.-K., Cha, J., Kim, D., An, J.-H., Kim, H.: SiteQ: engineering high performance QA system using Lexico-Semantic pattern matching and shallow NLP. In: Proceedings of the TREC 2010 Conference, pp. 437–446. NIST, Gaithersburg (2001)
14. Wang, B., Xu, H., Yang, Z., Liu, Y., Cheng, X., Bu, D., Bai, S.: TREC-10 experiments at CAS-ICT: filtering, web, and QA. In: Proceedings of the TREC-10 (2001)

Neural Networks Simulation of Distributed Control Problems with State and Control Constraints

Tibor Kmet$^{1(\boxtimes)}$ and Maria Kmetova^2

^{1} Department of Informatics, Constantine the Philosopher University,
Tr. A. Hlinku 1, 949 74 Nitra, Slovakia
tkmet@ukf.sk
^{2} Department of Mathematics, Constantine the Philosopher University,
Tr. A. Hlinku 1, 949 74 Nitra, Slovakia
mkmetova@ukf.sk
http://www.ukf.sk

Abstract. This paper is concerned with distributed optimal control problem. An adaptive critic neural networks solution is proposed to solve optimal distributed control problem for systems governed by parabolic differential equations, with control and state constraints and discrete time delay. The optimal control problem is discretized by using a finite element method in space and the implicit Crank-Nicolson midpoint scheme in time, then transcribed into nonlinear programming problem. To find optimal control and optimal trajectory feed forward adaptive critic neural networks are used to approximate co-state equations. The efficiency of our approach is demonstrated for a model problem related to a mixed nutrient uptake by phytoplankton with space diffusion and discrete time delay of nutrient uptake.

Keywords: Distributed control problem with discrete time delays · State and control constraints · Feed-forward neural network · Adaptive critic synthesis · Numerical examples · Ecological model

1 Introduction

We consider an optimal distributed control problem for systems governed by parabolic differential equations, with control and state constraints and discrete time delay. The problem is motivated by better understanding of real world systems eventually with the purpose of being able to influence these systems in a desired way. The solution of distributed control problem is characterised by the state (evolving forward in time) and co-state (evolving backward in time) equations with initial and terminal conditions, respectively. We pursue the one-shot multigrid startegy as proposed in [1]. A one-shot multigrid algorithm means solving the optimality system for the state, the co-state and the control variables in parallel in the multigrid process evolving forward in time. The finite

© Springer International Publishing Switzerland 2016
A.E.P. Villa et al. (Eds.): ICANN 2016, Part I, LNCS 9886, pp. 468–477, 2016.
DOI: 10.1007/978-3-319-44778-0_55

element approximation plays an important role in the numerical treatment of optimal control problems. This approach has been extensively studied in the papers e.g. [2,3,7,9] for parabolic optimal control problems. Through discretization the optimal control problem is transcribed into a finite-dimensional non-linear programming problem (NLP-problem). Optimal control problems have thus been a stimulus to develop optimization codes for large-scale NLP-problem [1,5,9]. Then neural networks are used as a universal function approximation to solve co-state variable forward in time with "adaptive critic designs" [10,12]. The paper presented extends adaptive critic neural network architecture proposed by [6] to the optimal distributed control problem for systems governed by parabolic differential equations with control and state constraints and discrete time delay. In this paper, we study discretization techniques for solving nonlinear optimal control problems with control and state constraints. In Sect. 2 we present a formal statement of first order necessary conditions for the general parabolic problem. These conditions turn out to be consistent with their counterparts for the discretized problem obtained from the KuhnTucker conditions (Sect. 3). The main focus is on the numerical solution of control and state constrained problems and on the verification of the optimality conditions. In Sect. 3, we discuss a space-time discretization approach in which both control and state variables are discretized. We use augmented Lagrangian techniques. The architecture of the proposed adaptive critic neural network synthesis for the optimal control problem with delays in state and control variables subject to control and state constraints is described also. We also present a new algorithm to solve distributed optimal control problems. Simulation and illustrative example are presented in Sect. 4. Finally, Sect. 5 concludes the paper.

2   The Optimal Control Problem

We consider the nonlinear control problem governed by parabolic equations with delays in state and control variables subject to control and state constraints. Let $x(p,t) \in R^n$ and $u(p,t) \in R^m$ denote the state and control variable, respectively in a given space-time domain $Q = [a,b] \times [t_0, t_f]$. The optimal control problem is to minimize

$$\mathcal{J}(u) = \int_a^b g(x(p,t_f))dp \tag{1}$$
$$+ \int_a^b \int_{t_0}^{t_f} f_0(x(p,t), x(p, t - \tau_x), u(p,t), u(p, t - \tau_u))dtdp,$$

subject to

$$\frac{\partial x(p,t)}{\partial t} = D\frac{\partial^2 x(p,t)}{\partial p^2} + f(x(p,t), x(p, t - \tau_x), u(p,t), u(p, t - \tau_u)), \quad (2)$$

$$\frac{\partial x(a,t)}{\partial p} = \frac{\partial x(b,t)}{\partial p} = 0, \quad t \in [t_0, t_f],$$

$$x(p,t) = \phi_s(p,t), \quad u(p,t) = \phi_c(p,t), \quad p \in [a,b], \quad t \in [t_0 - \tau_u, t_0],$$

$$\psi(x(p,t_f)) = 0, \quad c(x(p,t), u(p,t)) \le 0, \quad p \in [a,b], \quad t \in [t_0, t_f],$$

where $\tau_x \ge 0$ and $\tau_u \ge 0$ are discrete time delay in the state and control variable, respectively. The functions $g : R^n \to R$, $f_0 : R^{2(n+m)} \to R$, $f : R^{2(n+m)} \to R^n$, $c : R^{n+m} \to R^q$ and $\psi : R^n \to R^r$, $0 \le r \le n$ are assumed to be sufficiently smooth on appropriate open sets, and the initial conditions $\phi_s(p,t)$, $\phi_c(p,t)$ are continuous functions. The theory of necessary conditions for the optimal control problem of form (1) is well developed, see e.g. [5,9]. The augmented Hamiltonian function for problem (1) is given by

$$\mathcal{H}(x, x_{\tau_x}, u, u_{\tau_u}, \lambda, \mu) = \sum_{j=0}^{n} \lambda_j f_j(x, x_{\tau_x}, u, u_{\tau_u}) + \sum_{j=0}^{q} \mu_j c_j(x, u),$$

where $\lambda \in R^{n+1}$ is the adjoint variable and $\mu \in R^q$ is a multiplier associated to the inequality constraints. Assume that τ_x, $\tau_u \ge 0$, $(\tau_x, \tau_u) \ne (0,0)$ and $\frac{\tau_x}{\tau_u} \in \mathbb{Q}$ for $\tau_u > 0$ or $\frac{\tau_u}{\tau_x} \in \mathbb{Q}$ for $\tau_x > 0$. Let $(\hat{x}, \hat{u})$ be an optimal solution for (1). Then the necessary optimality condition for (1) implies [5] that there exist a piecewise continuous and piecewise continuously differentiable adjoint function $\lambda : Q \to R^{n+1}$, a piecewise continuous multiplier function $\mu : Q \to R^q$, $\hat{\mu}(p,t) \ge 0$ and a multiplier $\sigma \in R^r$ satisfying

$$\frac{\partial \lambda}{\partial t} = D\frac{\partial^2 \lambda}{\partial p^2} - \frac{\partial \mathcal{H}}{\partial x}(\hat{x}, \hat{x}_{\tau_x}, \hat{u}, \hat{u}_{\tau_u}, \lambda, \mu)$$

$$-\chi_{[t_0, t_f - \tau_x]}\frac{\partial \mathcal{H}}{\partial x_{\tau_x}}(\hat{x}_{+\tau_x}, \hat{x}, \hat{u}_{+\tau_x}, \hat{u}_{\tau_u + \tau_x}, \lambda_{+\tau_x}, \mu_{+\tau_x}), \quad (3)$$

$$\lambda(p, t_f) = g_x(\hat{x}(p, t_f)) + \sigma\psi_x(\hat{x}(p, t_f)), \quad \frac{\partial \lambda(a,t)}{\partial p} = \frac{\partial \lambda(b,t)}{\partial p} = 0, \quad (4)$$

$$0 = -\frac{\partial \mathcal{H}}{\partial u}(\hat{x}, \hat{x}_{\tau_x}, \hat{u}, \hat{u}_{\tau_u}, \lambda, \mu)$$

$$-\chi_{[t_0, t_f - \tau_u]}\frac{\partial \mathcal{H}}{\partial u_{\tau_u}}(\hat{x}_{+\tau_u}, \hat{x}_{\tau_x + \tau_u}, \hat{u}_{+\tau_u}, \hat{u}, \lambda_{+\tau_u}, \mu_{+\tau_u}). \quad (5)$$

Furthermore, the complementary conditions hold, i.e. in $p \in [a,b]$, $t \in [t_0, t_f]$, $\mu(p,t) \ge 0$, $c(x(p,t), u(p,t)) \le 0$ and $\mu(p,t)c(x(p,t), u(p,t)) = 0$. Herein, the subscript x, x_{τ_x}, u and u_{τ_u} denotes the partial derivative with respect to x, x_{τ_x}, u and u_{τ_u}, respectively and $x_{+\tau_x} = x(p, t+\tau_x)$, $x_{\tau_x + \tau_u} = x(p, t - \tau_x + \tau_u)$.

3   Discretization and Adaptive Critic Neural Networks Solution of the Optimal Control

The purpose of this section is to develop discretization techniques by which the distributed control problem (1) are transformed into a nonlinear programming problem (NLP-problem) [1,2,9]. We assume that $\tau_u = l\frac{\tau_x}{k}$ with $l, k \in \mathbb{N}$. Defining $h_{max} = \frac{\tau_x}{k}$ gives the maximum interval length for an elementary transformation interval that satisfies $\frac{\tau_x}{h_{max}} = k \in \mathbb{N}$ and $\frac{\tau_u}{h_{max}} = l \in \mathbb{N}$. The minimum grid point number for an equidistant discretization mesh $N_{min} = \frac{t_f - t_0}{h_{max}}$. Choose a natural number $K \in \mathbb{N}$ and set $N = KN_{min}$. Let $t_j \in \langle t_0, t_f \rangle$, $j = 0, \ldots, N$, be an equidistant mesh point with $t_j = t_0 + jh_t, i = 0, \ldots, N$, where $h_t = \frac{b-a}{N}$ is a time step and $t_f = Nh + t_0$. Assume that the rectangle $R = \{(p,t) : a \le p \le b, t_0 \le t \le t_f\}$ is subdivided into N by M rectangles with sides h_t and $h_s = \frac{b-a}{M}$. Start at the bottom row, where $t = t_0$, and the solution is $x(p_i, t_0) = \phi_s(p_i, t_0)$. A method for computing the approximations to $x(p,t)$ at grid points in successive rows $\{x(p_i, t_j) : i = 0, 1, \ldots, N, \ j = 0, 1, \ldots, M\}$, will be developed. An implicit scheme, invented by Jon Crank and Phyllis Nicholson, is based on numerical approximations for the solution of Eq. (2) at the point $(x, t + h_t/2)$ which lies between the rows in the grid. Let the vectors x_{ij}, $f_{i,j} \in R^n$, $u_{ij} \in R^m$, $i = 0, \ldots, N, \ j = 0, \ldots, M$, be an approximation of the state variable and control variable $x(p_i, t_j)$, $f(p_i, t_j)$ and $u(p_i, t_j)$, respectively at the mesh point (p_i, t_j). We will produce the difference equation, with $r = Dh_t/h_s^2 = 1$ results in the implicit difference formula

$$G_{i,j+1} = x_{i-1,j+1} - 4x_{i,j+1} + x_{i+1,j+1} + x_{i-1,j} + x_{i+1,j} + h_t f_{i,j} = 0. \quad (6)$$

for $i = 1, 2, \ldots, N - 1$. The terms on the right-hand side of the Eq. (6) are all known. When the Crank-Nicholson method is implemented with a computer, the linear system can be solved by their direct means or by iteration. Let $z := ((x_{ij}), (u_{ij}), \ i = 0, \ldots, N, \ j = 0, \ldots, M) \in R^{N_s}$, $N_s = (n+m)NM$ and $I(Q) = \{(i,j), \ i = 1, \ldots, N - 1, \ j = 1, \ldots, M - 1\}$. The optimal control problem is replaced by the following discretized control problem in the form of nonlinear programming problem with inequality constraints: Minimize

$$\mathcal{J}(z) = h_s h_t \sum_{(i,j)} f_0(x_{ij}, x_{\tau_x ij}, u_{ij}, u_{\tau_u ij}) + h_s \sum_{(i)} g(x_{iM}) \quad (7)$$

subject to

$$G_{i,j+1} = 0, \ x_{0j} = x_{1j}, \ x_{Nj} = x_{N-1j}, \quad (8)$$

$$x_{i,-j} = \phi_x(p_i, t_0 - jh), \ j = k, \ldots, 0, \ u_{i,-j} = \phi_u(p_i, t_0 - jh), \ j = l, \ldots, 0,$$

$$\psi(x_{i,N}) = 0, \ c(x_{ij}, u_{ij}) \le 0, \ i = 0, \ldots, N, \ j = 0, \ldots, M - 1.$$

In a discrete-time formulation we want to find an admissible control which minimizes objective function (7). Let us introduce the Lagrangian function for the nonlinear optimization problem (7):

$$\mathcal{L}(z, \lambda, \sigma, \mu) = h_s h_t \sum_{(i,j)} f_0(x_{ij}, x_{\tau_x ij}, u_{ij}, u_{\tau_u ij}) + h_s \sum_{(i)} g(x_{iM})$$

$$+ \sum_{(i,j) \in I(Q)} \lambda_{i,j+1}(G_{i,j+1})$$

$$+ \sum_{(i,j) \in I(Q)} \mu_{ij} c(x_{ij}, u_{ij}) + \sum_{(i)} \sigma_i \psi(x_{iN})$$

$$+ \sum_{(j)} \lambda_{0,j} \frac{x_{0,j+1} - x_{0,j}}{h_s} + \sum_{(j)} \lambda_{N,j} \frac{x_{N,j+1} - x_{N,j}}{h_s}. \tag{9}$$

The first order optimality conditions of Karush-Kuhn-Tucker for the problem (7) are:

$$0 = \mathcal{L}_{x_{ij}}(z, \lambda, \sigma, \mu) = \lambda_{i-1,j} - 4\lambda_{i,j} + \lambda_{i+1,j} + \lambda_{i-1,j+1} + \lambda_{i+1,j+1}$$
$$+ h_t \lambda_{i,j+1} f_{x_{ij}}(x_{ij}, x_{i,j-k}, u_{ij}, u_{i,j-l})$$
$$+ h_t \lambda_{i,j+k+1} f_{x_{ij\tau_x}}(x_{i,j+k}, x_{ij}, u_{i,j+k}, u_{i,j-l+k})$$
$$+ \mu_{ij} c_{x_{ij}}(x_{ij}, u_{ij}), \ j = 0, \dots, M - k - 1, \tag{10}$$

$$0 = \mathcal{L}_{x_{ij}}(z, \lambda, \sigma, \mu) = \lambda_{i-1,j} - 4\lambda_{i,j} + \lambda_{i+1,j} + \lambda_{i-1,j+1} + \lambda_{i+1,j+1}$$
$$+ h_t \lambda_{i,j+1} f_{x_{ij}}(x_{ij}, x_{i,j-k}, u_{ij}, u_{i,j-l}), \ j = M - k, \dots, M - 1,$$

$$\lambda_{0j} = \lambda_{1j}, \lambda_{Nj} = \lambda_{N-1,j}$$

$$0 = \mathcal{L}_{x_{iM}}(z, \lambda, \sigma, \mu) = g_{x_{iM}}(x_{im}) + \sigma_i \psi_{x_{iM}}(x_{iM}) - \lambda_{iM}, \tag{11}$$

$$0 = \mathcal{L}_{u_{ij}}(z, \lambda, \sigma, \mu) = h_t \lambda_{i,j+1} f_{u_{ij}}(x_{ij}, x_{i,j-k}, u_{ij}, u_{i,j-l})$$
$$+ h_t \lambda_{i,j+l+1} f_{u_{ij\tau_u}}(x_{i,j+l}, x_{i,j-k+l}, u_{i,j+l}, u_{i,j}) + \mu_{ij} c_{u_{ij}}(x_{ij}, u_{ij}),$$
$$j = 0, \dots, M - l - 1, \tag{12}$$

$$0 = \mathcal{L}_{u_{ij}}(z, \lambda, \sigma, \mu) = h_t \lambda_{i,j+1} f_{u_{ij}}(x_{ij}, x_{i,j-k}, u_{ij}, u_{i,j-l}) + \mu_{ij} c_{u_{ij}}(x_{ij}, u_{ij}),$$
$$j = M - l, \dots, N - 1.$$

Eqs. (10) – (12) represent the discrete version of the necessary conditions (4) – (5) for optimal control problem (1).

In the optimal control problems the objective is to devise a strategy of action, or control law, that minimizes the desired performance cost Eq. (7). In 1992, Werbos [12] introduced an approach for approximate dynamic programming, which later became known under the name of adaptive critic designs (ACD). A typical design of ACD consists of three modules action, model (plant), and critic. We need to determine three pieces of information: How to adapt the critic network; How to adapt the model network; and How to adapt the action network. The action consists of a parametrized control law. The critic approximates the value-related function and captures the effect that the control law has on the future cost. At any given time the critic provides guidance on how to improve the control law. In return, the action can be used to update the critic. An algorithm that successively iterates between these two operations converges to

---

Algorithm 1. Algorithm to solve the optimal control problem.

Input: Choose t_0, t_f, a, b, N, M - number of steps, time and space steps
h_t, h_s ε_a, ε_c - stopping tolerance for action and critic neural networks,
respectively, $x_{i,-j} = \phi_s(p_i, t_0 - jh_t)$, $j = k, \ldots, 0$,
$u_{i,-j} = \phi_c(i, t_0 - jh_t)$, $j = l, \ldots, 0$ -initial values.

Output: Set of final approximate optimal control $\hat{u}(p_i, t_0 + jh_t) = \hat{u}_{ij}$ and
optimal trajectory $\hat{x}(p_i, t_0 + (j+1)h_t) = \hat{x}_{i,j+1}$, $j = 0, \ldots, M-1$,
respectively

1 Set the initial weight $\mathbb{W}^a = (V^a, W^a)$, $\mathbb{W}^c = (V^c, W^c)$
  for $j \leftarrow 0$ **to** $M-1$ **do**
2   **for** $i \leftarrow 1$ **to** $N-1$ **do**
3   **while** $err_a \geq \epsilon_a$ **and** $err_c \geq \epsilon_c$ **do**
4   **for** $s \leftarrow 0$ **to** $max(k, l)$ **do**
5   Compute $u^a_{i,s+j}$, $\mu^a_{i,s+j}$ and $\lambda^c_{i,s+j+1}$ using action ($\mathbb{W}^a$) and
          critic ($\mathbb{W}^c$) neural networks, respectively and $x_{i,s+j+1}$ by Eq. (8)
6   Compute λ^t_{ij}, u^t_{ij}, and μ^t_{ij} using Eqs. (10) and (12)
        $\mathbb{F}(u_{ij}, \mu_{ij}) = (\mathcal{L}_{u_{ij}}(z, \lambda, \sigma, \mu), -c(x_{ij}, u_{ij})) = 0$
7   **if** $j = M-1$ **then**
8         $\mathbb{F}(u_{i,M-1}, \mu_{i,M-1}, \sigma_i) =$
          $(\mathcal{L}_{u_{i,M-1}}(z, \lambda, \sigma, \mu), -c(x_{i,M-1}, u_{i,M-1}), -\psi(x_{i,M}))$ with
          $\lambda_{iM} = \mathcal{G}_{x_{iM}}(x_{iM}) + \sigma_i \psi_{x_{iM}}(x_{iM})$
9       $err_c = \| \lambda^t_{ij} - \lambda^c_{ij} \|$
10      $err_a = \| (u, \mu)^t_{ij} - (u, \mu)^a_{ij} \|$
11   With the data set x_{ij}, λ^t_{ij} update the weight parameters $\mathbb{W}^c$
12   With the data set x_{ij}, $(u, \mu)^t_{ij}$ update the weight parameters $\mathbb{W}^a$
13   Set $\lambda^c_{ij} = \lambda^t_{i,j}$, $(u, \mu)^a_{i,j} = (u, \mu)^t_{i,j}$
14   Set $\hat{\lambda}_{i,j} = \lambda^t_{i,j}$, $(\hat{u}_{i,j}, \hat{\mu}_{i,j}) = (u, \mu)^t_{i,j}$
15   Compute $\hat{x}_{i,j+1}$ using Eq. (8) and $\hat{u}_{i,j}$
16 $\lambda_{0j} = \lambda_{1j}$, $\lambda_{Nj} = \lambda_{N-1,j}$
17 **return** $\hat{\lambda}_{i,j}$, $\hat{u}_{i,j}$, $\hat{\mu}_{i,j}$, $\hat{x}_{i,j+1}$

---

the optimal solution over time. The plant dynamics are discrete, time-invariant, and deterministic, and they can be modelled by a difference Eq. (8). The action and critic network are chosen as feed forward three-layer neural networks with input, hidden and output layer. The adaptive critic neural network procedure of the optimal control problem is summarized in Algorithm 1. In the adaptive critic synthesis, the action and critic network were selected such that they consist of $n + m$ subnetworks, respectively, each having $n - 3n - 1$ structure (i.e. n neurons in the input layer, $3n$ neurons in the hidden layer and one neuron in the output layer). The training procedure for the action and critic networks, respectively, are given by [10]. From the free terminal condition ($\psi(x) \equiv 0$) from Eqs. (10) – (11) we obtain that $\lambda_0 = -1$, and $\lambda_{iM} = 0$, $i = 1, \ldots, N$. We use this observation before proceeding to the actual training of the adaptive critic neural network.

4   Nitrogen Transformation Cycle

The aerobic transformation of nitrogen compounds [6] includes: Heterotrophic bacteria (x_1), bacteria from the genus Nitrosomonas (x_2), bacteria mainly from the genus Nitrobacter (x_3), phytoplankton (x_4), detritus (x_5), organic nitrogen compounds DON (x_6), ammonium (x_7), nitrites (x_8), and nitrate (x_9). The individual variables $x_1, \ldots, x_9$ represent nitrogen concentrations contained in the organic as well as in inorganic substances and living organisms presented in the model. The following system of partial differential equations is proposed as a model for the nitrogen transformation cycle:

$$\frac{\partial x_i(p,t)}{\partial t} = D\frac{\partial^2 x_i(p,t)}{\partial p^2} + x_i(t)U_i(x(t)) - x_i(t)E_i(x(t)) - x_i(t)M_i(x(t)), \ i = 1, 2, 3,$$

$$\frac{\partial x_4(p,t)}{\partial t} = D\frac{\partial^2 x_4(p,t)}{\partial p^2} + x_4(t-\tau)(U_4(x(t-\tau)) - E_i(x(t-\tau)) - M_i(x(t-\tau))),$$

$$\frac{\partial x_5(p,t)}{\partial t} = D\frac{\partial^2 x_5(p,t)}{\partial p^2} + \sum_{i=1}^{4} x_i M_i(x) - K_5 x_5(t),$$

$$\frac{\partial x_6(p,t)}{\partial t} = D\frac{\partial^2 x_6(p,t)}{\partial p^2} + K_5 x_5(t) - x_1(t)U_1(x(t)) + x_4(t)E_4(x(t)) - x_4(t)P_6(x(t)),$$

$$\frac{\partial x_7(p,t)}{\partial t} = D\frac{\partial^2 x_7(p,t)}{\partial p^2} + x_1(t)E_1(x(t)) - x_2(t)U_2(x(t)) - x_4(t)P_7(x(t)), \qquad (13)$$

$$\frac{\partial x_8(p,t)}{\partial t} = D\frac{\partial^2 x_8(p,t)}{\partial p^2} + x_2(t)E_2(x(t)) - x_3(t)U_3(x(t)),$$

$$\frac{\partial x_9(p,t)}{\partial t} = D\frac{\partial^2 x_9(p,t)}{\partial p^2} x_3(t)E_3(x(t)) - x_4(t)P_9(x(t)),$$

where $x_i(p,t)$ are the concentrations of the recycling matter in microorganisms, the available nutrients and detritus, respectively, and $\frac{\partial x(a,t)}{\partial p} = \frac{\partial x(b,t)}{\partial p} = 0$. Functions U_i, E_i and M_i describe uptake, excretion and mortality rate, respectively, and $U_4 = P_6 + P_7 + P_9$. The constant τ stands for the discrete time delay in uptake of nutrients by phytoplankton. Three variables $u = (u(1), u(2), u(3))$ express the preference coefficients for update of x_6, x_7, x_9. It can be expected that the phytoplankton will employ control mechanisms in such a way as to maximize its biomass over a given period t_f of time:

$$J(u) = \int_a^b \int_{t_0}^{t_f} x_4(p,t)dtdp \rightarrow max \qquad (14)$$

under the constraint

$$C(x,u) := b_1 U_4(x,u) + b_2 P_6(x,u) + b_3 P_9(x,u) + b_4 E_4(x,u) \leq W(I), \quad (15)$$
$$u_i \in [0, u_{imax}] \ \ for \ i = 1, 2, 3.$$

The last inequality expresses the fact that the amount of energy used for "living expenses" (synthesis, reduction and excretion of nutrients) by phytoplankton

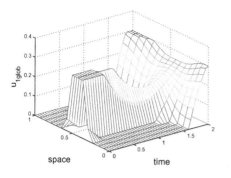 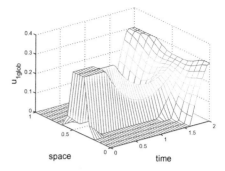

Fig. 1. Adaptive critic neural network simulation of optimal control $\hat{u}_1(t)$ and $\bar{u}_1(t)$ with initial condition $\psi_s(t) = (0.1, 0.1, 0.2, 0.8, 0.4, 0.5, 0.6, 0.7, .1)(1 + cos(2\pi p))$ and $\psi_c(t) = (0, 0, 0)$, respectively for $t \in [-1, 0]$.

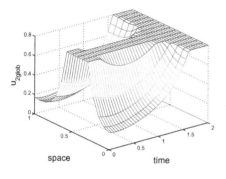 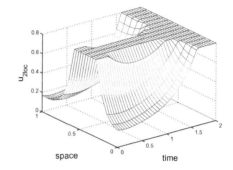

Fig. 2. Adaptive critic neural network simulation of optimal control $\hat{u}_2(t)$ and $\bar{u}_2(t)$ with initial condition $\psi_s(t) = (0.1, 0.1, 0.2, 0.8, 0.4, 0.5, 0.6, 0.7, .1)(1 + cos(2\pi p))$ and $\psi_c(t) = (0, 0, 0)$, respectively for $t \in [-1, 0]$.

cannot exceed a certain value $W(I)$ which depends on light intensity I (for detail explanation see [6]). We are led to the following optimal control problems:

(1) instantaneous maximal biomass production with respect to u:

$$\dot{x}_4 = x_4(U_4(x, u) - E_4(x, u) - M_4(x, u)) \rightarrow max \qquad (16)$$

under the constraint $C(x, u) \leq W(I)$, for all $t \in [t_0, t_f]$ and $u_i \in [0, u_{imax}]$, i=1, 2, 3,

(2) global maximal biomass production with respect to u:

$$J(u) = \int_{t_0}^{t_f} x_4(t)dt \rightarrow max \qquad (17)$$

under the constraint $C(x, u) \leq W(I)$, for all $t \in [t_0, t_f]$ and $u_i \in [u_{imin}, u_{imax}]$ for i=1,2,3.

4.1 Numerical Simulation

The solution of distributed optimal control problem (14) with state and control constraints using adaptive critic neural network and NLP methods are displayed in Figs. 1 and 2. In the adaptive critic synthesis, the critic and action network were selected such that they consist of nine and four subnetworks, respectively, each having 9-27-1 structure (i.e. nine neurons in the input layer, twenty seven neurons in the hidden layer and one neuron in the output layer). The proposed neural network is able to meet the convergence tolerance values that we choose, which leads to satisfactory simulation results. Simulations show that there is a very good agreement between short-term and long-term strategy and the proposed neural network is able to solve nonlinear optimal control problem with state and control constraints. The optimal strategy is the following. In the presence of high ammonium concentration, the uptake of DON and nitrate is stopped. If the concentration of ammonium drops below a certain limit value, phytoplankton starts to assimilate DON or nitrate dependently on values b_2, b_3. If the concentration of all three forms of nitrogen are low, all of them are assimilated by phytoplankton at the maximal possible rate, e.i. $\hat{u}_i(t) = u_{imax}$ for all $t \in [t_0, t_f]$ (Figs. 1 and 2). Our results are quite similar to those obtained in [6] by using Pontriagin's maximum principle.

5 Conclusion

In the current work, we presented an efficient optimization algorithm for distributed optimal control an inequality constraints on the controls and states. Using Crank-Nicolson's methods the optimal control problem is transcribed into a discrete-time high-dimensional nonlinear programming problem which is characterized by state and co-state equations involving forward and backward in time, respectively. The solution of co-state equations is approximated based on adaptive critic designs and is involved forward in time. This approach is applicable to wide class of nonlinear systems. The method was tested on the model of mixed substrate utilization by phytoplankton. Using MATLAB, a simple simulation model based on adaptive critic neural network was constructed.

Acknowledgments. The paper was worked out as a part of the solution of the scientific project number KEGA 010UJS-4/2014.

References

1. Borzi, A.: Multigrid methods for parabolic distributed optimal control problems. J. Comput. Appl. Math. **157**, 365–382 (2003)
2. Chryssoverghi, I.: Discretization methods for semilinear parabolic optimal control problems. Int. J. Numer. Anal. Model. **3**, 437–458 (2006)
3. Clever, D., Lang, J., Ulbrich, S., Ziems, J.C.: Combination of an adaptive multilevel SQP method and a space-time adaptive PDAE solver for optimal control problems. Procedia Comput. Sci. **1**, 1435–1443 (2012)

4. Hornik, M., Stichcombe, M., White, H.: Multilayer feed forward networks are universal approximators. Neural Netw. **3**, 256–366 (1989)
5. Gollman, L., Kern, D., Mauer, H.: Optimal control problem with delays in state and control variables subject to mixed control-state constraints. Optim. Control Appl. Meth. **30**, 341–365 (2009)
6. Kmet, T.: Neural network solution of optimal control problem with control and state constraints. In: Honkela, T. (ed.) ICANN 2011, Part II. LNCS, vol. 6792, pp. 261–268. Springer, Heidelberg (2011)
7. Knowles, G.: Finite element approximation of parabolic time optimal control problems. SIAM J. Control Optim. **20**, 414–427 (1982)
8. Marburger, J., Marheineke, N., Pinnau, R.: Adjoint-based optimal control using mesh free discretizations. J. Comput. Appl. Math. **235**, 3138–3150 (2011)
9. Mittelmann, H.D.: Solving elliptic control problems with interior point and SQP methods: control and state constraints. J. Comput. Appl. Math. **120**, 175–195 (2000)
10. Padhi, R., Unnikrishnan, N., Wang, X., Balakrishnan, S.N.: Adaptive-critic based optimal control synthesis for distributed parameter systems. Automatica **37**, 1223–1234 (2001)
11. Rumelhart, D.F., Hinton, G.E., Wiliams, R.J.: Learning internal representation by error propagation. In: Rumelhart, D.E., McClelland, D.E. (eds.) PDP Research Group: Parallel Distributed Processing: Foundation, vol. 1, pp. 318–362. The MIT Press, Cambridge (1987)
12. Werbos, P.J.: Approximate dynamic programming for real-time control and neural modelling. In: White, D.A., Sofge, D.A. (eds.) Handbook of Intelligent Control: Neural Fuzzy, and Adaptive Approaches, pp. 493–525 (1992)

The Existence and the Stability of Weighted Pseudo Almost Periodic Solution of High-Order Hopfield Neural Network

Chaouki Aouiti[1]([⊠]), Mohammed Salah M'hamdi[1], and Farouk Chérif[2]

[1] Faculty of Sciences of Bizerta, Department of Mathematics, University of Carthage, BP W, Zarzouna, 7021 Bizerta, Tunisia
chaouki.aouiti@fsb.rnu.tn, mohammedsalah.mhamdi@yahoo.com
[2] Laboratory of Math Physics; Specials Functions and Applications LR11ES35, ESSHS, University of Sousse, 4002 Sousse, Tunisia
faroukcheriff@yahoo.fr

Abstract. In this paper, by employing fixed point theorem and differential inequality techniques, some sufficient conditions are given for the existence and the global exponential stability of the unique weighted pseudo almost-periodic solution of high-order Hopfield neural networks with delays. An illustrative example is also given at the end of this paper to show the effectiveness of our results.

Keywords: Weighted pseudo almost-periodic solution · High-order Hopfield neural networks · Delays

1 Introduction

High order Hopfield neural networks (HOHNNs) have attracted many attentions in recent years due to the fact that they have stronger approximation property, faster convergence rate, greater storage capacity, and higher fault tolerance than lower-order neural networks. In particular, there have been extensive results on the problem of the existence and stability of equilibrium points, periodic solutions, and almost periodic solution of HOHNNs in the literature. We refer the reader to [1–5] and the references therein.

As is well known, both in biological and man-made neural networks, delays are inevitable, due to various reasons. For instance, time delays can be caused by the finite switching speed of amplifier circuits in neural networks. Time delays in the neural networks make the dynamic behaviors become more complex, and may destabilize the stable equilibria [2–5]. Thus, it is very important to study the dynamics of neural networks delay.

In this paper, we are mainly concerned with the existence of weighted pseudo almost periodic solutions to the following models for HOHNNs with delays:

$$x_i'(t) = -c_i x_i(t) + \sum_{j=1}^{n} d_{ij}(t) g_j(x_j(t)) + \sum_{j=1}^{n} a_{ij}(t) g_j(x_j(t-\tau))$$

$$+ \sum_{j=1}^{n} \sum_{l=1}^{n} b_{ijl}(t) g_j(x_j(t-\sigma)) g_l(x_l(t-\nu))$$

$$+ I_i(t), \quad i = 1, \ldots, n. \tag{1}$$

where n corresponds to the number of units in a neural network, $x_i(t)$ corresponds to the state vector of the ith unit at the time t, $c_i > 0$ represents the rate with which the ith unit will reset its potential to the resting state in isolation when disconnected from the network and external inputs at the time t, $d_{ij}(t), a_{ij}(t)$ and $b_{ijl}(t)$ are connection weights of the neural network, $\tau \geq 0, \sigma \geq 0$ and $\nu \geq 0$ correspond to the transmission delays, $I_i(t)$ denote the external inputs at time t, and g_j is the activation function of signal transmission.

For instance, we make the following assumptions:

(H1) For all $1 \leq i, j, l \leq n$, the functions $t \longmapsto d_{ij}(t)$, $t \longmapsto a_{ij}(t)$, $t \longmapsto b_{ijl}(t)$, $t \longmapsto I_i(t)$ are weighted pseudo almost-periodic functions.

(H2) Let $\rho : \mathbb{R} \longmapsto (0, +\infty)$, $\rho \in \mathbb{U}_\infty$ is continuous and assume

$$\sup_{s \in \mathbb{R}} \left[\frac{\rho(s+\delta)}{\rho(s)} \right] < \infty \text{ and } \sup_{T>0} \left[\frac{\mu(T+\delta, \rho)}{\mu(T, \rho)} \right] < \infty, \text{ for each } \delta \in \mathbb{R}$$

(H3) For each $j = \{1, 2, \ldots, n\}$, there exist nonnegative constants L_j^g and M_j^g such that for all $u, v \in \mathbb{R}$

$$\mid g_j(u) - g_j(v) \mid \leq L_j^g \mid u - v \mid, \ \mid g_j(u) \mid \leq M_j^g.$$

Furthermore, we suppose that for all $1 \leq j \leq n$, $g_j(0) = 0$.

Throughout this paper, we will use the following concepts and notations. $BC(\mathbb{R}, \mathbb{R}^n)$ denotes the set of bounded continued functions from $\mathbb{R}$ to $\mathbb{R}^n$. Note that $(BC(\mathbb{R}, \mathbb{R}^n), \| \cdot \|_\infty)$ is a Banach space where $\| \cdot \|_\infty$ denotes the sup norm

$$\| f \|_\infty = \max_{1 \leq i \leq n} \sup_{t \in \mathbb{R}} \mid f_i(t) \mid.$$

Furthermore, $C(\mathbb{R}, \mathbb{R}^n)$ denotes the class of continuous functions from $\mathbb{R}$ into $\mathbb{R}^n$. Let $(\mathbb{R}^n, \| \cdot \|_\infty)$ be Banach space. Let $\mathbb{U}$ denotes the collection of functions (weights) $\rho : \mathbb{R} \longmapsto (o, \infty)$ which are locally integrable over $\mathbb{R}$ such that $\rho > 0$ almost everywhere. From now on, if $\rho \in \mathbb{U}$ and for $T > 0$, we then set

$$\mu(T, \rho) = \int_{-T}^{T} \rho(x) dx.$$

As in the particular case when $\rho(x) = 1$ for each $x \in \mathbb{R}$, we are exclusively interested in those weights ρ, for which $\lim_{T \longrightarrow \infty} \mu(T, \rho) = \infty$.

Let $\mathbb{U}_\infty := \{\rho \in \mathbb{U} : \lim_{T \longrightarrow \infty} \mu(T, \rho) = \infty\}$

and $\mathbb{U}_B := \{\rho \in \mathbb{U}_\infty : \rho \text{ is bounded with } \inf_{x \in \mathbb{R}} \rho(x) > 0\}$.

Obviously, $\mathbb{U}_B \subset \mathbb{U}_\infty \subset \mathbb{U}$, with strict inclusions.

Definition 1. *[3]. A function $f \in C(\mathbb{R}, \mathbb{R}^n)$ is called (Bohr) almost periodic if for each $\varepsilon > 0$ there exists $L(\varepsilon) > 0$ such that every interval of length $L(\varepsilon) > 0$ contains a number τ with the property that $\| f(t + \tau) - f(t) \|_\infty < \varepsilon$, for each $t \in \mathbb{R}$. The number τ above is called an ε-translation number of f, and the collection of all such functions will be denoted as $AP(\mathbb{R}, \mathbb{R}^n)$.*

To introduce those weighted pseudo-almost periodic functions, we need to define the weighted ergodic space $PAP_0(\mathbb{R}, \mathbb{R}^n, \rho)$. Weighted pseudo-almost periodic functions will then appear as perturbations of almost periodic functions by elements of $PAP_0(\mathbb{R}, \mathbb{R}^n, \rho)$.

Let $\rho \in \mathbb{U}_\infty$. Define

$$PAP_0(\mathbb{R}, \mathbb{R}^n, \rho) := \{f \in BC(\mathbb{R}, \mathbb{R}^n) : \lim_{T \longrightarrow \infty} \frac{1}{\mu(T, \rho)} \int_{-T}^T \| f(\sigma) \| \rho(\sigma) d\sigma = 0\}.$$

Definition 2. *[3]. Let $\rho \in \mathbb{U}_\infty$. A function $f \in BC(\mathbb{R}, \mathbb{R}^n)$ is called weighted pseudo-almost periodic (or ρ-pseudo almost periodic) if it can be expressed as $f = g + \phi$, where $g \in AP(\mathbb{R}, \mathbb{R}^n)$ and $\phi \in PAP_0(\mathbb{R}, \mathbb{R}^n, \rho)$. The collection of such functions will be denoted by $PAP(\mathbb{R}, \mathbb{R}^n, \rho)$.*

The initial conditions associated with (1) are of the form

$$x_i(s) = \varphi_i(s), \quad s \in (-\theta, 0], i = 1, 2, \ldots, n,$$

The rest of this paper is organized as follow. In Sect. 2, the existence of weighted pseudo almost-periodic solutions of (1) are discussed. In Sect. 3, a numerical example is given to illustrate the effectiveness of our results. Finally, we draw conclusion in Sect. 4.

2   The Existence and the Global Exponential Stability of Weighted Pseudo Almost Periodic Solution

In this section, we establish some results for the existence of the weighted pseudo almost-periodic solution of (1). For convenience, we introduce the following notations, for $i, j, l = 1, 2, \ldots, n$, it will be assumed that $d_{ij}, I_i, a_{ij}, b_{ijl} : \mathbb{R} \longrightarrow \mathbb{R}$, and there exist constants $\overline{d}_{ij}, \overline{I}_i, \overline{a}_{ij}$ and $\overline{b}_{ijl}$ such that

$$\sup_{t \in \mathbb{R}}(| d_{ij}(t) |) = \overline{d}_{ij}, \quad \sup_{t \in \mathbb{R}}(| I_i(t) |) = \overline{I}_i,$$

$$\sup_{t \in \mathbb{R}}(| a_{ij}(t) |) = \overline{a}_{ij}, \quad \sup_{t \in \mathbb{R}}(| b_{ijl}(t) |) = \overline{b}_{ijl}.$$

Lemma 1. *Suppose that assumptions (H2) hold. If $\varphi(.) \in PAP(\mathbb{R}, \mathbb{R}^n, \rho)$, then $\varphi(. - h) \in PAP(\mathbb{R}, \mathbb{R}^n, \rho)$.*

Lemma 2. *If $\varphi, \psi \in PAP(\mathbb{R}, \mathbb{R}, \rho)$, then $\varphi \times \psi \in PAP(\mathbb{R}, \mathbb{R}, \rho)$.*

Lemma 3. *Suppose that assumptions (H1)–(H3) hold and for all $1 \leq i \leq n$*

$$(H4): \quad \sup_{T>0} \left\{ \int_{-T}^{T} e^{-c_i(T+t)} \rho(t) dt \right\} < \infty.$$

Define the nonlinear operator Γ as follows, for each $\varphi = (\varphi_1, \ldots, \varphi_n) \in PAP(\mathbb{R}, \mathbb{R}^n, \rho)$, $(\Gamma\varphi)(t) := x_\varphi(t)$ where

$$x_\varphi(t) = \left(\int_{-\infty}^{t} e^{-(t-s)c_1} F_1(s) ds, \ldots, \int_{-\infty}^{t} e^{-(t-s)c_n} F_n(s) ds \right)^T$$

and

$$F_i(s) = \sum_{j=1}^{n} d_{ij}(s) g_j(\varphi_j(s)) + \sum_{j=1}^{n} a_{ij}(s) g_j(\varphi_j(s - \tau))$$
$$+ \sum_{j=1}^{n} \sum_{l=1}^{n} b_{ijl}(s) g_j(\varphi_j(s - \sigma)) g_l(\varphi_l(s - \nu)) + I_i(s),$$

then Γ maps $PAP(\mathbb{R}, \mathbb{R}^n, \rho)$ into itself.

Theorem 1. *Suppose that assumptions (H1)–(H4) hold and (H5): there exist nonnegative constants L, p and q such that*

$$L = \max_{1 \leq i \leq n} \left\{ \frac{\overline{I}_i}{c_i} \right\}, p = \max_{1 \leq i \leq n} \left\{ c_i^{-1} \left[\sum_{j=1}^{n} \overline{d}_{ij} L_j^g + \sum_{j=1}^{n} \overline{a}_{ij} L_j^g + \sum_{j=1}^{n} \sum_{l=1}^{n} \overline{b}_{ijl} L_j^g M_l^g \right] \right\} < 1,$$

$$q = \max_{1 \leq i \leq n} \left\{ c_i^{-1} \left[\sum_{j=1}^{n} \overline{d}_{ij} L_j^g + \sum_{j=1}^{n} \overline{a}_{ij} L_j^g + \sum_{j=1}^{n} \sum_{l=1}^{n} \overline{b}_{ijl} (L_j^g M_l^g + M_j^g L_l^g) \right] \right\} < 1.$$

Then the delayed HOHNNs of (1) has a unique weighted pseudo almost periodic solution in the region $\mathbb{B} = \{ \varphi \in PAP(\mathbb{R}, \mathbb{R}^n, \rho), \| \varphi - \varphi_0 \|_\infty \leq \frac{pL}{(1-p)} \}$, where

$$\varphi_0(t) = \left(\int_{-\infty}^{t} e^{-(t-s)c_1} I_1(s) ds, \ldots, \int_{-\infty}^{t} e^{-(t-s)c_n} I_n(s) ds \right)^T.$$

Proof. One has

$$\| \varphi_0 \|_\infty = \sup_{t \in \mathbb{R}} \max_{1 \leq i \leq n} \left(\left| \int_{-\infty}^{t} e^{-(t-s)c_i} I_i(s) ds \right| \right)$$
$$\leq \max_{1 \leq i \leq n} \left(\frac{\overline{I}_i}{c_i} \right) = L.$$

After

$$\| \varphi \|_\infty \le \| \varphi - \varphi_0 \|_\infty + \| \varphi_0 \|_\infty$$
$$\le \| \varphi - \varphi_0 \|_\infty + L.$$

Set $\mathbb{B} = \mathbb{B}(\varphi_0, p) = \{\varphi \in PAP(\mathbb{R}, \mathbb{R}^n, \rho), \| \varphi - \varphi_0 \|_\infty \le \frac{pL}{(1-p)}\}$. Clearly, $\mathbb{B}$ is a closed convex subset of $PAP(\mathbb{R}, \mathbb{R}^n, \rho)$ and, therefore, for any $\varphi \in \mathbb{B}$ by using the estimate just obtained, we see that

$$\| \Gamma_\varphi - \varphi_0 \|_\infty$$
$$= \max_{1\le i\le n} \sup_{t\in\mathbb{R}}\{| \int_{-\infty}^{t} e^{-(t-s)c_i}[\sum_{j=1}^{n} d_{ij}(s)g_j(\varphi_j(s)) + \sum_{j=1}^{n} a_{ij}(s)g_j(\varphi_j(s-\tau))$$
$$+ \sum_{j=1}^{n}\sum_{l=1}^{n} b_{ijl}(s)g_j(\varphi_j(s-\sigma))g_l(\varphi_l(s-\nu))]ds \|\}$$
$$\le \max_{1\le i\le n} \sup_{t\in\mathbb{R}}\{\int_{-\infty}^{t} e^{-c_i(t-s)}[\sum_{j=1}^{n} \overline{d}_{ij}L_j^g \| \varphi \|_\infty + \sum_{j=1}^{n} \overline{a}_{ij}L_j^g \| \varphi \|_\infty$$
$$+ \sum_{j=1}^{n}\sum_{l=1}^{n} \overline{b}_{ijl}L_j^g M_l^g \| \varphi \|_\infty]ds\}$$
$$\le \max_{1\le i\le n} \{c_i^{-1}[\sum_{j=1}^{n} \overline{d}_{ij}L_j^g + \sum_{j=1}^{n} \overline{a}_{ij}L_j^g + \sum_{j=1}^{n}\sum_{l=1}^{n} \overline{b}_{ijl}L_j^g M_l^g]\} \| \varphi \|_\infty$$
$$= p \| \varphi \|_\infty \le \frac{pL}{1-p},$$

where $p = \max_{1\le i\le n} \{c_i^{-1}[\sum_{j=1}^{n} \overline{d}_{ij}L_j^g + \sum_{j=1}^{n} \overline{a}_{ij}L_j^g + \sum_{j=1}^{n}\sum_{l=1}^{n} \overline{b}_{ijl}L_j^g M_l^g]\} < 1$, it implies that $(\Gamma_\varphi)(t) \in \mathbb{B}$. So, the mapping Γ is a self-mapping from $\mathbb{B}$ to $\mathbb{B}$.

Next, we prove that the mapping Γ is a contraction mapping of the $\mathbb{B}$. In fact, in view of (H3), for $\forall \phi, \psi \in \mathbb{B}$, we have

$$| (\Gamma_\phi - \Gamma_\psi)_i(t) |$$
$$= | \int_{-\infty}^{t} e^{-(t-s)c_i}[\sum_{j=1}^{n} d_{ij}(s)(g_j(\phi_j(s)) - g_j(\psi_j(s))) + \sum_{j=1}^{n} a_{ij}(s)(g_j(\phi_j(s-\tau)) - g_j(\psi_j(s-\tau)))$$
$$+ \sum_{j=1}^{n}\sum_{l=1}^{n} b_{ijl}(s)(g_j(\phi_j(s-\sigma))g_l(\phi_l(s-\nu)) - g_j(\psi_j(s-\sigma))g_l(\psi_l(s-\nu)))]ds |$$
$$\le \int_{-\infty}^{t} e^{-(t-s)c_i}[\sum_{j=1}^{n} \overline{d}_{ij}L_j^g \sup_{t\in\mathbb{R}} | \phi_j(t) - \psi_j(t) | + \sum_{j=1}^{n} \overline{a}_{ij}L_j^g \sup_{t\in\mathbb{R}} | \phi_j(t) - \psi_j(t) |$$
$$+ \sum_{j=1}^{n}\sum_{l=1}^{n} \overline{b}_{ijl} | g_j(\phi_j(s-\sigma))g_l(\phi_l(s-\nu)) - g_j(\psi_j(s-\sigma))g_l(\phi_l(s-\nu))$$
$$+ g_j(\psi_j(s-\sigma))g_l(\phi_l(s-\nu)) - g_j(\psi_j(s-\sigma))g_l(\psi_l(s-\nu)) |]ds$$
$$\le \int_{-\infty}^{t} e^{-(t-s)c_i}[\sum_{j=1}^{n} \overline{d}_{ij}L_j^g \sup_{t\in\mathbb{R}} | \phi_j(t) - \psi_j(t) | + \sum_{j=1}^{n} \overline{a}_{ij}L_j^g \sup_{t\in\mathbb{R}} | \phi_j(t) - \psi_j(t) |$$

$$+ \sum_{j=1}^{n} \sum_{l=1}^{n} \overline{b}_{ijl}(L_j^g M_l^g + M_j^g L_l^g) \parallel \phi - \psi \parallel_\infty]ds$$

$$\leq c_i^{-1}[\sum_{j=1}^{n} \overline{d}_{ij}L_j^g + \sum_{j=1}^{n} \overline{a}_{ij}L_j^g + \sum_{j=1}^{n} \sum_{l=1}^{n} \overline{b}_{ijl}(L_j^g M_l^g + M_j^g L_l^g)] \parallel \phi - \psi \parallel_\infty,$$

where $i = 1, 2, \ldots, n$, it follows that

$$\parallel \Gamma_\phi - \Gamma_\psi \parallel_\infty \leq \max_{1 \leq i \leq n} \{c_i^{-1}[\sum_{j=1}^{n} \overline{a}_{ij}L_j^g + \sum_{j=1}^{n} \sum_{l=1}^{n} \overline{b}_{ijl}$$
$$\times (L_j^g M_l^g + M_j^g L_l^g)]\} \parallel \phi - \psi \parallel_\infty .$$

Notice that $q = \max_{1 \leq i \leq n} \{c_i^{-1}[\sum_{j=1}^{n} \overline{d}_{ij}L_j^g + \sum_{j=1}^{n} \overline{a}_{ij}L_j^g + \sum_{j=1}^{n} \sum_{l=1}^{n} \overline{b}_{ijl}(L_j^g M_l^g + M_j^g L_l^g)]\} < 1$, it is clear that the mapping Γ is a contraction. Therefore the mapping Γ possesses a unique fixed point $z^* \in \mathbb{B}, Tz^* = z^*$. So z^* is a weighted pseudo almost-periodic solution of system (1) in the region $\mathbb{B}$. The proof of Theorem 1 is now complete.

Theorem 2. *If the conditions (H1)–(H5) hold, then system (1) has a unique weighted pseudo almost periodic solution $z(t)$ which is globally exponentially stable.*

Proof. It follows from Theorem 1 that system (1) has at least one weighted pseudo almost periodic solution $z(t) = (z_1(t), \ldots, z_n(t))^T \in \mathbb{B}$ with initial value $u(t) = (u_1(t), \ldots, u_n(t))^T$. Let $x(t) = (x_1(t), \ldots, x_n(t))^T$ be an arbitrary solution of system (1) with initial value $\varphi^*(t) = (\varphi_1^*(t), \ldots, \varphi_n^*(t))^T$.
Let $y_i(t) = x_i(t) - z_i(t)$, $\varphi_i(t) = \varphi_i^*(t) - u_i(t)$ $i = 1 \ldots n$, then

$$y_i'(t) = -c_i(t)y_i(t) + \sum_{j=1}^{n} d_{ij}(t)(g_j(y_j(t-u) + z_j(t-u)) - g_j(z_j(t-u)))$$

$$+ \sum_{j=1}^{n} a_{ij}(t)(g_j(y_j(t-\tau) + z_j(t-\tau)) - g_j(z_j(t-\tau)))$$

$$+ \sum_{j=1}^{n} \sum_{l=1}^{n} b_{ijl}(t)(g_j(y_j(t-\sigma) + z_j(t-\sigma))g_l(y_l(t-\nu)$$

$$+ z_l(t-\nu)) - g_j(z_j(t-\sigma))g_l(z_l(t-\nu))), \quad i = 1, \ldots, n. \quad (2)$$

Let F_i be defined by

$$F_i(w) = c_i - w - \sum_{j=1}^{n} \overline{d}_{ij}L_j^g - \sum_{j=1}^{n} \overline{a}_{ij}L_j^g e^{w\tau} - \sum_{j=1}^{n} \sum_{l=1}^{n} \overline{b}_{ijl}(L_j^g e^{w\sigma} M_l^g + M_j^g L_l^g e^{w\nu}),$$

where $i = 1, \ldots, n$, $w \in [0, +\infty[$ and by (H5), we obtain that

$$F_i(0) = c_i - \sum_{j=1}^{n} \overline{d}_{ij}L_j^g - \sum_{j=1}^{n} \overline{a}_{ij}L_j^g - \sum_{j=1}^{n} \sum_{l=1}^{n} \overline{b}_{ijl}(L_j^g M_l^g + M_j^g L_l^g) > 0.$$

Since $F_i(.)$ is continuous on $[0, \infty[$ and $F_i(w) \longrightarrow -\infty; w \longmapsto +\infty$, there exist $\varepsilon_i^* > 0$ such that $F_i(\varepsilon_i^*) = 0$ and $F_i(\varepsilon_i) > 0$ for $\varepsilon_i \in (0, \varepsilon_i^*)$.

By choosing $\eta = \min\{\varepsilon_1^*, \ldots, \varepsilon_n^*\}$, we obtain that the weighted pseudo almost periodic solution of system (1) is globally exponentially stable. The globally exponential stability implies that the pseudo almost periodic solution is unique. We complete the proof.

3   Application

In order to illustrate some feature of our main results, we will apply the model for $n = 2$:

$$x_i'(t) = -c_i x_i(t) + \sum_{j=1}^{2} d_{ij}(t) g_j(x_j(t)) + \sum_{j=1}^{2} a_{ij}(t) g_j(x_j(t - \tau))$$

$$+ \sum_{j=1}^{2} \sum_{l=1}^{2} b_{ijl}(t) g_j(x_j(t - \sigma)) g_l(x_l(t - \nu)) + I_i(t), \ 1 \le i \le 2, \quad (3)$$

where $c_1 = c_2 = 2, g_1(t) = g_2(t) = \sin t, \tau = \sigma = \nu = 1, \rho(t) = e^t$

$$(d_{ij}(t))_{1 \le i,j \le 2} = \begin{pmatrix} 0.2\sin t + 0.1e^{-t} & 0.1\cos t \\ 0.1\sin\sqrt{2}t + 0.1e^{-t} & 0.2\cos\sqrt{2}t + 0.1e^{-t} \end{pmatrix}$$

$$(a_{ij}(t))_{1 \le i,j \le 2} = \begin{pmatrix} 0.1\cos t + 0.1e^{-t} & 0.2\sin t \\ 0.4\cos t + 0.1e^{-t} & 0.1\sin t + 0.1e^{-t} \end{pmatrix}, (I_i(t))_{1 \le i \le 2} = \begin{pmatrix} 0.8\cos\sqrt{5}t \\ 0.5\sin t + 0.1e^{-t} \end{pmatrix}$$

$$(b_{1jl}(t))_{1 \le j,l \le 2} = \begin{pmatrix} 0 & 0.3\sin\sqrt{3}t + 0.1e^{-t} \\ 0 & 0 \end{pmatrix}, (b_{2jl}(t))_{1 \le j,l \le 2} = \begin{pmatrix} 0 & 0.2\cos\sqrt{5}t + 0.1e^{-t} \\ 0 & 0 \end{pmatrix}$$

Then $L = 0.4, p = 0.75 < 1, q = 0.9 < 1$ and $\sup_{T>0}\{\int_{-T}^{T} e^{-c_i(T+t)} \rho(t) dt\} < \infty$.

Consequently, it is not difficult to verify that this example satisfies Theorem 1, then model (1) has a unique weighted pseudo almost periodic solution in the considered region. Figure 1 shows the oscillations of the solution of Eq. (1).

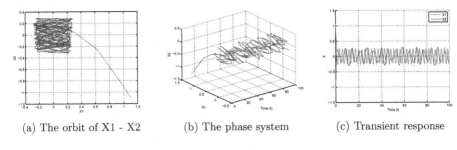

(a) The orbit of X1 - X2   (b) The phase system   (c) Transient response

Fig. 1. Example 1.

4   Conclusion

In nature there is no phenomenon that is purely periodic, and this gives the idea to consider the almost-periodic oscillation, the pseudo almost-periodic and weighted pseudo almost-periodic situations. So, in this paper, some sufficient conditions are presented ensuring the existence and uniqueness of weighted pseudo almost-periodic solutions of HOHNNs with delays (1). Finally, an illustrative example is given to demonstrate the effectiveness of the obtained results.

References

1. Xiao, B., Meng, H.: Existence and exponential stability of positive almost-periodic solutions for high-order Hopfield neural networks. Appl. Math. Model. **33**, 532–542 (2009)
2. Aouiti, C., M'hamdi, M.S., Touati, A.: Pseudo almost automorphic solutions of recurrent neural networks with time-varying coefficients and mixed delays. Neural Processing Letters (2016). doi:10.1007/s11063-016-9515-0
3. Diagana, T.: Weighted pseudo almost periodic solution to some différentiable equations. Nonlinear Anal. **68**, 2250–2260 (2008)
4. Yu, Y., Cai, M.: Existence and exponential stability of almost-periodic solutions for high-order Hopfield neural networks. Math. Comput. Model. **47**, 943–951 (2008)
5. Qiu, F., Cui, B., Wu, W.: Global exponential stability of high order recurrent neural network with time-varying delays. Appl. Math. Model. **33**, 198–210 (2009)

Sparse Extreme Learning Machine Classifier Using Empirical Feature Mapping

Takuya Kitamura[✉]

National Institute of Technology, Toyama College,
13, Hongo-cho, Toyama, Japan
kitamura@nc-toyama.ac.jp

Abstract. Usually, the solution of the conventional extreme learning machine, which is a type of single-hidden-layer feedforward neural networks, is not sparse.

In this paper, to overcome this problem, we discuss a sparse extreme learning machine using empirical feature mapping. Here, the basis vectors of empirical feature space are the linearly independent training vectors. Then, unlike the conventional extreme learning machine, only these linearly independent training vectors become support vectors. Hence, the solution of the proposed method is sparse. Using UCI bench-mark datasets, we evaluate the effectiveness of the proposed method over the conventional methods from the standpoints of the sparsity and classification capability.

Keywords: Empirical feature space · Extreme learning machine · Sparse · Support vector

1 Introduction

Recently, extreme learning machine (ELM) [1–3], which is a type of single-hidden-layer feedforward neural network (SLFNs), has been widely studied by many researchers. Unlike standard SLFNs, it is not necessary to tune the hidden layer. Namely, in training ELM, we can generate randomly hidden nodes if the activation functions are differentiable. And, we optimize only the weights $\beta = (\beta_1, \ldots, \beta_L)^\top$ between the hidden and output nodes, where L is the number of hidden nodes. Hence, the computational time of training ELM may be very faster than that of standard SLFNs. In determining β of ELM, we solve the optimization problem in order to minimize the training error and the norm of β. And furthermore, kernel method can be applied to ELM if we replace the random hidden nodes with feature mapping such as support vector machines (SVMs) [4]. However, as with least squares SVM (LS-SVM) [4,5] which is a type of SVM, the solution of the ELMs is not sparse. Hence, with huge training data, ELM entails huge storage space and the computational cost of test. To overcome these problems, in [6,7], support vectors (SVs) are chosen by adopting inequality constraints as with standard SVMs. Then, non-SVs in this method

© Springer International Publishing Switzerland 2016
A.E.P. Villa et al. (Eds.): ICANN 2016, Part I, LNCS 9886, pp. 486–493, 2016.
DOI: 10.1007/978-3-319-44778-0_57

are deleted. However, in training this type of ELM, the information of these data is lost. Hence, the solution of sparse ELM is difference from that of the conventional ELM.

In this paper, to overcome these problems, we propose sparse ELM (S-ELM), which is trained in the empirical feature space [8–12]. Namely, replacing ELM feature mapping with empirical feature mapping, we let the solution of ELM be sparse in the proposed method. First, empirical feature space, which is proposed in [9] by Xiong et al., is generated by solving eigenvalue problem of kernel matrix. Then, the values of kernel function in empirical feature space are equivalent to those in feature space. Here, to reduce the computational cost of generating empirical feature space, we use the reduced empirical feature space, which is proposed in [10] by Abe, in our work. Because the basis vectors of the reduced empirical feature space is linearly independent training vectors, we select these vectors without solving the eingenvalue problem. Then, to select these vectors, we use Cholesky factorization. Next, Using empirical feature mapping, $\boldsymbol{\beta}$ is determined by solving optimization problem in order to minimize the training error and norm of $\boldsymbol{\beta}$. Then, unlike ELM using kernel method, $\boldsymbol{\beta}$ is known to user because hidden nodes, which are empirical feature mapping, are known to user. In classification step, we need $\boldsymbol{\beta}$ and empirical feature mapping of input. To obtain this mapping, we need only linearly independent training vectors. Hence, because these training vectors can be defined as SVs, the solution of the proposed method is sparse. Furthermore, unlike ELM and SVMs using kernel method, hidden layer is not black-box.

This paper is organized as follows. In Sect. 2, we describe the conventional ELM. In Sect. 3, we propose S-ELM using empirical feature space. In Sect. 4, we demonstrate the effectiveness of the proposed method over the conventional methods through computer experiments using bench mark data sets. And we conclude our work in Sect. 5.

2 Conventional Extreme Learning Machines

In training ELM, unlike usual SLFNs, only output weights are optimized. The weights and bias terms of hidden node can be selected randomly, if the activiation functions are differentiable.

For binary classification problem, the number of training vectors and the set of m-dimensional training vectors and their labels be M and $\{\boldsymbol{x}_i, y_i\}$ ($i = 1, \ldots, M$), where $y_i = 1$ or $y_i = -1$ if the i-th training vector $\boldsymbol{x}_i$ belongs to class 1 or class 2. And, the weight vectors $\boldsymbol{a}_j$ ($j = 1, \ldots, L$) and bias terms b_j ($j = 1, \ldots, L$) between input and hidden nodes are determined randomly, where the activation function $f(\boldsymbol{a}_j^\top \boldsymbol{x}_i + b_j)$ is differentiable. The decision function $D(\boldsymbol{x})$ of ELM is given by

$$D(\boldsymbol{x}) = \text{sign}(\boldsymbol{\beta}^\top \boldsymbol{f}(\boldsymbol{x})), \tag{1}$$
$$\boldsymbol{f}(\boldsymbol{x}) = (f(\boldsymbol{a}_1^\top \boldsymbol{x} + b_1), \ldots, f(\boldsymbol{a}_L^\top \boldsymbol{x} + b_L))^\top. \tag{2}$$

Then, minimize the training errors by solving

$$F\beta = y, \tag{3}$$
$$F = (f(x_1), \ldots, f(x_M))^\top, \tag{4}$$
$$y = (y_1, \ldots, y_M)^\top. \tag{5}$$

The output weight vector β is obtained by

$$\beta = F^\dagger y, \tag{6}$$

where $F^\dagger$ is obtained by using Moore-Penrose generalized inverse of F.

And, according to [13], if the norm of output weights is small, the generalization capability is high for feedforward neural networks. Hence, instead of (3), the optimization problem is defined as follows:

$$\min \tfrac{1}{2}\beta^\top\beta + \tfrac{C}{2}\sum_{i=1}^{M}\xi_i^2 \tag{7}$$
$$\text{s.t. } \beta^\top f(x_i) = y_i - \xi_i \quad \text{for} \quad i = 1, \ldots, M, \tag{8}$$

where C and ξ_i is the hyper-parameter, which determines the trade-off between minimizing training error and the norm of β, and the slack variable for x_i In ELM, Using Kernel method, the random hidden node can be replaced with high dimension feature mapping. Then, the decision function $D(x)$ is given by

$$D(x) = f^\top(x)F^\top\left(\frac{I_{M\times M}}{C} + K\right)^{-1}y, \tag{9}$$
$$f^\top(x)F^\top = (K(x, x_1), \ldots, K(x, x_M)), \tag{10}$$
$$K_{ij} = K(x_i, x_j) \quad \text{for} \quad i, j = 1, \ldots, M, \tag{11}$$
$$K(x, x') = f^\top(x)f(x'), \tag{12}$$

where $I_{M\times M}$ ($\in \mathbb{R}^{M\times M}$) is unit matrix. In our following study, we use linear kernels: $x^\top x'$, polynomial kernels: $(x^\top x' + 1)^d$, where d is a positive integer, and radial basis function (RBF) kernels: $\exp(-\gamma\|x - x'\|^2)$, where γ is the width of the radius. Then, d and γ are kernel parameters while linear kernels do not have those. ELM using kernel method is similar to LS-SVM. As different points from LS-SVM, the dual optimization problem of ELM does not have the condition $\sum_{i=1}^{M}\alpha_i$, where α_i ($i = 1, \ldots, M$) are Lagrange multipliers, and ELM can unify for regression and classification (binary and multiclass) problems.

ELM using kernel method does not even need to determine the random hidden nodes. However, to obtain the decision function $D(x)$, it is necessary for this ELM to use all training vectors. Hence, the solution of ELM using kernel method is not sparse, and its ELM entails huge storage space and the computational cost of test.

3   Sparse Extreme Learning Machine

To overcome the above problems of ELM using kernel method, SELM training, which reduce the number of training vectors by adopting inequality constraints as with standard SVMs, has been proposed in [6,7]. However, the information of the reduced training vector is lost. In this paper, to overcome this problem, we train ELM in empirical feature space instead of reducing the number of training vectors.

3.1 Empirical Feature Mapping

Usually, the empirical feature space [9] is generated by solving the eigenvalue problem of kernel matrix K. However, it is time consuming to solve this problem and to transform input variables into variables in the empirical feature space. Hence, we use the reduced empirical feature space, which have proposed by Abe in [8]. The mapping function $h(x)$ into the reduced empirical feature space is given by

$$h(x) = (K(x, x_1^e), \ldots, K(x, x_N^e))^\top, \tag{13}$$

where x_i^e $(i = 1, ..., M')$ are the M' linearly independent training vector in the high dimension feature space. Namely, the basis vectors of the reduced empirical feature space are these training vectors, which are selected by Cholesky factorization. We assumed that the diagonal element in Cholesky factorization is zero if the argument of the square root in the diagonal element is less than or equal to a threshold value μ.

3.2 Training S-ELM Using Empirical Feature Mapping

The optimization problem of S-ELM in the reduced empirical feature space given by (7) and

$$\text{s.t.} \quad \beta^\top h(x_j) = y_i - \xi_j \quad \text{for} \quad j = 1, \ldots, M, \tag{14}$$

where β is N-dimensional vector. Then, unlike the conventional ELM, we solve the primal form of the optimization problem because $N \leq M$. β is given by

$$\beta = \left(\frac{I_{N \times N}}{C} + \sum_{i=1}^{M} h(x_i) h^\top(x_i)\right)^{-1} \sum_{i=1}^{M} y_i h(x_i), \tag{15}$$

where $I_{N \times N}$ $(\in \mathbb{R}^{N \times N})$ is unit matrix. The decision function is given by

$$D(x) = \beta^\top h(x). \tag{16}$$

Then, unlike the conventional ELM using kernel method, the β is known to user. Hence, to obtain decision function of input, we need only N' linearly independent training vector and they become SVs.

In the following, we show the proposed algorithm.

Algorithm of the Proposed S-ELM

Step 1. Select the linearly independent training data by Cholesky factorization of kernel matrix K.

Step 2. Using the selected linearly independent training data x_i^e $(i = 1, \ldots, N)$ in Step 1, calculate the reduced empirical feature mapping function $h(x)$ with (13).

Step 3. Using $h(x)$ determined in Step 2, calculate β by (15).

Step 4. Using β determined in Step 3, calculate $D(x)$ by (16).

4   Experimental Results

We compared the number of SVs and the generalization ability of ELM using kernel method, S-ELM, and LS-SVM, which is similar to the conventional ELM using kernel method, using two-class benchmark data sets [4,8,10–12,14,15] listed in the Table 1 that shows the number of inputs, training data, test data, and data sets. We measured training time using a personal computer (3.10 GHz, 2.0 GB memory, Windows 7 operating system).

Table 1. Two class Benchmark data sets

Data	Inputs	Training	Test	Sets
Banana	2	400	4900	100
B. cancer	9	200	77	100
Diabetes	8	468	300	100
German	20	700	300	100
Heart	13	170	100	100
Image	18	1300	1010	20
Ringnorm	20	400	7000	100
F. solar	9	666	400	100
Splice	60	1000	2175	20
Thyroid	5	140	75	100
Titanic	3	150	2051	100
Twonorm	20	400	7000	100
Waveform	21	400	4600	100

4.1   Selection of Hyper-Parameters

In the following study, we normalized the input ranges into [0, 1]. For ELM, S-ELM, and LS-SVM, we determined a kernel type, a kernel parameter of the selected kernels, and C by five-fold cross-validation for each problem. For S-ELM,

Table 2. Determined kernels and parameters values by five-fold cross-validation

	LS-SVM			ELM			S-ELM			
Data	kernels	d or γ	C	kernels	d or γ	C	kernels	d or γ	C	μ
Banana	RBF	$\gamma = 100$	0.1	RBF	$\gamma = 100$	0.1	RBF	$\gamma = 200$	0.1	10^{-2}
B. cancer	RBF	$\gamma = 10$	1	RBF	$\gamma = 50$	0.1	RBF	$\gamma = 50$	0.1	10^{-2}
Diabetes	RBF	$\gamma = 10$	5	RBF	$\gamma = 10$	5	Pol	$d = 3$	10	10^{-5}
German	RBF	$\gamma = 3$	50	RBF	$\gamma = 10$	10	RBF	$\gamma = 10$	5	10^{-5}
Heart	RBF	$\gamma = 1.5$	10	RBF	$\gamma = 1.5$	10	RBF	$\gamma = 1$	500	10^{-5}
Image	RBF	$\gamma = 1000$	100	RBF	$\gamma = 200$	5×10^3	RBF	$\gamma = 1000$	10^4	10^{-6}
Ringnorm	RBF	$\gamma = 100$	0.1	RBF	$\gamma = 50$	10	RBF	$\gamma = 50$	50	10^{-2}
F. solar	Pol	$d = 3$	1	Pol	$d = 4$	0.1	Linear	–	10^3	10^{-2}
Splice	RBF	$\gamma = 10$	50	RBF	$\gamma = 10$	10	RBF	$\gamma = 15$	10	10^{-2}
Thyroid	RBF	$\gamma = 100$	5	RBF	$\gamma = 100$	5	RBF	$\gamma = 100$	100	10^{-3}
Titanic	Linear	–	5	RBF	$\gamma = 100$	5	RBF	$\gamma = 100$	0.1	10^{-2}
Twonorm	Pol	$d = 2$	0.1	RBF	$\gamma = 0.5$	5	RBF	$\gamma = 1.5$	10	10^{-3}
Waveform	RBF	$\gamma = 15$	1	RBF	$\gamma = 15$	1	RBF	$\gamma = 10$	5	10^{-3}

we determined the threshold value μ of Cholesky factorization by five-fold cross-validation. We selected a kernel type from linear, polynomial, and RBF kernels. If we selected polynomial or RBF kernels, we selected d or γ from $\{2, 3, 4, 5\}$ or $\{0.1, 0.5, 1, 1.5, 3, 5, 10, 15, 20, 100, 200, 500, 1000\}$. And we selected C from $\{0.1, 1, 5, 10, 50, 100, 500, 10^3, 5 \times 10^3, 10^4\}$ and threshold value of Cholesky factorization μ from $\{10^{-2}, 10^{-3}, 10^{-4}, 10^{-5}, 10^{-6}\}$. Table 2 shows the selected type of kernels and parameters by the above procedure. In this table, "Pol." denote polynomial kernels.

4.2 Performance Comparison

Table 3 shows the average recognition rates of the test data sets, their standard deviations, which are denoted in columns of "Rec.", and the average number of support vectors which are denoted in columns of "SVs".

The Number of SVs. In Table 3, for all problems, LS-SVM and the conventional ELM are the same number of SVs as training vectors. Namely, their solution is not sparse. On the other hand, for all problems, the number of SVs of the proposed S-ELM is fewer than those of LS-SVM and the conventional ELM. And, for five problems, the number of SVs of the proposed S-ELM is fewer than half of those of LS-SVM and the conventional ELM. Especially, for F. Solar and Titanic datasets, the number of SVs of the proposed S-ELM is much fewer than one tenth of those of LS-SVM and the conventional ELM. According to the comparison with the conventional methods, we can affirm that the proposed S-ELM is effective from the standpoint of sparsity.

Table 3. Comparison of the average recognition rates in percent, standard deviations of the rates, and the average number of support vectors

	LS-SVM		ELM		S-ELM	
Data	Rec.	SVs	Rec.	SVs	Rec.	SVs
Banana	89.24 ± 0.53	400	89.27 ± 0.51	400	**89.51 ± 0.46**	**157**
B. cancer	73.61 ± 4.49	200	**74.65 ± 4.25**	200	73.96 ± 4.56	**164**
Diabetes	76.96 ± 1.56	468	76.94 ± 1.58	468	**77.19 ± 1.69**	**165**
German	76.23 ± 2.09	700	**76.26 ± 2.07**	700	75.93 ± 2.18	**689**
Heart	**84.21 ± 3.07**	170	84.16 ± 3.08	170	84.10 ± 3.04	**131**
Image	**97.34 ± 0.60**	1300	96.94 ± 0.42	1300	97.15 ± 0.61	**1197**
Ringnorm	**98.55 ± 0.11**	400	95.43 ± 0.62	400	96.30 ± 0.46	**399**
F. solar	66.63 ± 1.62	666	66.60 ± 1.73	666	**67.08 ± 1.71**	**9**
Splice	**89.38 ± 0.72**	1000	89.11 ± 0.69	1000	88.93 ± 0.75	**977**
Thyroid	**95.97 ± 2.17**	140	95.95 ± 2.22	140	95.77 ± 1.99	**85**
Titanic	77.34 ± 1.15	150	**77.57 ± 1.03**	150	77.29 ± 0.67	**11**
Twonorm	97.40 ± 0.18	400	**97.57 ± 0.13**	400	97.55 ± 0.13	**155**
Waveform	**90.31 ± 0.39**	400	90.28 ± 0.41	400	90.26 ± 0.43	**399**

Generalization Ability. In Table 3, through Welch's t-test whose level of significance is 5 (%), we can affirm that there is no significant difference between the average recognition rate of the proposed S-ELM and the conventional ELM for almost problems except Banana, Ringnorm, F. Solar, and Titanic datasets. And, for three problems, the proposed S-ELM performs better than the conventional ELM through Welch's t-test. Furthermore, for almost problems except Banana and Ringnorm and Twonorm dataset, we can affirm that there is no significant difference between the average recognition rate of the proposed S-ELM and LS-SVM through Welch's t-test. And, for two problems, the proposed S-ELM performs better than the conventional ELM through Welch's t-test. According to the comparison with the conventional methods, we can affirm that the proposed S-ELM performs the same or better than the conventional methods from the standpoint of the generalization ability.

5   Conclusion

In this paper, we proposed S-ELM using empirical feature mapping. Because, unlike the conventional ELM using kernel method, we require only linearly independent training vectors in order to obtain the decision function of input. Namely, the solution of S-ELM is sparse.

According to the computer experiments using two-class benchmark data sets, we can affirm that the proposed S-ELM performed much better than the conventional ELM and LS-SVM from the standpoint of sparsity. And we can affirm that the proposed S-ELM performed the same or better than the conventional ELM and LS-SVM from the standpoint of classification.

References

1. Huang, G.B., Zhu, Q.Y., Siew, C.K.: Extreme learning machine: a new learning scheme of feedforward neural networks. In: International Joint Conference on Neural Networks (IJCNN 2004), vol. 2, pp. 985–990 (2004)
2. Huang, G.B., Zhu, Q.Y., Siew, C.K.: Extreme learning machine: theory and application. Neurocomputing **70**(1–3), 489–501 (2006)
3. Huang, G.B., Zhou, H., Ding, X., Zhang, R.: Extreme learning machine for regression and multiclass classification. IEEE Trans. Cybern. **42**(2), 513–529 (2012)
4. Abe, S.: Support Vector Machines for Pattern Classification (Advances in Pattern Recognition). Springer-Verlag, London (2010)
5. Suykens, J.A.K., Vandewalle, J.: Least squares support vector machine classifiers. Neural Process. Lett. **9**(3), 293–300 (1999)
6. Huang, G.B., Ding, X., Zhou, H., Westover, M.B.: Sparse extreme learnin machine for classification. Neurocomputing **74**(1–3), 155–163 (2010)
7. Bai, Z., Huang, G.B., Wang, D., Wang, H.: Optimization method based extreme learning machine for classification. IEEE Trans. Cybern. **44**(10), 1858–1870 (2014)
8. Abe, S.: Sparse least squares support vector training in the reduced empirical feature space. Pattern Anal. Appl. **10**(3), 203–214 (2007)
9. Xiong, H., Swamy, M.N.S., Ahmad, M.O.: Optimizing the Kernel in the empirical feature space. IEEE Trans. Neural Netw. **16**(2), 460–474 (2005)
10. Kitamura, T., Sekine, T.: A novel method of sparse least squares support vector machines in class empirical feature space. In: Huang, T., Zeng, Z., Li, C., Leung, C.S. (eds.) ICONIP 2012, Part II. LNCS, vol. 7664, pp. 475–482. Springer, Heidelberg (2012)
11. Kitamura, T., Takeuchi, S., Abe, S., Fukui, K.: Subspace-based support vector machines for pattern classification. Neural Netw. **22**, 558–567 (2009)
12. Kitamura, T., Takeuchi, S., Abe, S.: Feature selection and fast training of subspace based support vector machines. In: International Joint Conference on Neural Networks (IJCNN 2010), pp. 1967–1972 (2010)
13. Bartlett, P.L.: The sample complexity of pattern classification with neural networks: the size of the weights is more important than the size of the network. IEEE Trans. Inf. Theor. **44**(2), 525–536 (1998)
14. Rätsch, G., Onda, T., Müller, K.R.: Soft margins for AdaBoost. Mach. Learn. **42**(3), 287–320 (2001)
15. http://archive.ics.uci.edu/ml

Three Approaches to Train Echo State Network Actors of Adaptive Critic Design

Petia Koprinkova-Hristova[⊠]

Institute of Information and Communication Technologies,
Bulgarian Academy of Sciences, Acad. G. Bonchev Street bl.25A,
1113 Sofia, Bulgaria
pkoprinkova@bas.bg

Abstract. The paper compares three approaches to train Echo state network (ESN) actors of Adaptive Critic Design (ACD): the classical gradient-based learning rule and two associative learning rules. First associative rule exploits the Hebbian learning law of the Adaptive Search Element from the seminal paper of Barto et al., while the the second one uses the Temporal Difference (TD) error for both critic and actor elements. The proposed learning approaches were applied to optimization of a complex nonlinear process for bio-polymer production. The comparison of the obtained results was done with respect to the convergence speed as well as to the reached local optima.

Keywords: Dynamic programming · Reinforcement Learning · Hebbian learning · Adaptive Critic Design · Echo State Network

1 Introduction

Adaptive Critic Designs (ACD) [14] are closely related to the behavioral model of "learning from experience" called Reinforcement Learning (RL) [1]. The core of these methods is in approximation of Bellman's equation [2] by a neural network called "adaptive critic" so that it is able to predict "future outcomes" of the current actions. Then the critic predictions are exploited to train an actor network by solving dynamic programming task in forward manner. During the last thirty years theoretical developments in this field led to numerous variations of optimal control approaches [11]. True on-line applications of ACD approaches, however, need very fast training algorithms [15]. That is why in [7,8] was proposed to use a recently developed class of Recurrent Neural Networks (RNNS) called Echo State Networks (ESNs) [4]. Their structure incorporates a randomly generated dynamic reservoir of neurons. The only trainable connections from the reservoir to the readout layer could be tuned on-line by Recursive Least Squares (RLS) method.

In case of ACD the critic and actor are trained by a gradient algorithm called "backpropagation of utility" [21]. In contrast, the RL from [1] uses associative (Hebbian) learning laws for both critic and actor networks. From biological point

© Springer International Publishing Switzerland 2016
A.E.P. Villa et al. (Eds.): ICANN 2016, Part I, LNCS 9886, pp. 494–501, 2016.
DOI: 10.1007/978-3-319-44778-0_58

of view, however, the gradient learning is considered as non-plausible while the associative learning algorithms are closer to the biological neurons behavior. That is why in [9,10] it was proposed to combine the ESN critic trained by RLS with the ESN actor trained by the associative learning law of Adaptive Search Element from [1].

In the present work another associative rule that exploits the states of the reservoir neurons as eligibility traces and TD error instead of critic prediction (reinforcement signal) was proposed and applied for training of both critic and actor. It is tested on the same optimization task (of a complex nonlinear process for bio-polymer production) as in [10]. The obtained results are compared with respect to the convergence speed as well as to the obtained solution, i.e. the reached local optima.

2   Problem Formulation

2.1   ACD Approach

The main scheme of ACD [16] is given on Fig. 1.

Here the dashed lines represent the training cycle. The vector $State(t)$ contains measurable object variables that are indicators of its current state, $a(t)$ is action (control) variable. The critic ESN has to be trained to predict the discounted sum of future utility $U(t)$, i.e. to approximate Bellman's equation as follows:

$$J\left(State(k), a(k)\right) = \sum_{t=0}^{k} \gamma^t U\left(State(t), a(t)\right) \tag{1}$$

where γ is discount factor taking values between 0 and 1. The critic network is trained so as to minimize the Temporal Difference (TD) error:

$$TDerror(k) = J(k) - U(k) - \gamma J(k+1) \tag{2}$$

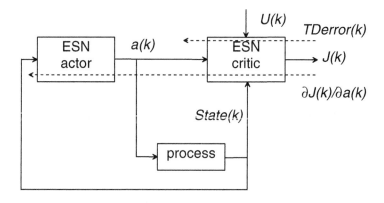

Fig. 1. ACD scheme with closed-loop control and ESN actor.

The actor ESN is the controller that has to be tuned so as to generate control actions that maximize (minimize) the utility. The feedback connection from the process state to the controller can include the full state vector or some of the state variables. The dashed lines represent the backpropagation of training signals for the critic (upper) and the actor (lower) respectively.

2.2   Echo State Network

Complete description of the ESN structure can be found in [4]. Here only basic mathematical notions used further in the paper are given. The ESN output vector denoted here by $out(k)$ (it will be $J(k)$ or $a(k)$ for critic and action network respectively) for the current time instance k is a function of its input and current state:

$$out(k) = f^{out} \left(W^{out} \left[in(k) \ R(k) \right] \right) \tag{3}$$

Here, $in(k)$ is a vector of network inputs and $R(k)$ a vector composed of the reservoir neuron states; f^{out} is a linear function (usually the identity), W^{out} is a $n_{out} \times (n_{in} + n_R)$ trainable matrix (here n_{out}, n_{in} and n_R are the sizes of the corresponding vectors out, in and R).

The neurons in the reservoir have a simple sigmoid output function f^{res} (usually hyperbolic tangent) that depends on both the ESN input $in(k)$ and the previous reservoir state $R(k-1)$:

$$R(k) = f^{res} \left(W^{in} in(k) + W^{res} R(k-1) \right) \tag{4}$$

Here W^{in} and W^{res} are $n_{in} \times n_R$ and $n_R \times n_R$ matrices that are randomly generated and are not trainable. There are different approaches for reservoir parameter production [12]. A recent approach used in the present investigation is proposed in [18]. It is called intrinsic plasticity (IP) and suggests initial adjustment of these matrices, aimed at increasing the entropy of the reservoir neurons outputs. For on-line training, the RLS algorithm [4] was used.

3   Three Training Algorithms

3.1   Gradient Training of ESN Actor

The details of backpropagation of utility and gradients calculations can be found in [8]. Here only the basic gradient training rule for ESN actor output weights W_a^{out} is reminded as follows:

$$W_a^{out}{}_i(k) = W_a^{out}{}_{i-1}(k) \pm \alpha \frac{\partial J_i(k)}{\partial a_i(k)} R_{ai}(k) \tag{5}$$

where i denotes the iteration number and $0 < \alpha < 1$ is the learning rate. The sign $(+ \text{ or } -)$ in the above equation depends on the optimization task (i.e. whether it is to maximize or to minimize the utility function).

3.2 Associative Training of ESN Actor

Following [1] learning rule of Associative Search Element (ASE) and formulas from [9] the associative learning rule for actor output weights W_a^{out} becomes:

$$W_a^{out}{}_i(k) = W_a^{out}{}_{i-1}(k) \pm \alpha J_i(k)e_{ai}(k) \tag{6}$$

where $e_{ai}(k)$ denotes the eligibility trace of all neurons in the reservoir of the action ESN. According to [1] and accounting for specificity of the ACD scheme used here, the eligibility traces become:

$$e_{ai}(k) = \delta e_{ai-1}(k) + (1 - \delta)a_i(k)R_{ai}(k) \tag{7}$$

where $0 < \delta < 1$ is decay rate of the trace.

3.3 TD Learning Algorithm for both ESN Critic and Actor

In most works that relate the RL elements onto neural correlates in the human brain, e.g. [13], the reinforcement signal is related to the dopamine activity and the TD error of its prediction is used for learning by both critic and actor elements. This motivated the idea to explore such kind of learning rule for both ESNs in the ACD scheme from Fig. 1.

The proposed rule is similar to the associative rule for training of the critic element from [1], but the reinforcement signal is replaced by the TD error. Another difference is that the eligibility traces are replaced by the current signal that enters the output layer of the ESN, i.e. a vector consisting of the current reservoir state and the current ESN input (see Eq. (3)). Motives for this change come form the fact that, due to dynamical nature of ESN, the current state of its reservoir depends not only on its current input but also on the history of reservoir states. Hence it could be considered as a "trace" of the ESN previous states. Thus the modified TD error-based learning rule become:

$$W_c^{out}{}_i(k) = W_c^{out}{}_{i-1}(k) \pm \alpha TDerror_i(k) \left[R_{ci}(k) \ in_{ci}(k) \right] \tag{8}$$

$$W_a^{out}{}_i(k) = W_a^{out}{}_{i-1}(k) \pm \alpha TDerror_i(k) \left[R_{ai}(k) \ in_{ai}(k) \right] \tag{9}$$

Here $in(k)$ denotes the corresponding ESN input and $R(k)$ corresponding reservoir current state. The $TDerror(k)$ is calculated according to Eq. (2). In all equations i denotes iteration number.

Further in the text this learning rule is briefly called TD learning in order to be distinguishable from the previously described associative learning approach.

4 Simulation Experiment Description

4.1 PHB Production Process

The test object under consideration here (PHB production process) is a biotechnological process for mixed culture cultivation. During it the sugars (glucose) are converted to lactate by the microorganism *L.delbrueckii* and then the lactate is converted to PHB (poly-β-hydroxybutyrate) by the microorganism *R.euthropha*. The target process product (PHB) is biodegradable polymer used as thermoplastic in food and drug industry. In [20] quite a complete mathematical model of the process has been developed and different control strategies were exploited separately or in combination. The model consists of seven nonlinear ordinary differential equations. More details can be found in [6,20]. This model was used as process simulator in our simulation experiment. The target product overall outcome is the subject of optimization in present study.

4.2   Optimization Task

The target product is measured by grams per liter and here was denoted by Q. The reactor volume in liters is denoted by V. Hence the utility function that is target product in grams at time step k is:

$$U(k) = Q(k)V(k) \tag{10}$$

and the aim of optimization procedure will be to maximize the overall outcome by the end of process, i.e.:

$$U_{sum} = \sum_{k=0}^{N} Q(k)V(k) \tag{11}$$

Vector $State(k)$ includes all main process state variables, i.e.:

$$State(k) = \begin{bmatrix} X_1(k) & S(k) & P(k) & X_2(k) & N(k) & Q(k) \end{bmatrix} \tag{12}$$

where X_1 and X_2 denote concentrations of two microorganisms; P is the intermediate metabolite (lactate) concentration; N is the nitrogen source concentration; S is sugar source concentration.

The applied control scheme is described in more details in [6,20]. We suppose that all concentration controllers work properly, i.e. they are able to follow the set points correctly. Hence the optimization task to be solved is to determine the proper values of the set points through time. The control vector consists of the three set points of the main controllers as follows:

$$a(k) = \begin{bmatrix} S^*(k) & N^*(k) & DO^*(k) \end{bmatrix} \tag{13}$$

Here DO is dissolved oxygen concentration in the cultural broth.

Following the ACD scheme from Fig. 1, for each control variable a corresponding ESN actor network was trained. In present work we choose to have only one input of each actor ESN - the key intermediate metabolite P since it is on-line measurable and its concentration is of crucial importance for the process.

All control variables have imposed restrictions in terms of the allowed minimum and maximum values. They were included in the utility function to be optimized by penalty terms as follows:

$$U^{opt}(k) = U(k) - \frac{1}{2}ra(k)^2 \tag{14}$$

Here $ra(k)$ is a kind of punishment signal in the case when calculated by the ESN control action is outside allowed interval $[a_{min}, a_{max}]$ as follows:

$$ra(k) = \begin{cases} a_{min} - a(k), & a(k) < a_{min} \\ 0, & a_{min} \le a(k) \le a_{max} \\ a(k) - a_{max}, & a(k) > a_{max} \end{cases} \qquad (15)$$

5 Results and Discussion

For simulation of ESNs the Matlab toolbox [17] was used. The critic network has 9 inputs (6 for the process state variables plus 3 for the control actions), 10 reservoir neurons and 1 output. All actor networks have one input, one output and 5 neurons in the reservoirs. All reservoir neurons have hyperbolic tangent output function. The initial set point time profiles were created using expert information given in [6]. Detailed optimization algorithm can be found in [5]. It consists of consecutive critic and actor training iterations. Initial value of the discounting factor γ was zero and it was gradually increased up to 0.5 during first 1000 iterations. During the last 200 iterations of the simulation γ remained constant.

Figure 2 represents changes of overall utility (Eq. (11)) through iteration steps. As can be seen from it, both associative and TD learning algorithms outperform the gradient one but the best outcome was achieved by the associative algorithm.

From the other hand, the associative algorithm behaves more like the gradient one with respect to big jumps up and down around the prospective optimal value during iterations. This similarity might be explained with the same training algorithm (RLS) of the critic element in both cases. However, by the end of

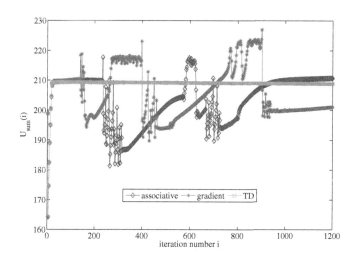

Fig. 2. Change of utility function value during iterative optimization.

iterations the associative algorithm is able to settle down and to approach the local optimum while the gradient one stacked into non-optimal valley, probably due to the bigger steps it did in the course of training. Hence the preliminary results demonstrate better stability of the associative algorithm in comparison with the gradient one.

In contrast, in the case of TD algorithm the critic is trained by the same TD error-based learning rule. This might be the reason why the TD algorithm reaches much faster the local optimum and slightly oscillates around it until the end of iterations. However, the preliminary investigations showed that TD algorithm is stable only for very small values of the learning rate and each attempt to increase it lead to oscillations through iterations, slow convergence and even inability to reach the optimum.

6 Conclusions

The presented comparative investigation of a gradient and two associative learning algorithms of ESN actors within ACD schemes having ESN for both critic and actor elements showed that no matter whether the critic element is trained with RLS or associative rule, the associative/TD training of the actors achieved much better results in comparison with the gradient one. Another interesting observation is that the ESN reservoir state can be successfully considered as a kind of eligibility trace like in seminal work of Barto et al. [1].

The reported results are preliminary. More exhaustive investigations using different test objects and variety of optimization tasks are needed to prove the advantages and disadvantages of all considered here algorithms.

Further theoretical investigations on the similarity between simple two neurons architecture form Barto et al. [1] and more complicated dynamic reservoir structures used in present work will be another direction of future work.

References

1. Barto, A.G., Sutton, R.S., Anderson, C.W.: Neuronlike adaptive elements that can solve difficult learning control problems. IEEE Trans. Syst. Man Cybern. **13**(5), 834–846 (1983)
2. Bellman, R.E.: Dynamic Programming. Princeton Universty Press, Princeton (1957)
3. Bertsekas, D.P., Tsitsiklis, J.N.: Neuro-Dymanic Programming. Athena Scientific, Belmont (1996)
4. Jaeger, H.: Tutorial on training recurrent neural networks, covering BPPT, RTRL, EKF and the "echo state network" approach. GMD Report 159, German National Research Center for Information Technology (2002)
5. Koprinkova-Hristova, P., Palm, G.: Adaptive critic design with ESN critic for bioprocess optimization. In: Diamantaras, K., Duch, W., Iliadis, L.S. (eds.) ICANN 2010, Part II. LNCS, vol. 6353, pp. 438–447. Springer, Heidelberg (2010)
6. Koprinkova-Hristova, P.: Knowledge-based approach to control of mixed culture cultivation for PHB production process. Biotechnol. Biotechnol. Equip. **22**(4), 964–967 (2008)

7. Koprinkova-Hristova, P., Oubbati, M., Palm, G.: Adaptive critic design with echo state net-work. In: Proceedings of 2010 IEEE International Conference on Systems, Man and Cybernetics, Istanbul, Turkey, 10–13 October 2010, pp. 1010–1015 (2010)
8. Koprinkova-Hristova, P., Oubbati, M., Palm, G.: Heuristic dynamic programming using echo state network as online trainable adaptive critic. Int. J. Adapt. Control Signal Process. **27**(10), 902–914 (2013)
9. Koprinkova-Hristova, P.: Adaptive critic design and heuristic search for optimization. In: Lirkov, I., Margenov, S., Waśniewski, J. (eds.) LSSC 2013. LNCS, vol. 8353, pp. 248–255. Springer, Heidelberg (2014)
10. Koprinkova-Hristova, P.: Hebbian versus gradient training of ESN actors in closed-loop ACD. In: Dimov, I., Fidanova, S., Lirkov, I. (eds.) NMA 2014. LNCS, vol. 8962, pp. 95–102. Springer, Heidelberg (2015)
11. Lenardis, G.G.: A retrospective on adaptive dynamic programming for control. In: Proceedings of International Joint Conference on Neural Networks, Atlanta, GA, USA, 14–19 June 2009, pp. 1750–1757 (2009)
12. Lukosevicius, M., Jaeger, H.: Reservoir computing approaches to recurrent neural network training. Comput. Sci. Rev. **3**, 127–149 (2009)
13. Niv, Y.: Reinforcement learning in the brain. J. Math. Psychol. **53**(3), 139–154 (2009)
14. Prokhorov, D.V.: Adaptive critic designs and their applications. Ph.D. dissertation. Department of Electrical Engineering, Texas Tech. Univ., (1997)
15. Prokhorov, D.: Training recurrent neurocontrollers for real-time applications. IEEE Trans. Neural Networks **18**(4), 1003–1015 (2007)
16. Si, J., Wang, Y.-T.: On-line learning control by association and reinforcement. IEEE Trans. Neural Networks **12**(2), 264–276 (2001)
17. Simple and very simple Matlab toolbox for Echo State Networks by H. Jaeger and group members. http://www.reservoir-computing.org/software
18. Schrauwen, B., Wandermann, M., Verstraeten, D., Steil, J.J.: Improving reservoirs using intrinsic plasticity. Neurocomputing **71**, 1159–1171 (2008)
19. Sutton, R.S.: Learning to predict by methods of temporal differences. Mach. Learn. **3**, 9–44 (1988)
20. Tohyama, M., Patarinska, T., Qiang, Z., Shimizu, K.: Modeling of the mixed culture and periodic control for PHB production. Biochem. Eng. J. **10**, 157–173 (2002)
21. Werbos, P.J.: Backpropagation through time: what it does and how to do it. Proc. IEEE **78**(10), 1550–1560 (1990)

Increase of the Resistance to Noise in Data for Neural Network Solution of the Inverse Problem of Magnetotellurics with Group Determination of Parameters

Igor Isaev[1]([⊠]), Eugeny Obornev[2], Ivan Obornev[1,2], Mikhail Shimelevich[2], and Sergey Dolenko[1]([⊠])

[1] D.V. Skobeltsyn Institute of Nuclear Physics,
M.V. Lomonosov Moscow State University, Moscow, Russia
isaev_igor@mail.ru, dolenko@srd.sinp.msu.ru
[2] S. Ordjonikidze Russian State Geological Prospecting University, Moscow, Russia

Abstract. When a multi-parameter inverse problem is solved with artificial neural networks, it is usually solved separately for each determined parameter (autonomous determination). In their preceding studies, the authors have demonstrated that joining parameters into groups with simultaneous determination of the values of all parameters within each group may in some cases improve the precision of solution of inverse problems. In this study, the observed effect has been investigated in respect to its resistance to noise in data. The study has been performed at the example of the inverse problem of magnetotellurics, which has a high dimensionality.

Keywords: Artificial neural networks · Perceptron · Multi-parameter inverse problems · Noise resistance · Group determination of parameters

1 Introduction

Inverse problems (IP) are an important class of problems. Almost any problem of indirect measurements can be considered to be one of them. Inverse problems include many problems from the domains of geophysics [1], spectroscopy [2], various types of tomography [3], and many others.

Among them is the IP of magnetotelluric sounding, where the purpose is to find the distribution of conductivity in the thick of the Earth by the components of electromagnetic field measured on its surface [4, p. 157]. Due to shielding of the underlying layers by the overlying ones, the contribution of the deeper-lying layers is smaller.

In general case, such problems have no analytical solution. So usually they are solved by optimization methods based on repeated solution of the direct

This study has been performed at the expense of the grant of Russian Science Foundation (project no. 14-11-00579).

A.E.P. Villa et al. (Eds.): ICANN 2016, Part I, LNCS 9886, pp. 502–509, 2016.
DOI: 10.1007/978-3-319-44778-0_59

problem with minimization of residuals [4, p. 158], or by matrix-based methods using regularization by Tikhonov [5, p. 304].

Optimization methods have several drawbacks, such as high computational cost, the need for good first approximation, and, most importantly, the need to have a correct model for solving the direct problem. For regularization based methods, the main difficulty is the necessity to choose a regularization parameter. In this study we consider artificial neural networks (ANN) as an alternative method of solving various IP [6–8] that is free from these shortcomings.

In practical tasks, it is often necessary to find the distribution of some parameter in one area of space by the values of some features measured in another area of space. Thus, the sought-for distribution has to be defined by a finite number of parameters, i.e. by introducing a so-called parameterization scheme with subsequent interpolation of the parameter values to the whole area. So there emerges a multi-parameter IP.

In ANN solution of multi-parameter IPs, the possible approaches are:

1. *Autonomous determination* - solution of a separate single-output IP, creating a separate ANN for each of the determined parameters. This approach is the most universal one, and it is used most often.
2. *Simultaneous determination* of all the sought parameters, creating a single ANN with the number of outputs N_O equal to the full number of the determined parameters. Efficiency of such approach rapidly degrades with increasing N_O.
3. *Group determination* - joining parameters into groups with simultaneous determination of parameters (creating a single ANN) within each group. The method of parameter grouping is imposed by physical sense of the determined parameters and by their known interconnections.

In [9], it has been demonstrated that when solving the IP of magnetotelluric sounding (MTS IP), group determination of parameters in some cases allows increasing the quality of problem solution compared to autonomous determination. Later, this effect was confirmed for other parameterization schemes [10]. It has been concluded that the observed effect was caused by fundamental properties of ANN rather than by properties of specific data.

The purpose of the present study was testing of the observed effect for resilience to noise in data.

2 Parameterization Scheme

In this study, we consider the 2D case, i.e. a vertical section of the Earth's surface. The electrical conductivity in the direction perpendicular to the plane of the section is assumed to be constant. We consider the most general model of medium parameterization - the so-called macro-grid. In this case, the distribution of conductivity is described by its values in the nodes of the macro-grid, and the conductivity values among the nodes are calculated by interpolation. A block

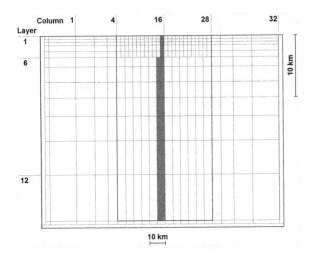

Fig. 1. Section parameterization scheme.

denoted by its column number and row number, corresponds to the node of the macro-grid, coinciding with the upper right corner of the block (Fig. 1).

The vertical size of the blocks is determined by the penetration depth of electromagnetic waves, limited by the skin effect. The lower border of each block corresponds to limiting penetration depth of an electromagnetic wave with definite measurement frequency. The number of blocks along the vertical equals the number of measurement frequencies - 13.

Horizontal size of blocks in the studied central ("anomalous") area is set according to the desired resolution. Most interesting is the central area from column 4 to 28 and from layer 1 to 12. Side areas are necessary to set border conditions for numeric solution of the direct problem, so their size gradually increases towards the edges.

As the conductivity ranges from 10^{-4} to $1\,\mathrm{S/m}$, the ANN was fed with decimal logarithm of the absolute conductivity values, ranging from -4 to 0.

3   Data

Work data were obtained by numerical solution of the direct problem [11, p. 213] by finite difference method. The initial data set contained 30,000 samples, divided into training, validation, and test sets in the ratio 70:20:10, respectively. The samples were obtained for random combinations of conductivity of blocks.

The values of 4 components of the electromagnetic field ρ^E, φ^E, ρ^H, φ^H were calculated for 13 frequencies in 126 pickets of the Earth's surface. So the input data dimensionality was $4 \times 13 \times 126 = 6552$. High input dimensionality requires data preprocessing by compression or selection of significant features.

The output data dimensionality corresponds to the number of nodes of the macro-grid $N_O = 336$. High output dimensionality also requires special approaches to the solution, which were the subject of this study.

4 Use of the Neural Network

The neural network was used as follows. Training was performed on the training data set. To prevent overtraining, it was stopped at 500 epochs without error improvement on the validation set. Independent estimation of the results was performed on the test (out-of-sample) sets (with various types and levels of noise described below).

For autonomous determination, significant input feature selection was performed for each determined parameter [12]. For group determination, the ANN is fed with the features significant for any of the determined parameters. The number of outputs of the ANN is determined by the size of grouping window.

In this study, the IP was solved with perceptrons with 3 hidden layers, having the following number of neurons: 24, 16, 8 for networks with 6 or less outputs; 26, 18, 10 for networks with output dimension from 7 to 9; 28, 20, 12 for the network with 10 outputs; 30, 22, 14 for networks with 11 or 12 outputs; 32, 24, 16 for the network with 13 outputs.

All hidden layers had a logistic activation function; the output layer had a linear one. For each considered configuration of the grouping window, 5 networks with various initializations of weights were trained. The statistical indicators of their performance were averaged.

ANN trained on the data without adding noise were applied to noisy test data sets, containing noise of various types and levels.

5 Description of the Noise

Two types of noise were considered: additive and multiplicative, and two kinds of statistics: uniform noise (uniform distribution) and Gaussian noise (normal distribution). The value of each observed feature was transformed as follows:

$$x_i^{agn} = x_i + norminv(random, \mu = 0, \sigma = noiselevel) \cdot max(x_i) \qquad (1)$$

$$x_i^{aun} = x_i + (1 - 2 \cdot random) \cdot noiselevel \cdot max(x_i) \qquad (2)$$

$$x_i^{mgn} = x_i \cdot (1 + norminv(random, \mu = 0, \sigma = noiselevel)) \qquad (3)$$

$$x_i^{mun} = x_i \cdot (1 + (1 - 2 \cdot random) \cdot noiselevel) \qquad (4)$$

for additive Gaussian (agn), additive uniform (aun), multiplicative Gaussian (mgn), and multiplicative uniform (mun) noise, respectively. Here, $random$ is a random value in the range from 0 to 1, $norminv$ function returns the inverse normal distribution, $max(x_i)$ is the maximum value of the given feature over all patterns, $noise\ level$ is the level of noise (the considered values were: 1 %, 3 %, 5 %, 10 %, 20 %).

To work with noise, each of the 300 patterns of the initial test set was used to produce 10 patterns with various noise implementations for each of the noisy data sets (with various types and levels of noise). Thus, each of the noisy test sets contained 3000 patterns.

6   Results

From Fig. 2, it can be seen that resistance of the neural network solution of the IP to additive noise is worse than that to multiplicative noise, and resistance to Gaussian noise is worse than that to uniform noise. At high noise levels, group determination allows significant improvement of the quality of the solution.

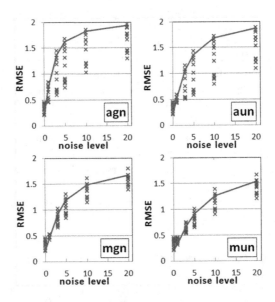

Fig. 2. Dependence of the solution quality (root mean squared error, RMSE) for determined parameter no. 17 (layer 1) on noise level for various noise types and statistics, for autonomous determination (line) and group determination (markers).

The effect of group determination can be also observed for all other parameters (Figs. 3, 4, 5 and 6), starting from some definite noise level depending on noise type. It should be noted that at increasing noise level, the size of parameter grouping window, at which group determination gives maximum effect, is shifted towards greater values (Figs. 4, 5 and 6).

Also note that for parameter no. 50 the effect of group determination is not observed without noise (Fig. 6). However, in presence of noise the effect is the more expressed, the stronger is the noise in data for any parameter (Figs. 2 and 6).

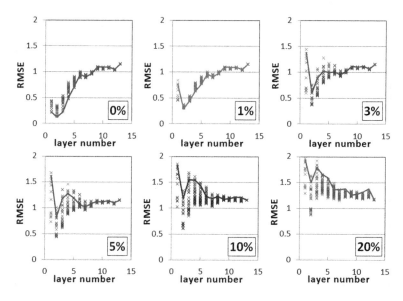

Fig. 3. Dependence of the solution quality (RMSE) on output (layer) number for additive Gaussian noise in data at various noise levels (0, 1, 3, 5, 10, 20%), for autonomous determination (line) and group determination (markers).

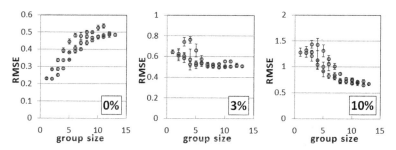

Fig. 4. Dependence of the solution quality (RMSE) on the size of grouping window for determined parameter no. 83, for additive uniform noise in data, at various noise levels (0, 3, 10%).

The observed effects can be explained with the properties of a multi-layer perceptron as a universal approximator. When a perceptron has several outputs, the composite features extracted in the hidden layers have to be optimal for approximation of all the outputs at once. This results in a more rigid approximating dependence, which is also more noise resistant. That is why the effect of group determination of parameters is more pronounced at higher levels of noise at the input (Fig. 2). On the other hand, higher level of noise requires a more rigid approximation provided with a greater number of grouped parameters (Figs. 4 and 6).

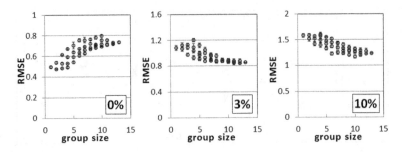

Fig. 5. Dependence of the solution quality (RMSE) on grouping window size for determined parameter no. 116, for multiplicative Gaussian noise in data, at various noise levels (0, 3, 10 %).

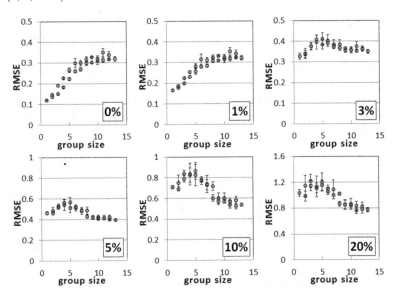

Fig. 6. Dependence of the solution quality (RMSE) on grouping window size for determined parameter no. 50, for multiplicative uniform noise in data, at various noise levels.

7   Conclusions

This study considered group determination of parameters for neural network solution of a multi-parameter inverse problem in presence of noise in data, at the example of the 2D inverse problem of magnetotellurics.

The ANN solution, both for autonomous and for group determination of parameters, is less resistant to additive noise than to multiplicative, and less resistant to Gaussian noise than to uniform.

The effect of group determination is observed starting from some definite noise level for all determined parameters and for any type of noise, and it is the more pronounced, the higher is the level of noise. Group determination is more noise resistant than autonomous determination. Possible reasons of the observed effects are discussed.

However, in the whole, noise resilience of ANN trained on "clean" data without noise is quite low. To improve it, in future studies, ANN should be trained on noisy data with various types and levels of noise.

So, in this study it has been demonstrated that use of group determination of parameters in neural network solution of multi-parameter inverse problems allows one not only to improve the quality of the solution of the inverse problem without noise, but also to increase noise resistance of the solution.

References

1. Zhdanov, M.: Inverse Theory and Applications in Geophysics, 2nd edn., 730 p. Elsevier, London (2015)
2. Yagola, A., Kochikov, I., Kuramshina, G.: Inverse Problems of Vibrational Spectroscopy, 297 p. De Gruyter, Boston (1999)
3. Mohammad-Djafari, A. (ed.): Inverse Problems in Vision and 3D Tomography, 468 p. Wiley, New York (2010)
4. Spichak, V.V. (ed.): Electromagnetic Sounding of the Earth's Interior. Methods in Geochemistry and Geophysics, vol. 40, 388 p. Elsevier, Amsterdam (2006)
5. Zhdanov, M.S.: Geophysical Electromagnetic Theory and Methods. Methods in Geochemistry and Geophysics, vol. 43, 848 p. Elsevier, Amsterdam (2009)
6. Spichak, V., Popova, I.: Artificial neural network inversion of magnetotelluric data in terms of three-dimensional earth macroparameters. Geophys. J. Int. **142**(1), 15–26 (2000)
7. Li, M., Verma, B., Fan, X., Tickle, K.: RBF neural networks for solving the inverse problem of backscattering spectra. Neural Comput. Appl. **17**(4), 391–397 (2008)
8. Yang, H., Xu, M.: Solving inverse bimodular problems via artificial neural network. Inverse Probl. Sci. Eng. **17**(8), 999–1017 (2009)
9. Dolenko, S., Isaev, I., Obornev, E., Persiantsev, I., Shimelevich, M.: Study of influence of parameter grouping on the error of neural network solution of the inverse problem of electrical prospecting. In: Iliadis, L., Papadopoulos, H., Jayne, C. (eds.) EANN 2013, Part I. CCIS, vol. 383, pp. 81–90. Springer, Heidelberg (2013). doi:10. 1007/978-3-642-41013-0_9
10. Dolenko, S., Isaev, I., Obornev, E., Obornev, I., Persiantsev, I., Shimelevich, M.: Elaboration of a complex algorithm of neural network solution of the inverse problem of electrical prospecting based on data classification. In: Proceedings of the 10th International Conference Problems of Geocosmos, St. Petersburg, Petrodvorets, pp. 11–16 (2014). http://geo.phys.spbu.ru/materials_of_a_conference_2014/ C2014/01_Dolenko.pdf
11. Zhdanov, M.S.: Geophysical Inverse Theory and Regularization Problems. Methods in Geochemistry and Geophysics, vol. 36, 633 p. Elsevier, Amsterdam (2002)
12. Dolenko, S., Guzhva, A., Obornev, E., Persiantsev, I., Shimelevich, M.: Comparison of adaptive algorithms for significant feature selection in neural network based solution of the inverse problem of electrical prospecting. In: Alippi, C., Polycarpou, M., Panayiotou, C., Ellinas, G. (eds.) ICANN 2009, Part II. LNCS, vol. 5769, pp. 397–405. Springer, Heidelberg (2009)

Convergence of Multi-pass Large Margin Nearest Neighbor Metric Learning

Christina Göpfert[✉], Benjamin Paassen, and Barbara Hammer

CITEC Universität Bielefeld, Inspiration 1, 33619 Bielefeld, Germany
{cgoepfert,bpaassen,bhammer}@techfak.uni-bielefeld.de
https://www.cit-ec.de/en/tcs

Abstract. Large margin nearest neighbor classification (LMNN) is a popular technique to learn a metric that improves the accuracy of a simple k-nearest neighbor classifier via a convex optimization scheme. However, the optimization problem is convex only under the assumption that the nearest neighbors within classes remain constant. In this contribution we show that an iterated LMNN scheme (multi-pass LMNN) is a valid optimization technique for the original LMNN cost function without this assumption. We further provide an empirical evaluation of multi-pass LMNN, demonstrating that multi-pass LMNN can lead to notable improvements in classification accuracy for some datasets and does not necessarily show strong overfitting tendencies as reported before.

Keywords: Metric learning · Large margin nearest neighbor · Multi-pass · Convergence

1 Introduction

Metric learning is concerned with inferring a metric from data that supports further processing of said data. The most common application of metric learning is the support of classification schemes. In simple terms this can be described as a distance that makes data points from the same class look more similar and data points from different classes look more dissimilar. Large margin nearest neighbor classification (LMNN) is one of the most popular techniques in the metric learning zoo [1,8,11], which specifically aims to improve the accuracy of a k-nearest neighbor classifier. It has been sucessfully applied in pattern recognition tasks such as pedestrian recognition [4], face identification [6] and movement classification [7].

As most other metric learning approaches, LMNN introduces a positive semidefinite matrix M to the standard Euclidean metric and optimizes this matrix according to a cost function that models the k-nearest neighbor classification error. This optimization is an instance of *semidefinite programming*, which implies that a global optimum can be found [2,11]. However, this desirable property only holds under the assumption that the closest k neighbors from the same class - the so-called *target neighbors* - remain constant. It is easy to imagine

© Springer International Publishing Switzerland 2016
A.E.P. Villa et al. (Eds.): ICANN 2016, Part I, LNCS 9886, pp. 510–517, 2016.
DOI: 10.1007/978-3-319-44778-0_60

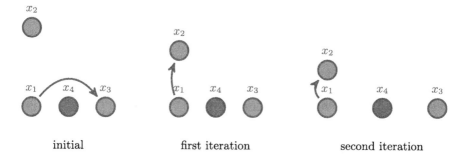

Fig. 1. A schematic illustration of a scenario where changes in the target neighborhood make the LMNN optimization easier. Left: the initial configuration where the data point x_1 is closest to x_3 within the same class. Middle: after a first metric learning step, x_2 becomes the target neighbor. x_1 would still not be correctly classified, because x_4 is closer to x_1 than x_2. Right: another metric learning step can now transform the space such that x_1 and x_2 are close but x_1 and x_4 are far apart.

a setting where this assumption is violated. Consider Fig. 1 (left and middle), for example. Here, the optimization of the convex problem does not find the global optimum in the LMNN cost function but a local one. The global optimum can only be found if neighborhood changes induced by the metric change are taken into account. This gives reason to suspect that classic LMNN might fail for data sets where changes in the neighborhood are likely to occur. Therefore it seems worthwhile to investigate the theoretical validity of LMNN in more detail.

In this contribution we show that the constant neighborhood assumption leads to an *overestimation* of the LMNN cost function, which implies that an update of the target neighborhood leads to an improvement in the cost function value. After updating the target neighbors, another LMNN run can be applied, resulting in a multi-pass LMNN scheme, converging to a local optimum (Sect. 5). We also demonstrate that such an iterative scheme does indeed improve the classification accuracy on artificial data (Sect. 6), and does not show strong overfitting tendencies on real data, that have been reported before [11].

2   Related Work

Several properties of large margin nearest neighbor classification (LMNN) have been investigated in the literature. For example, Do and colleagues have shown that LMNN can be regarded as learning a set of local SVM variants in a quadratic space [5]. Further, Ying and Li have reformulated LMNN as an Eigenvalue optimization problem [12]. Finally, several extensions of the original LMNN approach have been proposed, such as varied cost functions that support faster optimization [10], hierarchical LMNN [3], multi-task LMNN [9] and several more [1,8]. However, these extensions still assume a constant target neighborhood. To our knowledge, only Weinberger and Saul have attempted to adapt the target neighborhood in a multi-pass LMNN scheme [11]. However, they do not provide theoretical justification for this approach.

3   Quadratic Form Distances

Most metric learning schemes - LMNN among them - focus on a so-called *Mahalanobis metric* [1,8]. More precisely, assume that we have N data points $X = \{x_1, \ldots, x_N\} \subset \mathbb{R}^n$. We define d_M as a binary function

$$d_M(x_i, x_j) := \sqrt{(x_i - x_j)^T \cdot M \cdot (x_i - x_j)} \tag{1}$$

Note that d_M is a metric iff $M \in \mathbb{R}^{n \times n}$ is positive semidefinite. If M is the n-dimensional identity matrix, this is the standard Euclidean distance. Interestingly, positive-semi-definiteness of M also implies that M can be refactored into a product $M = L^T \cdot L$ for some matrix $L \in \mathbb{R}^{n \times n}$. L can then be interpreted as a linear transformation to a space, where d_M corresponds to the Euclidean metric. The challenge of a metric learning algorithm is to adapt M, such that the target task - e.g. classification - becomes simpler.

4   Large Margin Nearest Neighbor Classification

The aim of large margin nearest neighbor classification (LMNN) is to ensure good classification accuracy of a k-nearest neighbor classifier. A k-nearest neighbor classifier assigns the class label of the majority of the k nearest neighbors. Thus, to guarantee correct classification for each point, it has to be ensured that the majority of the k nearest neighbors belong to the correct class. LMNN formalizes this objective in a cost function with two parts: the first ensures that certain data points from the same class are close together, the second ensures that data points from different classes are *not* close together.

More precisely, given a data set $X = \{x_1, \ldots, x_N\} \subset \mathbb{R}^n$ with the respective class labels y_i, the LMNN cost function E is given as [11]:

$$E(M) := \sum_{i=1}^{N} \sum_{j \in \mathcal{N}_M^k(i)} d_M^2(x_i, x_j) + \sum_{l=1}^{N} (1 - y_i \cdot y_l) \cdot \left[d_M^2(x_i, x_j) + \gamma^2 - d_M^2(x_i, x_l) \right]_+ \tag{2}$$

where γ is a positive real number called the *margin*; $[\cdot]_+$ denotes the hinge-loss defined as $[r]_+ := \max\{0, r\}$; and $\mathcal{N}_M^k(i)$ are the indices of the k-nearest neighbors (regarding d_M) of point x_i that belong to the same class. $\mathcal{N}_M^k(i)$ is also called the *target neighborhood* of x_i.

Note that $\mathcal{N}_M^k$ depends on M. Therefore, a direct minimization of E by adapting M is infeasible. However, if the target neighborhood is fixed, a semidefinite program results, which can be solved efficiently [2,11]. We call this the *constant target neighborhood assumption*. It can be formalized as the minimization of $\tilde{E}$, where

$$\tilde{E}(M, \mathcal{N}^k) := \sum_{i=1}^{N} \sum_{j \in \mathcal{N}^k(i)} d_M^2(x_i, x_j) + \sum_{l=1}^{N} (1 - y_i \cdot y_l) \cdot \left[d_M^2(x_i, x_j) + \gamma^2 - d_M^2(x_i, x_l) \right]_+ . \tag{3}$$

and the second argument is fixed to some assignment of k target neighbors for each point. Note that $\tilde{E}(M, \mathcal{N}_M^k) = E(M)$.

5   Multi-pass LMNN

We intend to show that an indirect minimization of E is possible using an alternating optimization scheme. We proceed in two steps: First we prove that the classic LMNN solution *overestimates* E. Then we provide a convergence proof for our proposed alternating scheme.

Theorem 1. *Let M and M' be positive-semidefinite $n \times n$ matrices. Then it holds:*

$$\mathcal{N}_M^k = \mathcal{N}_{M'}^k \Rightarrow \tilde{E}(M', \mathcal{N}_M^k) = \tilde{E}(M', \mathcal{N}_{M'}^k) \tag{4}$$

$$\mathcal{N}_M^k \neq \mathcal{N}_{M'}^k \Rightarrow \tilde{E}(M', \mathcal{N}_M^k) > \tilde{E}(M', \mathcal{N}_{M'}^k) \tag{5}$$

Proof. If $\mathcal{N}_M^k = \mathcal{N}_{M'}^k$, then $\tilde{E}(M', \mathcal{N}_M^k) = \tilde{E}(M', \mathcal{N}_{M'}^k) = E(M')$ and the assertion in Eq. 4 is clear.

If $\mathcal{N}_M^k(i) \neq \mathcal{N}_{M'}^k(i)$ for some $i \in \{1, \dots, N\}$, then for each $j \in \mathcal{N}_M^k(i) \backslash \mathcal{N}_{M'}^k(i)$, $j' \in \mathcal{N}_{M'}^k(i)$, and $l \in \{1, \dots, N\}$, we have

$$d_{M'}(x_i, x_{j'}) < d_{M'}(x_i, x_j) \tag{6}$$

and

$$\left[d_{M'}^2(x_i, x_{j'}) + \gamma^2 - d_{M'}^2(x_i, x_l) \right]_+ \leq \left[d_{M'}^2(x_i, x_j) + \gamma^2 - d_{M'}^2(x_i, x_l) \right]_+ \tag{7}$$

Thus, the summand for i of $\tilde{E}(M', \mathcal{N}_M^k)$ is strictly larger than the corresponding summand of $\tilde{E}(M', \mathcal{N}_{M'}^k)$. As every other summand is either equal to or larger than the corresponding one in $\tilde{E}(M', \mathcal{N}_{M'}^k)$, the assertion in Eq. 5 follows.

If the constant target neighborhood assumption is guaranteed to lead to an overestimation of the actual cost function value, a minimization of $\tilde{E}$ under constant neighborhood assumption also decreases E. This suggests an alternating optimization scheme as shown in Algorithm 1, which is equivalent to multi-pass LMNN as proposed by Weinberger and Saul [11]. We optimize M w.r.t. $\tilde{E}$, then update the target neighborhoods. If at least one target neighborhood changes, we continue, otherwise the algorithm has converged.

Theorem 2. *Algorithm 1 is guaranteed to converge to a local optimum after a finite number of steps.*

Proof. Let $(M_t)_t$ be a sequence of matrices produced by a run of Algorithm 1. Then we know that $\tilde{E}(M_{t+1}, \mathcal{N}_{M_t}^k) \leq \tilde{E}(M_t, \mathcal{N}_{M_t}^k)$ due to the convex optimization step and $\tilde{E}(M_{t+1}, \mathcal{N}_{M_{t+1}}^k) \leq \tilde{E}(M_{t+1}, \mathcal{N}_{M_t}^k)$ due to Theorem 1. Thus, $E(M_{t+1}) \leq E(M_t)$ for all t.

If the algorithm terminates after T steps, then $\mathcal{N}_{M_T}^k = \mathcal{N}_{M_{T-1}}^k$. This implies that $\tilde{E}$ reached a local optimum because no change in the matrix can be made anymore that would decrease the value - otherwise it would have been chosen

Algorithm 1. An alternating optimization scheme for the LMNN cost function shown in Equation 2.

Initialize $M \leftarrow I^n$.
$converged \leftarrow false$
while $\neg converged$ **do**
    Optimize M w.r.t. $\tilde{E}(M, \mathcal{N}_M^k)$ via classic LMNN techniques.
    $converged \leftarrow true$
    for $i \in \{1, \ldots, N\}$ **do**
        Update $\mathcal{N}_M^k(i)$.
        if $\mathcal{N}_M^k(i)$ has changed **then**
            $converged \leftarrow false$.
        end if
    end for
end while
return M.

---

in the last step. This, in turn, implies a local optimum of E. Therefore, the stopping criterion of Algorithm 1 corresponds to a local optimum.

Now, assume that the algorithm does not stop. Since there is only a finite number of target neighborhoods to choose from, there must be t, t' with $t' > t$, such that $\mathcal{N}_{M_t}^k = \mathcal{N}_{M_{t'}}^k$. Since the optimization step of the algorithm finds a *global* optimum w.r.t. the current neighborhood it has to hold $\tilde{E}(M_{t'+1}, \mathcal{N}_{M_{t'}}^k) = \tilde{E}(M_{t+1}, \mathcal{N}_{M_t}^k)$. Because $\tilde{E}$ decreases monotonously, $\tilde{E}$ has to be constant for all iterations between t and t'. No two successive neighborhoods of $\mathcal{N}_{M_t}, \ldots, \mathcal{N}_{Mt'}$ are the same, otherwise the algorithm would stop. But according to Theorem 1, $\tilde{E}$ decreases strictly whenever the target neighborhood changes.

Therefore, we conclude that Algorithm 1 searches through the possible target neighborhoods without repetition, until a local optimum is achieved. As only a finite number of target neighborhoods exist, convergence is achieved after a finite number of steps.

6   Experiments

In order to assess multi-pass LMNN experimentally, we applied the current version (3.0) of the LMNN toolbox provided by Weinberger [11] in several iterative runs. Note that this recent version is a gradient-boosted variant of the optimization, unlike the original suggestion. As in the original paper, we set the neighborhood parameter to $k = 3$ for LMNN, and evaluated the performance of a k-nearest neighbor classifier on the learned metric after each iteration in a 10-fold cross-validation. For the sake of practicality, we did not run the algorithm until convergence but stopped after 5 iterations.

Artificial Data: To illustrate a typical situation where multi-pass LMNN is superior to single-pass LMNN we use a two-dimensional dataset suggested in Weinberger and Sauls original paper, namely a zebra-striped pattern, where

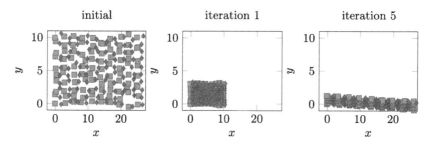

Fig. 2. The initial zebra stripes dataset, as well as the projected data points $L^T \cdot x_i$ after the first iteration and the last iteration.

stripes of points of the first and the second class alternate [11] (see Fig. 2, left). Such a dataset does not only highlight the value of a localized cost function, it also illustrates the importance of updating the target neighborhood. In the initial configuration, some of the target neighbors belong not to the same stripe, but to a different stripe, which makes the LMNN cost function under constant neighborhood assumption hard to optimize. However, after a first pass of LMNN metric learning, we expect that the learned metric "shrinks" the y dimension of the dataset, such that points in the same stripe move closer together. Thereby, more target neighbors belong to the same stripe and the LMNN cost function becomes easier to optimize.

Indeed, we observe this effect in the experimental evaluation. In each successive pass the y dimension shrinks, thereby increasing the accuracy of a k-NN classifier. In Fig. 2 we show the data as projected by the matrix L after each iteration. Figure 3 (left) displays the training and test error versus LMNN iteration, averaged in a 10-fold cross-validation.

Table 1. The number of data points N, the number of features/dimensions n, and the resulting classification error for each of the experimental data sets. The classification error is given for training and test set respectively, with standard deviation.

Dataset	N	n	Train error	Std.	Test error	Std.
zebra	200	2	0.019	0.004	0.015	0.023
iris	128	4	0.024	0.008	0.040	0.053
wine	152	13	0.000	0.000	0.021	0.028
bal	535	4	0.063	0.019	0.073	0.036
isolet	7,797	617	0.000	0.000	0.030	0.003
letters	20,000	16	0.002	0.000	0.027	0.005

Real datasets: In order to assess the performance on real data we also repeated most of the experiments with multi-pass LMNN reported in [11]. In particular,

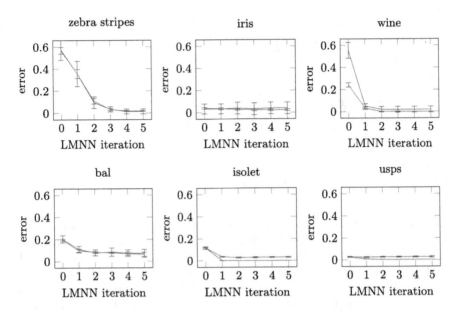

Fig. 3. The classification error on the training (blue) and on the test set (red) plotted for all datasets, averaged over 10 cross-validation trials. The x-axis shows the current LMNN iteration. The error bars signify the standard deviation across trials. (Color figure online)

we experimented on the USPS letter dataset, the isolet dataset, the iris dataset, the bal dataset and the wine dataset. Statistics regarding the datasets as well as the final classification error are shown in Table 1. The development of the classification error over time is displayed in Fig. 3.

All in all, we observe no strong benefit of multi-pass LMNN over 1-pass LMNN. However, we also did not observe noticeable over-fitting effects as reported by [11], which is likely due to relatively early stopping with five iterations.

7   Conclusion

We have shown that local optima of the LMNN cost function can be found using multi-pass LMNN. We have also demonstrated that data sets, for which an adapted metric changes the structure of the target neighborhood, can profit noticeably from multiple passes of LMNN metric learning. As a simple formula, multi-pass LMNN can be considered to be beneficial if the ideal target neighborhood is not obvious to the original metric. Interestingly, this benefit seems to be rather minor in the tested real datasets. Also, we did not notice (strong) over-fitting effects as reported by [11].

Overall, we conclude that multi-pass LMNN is a relatively risk-free and easy-to-use extension of classic LMNN approach that can be easily combined with other extensions of choice and comes with a theoretical convergence guarantee, which the original LMNN approach does not provide. Additionally, it might lead to noticeable performance improvements in datasets, where the initial target neighborhood leads to suboptimal learning impulses.

Acknowledgments. Funding by the DFG under grant number HA 2719/6-2 and the CITEC center of excellence (EXC 277) is gratefully acknowledged.

References

1. Bellet, A., Habrard, A., Sebban, M.: A survey on metric learning for feature vectors and structured data. arXiv e-prints (2013). http://arxiv.org/abs/1306.6709
2. Boyd, S., Vandenberghe, L.: Convex Optimization. Cambridge University Press, New York (2004)
3. Chen, Q., Sun, S.: Hierarchical large margin nearest neighbor classification. In: 2010 20th International Conference on Pattern Recognition (ICPR), pp. 906–909, August 2010
4. Dikmen, M., Akbas, E., Huang, T.S., Ahuja, N.: Pedestrian recognition with a learned metric. In: Kimmel, R., Klette, R., Sugimoto, A. (eds.) ACCV 2010, Part IV. LNCS, vol. 6495, pp. 501–512. Springer, Heidelberg (2011)
5. Do, H., Kalousis, A., Wang, J., Woznica, A.: A metric learning perspective of SVM: on the relation of LMNN and SVM. In: Proceedings of the 15th International Conference on Artificial Intelligence and Statistics (AISTATS), pp. 308–317 (2012)
6. Guillaumin, M., Verbeek, J., Schmid, C.: Is that you? metric learning approaches for face identification. In: 2009 IEEE 12th International Conference on Computer Vision, pp. 498–505, September 2009
7. Hosseini, B., Hammer, B.: Efficient metric learning for the analysis of motion data. In: 36678 2015 IEEE International Conference on Data Science and Advanced Analytics (DSAA), pp. 1–10, October 2015
8. Kulis, B.: Metric learning: a survey. Found. Trends Mach. Learn. **5**(4), 287–364 (2013)
9. Parameswaran, S., Weinberger, K.Q.: Large margin multi-task metric learning. In: Lafferty, J.D., Williams, C.K.I., Shawe-Taylor, J., Zemel, R.S., Culotta, A. (eds.) Advances in Neural Information Processing Systems, vol. 23, pp. 1867–1875. Curran Associates, Inc. (2010). http://papers.nips.cc/paper/3935-large-margin-multi-task-metric-learning.pdf
10. Park, K., Shen, C., Hao, Z., Kim, J.: Efficiently learning a distance metric for large margin nearest neighbor classification. In: Proceedings of the AAAI Conference on Artificial Intelligence (2011). http://www.aaai.org/ocs/index.php/AAAI/AAAI11/paper/view/3571
11. Weinberger, K.Q., Saul, L.K.: Distance metric learning for large margin nearest neighbor classification. J. Mach. Learn. Res. **10**, 207–244 (2009). http://dl.acm.org/citation.cfm?id=1577069.1577078
12. Ying, Y., Li, P.: Distance metric learning with eigenvalue optimization. J. Mach. Learn. Res. **13**(1), 1–26 (2012). http://dl.acm.org/citation.cfm?id=2503308.2188386

Short Papers

Spiking Neuron Model of a Key Circuit Linking Visual and Motor Representations of Actions

Mohammad Hovaidi Ardestani[1,2]([⊠]) and Martin Giese[1]

[1] Section for Computational Sensomotorics, Department of Cognitive Neurology, CIN and HIH, University Clinic Tübingen, 72076 Tübingen, Germany
martin.giese@uni-tuebingen.de
[2] IMPRS for Cognitive and Systems Neuroscience, University Clinic Tübingen, Tübingen, Germany
Mohammad.Hovaidi-Ardestani@uni-tuebingen.de
http://www.compsens.uni-tuebingen.de

Abstract. Action perception and the control of action execution are intrinsically linked in the human brain. Experiments show that concurrent motor execution influences the visual perception of actions and biological motion (e.g. [1]). This interaction likely is mediated by action-selective neurons in premotor and parietal cortex. We have developed a model based on biophysically realistic spiking neurons that accounts for such interactions. The model is based on two coupled dynamic neural fields [2], one modeling a representation of perceived action patters (vision field), and one representing associated motor programs (motor field), each implemented by 30 coupled spiking ensembles. Each ensemble contains 80 excitatory and 20 inhibitory adaptive Exponential Integrate-and-Fire (aEIF) neurons [3]. Within each field asymmetric recurrent connections between the ensembles stabilize a traveling pulse solution, which is stimulus-driven in the visual field and autonomously propagating in the motor field after initiation by a go-signal. Both fields are coupled by interaction kernels that results in mutual excitation between the fields of the traveling pulse propagate synchronously and in mutual inhibition otherwise. We used the model to reproduce the result of a psychophysical experiment that tested the detection of point-light stimuli in noise during concurrent motor execution [1], and for the simulation of the modulation of motor behavior by concurrent action vision [4]. The proposed model reproduces correctly the interactions between action vision and execution in these experiments and provides a link towards electrophysiological detailed models of relevant circuits.

Keywords: Action perception coupling · Neural fields

References

1. Christensen, A., Ilg, W., Giese, M.A.: Spatiotemporal tuning of the facilitation of biological motion perception by concurrent motor execution. J. Neurosci. (2011)

© Springer International Publishing Switzerland 2016
A.E.P. Villa et al. (Eds.): ICANN 2016, Part I, LNCS 9886, pp. 521–522, 2016.
DOI: 10.1007/978-3-319-44778-0

2. Amari, S.: Dynamics of pattern formation in lateral-inhibition type neural fields. Biol. Cybern. (1977)
3. Brette, R., Gerstner, W.: Adaptive exponential integrate-and-fire model as an effective description of neuronal activity. J. Neurophysiol. (2005)
4. Kilner, J.M., Paulignan, Y., Balkemore, S.J.: An interference effect of observed biological movement on action. Curr. Biol. (2003)

Analysis of the Effects of Periodic Forcing in the Spike Rate and Spike Correlation's in Semiconductor Lasers with Optical Feedback

Carlos Quintero-Quiroz[1](✉), Taciano Sorrentino[1,2], M.C. Torrent[1], and Cristina Masoller[1]

[1] Departament de Física, Universitat Politècnica de Catalunya,
Colom 11, 08222 Terrassa, Barcelona, Spain
carlos.alberto.quintero@upc.edu
[2] Departamento de Cincias Exatas e Naturais,
Universidade Federal Rural do Semi-rido,
Av. Francisco Mota 572, 59625-900 Mossor, RN, Brazil

Abstract. We study the dynamics of semiconductor lasers with optical feedback and direct current modulation, operating in the regime of low frequency fluctuations (LFFs) [1]. In the LFF regime the laser intensity displays abrupt spikes: the intensity drops to zero and then gradually recovers. We focus on the inter-spike-intervals (ISIs) and use a method of symbolic time-series analysis [2], which is based on computing the probabilities of symbolic patterns. We show that the variation of the probabilities of the symbols with the modulation frequency [3] and with the intrinsic spike rate of the laser allows to identify different regimes of noisy locking [4]. Simulations of the Lang-Kobayashi mode

Keywords: Semiconductor laser · Optical feedback · Diode laser modulation · Optical neuron · Low-frequency fluctuations · Excitability

References

1. Giudici, M., Green, C., Giacomelli, G., Nespolo, U., Tredicce, J.: Andronov bifurcation and excitability in semiconductor lasers with optical feedback. Phys. Rev. E **55**(6), 6414 (1997)
2. Bandt, C., Pompe, B.: Permutation entropy: a natural complexity measure for time series. Phys. Rev. Lett. **88**(17), 174102 (2002)
3. Sorrentino, T., Quintero-Quiroz, C., Torrent, M., Masoller, C.: Analysis of the spike rate and spike correlations in modulated semiconductor lasers with optical feedback. IEEE J. Sel. Top. Quantum Electron. **21**(6), 561–567 (2015)
4. Sorrentino, T., Quintero-Quiroz, C., Aragoneses, A., Torrent, M.C., Masoller, C.: Effects of periodic forcing on the temporally correlated spikes of a semicon- ductor laser with feedback. Opt. Express **23**, 5571–5581 (2015)

A.E.P. Villa et al. (Eds.): ICANN 2016, Part I, LNCS 9886, p. 523, 2016.
DOI: 10.1007/978-3-319-44778-0

Neuronal Functional Interactions Inferred from Analyzing Multivariate Spike Trains Generated by Simple Models Simulations Using Frequency Domain Analyses Available at Open Platforms

Takeshi Abe[1], Yoshiyuki Asai[1(✉)], and Alessandro E.P. Villa[2]

[1] Integrated Open Systems Unit, Okinawa Institute of Science and Technology,
Graduate University, Okinawa, Japan
{takeshi.abe,yoshiyuki.asai}@oist.jp
[2] Neuroheuristic Research Group, HEC-ISI, University of Lausanne,
Lausanne, Switzerland
avilla@neuroheuristic.org
http://www.neuroheuristic.org

Abstract. Functional interactions between neurons inferred on the analysis of frequency-domain analysis, such as coherence and partial coherence analyses, have been recognized for a long time as a necessary tool for the understanding of neural coding complementary to the time-domain analysis. Partial coherence analysis allows to determine the association between two spike trains as a function of an external stimulus or of another neuron's activity recorded simultaneously to the pair of spike trains [1]. We have implemented a simple neural network composed of MAT neurons [2] using Flint, a simulator concurrently developed with PhysioDesigner (http://www.physiodesigner.org). The algorithms for partial coherence analyses were implemented as tools available at OpenAdap.net [3] and Garuda platform [4] made freely available to a broad community. The results of the analyses presented here allow a user to infer functional interactions that can be tested against small changes in the simple neural network model. Moreover, users can easily access the methods of analyses presented here to process users' own multivariate spike trains.

Keywords: Neuronal connectivity · Coherence · Partial coherence · Frequency domain

References

1. Brillinger, D.R., Bryant Jr., H.L., Segundo, J.P.: Identification of synaptic interactions. Biol. Cybern. **22**(4), 213–228 (1976)
2. Kobayashi, R., Tsubo, Y., Shinomoto, S.: Made-to-order spiking neuron model equipped with a multi-timescale adaptive threshold. Front. Comput. Neurosci. **3**, e009 (2009)

© Springer International Publishing Switzerland 2016
A.E.P. Villa et al. (Eds.): ICANN 2016, Part I, LNCS 9886, pp. 524–525, 2016.
DOI: 10.1007/978-3-319-44778-0

3. Villa, A.E.P., Iglesias, J.: OpenAdap.net: evolvable information processing environment. In: Masulli, F., Mitra, S., Pasi, G. (eds.) WILF 2007. LNCS, pp. 227–236. Springer, Heidelberg (2007)
4. Ghosh, S., Matsuoka, Y., Asai, Y., Hsin, K., Kitano, H.: Software for systems biology: from tools to integrated platforms. Nat. Rev. Genet. **12**, 821–832 (2011)

Controlling a Redundant Articulated Robot in Task Space with Spiking Neurons

Samir Menon[1($\boxtimes$)], Vinay Sriram[1], Luis Kumanduri[1], Oussama Khatib[1], and Kwabena Boahen[2]

[1] Departments of Computer Science, Stanford University, Stanford, CA 94305, USA
{smenon,ok}@cs.stanford.edu, {vsriram,luisk}@stanford.edu
[2] Bioengineering, Stanford University, Stanford, CA 94305, USA
boahen@stanford.edu

Abstract. Using spiking neural network (SNN) controllers [3] to implement multiple motor tasks for complex redundant robots requires efficient methods to compute complex kinematic and dynamic functions with spiking neurons. Three fundamental problems arise while using SNNs to compute high-dimensional robot kinematics using steady-state spike rate decoding (following the neural engineering framework [2]): first, differential maps from the generalized coordinates to task-space, task control Jacobians, cease to be humanly factorizable into sub-functions with low-dimensional domains; second, efficient Jacobian factorizations require multiple neuron layers, exacerbating neuron spike noise and latency; and third, function-agnostic sampling strategies require an exponential growth in the number of neural response samples as the number of input dimensions increases. Here, we present an SNN implementation that overcomes these problems to compute kinematic functions (Jacobians) for the *Kuka LBR iiwa*, and *Kinova JACO*, which have seven and six degrees-of-freedom respectively. Both robots are redundant for task space motion control. To control them, we developed a multi-task control system where task Jacobians, and a part of the Jacobian's dynamically consistent generalized inverse, were implemented with SNNs. Our SNN was an asynchronous spiking neural simulation with dynamical neurons modeled using the Neurogrid neuromorphic system's soma equations [1]; it thus serves as a model of what neuromorphic computers can achieve.

Keywords: Neurobotics · Spiking neural networks · Multi-task control

References

1. Benjamin, B.V., Gao, P., McQuinn, E., Choudhary, S., Chandrasekaran, A., Bussat, J.M., Alvarez-Icaza, R., Arthur, J., Merolla, P., Boahen, K.: Neurogrid: A mixed- analog-digital multichip system for large-scale neural simulations. Proc. IEEE **102**(5), 699–716 (2014)

© Springer International Publishing Switzerland 2016
A.E.P. Villa et al. (Eds.): ICANN 2016, Part I, LNCS 9886, pp. 526–527, 2016.
DOI: 10.1007/978-3-319-44778-0

2. Eliasmith, C., Anderson, C.: Neural Engineering: Computation, Representation, and Dynamics in Neurobiological Systems. MIT Press (2004)
3. Menon, S., Fok, S., Neckar, A., Khatib, O., Boahen, K.: Controlling articulated robots in task-space with spiking silicon neurons. In: 2014 5th IEEE RAS EMBS International Conference on Biomedical Robotics and Biomechatronics, pp. 181–186, August 2014

Onset of Global Synchrony by Application of a Size-Dependent Feedback

August Romeo[1] and Hans Supèr[1,2,3]

[1] Department of Cognition, Development and Educational Psychology,
Faculty of Psychology, University of Barcelona (UB), Barcelona, Spain
[2] Institut de Neurociències, Barcelona, Spain
[3] Catalan Institution for Research and Advanced Studies (ICREA), Barcelona, Spain

Abstract. We introduce a two layer network of spiking neurons with a regulated feedback between both layers determined by a unit functioning as a gating element. Its activity, which ultimately influences the synchrony regime, depends on the processing of the sensory inputs through a receptive field of time-varying radius. The time evolution of this scale affects the length of the intervals which are relevant to attentional effects.

Attention can be regarded as an attempt to reduce variability in the difference between expected and actual sensory input. Cognitive processing of sensory stimuli is represented by spike rate as well as by spike timing and the ensuing degree of synchrony. The fact that feedback modifies spike rates by changing spike timing may highlight new aspects of the neural correlates in cognitive processing. That was one of the motivations for the present network, after realizing that the synchrony of global oscillation can be described by changes in feedback signals.

We try to model the degree of readiness for success in an visual attentional task using a changing length scale, i.e., a single variable with dimension of length which evolves in time. Our considered stimuli are circles and the internal states of the system are represented by the radius of a visual receptive field (RF), which is also circular and evolves in time. Next, going on to neurons themselves, time oscillation and synchrony properties supply pictures of their global states, and may reflect the variations which take place during a cognitive task.

Taking advantage of a gated feedback mechanism, we propose a model for how oscillations can occur sooner at cued regions, and also, with longer delays, at uncued regions. A two-layer network causes a delay in global oscillations when the cue is 'invalid', i.e., occurs at a different region than the target. Further, an evolution rate parameter for the RF scale determines the efficiency of the system's adaptation to new stimuli, to the extent that different degrees of success depend on the value of that rate, which we may interpret as an indirect measure of attention.

Our obtained values show rough agreement with experimental measures of typical 'consolidation' times. The model provides changing pictures when evolution rates increase by an order of magnitude. On top of lapse lengths, differences in global oscillation onsets between 'valid-cue' and 'invalid-cue' cases are present. These differences may vary from 200 ms to 25–50 ms when applying such modifications.

Keywords: Attention · Global oscillation · Gated feedback

© Springer International Publishing Switzerland 2016
A.E.P. Villa et al. (Eds.): ICANN 2016, Part I, LNCS 9886, p. 528, 2016.
DOI: 10.1007/978-3-319-44778-0

Identification of Epileptogenic Rhythms in a Mesoscopic Neuronal Model

Maciej Jedynak[1,2], Antonio J. Pons[1], Jordi Garcia-Ojalvo[2],
and Marc Goodfellow[3]

[1] Departament de Física, Universitat Politécnica de Catalunya, Barcelona, Spain
maciej.jedynak@upf.edu, a.pons@upc.edu
[2] Department of Experimental and Health Sciences, Universitat Pompeu Fabra,
Parc de Recerca Biomedica de Barcelona, Barcelona, Spain
jordi.g.ojalvo@upf.edu
[3] College of Engineering, Mathematics and Physical Sciences,
University of Exeter, Exeter, UK
m.goodfellow@exeter.ac.uk

Abstract. Biological neuronal networks are capable of displaying various types of activity, such as oscillatory behaviour, irregular excitations, or bursting. These dynamical patterns are often linked to different brain states and functions, such as perception, awareness, or cognition. A prominent example of a discernible dynamical pattern is epileptic activity that shows as series of high-amplitude excessively synchronous discharges in the EEG recordings and entails impairment of brain functionality that may include brief losses of consciousness.

Mechanisms of initiation of epileptic activity are nowadays elusive. Considerations based in the methods of nonlinear dynamics suggest that the routes to epilepsy could include instantaneous switching between multistable states, fast excitations, or slow passing through a bifurcation. Here, we theoretically study these initiations in a neuronal population subjected to background activity of the cortical network, which combines rhythms from a wide range of frequencies. We approximate this background activity with a single source of temporally correlated noise, which bears resemblance to spectral properties of the brain activity known from the EEG recordings.

To study these effects we employ a stochastically driven mesoscopic neuronal model, which is capable of displaying both healthy and epileptic behaviour and it features bistability, bifurcation and excitability. By varying spectral characteristics of the driving signal we find conditions favourable for initiations of epileptic activity and by characterizing the system's response to harmonic driving, we identify epileptogenic rhythms.

In summary, our work demonstrates potential mechanisms by which pathological, epileptic-like dynamics can be initiated and spread due to the presence of certain rhythms in an ongoing activity of the brain. We also link our theoretical results to the experimental findings on precursors of epileptic activity.

Keywords: Brain · Noise · Neural mass models · Epilepsy

A.E.P. Villa et al. (Eds.): ICANN 2016, Part I, LNCS 9886, p. 529, 2016.
DOI: 10.1007/978-3-319-44778-0

Modulation of Wave Propagation in the Cortical Network by Electric Fields

Pol Boada-Collado[1]([⊠]), Julia F. Weinert[1], Maurizio Mattia[2],
and Maria V. Sanchez-Vives[1,3]

[1] IDIBAPS, Barcelona, Spain
boada.pol@gmail.com, j.f.weinert@gmail.com, msanchez3@clinic.ub.es
[2] Instituto Superiore di Sanita (ISS), Rome, Italy
mattia@iss.infn.it
[3] ICREA (Institucio Catalana de Recerca i Estudis Avancats), Barcelona, Spain

Abstract. Slow waves propagate in the cortical network and their spatio- temporal patterns provide valuable information about the underlying circuitry. In a previous study [1] done in an isolated cortical network *in vitro*, we found that propagation is lead by the most excitable layers of the network. Here we experimentally probe the network by applying DC electric fields of different intensities (between -2 and $+5\,\mathrm{V/m}$) oriented perpendicular to cortical layers and explore the resulting modulation of slow wave propagation. To this end, we recorded with 16-electrode arrays covering supra and infragranular layers of $400\,\mu\mathrm{m}$ thick cortical slices. We next inferred the optimal set of speeds that most accurately explained the patterns and the delays observed in the electrophysiological data. As previously reported [2], the vertical (columnar) propagation was faster ($10.3 \pm 4.3\,\mathrm{mm/s}$) than horizontal (laminar) propagation ($5.4 \pm 1.9\,\mathrm{mm/s}$). Our main finding was that DC fields induced a strong modulation of horizontal propagation, while no significant changes were measured on vertical propagation. Besides, positive DC fields decreased the refractory period, thus increasing the probability of propagation of subsequent waves, while the opposite occurred with negative DC fields. This differential impact of DC fields on wave propagation suggests that different mechanisms are regulating both processes. In this study we explore experimentally and theoretically the possibility that excitation/inhibition are differently involved in the regulation of horizontal and vertical propagation in the network.

Keywords: Propagation · Electric fields · Slow waves · Cortical network · Up states

Acknowledgments. Supported by EU CORTICONIC contract 600806 and FlagEra SloW-Dyn.

© Springer International Publishing Switzerland 2016
A.E.P. Villa et al. (Eds.): ICANN 2016, Part I, LNCS 9886, pp. 530–531, 2016.
DOI: 10.1007/978-3-319-44778-0

References

1. Capone, C., et al.: Slow-waves in cortical slices: how spontaneous activity is shaped by laminar structure. BMC Neurosci. **16**(Suppl 1), P161
2. Sanchez-Vives, M.V., McCormick, D.A.: Cellular and network mechanisms of rhythmic recurrent activity in neocortex. Nat Neurosci. **3**(10), 1027–34 (2000)

Investigation of SSEP by Means of a Realistic Computational Model of the Sensory Cortex

Elżbieta Gajewska-Dendek$^{(\boxtimes)}$ and Piotr Suffczyński

Department of Biomedical Physics, Institute of Experimental Physics,
University of Warsaw, 02-093 Warsaw, Poland
{Elzbieta.Gajewska-Dendek,Piotr.Suffczynski}@fuw.edu.pl

Abstract. Steady State Evoked Potentials (SSEP) are emerging in the EEG signals in response to periodically changing stimulus. Their frequencies correspond to stimulus frequency, its harmonics and subharmonics. The SSEP can be observed in visual, auditory and somatosensory modalities. Despite applications of SSEP in cognitive neuroscience, clinical neuroscience and brain computer interfaces (BCI), physiological mechanisms of SSEP generation are unknown. The aim of this study was investigation of SSEP mechanisms with a realistic computational model. The model consisted of single compartment excitatory and inhibitory cells arranged in multiple cortical columns, based on data from cat's primary visual cortex. The modelled neurons received three kinds of Poisson inputs, which represent: background sensory input from the thalamus, background top-down input from higher order cortical regions and periodic stimulus from the thalamus, representing sensory stimulation. The sensory stimulus was modelled by Poisson process, with mean rate modulated periodically in time by square or sinusoidal function at frequency in 7 to 50 Hz range. The EEG signal was modelled as a sum of synaptic currents of pyramidal neurons. We compared the simulation data with experimental EEG recordings obtained in somatosensory cortex during vibrotactile stimulation. The spectra of modeled SSEP signals exhibited fundamental and higher harmonic frequencies similarly to experimental observations. The first harmonic was stronger than fundamental response for the driving frequencies smaller than network natural frequency (15–20 Hz) as observed experimentally. When the driving frequency coincided with network natural frequency the model exhibited resonance behaviour, visible in power spectrum, firing rate and synchronicity measures. The neurons firing rates were approximately constant and much lower than stimulus frequencies (except from around natural frequency). The network oscillation emerged from irregular and sparse firing of individual neurons but in phase with the population rhythm. Preservation of connections between excitatory and inhibitory cells was necessary for the oscillations to emerge. We conclude that (i) the observed SSEP oscillations are caused by firing-rate synchrony (ii) emergence of driven oscillatory synchrony patterns is mediated by mutual interactions between excitatory and inhibitory cells (iii) SSEP oscillations correspond to oscillatory process and cannot be fully explained by superposition of the transient event related responses.

© Springer International Publishing Switzerland 2016
A.E.P. Villa et al. (Eds.): ICANN 2016, Part I, LNCS 9886, p. 532, 2016.
DOI: 10.1007/978-3-319-44778-0

Exploration of a Mechanism to Form Bionic, Self-growing and Self-organizing Neural Network

Hailin Ma[1], Ning Deng[1], Zhiheng Xu[1], Yuzhe Wang[1], Yingjie Shang[1], Xu Yang[2(✉)], and Hu He[1(✉)]

[1] Institute of Microelectronics, Tsinghua University, Beijing, China
mhl1991@163.com, {ningdeng,hehu}@tsinghua.edu.cn,
{1534305830,291087211}@qq.com, syjyingjieshang@163.com
http://dsp.ime.tsinghua.edu.cn/
[2] School of Software, Beijing Institute of Technology, Beijing, China
yangxu@tsinghua.edu.cn

Abstract. Neural network is one of the mainstream interests in artificial intelligence research. However, neurons in most artificial neural networks are in a fixed connection with each other at this stage, making it impossible to achieve self-learning ability. In this paper, we present our approach to build a self-growing and self-organizing neural network. We try to imitate the way in biological neural network, where neurons would form connections as a response to external stimulates, and evolve, thus to build a self-growing, self-organizing neural network. The neuron model in our work is built based on Leaky I&F model [1]. The inputs of our model are digital pulse signals. A counter was added into the neuron model, so that it could calculate the changing rate of outputs, called the output intensity of a neuron. Only when the output intensity of a neuron meets a certain condition, it can exchange information with other neurons. The distance of the forming connection is decided by the output intensity. While the target of connection is picked through calculation of a Probability Matrix C, the values in which are generated by training. Matrix C could learn from the input data, thus to optimize the generation of neural networks. We verify the generated neural network with different inputs. Those could generate different outputs with respect to different inputs would be treated as successful ones. Redundant connections is then deleted. We have exploited a CPU+GPU way to build the simulation environment. CPU is used to control, while GPU is used for all the computation of neurons. 2-bits input is first used to stimulate the network, and prompted it to grow. After verification and optimization, those generated seeds are used to build more complex ones. The result shows that, neural network built by our method can self-grow and self-organize as the complexity of the input external signals increase. Also our neural network can show some level of intelligence.

Keywords: Neural network · GPU · Parallel processing

Reference

1. Abbott, L.F.: Lapicque introduction of the integrate-and-fire model neuron(1907). Brain Res. Bull. **50**(5–6), 303–304 (1999)

© Springer International Publishing Switzerland 2016
A.E.P. Villa et al. (Eds.): ICANN 2016, Part I, LNCS 9886, p. 533, 2016.
DOI: 10.1007/978-3-319-44778-0

Living Neuronal Networks in a Dish: Network Science and Neurological Disorders

Sara Teller[✉], Elisenda Tibau, and Jordi Soriano

Departament de Física de la Matèria Condensada, Universitat de Barcelona,
Av. Diagonal 645, 08028 Barcelona, Spain
jordi.soriano@ub.edu
http://soriano-lab.eu

Abstract. The flexibility and relative simplicity of neuronal cultures make them excellent tools to investigate open questions in living neuronal networks, and offer a unique scenario to tackle important questions in network theory. In our research group we use different configurations of neuronal cultures and monitor their spontaneous activity. Two kinds of preparations are of special interest, namely homogeneous and aggregated. For the former, neurons cover uniformly the substrate, leading to a connectivity blueprint in which neurons also connect in a uniform manner [1]. For the latter, neurons form compact aggregates (*clusters*) connected to one another, leading to a network in which nodes (the clusters) and links (connections among clusters) are well visible and accessible [2].

For the homogeneous cultures, and using modeling scenarios from dynamical systems and information theory, we were able to unveil the functional connectivity of the network and ascribe the macroscopic properties of the observed activity patterns with the microscopic, network-level traits [1, 3]. For the aggregated networks, we observed that they exhibit a particular dynamics in which clusters tend to fire together in small groups, shaping dynamic modules of varying size. Such a trait leads to functional networks that are both modular and hierarchical. Additionally, network dynamics showed a strong sensitivity to the details of the connectivity among aggregates. We have exploited this observation to monitor the changes in the functional network before and after physical damage, to quantify the re-organization of the modules upon circuitry degradation, and to assess which circuit configuration is more resilient to damage [2].

Keywords: Neuronal cultures · Complex networks · Functional graphs

References

1. Orlandi, J.G.: Noise focusing and the emergence of coherent activity in neuronal cultures. Nat. Phys. **9**, 582–590 (2013)
2. Teller, S., et al.: Magnetite-Amyloid-β deteriorates activity and functional organization in an in vitro model for Alzheimer's disease. Sci. Rep. **5**, 17261 (2015)
3. Tibau, E., et al.: Identification of neuronal network properties from the spectral analysis of calcium imaging signals in neuronal cultures. Front. Neur. Circ. **7**, 199 (2013)

A.E.P. Villa et al. (Eds.): ICANN 2016, Part I, LNCS 9886, p. 534, 2016.
DOI: 10.1007/978-3-319-44778-0

Does the Default Network Represent the 'Model' in Model-Based Decision-Making?

Raphael Kaplan[1,2](✉) and Gustavo Deco[2]

[1] University College London, London, UK
{raphael.kaplan,gustavo.deco}@upf.edu
[2] Universitat Pompeu Fabra, Barcelona, Spain

Abstract. The past decade has witnessed a rapid growth in the amount of human brain imaging papers investigating what goes on while we are at rest and other internally directed mental states. In parallel, the field of decision-making has investigated how these same medial parietal, prefrontal, and temporal lobe regions, collectively known as the default network, also contribute to an internal model of the world that guides our decisions- i.e. model-based decision-making.

In this talk, I will discuss how this neural system might guide internally oriented behaviours like mental exploration, generalization, imagination, and transitive inference that contribute to model-based decision-making. Specifically, I will present a variety of evidence supporting a framework, where endogenous oscillations across different brain regions might help coordinate hippocampal reactivation of memories and subsequently guide rapid prefrontal inferences about novel decisions. I will present a task adapted from rodent spatial decision-making that enabled us to elucidate core neural computations underlying the human capacity to make fast and robust inferences in complex environments with little or no learning. These findings highlight a unique contribution of medial prefrontal cortex when making choices that require deep prospection and counterfactual processing.

Drawing from research conducted in the laboratory of Gustavo Deco, I will show offline functional magnetic resonance imaging signal fluctuations throughout the default mode network (DMN), which includes frontal and parietal midline regions, are uniformly influenced by hippocampal sharp-wave ripples. These data help relate ongoing DMN fluctuations to the consolidation of past experience and preparation for future behaviour. Lastly, I will discuss how interregional oscillatory interactions between these same medial prefrontal cortex and medial temporal/parietal lobe areas contribute to how we mentally explore and imagine learned representations.

Taken together, these data contribute to a framework that could potentially reveal the neural mechanism underlying rapid and robust mental simulation, where interareal coordination between medial prefrontal, parietal, and temporal regions allows the brain to explore past experience in order to prepare for novel decisions.

Keywords: Planning · Cognitive neuroscience · Prefrontal cortex

© Springer International Publishing Switzerland 2016
A.E.P. Villa et al. (Eds.): ICANN 2016, Part I, LNCS 9886, p. 535, 2016.
DOI: 10.1007/978-3-319-44778-0

Experimental Approaches to Assess Connectivity in Living Neuronal Networks

Lluís Hernández-Navarro, Javier G. Orlandi, Jaume Casademunt, and Jordi Soriano[✉]

Departament de Física de la Matèria Condensada, Universitat de Barcelona, Av. Diagonal 645, 08028 Barcelona, Spain
jordi.soriano@ub.edu
http://soriano-lab.eu

Abstract. The complexity of the connectivity blueprint in living neuronal circuits has motivated the development of theoretical and computational tools to infer their major characteristics. Three major descriptors are of interest, namely the average number of connections, the distribution of connections, and high-order topological features such as clustering. In our study we have explored them by analyzing the activity in neuronal cultures, and considered approaches that include the analysis of the network as a dynamical system, percolation, and spin models.

For the first approach, we recorded spontaneous neuronal activity and resolved the ignition times of all the monitored neurons. The analysis shows that activity takes place in the form of *bursts*, events of fast activation of all the neurons in a short time window. These bursts occur quasi-periodically along time and initiate in a few, well-defined locations in the culture, which we call nucleation points [1]. The number of nucleation points, as well as the characterisitics of the propagating fronts, strongly depend on the circuitry of the network. Hence, by carrying out experiments with different perturbations of the neuronal circuitry (e.g. by chemical or electrical action), we can extract interesting properties of the underlying connectivity map.

For the second and third approaches, we considered a global bath excitation protocol combined with a progressive weakening of the connections among neurons [2]. This protocol leads to a percolative scenario, in which the largest group of connected neurons defines a *giant component* that decreases in size as the network is gradually disconnected. At a critical disconnection degree, the giant component disappears. The properties of this critical point are tightly related with the topology of the circuit, particularly the average number of connections.

Keywords: Neuronal cultures · Complex networks · Percolation

References

1. Orlandi, J.G., et al.: Noise focusing and the emergence of coherent activity in neuronal cultures. Nat. Phys. **9**, 582–590 (2013)
2. Soriano, J., et al.: Development of input connections in neural cultures. PNAS **105**, 13758–13763 (2008)

© Springer International Publishing Switzerland 2016
A.E.P. Villa et al. (Eds.): ICANN 2016, Part I, LNCS 9886, p. 536, 2016.
DOI: 10.1007/978-3-319-44778-0

Spectral Analysis of Echo State Networks

Pau Vilimelis Aceituno[1]([⊠]), Gang Yan[2], and Yang-Yu Liu[1]

[1] Harvard Medical School, Brigham's and Women's Hospital, Boston, USA
pv960@partners.org,spyli@channing.harvard.edu
[2] Northeastern University, Boston, USA
g.yan@neu.edu

Abstract. Echo State Network (ESN) is a classical recurrent neural network architecture with a wide range of applications, from robot control to biological data analytics and stock market prediction. The key feature of ESN paradigm is the reservoir, i.e., a random directed network of neurons, which is left unaltered once constructed. Despite previous efforts dedicated to improving the performance of ESN over Erdős-Rényi random graphs, we still lack a general framework to reveal the relationship between ESN performance and network structure. Here we systematically explore the impact of various network properties, leading to the discovery that the eigenvalue distribution of reservoir network determines the performance of ESN. Following that initial insight, we found that in the state-of-the-art ESN all reservoir networks are created asymmetrically ($\rho = 0$). Yet, we find that the network symmetry parameter ρ allows for further optimization of the reservoir topology. Our findings not only provide novel insights to artificial intelligence optimization, but also show key relationships between the trade-off in memory and computational capacity of neural networks.

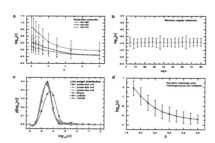 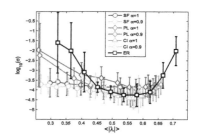

(a) Here we present the effects of various network parameters for the most common network classes. It is clear that heterogeneity in both degree distribution and link weights is detrimental.

(b) This figure shows that for various parameters and network types, the average eigenvalue modulus predicts the optimal ESN performance.

Keywords: Reservoir computing · Echo state network · Network science · Network spectra

© Springer International Publishing Switzerland 2016
A.E.P. Villa et al. (Eds.): ICANN 2016, Part I, LNCS 9886, p. 537, 2016.
DOI: 10.1007/978-3-319-44778-0

Adaptive Hierarchical Sensing

Henry Schütze[✉], Erhardt Barth, and Thomas Martinetz

Institute for Neuro- and Bioinformatics, University of Lübeck, Lübeck, Germany
{schuetze,barth,martinetz}@inb.uni-luebeck.de

Abstract. Compressive Sensing (CS) is a signal acquisition technique by which an unknown, continuous signal of interest is simultaneously sampled and compressed. With CS, inner products between the signal and random sensing vectors are collected. The objective is to perform only few of such non-adaptive measurements while capturing the bulk of information. CS theory states that if the signal is K-compressible in a transform domain, and the sensing vectors satisfy certain incoherence conditions, then the number of measurements required to reconstruct the signal is of order $\mathcal{O}(K \log \frac{N}{K})$, where N is the signal dimensionality. To reconstruct the signal an inverse optimization problem has to be solved.

We propose the novel compressive sensing algorithm K-AHS that adaptively performs measurements by selecting sensing vectors from a predefined collection. K-AHS is adaptive because the selection of a sensing vector depends on previous measurements. The key concept is that relevant measurements are more and more refined, and gradually emerge to significant transform coefficients of the signal, whereas irrelevant measurements cause the omission of large subsets of the collection and thus the underlying insignificant coefficients. Like CS, the K-AHS sampling complexity is of order $\mathcal{O}(K \log \frac{N}{K})$. However, it is not necessary to incorporate incoherence, or to solve an optimization problem, because the signal is reconstructed simply by a synthesis transform.

On standard test images, K-AHS attains higher PSNR than ℓ_1-based CS for small to intermediate numbers of measurements. Figure 1 shows a corresponding rate distortion analysis. The transform domain is the CDF97 wavelet basis. CS measurements are performed using randomly selected real-valued noiselet basis vectors.

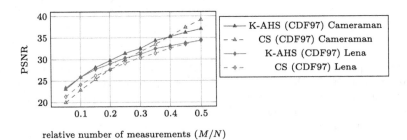

relative number of measurements (M/N)

Fig. 1. Rate distortion of K-AHS and ℓ_1-based CS for test images (512×512).

Keywords: Compressed sensing · Compressive imaging

© Springer International Publishing Switzerland 2016
A.E.P. Villa et al. (Eds.): ICANN 2016, Part I, LNCS 9886, p. 538, 2016.
DOI: 10.1007/978-3-319-44778-0

Across-Trial Dynamics of Stimulus Priors in an Auditory Discrimination Task

Ainhoa Hermoso-Mendizabal[1]([⊠]), Alexandre Hyafil[1,2],
Pavel Ernesto Rueda-Orozco[3], Santiago Jaramillo[4], David Robbe[5],
and Jaime de la Rocha[1]

[1] IDIBAPS, Barcelona, Spain
ainhoahem@gmail.com, alexandre.hyafil@gmail.com
[2] Center for Brain and Cognition, Universitat Pompeu Fabra, Barcelona, Spain
[3] Universidad Nacional Autonoma de México, Mexico City, Mexico
pavel.rueda@gmail.com
[4] University of Oregon, Eugene, USA
sjara@uoregon.edu
[5] Institut de Neurobiologie de la Méditerranée, Marseille, France
david.robbe@inserm.fr, jrochav@clinic.cat

Abstract. Just as our experience has its origin in our perceptions, our perceptions are fundamentally shaped by our experience. How does the brain build expectations from experience and how do expectations impact perception?

We aim to understand how neural circuits integrate the recent history of stimuli and rewards in order to generate priors, and how these priors are combined with sensory information across the processing hierarchy to bias decisions. We trained rats in a reaction-time two-alternative forced-choice (2AFC) task with stimuli consisting in a parametric superposition of two amplitude-modulated tones. Rats had to discriminate the dominant tone and seek reward in the associated port. We used partially predictable stimulus sequences that, once learned, could be used to generate adaptive priors that maximize the performance. These sequences were introduced by defining Repeating trial blocks, in which the probability to repeat the previous stimulus category was 0.7, and Alternating blocks with probability 0.2.

We found that animals adapted their behavior to the statistics of each block and showed a repeating choice bias after several correct repetitions and a weaker but reliable alternating bias after correct alternations. The magnitude of the bias built up after each correct response but reset to zero after error trials. Moreover, animals reaction time was shorter for expected compared to unexpected stimuli, and stimulus impact on choice was smaller when the choice matched the expectation, than when it went against it.

Our findings show that priors show build-up-and-reset dynamics across trials allowing animals to capitalize on the predictability of the stimulus sequence.

Keywords: Decision making · Expectation · Perception

© Springer International Publishing Switzerland 2016
A.E.P. Villa et al. (Eds.): ICANN 2016, Part I, LNCS 9886, p. 539, 2016.
DOI: 10.1007/978-3-319-44778-0

Artificial Neural Network-Based Control Architecture: A Simultaneous Top-Down and Bottom-Up Approach to Autonomous Robot Navigation

Dalia-Marcela Rojas-Castro[✉], Arnaud Revel, and Michel Ménard

Computing Science Department, Laboratory L3i, La Rochelle University,
17000 La Rochelle, France
{dalia_marcela.rojas_castro,arnaud.revel,michel.menard}@univ-lr.fr

Abstract. This paper presents an artificial neural network-based control architecture allowing autonomous mobile robot indoor navigation by emulating the cognition process of a human brain when navigating in an unknown environment. The proposed architecture is based on a simultaneous top-down and bottom up approach, which combines the *a priori* knowledge of the environment gathered from a previously examined floor plan with the visual information acquired in real time. Thus, in order to take the right decision during navigation, the robot is able to process both set of information, compare them in real time and react accordingly. The architecture is composed of two modules: (a) *A deliberative module*, corresponding to the processing chain in charge of extracting a sequence of navigation signs expected to be found in the environment, generating an optimal path plan to reach the goal, computing and memorizing the sequence of signs [1]. The path planning stage allowing the computation of the sign sequence is based on a neural implementation of the resistive grid. (b) *A reactive module*, integrating the said sequence information in order to use it to control online navigation and learning sensory-motor associations. It follows a perception-action mechanism that constantly evolves because of the dynamic interaction between the robot and its environment. It is composed of three layers: one layer using a cognitive mechanism and the other two using a reflex mechanism.

Experimental results obtained from the physical implementation of the architecture in an indoor environment show the feasibility of this approach.

Keywords: Neural control architecture · Robot navigation · Hybrid (top-down and bottom-up) approach · Neural path planning

Reference

1. Rojas Castro, D.M., Revel, A., Menard, M.: Document image analysis by a mobile robot for autonomous indoor navigation. 2015 13th International Conference on Document Analysis and Recognition (ICDAR). IEEE (2015)

Research work supported by European regional development Funds (Contract35053) and the Poitou Charente Region.

A.E.P. Villa et al. (Eds.): ICANN 2016, Part I, LNCS 9886, p. 540, 2016.
DOI: 10.1007/978-3-319-44778-0

Realization of Profit Sharing by Self-Organizing Map-Based Probabilistic Associative Memory

Takahiro Katayama and Yuko Osana[(⊠)]

Tokyo University of Technology, Tokyo, Japan
osana@stf.teu.ac.jp

Abstract. In this paper, we realize a Profit Sharing [2] using Self-Organizing Map-based Probabilistic Associative Memory (SOMPAM) [1]. The SOMPAM whichis used in the proposed method is based on Self-Organizing Map and it has an Input/Output Layer and a Map Layer. In this model, probabilistic associations based on brief degree for binary/analog patterns including common term(s) can be realized. Moreover, it can also realize additional learning by adding new neuron if needed. In the proposed method, patterns corresponding to the pairs of observation and action are memorized to the SOMPAM, and the brief degree is set to value of the rule. We carried out a series of computer experiments for prey capture problem and confirmed that the proposed method can learn appropriate actions even when observation includes noise. Figure 1 shows transition of the number of steps per episode of the proposed method and the conventional Profit Sharing [2]. This figure shows the average of 10 trials (400 trials × 10). As shown in this figure, in early stage of learning, the agent needs about 6000~8000 steps to capture the prey. In contrast, after 200~250 trials, the agent needs only 100~300 steps to capture the prey.

Keywords: Reinforcement learning · Self-Organizing Map-based Probabilistic Associative Memory

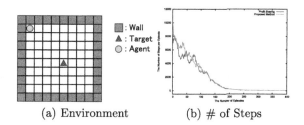

(a) Environment (b) # of Steps

Fig. 1. Transition of the number of steps per episode (with noise).

References

1. Osana, Y.: Self-organizing map-based probabilistic associative memory. In: Proceedings of International Conference on Neural Information Processing, Kuching (2014)
2. Grefenstette, J.J.: Credit assignment in rule discovery systems based on genetic algorithms. Mach. Learn. **3**, 225–245 (1988)

© Springer International Publishing Switzerland 2016
A.E.P. Villa et al. (Eds.): ICANN 2016, Part I, LNCS 9886, p. 541, 2016.
DOI: 10.1007/978-3-319-44778-0

State-Dependent Information Processing in Gene Regulatory Networks

Marçal Gabaldà-Sagarra$^{(\boxtimes)}$ and Jordi Garcia-Ojalvo

Universitat Pompeu Fabra, Barcelona, Spain
{marcal.gabalda,jordi.g.ojalvo}@upf.edu

Abstract. Cells monitor the dynamics of multiple features in their environment to adapt to present and foreseeable future changes. The interaction of the elements of their regulatory networks allows them to integrate different inputs and, even more, process temporal information. However, the general mechanism by which they encode their history to extract temporal information is still unknown.

We aim to describe the general framework through which cellular regulatory networks can integrate temporal information.

We analyzed the gene regulatory networks of five distant organisms and identified cyclic recurrent structures, as these recurrences are essential for dynamical encoding and integration of temporal information in networks. In each network, we found a single group of nodes, a core, forming a recurrent structure. These recurrent cores are upstream of most of the other nodes. This network organization resembles the Reservoir Computer paradigm. In networks that adjust to this paradigm, the transient dynamics of a recurrent group of nodes encode the recent history of the system and the rest of the network reads these dynamics. However, although it is similar to a Recurrent Neural Network, in Reservoir Computing there are no recurrences from the output nodes back to the rest of the system. The benefit of this difference is that only the links from the recurrent core to the output nodes need to be trained. This facilitates the learning of new environmental conditioning and prevents catastrophic interferences [1].

We show that the topology of the recurrent cores of the biological networks perform well in standard memory demanding tasks used in Reservoir Computing. We also show that these results hold when considering different biological stress signaling pathways as inputs. Furthermore, we show that the connectivity of these networks is optimized to encode temporal information given the constraint of the number of transcription factors. Finally, we prove the output nodes of a network can learn to interpret the dynamics of the reservoir, to perform memory-demanding tasks, through evolutionary processes. Our work suggests that cells can process information in a state-dependent manner: it is the transient dynamics of a small part of the regulatory networks that codifies the recent history.

Keywords: Reservoir computing · State-dependent computation · Temporal information processing · Gene regulatory networks

Reference

1. Buonomano, D.V., Maass, W.: Nat. Rev. Neurosci. **10**(2), 113–125 (2009)

© Springer International Publishing Switzerland 2016
A.E.P. Villa et al. (Eds.): ICANN 2016, Part I, LNCS 9886, p. 542, 2016.
DOI: 10.1007/978-3-319-44778-0

Patent Citation Network Analysis: Topology and Evolution of Patent Citation Networks

Péter Érdi[1,2]($\boxtimes$)

[1] Center for Complex Systems Studies, Kalamazoo College, Kalamazoo, MI, USA
perdi@kzoo.edu
[2] Wigner Research Centre for Physics, Hungarian Academy of Sciences,
Budapest, Hungary

Abstract. The network of patents connected by citations is an evolving graph, which represents the innovation process. A patent citing another implies that the cited patent reflects a piece of previously existing knowledge that the citing patent builds upon. We review models evolution of the patent citation network both at the "microscopic" level of individual patents [1–5] and at "mesoscopic" [6] levels. Microscopic level studies helped to measure the "attractivness" of a patent, as the function of its age and the number of citation already has obtained. A somewhat similar approach was given here: [7]. At mesoscopic level the analysis has been extended to subclasses, and it was demonstrated by adopting clustering algorithms that it is possible to detect and predict emerging new technology clusters.

Keywords: Evolving networks · Patent citation analysis

References

1. Csardi, G., Strandburg, K.J., Zalanyi, L., Tobochnik, J., Erdi, P.: Modeling innovation by a kinetic description of the patent citation system. Physica A **74**(12), 783–793 (2007)
2. Csardi, G., Strandburg, K.J., Tobochnik, J., Erdi, P.: Chapter 10. The inverse problem of evolving networks with application to social nets. In: Bollobas, B., Kozma, R., Miklos, D. (eds.) Handbook of Large-Scale Random Networks, pp. 409–443. Springer-Verlag (2009)
3. Erdi, P.: Complexity Explained. Springer-Verlag (2007)
4. Strandburg, K., Csardi, G., Tobochnik, J., Erdi, P., Zalanyi, L.: Law and the science of networks: an overview and an application to the patent explosion. Berkeley Technol. Law J. **21**, 1293 (2007)
5. Strandburg, K., Csardi, G., Tobochnik, J., Erdi, P., Zalanyi, L.: Patent citation networks revisited: signs of a twenty-first century change? North Carol. Law Rev. **87**, 1657–1698 (2009)
6. Erdi, P., Makovi, K., Somogyvari, Z., Strandburg, K., Tobochnik, J., Volf, P., Zalanyi, L.: Prediction of emerging technologies based on analysis of the U.S. patent citation network. Scientometrics **95**, 225–242 (2013)
7. Valverde, S., Sole, R.V., Bedau, M.A., Packard, N.: Topology and evolution of technology innovation networks. Phys. Rev. E **76**, 056118 (2007)

© Springer International Publishing Switzerland 2016
A.E.P. Villa et al. (Eds.): ICANN 2016, Part I, LNCS 9886, p. 543, 2016.
DOI: 10.1007/978-3-319-44778-0

Patent Citation Network Analysis: Ranking: From Web Pages to Patents

Péter Érdi[1,2(✉)] and Péter Bruck[1,2]

[1] Center for Complex Systems Studies, Kalamazoo College,
Kalamazoo, MI, USA
[2] Wigner Research Centre for Physics,
Hungarian Academy of Sciences, Budapest, Hungary
perdi@kzoo.edu

Abstract. Ranking of nodes in a network of diverse number of connections (degree) is an extensively studied field. In the theory of social networks centrality measures were constructed to rank nodes of networks based on their (not unique) topological importance, Another family of measures is related to the spectral properties of the adjacency matrix [1], which takes into account the importance of the influence of a neighbor. Importance can be defined recursively. Brin and Page [2] introduced a matching recursive centrality measure called PageRank. The relevance of this algorithm to citation networks was expressed by [3]. By adopting a citation-based recursive ranking method for patents the evolution of new field of technologies can be traced. Specifically, the laser/inkjet printer technology emerged from the recombination of existing technologies, such as sequential printing and static image production. The dynamics of the citations coming from the different precursor classes illuminate the mechanism of the emergence of new fields and give the possibility to make predictions about future technological development [4]. The combination of using clustering algorithms with ranking algorithms give more insight about the dynamics of the patent citation network [5].

Keywords: Ranking · PageRank · Patent citation analysis

References

1. Perra, N., Fortunato, S.: Spectral centrality measures in complex networks. Phys. Rev. E **78**, 036107 (2008)
2. Brin, S., Page, L.: The anatomy of a large-scale hypertextual web search engine. Comput. Netw. ISDN Syst. **30**, 107–117 (1998)
3. Maslov, S.: Promise and pitfalls of extending googles pagerank algorithm to citation networks. J. Neurosci. **29**, 1103–1105 (2009)
4. Bruck, P., Rethy, I., Szente, J., Tobochnik, J., Erdi, P.: Recognition of emerging technology trends. class-selective study of citations in the U.S. patent citation network. Scientometrics **107**, 1465–1475 (2016)
5. Fulop, A., Beltz, H., Hochster, L., Pennington, M., Wadhwa, R., Erdi, P.: in preparation

© Springer International Publishing Switzerland 2016
A.E.P. Villa et al. (Eds.): ICANN 2016, Part I, LNCS 9886, p. 544, 2016.
DOI: 10.1007/978-3-319-44778-0

Multistable Attractor Dynamics in Columnar Cortical Networks Transitioning from Deep Anesthesia to Wakefulness

Cristiano Capone[1,2], Nuria Tort-Colet[3], Maurizio Mattia[1(✉)],
and Maria V. Sanchez-Vives[3,4]

[1] Istituto Superiore di Sanità (ISS), 00161 Rome, Italy
[2] PhD Program in Physics, Sapienza University, 00185 Rome, Italy
maurizio.mattia@iss.it
[3] IDIBAPS, 08036 Barcelona, Spain
[4] Institució Catalana de Recerca i Estudis Avançats (ICREA),
08010 Barcelona, Spain

Abstract. Slow rhythms of activity ($\sim 1\,Hz$) are a universal hallmark of slow-wave sleep and deep anesthesia across many animal species. A remarkably reproducible default mode with a low degree of complexity which opens a window on the brain multiscale organization, on top of which cognitive functions emerge during wakefulness. Understanding how such transition takes place starting from the characterization of a stereotyped state like the slow-wave activity [1], might shade light on the emergence of the rich repertoire of neuronal dynamics underlying brain computation. Sleep-wake transition is a widely studied phenomenon [2], however it is still debated how brain state changes occur. Here we show from intracortical recordings in anesthetized rats, that sleep-like rhythms fade out when wakefulness is approached giving rise to an alternation between slow Up/Down oscillations and awake-like activity periods. This phase of activity pattern bistability is captured by a mean-field rate-based model of a cortical column, in which for a transient range of anesthesia levels the coexistence of two metastable attractor states emerges. Alternation between these two states is granted by the ongoing competition of local features and exogenous modulations governing both the excitability and the fatigue level of the modeled column. Our results highlight a brain state transition which is not a continuous smooth change but rather a progressive modulation of the stability of two coexistent activity regimes, which in turn leave different fingerprints across cortical columns. Guided by this mean-field model, spiking neuron networks are devised to reproduce the electrophysiological changes displayed during the transition.

Keywords: Sleep awake transition · Multistable system

Supported by EC FP7 CORTICONIC Grant 600806 and WaveScalES EC FET Flagship HBP SGA1 720270.

A.E.P. Villa et al. (Eds.): ICANN 2016, Part I, LNCS 9886, pp. 545–546, 2016.
DOI: 10.1007/978-3-319-44778-0

546   C. Capone et al.

References

1. Sanchez-Vives, M.V., Mattia, M.: Arch Ital Biol **152**, 147–155 (2014)
2. Bettinardi, R.G., Tort-Colet, N., Ruiz-Mejias, M., Sanchez-Vives, M.V., Deco, G.: Neuroimage **114**, 185–198 (2015)

Modulation of Cortical Intrinsic Bistability and Complexity in the Cortical Network

Maria V. Sanchez-Vives[1,4], Julia F. Weinert[1], Beatriz Rebollo[1],
Adenauer G. Casali[2], Andrea Pigorini[3], Marcello Massimini[3(✉)],
and Mattia D'Andola[1]

[1] IDIBAPS, Barcelona, Spain
mattia.dandola@gmail.com
[2] Institute of Science and Technology, USP, Sao Jose dos Campos, SP, Brazil
[3] Department of Biomedical and Clinical Sciences 'L. Sacco', UNIMI, Milano, Italy
msanche3@clinic.ub.es
[4] ICREA (Institucio Catalana de Recerca i Estudis Avancats), Barcelona, Spain

Abstract. Slow waves emerge from the cortical network during states
of functional disconnection (non-REM sleep, anesthesia) and anatomical
disconnection (slices, deafferented cortex) as if it were its default activity
[1]. Such emergent activity and its spatiotemporal patterns reveal features about the underlying network. By using an observational approach
of these emergent slow waves we have identified alterations in the cortical emergent patterns in transgenic models of neurological disease [2].
Here, we present a perturbational approach where we probe the network
by electrical stimulation using two different approaches: (1) By means
of DC electric fields we explore the modulation of the emergent activity,
(2) By means of electric pulses we measure the complexity of the cortical
network's responses. To this end we have adapted to cortical slices the
perturbational complexity index (PCI) recently introduced in humans
to quantify the information content of deterministic patterns evoked in
the brain by transcranial magnetic stimulation [3]. Our *in vitro* perturbational study reveals that the spontaneous intrinsic cortical bistability
breaks-off complexity in the neural network. We also explore the mechanisms modulating network complexity under different brain states.

Keywords: Complexity · Cerebral cortex · Oscillations · Synchronization · Electric fields · Slow waves · Cortical network · Up states

Acknowledgments. Supported by EU CORTICONIC contract 600806 and PCIN-
2015-162-C02-01 (FLAG ERA) del MINECO.

References

1. Sanchez-Vives, M.V., Mattia, M.: Slow wave activity as the default mode of the
cerebral cortex. Arch. Ital. Biol. **152**, 147–155 (2014)
2. Ruiz-Mejias, M., et al.: Overexpression of Dyrk1A, a down syndrome candidate,
decreases excitability and impairs gamma oscillations in the prefrontal cortex. J.
Neurosci. **36**(13), 3648–3659 (2016)
3. Casali, A., et al.: A theoretically based index of consciousness independent of sensory
processing and behavior. Sci. Transl. Med. **5**(198) (2013)

A.E.P. Villa et al. (Eds.): ICANN 2016, Part I, LNCS 9886, p. 547, 2016.
DOI: 10.1007/978-3-319-44778-0

A Neural Network for Visual Working Memory that Accounts for Memory Binding Errors

João Barbosa[✉] and Albert Compte

IDIBAPS, 08036 Barcelona, Spain
palerma@gmail.com, acompte@clinic.cat

Abstract. Binding errors, also called swap errors, occur in working memory (WM) tasks when the participant fails to report the feature of a previously presented target but the response is accurate relative to a non-target stimulus [1]. These errors reflect the failure of the system to maintain bundled through memory the conjunction of features that define one object. The brain mechanisms that maintain integrated several features of an item in one memory remain unknown. We explore the hypothesis that synchrony of different neural assemblies coding each for a feature of an item plays the main role [2]. To test the synchrony hypothesis, we built a network model for the storage of multiple items defined by one color and one location in WM. The model is composed of two networks for WM [3], one representing colors and the other one locations. These two networks are then connected via weak cortico-cortical excitation. With this model we are able to maintain persistent memory bumps that encode colors and locations in each respective network. Fast recurrent excitation within each network induced γ oscillations during bump activity through the interplay of fast excitation and slower feedback inhibition [3]. Spectral power of network activity in the γ range of frequencies increased with the number of stored items, as it has been reported both in humans and monkey studies [4]. Binding between features was effectively accomplished through the synchronization of γ oscillations between bumps across the two networks. As a result, different memorized items were held at different phases of a global network oscillation, whose frequency increased with WM load. In some simulations swap errors arose: color bumps abruptly changed their phase relationship with location bump. Furthermore, by systematically decreasing the distance between different memory items, thus increasing potential interference within trials [5], the model predicts that swap errors should increase.

Keywords: Working memory · Spiking network · Gamma oscillations

References

1. Bays, P., Catalao, F., Husain, M.: J. Vis. **9**, 7 (2009)
2. Singer, W.: Neuron **24**, 49 (1999)
3. Compte, A., et al.: Cereb Cortex **10**, 910 (2000)
4. Kornblith, S., Buschman, T., Miller, E.: Cerb Cortex (2015)
5. Almeida, R., Barbosa, J., Compte, A.: J. Neurophisiol (2015)

© Springer International Publishing Switzerland 2016
A.E.P. Villa et al. (Eds.): ICANN 2016, Part I, LNCS 9886, p. 548, 2016.
DOI: 10.1007/978-3-319-44778-0

Single-Neuron Sensory Coding Might Influence Performance in a Monkey's Perceptual Discrimination Task

Pau de Jorge[1]([✉]), Verónica Nácher[2], Rogelio Luna[3], Jordi Soriano[1], Ranulfo Romo[4,5], Gustavo Deco[6,7], and Adrià Tauste Campo[7,8]

[1] Universitat de Barcelona, Barcelona, Spain
[2] York University, Toronto, Canada
[3] The University of Western Ontario, London, Canada
[4] Universidad Nacional Autónoma de Mexico, Mexico, D.F., Mexico
[5] El Colegio Nacional, Mexico, DF, Mexico
[6] Institució Catalana d'Estudis Avançats, Barcelona, Spain
[7] Universitat Pompeu Fabra, Barcelona, Spain
[8] Hospital del Mar Medical Research Institute, Barcelona, Spain

Abstract. During the process of making a perceptual decision, a number of cognitive processes are sequentially involved, whose interplay determines the subject's final response. To help disentangling the intermingling effect of these processes into behaviour, we studied how an initial process such as stimulus encoding influences the response accuracy during a perceptual discrimination task in monkeys. We examined this hypothesis by analysing single-cell recordings from a monkey's somatosensory area 1 (S1) during a vibrotactile discrimination task, in which the monkey compared two tactile vibrations delivered at different times and reported which vibration had a higher frequency [1].

We quantified sensory coding accuracy during the first stimulation period by estimating the significance of the mutual information between each neuron's mean firing rate and the first stimulus frequency. We evaluated this measure in trials in which the monkey correctly reported the decision (correct trials) and trials in which it did not (incorrect trials). The results of this analysis applied over nearly 100 neurons revealed that sensory coding accuracy had a significant effect on task performance. Indeed, among all neurons that exhibited coding accuracy differences across both sets of trials (36 % of the population), 86 % of those neurons were only encoding stimulus information during the correct trials. These preliminary results suggest that initial sensory coding may greatly affect performance in a perceptual discrimination task.

Keywords: Discrimination task · Neural coding · Information theory

Reference

1. Hernández, A., Nácher, V., Luna, R., Zainos, A., Lemus, L., Alvarez, M., Romo, R.: Decoding a perceptual decision process across cortex. Neuron **66**, 300–314 (2010)

© Springer International Publishing Switzerland 2016
A.E.P. Villa et al. (Eds.): ICANN 2016, Part I, LNCS 9886, p. 549, 2016.
DOI: 10.1007/978-3-319-44778-0

Modelling History-Dependent Perceptual Biases in Rodents

Alexandre Hyafil[(✉)], Ainhoa Hermoso Mendizabal, and Jaime de la Rocha

Idibaps, Barcelona, Spain
alexandre.hyafil@gmail.com

Abstract. Higher order cognition relies on selecting actions based on current sensory information and on the outcome of previous experiences. While humans can flexibly learn the statistical regularities of the sensory environment and use them to guide behavior, little is known about whether rodents display comparable abilities. We studied the capacity of rats to use the history of recent actions and outcomes to bias future perceptual decisions. Rats performed a novel acoustic discrimination task (with two-alternative forced choice) in which we introduced correlations in the rewarded choice sequence that could be used to guide decisions. Specifically, blocks of trials in which the probability to repeat the previous stimulus category was $P_{rep} > 0.5$ (repeating environment) alternated with blocks where it was $P_{rep} < 0.5$ (alternating environment). Rats were able to accumulate acoustic evidence across the stimulus duration, as well as integrate recent history of rewards and errors. Combining these two sources of information to guide their choices they could improve their discrimination performance by adapting their history-dependent choice biases to the statistics of each environment.

We performed a probit regression analyses to show that rats, as previously described in primates, used recent history of responses to guide action selection: they positively weighted Left and Right responses in the last few trials to favor upcoming choice to the Left and Right ports, respectively. More interestingly they also weighted previous response transitions, i.e. Alternations and Repetitions, that lead them to bias upcoming choices to Alternate or Repeat the last choice, respectively. While sequences of successful alternations could lead to gradual build-up of such history-dependent bias, importantly, erroneous alternations lead to a reset of such biases.

Given this evidence we fitted a Reinforcement Learning model of behavior to detail the mechanisms at play in integration of sensory evidence with recent history. Our model includes build-up of both laterality (left/right) and transition (alternate/repeat) biases as latent (autoregressive) variables, each of them containing different learning rates for correct and incorrect responses. Fitting parameters indeed showed opposing effects of correct left vs. right responses onto the laterality bias, and opposing effects of correct alternate vs. repeat responses onto the transition bias, while errors lead to a complete reset of such biases. Our work provides a normative framework to describe how organisms flexibly adapt to regularities in the environment by updating their choice bias according to the history of past rewards and errors.

© Springer International Publishing Switzerland 2016
A.E.P. Villa et al. (Eds.): ICANN 2016, Part I, LNCS 9886, p. 550, 2016.
DOI: 10.1007/978-3-319-44778-0

Applicability of Echo State Networks to Classify EEG Data from a Movement Task

Lukas Hestermeyer$^{(\boxtimes)}$ and Gordon Pipa

Institute of Cognitive Science, University of Osnabrueck, Osnabrück, Germany
{lhestermeyer,gpipa}@uos.de

Abstract. Prosthetic devices have come a far way from being just mechanical devices. In recent years, neuroprosthetic devices have been developed, that directly infer movements commands from neuronal activities. Amongst these, hand prostheses require a more precise detection of different hand motions than other body parts. However, detection of such precise movements in EEG data is a non-trivial task due to the noisiness. To challenge this problem, the WAY consortium created a classification challenge on the Kaggle platform in the summer 2015.

The winners used a recurrent convolutional neural network that scored 0.98 AUC. Since training such a network is computationally demanding, we applied an echo state network to the same dataset, to see whether this faster approach can compete with the RCNN. The dataset originates from grasp and lift trials recorded by the WAY consortium [1]. They labeled the data with six different events, occurring in the same order for each trial. Further, each of the events are labeled ± 75 ms around the onset of the event. Lastly, the dataset is imbalanced, as most of the time no event occurs.

To challenge this imbalanced, we used a weighted ridge regression to learn the weights of the output layer. We further tried subsampling the frames where no event occurred. Preliminary results suggest no significant difference between these two methods. Additionally, we used different activation functions including hyperbolic tangent and rectified hyperbolic tangent. Lastly, we set up the reservoir in three "bubbles" that were highly connected, whilst between bubbles only few connections were active. Other than that, the original approach of Jaeger was used [2]. To preprocess the data, we used common spatial patterns. We applied these to each event separately against the rest time, leading to six different preprocessed datasets. For each of these datasets, we classified the corresponding event using one ESN. Afterwards, we concatenated the predictions to form the original six events. We have not yet fully evaluated this approach. However, preliminary results (ca. 0.76 AUC) are promising, although they do not compete with the results of the competition winners.

Keywords: Echo state network · Recurrent neural network · EEG classification · Brain computer interface · Kaggle

© Springer International Publishing Switzerland 2016
A.E.P. Villa et al. (Eds.): ICANN 2016, Part I, LNCS 9886, pp. 551–552, 2016.
DOI: 10.1007/978-3-319-44778-0

References

1. Luciw, M.D., Jarocka, E., Edin, B.B.: Multi-channel EEG recordings during 3,936 grasp and lift trials with varying weight and friction. Sci. Data 1 (2014)
2. Jaeger, H.: The "echo state" approach to analysing and training recurrent neural networks-with an erratum note. German National Research Center for Information Technology GMD Technical Report, Bonn, Germany, vol. 148 (2001)

Data Assimilation of EEG Observations by Neural Mass Models

Lara Escuain-Poole[1]([✉]), Jordi Garcia-Ojalvo[2], and Antonio J. Pons[1]

[1] Department of Physics, Universitat Politècnica de Catalunya – BarcelonaTech,
Barcelona, Spain
[2] Department of Experimental and Health Sciences, Universitat Pompeu Fabra,
Barcelona, Spain

Abstract. Brain modelling in the mesoscopic scale deals with functional groups of thousands of neurons in the cerebral cortex, the cortical columns, which represent the source of the electrical currents that can be detected in the brain. These cortical columns can be modelled theoretically with neural mass models, whose dynamics are determined by a set of parameters with biological meaning. Changes in the values of these parameters may point to variations in the behaviour or structure of the system. The averaged activity of the neurons in the cortical column results in dipole currents that can be measured with electroencephalography (EEG).

EEG is a non-invasive and fairly cost-efficient way of detecting healthy or pathological brain activity, and its use is currently widespread and well established. Nevertheless, it is a descriptive technique, which cannot explain the underlying causes that may lead to a specific functional state. Linking brain structure and function can be done by neural mass models, but these computational descriptions are hardly applicable in a clinical setting due to lack of knowledge of the biological constraints that affect the model parameters in specific brain states.

To address these shortcomings, we aim to bring computational models and experimental measurements together with data assimilation algorithms. In particular, we use the Unscented Kalman Filter to feed synthetic EEG data to a neural mass model, and estimate the state of the system and the parameters of the model therewith. Preliminary results show the advantages of using several extracranial electrodes as opposed to a single intracortical measurement, information-wise. We also discuss the influence of the number of electrodes on the quality of the estimation.

Keywords: Data assimilation · Neural mass modelling · Kalman filtering · Electroencephalography

A.E.P. Villa et al. (Eds.): ICANN 2016, Part I, LNCS 9886, p. 553, 2016.
DOI: 10.1007/978-3-319-44778-0

Functional Reorganization of Neural Networks Prior to Epileptic Seizures

Adrià Tauste Campo[1,2,3], Alessandro Principe[2,3], Rodrigo Rocamora[2,3], and Gustavo Deco[1,4]

[1] Universitat Pompeu Fabra, Barcelona, Spain
[2] Epilepsy Unit, Hospital del Mar, Barcelona, Spain
[3] Hospital del Mar Medical Research Institute, Barcelona, Spain
[4] Institució Catalana d'Estudis Avançats, Barcelona, Spain

Abstract. Epilepsy is among the most common neurological disorders with an estimated prevalence of about 1% of the world's population. Around a third of all epileptic subjects are resistant to anticonvulsant therapy and could benefit from therapeutic closed-loop interventions (e.g. electrical stimulation) based on an accurate prediction of seizure occurrences. Over the last decades, a large number of algorithms have been tested to predict seizures. Although the performance of these algorithms has improved over time [1], a clear understanding of the mechanisms by which epileptic networks generate seizures is still missing, which questions their current applicability.

To take this question we studied emerging properties of epileptic networks during pre-seizure activity periods. Specifically, we analyzed the temporal evolution of functional connectivity networks using long-lasting (up to 12 h) periods of setereoencephalography (SEEG) intracranial recordings from epileptic patients before a seizure occurred. Functional networks were dynamically characterized by inferring sequential connectivity graphs in non-overlapping short time windows (0.6 s) and extracting time-varying network measures (e.g. strength, centrality) for each channel of interest. Pre-seizure specificity of our findings was assessed via a control analysis on the same time period from a precedent seizure-free day.

The results of our analysis applied to 10 patients with different clinical prognosis show that seizures were preceded by long (3–8 h) periods of decreased functional network variability. These findings may open new roads to explain the underlying network mechanisms of previously reported pre-ictal EEG features [1] and eventually guide data-driven seizure prediction algorithms.

Keywords: Intracranial EEG · Epileptic networks · Network centrality

Reference

1. Gadhoumi, K., et al.: Seizure prediction for therapeutic devices: a review. J. Neurosci. Methods (2015)

© Springer International Publishing Switzerland 2016
A.E.P. Villa et al. (Eds.): ICANN 2016, Part I, LNCS 9886, p. 554, 2016.
DOI: 10.1007/978-3-319-44778-0

Attractor Models of Perceptual Decisions Making Exhibit Stochastic Resonance

Genis Prat-Ortega[1,2]([✉]), Klaus Wimmer[1], Alex Roxin[2],
and Jaime de la Rocha[1]

[1] Institut dinvestigacions Biomèdiques August Pi i Sunyer, Barcelona, Spain
[2] Centre de Recerca Matemàtica, Barcelona, Spain
gprat@crm

Abstract. Several computational models have been proposed to describe the integration of sensory evidence in perceptual 2-Alternative Forced-Choice (2AFC) tasks. Although these disparate models can account for the behavior of subjects performing such tasks, for example their performance or reaction time, they rely on different dynamical mechanisms.

Here, we investigate the dynamics of evidence integration in models with attractor dynamics during a fixed duration 2AFC task. We studied a spiking network and a diffusion process in a DW potential (the one dimensional potential equivalent to the spiking network). We have found two interesting properties of these models when we consider a fluctuating stimulus in which evidence is drawn in each time step from a noisy distribution with mean μ and variance σ. Both rely on the same underlying mechanism, the stochastic transitions between wells that can be correcting if the final well is deeper than the initial or error in the opposite case. In particular, the predictions are: (1) As σ increases the fluctuations with a higher impact on choice shift from the beginning (transient integration) to the end of the stimulus (leaky integration). For small σ, when the system reaches an attractor it is unlikely to escape, thus the fluctuations with a higher impact on the choice are at the beginning of the stimulus. As σ is increased, more transitions occur, and the fluctuations at the end determine the final decision. (2) The categorization performance shows a resonance with a local maximum at $\sigma_{max} > 0$. The Kramers transition rates are higher for the correcting than error transition because the correct well is deeper. As a consequence, there is a range of σ where the benefit of having more correction than error transitions offsets the decrease in signal-to-noise ratio (stochastic resonance).

Importantly, these predictions are robust for a wide range of model parameters and specific for a model with attractor dynamics. Other models that consider optimal evidence integration yield different predictions. Our analysis makes specific predictions that can be tested in psychophysical 2AFC tasks, which would clarify some fundamental aspects of sensory integration dynamics.

Keywords: Attractor network models · Decision making · Stochastic resonance

© Springer International Publishing Switzerland 2016
A.E.P. Villa et al. (Eds.): ICANN 2016, Part I, LNCS 9886, p. 555, 2016.
DOI: 10.1007/978-3-319-44778-0

VLSI Design of a Neural Network Model for Detecting Planar Surface from Local Image Motion

Hisanao Akima[✉], Satoshi Moriya, Susumu Kawakami, Masafumi Yano, Koji Nakajima, Masao Sakurabah, and Shigeo Sato

Research Institute of Electrical Communication,
Tohoku University, Sendai, Japan
akima@riec.tohoku.ac.jp

Abstract. The spatial perception, in which objects motion and position are recognized in 3-D like humans, has been demanding for applications such as an autonomous mobile robot and an autonomous car. Biologically inspired methods with dedicated hardware have been attractive because of its high energy efficiency compared with image processing algorithms performed on a CPU. We have focused on planar surface detection by using a neural network model proposed by Kawakami et al. [1, 2] and implemented this model on a VLSI.

In the Kawakami model, the orientation and time-to-contact (TTC) of a planar surface are detected in two steps. First, local image motions are detected in motion detection cells (MDCs) from local retinal images. Second, the local image motions are integrated by accumulating MDC responses in medial superior temporal (MST) cells. In this study, we focused on the second step. The MDC responses are given as inputs to a VLSI. The neural connections between MDCs and MST cells are determined by using polar and cross-ratio transforms [2]. One of the main issues in implementing this step on a VLSI is wiring of these huge connections. We solved this by using virtual connection scheme with connection tables and packet-based communication.

We designed a VLSI chip by using TSMC 65 nm CMOS standard cell library in 1.32 mm × 1.32 mm core area. The chip includes 64 processing elements (PEs) and each PE corresponds to an MST cell. Each PE has a connection table stored in a local memory, and a register to accumulate MDC responses. The orientation and TTC of a planar surface are detected from a location of the PE which has the maximum value. The latency required to accumulate all MDC responses and retrieve all PEs' register values was estimated as 2.2 ms in a 100 MHz operation by using gate-level HDL simulation. The power consumption was also estimated as 36 mW. The operation speed of the designed VLSI is comparable with a C++ program performed on a CPU (Intel Core i7-3770, 3.4 GHz, TDP 77 W), while its power consumption is smaller than the CPU by less than 1 %.

Keywords: VLSI · Neural network · Vision processing

A.E.P. Villa et al. (Eds.): ICANN 2016, Part I, LNCS 9886, pp. 556–557, 2016.
DOI: 10.1007/978-3-319-44778-0

References

1. Kawakami, S., Okamoto, H.: A cell model for the detection of local image motion on the Magnocellular pathway of the visual cortex. Vision Res. **36**, 117–147 (1996)
2. Kawakami, S., Matsuoka, M., Okamoto, H., Hosogi, S.: A neural network model for detecting a planar surface spatially from the optical flow in area MST of the visual cortex. Syst. Comput. Jpn. **34**, 46–59 (2003)

Learning Method for a Quantum Bit Network

Yoshihiro Osakabe[1]($^{\boxtimes}$), Shigeo Sato[1], Mitsunaga Kinjo[2], Koji Nakajima[1], Hisanao Akima[1], and Masao Sakuraba[1]

[1] Research Institute of Electrical Communication, Tohoku University, Sendai, Japan
osakabe@riec.tohoku.ac.jp
[2] Department of Electorical and Electronic Engineering,
University of the Ryukyus, Nishihara, Japan

Abstract. Quantum computing (QC) has attracted much attention due to its enormous computing power, but proposed algorithms so far are not sufficient for practical use. Therefore, if a quantum computer could obtain algorithms by itself, the applicable field of QC would be extended greatly. In this study, we investigate a learning method for a quantum bit network (QBN) by utilizing the analogy between an artificial neural network and a QBN as described in the previous reports [1, 2]. According to this analogy, we can relate a synaptic weight matrix with a Hamiltonian.

We propose a quantum version of Hebb learning as follows; we enhance both excitatory and inhibitory couplings according to the probability that arbitrary two quantum bits (qubits) take the same or opposite states when a QBN outputs a desired pattern. As a first step, we trained a QBN shown in Fig. 1 to learn the XOR problem. We updated the Hamiltonian only when the hidden qubit took the state "1" in order to break symmetry because the network always learns a pair of symmetric patterns whether these patterns are desired or not. A typical successful learning result is shown in Fig. 2. Though the success rate of learning with various initial Hamiltonians reaches only 50 %, this preliminary result indicates certain possibility for implementing learning function with a QBN.

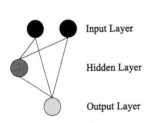

Fig. 1. Quantum bit network

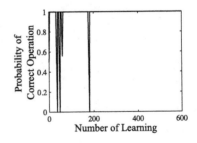

Fig. 2. Probability of the correct operation as function of the number of learning

Keywords: Quantum computing · Hebb learning

© Springer International Publishing Switzerland 2016
A.E.P. Villa et al. (Eds.): ICANN 2016, Part I, LNCS 9886, pp. 558–559, 2016.
DOI: 10.1007/978-3-319-44778-0

References

1. Sato, S., Kinjo, M., Nakajima, K.: An approach for quantum computing using adiabatic evolution algorithm. Jpn. J. Appl. Phys. **42**, 7169–7173 (2003)
2. Kinjo, M., Sato, S., Nakamiya, Y., Nakajima, K.: Neuromorphic quantum computation with energy dissipation. Phys. Rev. A **72**, 052328 (2005)

Information-Theoretical Foundations
of Hebbian Learning

Claudius Gros[1($\boxtimes$)] and Rodrigo Echeveste[1,2]

[1] Institute for Theoretical Physics, Goethe University Frankfurt, Frankfurt, Germany
{gros07,echeveste}@itp.uni-frankfurt.de
http://itp.uni-frankfurt.de/~gros/
[2] Department of Engineering, University of Cambridge, Cambridge, UK

Abstract. Neural information processing includes the extraction of information present in the statistics of afferent signals. For this, the afferent synaptic weights w_j are continuously adapted, changing in turn the distribution $p_\theta(y)$ of the post-synaptic neural activity y. Here θ denotes relevant neural parameters. The functional form of $p_\theta(y)$ will hence continue to evolve as long as learning is on-going, becoming stationary only when learning is completed. This stationarity principle can be captured by the Fisher information

$$F_\theta = \int p_\theta(y) \left(\frac{\partial}{\partial \theta} \ln \left(p_\theta(y) \right) \right)^2 dy, \qquad \frac{\partial}{\partial \theta} \rightarrow \sum_j w_j \frac{\partial}{\partial w_j}$$

of the neural activity with respect to the afferent synaptic weights w_j. It then follows, that Hebbian learning rules may be derived by minimizing F_θ. The precise functional form of the learning rules depends then on the shape of the transfer function $y = g(x)$ relating the membrane potential x with the activity y.

The learning rules derived from the stationarity principle are self-limiting (runaway synaptic growth does not occur), performing a standard principal component analysis, whenever a direction in the space of input activities with a large variance is present. Generically, directions of input activities having a negative excess Kurtosis are preferred, making the rules suitable for ICA (see figure). Moreover, when only the exponential foot of g is considered (low activity regime), the standard Hebbian learning rule, without reversal, is recovered.

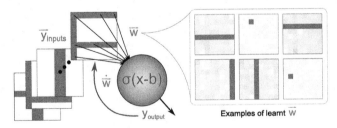

Examples of learnt $\overline{w}$

Keywords: Information theory · Hebbian learning · Stationarity principle

© Springer International Publishing Switzerland 2016
A.E.P. Villa et al. (Eds.): ICANN 2016, Part I, LNCS 9886, p. 560, 2016.
DOI: 10.1007/978-3-319-44778-0

Artificial Neural Network Models for Forecasting Tourist Arrivals to Barcelona

Bulent Alptekin[1]([✉]) and Cagdas Hakan Aladag[2]

[1] Department of Statistics, Middle East Technical University, Ankara, Turkey
`albulent@metu.edu.tr`
[2] Department of Statistics, Hacettepe University, Ankara, Turkey
`aladag@hacettepe.edu.tr`

Abstract. In order to reach accurate tourism demand forecasts, various forecasting methods have been proposed in the literature [1]. These approaches can be divided into two subclasses. One of them is conventional methods such as autoregressive moving average (ARIMA) or exponential smoothing. And, the other one is advanced forecasting techniques such as fuzzy time series, artificial neural networks (ANN) or hybrid approaches. The main purpose of this study is to develop some efficient forecasting models based on ANN for tourism demand of Barcelona in order to reach high accuracy level.

Different ANN models are constructed by changing architectures and activation functions used in neurons of hidden layer. Three activation functions such as stepwise, logistic and hyperbolic tangent functions are utilized for neurons of hidden layer. The number of neurons in the input layer is changed from 1 to 6 and the number of neurons in the hidden layer is changed from 1 to 15. Thus, 90 architectures are examined for each activation function since one neuron is used in the output layer. In the implementation, 270 different ANN model constructed and applied to tourism demand of Barcelona.

The tourist arrival to Barcelona between 2000 and 2014 has 15 yearly observations. When this time series was analyzed by ANN models, the first 12 observations were used as training data and the rest of them as test data. First of all, all models are trained and model parameters are determined by using the training set. Then, the forecasting performances of the models are evaluated by using a performance measure. Then, the best architecture that has the minimum performance measure value calculated over the test set is selected. All obtained forecasting results are presented and discussed.

Keywords: Forecasting · Feed forward neural networks · Time series

References

1. Aladag, C.H., Egrioglu, E., Yolcu, U.: Robust multilayer neural network based on median neuron model. Neural Comput. Appl. **24**, 945–956 (2014)
2. Aladag, C.H., Egrioglu, E., Yolcu, U., Uslu, V.R.: A high order seasonal fuzzy time series model and application to international tourism demand of Turkey. J. Intell. Fuzzy Syst. **26**(1), 295–302 (2014)

© Springer International Publishing Switzerland 2016
A.E.P. Villa et al. (Eds.): ICANN 2016, Part I, LNCS 9886, p. 561, 2016.
DOI: 10.1007/978-3-319-44778-0

Experimental Study of Multistability and Attractor Dynamics in Winnerless Neural Networks

Ashok Chauhan[(✉)] and Alain Nogaret

Department of Physics, University of Bath, Bath BA2 7AY, UK
{a.s.chauhan,a.r.nogaret}@bath.ac.uk

Abstract. We report on the experimental observation and study of dynamic attractors in chaotic neural networks, probed by timed current stimuli. We observed multistability in chaotic networks and demonstrate how systematically controlling the timing of stimulation selects the spatiotemporal sequences of voltage oscillations of neurons.

We have developed a network of N neurons interconnected with mutually inhibitory gap junctions, using silicon chips. This neural network is based on the Hodgkin-Huxley model. We then generated phase-lag maps of neuronal oscillators by varying the timing of current stimulation to individual neurons [1]. We observed multiple attractors that consists of N-phasic sequences of unevenly spaced pulses, propagating clockwise and anti-clockwise. Our results validate the command neuron hypothesis and the control of adaptation of motor patterns to stimulation.

The proposed approach may find application for modulating heart rate and providing therapy for heart failure [2].

Keywords: Winnerless chaotic network · Dynamic attractors

References

1. Zhao, L., Nogaret, A.: Experimental observation of multistability and dynamic attractors in silicon central pattern generators. Phys. Rev. E. **92**, 052910 (2015)
2. O'Callaghan, E.L., Chauhan, A.S., Zhao, L., Lataro, R.M., Salgado, H.C., Nogaret, A., Paton, J.F.R.: Utility of a novel biofeedback device for within-breath modulation of heart rate in rats: a quantitative comparison of vagus nerve vs. right atrial pacing. Frontiers Physiol. **7**, 27 (2016)

© Springer International Publishing Switzerland 2016
A.E.P. Villa et al. (Eds.): ICANN 2016, Part I, LNCS 9886, p. 562, 2016.
DOI: 10.1007/978-3-319-44778-0

Author Index

Abdullatif, Amr II-216
Abe, Takeshi I-524
Aboudib, Ala II-439
Agathocleous, Michalis I-123
Agelidis, Vassilios G. II-299
Akima, Hisanao I-556, I-558
Aksenova, Tetiana I-288
Al Moubayed, Noura II-423
Aladag, Cagdas Hakan I-561
Alexandre, Frédéric I-214
Alptekin, Bulent I-561
Alpay, Tayfun I-132
Altahhan, Abdulrahman II-38, II-535
Amari, Shun-ichi I-427
Ambroszkiewicz, Stanisław II-145
Andrés-Merino, Jaime II-208
Antonik, Piotr I-374
Aouiti, Chaouki I-478
Araújo, Daniel II-388
Arie, Hiroaki I-339
Arjannikov, Tom II-199
Arratia, Argimiro II-336
Arsiwalla, Xerxes D. I-83, I-107, I-184
Asai, Yoshiyuki I-524

Baba, Yukino I-453
Baccouche, Moez II-161
Backhus, Jana I-444
Baladron, Javier I-248
Balagué, Marta I-264
Balaguer-Ballester, Emili I-314
Banquet, Jean-Paul I-238
Barbosa, João I-548
Barros, Pablo II-80
Barth, Erhardt I-538
Bauer-Wersing, Ute II-489
Belanche, Lluís A. II-208, II-336
Belić, Jovana J. I-72
Berlemont, Samuel II-406
Berzish, Murphy I-349
Beuth, Frederik II-447
Bezerra, Sabrina G.T.A. II-308
Bhattacharya, Basabdatta Sen II-225
Bicho, Estela I-411

Billard, Aude I-205
Binder, Alexander II-63
Boada-Collado, Pol I-530
Bolaños, Marc II-3
Boahen, Kwabena I-526
Bologna, Guido II-537
Bolzoni, Alberto II-291
Botsch, Mario II-506
Boutefnouchet, Abdelatif II-542
Boukabou, Abdelkrim II-544
Breckon, Toby II-423
Breuel, Thomas M. II-347
Bruck, Péter I-544
Burikov, Sergey II-355
Byeon, Wonmin II-347

Cabessa, Jérémie I-115
Canuto, Anne M.P. II-275
Capone, Cristiano I-545
Carrere, Maxime I-214
Carrino, Casimiro Pio II-539
Casademunt, Jaume I-536
Casacuberta, Francisco II-3
Casali, Adenauer G. I-547
Castellano, Marta I-306
Çelikok, Sami Utku I-256
Cerezuela-Escudero, Elena I-45, II-363
Chappet de Vangel, Benoît I-357
Chauhan, Ashok I-562
Che, Xiaoyin II-187
Chen, Jun II-225
Chérif, Farouk I-478
Chettibi, KheirEddine II-542
Chernodub, Artem II-533
Christodoulou, Chris I-123
Cohen, Laura I-205
Compte, Albert I-548
Coombes, Stephen I-411
Coppin, Gilles II-439

D'Andola, Mattia I-547
Dalmazzo, David I-83
Davey, Neil II-372

David, Omid E.   II-20, II-88, II-170
de Andrade, Camila B.   II-308
de Sousa, Giseli   II-372
de Jorge, Pau   I-549
de la Rocha, Jaime   I-539, I-550, I-555
Deco, Gustavo   I-535, I-549, I-554
Dempere-Marco, Laura   I-264
Deng, Ning   I-533
Dengel, Andreas   II-347
Dolenko, Sergey   I-502, II-317, II-355, II-541
Dolenko, Tatiana   II-355
Dominguez-Morales, Juan Pedro   I-36, I-45, II-363
Dominguez-Morales, Manuel J.   I-36, I-45, II-363
Dörr, Alexander   I-140
Dorronsoro, José R.   II-243
Duan, Tiehang   II-105
Duffner, Stefan   II-406
Dunne, Stephen   I-306

Echeveste, Rodrigo   I-560
Efitorov, Alexander   II-355
Eliasmith, Chris   I-349
Elleuch, Mohamed   II-136
Ellouze, Marieme   I-461
Elshaw, Mark   II-38, II-535
Érdi, Péter   I-543, I-544
Erlhagen, Wolfram   I-411
Escuain-Poole, Lara   I-553

Faigl, Jan   II-497
Farah, Nadir   II-542
Farfar, Kheir Eddine   II-415
Feldbauer, Roman   I-175
Fischer, Andreas   II-113
Fleischer, Andreas G.   I-158
Flexer, Arthur   I-175
Fontenla-Romero, Oscar   II-398
Foroutan, Marzieh   II-545
Fouss, François   I-192
Franzius, Mathias   II-489

Gabaldà-Sagarra, Marçal   I-542
Gandhi, Vaibhav   II-550
Gajewska-Dendek, Elżbieta   I-532
Garcia, Christophe   II-161, II-406
Garcia-Ojalvo, Jordi   I-529, I-542, I-553
Gaussier, Philippe   I-238

Geng, Tao   II-550
Gepperth, Alexander   II-121, II-179
Ghosh, Rohan   II-455
Giese, Martin A.   I-222, I-521
Girau, Bernard   I-357
Giuffrida, Mario Valerio   II-480
Goodfellow, Marc   I-529
Göpfert, Christina   I-510, II-251
Gros, Claudius   I-560
Gripon, Vincent   II-153, II-439
Gu, Xiaodong   II-547
Gutierrez-Galan, Daniel   I-45
Guy, Tatiana V.   I-230

Hadrich Belguith, Lamia   I-461
Haelterman, Marc   I-374
Hamker, Fred H.   I-248, II-447
Hammer, Barbara   I-510, II-251, II-506
Handmann, Uwe   II-179
Hanoune, Souheïl   I-238
Hanten, Richard   I-149, II-29
Hara, Kazuyuki   II-72
Harkin, Jim   I-382
Haschke, Robert   II-12
Hasegawa, Mikio   I-91
Hashiguchi, Riku   II-537
Hayashi, Yoichi   II-537
Hecht, Thomas   II-121
He, Hu   I-533
Hedley, Yih-Ling   II-535
Heinrich, Stefan   I-132
Hellgren Kotaleski, Jeanette   I-72
Hennebert, Jean   II-113
Hermans, Michiel   I-374
Hermoso-Mendizabal, Ainhoa   I-539
Hernández-Navarro, Lluís   I-536
Hernández, Nicolás   II-235
Herreros, Ivan   I-272
Hesse, Evelyn   II-372
Hestermeyer, Lukas   I-551
Hicks, Luke   II-535
Hinakawa, Nobuhiro   I-11
Hinz, Tobias   II-80
Hori, Sansei   I-391
Hyafil, Alexandre   I-539, I-550
Hosseini, Babak   II-506
Hovaidi Ardestani, Mohammad   I-521
Huang, Moyuan   II-199
Hůla, František   I-230, I-330
Hülsmann, Felix   II-506

Ibañez, David   I-306
Imai, Hideyuki   I-444
Irastorza-Landa, Nerea   II-47
Isaev, Igor   I-502

Jamalian, Amirhossein   II-447
Jedynak, Maciej   I-529
Jaramillo, Santiago   I-539
Jensen, Joris   II-251
Jesus, Jhoseph   II-388
Jiang, Liangxiao   I-419
Jiang, Nan   II-199
Jimenez-Fernandez, Angel   I-36, I-45, II-363
Jimenez-Moreno, Gabriel   I-45
Jörger, Patrick   I-453

Kacalak, Wojciech   II-523
Karakida, Ryo   I-427
Kárný, Miroslav   I-230, I-330
Kalyani, Ganesh Kumar   II-550
Kaplan, Raphael   I-535
Katayama, Takahiro   I-541
Kawakami, Susumu   I-556
Kashima, Hisashi   I-453
Keil, Matthias S.   II-549
Khadir, Mohamed Tarek   II-415
Khatib, Oussama   I-526
Khelifa, Mohammed Amin   II-544
Kherallah, Monji   II-136, II-259, II-431
Kinjo, Mitsunaga   I-558
Kitamura, Takuya   I-486
Kitano, Katsunori   I-11, I-63
Kmet, Tibor   I-468
Kmetova, Maria   I-468
Koike, Chieko   I-63
Kopinski, Thomas   II-179
Koprinkova-Hristova, Petia   I-494
Koprinska, Irena   II-299
Kountouris, Petros   I-123
Kudo, Mineichi   I-444
Kukreja, Sunil L.   II-455
Kumanduri, Luis   I-526
Kummert, Johannes   II-251
Kuravi, Pradeep   I-222
Kuroda, Kaori   I-91
Kuyumcu, Arden   II-515

Laptinskiy, Kirill   II-355
Lapuschkin, Sebastian   II-63
Le, Hoang   I-107

Lefebvre, Grégoire   II-406
Lerer, Alejandro   II-549
Leva, Sonia   II-291
Li, Chaoqun   I-419
Li, Haiteng   II-128
Liang, Xun   II-326
Linares-Barranco, Alejandro   I-36, II-363
Liu, Jia   II-128
Liu, Junxiu   I-382
Liu, Yang-Yu   I-537
Liwicki, Marcus   II-347
Louis, Matthieu   II-552
Luna, Rogelio   I-549
Low, Sock Ching   I-28
Luo, Sheng   II-187

Ma, Hailin   I-533
M'hamdi, Mohammed Salah   I-478
Maalej, Rania   II-431
Madai-Tahy, Lorand   II-29
Madrenas, Jordi   I-365, I-399
Maffei, Giovanni   I-272
Mahmoud, Hassan   II-216
Majewski, Maciej   II-523
Malagarriga, Daniel   II-552
Martin, George   I-382
Martins, Allan   II-388
Martinetz, Thomas   I-538
Masoller, Cristina   I-523
Massar, Serge   I-374
Massimini, Marcello   I-547
Masulli, Francesco   II-216
Masulli, Paolo   I-99
Matthews, Peter   II-423
Mattia, Maurizio   I-530, I-545
McDaid, Liam   I-382
McGough, A. Stephen   II-423
Medeiros, Inácio G.   II-275
Meier, Martin   II-12
Meinel, Christoph   II-187
Mendizabal, Ainhoa Hermoso   I-550
Menon, Samir   I-526
Mekki, Yasmina Nozha   II-542
Ménard, Michel   I-540
Metka, Benjamin   II-489
Mici, Luiza   II-472
Mokni, Raouia   II-259
Montavon, Grégoire   II-63
Morie, Takashi   I-391
Moriya, Satoshi   I-556

Müller, Klaus-Robert   II-63
Muñoz, Alberto   II-235
Muñoz-Almaraz, Javier   II-55
Murata, Shingo   I-339
Mussetta, Marco   II-291
Myagkova, Irina   II-317, II-541

Nácher, Verónica   I-549
Nallapu, Bhargav Teja   I-322
Nakajima, Koji   I-556, I-558
Neji, Zeineb   I-461
Netanyahu, Nathan S.   II-20, II-88, II-170
Neto, Adrião Dória   II-388
Ninomiya, Hiroshi   II-540
Nogaret, Alain   I-562
Nowicki, Dimitri   II-533
Nowotny, Thomas   I-54

Oberleiter, Sabine   II-463
Obornev, Eugeny   I-502
Obornev, Ivan   I-502
Ogata, Tetsuya   I-166, I-339, II-283
Ogliari, Emanuele   II-291
Okada, Masato   I-427
Oliva, Jefferson Tales   I-297
Orlandi, Javier G.   I-536
Osakabe, Yoshihiro   I-558
Osana, Yuko   I-3, I-541
Otte, Sebastian   I-140, I-149, II-29

Paassen, Benjamin   I-510, II-251
Palacio, Sebastian   II-347
Palade, Vasile   II-38, II-535
Pardo, Juan   II-55
Parisi, German I.   II-472
Patzelt, Florian   II-12
Paz-Vicente, Rafael   II-363
Peña, Mauricio   II-336
Pérez-Sánchez, Beatriz   II-398
Peris, Álvaro   II-3
Peyrard, Clément   II-161
Piater, Justus   II-380, II-463
Pipa, Gordon   I-551
Pigorini, Andrea   I-547
Plastino, Angel R.   I-19
Pons, Antonio J.   I-529, I-553
Popa, Călin-Adrian   I-435
Prat-Ortega, Genis   I-555

Principe, Alessandro   I-554
Priori, Daniel   II-372
Promponas, Vasilis   I-123
Puigbò, Jordi-Ysard   I-28

Quintero-Quiroz, Carlos   I-523
Quoy, Mathias   I-238

Radeva, Petia   II-3
Ramos-Murguialday, Ander   II-47
Rana, Mashud   II-299
Rasouli, Mahdi   II-455
Raue, Federico   II-347
Revel, Arnaud   I-540
Rebollo, Beatriz   I-547
Rios-Navarro, Antonio   I-36, I-45
Ritter, Helge J.   II-12
Robbe, David   I-539
Robert, Maëlys   II-153
Rocamora, Rodrigo   I-554
Rodríguez-Sánchez, Antonio   II-380, II-463
Roisenberg, Mauro   II-372
Romeo, August   I-528
Romo, Ranulfo   I-549
Rojas-Castro, Dalia-Marcela   I-540
Rong, Wenge   II-199
Rosa, João Luís Garcia   I-297
Rougier, Nicolas P.   I-322
Rovetta, Stefano   II-216
Roxin, Alex   I-555
Rubinov, Mikail   I-107
Ruffini, Giulio   I-306
Rueda-Orozco, Pavel Ernesto   I-539
Ruiz-Garcia, Ariel   II-38
Ruman, Marko   I-230, I-330
Rupp, André   I-314

Sachara, Fabian   II-179
Saerens, Marco   I-192
Saitoh, Daisuke   II-72
Saitoh, Fumiaki   II-267
Salawu, Emmanuel   II-372
Samek, Wojciech   II-63
Sanchez-Fibla, Marti   I-272
Sánchez-Maroño, Noelia   II-398
Sakuraba, Masao   I-558
Sakurabah, Masao   I-556
Sanchez-Vives, Maria V.   I-530, I-545, I-547
Sarasola-Sanz, Andrea   II-47
Sasaki, Kazuma   II-283

Sato, Hiroki   I-3
Sato, Shigeo   I-556, I-558
Schaeffer, Marie-Caroline   I-288
Schütze, Henry   I-538
Sekiguchi, Kana   II-283
Şengör, Neslihan Serap   I-256, II-515
Shang, Yingjie   I-533
Sharma, Sugandha   I-280
Sharpe, James   II-552
Shen, Hua   II-326
Shimelevich, Mikhail   I-502
Shiroky, Vladimir   II-317, II-541
Sholomon, Dror   II-170
Shouno, Hayaru   II-72
Silva, Huliane M.   II-275
Siyi, Tang   II-455
Slavkov, Ivica   II-552
Sommer, Felix   I-192
Soria-Frisch, Aureli   I-306
Soriano, Jordi   I-534, I-536, I-549
Sorrentino, Taciano   I-523
Soulié, Guillaume   II-153
Spüler, Martin   II-47
Sriram, Vinay   I-526
Srihari, Sargur N.   II-105
Stabinger, Sebastian   II-380
Stopford, Christopher   II-372
Stramaglia, Sebastiano   II-539
Suffczyński, Piotr   I-532
Sugano, Shigeki   I-166
Sugimoto, Masanori   I-444
Sun, Shangdi   II-547
Supèr, Hans   I-528, II-549
Sun, Yi   II-372

Tabas, Alejandro   I-314
Takahashi, Kuniyuki   I-166
Takigawa, Ichigaku   I-444
Tamukoh, Hakaru   I-391
Taniguchi, Kanako   I-63
Tapiador-Morales, Ricardo   I-36
Tauste Campo, Adrià   I-549, I-554
Teller, Sara   I-534
Thakor, Nitish V.   II-455
Tjandra, Hadi   I-166
Tibau, Elisenda   I-534
Torrent, M.C.   I-523
Torres-Barrán, Alberto   II-243
Tort-Colet, Nuria   I-545
Tripp, Bryan P.   I-280, I-349, II-97

Troncoso, Alicia   II-299
Tsaftaris, Sotirios A.   II-480

Valença, Mêuser J.S.   II-308
van Wijngaarden, Joeri   I-28
Váňa, Petr   II-497
Vassiliades, Vassilis   I-123
Verschure, Paul F.M.J.   I-28, I-83, I-107, I-184, I-272
Villa, Alessandro E.P.   I-99, I-115, I-524
Villagrasa, Francesc   I-248
Vilimelis Aceituno, Pau   I-537
Vogels, Rufin   I-222

Wang, Cheng   II-187
Wang, Nanyue   II-128
Wang, Yuzhe   I-533
Wedemann, Roseli S.   I-19
Weinert, Julia F.   I-530, I-547
Wermter, Stefan   I-132, II-80, II-472
Wicht, Baptiste   II-113
Wimmer, Klaus   I-555
Wojtak, Weronika   I-411
Wolf, Lior   II-88

Xavier-Júnior, João C.   II-275
Xiong, Hanchen   II-463
Xiong, Zhang   II-199
Xu, Bin   II-128
Xu, Zhiheng   I-533

Yamada, Tatsuro   I-339
Yamakawa, Madoka   II-283
Yan, Gang   I-537
Yano, Masafumi   I-556
Yang, Xu   I-533
Yang, Haojin   II-187
Yang, Zhijun   II-550
Yavuz, Esin   I-54

Zamora-Martínez, Francisco   II-55
Zapata, Mireya   I-365, I-399
Zareian, Elham   II-225
Zegarek, Gregory   I-83
Zell, Andreas   I-140, I-149, II-29
Zhang, Lungan   I-419
Zouari, Ramzi   II-136
Zucca, Riccardo   I-107
Zwiener, Adrian   I-149

Printed in the United States
By Bookmasters